# Social Problems

# Social Problems

## A Service Learning Approach

Corey Dolgon
*Stonehill College*

Chris Baker
*Walters State Community College*

Los Angeles | London | New Delhi
Singapore | Washington DC

*For information:*

Pine Forge Press
An Imprint of SAGE Publications, Inc.
2455 Teller Road
Thousand Oaks, California 91320
E-mail: order@sagepub.com

SAGE Publications Ltd.
1 Oliver's Yard
55 City Road
London EC1Y 1SP
United Kingdom

SAGE Publications India Pvt. Ltd.
B 1/I 1 Mohan Cooperative Industrial Area
Mathura Road, New Delhi 110 044
India

SAGE Publications Asia-Pacific Pte. Ltd.
33 Pekin Street #02-01
Far East Square
Singapore 048763

Printed in the United States of America.

*Library of Congress Cataloging-in-Publication Data*

Dolgon, Corey.
 Social problems : a service learning approach / Corey Dolgon, Chris Baker.
   p. cm.
 Includes bibliographical references and index.
 ISBN 978-0-7619-2947-5 (pbk.)
   1. Sociology. 2. Sociology—Methodology. I. Baker, Chris. II. Title.

HM585.D66 2011
301—dc22                                   2010020622

This book is printed on acid-free paper.

10   11   12   13   14   10   9   8   7   6   5   4   3   2   1

| | |
|---|---|
| *Acquisitions Editor:* | David Repetto |
| *Editorial Assistant:* | Maggie Stanley |
| *Production Editor:* | Karen Wiley |
| *Copy Editor:* | Teresa Herlinger |
| *Proofreader:* | Laura Webb |
| *Typesetter:* | C&M Digitals (P) Ltd. |
| *Indexer:* | Rick Hurd |
| *Cover Designer:* | Bryan Fishman |
| *Marketing Manager:* | Erica DeLuca |

# Contents

# Acknowledgments

Putting together a book like this requires the help of many people. We would like to thank the many good folks at Pine Forge Press who have stuck with us through this process and nurtured us along every big and small step of the way. We would also like to express our professional gratitude to the many kind and insightful reviewers whose comments kept us energized, committed, and made us look a lot smarter than we are. On a more personal note, Chris Baker would like to thank his wonderful wife, JoBeth Bradley, and Corey Dolgon would like to thank his wife, Deborah Milbauer, and his daughters, Bailey and Ruby. Their love and support not only enable us to do the academic and political work we do, but remind us why living a life in the struggle to solve social problems will always be the right path. And finally, we would like to acknowledge all of the faculty and students and especially their community partners who have done so much of the excellent work that we have only partially chronicled in this book. While we don't have space to mention everyone involved, we would especially like to thank those listed below whom we interviewed and wrote about, and who gave us permission to use their ideas, experiences, and pictures, and sometimes even read and commented on sections of the work that involved their organizations, courses, and written materials. It is their efforts that comprise the heart and soul of this book and make an intellectually engaged study of social problems so exciting and powerful.

| | | |
|---|---|---|
| Robert Sanders | Daphne Renee | Amy Schulz |
| Rienhard Heinisch | Eric Hartmann | Michael Kline |
| Miguel Centeno | Melinda Wiggins | Valerie Mapstone Ackerman |
| Michael Kline | Jason Pramas | |
| Martin Espada | José Calderón | David Gilvin |
| John Reiff | Cassie Waters | Mary Chayko |
| Steve Corey | Bob Zellner | Woody Doane |
| Ann Rafferty | Kristine Donnelly | Jason Pramas |

Barbara Vann

James Russell

Jerry Lembcke

Adam Boyle

Melissa Arch-Walton

Steve Cooper

Dave McMahon

Lawrette Axley

Christie Ochoa

Glenn Johnson

John David

Highlander Folk School

Anthony Collatos

Lori Campbell

Evelyn Dortch

Andrew McNamara

# Introduction: What Are Social Problems and What Do Sociologists Do About Them?

> *The core of the social problem is a multisided clash of social interests. The job of the sociologist is to isolate and define these conflicting value judgments which are the modus operandi of the problem. He need no longer hold himself out as an expert on social problems but as an expert on the* sociology of social problems. *As a scientist* he must avoid making value judgments; *but moral judgments in themselves are the content of a true sociology of social problems.*
>
> —Richard Fuller, "The Problem of Teaching
> Social Problems" (1938, emphasis original)

> *The humanist-scholar activist* eschews the arm chair model of research, but also the objective field researcher model, *and instead works together with progressive groups struggling to create alternative economic and social forms of existence and writes from a perspective that confronts power and nurtures social change. The humanist scholar-activist* doesn't simply "study" disadvantaged groups, but interacts with them *in an effort to understand the processes that foster social inequality and the psychological consequences that result from [them], all in the effort to better inform human struggle.*
>
> —Timothy Black, "Humanist Sociology in the
> Wake of Al Lee" (2004, emphasis original)

When I (Corey Dolgon) was in graduate school at the University of Michigan, I joined a group called HAC (the Homeless Action Committee). This collection of community activists, students, homeless, and formerly homeless people had come together to address the growing problem of homelessness in Ann Arbor, Michigan. Over the years, city officials had invested hundreds of millions of dollars in high-tech research parks, luxury office buildings, and in projects to beautify the downtown shopping district. Yet skyrocketing property taxes and the disappearance of affordable housing resulted in poorer residents being squeezed out. For people without homes, upscale townhouses and boutique specialty shops had replaced low-rent apartments and inexpensive, single-room occupancies (Dolgon 1999).

Some people in the city, including a few political leaders and social service providers, *did* believe that homeless people needed more help. They supported things like employment counseling and more shelter beds. HAC, however, argued that homelessness would not go away until the city built low-income housing for poor people. We studied wage rates, housing trends, economic development policies, and the overall cost of living. Even with full-time employment, we concluded, most poor people could not afford to live in downtown Ann Arbor or its environs.

HAC also discovered that the University of Michigan itself was the driving force behind these local economic and social trends. Institutional expansions after World War II had inspired a huge population growth of professional middle- and upper-class faculty, staff, and students. In an effort to compete with other cities, Ann Arbor's city government teamed up with university administrators and the chamber of commerce. They designed projects using tax dollars to attract hi-tech industries and expand the university. But successful development policies to support scientific research and upscale consumer tastes had resulted in the displacement of poor people (Dolgon 1995, 1998).

I decided to write my dissertation about HAC and the economic and social dynamics of a "university city," but some of my mentors balked. One explained that scholars shouldn't base their intellectual work on political projects. Our job, he said, was to develop useful analyses and theories that could inform the practical work of others. Another advisor thought that the issue was too provincial and lacked the possibility of providing significant scientific data or theory. And a third faculty member questioned HAC's premise to begin with, arguing that the city couldn't build low-income housing without more revenue, and it needed to cater to an upper class in order to attract that revenue. We were four social scientists and we managed to disagree about my project in at least four different ways.

## DEFINING SOCIAL PROBLEMS: ARGUMENTS VERSUS OPINIONS

Thinking about the quotations at the beginning of the chapter reminded me of this personal experience with the subjectivity of social science and social scientists. I realize that telling students that sociologists can't completely agree on what social problems are, how they come about, or what we as sociologists can or should do about them may not be the best way to start this book. Students often look to professors for answers. Soon, they find out that so-called "experts" disagree and that a variety of possible explanations might be viable for any one particular social phenomenon. In response, they might wonder if thinking about the world isn't just a matter of different *opinions*. Maybe our actions are just a matter of *individual choices*.

Of course, one thing all sociologists would agree on is that, despite disagreements over definitions and causation, social phenomena *can* be studied scientifically, understood theoretically, and acted upon effectively. Thus, while there are many sociological definitions for what a social problem is, most vary only a little. A **social problem** is a *condition that harms a significant number of people or results in the structural disadvantage of particular segments in any given society.* Many sociologists would add to this definition that such problems exist "when there is a sizable difference between the ideals of a society and its actual achievement" (Merton and Nisbet 1966:780). For example, in a society where equality is valued, poverty and discrimination would be social problems. But in a society that cherishes strict hierarchies, inequalities of various sorts may not only be tolerated, they may also be encouraged and enforced.

Such relativity leads us to a third variation of the definition: A social problem exists only when a *significant portion of a given population* believes *there is a problem or that at least some public controversy takes place over an issue.* In part, this perspective developed out of a symbolic interactionist or social constructionist approach (see Chapter 1) where the reality of a social problem depends on its having been *labeled* a social problem. Sociologist Herbert Blumer (1971) argued that social problems are "a product of a process of collective definition," not the "objective conditions and social arrangements" of a society (p. 298). In other words, because the existence of a problem requires some value judgment about what is good or bad, how societies *construct* and *use* their values determines what a problem is, not the actual conditions that might cause it. For example, contemporary problems such as "date rape" and "global warming" were not mentioned in social problems textbooks before the late 1970s. They existed, but it took the women's movement and the environmental movement to educate the public and organize pressure on officials to recognize and address these problems.

C. Wright Mills (1959) also emphasized the importance of size and relativity in determining what counts as a social problem. He distinguished between what he called "**personal troubles** of milieu and the **public issues** of social structure." "Troubles," according to Mills, "occur within the character of the individual and within the range of his immediate relations with others," while issues "transcend the local environments of the individual and . . . involve crises of institutional arrangements" and larger structures (p. 9). For example, he argued that in the case of unemployment, "if only one man is unemployed in a city of 100,000, "we properly look to the *character* of the man, his skills and his immediate opportunities. But when in a nation of 50 million employees, 15 million men are unemployed, that is an *issue* . . . the very structure of opportunity has collapsed" (p. 9, emphasis added). Mills defines social problems as relative to how many people are affected. Unlike the symbolic interactionists, though, he contends there *is* an objective, material foundation that causes large numbers of people to be harmed regardless of whether a majority of people label it a problem. To best analyze the intersection of personal and social, Mills advocates what he calls the "sociological imagination."

**Image I.1**    This photo of urban tenement life comes from Jacob Riis's *How the Other Half Lives*, published in 1890. His experience as a police reporter led him to depict the lives of New York City's poor (especially immigrants) in hopes of bringing their conditions to the public light. Riis argued that the misery, poverty, and overcrowding were signs that "the poor were the victims rather than the makers of their fate" (p. 7). Riis's work resulted in major public policy changes and helped shape the debate over poverty for many years. The problem of poverty has always been pervasive, but because its victims live on the margins of mainstream society or are demonized by popular culture, it often takes someone like Riis to make the problem "public."

*Source:* © Corbis/Bettmann.

Each of these approaches to social problems has its flaws. For those who focus on the objective existence of harm or disadvantage, there is the subjective consideration of who *defines* what harm is or who is disadvantaged by it. For instance, a majority of white college students agree (although sometimes reluctantly) that racism is a social problem. But many of them identify "reverse discrimination" (white people denied privilege or access because of affirmative action) as the most prevalent form of systemic racism. Yet there is no scholarly evidence that proves affirmative action has had *any significant discriminatory impact* on white people's collective opportunities. Still, conservative political interests have been able to use white (especially white males') fears over declining employment and college enrollment rates to claim that affirmative action is to blame for *any* instance where a white person is denied a job, a college placement, and so on. According to John Moland, Jr. (1996), the narrative of "affirmative action as reverse discrimination" reflects "faulty assumptions and misleading implications based upon the use of limited information" (p. 404; see also Doane and Bonilla-Silva 2003; Feagin and Vera 1995). Thus, harm and disadvantage are not only subjective, but one group's perceptions of them can be manipulated to claim that they themselves are being overburdened by attempts to ameliorate previous inequities.

Who Burns for the Perfection of Paper

by Martin Espada

At sixteen, I worked after high school hours

at a printing plant

that manufactured legal pads

Yellow paper stacked seven feet high

and leaning

as I slipped cardboard

between the pages,

then brushed red glue

up and down the stack.

No gloves: fingertips required

for the perfection of paper,

smoothing the exact rectangle.

Sluggish by 9 PM, the hands

would slide along suddenly sharp paper,

and gather slits thinner than the crevices

of the skin, hidden.

Then the glue would sting,

hands oozing

**Image I.2**   In 1963, Martin Luther King Jr. was arrested for protesting segregation in Birmingham, Alabama. He was criticized, not only by the Southern white power structure, but by members of black and white religious communities as well.

*Source:* © Corbis/Bettmann.

till both palms burned
at the punchclock.

Ten years later, in law school,
I knew that every legal pad
was glued with the sting of hidden cuts,
that every open lawbook
was a pair of hands
upturned and burning.

Meanwhile, there are few societies with such unified sets of values and ideals that a widespread consensus could determine effectively and objectively what a social problem is, nor do controversies usually mark the first stages of a social problem. On the contrary, they are most likely the result of a long-term simmering of marginalized or repressed anger and mainstream ignorance or apathy. In fact, by the time the public recognizes that a social problem exists and warrants some form of redress, the group experiencing disadvantage or harm has often been aware of it for some time. In the 1960s, Martin Luther King Jr. (1963) was accused of creating tensions by protesting racial segregation. He responded, "Nonviolent direct action seeks . . . to dramatize the issue that it can no longer be ignored. . . . Actually, we who engage in [it] are not the creators of tension. We merely bring to the surface the hidden tension that is already alive" (p. 2). King continued,

> I have tried to say that this normal and healthy discontent can be channelized through the creative outlet of nonviolent direct action. Now this approach is being dismissed as extremist. . . . I gradually gained a bit of satisfaction from being considered an extremist. Was not Jesus an extremist for love—"Love your enemies, bless them that curse you, pray for them that despitefully use you." . . . Was not Abraham Lincoln an extremist—"This nation cannot survive half slave and half free." Was not Thomas Jefferson an extremist—"We hold these

truths to be self-evident, that all men are created equal." So the question is not whether we will be extremist but what kind of extremist will we be. Will we be extremists for hate or will we be extremists for love? Will we be extremists for the preservation of injustice or will we be extremists for the cause of justice? (pp. 2–3).

Despite the shortcomings of each definition, they do help us to think critically, if not always uniformly, about the origins, existence, and impact of social problems. If we go back to my own experience with homelessness in Ann Arbor, we can see that all of these approaches and critiques assist in understanding various aspects of the problem. "Homelessness," both in Ann Arbor and around the country, was first labeled a social problem in the early to mid-1980s as a variety of conditions converged to create a crisis for people in need of low-income housing (Campbell and Reeves 1999).

The odd street person whose homelessness may have appeared an individual matter had become more notably a structural and public issue of fewer housing opportunities for poor people. Still, most of Ann Arbor's officials and local media refused to acknowledge this growing problem. Thus, HAC organized, in part, to publicize the issue and educate the wider community (Dolgon 2000).

HAC's demonstrations at City Hall, its direct action events in parking lots and vacant buildings, and its publicity campaign about government spending for the rich and neglect toward the poor, all brought to the surface "hidden tensions . . . already alive" in Ann Arbor. Eventually, HAC succeeded in organizing enough support to change some local economic policies that resulted in more services for homeless people and more low-income housing. This achievement came primarily from political pressure on officials who could not justify building parking lots and office buildings while a growing number of local citizens had no place to live. In essence, HAC manipulated the "sizable difference between the ideals of a society and its actual achievement" (Merton and Nisbet 1966:780) by exposing just how many people were actually harmed by homelessness and poverty. Eventually, the larger society recognized homelessness as a social problem, not a personal trouble.

## A HISTORY OF SOCIOLOGY AND SOCIAL PROBLEMS

One way to understand the relationship between **sociology** and social problems is to explore how the desire to address social ills has been at the very heart of the field's development. From the beginning, sociology was both an intellectual and a practical pursuit. Although we are interested in sociology as a specific and professional *discipline,* we want to recognize, as Roger Straus (2002) has, that "thoughtful men and women have always sought to understand the workings of society and its effects on people" (p. 4). Specifically, Straus notes the work of Rahman Ibn Khaldun, the 14th-century Arab historian and statesman. Khaldun not only initiated a systemic application of science for studying **society**, but also believed such an approach could be *applied* to social policies., Antonio Gramsci's (1971) dictum that "*all* people carry on some form of intellectual activity" (p. 223, emphasis original) also recognized that sociological thinking could help keep the world as it is or help people work to change it. To some degree, therefore, we are all intellectuals. The great hope of sociologists has always been that the application of Mills's sociological imagination would help us *all* to solve social problems.

Most historians of sociology site the beginnings of a formal, scientific approach to the study of society in 18th- and 19th-century Europe. Social intellectuals of the period witnessed revolutions in both industrial production and scientific thinking. On the one hand, early sociologists saw the poverty, despair, and bewilderment brought on by rapid urban and industrial development. On the other hand, they found that science and reason promised the possibility of discovering how society worked and using that knowledge to improve it. French philosophers such as Henri De Saint-Simon and Auguste Comte argued that scientific principles could be used to study social dynamics and reform social policy. Comte, in particular, thought that sociology "would help us 'live the dream' better than it was lived in the Middle Ages. . . . [Sociology was] a science that would seek to develop the conditions of life enhancement" (quoted in Becker 1968:24).

Later in the 19th century, German writers Karl Marx and Friedrich Engels documented the historical evolution and social impact of capitalism. They argued that changes in the forms of economic production resulted in both political and social upheavals. When economic conditions changed, such as the transformation from agricultural to industrial production, new groups—or **classes,** as they called them—vied for power. These struggles resulted in new political systems, such as the rise of democracy (Marx 1933); new intellectual paradigms, such as the triumph of science over religion (Marx 1972); and new social relationships, such as the nuclear versus the extended family, growing individualism, and increased alienation. Ultimately, Marx and Engels (1955) claimed that the "history of all hitherto societies is the history of class struggles" (p. 8) and their outcomes.

Like Saint-Simon and Comte, however, Marx and Engels thought that social analyses could and should be focused on solving social problems. For them, industrial capitalism exploited, degraded, and impoverished workers. It left them as mere appendages to machinery in the factory, and as victims of poor, overcrowded, crime-ridden streets at home. Yet the class in power maintained these conditions for its own benefit. In fact, Marx (1972) claimed that "the ruling ideas of any age are the ideas of the ruling class" (p. 138). Those in power, therefore, generally justified inequality by shaping political issues, cultural values, and ideology to either rationalize inequality or blame poverty on the poor themselves.

Thus, instead of trying to work toward reforming social policies at the top of society, the duo laid their hopes for social change on the working class, or *proletariat*. They envisioned their analytical work as part of an international movement to raise workers' consciousness and create the solidarity and political strength necessary for a revolution. For Marx (1972), examining the workings of the social world and creating a more just society were part of the same enterprise. They concluded, "Social life is essentially *practical*. All mysteries which mislead theory into mysticism find their rational solution in human practice and in the comprehension of this practice. . . . The philosophers have only *interpreted* the world in various ways; the point, however, is to *change* it" (p. 107, emphasis added).

Émile Durkheim (1947), arguably the founder of modern sociology, also wanted to understand the instability, violence, and social decay of late 19th-century industrialized Europe. While he lacked some of Comte's optimism about the inevitable progress and reform of modern society, he felt more compelled than Marx by the possibilities of bourgeois democracy. Even though he studied what he called the "devious forms" of social life—such as crime and suicide—he saw promise in the period's rise of mass public education, increased individual freedoms, and the triumph of science and reason.

Durkheim (1961) was particularly interested in education. He taught in high schools and worked on committees to reform and update the national curriculum of France. For him, educational theories had "the immediate aim of guiding conduct." Although these theories did not constitute action in and of themselves, they "were a preparation for it. . . . Their *raison d'être* is in action" (p. 2). Durkheim believed firmly that sociological analyses could strengthen educational theory and practice. Better schools, better teachers, and a better curriculum would result in a better society.

In the United States, some of sociology's first leaders focused their efforts on **applied sociology**. Early presidents of the American Sociological Society (ASA) such as Lester Ward (1906–1907) and Albion Small (1912–1913) promoted a field of study engaged with the social problems of the day. Ward (1906), in particular, detailed a "necessary" movement from *pure* sociology (research that created new knowledge) to *applied* sociology (research deployed to improve the human condition). He explained that pure sociology, "teaches man what he is and how he came to be so. . . . With a clear comprehension of what constitutes achievement [man] is able to see what will constitute improvement. The purpose of applied sociology is to harmonize achievement with improvement" (p. 21).

Under Small's initial direction, the University of Chicago's Sociology Department built a reputation as a kind of "city lab" that used the social problems caused by rapid industrialization, urbanization, and immigration as subjects for research. Many of their studies examined the difficulties that poor and ethnically isolated immigrant communities had in assimilating into American mainstream life. According to Straus (2002), however, "some Chicago school sociologists went beyond applied research to intervene in social problems through social activism or involvement with clinics and Settlement Houses." (p. 11). The most important of these houses was **Hull House,** run by Jane Addams.

**Image I.3** Women's Peace Committee delegation to the International Congress of Women's Anti-War protest at The Hague in the Netherlands, 1915. (Jane Addams is behind the banner, second from the left.)

*Source:* © Corbis.

Scholars have argued that formal sociology overlooked Addams in part because she was a woman, in part because she was a practitioner, and in part because she was an activist (Deegan 1988; Scimecca and Goodwin 2003). All are probably true, but it is undeniable that her work at Hull House had an immense impact on sociologists such as W. I. Thomas and George Herbert Mead, as well as the philosopher John Dewey. Hull House integrated service provision with community organizing. It became both a place for neighborhood political activity and a laboratory for applying social research to social problems. Addams (1910) wrote that student volunteers felt "a fatal want of harmony between their theory and their lives, a lack of coordination between thought and action. . . . The settlement house is an out-let for that sentiment of universal brotherhood" (p. 115). Addams should be recognized not only as a significant influence on the development of applied sociology, but also as one of the first pioneers in **service learning.**

Similarly, African American sociologist and political activist W. E. B. Du Bois' work has often been overlooked, both for its impact on the field of sociology as well as its significance for strengthening the relationship between scholarship and social action. Du Bois (1998,

1999) studied the ways in which race shaped the contours of U.S. history and politics. As early as 1903, he concluded that "The problem of the 20th century is the problem of the color line" (p. 7). He also wrote about the everyday struggles of African Americans to challenge racism and oppression. Du Bois (1903) demonstrated that "the Black men and women who fought to reconstruct the South were more than servants and cotton pickers" (p. 7). According to historian Robin D. G. Kelley (1994) "they were Negroes with a capital N, they belonged to families and churches and they brought with them a powerful millenarian vision of fairness and equality" (p. 47). Du Bois' work corrected the historical and sociological record that had portrayed African Americans as passive victims.

But Du Bois himself was an activist as well as a scholar. He believed that "knowledge based on scientific investigation" and "carefully gathered scientific proof" would demonstrate and ensure that "neither color nor race determined the limits of a man's capacity or desert" (quoted in Levering 1993:160). Even armed with the best science, however, Du Bois understood that organized political power was necessary to change society. He used his research to inform struggles against segregation and racism, and used his academic posts to improve educational resources at black colleges. In 1909, Du Bois founded the National Association for the Advancement of Colored People (NAACP), and through his editorship of its magazine, *The Crisis*, helped inform, educate, and organize the nation's earliest civil right movement.

World War II, the Cold War, and McCarthyism quieted some of the academy's more progressive teachers and scholars (Schrecker 2002). The period encouraged scholars to be less critical and more committed to patriotism, imperialism, and corporate capitalism. Sociology, in particular, became a conservative discipline whose major practitioners looked to government and corporate grants to conduct research. The result was "knowledge" that often legitimized or apologized for domestic inequality, global militarism, and the rise of what Senator J. William Fulbright (1970) called the **military-industrial-academic complex.** This institutional and ideological triumvirate preached conformity and threatened academic freedoms of speech and inquiry. Although applied sociology remained popular, much of it was linked to research for government defense projects and private industry.

In response, sociologists like Betty and Alfred McClung Lee formed the Society for the Study of Social Problems (SSSP), an alternative professional organization that challenged the rising conservatism and rigid hierarchy of the major sociology group, the ASA. The SSSP would be more activist oriented in support of faculty who criticized conservative trends, corporate interests, and U.S. policies at home and abroad. The group's stated objective was to "promote and protect sociological research and teaching on significant problems of social life and . . . to foster higher quality of life, social welfare, and positive social relations in society."[1] In other words, the SSSP started with social critique as its goal, not currying favor with government, industry, or grant makers.

---

[1]See the Society for the Study of Social Problems website at http://sssp1.org/.

The civil rights movement, as well as other **social movements** in the 1950s and 1960s, inspired new attempts to develop a sociology that could analyze social problems and foster fundamental social change. Asking questions like, "knowledge for whom?" and "knowledge for what purpose?" a group of sociologists formed the Sociology Liberation Movement (SLM) in 1968. On the one hand, the SLM criticized their profession for not speaking out against oppression. They blamed their colleagues for "letting the development of our field be guided by the needs of those who can pay for our time. . . . In the name of value-neutrality, we have failed [to help] the poor, the powerless, or the unorganized" (Brown 1991:44; Feagin and Vera 2008).

On the other hand, more and more sociology students *and* faculty around the country were finding that their intellectual and scholarly interests could be deeply impacted by their **civic engagement**—especially their involvement in social movements. C. Wright Mills's work had inspired Tom Hayden and other Students for a Democratic Society (SDS) to speak out against the Vietnam War and segregation in the South. But these student activists' experiences in political organizing led them to critique Mills, too. Future SDS officer (and sociology professor) Robert J. S. Ross (1991) wrote in his honors thesis, "Mills did neglect the potential of organizing power from below the heights of the elite. . . . Social movements can (and do) generate power; some elections do (and more can) have importance" (p. 198).

Young people from the Student Nonviolent Coordinating Committee (SNCC) had similar experiences in integrating their civic engagement in the grassroots politics with the theoretical or academic work they learned in class. Students conducted sit-ins at segregated lunch counters and marched through the streets to protest police brutality. For student activist Chuck McDew (1966), these actions "offered students a chance for the word to become flesh . . . [and] promoted a challenging philosophy—the philosophy of love overcoming hate, of nonviolence conquering violence, of offering oneself as a sacrifice for a valuable cause" (p. 57). For Bob Zellner, sociology major at Huntingdon College in Montgomery, Alabama, it was a sociology class assignment that gave him the idea to interview Martin Luther King Jr. at the nearby Dexter Avenue Baptist Church. Zellner eventually became one of the first *white* leaders within SNCC.

University of California Sociology Professor Emeritus Hardy Frye has written that his "political consciousness" as a SNCC activist also influenced his academic studies. As an undergraduate at Sacramento State College in California, Frye worked as a community organizer. In response to complaints of police brutality, he helped create a "community alert patrol" in black neighborhoods to monitor police behavior toward black youth. Eventually, the group formed a coalition with other community residents called the Oak Park Service and Action Committee. The group addressed community grievances, acting as a liaison to the school board and the police department. According to Frye (1991), his community work "allowed me to better understand the issues under sociological scrutiny in class, and that in turn gave me a deeper insight into the problems we faced in our attempts to organize the community" (p. 183).

More recently, sociologists have been inspired by global innovations in something called **participatory action research (PAR).** Russell Schutt (2003) defines PAR as "a type of research in which the researcher involves some organizational members as active participants throughout the process of studying an organization; the goal is making changes in the organization" (p. 420). William F. Whyte (1989), one of PAR's initial advocates, was inspired by Industrial Democracy Projects in Norway. Norwegian shippers and their unionized crews had worked successfully with scholars from the Norwegian Work Research Institute to compete more effectively with foreign companies while simultaneously improving working conditions.

Whyte himself worked with Cornell University's Industrial and Labor Relations Program in a project that developed a Cost Study Team (CST) at Xerox Corporation. The CST, composed of six workers and two managers working full time (on regular wages and salaries), spent up to 6 months with Cornell researchers preparing a report to address the company's declining market share and threats of mass layoffs. "The payoffs," according to Whyte (1989), "were spectacular." CSTs documented cost savings that kept management from outsourcing jobs at the same time that the company was able to reduce costs and increase market share.

Other sociologists have been influenced by activist researchers in third-world countries. These researchers experimented with new forms of community-based development designed to help indigenous communities conduct projects on their own terms. Such efforts, according to sociologist Peter Park (Park, Brydon-Miller, Hall, and Jackson 1993), put "research capabilities in the hands of the deprived and disenfranchised people so that they can transform their lives for themselves" (p. 17). In these cases, PAR is not just organizationally based, but community based; the goals are not just group change, but large-scale social change. "Gradually," says Randy Stoecker (1996), "this philosophy of 'participatory research' made its way to the developed world through sociologists and other academics attempting to link their academic skills with grassroots social change efforts" (p. 5). For example, Stoecker cites the involvement of sociologists like John Gaventa and others from the Highlander Center, a grassroots organizing and education center in Tennessee. Highlander organized educational programs for the civil rights movement and, more recently, directed a land ownership study in Appalachia that exposed how mining companies damaged local communities (Appalachian Landownership Task Force 1983; Stoecker 2005).

The Highlander Center was founded in 1932 to serve as an adult education center for community workers involved in social and economic justice movements. The goal of Highlander was and is to provide education and support to poor and working people fighting economic injustice, poverty, prejudice, and environmental destruction. The center helps grassroots leaders create the tools for building broad-based movements for change. The founding principle and guiding philosophy of Highlander is that the answers to the problems facing society lie in the experiences of ordinary people. Those experiences, so often belittled and denigrated in our society, are the keys to grassroots power.

Participatory action research and community-based research are only the latest efforts to practice a sociology engaged with the problems of the world. These approaches to "doing sociology" have tried to formalize how sociologists conduct research that embraces social problems as well as the people who are victimized by them. But until recently, few people have been able to formalize any particular method for *teaching and learning* in the same way. What Jane Addams did at Hull House in the 1900s and what students involved in social movements were doing in city streets and Southern hamlets during the 1960s had yet to result in a pedagogical movement. The growth of service learning, however, has had the potential to reshape how we teach, how we learn, as well as how we *do* sociology.

## THE PROMISE OF SERVICE LEARNING

Although a relatively young field, service learning has yielded many definitions. For our purposes, a good working definition comes from two of the field's most prolific chroniclers, Janet Eyler and Dwight Giles (1999). They explain,

> Service-learning is a form of **experiential education** where learning occurs through a cycle of action and reflection as students work with others through a process of applying what they are learning to community problems and, at the same time, reflecting upon their experiences as they seek to achieve real objectives for the community and deeper understanding and skills for themselves. (p. 3, emphasis added)

In other words, service learning encourages students and faculty to learn about social problems while engaged in activities that might help to ameliorate them. Along with this definition is a set of criteria that most service learning advocates would agree comprise the field's best practices. These elements include "relevant and meaningful service within the community, enhanced academic learning, and purposeful civic learning" (Saltmarsh, Giles, Ward, and Buglione 2009:26).

Service learning comes out of a tradition of experience-based education where teachers developed curriculum around a variety of types of field work. John Dewey, an American philosopher of education, argued that such experiences enriched course content and outcomes because "genuine learning . . . occurs when human beings focus their attention, energies and abilities on solving genuine dilemmas and perplexities—and when they reflect on their experiences and therefore, increase their capacity for future intelligent thought and action" (quoted in Harkavy and Benson 1998:12). Inspired by his own experience working with Jane Addams at Hull House, Dewey believed that guided experiences and proper reflection created a "habit of mind" that gave students the best tools to become thoughtful and engaged democratic citizens. Such experiential approaches can be found in a variety of teaching and research methodologies such as participatory and action research, community-based learning and research, and so forth. All of these teaching and research methods embrace what practitioners would call "civic engagement."

Service learning should not, however, be perceived as a panacea for solving the controversies and problems that plague today's colleges and universities. Many effective critiques have taken practitioners to task for everything from "watering down the rigor of traditional curriculum" to exploiting local communities for the benefit of student learning. But few of these critiques suggest service learning is so problematic that it should be cast aside as a pedagogical pariah. If projects are designed with proper concern for academic sophistication and community reciprocity, service learning has proven to be an effective mechanism for integrating intellectual inquiry with civic engagement and social action (Giles 1994; Hesser 1995).

As such, service learning is a "natural" for teaching social problems, especially from a sociological perspective. Service learning facilitates the teaching of sociology's theoretical emphasis on themes of structure and agency by promoting a "praxis-based" curriculum. By *praxis,* we mean that students combine academic work with practical community service by learning about the history and politics of particular social problems in the classroom and then participating in efforts to address those problems in the community. Such pedagogical strategies also return sociology to its historical roots as a discipline whose study of society is integrally linked to the goals of applying knowledge to intervene in social problems.

As we will see in the many case studies that follow, a curriculum based in service learning or civic engagement breaks down those dichotomies of classroom and community even more by recognizing that theory, history, and politics can also be learned in the field. The project of sociological inquiry as framed by service learning

---

John Reiff presents five core elements to good service learning.

1. *Preparation*—not only do faculty need to identify goals, but students should learn about the community they enter and about the work in which they will engage.

2. *Action*—is there reciprocity for community and is their voice included in designing service?

3. *Reflection*—faculty and students should understand action and reflection as a recursive cycle and an ongoing conversation.

4. *Evaluation*—while goals should be set initially and assessed throughout, new issues and goals emerge as well.

   Evaluation should be comprehensive and all players should have a role and a stake.

5. *Celebration and Acknowledgement*—all projects should offer all participants an opportunity to recognize their growth and engagement.

*Source:* John Reiff, Director, Office of Community Service Learning, Commonwealth College, University of Massachusetts Amherst, and former scholar-in-residence for the Massachusetts Campus Compact.

or civic engagement argues that what James Ostrow (1999) has called a "sociological habit of mind" necessitates an integrated experience. A sociological habit of mind begins by integrating Dewey's "habit of mind" with Mills's "sociological imagination." It then goes beyond just an analytical thought process about the world, to promoting a *critical engagement* with the world's social problems. By an "integrated experience," we mean those community-based encounters that give students firsthand knowledge of both the critical issues to be analyzed sociologically and the social action possibilities to be engaged in critically.

Finally, using service learning and civic engagement to teach social problems fulfills "the promise" that C. Wright Mills wrote so eloquently about almost half a century ago. Mills (1959) declared,

> The moral and intellectual promise of the social sciences is that freedom and reason will remain cherished values, that they will be used seriously and consistently and imaginatively in the formulation of problems. . . . Freedom is, first of all, the chance to formulate the available choices, to argue over them—and then the opportunity to choose. That is why freedom cannot exist without the enlarged role of human reason in human affairs. Within the individual's biography and within society's history, the social task of reason is to formulate choices, to enlarge the scope of human decisions in the making of history. (p. 174)

## GOALS, ORGANIZATION, AND HOW TO USE THIS BOOK

The goal of this book is to present information and analytical frameworks for both understanding social problems and taking action to address them. Thus, each chapter describes and defines particular sets of social problems ranging from economic inequality and identity-based discrimination, to the degradation of institutions such as schools and families, to the failings of systems such as criminal justice and health care, to the destruction of our most vital natural resources and environments. We convey these things primarily through the presentation of case studies. These cases include examples where students have:

- performed service learning assignments or become civically engaged with campus and community groups;

- worked with faculty conducting community-based research projects;

- worked with organizations using the tools of social science research to improve the living and working conditions of citizens.

We believe these examples represent both sociology and service learning at their best.

Each chapter begins with an overview of particular problems including some statistical portraits of related issues. Next, we present some theoretical approaches to understanding the problems from varying perspectives. It should be noted that we don't include the same theoretical approaches in every chapter as we believe some are more suited to particular problems than others. While we do want to depict the range of analyses and possible interventions that different theories offer, we don't think it necessary to present each approach regardless of its efficacy in different situations.

Finally, we present a variety of case studies that demonstrate how theoretical approaches and descriptions of social problems can be understood and acted on by students in service learning and civic engagement projects. Each case study is followed by some basic questions about it, but also a question or two that ask students to relate particular cases to their own experiences. We also include a variety of "voices from the field" where we (or others) have interviewed faculty, students, and community activists whose work integrates intellectual analysis and practical applications. We conclude each chapter with questions that summarize approaches to understanding problems as well as various ways of addressing problems. We also have a glossary of important terms and a list of websites and organizations that students can examine to either get involved themselves or view how others are addressing social problems.

In the end, this book may be best suited for classes where students are engaging in some form of service learning for themselves. However, we believe the cases here are rich enough to stand on their own, and students can engage with both analytical and practical materials without necessarily being "in the streets" themselves. While we are strong advocates of rigorous and integrated community-based learning, we realize that such pedagogy is not for everyone. This book's own presentation of such engagements should provide enough practical examples to be effective.

## SUMMARY QUESTIONS

1. How do sociologists define social problems?

2. What is applied sociology and what are the goals of its advocates?

3. How does applied sociology differ from formal sociology?

4. What is participatory action research (PAR)?

5. Discuss the advantages of service learning for understanding and addressing social problems.

## GLOSSARY

**Applied Sociology:** Employing sociological tools, devices, methods, findings, techniques, principles, insights, concepts, and so on to analyze and impact practical problems and situations.

**Civic Engagement:** Ways in which people work with their communities and larger social groupings to participate in the cultural and political lifeblood of their fellow men and women.

**Classes:** From a Marxist perspective, class reflects an individual or group relation to the ownership of the means of production (i.e., lord/serf, capitalist/proletariat), but for other sociologists, class also relates to a hierarchy of social and cultural indicators such as education credentials, family lineage, and so forth.

**Experiential Education:** As formulated by John Dewey, students were encouraged to learn through guided engagements with and reflections of lived world reality and the problems of the human condition.

**Hull House:** Founded by Jane Addams and Ellen Gates Starr on the Near West Side of Chicago, its innovative programs for immigrants and the poor made it the most famous Settlement House in the United States. Many of America's early Chicago School Sociologists (and other educators such as John Dewey) volunteered at Hull House and used it as a kind of laboratory for social science research.

**Military-Industrial-Academic Complex:** Originally referring to the interlocking interests and elites who simultaneously governed and benefitted from collaborations among government, corporate, and military elites. J. William Fulbright, noting the increasing role of researchers and other knowledge producers, coined the term.

**Participatory Action Research (PAR):** Research that involves all relevant parties in actively examining current problems in order to change them. PAR advocates reflect critically on the historical, political, cultural, economic, geographic, and other contexts in order to understand problems and to act successfully to address them.

**Personal Troubles:** These are concerns experienced by individuals within a society. They rarely reflect problems in the overall social structure or ideology of a society, instead reflecting individual idiosyncrasies.

**Public Issues:** These are concerns that are experienced by many in a society and often relate to structural problems such as inequality.

Service Learning: A pedagogy of active participation in service that is coordinated with classroom content to simultaneously improve students' critical engagement with course curriculum while fostering civic responsibility and citizenship.

Social Movement: A collective effort aimed at either changing or preserving some aspect of social systems.

Social Problem: Often defined by groups in power or those coming to power, social problems represent the distinction between a society's stated values and its actual behavior and outcomes.

Society: A complex form of social life made up of a matrix of social networks and institutions, each with a division of labor and, often, hierarchy of governance.

Sociology: The use of theory, methods, and concepts to study the relationships between people; the study of human action and collective behavior, institutions, and the ways in which people construct reality.

## WEBSITES FOR INFORMATION AND IDEAS ABOUT SERVICE LEARNING

Campus Activism: http://www.campusactivism.org/

Campus–Community Partnerships for Health: http://www.ccph.info/

Campus Compact: http://www.compact.org/

Community Works Institute: http://vermontcommunityworks.org/

International Association for Research on Service-Learning and Community Engagement: http://www.researchslce.org/

The International Partnership for Service-Learning and Leadership: http://www.ipsl.org/

Learn and Serve America's National Service-Learning Clearinghouse: http://www.servicelearning.org/

National Service-Learning Partnership: http://www.service-learningpartnership.org/

National Society for Experiential Education: http://www.nsee.org/

National Youth Leadership Council: http://www.nylc.org/

Student Activism: http://studentactivism.net/

# REFERENCES

Addams, Jane. 1910. *Twenty Years at Hull House*. New York: New American Library.

Appalachian Landownership Task Force. 1983. *Who Owns Appalachia: Landownership and Its Impact*. Lexington, KY: University of Kentucky Press.

Becker, Ernst. 1968. *The Structure of Evil*. New York: The Free Press.

Black, Timothy. 2004. "Humanist Sociology in the Wake of Al Lee." *Humanity and Society,* 27.

Blumer, Herbert. 1971. "Social Problems as Collective Behavior." *Social Problems,* 18:298–306.

Brown, Carol. 1991. "The Early Years of the Social Liberation Movement." Pp. 43–54 in *Radical Sociologists and the Movement: Experiences, Lessons, and Legacies,* edited by Martin Oppenheimer, Martin J. Murray, and Rhonda F. Levine. Philadelphia, PA: Temple University Press.

Campbell, Richard and Jimmie L. Reeves. 1999. "Covering the Homelessness: The Joyce Brown Story." Pp. 23–44 in *Reading the Homeless: The Media's Image of Homeless Culture,* edited by Eungjun Min, Westport, CT: Praeger.

Deegan, Mary Jo. 1988. *Jane Addams and the Men of the Chicago School, 1892–1918.* New Brunswick, NJ: Transaction.

Doane, Ashley and Eduardo Bonilla-Silva. 2003. White Out: The Continuing Significance of Racism. New York: Routledge.

Dolgon, Corey. 1998. "Rising From the Ashes: The Michigan Memorial Phoenix Project and the Corporatization of University Research." *Educational Studies,* 23:5–31.

_____. 1999. "Ann Arbor—The Cutting Edge of Discipline: Postfordism, Postmodernism, and the New Bourgeoisie." *Antipode,* 31:129–162.

Dolgon, Corey, with Michael Kline and Laura Dresser 1995. "'House People, Not Cars!' Economic Development, Political Struggle, and Common Sense in a City of Intellect." Pp. 1–36 in *Marginal Spaces: Comparative Urban and Community Research,* edited by Michael P. Smith. New Brunswick, NJ: Transaction Publishers.

Dolgon, Corey, with Michael Kline and Laura Dresser. 2000. "The Politics of Empowerment: Homelessness, Development, and Resistance in Ann Arbor, Michigan." *Journal of Community Practice,* 8:23–38.

Du Bois, W. E. B. 1903. The Souls of Black Folk. Chicago: A.C. McClurg.

_____. [1935]1998. Black Reconstruction in America 1860-1880. New York: The Free Press.

_____. 1999. The Souls of Black Folk: Authoritative Text, Contexts, Criticism (Edited by Henry Louis Gates). New York: Norton.

Durkheim, Émile. 1947. *The Division of Labor in Society*. Glencoe, IL: The Free Press.

_____. 1961. *Moral Education: A Study in the Theory and Application of the Sociology of Education*. Glencoe, IL: The Free Press.

Espada, Martin. 1993. *City of Coughing and Dead Radiators*. New York: Norton.

Eyler, Janet and Dwight E. Giles. 1999. *Where's the Learning in Service Learning?* San Francisco, CA: Jossey-Bass.

Feagin, Joe and Hernan Vera. 1995. *White Racism*. New York: Routledge.

_____. 2008. *Liberation Sociology.* 2nd ed. Boulder, CO: Paradigm Publishers.

Frye, Hardy T. 1991. "Living and Learning Sociology: The Unorthodox Way." Pp. 114–126 in *Radical Sociologists and the Movement: Experiences, Lessons, and Legacies,* edited by Martin Oppenheimer, Martin J. Murray, and Rhonda F. Levine. Philadelphia, PA: Temple University Press.

Fulbright, J. William. 1970. "The War and Its Effects: The Military-Industrial-Academic Complex." Pp. 171–178 in *Super-State: Readings in the Military-Industrial Complex,* edited by Herbert I. Schiller and Joseph D. Phillips. Urbana, IL: University of Chicago.

Fuller, Richard. 1938. "The Problem of Teaching Social Problems." *American Journal of Sociology,* 44:415–435.

Giles, Dwight E. 1994. "The Impact of a College Service Laboratory on Student's Personal, Social and Cognitive Outcomes." *Journal of Adolescence,* 17:327–339.

Gramsci, Antonio. 1971. *The Prison Notebooks.* New York: International Publishers.

Harkavy, Ira and Lee Benson. 1998. "De-Platonizing and Democratizing Education as the Bases of Service Learning." *New Directions for Teaching and Learning,* 73:11–19.

Hesser, Gary. 1995. "Faculty Assessment of Student Learning: Outcomes Attributed to Service Learning and Evidence of Changes in Faculty Attitudes About Experiential Education." *Michigan Journal of Community Service-Learning,* 2:33–42.

Kelley, Robin D. G. 1994. *Race Rebels: Culture, Politics, and the Black Working Class.* New York: The Free Press.

King, Martin Luther Jr. 1963. "Letter From Birmingham Jail." Martin Luther King, Jr. Research and Education Institute, Stanford University. Retrieved February 19, 2010 (http://www.stanford.edu/group/King/liberation_curriculum/pdfs/letterfrombirmingham_wwcw.pdf).

Levering, David. 1993. *Biography of a Race, 1868-1919.* New York: Henry Holt.

Marx, Karl. 1933. "The Class Struggles in France, 1848-1850." Pp. 401–432 in *Karl Marx: Selected Works, Volume 2,* edited by V. V. Adoratsky. New York: International Publishers.

———. 1972. "The Economic and Philosophic Manuscripts of 1844: Selections." Pp. 66–125 in *The Marx-Engels Reader,* edited by Robert Tucker. New York: Norton.

Marx, Karl and Friedrich Engels. 1955. *The Communist Manifesto.* New York: Meredith Corporation.

McDew, Chuck. 1966. "Spiritual and Moral Aspects of the Student Nonviolent Struggle in the South." Pp. 258–270 in *The New Student Left*, edited by Mitchell Cohen and Dennis Hale. Boston, MA: Beacon Press.

Merton, Robert, and Robert Nisbet. 1966. "Social Problems and Sociological Theory." Pp. 775–823 in *Contemporary Social Problems,* edited by Robert Merton. New York: Harcourt, Brace & World.

Mills, C. Wright. 1959. *The Sociological Imagination.* New York: Oxford University Press.

Moland, John, Jr. 1996. "Social Change, Social Inequality, and Intergroup Tensions." *Social Forces,* 75:403–421.

Ostrow, James. 1999. "Service-Learning and the Teachability of Sociology." Pp. 21–32 in *Cultivating the Sociological Imagination: Concepts and Models for Service-Learning in Sociology,* edited by James Ostrow, Garry Hesser, and Sandra Enos. Washington, DC: American Association for Higher Education & Accreditation.

Park, Peter, Mary Brydon-Miller, Budd Hall, and Ted Jackson, eds. 1991. *Voices of Change: Participatory Research in the United States and Canada.* Westport, CT: Bergin & Garvey.

Riis, Jacob. 1890. *How the Other Half Lives:* Studies Among the Tenements of New York. New York: Scribner.

Ross, Robert J. S. 1991. "At the Center and the Edge: Notes on a Life in and Out of Sociology and the New Left." Pp. 197–215 in *Radical Sociologists and the Movement: Experiences, Lessons and Legacies,* edited by Martin Oppenheimer, Martin J. Murray, and Rhonda F. Levine. Philadelphia, PA: Temple University Press.

Saltmarsh, John, Dwight E. Giles, Elaine Ward, and Suzanne Buglione. 2009. "Rewarding Community-Engaged Scholarship." *New Directions for Higher Education,* 2009:25–35. New York: Periodicals, Inc.

Schrecker, Ellen W. 2002. *The Age of McCarthyism: A Brief History With Documents*, 2nd ed. New York: Bedford/St. Martin's.

Schutt, Russell. 2003. *Investigating the Social World: The Process and Practice of Research*. Thousand Oaks, CA: Pine Forge Press.

Scimecca, Joseph and Glenn Goodwin. 2003. "Jane Addams: The First Humanist Sociologist." *Humanity and Society,* 27:143–157.

Stoecker, Randy. 1996. "Sociology and Social Action." *Sociological Imagination,* 33:91–93

____. 2005. *Research Methods for Community Change*. Thousand Oaks, CA: Sage.

Straus, Roger. 2002. "Using What? The History and Nature of Sociology." Pp. 3–20 in *Using Sociology: An Introduction to the Applied and Clinical Perspectives,* 3rd ed., edited by Roger Straus. Lanham, MD: Rowman & Littlefield.

Ward, Lester. 1906. *Applied Sociology: A Treatise on the Conscious Improvement of Society by Society*. Boston, MA: Ginn and Company.

Whyte, William F. 1989. "Advancing Scientific Knowledge Through Participatory Action Research." *Sociological Forum,* 4:367–385.

# Do We Make the World or Does the World Make Us?

*Concepts and Theories*

*The social world as we know it and have known it is mostly an illusion. Yet, if we were all completely deluded, there would be no point in trying to investigate and explain, and this writing, as well as any other, would be worthless. The existence of illusions is not incompatible with the existence of facts and of the principles of logic. But facts and logic are inextricably mixed with concepts and theories, and in the study of society the concepts and theories involved are the ones that we daily act upon as well as use to explain how things are and why. . . . As was once said of philosophy, sociology is like rebuilding a boat, plank by plank, while floating on it in the middle of the ocean.*

—Randall Collins, *The Discovery of Society*
(Collins and Makowsky 1998)

Graduate students in a communications course at California State University, Sacramento (Perkins, Kidd, and Smith 1999), were asked to participate in a local service organization and provide a qualitative analysis of the organization. The course, Assessing Communications in Organizations, integrated classroom readings on theory and applied field research with students' actual experiences in the community. Students worked with groups ranging from women's homeless and domestic violence shelters to a teen conference sponsored by the Camp Fire Boys and Girls. Students also compiled annotated bibliographies on the particular social issues that the organizations addressed.

According to the faculty, students benefited from the service learning framework by gaining an increased awareness of and a direct exposure to particular social problems. One student worked at a domestic violence shelter that used "creative arts" to help women both as therapy and as a form of self-empowerment. This student decided to actually take the arts courses as well as provide services for the shelter. She wrote of her experiences, "I personally benefited by feeling the expansion of and power of my own creativity" (Perkins et al. 1999:40). But her strongest reflections concerned who the women in the program were and what actual conditions *they* faced. She explains,

> My research has taught me that they are usually subject to harsh and stereotypical judgments. While I do not think I judged them harshly, I had no idea I would find the women thoughtful, articulate, and friendly. The women I met have been working very hard on themselves to improve their lives and it shows. (p. 41)

Eventually, this student was asked to join the organization's board of directors and continued to participate and serve in integral ways.

Another student who worked at a shelter for homeless women experienced a similar integrated engagement with both the individuals who needed services and the social conditions that created their need. She remembered "driving home upset and distraught . . . horrified and repulsed at the levels of social and economic deprivation that I was witnessing" (Perkins et al. 1999:41). She continued,

> I spent a lot of time asking myself why I had been so blissfully unaware of these problems previously. In the end, I realized that these experiences were necessary. Talking to the women and hearing their stories has raised my awareness in a way that would be impossible to experience without having served them. (p. 41)

According to these students' teachers, "they challenged their preconceived notions by engaging in self-reflection and ultimately experienced personal growth as a result of their service-learning activities" (p. 41). By doing so, students changed their own perceptions of society at the same time that they acted to change society itself.

*Society* is socially constructed. As Randall Collins suggests in the opening quotation, when we talk about society, we may be referring to an *illusion* of sorts. Unlike some natural sciences, sociologists cannot literally dissect society under a microscope or measure it in a beaker. Society is really a narrative device we use to represent a large number of people who share enough values, behaviors, languages, and material things to consider them as a group. Studying society is not exactly the same as examining a cell under a microscope or the interaction between two chemical compounds. But the people do exist. Their activities can be observed. What they think can be documented. They live in families and prepare meals; build schools and churches; elect, obey, or protest governments; and work in myriad ways to produce what they need to survive. Émile Durkheim (1982) called these phenomena **social facts.** Society may be a social construction, even an illusion, but that does not mean it isn't real.

In many ways, we make the world. Like the boat that Collins refers to, each day we rebuild society, sometimes plank by plank. Part of the sociologist's job is to examine closely how we go about making and remaking society. In contemporary sociological lingo, we call the human activity of making the world **agency.** Sociologists define agency as the ability to change the institutions in which [people] live."[1] We might expand that to include all social relationships both *macro* or large (economies and governments) as well as *micro* or small (personal intimacies, relationships, and encounters). The ways in which we control and change our interactions with institutional structures and other people represent our agency. For the two California State students, getting involved with attempts to solve social problems not only changed their own understandings of the problems and themselves, but also helped to change the conditions creating the problems.

But the world surely makes us, too. We are born into a world where both macro and micro systems have already determined what language we learn, what foods we might eat, and what belief systems we adopt. The economic and social class systems and our position within them are already in place by the time we arrive. Sociologists refer to these material and cultural conditions as the **social structure.** Despite our best intentions and strongest will, where we are born, what socioeconomic class we occupy, and what values and ideas are discussed by the people around us heavily shape who we are and what we become. As Karl Marx (Marx and Engels 1955) wrote, people "make their own history, but they do not make it just as they please; they do not make it under circumstances chosen by themselves, but under circumstances directly found, given and transmitted from the past" (p. 1).

Sociologists develop concepts and theories as tools to help examine social structure, human agency, and their impact on one another. This dynamic of structure and agency is crucial for understanding both the origin of social problems and the possibilities of acting in the world to change them. To better grasp how sociologists approach society, we should take a closer look at the most basic and popular tools they use. After looking at particular concepts, each major theoretical approach will be followed by a service learning case study that illuminates how one might apply such concepts and theories to practice.

## SOCIAL CONCEPTS

Sociologists use a number of concepts to help them understand and engage with society. On a structural level, **institutions** are one of the most important concepts for students to comprehend. While definitions vary somewhat, most sociologists would agree that institutions represent *patterns of behavior that become formalized as structural or cultural entities.* Groups and collective phenomena such as family, church, schools, legislatures,

---

[1] T. R. Young, *The Red Feather Dictionary of Critical Social Science* (http://uwacadweb.uwyo.edu/red_feather/).
T. R. was a prolific writer whose website is a vital resource for students, teachers, and researchers alike.

hospitals, and prisons can all be described as social institutions. Gordon Marshall (1998) refers to institutions as "super-customs," which are "sets of mores, folkways, and patterns of behavior" that address major social interests. These include people's practices as institutions, not just the structural unit or physical place. Thus, religion, law, and education can also be thought of as general institutions, regardless of any specific church, court, or school.

Sociologists agree that institutions establish a structural or cultural setting wherein people learn and act out the values and norms of a given society. By **values,** we generally mean those *strong, seemingly permanent dispositions shared by groups of people*. Values represent what societies define as good and bad, right and wrong, beautiful and ugly, smart or stupid, and so forth. Sometimes values are openly celebrated and promoted. Other times they are underlying and so ingrained that we don't even recognize their taken-for-granted status as part of our culture. Similarly, **norms** are *shared expectations of behavior*—what people consider to be doing the right thing. Thus, values and norms are intimately related, as norms require and reflect some sense of a culture's values. Yet, as we will see when we examine labeling theory, for example, sometimes expected behaviors are stigmatized, thus representing negative, not positive values. In either case, institutions help reproduce and enforce both social values and social norms.

Institutions can, however, represent or become sites where people contest various cultural values and social norms. Marriage and family remain strong institutions in the United States and, as progenitors of traditions, they often reflect the culture's more conservative values. Yet, even within these institutions, groups struggle to redefine values and norms. Gay male and lesbian marriages or civil unions; single-parent families; and interracial, interethnic, and even interreligious marriages all challenge more traditional sets of institutional values and norms that come from families or churches. In fact, institutions often become the sites where social problems that have been hidden or obscured seem to burst onto the scene. Implicit or latent conflicts and tensions over values and norms eventually break through the seemingly stable sense of shared actions and beliefs.

The family, for example, despite its image as an institution of traditional customs, cooperation, and socialization, has always been a site of conflict. According to historian Linda Gordon (2002), family members have traditionally used violence as a method for controlling conflicts. The rise of *domestic violence as a social problem* tells the story of changing politics and culture (values and norms), not the sudden appearance of physical force employed by fathers and mothers, and husbands and wives. She explains,

> [F]amily violence has been historically and politically constructed. . . . First, the very definition of what constitutes unacceptable domestic violence . . . developed and then varied according to political moods and the force of certain political movements. Second, violence among family members arises from family conflicts which are historically influenced but political in themselves, in the sense of that word as having to do with power relations. (p. 18)

The institution of the family and marriage represent, for many, sacred values and power-ful normative expectations. But the values and norms associated with these practices change over time.

## Values, Norms, and Institutions in Action: Abby's House

At Worcester State College in Massachusetts, some students have participated in service learn-ing projects at Abby's House, a domestic violence shelter for women and their children. Domestic violence or battered women's shelters (sometimes known as Safe Houses) started to appear in the mid-1970s, "not because of an increase in [domestic violence's] frequency or because the public has become more concerned, but because a social movement developed in the 1970s to help battered women" (Rafferty 2001:1). This movement was itself an outgrowth of the 1960s and 1970s women's movement that challenged traditional cultural values and norms (such as wives' subservience to husbands) and legal rights (such as wives' inability to sue husbands for violence and rape). Abby's House was founded in 1976, as "one of the first overnight emergency shelters for women with or with-out children in the U.S." (Rafferty 2001:1).

Here, students met and worked with women who made difficult choices based on conflicting values about caring for their children's (and their own) health and safety. Most had spent tortured weeks, months, and years experiencing abuse before they left their homes and husbands, with or without their children. Their dilemmas were heightened by traditional norms that taught wives to be def-erent to husbands, and traditional values that celebrate family unity above all outcomes. According to sociologist Sam Marullo (1999), students engaged in service learning projects are uniquely situated not only to learn what values and norms *are,* but also to understand the existence of struggles over what values and norms *should be.* Sociologists' "explicit elaboration of values helps our students with their own values clarification" (p. 897) as they are challenged to take on others' roles, reflect on the social structuring of others' choices, and weigh questions of value conflicts and social justice.

**Image 1.1**   Photo of Abby's House dining hall and cafeteria.

*Source:* Copyright © Abby Kelley Foster House, Inc.

According to founder Annette Rafferty (2001), Abby's House exists "to be the comfort, to be the decent place. To help women shape something meaningful from absolutely nothing, to offer resources and much needed understanding" (p. 2). Rafferty believes that students' experiences here challenge their inherited sense of middle-class values. On the one hand, students witnessed the need for women to take action for themselves and their children's safety by leaving violent situations in the home. Cultural and class judgments about women's roles and responsibilities were shaken by the lived reality of these women in crisis. On the other hand, the House's mission is to allow people in crisis to "gain control, to be empowered." Thus, it's crucial for volunteers and staff to be "aware of what [a guest] is capable of doing for herself . . . to do for a person what she is capable of doing is to disempower" (p. 72). Rafferty explains, "Of necessity we make judgments, but judgments are always open to revision. We provide support, back-up. We intervene when appropriate. We share information, resources, and skills" (p. 72). While students learn about the particular issues involved in domestic violence, homelessness, and other things, they also learn the various dimensions of power and how important it is to work collaboratively and collectively. They learn that the process of service involves an awareness of power dynamics and politics, as well as simple kindness and compassion.

At Abby's House, students helped care for children and participated in the daily upkeep of the premises. Some took training courses to help counsel women in abusive relationships. But in working to provide a safe place for women who chose to leave their marriages and "break up" their families in order to protect their children and themselves, students grappled with the definitions of values, norms, and institutions. They not only encountered how social problems evolve from conflicts within institutions, but they also experienced how organizations and new kinds of institutions evolve to impact changes in values, norms, and institutions themselves.

## MEDIA BOX: SOCIOLOGISTS ON THE BIG SCREEN

Unless you are watching some sort of talking heads documentary, you don't see sociologists in films very often. According to John Conklin (2009), his study of 32 Hollywood films released between 1915 and 2006 "shows that sociology is often portrayed as a discipline that focuses on the useless, the trivial, and the obscure. Undergraduate students of sociology are sometimes presented as academically untalented and weakly motivated, but at other times as thoughtful and capable of good work. Graduate students are depicted as flawed researchers who are more interested in romance than the completion of their degrees. . . . Sociologists occasionally appear in brief classroom scenes that contain little of substance" (p. 199). Typical examples of this perspective appear in films such as *R.P.M.* (Revolutions per Minute) (1970), where a drunken and despondent sociology professor asks his graduate student what her field of study is. She answers, "Sociology," and he replies, "Sociology. What the hell good is that? You should have chosen something relevant, like auto mechanics." Another college senior in *The One and Only* (1978) asks her boyfriend, "So I have this degree in sociology and, um, well, what'll I do with it?" He answers, "Open a sociology store" (p. 199).

**Image 1.2**   Sociology grad student Helen Lyle (Virginia Madsen) and the Candyman (Tony Todd) await the spoils of research.

*Source:* © Bureau L.A. Collection/CORBIS.

Our favorites are the horror genre, though, where you often find faculty, in general, as either the progenitors of slasher mania, as in *The Faculty*, or as casual victims in movies like *SAW*. In *Candyman*, a sociology graduate student unwittingly unearths the legend of a serial killer—a dead artist who now kills urban youth with a hook. But she ends up getting framed as the killer herself. She dies along with the Candyman killer in a climactic funeral pyre. Beware of the revenge of the sociology professors!

## SOCIAL THEORIES

Social theories are analytical frameworks that help us interpret the meaning of social life and determine how and why the world works the way it does. For example, we may look at data on increasing poverty rates in the United States, but they don't explain what causes them to increase or why we have poverty to begin with. Theories give us a systematic way to create a story (hopefully nonfiction) using data and research to explain the social world around us. It is important to note that no theory is perfect or explains everything, and that most sociologists use different theories to address different aspects of examining the world around them.

Sociologists have long divided their discipline into three major *paradigms* (or ways of thinking) about society: *functionalism, conflict sociology,* and *symbolic interactionism*. These are not the only theoretical approaches, nor are they mutually exclusive. Again, most sociologists recognize that different theories can be integrated or combined to analyze a particular social problem or phenomenon more effectively. By separating them here, we hope to offer a clearer explanation of these approaches and how they differ from one another. Students should feel free to explore all manner of mixing and matching these ideas to best grapple with the social world.

## Functionalism

Inspired by the early works of Comte, the later works of Durkheim, and the more recent works of Talcott Parsons and Robert Merton, **functionalism** *is based on the idea that society is an increasingly complex organism that must fulfill certain basic functions to continue its survival.* These functions include the economic, political, and social realms of the social world and are experienced by people primarily through institutions (Merton 1978), as described below.

- *Economic*—sometimes called the *adaptive* function because it represents how a society adapts to its physical environment and produces its survival. All societies have an "economy," and they must be able to make and distribute the food, clothing, and shelter necessary to keep people alive and healthy. Historically, societies have moved from hunting and gathering to agricultural to industrial means of economic production. They have also shifted from slave systems to feudal systems to capitalist forms of organizing economic activity.

- *Political*—sometimes called the *goal attainment* function because it represents how societies act collectively and make decisions for the entire group. Societies establish some form of government to make decisions and manage the ongoing integration of various institutions. The forms of government may differ, but every society must have some formal mechanisms for choosing social policies, maintaining social values, and regulating social norms of behavior.

- *Social*—individuals must be socialized into the values and norms of any given society. Functionalists often divide this category into two kinds of socialization. The first—*latent pattern maintenance* functions—relates to *ways that institutions like the family and church pass on their values and norms*. The second—*integrative* functions—entails institutions like schools and courts where the values and norms of a larger society are taught or enforced. Values represent shared ideas of good and bad, right and wrong, beautiful and ugly. Norms represent the shared expectations for behavior that a society would consider appropriate or not. In smaller, homogenous societies, families and churches play the dominant role in socializing young people. In larger, diverse, and more complex societies, schools and the justice system must step in to teach appropriate behaviors or at least enforce compliance (Parsons 1966).

The most important aspect of these functions, especially of the socialization functions, is to create the solidarity necessary for social order to continue. Functionalists often assume solidarity comes naturally from a shared sense of values that emanate from mutual interests in economic competition or success; political unity; and the common set of values produced by family, church, and state. However, functionalists also recognize that solidarity can be created, maintained, or even coerced by social regulation and control.

Functionalism's approach to social problems involves three basic ideas. The first is that of **social dysfunction.** According to Robert Merton (1966), social dysfunction *"refers to a designated set of consequences of a designated pattern of behavior, belief, or organization that interfere with a designated functional requirement of a designated social system"* (p. 780, emphasis added). In other words, while various institutions fulfill the role of meeting a particular set of social needs, actions that interfere with the effort to carry out these essential functions would be dysfunctional. For example, an economic market system that resulted in the poverty and hunger of many could be thought of as dysfunctional given that the job of an economy is to produce and distribute food, clothing, and shelter to everyone.

A second source of social problems (from a functionalist perspective) comes from the **unintended or hidden functions** that institutions produce. Distinguished as *manifest* (overt) and *latent* (covert or hidden), these two types of functions contribute to a system's adaptation to various conditions. Yet latent functions are often unintended and unrecognized. For example, education in the United States serves three overt purposes—teaching students social skills, intellectual skills, and career skills—with the ultimate goal being a democratic society with equal opportunities. Schools not only serve the *integrative* function of providing students with the knowledge and experiences they need, but they also aid in the *adaptive* function by providing increasingly skilled workers for the economy (Merton 1978). Such institutional goals lead politicians and pundits to claim that education produces social mobility and democracy. Yet schools also produce latent functions that further inequality and limit opportunity. As researchers such as Jonathan Kozol (1992), Caroline Hodges Persell (1977), and Stanley Aronowitz (2001) have demonstrated, unequal funding and biased expectations based on race, class, and gender often result in reinforcing discrimination and disadvantages.

Our experiences teaching simultaneously at Worcester State College and at Harvard University demonstrated that students' expectations of college have been almost completely shaped by their class backgrounds. Working- and middle-class students, by and large, want to get direct training for middle-class jobs, while wealthy students expect a broader education that prepares them for professional careers and a culture of leadership (Trumpbour 1989). The latent function of education is to reproduce a stratified society where upper-class students are trained with the knowledge, skills, and expectations to be upper class, and lower-class students with the knowledge, skills, and expectations to be lower class. Social problems arise from the contradictions between the dominant ideological role that education serves (that of democracy and equal opportunity) and the actual structural impact of unequal schools.

Finally, the Chicago School of Sociology coined the term **disorganization** to explain the phenomena of social problems that come about when rapid changes overwhelm people and their institutions. The industrial revolution, urbanization, and massive waves of immigration all radically transformed traditional ways of life. Dirty, overcrowded city streets with poor workers and their families living in unhealthy conditions and struggling for survival resulted in a variety of social problems including poverty, crime, and disease. The social systems and policies necessary to address these problems did not yet exist. William Fielding Ogburn (1950) coined the phrase "cultural lag" to describe this situation where the technological developments of a society have surpassed its moral and legal institutions. Of course, many of the Chicago School Sociologists thought that policy changes could address these problems and became active reformers (Fischer 1975).

## CASE STUDY #1

### Applying Functional Analysis: The Policy Research Action Group

For many poor, urban communities, reinvestment results in displacement. Gentrification, neighborhood beautification, and upscale commercial development often have the unintended consequences of forcing poor people and people of color out of communities in transition. From a functionalist perspective, even a successful market has dysfunctions, and rapid redevelopment can result in a variety of disorganization. In fact, displacing poor people and people of color could be considered one of the latent functions of the capitalist market system as it reinvests in poorer communities.

Thus, in cities around the United States, the story of economic development has also been a story of "urban removal," "white flight," and rising homelessness. Working-class, Chicago neighborhoods were particularly hard hit during the post–World War II period of suburbanization, the post-1970s period of deindustrialization, and the post-1990s cuts in social welfare spending (Herring 1998). Since the early 1990s, the Policy Research Action Group (PRAG) has brought university faculty and students together with community organizations in Chicago to work on research projects developed by neighborhood groups. Many of the projects involve opposing gentrification; preserving racially diverse communities, determining effective strategies for community-led economic development, and studying the impact of the transition from industrial to service employment. The goal of these projects is to make the economic system work in favor of those who already live in the community and not result in the dysfunctions of displacement and disempowerment.

One project in particular has involved Loyola University and the Organization of the Northeast (ONE)—an umbrella association for community-based groups on Chicago's northern lakefront. These are working- and middle-class neighborhoods whose populations are increasingly diverse. Their proximity to downtown, however, marks them as easy targets for gentrification and upscale commercial development. To help fight off these phenomena and respond with a local development plan that is built on the human capital already present in the community, Loyola and ONE embarked on a variety of collaborative research and service projects to strengthen the organizing and policy efforts (Axel-Lute 1999; Nyden, Adams, and Zalent 1997).

The work began with meetings between Professor Phil Nyden from Loyola and Josh Hoyt from ONE who designed a study of race and ethnic relations in three local subsidized apartment buildings. The research, carried out by a graduate sociology class in qualitative methods, included 43 in-depth interviews and a telephone survey. The findings were eventually published as *Racial, Ethnic, and Economic Diversity in Uptown's Subsidized Housing: A Case Study of Its Present Character and Future Possibilities* (Nyden et al. 1990). Some of the findings included the following:

1. Affordable housing provided families with the financial and social foundation upon which to build self-sufficiency.

2. Residents were attracted to the neighborhood's diversity and found it a comfortable place to live because people were tolerant of one another.

3. Community institutions—ranging from churches to community-based groups—increase the interactions among different racial and ethnic groups.

4. Tensions did exist between renters and middle-income homeowners, single adult families and families with children, and African Americans and newly arrived African immigrants.

The collaborative effort led to other long-term research projects that studied youth and diversity, the impact of diversity on local economic development, and the struggle to save affordable housing. Nyden et al. (1997) conclude that these research efforts had three notable impacts: They

provided documentation of the ways in which different racial and ethnic groups were already cooperating and the areas where community organization intervention could improve relations. . . . [They] enhanced the capacity of the community to use research for its own benefit . . . [and they presented] documentation of community organization struggles and the analysis of the effectiveness of these struggles. (p.16)

Other projects emanating from PRAG included Loyola educators working with inner-city schools to develop a science curriculum that incorporated collaborations with community organizations to do soil sampling near a solid waste incinerator. Another collaborative effort provided the groundwork for saving Theresa's, an old blues club, targeted to be an anchor for the creation of a Black Historic District. The overall goal remains to demonstrate that successful economic development can be achieved with the cultural and human capital already present in the community. In addition, hundreds of students every semester conduct internships and fieldwork through PRAG, helping neighborhood development groups, immigrant aid organizations, environmental and land-use agencies, and a host of other locally based service and political action efforts. PRAG's work challenges the latent functions and dysfunctions of economic development and urban revitalization by working with community-based groups to develop knowledge, strategies, and actions that protect the integrity of poor and working-class communities while still trying to improve their conditions. Although rapid economic and demographic changes continue to threaten the stability of these neighborhoods, PRAG has remained a powerful source for organizing and solidarity, as well as student learning and community building.

*(Continued)*

(Continued)

Case Study Questions

1. How did theory help explain the causes of displacement and disempowerment?

2. How did these explanations help inform strategies to address social problems?

3. How did projects challenge the latent functions or dysfunctions of the mainstream market system? Were they successful?

## Symbolic Interaction

Unlike the more macro sociological approaches of functionalism and conflict sociology, symbolic interaction examines the social world from the small-scale perspective of how people interact with one another on an everyday level. The basic element of **symbolic interactionism** *is the individual and his or her own construction of identity that takes place in small groups and organizations.* Larger structures such as institutions are important primarily for the ways in which they shape and condition peoples' interactions. But institutions and structures only exist, according to symbolic interactionists, because people continue to recreate them through ritual activities, conversations, and encounters.

On the symbolic level, the interactionist approach relies on the notion that people participate in patterns of behavior governed by what W. I. Thomas (Thomas and Thomas 1928) called the "definition of a situation." Here, *individuals think and act in coordination with the traditions, customs, values, and beliefs of the social life surrounding them.* For example, people who live in poor communities with few job opportunities and little access to public services tend to vote in smaller numbers than do people in middle-class or wealthy communities who have good schools and clean, safe neighborhoods. People who historically see little improvement in their family's living conditions do not define the democratic procedure of voting as empowering. For African Americans who, until the 1960s, were often prohibited from voting by law, and who have more recently been victimized by efforts to hinder their electoral efforts through intimidation, misinformation, and a variety of other "dirty tricks," voter participation levels remain disproportionately low (Piven and Cloward 1989, 2002). For middle- and upper-class individuals with greater access to politicians and their policies, voting seems to be an opportunity to influence decisions that do affect their lives. Different histories, experiences, and identities impact how people define situations and engage in public activities.

According to another interactionist, George Herbert Mead (1940), these definitions are learned through the process of **socialization.** *Socialization represents the ways in which we internalize cultural values and norms, as well as come to know the social expectations we must* *meet and the roles we must play.* Thus, like functionalism, families, churches, and schools teach people social norms and behaviors—giving them the tools to know how to act. Unlike functionalism, however, most symbolic interactionists recognize that microanalysis demonstrates a variety of tensions and struggles that characterize these encounters.

For symbolic interactionists, social problems come from a variety of these tensions. Georg Simmel (1964) studied the effects of rapid urbanization. He noticed how drastically the increased pace, density, and rationalization of city life altered the quantity and intensity of people's social interactions. At the same time that they encountered a rapidly growing and increasingly diverse population, their relationships grew less emotionally intense and personally satisfying. Combined with the increased stimuli of urbanization, the loss of significant interpersonal connections left people with what Simmel called a "blasé" attitude. For him, social alienation resulted from a dramatic change in the day-to-day interactions of individuals that remarkably shaped their own sense of the social world.

Interactionists also look at how individual behavior becomes problematic. Howard Becker (1997) argues that deviance comes from the ways in which social groups make rules about appearance and behavior and then "label" people who can't or won't conform. Such labeling *stigmatizes individuals or small groups, often resulting in their social alienation.* Isolation often leads to the amplification of nonconformity or deviance, as those labeled begin to define themselves by whatever characteristics have been deemed "different." In the book *Teenage Wasteland*, Donna Gaines (1998) studies a group of youth that have been labeled as "burnouts." This designation stigmatized the youth as "losers," resulting in teachers giving up on them in school and police harassing them in town. Eventually, these youth used the term themselves, but proudly, creating a subculture based on their experience of alienation and sense of "difference." After some of these burnouts carried out suicide pacts, leaving notes about how isolated and outcast they felt, Gaines wondered whether they hadn't been "labeled to death."

## CASE STUDY #2

### Applying Symbolic Interactionist Analysis and Solutions: A Self and Society Course Assignment

Professor Barbara Vann of Loyola University in Maryland teaches a course called Self and Society.[2] In the course, Dr. Vann's students explore how power and deference, especially as they are shaped by race, gender, ethnicity, and class, impact social interactions. Vann (1999) gives students the following assignment:

*(Continued)*

---

[2]All of the information on this assignment comes from Dr. Vann's (1999) article "Service Learning as Symbolic Interaction," as well as from e-mail discussions with Dr. Vann.

(Continued)

> Assignment: Gender, Class, and Racial Ethnic Inequality: The Effect of Position in the Stratification Structure of Interaction
>
> For this assignment, choose a setting in which to observe interaction among individuals of different backgrounds based on gender, race/ethnicity, or social class. A likely setting would be a meal program such as Beans and Bread or Our Daily Bread, or some setting in which people who are "cultural strangers" meet. Observe long enough to determine what patterns of behavior, norms, etc., are in operation. After gathering your data, write up your analysis in terms of how position in the stratification structure affected interaction. Pay particular attention to such things as demeanor, appearance, setting, props, gestures, and language. Be sure to address the role power plays.

While doing Vann's assignment, students experience the ways in which physical and behavioral "cues" inform how they judge poor people they meet at meal programs, and how their interactions with them proceed from that initial encounter. Thus, as one student explained, "The first subject I observed was a white, working-class male, in his mid-40s, dressed in dirty clothes and rather unkempt. He wore a cheap, stained baseball cap and filthy generic tennis shoes" (p. 86). Without any intimate knowledge of this person, Vann's student had no problem in using such negative terms as "dirty, unkempt, cheap, filthy, and stained" to label the first meal recipient. His depiction relies on prevailing assumptions and labels.

Through Vann's assignment, students gain an analytical framework that helps them understand how appearance, props, and demeanor might impact interactions. Vann contends that these students develop "more empathy, and engage in less judgment and negative stereotyping." In fact, some students understood how "they themselves manage others' impressions" (p. 87). Thus, one white male student explained,

> When a group of African-American men were talking while eating their sandwiches, I approached them and asked how they were doing. At first, they were fairly reticent in talking to me, but as the conversation continued, I found that they had tried to bring me in. I found that I was talking in a streetwise fashion rather than a more refined and educated manner than I usually did. (p. 87)

This student not only recognizes the potential that stereotypes might have in limiting conversation and relationships, but he also understands all the participants' ability to manipulate the situation's cues and cultural frameworks.

Overall, Vann suggests that students working with poor and homeless people begin to understand the power inherent in different "symbolic backgrounds." Thus, students could "view themselves as those they are serving view them" and begin to comprehend, if not actually take on, the role of "the other" (p. 90). More importantly, Vann argues that students start to overcome the limitations on both learning and political engagement that result from differences in status positions. By grasping the way that power is exercised in being able to control what Thomas and Thomas (1928) called the "definition of a situation," students also captured "not only the power inherent in roles in this particular context but also interactional struggles for power that play out through language and demeanor" (Vann 1999). For example, one student describes the soup kitchen by claiming that

> it was evident that the volunteers and the security guards were in power in this structure. . . . [S]ome guests tried to reverse the power by their use of language and bearing a demeanor that put them in charge. But in the end, the security guards would have the last word, having ultimate power in being able to tell people to leave (p. 90).

Service learning projects such as Vann's not only make theory and concepts of symbolic interactionism "come alive," but they also help students examine how such interpretations can be applied to change social conditions and human relationships. Such an analysis, however, leads us to ask whether students who worked in these projects didn't, in the end, get more out of the encounters than those served. In fact, their ability to understand the elements of manipulating roles and symbolic resources may only enhance the status power they held to begin with. Vann responds to this situation by hoping that "students are better citizens for their experience" (p. 91). Whether students have challenged their own blasé attitudes, become more adept at deconstructing discriminatory and demeaning social labels, or been inspired to take political action to break down the structure of status inequalities and their ramification, Vann's hopes do not seem unreasonable.

### Case Study Questions

1. How did theory help explain the limitations students experienced while providing services?

2. How did the explanation help inform Professor Vann's strategies for teaching social problems?

3. How did these assignments attempt to challenge students' and society's labels? Were they successful? If so, how?

4. What are the advantages and limitations of such projects?

## Conflict Sociology

Conflict sociology works from a different premise than functionalism. Functionalists focus on the social integration of institutions and the shared sense of values and norms within a society. Instead, **conflict sociology** contends that *inequality and the struggle over resources, different interests, and different values shape society.* Social order comes not from consensus but through the authority and the power of a ruling class to bring about compliance. Such management can take the form of rewards or punishment, ideological indoctrination or seduction, promises of good things or threats, persuasion, intimidation, or force. Collins (1975) concludes that conflict sociology's vision of social order "consists of groups and individuals trying to advance their own interests over others whether or not overt outbreaks take place. . . . What occurs when conflict is not openly taking place is a process of domination" (p. 114).

Most sociologists consider Marx and Engels (1955) to be the founders of conflict sociology. This duo argued that *those who owned the means of economic production were in a constant struggle to maintain and increase their power over those who did not.* The shape of society evolves from the ways in which those in power negotiate their control. Those without such power struggle too, and their efforts also impact social structure and ideology. For example, capitalists own the means of production, and workers generally have to accept wage-labor jobs in order to survive. Owners and their managers set wages and compensation at the lowest level possible in order to maximize profits. Workers, meanwhile, organized unions, which effectively increased pay, benefits, and worker safety. While most unions have contracts that regulate the wages and conditions of their members' employment, these agreements must be constantly negotiated. Thus, even though strikes and lockouts occur only from time to time, labor relations are marked by constant conflicts of class interest.

Max Weber (1978), one of the most sophisticated sociologists on the nature of power, expanded the idea of **social stratification.** First, Weber argued that, despite the significance of economic stratification in determining social order, *political power and social status were also important forms of social hierarchy.* Political power can be gained through election, selection, or through mass organization. While financial resources certainly help facilitate political power, the opposite could also occur where a person uses his or her political power to gain economic resources. Similarly, cultural stratification can result in people having significant social status and then using this status to gain either political or economic resources or both. For example, church leaders have social status in certain communities. These leaders often try to influence their constituents' political activities. The more they can guarantee their followers' support, the more political power they wield. The more social status and political clout they acquire, the more likely they are to successfully increase institutional fund-raising, grant writing, and their own public appearances complete with paid honoraria and even television shows.

Second, Weber (1978) dissected how modern organizations distribute power along all three of these axes—economic, political, and social or cultural power. Like the functionalists, Weber recognized that people experience social dynamics primarily through organizations and institutions. As a conflict sociologist, however, Weber argued that these *sites for collective behavior were all sites for conflict over power and authority.* On the one hand, corporations, schools, and social agencies all have an organizational chart that clearly demarcates who has what power over whom. Yet both formal and informal networks within the organization allow for subordinates to gain either social or political power that might transcend their position. Similarly, subordinates often have control over materials or processes that empower them with either specialized knowledge or simply the trust of coworkers. Despite the fact that bureaucracies represent highly efficient and rationalized entities for distributing power, struggles over power remain an inherent part of all social life and social organizations.

C. Wright Mills (1956) effectively synthesized Marx and Weber in his discussion of the "power elite." Mills described how "ordinary" people live in "everyday worlds" where modern society "confines them to projects not their own." Most people "feel that they are without purpose in an epoch in which they are without power" (p. 3). In contrast, however, Mills explains that some people come to occupy positions of great power and control over the major hierarchies and organizations of modern society. He concludes,

> [T]hese people rule the big corporations. They run the machinery of the state and claim its prerogatives. They direct the military establishment. They occupy the strategic command posts of the social structure in which are now centered the effective means of the power and the wealth and the celebrity which they enjoy. (pp. 3–4)

Power, although partly diffused throughout society and always being recast by various kinds of struggles, rests primarily with elite members of economic, political, and cultural institutions. The stronger the consolidation of power, the more that ordinary people lack control over their conditions and life chances.

In general, conflict sociology argues that social problems develop from an inequality of resources and power. Whether the problem is poverty or illness, conflict sociologists begin from the premise that one's relation to power and resources will determine the likelihood that one suffers from such problems. In fact, such an approach generally assumes that the source of social problems begins with the notion that those in power work to maintain their control and privilege. Yet those without power can organize and strategize to gain power in a variety of ways.

More recently, sociologists interested in race, ethnicity, and gender have applied the precepts of conflict sociology to look at the impact of social stratification by personal, cultural, or institutionalized identity. In the United States, race has always been a category that privileges one group and discriminates against another—even ethnic groups, such as Irish and Jewish immigrants, that were considered neither white nor black. But over time, these groups have negotiated mainstream identities and acquired power by "becoming" white (Brodkin 1998; Ignatiev 1996). Despite affirmative action and other remedial policies, the distribution of power, money, and other resources in the United States remains disproportionately in the hands of white people. Similarly, men have historically controlled both the institutions of power and the social conditions of everyday life. Whether women were disenfranchised because they couldn't vote, possessed no property rights, or simply had to defer to men when making major decisions, patriarchy limited their access to power.

But ordinary people and those discriminated against based on race, ethnicity, or gender do resist and challenge the power elite and their institutions. Sometimes these protests are individual acts of bravery, subversive acts of theft or sabotage, or simple moments of saying "no" in desperation or exhaustion. Sociologists, however, focus more on *the collective efforts of subordinate groups to organize and challenge for power—a social phenomenon we call "social movements."* The term *social movements* encompasses the study of everything from abolitionism and labor unions to the civil rights movement and the moral majority. Recently, sociologists have coined the phrase "social movement organizations" (SMOs) to refer to organized efforts by smaller groups who may not be affiliated with large-scale movements but still represent collective attempts to empower subordinate groups and change public policy or institutional conditions. Regardless of size, however, the key aspect in all social movement cases is that they recognize the inherent nature of conflict within society and represent the intersection of collective agency and social structure (Fitzgerald and Rodgers 2000; Morris and Mueller 1992).

## CASE STUDY #3

### Applying Conflict Theory to Solutions: United Students Against Sweatshops

By the end of World War II, most people thought sweatshops were a thing of the past. Yet in the mid-1990s, the problem of worker exploitation in the garment industry reappeared with a vengeance. In 1995, the U.S. Department of Labor raided a sweatshop in El Monte, California, where, according to Medea Benjamin (2000), 72 Thai immigrants made garments in a "state of virtual slavery." A year later, the National Labor Committee went public with evidence that underpaid child laborers in Honduras made Kathie Lee Gifford's line of clothing for Wal-Mart. Her "teary denial on national TV would help reintroduce 'sweatshop' to the global vocabulary. After that, media exposes about sweatshops swept the nation" (p. 3).

Anti-sweatshop campaigns followed as workers and consumers pressured corporations to change policies to improve workers' conditions. Students played a crucial role in these campaigns, arguing that they should have "the power and the right" to influence how school logos were used in the production and marketing of college-branded clothing—a $2.5 billion industry in the late 1990s. Companies responded quickly by creating "codes of conduct" prohibiting child labor and forced labor, while improving health and safety standards and wage rates. But most codes ended up being weak and poorly enforced. Soon, labor and religious groups, who had initially supported these attempts at corporate responsibility, backed out. Students around the country moved into the void, and the organization United Students Against Sweatshops (USAS) erupted on the scene (Featherstone 2002).

This group successfully linked local and global issues by demonstrating the integral connection between what students wore on campus and the people who made those products, often halfway around the world. An activist student from Princeton University, David Tannenbaum, explained, "This is an issue that really moves a lot of people. The workers making our clothes are thousands of miles away, but in other ways we're so close to it—we're wearing these clothes every day" (quoted in Benjamin 2000:238). In fact, as Rachel Paster from the University of Michigan stated,

> One reason we've been so successful is that opposition to sweatshops isn't that radical. Although I'm sure lots of us are all for overthrowing the corporate power structure, the human rights issues are what make a lot of people get involved and put their energies into rallies, sit-ins, etc. (p. 238)

But students who got active in the anti-sweatshop campaigns did more than go to rallies. Students constructed mock sweatshops in central campus locations to illustrate the actual conditions. They organized mock fashion shows where students modeled "college apparel" while voiceovers described the working conditions under which the clothing was made. Student leaders, along with groups like the National Labor Committee, have visited factories around the world to examine the actual conditions and report back to campuses as well as policy makers. But the most effective tool to pressure college campuses and corporations alike has been the boycott.

As part of a national strategy to have college administrations pressure apparel makers into full disclosure of working conditions, students coordinated campus-by-campus boycotts of clothing with college logos. Despite the claim by university officials at places like Duke University that their "hands were tied . . . because the U.S. companies would never agree to full public disclosures" (Benjamin 2000: 239–240), Duke students won just such a demand from the corporations that produced their university's clothing line. In fact, by the spring of 1999, "every university where students organized a sit-in (Duke, Georgetown, Arizona, Michigan and Wisconsin) . . . wrested agreements to require licensees to disclose the specific location of their factory sites" in order to allow for independent monitoring (pp. 239–240).

United Students Against Sweatshops recognized that a conflict over power lay at the heart of economic production and global commercial relationships. American corporations moved their factories overseas to avoid union-negotiated wages, safety and health laws, as well as environmental safety regulations. Corporations used their power and wealth to reduce costs and increase profits, as foreign workers were kept from organizing by the governments and militaries in their own countries. Students therefore decided to intervene in corporate profit-making by using the power that consumers could generate by refusing to purchase certain products, and thereby making sure the institutions they were a part of didn't buy sweatshop-made goods. While individual or small-group boycotts would have had little impact, institutional boycotts along with large-scale and highly publicized tactics such as demonstrations and sit-ins could have great impact and change university purchasing policies. Thus, United Students Against Sweatshops formed a social movement organization that mobilized enough power to counter the economic, political, and even military power of corporations and foreign nations to impact the labor conditions of workers around the world.

Traditionally, social movements concerning labor conditions and workers' rights have emerged from what's called the "point of production." In other words, the workers themselves have organized unions to battle poor wages and working conditions. However, the anti-sweatshop movement has recognized that students as consumers not only shoulder responsibility for contributing to the profitability of sweatshops by buying clothes made in them, but they also possess a substantive amount of power as a collective force to change college and corporate ways of doing business. In countries where unions are illegal and organizing efforts are met with death threats, workers must rely on the conscience and political will of consumers. Students, recognizing the complexity of global capitalism and power relations within the global marketplace, have stepped up the work of challenging corporate powers and the college administrations that make deals with them. Their efforts have significantly changed the lives of thousands of workers around the world.

*(Continued)*

(Continued)

The long-term success of these workers will depend on their own ability to control working conditions for themselves. Such efforts have been limited by the ability of factory sites to garner government support for using military force to repress and intimidate workers, as well as by the fact that most sweatshop labor is composed of young women in cultures where patriarchy is strong. But student efforts to gain disclosure and improve international workers' rights have begun to help these women gain the ability to organize and protect themselves. By analyzing the specific structure of new global markets and using collective forms of pressure to challenge both corporate and university power elite, students have demonstrated a powerful understanding of social problems, as well as the possibility for social solutions.

## Case Study Questions

1. How does conflict theory help explain sweatshops and labor rights violations?

2. How does this explanation inform strategies to address these social problems?

3. Did USAS challenge relations of production, consumption, or both? Did it do so successfully? Explain your answer.

## VOICES FROM THE FIELD

Interview with Camilo Romero, the USAS National Organizer for Outreach. He began working for USAS in July of 2004, after receiving his undergraduate degree in sociology from the University of California - Berkeley. Camilo led the campaign to have the University of California system cut its contract with Coca-Cola due to extensive human rights abuses in its bottling plants in Colombia. These excerpts come from an interview with *Fellowship Magazine*, a publication of the Fellowship For Reconciliation—For a World of Peace, Justice, and Non-Violence.

Fellowship: What are some of the major successes USAS has achieved with these campaigns?

Romero: One was last March, when students were organizing in favor of workers in Immokalee, Florida, with the campaign against Taco Bell. These were mostly migrant and undocumented workers from Mexico, Guatemala, and Haiti [seasonal workers] who pick tomatoes for Taco Bell suppliers. [Workers] asked for a one-penny increase per bucket of tomatoes—a minuscule increase, yet the growers said no. So these workers partnered with the Coalition of Immokalee Workers (CIW), USAS, Student/Farmworker Alliance, MECHA (Movimiento Estudiantil Chicano de Aztlán), and other community groups to put pressure on Taco Bell. . . . Taco Bell was chosen since they are the ones with the power, who make the big bucks. It was a campaign that took several years. The student side focused on kicking Taco Bell off campuses because (1) they were abusing workers and (2) they were making money by exploitation. It was called "Boot the Bell." The University of California at Los Angeles, the University of Chicago, and California State University at San Bernardino, among others, all kicked Taco Bell off their campuses. In March 2005, the campaign forced Taco Bell to sign a historic agreement with CIW recognizing all demands and setting a precedent for other companies like McDonald's, Burger King, and Subway to respect those rights.

**Fellowship:**    What are some challenges that USAS faces in these campaigns?

**Romero:**    The funny thing is that initially it was the same with me. I was, like, "How do we take on such a huge company that invests millions of dollars in things like checking our website each day and trying to have interns hack into it?" I was, like, "Wow, this is too much!" But these companies are like anyone else and tend to screw up a lot as well. In the case of Coca-Cola, as well as with Nike, Reebok, and others, they have that big façade of being impenetrable, but there are several loopholes for targeting them. For example, with Coca-Cola, they were terrible when dealing with our campaign because they were addressing it as a PR [public relations] problem. They just brushed off not only the requests of students, but also the requests of institutions, the so-called "respected" individuals such as university administrators and city government officials. This showed clearly that Coca-Cola had never been challenged in this way. The bigger challenge is dealing with the larger culture. In activism, there are only a certain few who can get involved—but a type of movement that will truly change things around will be led by people who otherwise don't have the time. Activism takes time and community: That's one challenge. A second challenge is that in general, activism is almost a dirty word. People associate it with young hippie tree-huggers who don't shower and eat granola, and that is certainly not true. The fact is that people construe activism as something kind of far-fetched, something you have to become—while I believe that all of us, to some extent, are activists. We all have values, morals, and ideals that, when they are challenged or hit by injustice, send us into action. When we put those thoughts, those passions into motion, that is really what activism is.

**Fellowship:**    Was there a specific experience in college that sparked an interest in social justice work?

*(Continued)*

(Continued)

Romero:    Certainly the person that went into school and the one that left it were quite different—in terms of outlook on life, and perspective on how the world works, and politics and such. When I graduated and looked back on what I accomplished, I had the idea that, first, I was very lucky, very fortunate, very privileged to have had all these experiences, and second, that it was really a chance to get other people involved—to get them to realize that there is a heck of a lot that you can do inside the classroom, but there is a whole lot more you can do outside it. The message for getting other young people involved, whether they go to a four-year college or not, is that they must see there is a place for them to engage. Just as important as the work we do is the way we do it. It is critical to do our work in a way that is welcoming and inclusive. Our work needs to truly represent the realization that we all someday hope to achieve for people of the working class, women, people of color, people of different sexual orientations. We need to realize the struggles we have ahead of us—but the more people we have on board, the more likely we are to achieve success sooner.

Fellowship: A comment I often hear about students today is that they seem so apathetic, especially compared to students 30 or 40 years ago. How would you respond, and how do you get students interested and involved?

Romero:    You have to make the campaign accessible and a little more real. If you show that activism isn't anything but people with conscientiousness about what is right and wrong putting this into action—that is the key.

*Photo Source:* Used by permission of the Fellowship of Reconciliation-USA. All Rights Reserved. Website: www.forusa.org. 521 North Broadway, Nyack, NY 10960.

## SUMMARY

In this chapter, we have examined social problems and society from three major theoretical frameworks that sociologists use to understand the world. Different theoretical perspectives may yield different understandings about what the root causes of social problems are, as well as what kinds of social actions or services might be effective to address those causes. By bringing these theories into the field, sociologists can also evaluate their effectiveness both as theories and as guides to action.

We have also explored particular service learning, action-oriented, and community-based projects where students were able to bring together intellectual and experiential work. In each case, sociological concepts and theories gave students certain tools to understand the social problems they witnessed as well as to evaluate the significance and depth of their actions, both personally and for the larger society. The rest of the book will continue to present such case studies as a way to both analyze particular social problems and think about how to address them.

In the end, sociology does not promise to change the world. The promise is that it will help us to understand how the world makes us who we are as individuals and societies. But the goal of sociological analysis and practice does not stop at understanding. The history of sociology is the history of efforts to move from theory and research to practical application and social action. Service learning pedagogy and civic engagement call on students and teachers to integrate analysis with action in order to address social problems.

## SUMMARY QUESTIONS

1. What is meant by the term *social construction?* How would sociologists explain that both society and the self are socially constructed?

2. What is an institution? How do institutions shape social life?

3. What are values, norms, and beliefs? How do they compare/contrast with one another?

4. What is a social theory? How do different theories work to emphasize different aspects of the social world around us?

## GLOSSARY

Agency: The ability to change the institutions in which people live. We might expand that to include all social relationships, both macro or large (economies and governments) and micro or small (personal intimacies, relationships, and encounters).

Conflict Sociology: A theory that contends societies are not unified single entities, but reflect and are shaped by inequality and the struggle over resources, competing interests, and different values. Any given society generally reflects the ability of one group to exert and maintain power over others, as well as the level of resistance against that bloc.

Disorganization: Social problems that come about when rapid changes overwhelm people and their institutions.

Functionalism: A theory premised on the basic idea that society is an increasingly complex organism that must fulfill certain basic functions to continue its survival. These functions include the economic, political, and social realms of the social world and are experienced by people primarily through institutions.

Institutions: Patterns of behavior that become formalized as structural or cultural entities. Examples are collective phenomena such as family, church, schools, legislatures, hospitals, and prisons. Some sociologists refer to institutions as "super-customs" and include the practices—not just the structural unit or physical place—as institutions. Thus, religion, law, and education can also be thought of as general institutions regardless of any specific church, court, or school.

Norms: The shared expectations of behavior—what people consider as doing the right thing.

Social Dysfunction: This refers to a designated set of consequences of a designated pattern of behavior, belief, or organization that interfere with a designated functional requirement of a designated social system. These can be manifest (overt) in or latent (hidden) from the everyday experience of social processes.

Social Facts: According to Émile Durkheim, a social fact is any way of acting, whether fixed or not, capable of exerting over the individual an external constraint; or, which is general over the whole of a given society whilst having an existence of its own, independent of its individual manifestations. In any given society, these facts may be exemplified through money, rules, laws, particular beliefs, institutions, and so forth.

Social Stratification: The process by which some people in a society are guided or forced into inferior (or superior) social positions; usually class, race, and gender inequality, but sometimes based on caste or other social and cultural identities.

Social Structure: The material and cultural conditions, such as economic and political systems, institutional networks, family, and religious practices, that shape our lives and our choices.

Socialization: The process through which people learn to think, feel, evaluate, and behave as individuals in relation to others and institutions within a given society.

Symbolic Interactionism: A theory focusing on the approach that has evolved from social behaviorism and that stresses the symbolic nature of human interaction; linguistic and gestural communication; and particularly the role of language in the formation of mind, self, and society.

Values: The strong, seemingly permanent dispositions shared by groups of people.

## WEBSITES TO LEARN MORE ABOUT SOCIOLOGY, SERVICE LEARNING, AND SOCIOLOGY "IN ACTION"

American Sociological Association (ASA): http://www.asanet.org

Association for Applied and Clinical Sociology: http://www.aacsnet.org/wp/

Association for Humanist Sociology (AHS): http://www.humanistsociology.org

*Contexts*—ASA journal of "interesting and relevant" sociology: http://contexts.org/

Project South: http://projectsouth.org/

Public Sociology: http://www.publicsociology.com

Society for the Study of Social Problems (SSSP): http://www.sssp1.org

Sociologists Without Borders: http://www.sociologistswithoutborders.org/

Transformative Studies Institute: http://www.transformativestudies.org/

## REFERENCES

Aronowitz, Stanley. 2001. *The Knowledge Factory: Dismantling the Corporate University and Creating True Higher Learning.* Boston, MA: Beacon Press.

Axel-Lute, Miriam. 1999. "Town & Gown: Making Research Serve Communities' Needs." *Shelterforce,* 108. Retrieved February 18, 2010 (http://www.nhi.org/online/issues/108/towngown.html).

Becker, Howard. 1997. *Outsiders: Studies in the Sociology of Deviance.* New York: The Free Press.

Benjamin, Medea. 2000. "Toil and Trouble: Student Activism in the Fight Against Sweatshops." Pp. 237–252 in *Campus Inc.,* edited by Geoffry White. Amherst, NY: Prometheus Books.

Brodkin, Karen. 1998. *How Jews Became White Folks and What That Says About Race in America.* New Brunswick, NJ: Rutgers University Press.

Collins, Randall. 1975. *Conflict Sociology: Toward an Explanatory Science.* New York: Academic Press.

Collins, Randall and Michael Makowsky. 1998. *The Discovery of Society.* 6th ed. Boston, MA: McGraw-Hill.

Conklin, John. 2009. "Sociology in Hollywood Films." *American Sociologist,* 40:198–213.

Durkheim, Émile. 1982. *The Rules of Sociological Method.* Translated by W. D. Hallis; edited by Steven Lukes. New York: The Free Press.

Featherstone, Liza. 2002. *Students Against Sweatshops: The Making of a Movement.* New York: Verso.

Fischer, Claude. 1975. "Towards a Subcultural Theory of Urbanism." *American Journal of Sociology,* 80:1319–1341.

Fitzgerald, Kathleen and Diane Rodgers. 2000. "Radical Social Movements Organizations: A Theoretical Model." *Sociological Quarterly,* 41:573–592.

Gaines, Donna. 1998. *Teenage Wasteland: Suburbia's Dead End Kids.* Chicago, IL: University of Chicago Press.

Gordon, Linda. 2002. *Heroes of Their Own Lives*: The Politics and History of Family Violence—Boston, 1880–1960. Champaign, IL: University of Illinois Press.

Herring, Cedric. 1998. *Empowerment in Chicago: Grassroots Participation in Economic Development and Poverty Alleviation.* Chicago, IL: Scholarly Audio.

Ignatiev, Noel. 1996. *How the Irish Became White.* London, UK: Routledge.

Kozol, Jonathan. 1992. *Savage Inequalities: Children in America's Schools.* New York: Perennial.

Marshall, Gordon. ed. 1998. *A Dictionary of Sociology.* 2nd ed. New York: Oxford University Press.

Marullo, Sam. 1999. "Sociology's Essential Role: Promoting Critical Analysis in Service Learning." Pp. 11–28 in *Cultivating the Sociological Imagination: Concepts and Models for Service Learning in Sociology,* edited by James Ostrow, Garry Hesser, and Jim Enos. Washington, DC: American Association for Higher Education & Accreditation.

Marx, Karl and Friedrich Engels. 1955. *The Communist Manifesto*. New York: Meredith Corporation.

Mead, George Herbert. 1940. *Mind, Self, and Society From the Standpoint of a Social Behaviorist*. Chicago, IL: University of Chicago Press.

Merton, Robert. 1966. *Contemporary Social Problems*. New York: Harcourt, Brace & World.

———. 1978. "A Paradigm for Functional Analysis in Sociology." Pp. 104–108 in *Contemporary Sociological Theories,* edited by Alan Wells. Santa Monica, CA: Goodyear.

Mills, C. Wright. 1956. *The Power Elite*. London, UK: Oxford University Press.

Morris, Aldon and Carol Mueller. 1992. *Frontiers in Social Movement Theory.* New Haven, CT: Yale University Press.

Nyden, Philip, Joanne Adams and Kim Zalent. 1997. "Creating and Sustaining Racially and Ethnically Diverse Communities." Pp. 32–42 in *Building Community: Social Science in Action*, edited by Nyden et al. Thousand Oaks, CA: Pine Forge Press.

Nyden, Philip, Diane Binson, Sr. Mary Paul Asoegwu, Roger Atreya, Ronald Gulotta, Gayle Hooppaw Johnson, et al. 1990. Racial, Ethnic, and Economic Diversity in Uptown's Subsidized Housing: A Case Study of Its Present Character and Future Possibilities. Chicago: Human Relations Task Force of Chicago Community Trust.

Nyden, Philip, Anne Figert, Mark Shibley, and Darryl Burrows, eds. 1997. *Building Community: Social Science in Action*. Thousand Oaks, CA: Pine Forge Press.

Ogburn, William F. 1950. *Social Change With Respect to Cultural and Original Nature.* New York: Viking Press.

Parsons, Talcott. 1966. Societies: Evolutionary and Comparative Perspectives. Englewood Cliffs, NJ: Prentice Hall.

Perkins, Sally, Virginia Kidd, and Gerri Smith. 1999. *Voices of Strong Democracy: Concepts and Models for Service Learning in Communication Studies.* Washington, DC: American Association for Higher Education & Accreditation.

Persell, Caroline Hodges. 1977. *Education and Inequality: A Theoretical and Empirical Synthesis.* New York: Free Press.

Piven, Frances Fox and Richard Cloward. 1989. *Why Americans Don't Vote*. New York: Pantheon.

———. 2002. *Why Americans Still Don't Vote*. Boston, MA: Beacon Press.

Rafferty, Annette. 2001. *Wearing Smooth the Path: 25 Years at Abby's House, an Unfinished Memoir*. Worcester, MA: Ambassador Books.

Simmel, Georg. 1964. *The Sociology of Georg Simmel*. Edited by Kurt H. Wolff. New York: The Free Press.

Thomas, William I. and Dorothy Swaine Thomas. 1928. *The Child in America: Behavior Problems and Programs*. New York: Knopf.

Trumpbour, Jack. 1989. *How Harvard Rules*. Boston, MA: South End Press.

Vann, Barbara. 1999. "Service Learning as Symbolic Interaction." Pp. 83–92 in *Cultivating the Sociological Imagination*, edited by James Ostrow, Garry Hesser, and Jim Enos. Washington, DC: American Association for Higher Education & Accreditation.

Weber, Max. 1978. *Economy and Society*. Berkeley, CA: University of California Press.

# Who Has, Who Doesn't?

## Looking for Answers to Poverty, Inequality, and Homelessness

*The curse of poverty has no justification in our age. It is socially as cruel and blind as the practice of cannibalism at the dawn of civilization, when men ate each other because they had not yet learned to take food from the soil or to consume the abundant animal life around them. The time has come for us to civilize ourselves by the total, direct and immediate abolition of poverty.*

—Martin Luther King Jr., *Where Do We Go From Here?* (1967)

Professor Robert Rhoads created a service learning class at Pennsylvania State University where students spent a week over winter break working with homeless citizens in Washington, D.C. While spending their nights sleeping in the basement of a local church, students volunteered at a variety of soup kitchens. According to Rhoads (1998), the project "enabled students to learn about the lives of homeless people and in this way helped students to see homeless citizens as real people with real problems and concerns" (p. 43). As one student explained, "I learned that the homeless in general do not earn their predicament. Instead, their problems are brought on by a series of events that are largely beyond their control. Such events could make me or anyone wind up homeless" (p. 44).

Inequality exists in all societies, and **poverty** in most. Sociologists argue that both result primarily from social and structural conditions. While individuals' behaviors may contribute to their own particular circumstances, *poverty itself comes from a society's unequal distribution of resources—money, food, clothing, shelter, and so on.* Inequality derives from various groups possessing different amounts of wealth and power. Thus, while some people may have particular talents or skills, or might work very hard, their success in obtaining wealth or status is more often determined by the larger economic, social, or political conditions that surround them, *not* by their own individual actions.

Although inequalities seem basic to all forms of social organization, what they are and how they impact people vary tremendously across time and space. Thus, the social problems that come from inequality can differ widely depending on any particular society's economic system, political composition, and set of cultural norms and values. As you will see later in the chapter, some sociologists even argue that inequality is *not* a social problem. For them, wealth and power inspire competition and result in the most skilled and talented people reaching the positions they are best suited for. But even these sociologists would agree that huge inequalities either represent significant social problems or can be the root cause of them.

The student quoted earlier, in fact, implies that homelessness is not simply about a person's inability to compete for rewards. Homeless people don't necessarily "choose" their conditions, nor do they become homeless because of laziness or a lack of natural aptitudes. The phenomenon of **homelessness** has two major causes: poverty and the lack of affordable housing for poor people. Individual homeless people have little power to impact falling wage rates, change tax policies that benefit rich people and reduce subsidies for the poor, or alter real estate markets that make it more profitable to tear down cheap apartments and build luxury townhouses.

In spite of how little control most homeless people have in determining the larger causes of poverty, they often work very hard to improve their own and their family's lives. According to Gaetz and O'Grady (2004), there is little evidence that homeless people avoid work. In fact, just the opposite is true: "[M]any hours are spent toiling for, in many cases, limited dollars. . . . The problem is not about motivation, a rejection of the world of work, or the attractiveness of government benefits (in many jurisdictions the homeless are not eligible for welfare)" (p. 607). Similarly, Robert Rosenthal (1994) has argued, *social stigma*—the ways in which people discriminate against and devalue others based on physical or behavioral attributes—actually hinders anyone who has become homeless from ever rejoining the ranks of the housed. Because they look poor or unkempt or "scary," no one gives them a chance. As another student in Professor Rhoads's (1998) service projects announced,

> I feel entirely different about homeless people than I did previously. I understand better some of the circumstances that contribute to people losing their jobs, or their homes. But I also understand that many of the people I've met through this work are not helpless victims. They are more than capable of working and maintaining a normal life if there were just more opportunities. (p. 40)

In most cases, to be homeless in America is not a sign of laziness or incapacity, but an indicator of people who struggle immensely, both physically and emotionally, to survive against the odds.

**Image 2.1**   Despite a C average in college and a sketchy performance in graduate school; a series of failed business deals; serious violations of duties while a member of the military; and almost two decades (age 17–35) of "nomadic" behavior that included heavy drinking, partying, and drug use, George W. Bush became the 43rd president of the United States. While pundits and others have debated Bush's political skills and overall intelligence, sociologists would argue that his success can only be explained by the wealth and power of his family. Each time he failed, or performed poorly, or misbehaved socially, he was able to avoid the economic or social ramifications that poor, working-, and middle-class people normally experience. While the United States of America promotes and cherishes an ideology of rugged individualism, the majority of our most successful people began with a disproportionate cache of wealth and power, and benefited from familial, peer, institutional, and even governmental support in gaining or maintaining their success. Sociologists use the term *social stratification* to explain the shape of structural inequalities and the varying levels of economic wealth, political power, and social status that different people have.

*Source:*© Reuters/CORBIS.

In the United States, mainstream values and ideas now celebrate individual achievement almost to the exclusion of concern for the collective or public good. Such cultural shifts have resulted in strong sentiments to cut taxes and reduce the size and power of government agencies once charged with redistributing various resources to poor people. These policies actually increase inequality by giving those with more wealth and power greater opportunities to make it and retain it, while simultaneously taking away support, not just from social welfare programs like food stamps and Medicaid, but also from traditionally espoused public institutions such as schools, hospitals, and police and fire departments. For example, tax cuts since 2001 have returned over $100,000 to each person making over $1 million per year. These same tax cuts have returned less than $100 dollars per year to those making less that $50,000 annually. For those earning $51,000 to $99,000, the percentage of federal income paid in taxes has actually increased from 18.7% to 19.5% during that period. In the eyes of many critics, most tax cuts have shifted the burden of public funding from the wealthy to the middle class (Krugman 2004).

Meanwhile, the costs of health care and education—services whose costs were historically offset by large public infusions of tax revenue—have risen as government funding has diminished. Thus, whatever tax savings may have been experienced by working- and middle-class people, they were easily wiped out by the increases to the costs of health; education; and a host of local services like sanitation, roads, and police and fire protection. In other words, recent tax policies have cost the middle and working class more money in the long run, while those in the top levels of wealth and income have benefited from getting more money back. Inequality continues to grow in our society, as those with resources acquire more and those without find fewer opportunities to succeed.

This chapter on inequality begins with a brief look at data on wealth, poverty, and inequality in the United States. Next, we present a brief historical look at the nation's broadest and most formalized policy attempt to address poverty: the welfare system. We will then examine how various sociological theories and concepts help explain inequality. *Despite different theories about the origins and impact of inequality, each intellectual approach provides potential strategies for addressing the social problems that arise from inequality.* By presenting how people with contrasting ideas might organize programs and projects that address similar issues, we hope to encourage a more broad-based understanding of both the discipline of sociology and its commitment to ameliorating social problems, thus making the world a better place. We should also note that data and analysis on global poverty and inequality will be addressed in the final chapter on globalization. However, we also need to recognize that many of the same social dynamics are at work in poverty and inequality on both domestic and international levels, and thus the same theoretical analyses are used to understand them.

# PAINTING INEQUALITY BY THE NUMBERS:
# A STATISTICAL PORTRAIT OF U.S. WEALTH AND POVERTY

In 2003, the median household income in the United States was $43,318. However, if we break down the population into quintiles (fifths), we see that incomes range dramatically among the nation's population. Even more notable is the trend toward increasing income inequality. Between 1979 and 2002, the middle 20% of American income earners saw their after-tax income rise 15% or $5,700, while the lowest quintile rose only 4.5% or about $600. Yet income levels for the top fifth of the nation rose almost 50% or just over $42,000. *For those in the top 1% of the nation's population, their incomes skyrocketed over 111% or more than $333,000* (see Table 2.1). In 1979, the average income for the top 1% was 33.1 times the average income of the lowest 20% and 10.1 times the middle fifth. By 2000, the top 1% had an average income that was *88.5 times higher* than the bottom fifth.[1]

Table 2.1   Average After-Tax Income by Income Group (in 2002 dollars)

| Income Category | 1979 | 2002 | Percent Change 1979–2002 | Dollar Change 1979–2002 |
|---|---|---|---|---|
| Lowest fifth | $13,200 | $13,800 | 4.5% | $600 |
| Second fifth | $26,700 | $29,900 | 12.0% | $3,200 |
| Middle fifth | $38,000 | $43,700 | 15.0% | $5,700 |
| Fourth fifth | $49,800 | $61,700 | 23.9% | $11,900 |
| Top fifth | $87,700 | $130,000 | 48.2% | $42,300 |
| Top 1 Percent | $298,900 | $631,700 | 111.3% | $332,800 |

*Source:* Congressional Budget Office, *Effective Federal Tax Rates: 1979–2002,* March 2005.

This increasing inequality results in some startling numerical juxtapositions. On the one hand, the number of millionaires (those with financial assets totaling $1 million) has risen from almost 84,000 in 1983 to nearly 2.5 million in 2004. Households with a net worth of over $1 million rose to almost 7.5 million. On the other end of the economic spectrum, less than 10% of Americans, or about 23 million, lived below the poverty threshold in 1983. By 2004, nearly 12.5 % of the population, or almost 36 million, lived below the poverty line.

---

[1]These statistics were compiled from a number of sources including Edward N. Wolff, *Top Heavy* (Washington, DC: The Century Foundation, 2002).

## WHO DREW THE POVERTY LINE AND WHAT DOES IT MEAN?

*Source:* © BananaStock/Thinkstock.

Almost unchanged since its inception in 1965, the *poverty line* came from an article published by Mollie Orshansky of the Social Security Administration. Established research showed that families of three or more persons spent about a third of their income on food. Orshansky then calculated the dollar amount for a family of three based on the Department of Agriculture's "Economy Food Plan" and multiplied it by three. Although she argued that such an amount would never be sufficient for an actual family of three to live on, she thought it might be effective as an amount by which to measure inadequacy, explaining, "if it is not possible to state unequivocally 'how much is enough,' it should be possible to assert with confidence how much, on an average, is too little" (quoted in Fisher 1992). The poverty line has become a demarcation of who is or is not poor. Since 1965, however, the cost of living has changed dramatically. Food is no longer the most expensive budget item for families. The costs of housing, health care, child care, and transportation have risen exponentially, while food expenditures have declined significantly.

The growing concentration of wealth shows an even greater economic disparity than does income. **Income** is what one earns through wages. According to Oliver and Shapiro (1997),

> Income refers to a flow of money over time, like a rate per hour, week, or year; wealth is a stock of assets owned by an individual at a particular time. **Wealth** is what people own, while income is what people receive for work, retirement, or social welfare. Wealth signifies command over financial resources that a family has accumulated over its lifetime along with those resources that have been inherited across generations. (p. 259, emphasis added)

They conclude that wealth is "more encompassing" than income in determining life chances. In 1976, the richest 10% of families in the United States held 50% of the country's wealth; by 1995, they held 70% of all wealth. In 1995, the top 20% of families owned 83% of wealth, while the remaining 80% of families held only 17%. The figures below (Figure 2.1) show that between 1989 and 2004, during both economic upturns and downturns, the richest 1% moved from having just below 30% of the wealth to almost 35%, while the poorest 50% went from a high of over 4% in 1995 to under 3% in 2004 (Collins et al. 2004; Wolff 2002).

**Figure 2.1**   Proportions of Total Net Worth Held by Various Percentile Groups, 1989–2004

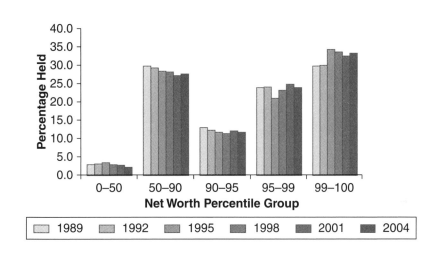

*Source: Currents and Undercurrents: Changes in the Distribution of Wealth, 1989–2004,* by Arthur B. Kennickell, 2006 (cited in http://www.stephenkinsella.net/2006/04/06/changes-in-the-distribution-of-wealth-between-1989-and-2004/).

The difference between wealth and income is also notable when it comes to issues of race and gender. Just in the last decade or so, the median income of families of color has risen by approximately 12%, while that of white families has risen 18% (see Table 2.2). However, if we look at the wealth difference between white and non-white families during same period, the gap is much more stark and growing. Median net worth for families of color actually decreased 7% from 1995 to 2001 while white families saw their median net worth rise 37%.

**Table 2.2**   Changing Median Incomes and Net Worth by Race (1995–2001)

| Median Income | 1995 | 1998 | 2001 | $ change | % |
|---|---|---|---|---|---|
| Families of Color | $23,000 | $25,400 | $25,700 | $2,700 | 12% |
| White Families | $38,200 | $41,100 | $45,200 | $7,100 | 18% |
| Median Net Worth | 1995 | 1998 | 2001 | $ change | % |
| Families of Color | $18,300 | $17,900 | $17,100 | –$1,200 | –7% |
| White Families | $88,000 | $103,400 | $120,900 | $32,400 | 37% |

*Source:* "Recent Changes in U.S. Family Finances," by Ana M. Aizcorbe, Arthur B. Kennickell, and Kevin B. Moore. In *The Wealth Inequality Reader,* edited by Dollars & Sense and United for a Fair Economy, 2004, Boston, MA: Economic Affairs Bureau.

Economic inequalities along gender lines are a bit more complicated. While income differentials between men and women have been well documented (Tomaskovic-Devey 1993; Wilson 2003), wealth differentials are impacted by other variables. For example, marriage makes it difficult to measure inequalities between genders. However, among non-married men and women, large differentials exist, as the median net worth for female-headed households was $28,000 in 2001 and for male-headed households it was $47,000 in the same year. There is an even greater gap between white and non-white women, as single white female households' median net worth was $56,590 in 2001, while that of single African American female households was $5,700 and that of single Hispanic women was $3,900. According to Amy Gluckman (2004), however, the gap among younger men and women seems to be disappearing. She says, "this should not be surprising as women are moving toward parity with men in several of the factors correlated with higher net worth, such as education and income" (p. 63). Still, she cautions, "the income gap has long been smaller between young women and men than between older women and men, at least in part because the workforce participation of women—who typically bear greater parenting responsibilities than men—becomes more uneven over time" (p. 63).

The impact of an increasing bifurcation of wealth can be best witnessed in the difficulties even middle-class Americans have in paying for basic commodities such as housing and health care. In urban areas, property and real estate have become such lucrative industries that both housing costs and rental rates have gone through the roof. The following chart (Table 2.3) shows just how much the average family would pay for a modest, two-bedroom apartment in the cities listed. Also included are the average salaries for selected working- and middle-class professions in those cities and how much annual income would be needed to pay for housing based on a family spending 30% of its income on it.

**Table 2.3**   Middle- and Working-Class Rental Affordability in Major U.S. Cities

|  | San Francisco | Boston | Washington | San Diego | Chicago | Dallas |
|---|---|---|---|---|---|---|
| Apartment rent* | 1,362 | 942 | 840 | 805 | 762 | 749 |
| Income needed to pay for rent** | 54,480 | 37,680 | 33,680 | 32,200 | 30,480 | 29,960 |
| Median teacher's income | 38,293 | 38,584 | 32,781 | 38,584 | 36,733 | 34,800 |
| Median nurse's income | 39,603 | 39,541 | 32,280 | 31,990 | 31,990 | 38,930 |
| Median janitor's income | 20,800 | 20,987 | 15,787 | 16,536 | 18,824 | 14,830 |

*Source:* Joint Centre for Housing Studies, as reported by *The Economist* (available at http://www.pbs.org/now/politics/middleclass.html).

*Monthly rent for modest two bedroom

**Assuming 30% of income spent on housing

Middle-class professionals like teachers and nurses either barely make enough money or in some cities fall just below what is needed. For janitors and other working-class families, it is virtually impossible to find adequate housing without either paying well above 30% of one's salary or moving far enough out of urban centers to find cheaper housing. The latter strategy usually results in even higher transportation costs. These are the dynamics at work as more and more working people must choose which commodities to purchase among health care, housing, and food.

Economic inequality also affects health and health care. The table below demonstrates the impact financial resources have on who has health insurance.

| Annual Income | % Not Covered by Health Insurance |
|---|---|
| Under $25,000 | 24.3 |
| $25,000–$49,999 | 18.8 |
| $50,000–$74,999 | 13.0 |
| More than $75,000 | 8.2 |

Studies continue to show that the more wealth you have, the more likely you are to stay healthy, get adequate medical attention when you're sick, and live longer. However, the greater income inequality that exists in a given society may also contribute to poorer health for *everyone,* not just the impoverished. According to social epidemiologist Richard Wilkinson (Wilkinson and Pickett 2006), the lack of access to health and health care results in poor health for those without resources, but a society's overall health also is negatively impacted by levels of economic inequality. He explains that "relative inequality" creates an overall sense that particular individuals are "failing," and these people are much more likely to die of cancer or coronary disease, infectious diseases, or (of course) suicide than are people who rate themselves as successful. Wilkinson points toward higher mortality rates in the United States than in poorer countries that have greater equality as evidence for his theory. In other words, while the United States may have more wealth, greater economic and social disparity results in more stress, illness, conflict, and crime. Thus, the United States has higher mortality rates than countries with less wealth but also less *disparity.*[2]

Whether Wilkinson is right or not about the overall impact of inequality on health, concentrations of wealth have indisputably resulted in a variety of social problems, especially in communities characterized by concentrations of poverty. To address these problems, the United States has embarked on many different solutions to poverty, but none as formal or expansive as our system of welfare.

## CORPORATE WELFARE

Copyright © 2002 United Feature Syndicate, Inc.

---

[2]Other arguments for the impact of economic disparity on everyone's health include the following: (1) Very contagious diseases including STD's fester when people receive neither preventive care nor treatment. These diseases spread among an *entire* population, not just the poor. (2) Vast inequality obscures the problems of the poorest, and those with the resources and power to establish health care for poor people understand these issues less and less. The more distance between rich and poor, the less likely the rich are to address poverty. Again, without redress, health issues among the poor quickly become health issues for the mainstream. See Robert H. Frank, *Falling Behind: How Rising Inequality Harms the Middle Class* (University of California Press, 2007).

The Cato Institute, a conservative Washington, DC, think tank, defines corporate welfare as "any government spending program that provides unique benefits or advantages to specific companies or industries . . . [including] programs that provide direct grants to businesses, programs that provide research and other services for industries, and programs that provide subsidized loans or insurance to companies." Supporters of these programs argue that government aid boosts the economy, and company profits eventually create more jobs and trickle down to the general public. Congressman Bernie Sanders (2002) has demonstrated, however, that some programs like the Export–Import Bank show corporate welfare at its worst. He explains, "General Electric has received over $2.5 billion in direct loans and loan guarantees from the Ex-Im Bank. And what was the result? From 1975–1995 GE reduced its workforce from 667,000 to 398,000, a decline of 269,000 jobs. . . . [This included insuring] a $3-million loan to . . . [help] General Electric build a factory where Mexican workers will make parts for appliances to export back to the United States. This project is responsible for the loss of 1,500 jobs in Bloomington, Indiana" (n.p.).

## A BRIEF HISTORY OF WELFARE IN THE UNITED STATES

The history of a national **welfare** system in the United States begins during the Great Depression, although programs to address the problems of poverty date back to the early use of poorhouses and outdoor relief aid in the 1700s and 1800s (Katz 1986). All relief programs, however, reflect a long-standing *ideological suspicion over subsidies* for poor people. In essence, what sociologist Robert Bellah has called Americans' belief in "hyper-individualism" and myths of the "self-made man" run counter to social welfare efforts. This distrust has resulted in the requirement that any public aid program prove the *worthiness* of potential recipients. For example, in the late 19th and early 20th century, state and local governments established aid programs that responded to a perceived crisis in the rise of single motherhood. Most supporters "saw single mothers as victims, either of death [of husbands] or other undesirable mishaps, or of male irresponsibility" (Gordon 1994:160). Historian Linda Gordon argues that such images were necessary to legitimize the aid on a moral level. Eventually, these local "Mothers' Aid" programs "became the model not only for ADC (Aid to Dependent Children) but for most of the programs today called 'welfare'" (p. 160). Yet the ideological apprehensions of a devoutly individualistic citizenry remained constant as well.

After the stock market crash of 1929, the United States witnessed some of its worst economic conditions ever. Unemployment rates reached record highs as over 25% of the population couldn't find work. Evictions skyrocketed, leaving between 1 and 5 million people homeless. From bread lines to shanty towns, the signs of poverty were everywhere. By the early 1930s, local and state governments had broken their budgets on public aid and could not meet basic relief needs (Leuchtenberg 1963; McIlvane 1993).

In 1932, President Franklin Roosevelt declared that "every man has a right to life; and this means that he has also a right to make a comfortable living. He may by sloth or crime decline to exercise that right; but it may not be denied him" (quoted in Zinn 1966:50–51). The federal government thus designed a wide range of relief efforts—commonly known as the **New Deal**—that included a $500 million federal emergency aid program, a national employment service, the Commodity Credit Corporation for farm loans, and a variety of public works projects through the Civilian Conservation Corps (CCC) and the Public Works Administration (PWA).

The largest Depression-era aid programs came under the Social Security Act, which established unemployment insurance, old age and survivors' insurance for pensions, and aid to dependent children or ADC. But, as historian Michael Katz (1986) has argued, these programs only further entrenched the deep ideological distinction between those worthy and not worthy of support. "There remains a lurking assumption," Katz writes, "that many of those who ask for help neither need nor deserve it" (p. 246). Thus, despite FDR's recognition that poverty could very well be a systemic problem and not one of individual failings or weaknesses, America's myth of rugged individualism continued to stigmatize most poor people who needed help.

But FDR's New Deal also represented a response to tremendous social and political upheaval brought about through grassroots organizing around the country. The Depression had inspired a host of collective activity and protest that sociologists Frances Fox Piven and Richard Cloward (1979) have referred to as "poor people's movements." They argue that poor people "began to define their personal hardship not just as their own individual misfortune but as misfortune they shared with many of their own kind. . . . [and] maybe it wasn't they who were to blame, but 'the system'" (p. 32). Demonstrations, marches, and rent riots as well as increased pressure from labor strikes and sit-ins eventually forced the federal government to develop more support programs and larger financial subsidies for the poor and unemployed. Piven and Cloward conclude, however, that the expansion of relief programs and the mainstreaming of dissent eventually reduced pressure on the system. As protest alliances waned and leaders moved from militancy to legislative lobbying and agency building, the relief rolls were cut back and millions were left unemployed and destitute again.

Still, these benefits comprised the bulk of the welfare system until the 1960s when ADC was changed to ADFC (Aid to Dependent Families with Children), and the number of recipients more than doubled. President Lyndon Johnson's **"war on poverty"** programs increased the wide variety of services available to poor people, including expanded health care, legal services, and social work. Once again, Piven and Cloward (1979) argue that such federal programs were responding to growing social movements and the political upheavals of poor people, not simply to the feelings of sympathy and goodwill among political leaders. By the end of the 1960s and the beginning of the 1970s, protest alliances again gave way to institutionalized service agencies and community organizations. And once again, the money for programs and services was cut.

But the backlash against such programs and the "undeserving poor" had, according to historian Premilla Nadasen (2005), "come to be dominated by discussions of cultural values, 'illegitimacy,' and immorality, all cast through a racial lens" (p. 37). State and local officials used such stereotypes to justify benefit cuts, limited access, and more invasive monitoring procedures. These changes made a hard life for poor people even harder. The distrust of poor people also led to shifts in how money was spent, as more went toward *administering* programs and *managing* or *supervising* recipients instead of directly to poor people themselves. Large layers of bureaucracy now stood between economic resources and the people who needed them. Agency staff and social workers took on the intermediary role of determining who deserved aid and who didn't, resulting in even more moralizing and stigmatizing of poor people.

Since the 1970s, most federal and state welfare policies have consistently cut welfare benefits and limited eligibility. In the 1980s, President Ronald Reagan made cutting welfare one of his major domestic policy initiatives. Citing the story of a Chicago "welfare queen" (a euphemism for a welfare cheat) driving a "welfare-paid-for Cadillac," he suggested that this particular woman had "ripped off" the government for more than $150,000, and was representative of rampant fraud within the system. Although no researcher ever found this woman, and most reputable studies showed that fraud was actually a minor problem at most, Reagan succeeded in initiating deep cuts to public aid. Politicians again found that they could gain popular support by ridiculing the supposed behavioral problems and character flaws of the poor.

From a conflict theoretical perspective, the history of welfare can be seen as a long *struggle between rich and poor.* When poor and working-class people create effective social movements, they are successful in bringing about public policies that redistribute certain amounts of wealth. When the movements wane or don't exist at all, government policies generally benefit the wealthy with tax breaks, corporate subsidies and bailouts, and so on. In fact, as Piven and Cloward (1993) have argued, most welfare policies are intended to "regulate the poor." For the economy, welfare maintains a surplus labor force at barely subsistence levels during periods of slow production. On a cultural and political level, welfare maintains a group of social scapegoats whose behavior and capacities can be ridiculed to reinforce the moral legitimacy of an unequal system. But even the words and language used to talk about poverty change when poor people organize and speak for themselves. As Nadeasen (2005) explains about the national welfare rights movements of the 1960s and 1970s, "empowering individuals as agents of social change, movements gave a voice to the disenfranchised and articulated a moral code of human rights, racial equality and social justice that superseded the law and custom" (p. 39) that discriminated against them.

## MEDIA BOX: POVERTY AND INEQUALITY IN THE MEDIA

According to sociologist Kate Butler (2007), "The mainstream media presents those who live in poverty as being inherently different from the rest of society by creating artificial divisions and dissimilarities." She continues, "Few stories about issues surrounding the debate on poverty make it to the mainstream, and when articles about those living in poverty do appear, these stories are too often negative and have no contextual information" (n.p.). She cites three reasons for these stories and their focus:

1. The feminization and racialization of poverty in the media;

2. The complexity of the issue itself;

3. The unpopular nature of these types of stories with elites in society.

The result, according to the media research group FAIR (Fairness and Accuracy in Reporting), argues that "despite being an issue that directly or indirectly affects a huge chunk of the U.S. population, poverty and inequality receive astonishingly little coverage on nightly network newscasts. An exhaustive search of weeknight news broadcasts on CBS, NBC, and ABC found that with rare exceptions, such as the aftermath of Katrina, poverty and the poor seldom even appear on the evening news—and when they do, they are relegated mostly to merely speaking in platitudes about their hardships" (deMause and Rendall 2007:2). In the 3 years between 2001 and 2004, only 58 segments on poverty appeared on the major news networks and over half of them followed the Katrina disaster in New Orleans (p. 2). Perhaps media corporations hope that if poor people aren't on TV, people won't think poverty is much of a social problem at all—out of sight, out of mind. Or maybe, as Gil Scott-Heron proclaimed in his poem of the same name, "The Revolution will not be televised":

> The revolution will not be right back after a message
> > about a white tornado, white lightning, or white people.
> You will not have to worry about a dove in your
> > bedroom, a tiger in your tank, or the giant in your toilet bowl.
> The revolution will not go better with Coke.
> The revolution will not fight the germs that may cause bad breath.
> The revolution will put you in the driver's seat.
> The revolution will not be televised, will not be televised,
> > will not be televised, will not be televised.
> The revolution will be no re-run brothers;
> The revolution will be live.

## CASE STUDY #1

Speaking Truth to Power: Conflict Sociology and the Welfare Warriors

In 1996, the U.S. government passed sweeping welfare reform legislation that included cutting sub-sidies and reducing the time period during which poor people could receive benefits. The bill also forced many recipients to work for their benefits and made it increasingly difficult for them to attend college, study for GEDs (General Educational Development certificates, equivalent to high school diplomas), find alternative job training programs, and raise their children. The rhetoric supporting the legislation seemed even harsher. Although negative images of welfare recipients had been common since the beginning of government support for the poor, politicians in 1996 got downright nasty. Congressman John Mica (R-FL) compared aid recipients to animals as he held up a sign on the house floor reading, "Don't Feed the Alligators." He explained that "we post these warnings because unnat-ural feeding and artificial care create dependency." While equations between poor people and ani-mals may have been extreme, such comments found acceptance with a public that believed people receiving welfare were lazy, fraudulent, immoral, and unwilling to work.

In response to cuts in aid and the increasingly hostile climate that supported them, a group of Suffolk County, New York, welfare recipients (or *participants,* as they preferred to be called) organized to challenge unfair policies for, and images of, the poor. Calling themselves the Suffolk County Welfare Warriors (SWW) and modeled after a similar group of poor women activists in Milwaukee, Wisconsin, these women began as a kind of speakers bureau. As lecturers, they countered stereotypes of laziness, ignorance, irresponsi-bility, and lack of ambition with stories of hard work, close families, and serious dreams. SWW spoke to religious groups and civic organizations and gave testimony at public hearings about the social disen-franchisement of poverty, the widespread impact of domestic abuse, the lack of economic opportunities for single women, and the dearth of child and health care available to low-income mothers. By debunk-ing myths about who they were and how they became poor, SWW hoped to educate the public and change policies. The group also lobbied against a local policy that stopped child care benefits for women attend-ing college, which led to a successful lawsuit. Eventually, the warriors also used direct action techniques such as hijacking programs at government meetings and public events in order to get their messages heard.

A group of undergraduate students from Southampton College started working with the organi-zation in 1994 and for almost 2 years participated in a range of events, from educational to direct action, in order to help. One student, an older African-Native American woman with three children who herself had been on and off welfare support, became a member of the speakers bureau. Another student, a white Navy veteran whose mother had been on welfare for a short time after his parents divorced, attended meetings and helped organize a variety of direct action events. And another student, an 18-year-old woman from a white, upper-middle-class family in the Philadelphia suburbs, helped run an art program that acted as an informal day care for the children of some of the women who participated in the organization. In each case, students gained insights into the everyday lived

*(Continued)*

(Continued)

experiences of people in poverty, as well as experience in working together with poor people them-selves to change policies that maintained and intensified poverty.

Terri Scofield, the founder of SWW, believed that a group of women receiving welfare benefits could debunk mean-spirited myths about poor people at the same time that they organized to advocate for others suffering from what she called "systemic problems" of economic abuse and neglect (deMause 1995). For Melissa Arch-Walton, the Southampton College student, a single mother of three children and a welfare recipient, SWW "reframed the whole welfare reform debate from 'the welfare problem' to the problem of the disparity between the poor and the wealthy." In other words, she continued, "welfare exists to address inequality, so you can't reform welfare without doing something more about inequality."[3]

In fact, SWW argued that poor people should be shaping welfare reforms since they were the experts on what resources they needed to better raise their families. Scofield explains,

> [The government] does a business bill, they talk to businessmen. They do an environmental bill, they talk to environmentalists. Why when they write a poverty bill, don't they talk to poor people? We are the experts on poverty. We can tell you exactly what we need. And it ain't ser-vices. The only thing keeping us from a decent life is money, income. We don't need parenting classes, we don't need supervision, we don't need training in self-esteem. What we need is edu-cation, what we need is good paying jobs. (Quoted in deMause 1996:16)

In other words, SWW allowed poor women to represent themselves. These women knew they worked hard, parented well, and were intelligent enough to succeed in higher education. Their stories described how a host of life circumstances, primarily linked to their class positions and public poli-cies, kept them in poverty.

Students who worked with SWW not only learned these stories (for Melissa, it was already her own experience), but they also learned about strategies to impact public perceptions and public policies. For the student who led the arts and crafts workshop for the children of some of the activists, she pro-vided an important service for the women who needed time to give talks, support other welfare recip-ients who were dealing with red tape, or just run errands. She also wrote that the experience taught her how few opportunities children in poverty have for enrichment programs—something she always took for granted growing up in an upper-middle-class suburb.

Adam Boyle (personal communication, June 2005), the Navy veteran, explains that he learned how systemic inequalities impacted people on an everyday level. In an interview, he remembers thinking that he "could have learned the specifics of welfare policies and how agencies work, but without

---

[3]Quotation from personal interview with Melissa Arch-Walton, March 1998. For more on the backlash against welfare mothers, see Ellen Reese, *Backlash Against Welfare Mothers: Past and Present* (University of California Press, 2005) and Angie-Marie Hancock, *The Politics of Disgust: The Public Identity of the Welfare Queen* (NYU Press, 2004).

getting to know and work with SWW I would never have experienced how these policies and procedures work to impact people's daily lives." He continues,

> When Beth lost a whole day of work because a case worker lost her file and she needs to fill out paperwork again; or when Terri spent an afternoon defending someone whose benefits were cut unfairly, you can see how the system works to degrade people, puts stumbling blocks in front of them and makes it harder to get off of welfare. On top of that, these women were vilified—they were an easy target to deflect attention from issues of government and corporate malfeasance by turning them into "lazy people with 10 kids living off the government's dime." When you meet them you would see how comical this caricature was. They didn't want to be on welfare. Who would, considering the hardships? Yet, if they did manage to make a decent life for their family they'd be vilified for that, too ("how come you can buy meat and your kids are dressed nice?" when checking out at the grocery store using food stamps). To make matters worse, the government wants to *look* like they're doing something to solve this "problem" and comes up with unworkable solutions to get them off welfare and into the workplace, forgetting that most of them already work, go to school, or both and that there are often children to care for, no money for transportation, and the government-sponsored jobs were dead-end, low wage ones. These women went though life just trying to eke out a living for themselves and their children, facing scorn at every turn. (n.p.)

SWW understood their poverty as being caused by systemic inequalities resulting from rich and powerful people promoting policies that increased their own wealth and power while demonizing those on welfare. Students who worked with SWW learned how policies and structural inequalities caused poverty in general, and they also learned how people in poverty could fight back to challenge both structures and ideologies that oppressed them.

Conflict sociology has long looked at inequality, not as a necessary function of social organization like the functionalists do, but as a result of unequal struggles for power in society. From a conflict perspective, poverty exists because people in power create policies and institutions to maintain and increase their power and wealth, while those with little power struggle to organize and change those conditions. Policies and programs to improve the lives of poor people arise only when serious grassroots movements force people in power to respond.

## Case Study Questions

1. How might welfare policies be designed differently if their architects were composed of people who participated in the welfare system?

2. What kinds of organizing methods did the Welfare Warriors use to challenge the power of state legislators and others?

3. What roles do you think students could or should play in addressing issues such as welfare reform?

## VOICES FROM THE FIELD

### The Welfare Warriors and the Direct Action Welfare Group

Headquartered in Milwaukee, Wisconsin, the Welfare Warriors have been fighting for the rights of poor women since 1986. According to its mission, "The Welfare Warriors are mothers and children in poverty who have joined together to make our voices heard in all policies affecting families in poverty, the larger community, and the Earth." Aside from marches, demonstrations, lobbying, and other grassroots activist tactics and organizing strategies, the Welfare Warriors produce the *Welfare Mothers Voice,* a newsletter with national distribution in the tens of thousands.

One recent edition featured the group DAWG (Direct Action Welfare Group) from West Virginia. According to Evelyn Dortch, one of DAWG's leaders, "Direct Action Welfare Group (DAWG) was founded by welfare mothers in college. We were fighting to make sure education counted as a work activity. To this day higher education and the right to an education are a big part of DAWG.

In 2000, the West Virginia Legislature passed Senate Bill 577, which was widely viewed as landmark legislation in the wake of welfare reform. The bill allowed West Virginia TANF [Temporary Assistance for Needy Families] recipients to count education and training as a work activity. This bill allowed people to pursue college degrees and still receive welfare benefits. West Virginia was one of the first states to allow this.

DAWG continues to fight to ensure that everyone who wants to pursue higher education has that right. West Virginia is still one of the few states that allows postsecondary (college) education to count toward work requirements for a welfare check. But we are in danger of no longer having this option. Due to the recent Deficit Reduction Act (DRA) the federal government has changed what can count as a work activity. And one of the things that no longer counts is higher education. This means people who receive welfare can *not* go to college."

*Source:* Welfare Warriors website at www.welfarewarriors.org. Photos courtesy of Evelyn Dortch (DAWG).

## CASE STUDY #2

### To Market: Functionalism and the East St. Louis Farmers' Market

Kenneth Reardon (1997), former professor of urban planning at the University of Illinois at Urbana-Champaign and director of the East St. Louis Action Research Project (ESLARP), writes that the idea for a farmers' market in East St. Louis came from a door-to-door survey of 550 households conducted by a group of college students and community members. The survey found that most people spent more money on food than any other regular consumer item, yet they were often forced to shop outside of their neighborhoods or pay inflated prices for poor selections at local "convenience" stores. According to a University of Connecticut's Food Marketing Policy Center report, low-income urban neighborhoods across the United States have 30% fewer supermarkets than their wealthier suburban neighbors (Brownell & Horgen 2004; Cotterill & Franklin 1995). When it comes to groceries, *poor people pay more for less.*

The lack of access to adequate and healthy food results in something economists and hunger analysts call **food insecurity.** According to Kathleen Walker (2005),

> Food insecurity is best defined as the uncertain ability of acquiring adequate nutritional food in a safe and acceptable manner. Household food security is defined as the ability of a household to have permanent and secure access of sufficient amounts and variety of foods. In food security all individuals in the household live a healthy, active and productive life. (p. 2)

Poor people suffer a variety of health problems because of the inaccessibility of nutritional food in adequate quantities. Changing their lack of access, however, seems out of their hands.

For major retailers, it only makes sense to locate in areas where people have more money to shop. The old joke states that three things determine a retail business's success: "location, location, location." Thus, Just-Food.com (2001) found, "it was no surprise that, on average, the top stores in the 2001 Supermarket Panel were in locations with unusually high median household income" (n.p.). Along with poorer people, low-income urban neighborhoods usually have higher crime rates that result in more security costs, higher utility rates, and older infrastructures that require frequent and expensive repairs. A lack of adequate transportation for consumers results in more people taking shopping carts home, further increasing retailers' costs. In essence, it doesn't make good business sense for grocery stores to locate in poor urban neighborhoods.

Perceived "good sense" based on such cost-benefit analyses pervades contemporary logic and morality. Such premises, however, also dominated sociological thinking for many years. Functionalism gained ascendancy in the United States right after World War II. As described earlier, the theory argues that society is an increasingly complex organism that must fulfill certain basic functions to survive and thrive. While functionalists usually claim that social problems are "dysfunctions" that eventually get addressed, many believe that the continued existence of certain social ills must mean that so-called "problems" actually have positive functions, too. In other words, a cost-benefit analysis would reveal that some social problems actually benefit much of society and, therefore, societies have a functional interest in maintaining, not ameliorating them.

In a famous article entitled "The Uses of Poverty: The Poor Pay All," Herbert Gans (1971) claimed that the historical persistence of poverty forces social scientists to consider the possibility that it serves

*(Continued)*

(Continued)

some undeniable role in fulfilling some of society's basic functions. Gans realized such a claim, that poverty may be good (or at least necessary) for society, might be seen as controversial. He explained,

> Associating poverty with positive functions seems at first glance to be unimaginable. Of course, the slumlord and the loan shark are commonly known to profit from the existence of poverty, but they are viewed as evil men, so their activities are classified among the dysfunctions of poverty. However, what is less often recognized, at least by the conventional wisdom, is that poverty also makes possible the existence or expansion of respectable professions and occupations, for example, penology, criminology, social work, and public health. (p 20)

Gans continued his list, contending that poverty also created jobs for people who provide services for the poor and presented career-making subject matter for journalists and social scientists. He concluded that "poverty and the poor may well satisfy a number of positive functions for many nonpoor groups in American society" (p. 20).

Gans (1971) went on to argue that poor people serve important economic functions, as they do the "dirty work" no one else wants to do, they do it cheaply enough to subsidize the middle and upper class who hire them, and they create jobs for middle-class service professionals ranging from social workers and health care providers to police and prison officials. On a social level, poverty serves to guarantee the social status of non-poor people, it provides an easily stigmatized group, and it helps to maintain economic and cultural discipline among those of higher classes who might fear falling into poverty.

Some sociologists believe that Gans's article was written "tongue-in-cheek" as a sarcastic critique of functionalism. For some, the idea that a system's functioning depended on a group's poverty and suffering seemed absurd, morally and theoretically. Yet, from a macro-functionalist perspective, Gans shed light on the many interests that *are* served by poverty's persistence. Certainly, poverty does not serve many positive functions for the poor themselves. Poor people often find that their own "cost-benefit analyses" of their condition require them to organize and act on their own behalf against what might be financially or socially profitable for others in society.

In the early 1990s, East St. Louis was one of the poorest communities in the nation with almost 40% of the population living below the poverty line. The city's once-thriving industrial base had disappeared as businesses sought to maximize their profits by seeking cheaper labor and production costs elsewhere. Meanwhile, the city also experienced a rapid evacuation of upper- and middle-class residents (mostly white) to the suburbs. With them went major department stores and other retail outlets. Traditional economic development plans had not succeeded in recruiting either major retailers or manufacturers back to the city. In an effort to take control of their own local economic and social development, the Winstanley/Industry Park Neighborhood Organization (WIPNO) contacted ESLARP to bring in university resources and expertise in hopes that more collaborative and community-based planning projects could be successful.

The ensuing project brought together University of Illinois students and faculty with religious leaders and local officials. They investigated job-creation strategies that might also keep consumer spending inside the local community. As Reardon (1997) explains, "*recaptured* purchases provide direct sales to local businesses, enabling them to expand their activities and increase city revenues from local sales taxes" (p. 63, emphasis original). The aforementioned household survey was then conducted to see what kinds of businesses might be most successful in attracting people to shop locally. The emphasis on groceries, and particularly fresh and affordable produce, led the task force to consider the potential of a community-owned farmers' market.

In 1993, local residents and students examined a dozen other similar midwestern cities that had municipally operated farmers' markets. They interviewed customers, vendors, and managers to find out what made markets successful. Eventually, the group recommended that WIPNO develop a market in or near the East St. Louis central business district (Axel-Lute, 1999). Reardon (1999) describes the kinds of student involvement that ensued:

> In the spring of 1994, the task force, with the assistance of a graduate planning student and faculty member, developed funding for such a facility. The task force collaborated with three graduate architecture, landscape architecture, and urban and regional planning studios to identify the most appropriate site for the market, design an attractive yet inexpensive market structure, and secure the necessary local and state building and health permits to establish a facility where fresh foods could be sold. . . . When the physical rehabilitation of the market structure was completed, these graduate students helped the task force recruit fourteen local residents interested in operating stands in the new market, and worked with WIPNO to design and offer a sixteen-hour small business training program to provide would-be merchants with basic skills in purchasing, marketing, merchandising, pricing, customer relations, and accounting. (p. 65)

Ultimately, between 1994 and 1996, the market generated almost $395,000 in direct sales and helped the city recapture over $900,000 that would have gone to nearby suburban towns if the farmers' market had not been there.

Gans's (1971) argument, that some social problems persist because they serve a range of social functions, is persuasive. But a functionalist approach to social problems also requires that we recognize how groups strive to meet their *own* needs. By tapping into the resources of local institutions such as universities and churches, WIPNO was able to move toward improving local economic conditions and even improve the community's nutritional choices. ESLARP's primary political goals target such opportunities and aim to offer resources, research, and expertise in the cause of community-led local development.

But ESLARP also has important educational objectives. Students participating in local development and improvement projects learn that social science research can be done in collaboration with nonacademic organizations and be applied to making the community a better place. They've learned and applied knowledge in a variety of fields: research methods, urban planning, community organizing, and landscape architecture. Reardon (1999) believes that examples such as the East St. Louis Farmers' Market highlight "the reciprocal learning that occurs in participatory action research projects in which the local knowledge of community residents is joined with the professional knowledge offered by university faculty and students to arrive at innovative solutions to community problems" (p. 65).

In essence, social problems become the subject and object of study as students use particular social problems as their curriculum, and use their course work to try and understand *and* address these very

*(Continued)*

(Continued)

same problems. In the case of the East St. Louis Farmers' Market, students learned that poverty can impact a variety of issues, from consumer practices to nutrition. They also discovered that these disparities were not just a sign of social dysfunctions, but could also appear because economic institutions made cost-benefit analyses that seemed logical—at least for some. Ultimately, students learned that sociological theories could be marshaled to analyze a situation and develop strategies for change. Sociological research and knowledge could then be applied to make that change.

### Case Study Questions

1. What difference do you think it makes to have people in the neighborhoods decide what the local problems are that need to be addressed?

2. Many sociologists consider functionalism a "conservative" theory that merely legitimizes the system "as it is." Do you agree? How might this example challenge such a perspective?

3. What local businesses or groups would you create to address community problems?

## VOICES FROM THE FIELD

### Mimi Arnstein, Wellspring Farm CSA

Mimi Arnstein is a farmer in Marshfield, Vermont. She runs the Wellspring Farm CSA (Community Supported Agriculture). CSAs allow people who might not have access to fresh (and often organic) produce to get them straight from the farm. According to Arnstein, "they reconnect people with the farms producing their food, while using 'members' or 'shareholders' fees to meet the farm's early season expenses." In exchange, members receive a weekly share of the season's harvest direct from the farm. CSAs address a variety of social problems by educating people about the environment and nutrition; helping the local economy and preserving farm land; and bringing people together to build community. Arnstein says, "CSA connects members with the land, seasonal change, and the people growing their food. Members support local farmers by keeping their food dollars in the community and contribute toward stewardship of local land and agricultural viability on a small scale." CSAs often depend on volunteer labor and student internships.

*Source: Personal communication, April 2008.*

## CASE STUDY #3

Cultures of Poverty and Power: Symbolic Interactionism, or "Who You Callin' Homeless?"

Poverty impacts children the most. In 2004, an estimated 38% of children (almost 27 million) lived in a low-income home, and 17% lived in families below the poverty line.[4] These children suffer from hunger, homelessness or inadequate shelter, and poor medical care. The 1994 Children's Defense Fund report, *Wasting America's Future,* documents what a lack of money does to poor children. Without proper food, poor children have high rates of iron deficiency, malnutrition, stunted growth, and lack of energy. Without adequate housing, youth suffer from transience; overcrowding; allergies and illness caused by cold, dampness, mold, cockroaches, and so on; and the disruption of sleep and study. Without sufficient health care, many chronic illnesses go untreated and serious diseases go undetected. Meanwhile, these children have little hope of improving their conditions through education, hard work, or some form of creative self-expression or intellectual activity. As one of the SWW student volunteers learned, kids who grow up in poverty have fewer resources and opportunities to experience the kinds of enrichment programs that often allow middle- and upper-class children to explore creative interests, occupations, or dreams.

In 1991, Valerie Ackerman, a social worker and local activist in Ann Arbor, Michigan, wrote a successful grant for McKinney Act funding for homeless youth. Passed in 1986, the McKinney-Vento Homeless Assistance Act originally consisted of 15 programs providing a range of services to homeless people, including emergency shelter, transitional housing, job training, primary health care, education, and some permanent housing. Ackerman wanted money to address the educational deficiencies of youth whose transience from shelter to relatives' homes to public housing to shelter severely impacted their schooling. As part of her work, she enlisted me (Corey Dolgon, then a University of Michigan graduate student and composition teacher) to design a summer writing and enrichment program for her students. I had been involved with summer writing programs for high school students at the university and had worked with colleagues who were nationally known for designing community-based literacy programs for "at-risk" youth (Fleischer 1995; Schaafsma 1993).

To develop the curriculum, I enlisted a group of graduate students he had worked with as writing teachers and as community activists involved with anti-poverty, anti-racism and homelessness issues. We wanted to give students a chance to write creatively about their lives and experiences at the same time that we offered them basic literacy skills, computer skills, and a chance to publish work at the end of the 6-week program. We knew that homeless youth were stigmatized by teachers, welfare case workers, and the community at-large (Polakow, 1994). Many of us had already experienced, either through observation or our own backgrounds, how people assumed that poor youth grew up in cultures of poverty where education had little value.

*(Continued)*

[4]These numbers are from the federal poverty guidelines issued by the U.S. Department of Health and Human Services. The demographic findings in this fact sheet were calculated using a more complex version of the federal poverty measure—the thresholds issued by the U.S. Census Bureau. More information about federal poverty measures is available at http://aspe.hhs.gov/poverty/04poverty.shtml.

(Continued)

These assumptions led to the kind of labeling that lowered expectations of the youth and limited the motivations of the youth themselves. We thought our program could challenge these dynamics.

From a cultural perspective, some sociologists and anthropologists have proposed the **culture of poverty** theory (Lewis 1966). In brief, this idea recognizes that different classes have different sets of cultural values and practices. Poor people develop a *subculture* that includes unstable family structures, personal irresponsibility, and a lack of faith and investment in education and other public institutions. These values and behaviors get passed down from generation to generation and make it almost impossible to get out of poverty.

Many sociologists (Coward, Feagin, Williams 1974), however, argue that these cultures are a response to social conditions and are shaped as much, if not more, by the choices allotted by society as by individuals' choices. Sociologist Elijah Anderson's (1989, 1992) work on the sexual practices and family structures of inner-city teenagers offers an example of these dynamics. He explains that the sexual conduct among poor, black, inner-city adolescents often results in growing numbers of unwed parents. Partly, this comes from young men whose peer groups boast about sexual exploits and denounce conventional family life. Yet Anderson (1989) argues that their "realities are born of the extremely difficult socioeconomic situation prevailing in ghetto communities. The lack of family-sustaining jobs or job prospects denies young men the possibility of forming economically self-reliant families, the traditional American mark of manhood" (p. 25). While these young males' peer groups emphasize sexual prowess as a mark of manhood, girls may be lured by promises of love and marriage. As girls submit, they "often end up pregnant and abandoned, eligible for a limited but sometimes steady income in the form of welfare which may allow them to establish their own households, and at times, attract other men, in need of money" (p. 25). A culture of poverty results, but it is a culture that is highly structured by the opportunities and values that impact the possibilities and choices of poor urban youth.

Similarly, labeling theory helps explain how the expectations and treatment of poor youth further influence their cultural practices and social behaviors. We've seen how stereotyping and social stigma worked to impact the lives of poor women on welfare. The process of labeling has even more detrimental effects on children. Poor youth face lower expectations at school; experience higher rates of arrest; and suffer a barrage of media images that demonize their music, fashion, and other means of expression (Males 1996). Writer Jonathan Kozol (1996) interviewed a poor teenage girl from New York's South Bronx who explained the impact of these dynamics:

> If you weave enough bad things into the fibers of a person's life—sickness and filth, old mattresses and other junk thrown in the streets and other ugly ruined things, and ruined people, a prison here, sewage there, drug dealers here, the homeless people over there, then give us the very worst schools anyone could think of, hospitals that keep you waiting for ten hours, police that don't show up when someone's dying . . . you can guess that life will not be very nice and children will not have much sense of being glad of who they are. Sometimes it feels like we've been buried six feet under their perceptions. (p. 123)

Our summer writing program hoped to address these cultural conditions. First, we would offer poor youth the chance to change their own self-perceptions by giving them an opportunity to be published authors. At the same time, we hoped to challenge the community's perceptions of these youth as they became the public experts on their own lives.

In two summers, students produced two different volumes of writing and art work (*Life Stories* and *Minds at Work*) and each summer we held book signings at local bookstores. Some wrote about their work experiences. Lanier, an 18-year-old junior at Willow Run High School, wrote "A Day at Work":

> When I come in McDonald's I be wanting to be like, "Damn, another day in this bitch!" So I just, you know, go and do my original job: I go wash my hands, punch in and get my apron, and I begin working.
>
> I go check the meat setting to see if everything is all right. The meat patties are very cold. I grab a few and begin cooking meat and wrapping burgers for about six hours.
>
> The heat from the grill is very hot. The grease from the burgers was popping on me, burning me a little bit while I was cleaning the grill.
>
> For about six hours I wrapped burgers and thought about stuff like them not giving me enough hours, about my pay, and about getting me another job.
>
> Two weeks later I got twenty dollars for that day's pay.

Many of us had read ethnographies of factory and service work, but Lanier's words captured so much of the sensory experience—the range from frozen meat on the fingers to burning oil on the arms—of fast food labor. Lanier poignantly exposes the awful dilemma of such drudgery—hating the tediousness but wanting more hours.

Other students wrote about their lives in the streets. Guns and shootings, drugs and illness, welfare services and prisons, violence and despair filled the pages of both books. But students also wrote tremendous fantasy stories about knights and football players, about haunted houses and graveyards, about hard-nosed crime detectives and superheroes. Some of the most powerful writing reflected the dichotomy of being both children and people struggling to survive poverty. Poems from student David Gilvin-Heath depict the heart-wrenching truths of innocence amidst the degradation and horror.

> **Bear**
>
> I am a bear, large and fierce
>
> Yet somehow only a cub
>
> My fellow people surround me with knowledge
>
> I eat this sweet fruit with nectar and am poisoned

*(Continued)*

(Continued)

Poisoned by my own fear and ignorance

But yet I am a bear and am compelled by tradition to fight

My own bitter hemlock now makes me weak

No I must fight! Fight! Until there is nothing left to do

But to die in shame and unknowing, a bear.

Cat

I chase birds; I must be strong

I run from dogs, could I be weak?

I am a cat: no one's beast of burden

I am a cat: not like a dog

I am a cat: use me only as directed.

In the introduction to the first volume, Dave Schaafsma (quoted in *Life Stories* 1993:8) reminded readers that "despite all that [these students have] seen and done they are still children." He concluded,

Dancing with hope on these pages for a future where they are loved, where they are accepted, where they are not living in fear, hunger, despair, the voices of these proud and defiant and vulnerable children speak to us. What emerges, finally, is that these children become our teachers, speaking to us about what it means to live their lives. (p. 9)

And I believe that is exactly what Gilvin-Heath had in mind when he invited us to read,

**Being a Fruit**
Lying idle waiting for you
Waiting
Unwrap my gentle skin
Eat my sweet and lush insides
Swallow me
Let me provide for you

Students surprised us in other ways, too. Whenever we discussed the project in general terms, youth resisted the program's reference to "homeless" or "poor" youth. One student exhorted, "Who you callin' homeless? My mom has a home now." The youth themselves had accepted the social stereotypes of poor and homeless people to such a degree that they were offended by the reference. Such ingrained hostility to their own social conditions and position helps explain why so many of them actually resisted relating personal experiences and often chose to create fantasy pieces or fictional characters who experienced similar conditions. But even in these fantasies, they demanded a kind of respect and dignity, even if they couldn't reflect critically on the social and structural conditions that stigmatized and even demonized being poor.

Ultimately, the writing project was only a momentary blip on the radar screens of these youths' lives. But for a short time, these youth got a variety of opportunities: educational, personal, and political. The program gave students intense tutoring in writing and computer literacy, and it helped them develop a host of skills that would enhance their learning potential in school. Today, Gilvin says the program encouraged him to keep reading and writing and trying to better understand himself and the world around him. "It was an opportunity to think and dream about a better world, something that remains important to me today." I recently received an e-mail request from David to sign a petition and forward an announcement concerning a multinational corporation's plan to destroy two glaciers in Chile (thus destroying the local water resource) in order to mine for precious minerals discovered below the glaciers. He explained, "The problem we face with greed is out of control. This sort of ecological destruction should never be condoned."

Students also got an opportunity to build relationships with staff and one another in a noninstitutional academic context. In other words, youth experienced education in an empowering and encouraging framework—very different from the stereotyping or negligence they were used to. And, finally, as they became "published" experts in communicating their lives, their insights and ideas entered the public debate about policies for youth in poverty. Many of the staff members who have gone on to work in education and policy fields claim to have been impacted by these stories. Some of us use them frequently when promoting the power of intense, noninstitutional educational opportunities for children in poverty.

## Case Study Questions

1. Why did some of the young people respond negatively to being called "homeless"?

2. How did having the opportunity to express themselves formally and creatively change at least some of the hardships facing these youth?

3. Can you think of any experiences in your own life where your own sense of identity and pride was challenged by being stereotyped?

## VOICES FROM THE FIELD

Neil Donovan, Executive Director, National Coalition for the Homeless

(Excerpt from interview with Andy Freeze, Street News Service)

**Andy Freeze:** How did you get started working on the issue of homelessness?

**Neil Donovan:** In my early twenties, I was studying to be a brother of religious orders, with the Xaverian Brothers. It was an important and life-changing period in my life. My first internship involved working at Common Life, a drop-in center for homeless and run-away youth. As a new intern, I asked a young girl in the shelter if she wanted to talk. She said, "Only if you promise to come back tomorrow." I agreed to return, hoping that our conversations could help her in some small way and maybe turn into something lasting. The Xaverian Brothers' motto is, "In harmony small things grow." So I guess in a way, I've just never stopped, "coming back tomorrow."

**AF:** You have worked with and for people who are homeless over 26 years, working at a variety of agencies, from what you have learned, what will help the National Coalition for the Homeless [NCH] move forward with their plan/agenda?

ND:        Everywhere I've worked and everything I've learned, from working with and for people experiencing homelessness, has taught me about the importance of justice. The Coalition's mission, strategic plan and stand on justice is clear and direct: Bring America Home. It's the cornerstone of our beliefs and the engine that drives our advocacy. The only way that we can work toward ending homeless[ness], either as a coalition or as a nation, is through: housing justice, health care justice, economic justice and civil rights. . . .

AF:        You then went to the National Alliance to End Homelessness to start up the Center for Capacity Building, which works with communities across the country. What did you learn from this experience and what else do you think is needed to help communities accomplish the goals contained in their Ten Year Plans to End Homelessness?

ND:        I think there was a lot to learn from the Ten Year Plan to End Homelessness experience. National advocacy groups learned that a call-to-action must consider the overall capacity of local communities to respond. The federal government learned that top down guidance only works if that guidance takes into consideration the needs and characteristics of local communities. And local communities learned about the importance of building capacity to a level that would allow them to end homelessness and not merely maintain a level of support. I think two things are needed to help communities accomplish the goals contained in their Ten-Year Plan to End Homelessness. First, include current and former homeless people at every level of planning, development and execution. At the Coalition, we ask all groups—public and private, local, state, and federal—to begin every meeting by asking the basic question "Is everyone here, who needs to be here?" If there isn't a first-person representative stakeholder representing homelessness at your meetings and convenings, your plan has a greater potential to fail. Second, local communities can not and will not end homelessness without a greater federal commitment. There's an expression: "Homelessness is a national problem with local solutions." The end of that sentence should be, ". . . and a greater federal commitment."

AF:        NCH has been around over 25 years, what do you see the role of the coalition as the organization moves forward?

ND:        The original purpose or role of the National Coalition for the Homeless remains its only purpose: The Coalition exists as a national network of current and former homeless people, activists and advocates, community-based and faith-based service providers, and other dedicated individuals and organizations committed to ending homelessness in America. It's what attracted me to the Coalition and more importantly it's what will Bring America Home. The power is in its simplicity.

## SUMMARY

While some believe that "the poor will always be with us," history has demonstrated that the rates and impact of poverty change significantly over time. How many people are poor and what quality of life poor people can expect are malleable social conditions, effectively impacted by humane public policies and committed public efforts. This chapter has demonstrated how a wide range of projects and programs has challenged the structural and cultural impediments that face poor people. Students working with neighborhood organizations, direct action groups, and educational programs have helped to make a serious difference in the lives of people with fewer resources. These collaborations taught all involved about the power of collective engagement in changing individual lives, but more importantly social institutions and public policies. Perhaps even more importantly, this work also exposed the limitations of these efforts and the continuing need to integrate local and regional work with large-scale political attempts to change the basic conditions of resource distribution in the country and around the world.

## SUMMARY QUESTIONS

1. What is social stratification? How does it shape and support the existence of poverty?

2. What is the poverty line? Why was it created? How has its impact changed?

3. How does an ideology like individualism impact our understanding and treatment of poverty in general and poor people in particular?

4. What is a social stigma? How does stigma influence social policy and individual treatment of poor people?

5. How do different theories of social life influence the kinds of approaches society takes to addressing poverty?

## GLOSSARY

Corporate Welfare: Government funding to corporations so as to enhance their profit-making capabilities through international trade subsidies, tax breaks, grants for advertising and marketing, and so on.

**Culture of Poverty:** This theory contends that poor people share deviant cultural characteristics and maintain lifestyles that perpetuate their own poverty.

**Food Insecurity:** When people lack physical, social, and economic access to sufficient, safe, and nutritious food that meets their dietary needs and preferences for an active and healthy life.

**Homelessness:** An extreme form of poverty in which families and individuals do not have access to affordable shelter.

**New Deal:** A series of policies and programs enacted by Franklin Delano Roosevelt's administration that addressed the severe economic hardships caused by the Great Depression. These included jobs programs, Social Security, and Medicare.

**Poverty:** The World Bank contends that poverty is hunger; not having a job; and lack of access to schools, health care, adequate shelter, and so on. However, a more comprehensive definition understands poverty as a relative term: Individuals, families, and groups in the population can be said to be in poverty when they lack the resources to obtain the types of diet, participate in the activities, and have the living conditions and amenities that are customary, or are at least widely encouraged and approved, in the societies in which they belong.

**War on Poverty:** A series of policies and programs enacted by the Lyndon Baines Johnson administration to address the problems of poverty during the 1960s.

**Wealth vs. Income:** *Income* is what one earns through wages, while *wealth* is what people own.

**Welfare:** Government funding programs that include food stamps and direct payments to poor people, unemployment compensation and workman's compensation, and other aid that helps people when economic hard times occur.

## WEBSITES TO LEARN MORE ABOUT INEQUALITY AND SERVICE LEARNING PROJECTS

Alliance of Students Against Poverty: http://www.asap2025.org/

Beyond Shelter: Combating Chronic Poverty, Welfare Dependency & Homelessness: http://www.beyondshelter.org/home.html

Food First: http://www.foodfirst.org/

Institute for Research on Poverty: http://www.irp.wisc.edu/

National Coalition for the Homeless: http://www.nationalhomeless.org/

National Student Campaign Against Hunger and Homelessness: http://www.studentsagainst hunger.org/

Oxfam America: http://www.oxfamamerica.org/

Project South: http://www.projectsouth.org/

Spotlight on Poverty and Opportunity: http://www.spotlightonpoverty.org/

US Census Bureau—Poverty: http://www.census.gov/hhes/www/poverty/poverty.html

Welfare Warriors: http://www.welfarewarriors.org/

## REFERENCES

Anderson, Elijah. 1989. "Sex Codes and Family Life Among Poor Inner-City Youths." *Annals of the American Academy of Political and Social Science,* 501:59–78.

_____. 1992. *Streetwise: Race, Class, and Change in an Urban Community.* Chicago, IL: University of Chicago Press.

Axel-Lute, Miriam. 1999. "Town & Gown: Making Research Serve Communities' Needs." *Shelterforce,* November/December.

Brownell, Kelly and Katherine Horgen. 2004. *Food Fight.* New York: McGraw-Hill.

Butler, Kate. 2007. "Portraying Poverty in the News: Media Outlets Represent the Poor as Essentially Different." *Suite101.com.* Retrieved February 18, 2010 (http://mainstreamjournalism.suite101.com/article.cfm/ portraying_poverty_in_the_news#ixzz0ceMKjWC5).

Children's Defense Fund. 1994. *Wasting America's Future.* Boston, MA: Beacon Press.

Collins, Chuck, Amy Gluckman, Meizhu Lui, Betsy Londar-Wright, Amy Offner, and Adria Scharf. eds. 2004. *The Wealth Inequality Reader.* Cambridge, MA: Dollars & Sense Economic Affairs Bureau.

Cotterill, Ronald W. and Andrew W. Franklin. 1995. *The Urban Grocery Store Gap.* Food Marketing Policy Issue Paper No. 8. Storrs, CT: Food Marketing Policy Center, University of Connecticut.

Coward, Barbara, Joe R. Feagin, and J. Allen Williams Jr. 1974. "The Culture of Poverty Debate: Some Additional Data." *Social Problems,* 21:621–634.

deMause, Neil. 1995. "Trouble in Riverhead." *Here.* Retrieved February 18, 2010 (http://www.heremagazine .com/riverhead.html).

_____. 1996. "Mobilizing the Welfare Vote." *Progressive,* 60:16.

deMause, Neil and Steve Rendall. 2007. "The Poor Will Always Be With Us—Just Not on the TV News. *FAIR: Fairness & Accuracy in Reporting,* September/October. Retrieved February 18, 2010 (http://www .fair.org/index.php?page = 3172).

Fisher, Gordon M. 1992. "The Development and History of the Poverty Thresholds," *Social Security Bulletin,* 55:3–14.

Fleischer, Cathy. 1995. *Composing Teacher-Research: A Prosaic History.* Albany, NY: State University of New York Press.

Gaetz, Stephen and Bill O'Grady. 2004. "Work on the Streets." Pp. 606–609 in *Encyclopedia of Homelessness,* edited by David Levinson. Thousand Oaks, CA: Sage.

Gans, Herbert J. 1971. "The Uses of Poverty: The Poor Pay All." *Social Policy,* July/August:20–24.

Gluckman, Amy. 2004. "Women and Wealth: A Primer." Pp. 62–68 in *The Wealth Inequality Reader,* edited by Dollars & Sense and United for a Fair Economy. Boston, MA: Economic Affairs Bureau.

Gordon, Linda. 1994. *Pitied But Not Entitled: Single Mothers and the History of Welfare.* New York: The Free Press.

Just-Food.com. 2001, December 18. "USA: The Results of the 2001 Supermarket Panel." Retrieved January 8, 2010 (http://www.just-food.com/article.aspx?id = 74410&lk = s).

Katz, Michael. 1986. *In the Shadow of the Poorhouse: A Social History of Welfare in America.* New York: Basic Books.

King, Martin Luther Jr. 1967. *Where Do We Go From Here: Chaos or Community?* New York: Harper & Row.

Kozol, Jonathan. 1996. *Amazing Grace: The Lives of Children and the Conscience of a Nation.* New York: Harper Perennial.

Krugman, Paul. 2004. *The Great Unraveling: Losing Our Way in the New Century.* New York: Norton.

Leuchtenberg, William. 1963. *Franklin D. Roosevelt and the New Deal.* New York: HarperCollins.

Lewis, Oscar. 1966. *La Vida: A Puerto Rican Family in the Culture of Poverty—San Juan and New York.* New York: Wiley.

*Life Stories: Expressions from the Students of the Willow Run/Ann Arbor Project for Homeless Youth Summer Writing Program 1993.* 1993. Ann Arbor, MI: Great Copy.

Males, Mike. 1996. *The Scapegoat Generation: America's War on Adolescents.* Boston, MA: Common Courage Press.

McIlvane, Robert S. 1993. *The Great Depression: America 1929–1941.* Pittsburgh, PA: Three Rivers Press.

Nadasen, Premilla. 2005. *Welfare Warriors: The Welfare Rights Movement in the United States.* New York: Routledge.

Oliver, Melvin and Thomas Shapiro. 1997. "Black Wealth/White Wealth: A New Perspective on Racial Inequality." Pp. 258–276 in *The Inequality Reader: Contemporary and Foundational Readings in Race, Class, and Gender,* edited by David Grusky and Szonja Szelényi. Boulder, CO: Westview Press.

Piven, Frances Fox and Richard Cloward. 1979. *Poor People's Movements: Why They Succeed, How They Fail.* New York: Vintage Press.

____. 1993. *Regulating the Poor: The Functions of Public Welfare.* New York: Vintage Press.

Polakow, Valerie. 1994. *Lives on the Edge: Single Mothers and Their Children in the Other America.* Chicago, IL: University of Chicago Press.

Reardon, Kenneth. 1997. "East St. Louis Action Research Project." Pp. 52–57 in *Grassroots Participatory Research: A Working Report From a Gathering of Practitioners,* edited by Lee Williams. Knoxville, TN: University of Tennessee.

____. 1999. "Promoting Community Development Through Empowerment Planning: The East St. Louis Action Research Project." Pp. 124–139 in *Rebuilding Urban Neighborhoods,* edited by W. Dennis Keating and Norman Krumholz. Newbury Park, CA: Sage.

Rhoads, Robert A. 1998. "Critical Multiculturalism and Service Learning." Pp. 7–14 in *Academic Service Learning: A Pedagogy of Action and Reflection,* edited by Robert A. Rhoades and Jeffrey P. F. Howard. San Francisco, CA: Jossey-Bass.

Rosenthal, Robert. 1994. *Homeless in Paradise: A Map of the Terrain.* Philadelphia, PA: Temple University Press.

Sanders, Bernie. 2002. "The Export-Import Bank: Corporate Welfare at Its Worst." *The Nation.* May 22.

Schaafsma, David. 1993. *Eating on the Street: Teaching Literacy in a Multicultural Society.* Pittsburgh, PA: University of Pittsburgh Press.

Tomaskovic-Devey, David. 1993. *Gender & Racial Inequality at Work: The Sources & Consequences of Job Segregation.* Ithaca, NY: ILR Press.

Walker, Kathleen C. 2005. "Management of Hunger in the United States." Retrieved January 8, 2010 (http://www.case.edu/med/epidbio/mphp439/Hunger.htm).

Wilkinson, Richard G. and Kate E. Pickett. 2006. "Income Inequality and Population Health: A Review and Explanation of the Evidence." *Social Science and Medicine,* 62:1768–1784.

Wilson, Andrea. 2003. "Race and Women's Income Trajectories: Employment, Marriage, and Income Security over the Life Course." *Social Problems,* 50:87–110.

Wolff, Edward N. 2002. *Top Heavy: The Increasing Inequality of Wealth in America and What Can Be Done About It.* 2nd ed. New York: The New Press.

Zinn, Howard. 1966. *New Deal Thought.* New York. Dobbs-Merrill.

# On the Job

*Work, Workers, and the Changing Nature of Labor*

> *When someone works for less pay than she can live on—when, for example, she goes hungry so that you can eat more cheaply and conveniently—then she has made a great sacrifice for you, she has made you a gift of some part of her abilities, her health, and her life. The "working poor" . . . are in fact the major philanthropists of our society. They neglect their own children so that the children of others will be cared for; they live in substandard housing so that other homes will be shiny and perfect. . . . To be a member of the working poor is to be an anonymous donor, a nameless benefactor, to everyone else.*
>
> —Barbara Ehrenreich, *Nickel and Dimed* (2002)

> *[W]e found my old man down on the trim line. His job was to install windshields using this goofy apparatus with large suction cups that resembled an octopus being crucified. A car would nuzzle up to the old man's work area and he would be waiting for it, a cigarette dangling from his lip. . . . Car, windshield. Car, windshield. Car, windshield. Drudgery piled atop drudgery. Cigarette to cigarette. Decades rolling through the rafters, bones turning to dust, stubborn clocks gagging down flesh, another windshield, another cigarette, that mechanical octopus squirming against nothing, nothing, NOTHINGNESS. I wanted to shout at my father, "Do something else!"*
>
> —Ben Hamper, *Rivethead* (1992)

On May 3, 2007, students at Harvard University began a hunger strike in support of campus security guards who were trying to bargain for a new contract. Fifteen years earlier, Harvard had outsourced its security guards to a management company. **Outsourcing** is a process in which employers hire other companies to provide ancillary service personnel in areas such as maintenance, food services, security, and so on, instead of hiring and managing them internally. Management companies generally promise employers better quality services at cheaper costs. To accomplish this, they reduce wages and benefits, often fighting to break unions or keep them from being organized in the first place. Although Harvard's security guards were represented by SEIU (Service Employees International Union) Local 615, the union had been unable to negotiate decent contracts with the management company—Allied Barton. To strengthen the union's efforts, Harvard students organized a campaign pressuring the university itself to play a role in forcing Allied Barton to negotiate fairly. As one student, Alyssa Aguilera, explained, "Because Harvard pays Allied Barton, Harvard does have the final say in the contract . . . [and] the capability [to ensure] that Harvard workers receive good pay and benefits. We're holding them responsible for that" (quoted in Benitez 2007a:n.p.).

Harvard students had been active on a number of campus worker issues throughout the late 1990s and early 2000s, supporting the organizing efforts of clerical workers and janitors (Featherstone 2002). In 2005, they established the Student Labor Action Movement (SLAM) and then coordinated a coalition of other campus groups called the Stand for Security Coalition to support the security guards. SLAM explained its work this way:

> The coalition was formed in order to establish a more broad support network for security officers. Although this campaign is one based on worker's rights, it is also a campaign simply to support fellow members of the Harvard community as they strive for social justice.
>
> As students, the security officers we see everyday are just as much a part of our lives as our professors or deans. We support our security officers, and all Harvard workers, in their efforts to improve their workplaces and will not sit idly as Harvard refuses to comply with these basic demands. (Stand for Security Coalition 2007:n.p.)

Students adopted a platform and began organizing activities to support the security guards' four basic demands: (1) fair wages, (2) regular, full-time hours, (3) union status and recognition, and (4) a grievance procedure.

Throughout 2006, students attended rallies, released statements of support, and gathered petitions calling on Harvard to take responsibility for how its contractor treated employees. Then, in April of 2007, students held their own rally to "turn up the pressure" on the university. As Aguilera, a Harvard sophomore and SLAM organizer, explained, "I know that, as a student, I have a lot of privilege, and I want to use that privilege to lend a hand to the workers who are also a part of the Harvard community" (Benitiz 2007b:n.p.). A month later, students held a one-day fast to intensify the pressure on Harvard's administration. When that failed, they began the hunger strike a few weeks later. In June of 2007, security guards ratified a contract that met almost all of their demands.

Work is not inherently a social problem. Labor to furnish the necessities of food, clothing, and shelter has always been an inherent part of the human condition. The goals of work, however, changed over time from survival, self-sufficiency, and community sustainability to creating large surpluses for royal families or massive profits for global corporations. Poverty, suffering, and dissatisfaction grew along with inequality and exploitation. As the content and control of labor moved from the hands of the worker to the purview of landowners and then factory managers, discontent and **alienation** quickly followed. Moreover, as compensation for labor became increasingly stratified by market dynamics; racial, ethnic, and gender biases; and a host of other cultural and social forces, the world of the worker grew more difficult. The evolution of labor has, therefore, resulted in a variety of social problems.

Service workers like security guards, custodians, clerical workers, and others occupy some of the most vulnerable positions in today's economy. The students at Harvard understood that their participation would be crucial to support workers whose union seemed relatively powerless to impact new economic conditions and management strategies such as outsourcing. Analyzing why these historically low-wage, nonunion jobs have become increasingly precarious in the new economy requires a broad sociohistorical context. This chapter begins with a brief statistical portrait of today's labor force that describes the social problems facing most workers. We then offer a short historical overview of how economic, cultural, and technological changes have impacted the way society has organized work and the way individuals have experienced labor conditions. Finally, we look at three case studies to examine how contemporary labor is being transformed, and how students are involved in addressing the social problems that surround the world of work.

## LABOR BY THE NUMBERS: A STATISTICAL PORTRAIT OF WORKERS IN THE UNITED STATES

Statistics can't tell us everything. At best, they offer us various snapshots that, when woven together artfully, create stories that are both accurate and meaningful. Yet they can easily be distorted, too. As Joel Best explained in his book, *Damned Lies and Statistics* (2001), "People use statistics to support particular points of view, and it is naïve simply to accept numbers as accurate without examining who is using them and why" (p. 13). Maintaining a critical perspective on statistics is crucial when studying social problems.

But when statistics can be compiled into a compelling narrative, and they overwhelmingly point toward particular conditions and trends, social scientists use them to explain both what is and how it came to be. For instance, the statistical portrait of inequality from the previous chapter paints a picture of growing disparities between wealth and poverty so striking that the problems are almost indisputable—even for those who argue that some inequality is necessary and useful. While different sociological theories make different causes and solutions debatable, the problems and scope are not.

The same kind of portrait can be constructed of the current conditions and trends for U.S. workers. This first figure (Figure 3.1) illustrates the average hourly wages and compensation of American workers from 1959 to 2004.

**Figure 3.1** Hourly Wage and Compensation for Production/Nonsupervisory Workers, 1959–2005

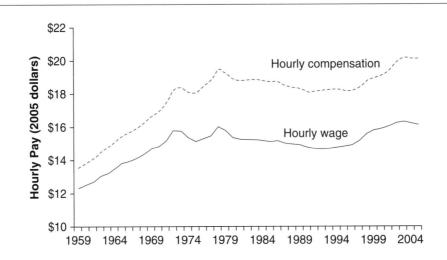

*Source:* Author's analysis.

As the graph indicates, while wages and benefits rose throughout the 1960s and even for a few years during the 1970s, from 1978 until 1997, wages declined or remained relatively flat for workers in nonsupervisory positions. And while they went up some in the late 1990s and early 2000s, they have since declined again. In fact, average wages and compensation are pretty much the same now as they were in the late 1970s. Yet the average cost of living in the United States has risen about 250% during this same period. What an hour of paid wages bought in 1979 ($16.00), an employee now has to work over 2.5 hours to purchase ($41.63). Thus, *real wages* (that is, wages adjusted for inflation to accurately measure purchasing power) have continued to decline steadily, sometimes dramatically, since the early 1970s.

Along with wages, the most dramatic change in compensation has been in the area of health care. Most workers were covered by employer insurance plans after World War II, but as health care costs skyrocketed in the 1970s and 1980s, more and more employers shifted costs to employees or imposed cost-cutting mechanisms such as "managed care," which limited services and often refused care outright to people with "pre-existing conditions." By the 1990s, fewer and fewer employers offered free, comprehensive health plans as part of compensation packages, and most began either increasing shared costs for employees or terminating plans altogether. In 2005, less than 56% of employers offered any kind of health insurance plans for their workers (Gould 2005; Skocpol 1997).

While wages and benefits have decreased, the amount of time workers spend on the job has increased dramatically. Historically, the average hours Americans worked per week decreased from the mid-60s in the late 19th century to the high 30s in the late 1960s.

Despite post–World War II predictions that Americans might have a 22-hour work week, a 6-month work year, or actually set a standard retirement age of 38, work hours have actually risen steadily since 1967. By the year 2000, workers in the United States put in about 200 hours (or 5 weeks) more per year than they did 30 years earlier. By 2006, almost 30% of nonagricultural workers and nearly 45% of agricultural workers put in more than 40-hour weeks at one job. This statistic does not include those working second or third jobs in different industries or "off the books" (Schor 1992).

Most sociologists argue that two major factors have caused workers' increased hours and decreased compensation. The first has been the changing nature of work. Table 3.1 demonstrates that since 1950, the majority of jobs available to Americans shifted from the manufacturing sector to the service sector. While minor shifts have occurred in transportation, trade, and government employment, the most drastic changes have occurred in the diminishing percentage of jobs in mining, construction, and manufacturing (Table 3.2), (from 41.5% in 1950 to 19.5% in 2000) and the rising proportion of work in the service industries (from 16% in 1950 to 36.5% in 2000).

**Table 3.1**   U.S. Labor Sector Breakdown 1950–2000

| Year | Total non-agricultural employment | Mining, construction, and manufacturing | Transportation | Trade (retail and wholesale) | Services (inc. real estate and financial) | Government |
|---|---|---|---|---|---|---|
| 1950 | 45,197 | 18,506 | 4,034 | 9,386 | 7,244 | 6,026 |
|  | 100% | **41.5%** | **8%** | **21%** | **16%** | **13.5%** |
| 1960 | 54,189 | 20,434 | 4,004 | 11,391 | 10,006 | 8,353 |
|  | 100% | **38%** | **7%** | **22%** | **18%** | **15%** |
| 1970 | 70,880 | 23,578 | 4,515 | 15,040 | 15,193 | 12,554 |
|  | 100% | **33%** | **7%** | **22%** | **20.5%** | **17.5%** |
| 1980 | 90,406 | 25,658 | 5,146 | 20,300 | 23,050 | 16,241 |
|  | 100% | **28.5%** | **6%** | **22%** | **25.5%** | **18%** |
| 1990 | 109,403 | 24,905 | 5,777 | 25,774 | 34,643 | 18,304 |
|  | 100% | **23%** | **5.5%** | **23.5%** | **31.5%** | **16.5%** |
| 2000 | 131,759 | 25,760 | 7,019 | 30,331 | 48,020 | 20,681 |
|  | 100% | **19.5%** | **5.5%** | **23.5%** | **36.5%** | **16%** |

*Source:* Data compiled from Bureau of Labor Statistics Report 2001 (http://www.bls.gov/opub/rtaw/pdf/table12.pdf).

The numbers are even more striking if we factor out construction, which has actually increased over that time. Without construction, manufacturing went from 38% of all nonagricultural employment to 14.5%. The loss of manufacturing jobs and the rise of a service economy comprise the defining characteristic of what sociologists and economists have called **deindustrialization.**

The "problems" with the loss of manufacturing jobs and the rise of service sector jobs are many. Most notable is that, while the service sector has produced some very high-wage positions, most service-oriented jobs have low wages and poor, if any, benefits. This next table demonstrates exactly how much worse service and retail sector jobs are relative to manufacturing and other employment.

Table 3.2   U.S. Labor Sector Breakdown and Related Wages and Benefits

| | Service jobs | Retail jobs | Manufacturing/ other | % diff (service) | % diff (retail) |
|---|---|---|---|---|---|
| Median wages | 456 | 343 | 542.3 | −16 | −37 |
| Health benefits | 49 | 38.4 | 71.5 | −36 | −46 |
| Pension benefits | 35.2 | 25.7 | 56.8 | −38 | −55 |
| Sick leave | 55.1 | 35.3 | 61.3 | −10 | −42 |
| Disability | 31.4 | 22.3 | 48.2 | −35 | −54 |

*Source:* "Inequality in Earnings at the Close of the Twentieth Century," 1999, by Martina Morris and Bruce Western *(Annual Review of Sociology*, 25:623–657).

Wages in service sector jobs averaged almost $100 less per week than manufacturing jobs and were 35–40% less likely to have health, pension, or disability benefits. Retail jobs measured even worse in comparison. The old adage that regardless of position, hard work will result in better compensation doesn't necessarily hold true for service sector jobs. In fact, economists have argued that, since the majority of service positions are in areas of low productivity growth such as education, health care, personal services, food services, and leisure, wages and benefits rarely increase, regardless of the quantity or quality of service provided (Iverson and Wren 1998).

Furthermore, as Barbara Ehrenreich documented in her book *Nickel and Dimed: On (Not) Getting By in America* (2002), service sector jobs tend to be the hardest physically and mentally, offer the least amount of autonomy or dignity, and present the strictest codes of behavior often enforced by threats of termination. From having her purse searched while waitressing to routine drug tests and even rules against gossiping or talking with coworkers, Ehrenreich concludes,

> When you enter the low-wage workplace . . . you check your civil liberties at the door, leave America and all it supposedly stands for behind, and learn to zip your lips for the duration of the shift. The consequences of this routine surrender go beyond the issues of wages and poverty. We can hardly pride ourselves on being the world's preeminent democracy, after all, if large numbers of citizens spend half their waking hours in what amounts, in plain terms, to a dictatorship. (p. 201)

Perhaps the most important civil liberty lost in service workplaces has been the right to organize. Deindustrialization has been accompanied by a severe decline in union membership, and the loss of union representation is the second largest factor in the decline of workers' compensation and the increase of their hours. The following figures chart the demise of unions, beginning slowly in the late 1950s and then declining rapidly since the 1970s. Table 3.3 demonstrates that unions represented over 33% of all U.S. workers in 1954, but by 1995, only 14.9% belonged to unions. In the following decade, as Figure 3.2 shows that union membership continued to fall steadily over the next decade reaching a low of 12% in 2006.

Sociologists debate the reasons for union decline, some claiming that deindustrialization weakened traditional unions tied to manufacturing, and membership fell as jobs disappeared. Others argue that the service sector is inherently more difficult to organize because work is more flexible and less skilled—without specialized skills or a permanent workforce, workers

**Table 3.3**   Percentage of U.S. Workers With Union Membership, 1954-2006

| Year | % of union membership, U.S. workers |
|------|-------------------------------------|
| 1954 | 35.0% |
| 1970 | 23.5% |
| 1980 | 19.5% |
| 1990 | 15.5% |
| 1995 | 14.9% |
| 2006 | 12.0% |

**Figure 3.2**   Steady Decline of Union Membership in United States, 1995–2006

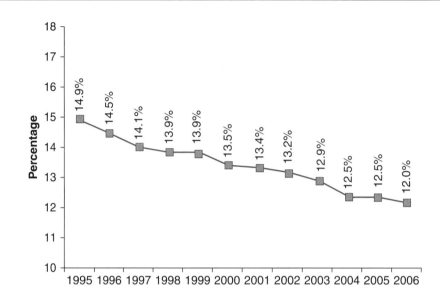

*Source:* Date from U.S. Bureau of Labor Statistics (2006).

have little power to negotiate because they are easily replaceable. As we saw in the United Students Against Sweatshops case in Chapter 2 and the Harvard case earlier in this chapter, organized labor looked to consumers and other supporters to enhance their organizing capability. Some sociologists and historians blame unions themselves for becoming apathetic, elitist, too cozy with management, and too reluctant to make transitions from organizing predominantly white men in factories to predominantly women and immigrant people of color in the service industries. Others argue that employers have intensified their campaigns against union organizing, hiring highly paid consultants who specialize in sometimes brutal tactics to defeat labor organizing.

Regardless of the causes for union decline, its impact is undeniable. The next figure and table show that no matter the race, gender, or occupation, unionized workers get paid more and are more likely to have better benefits. Figure 3.3 demonstrates that union members earn more weekly on average than nonunion workers by 28%. In fact, the difference between union and nonunion wages is even higher for women (about 30%), African Americans (30%), and Latino workers where union membership earns a worker almost 50% more than Latino workers without representation.

Table 3.4 shows that similar dynamics occur across a variety of occupations. Although there is little difference in sales, executive, and managerial positions and the professions, every other occupational field demonstrates that union workers earn from 14% to 58% more than nonunion workers—the largest difference being in the service sector and among security personnel.

**Figure 3.3**   Median Weekly Earnings for Union and Nonunionized Workers by Race and Gender

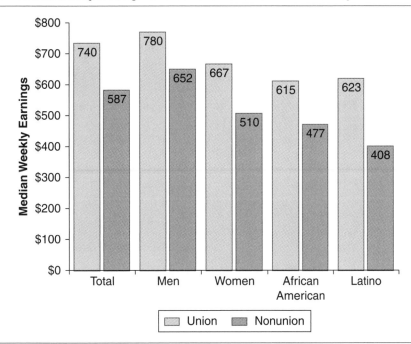

*Source:* Data from U.S. Bureau of the Census (2003a). *Current Population Reports,* Series P-60, no. 221. Income in the United States: 2002. Washington, DC: Government Printing Office.

**Table 3.4**   Union and Nonunion Earnings by Occupation, 2002 (Full-Time Wage and Salary Workers' Median Weekly Earnings)

| Occupation | Union | Non-union | % Difference |
|---|---|---|---|
| Administrative-clerical | $613 | $490 | 25 |
| Exec., administrative, mgr. | $892 | $889 | 0.3 |
| Farm, forestry, fish | $548 | $357 | 54 |
| Handlers, laborers | $555 | $381 | 46 |
| Machine operators | $616 | $490 | 26 |
| Precision, craft, repair | $821 | $590 | 39 |
| Professional | $889 | $879 | 1 |
| Sales | $572 | $601 | −5 |
| Service, protective | $820 | $519 | 58 |
| Service, other | $448 | $341 | 31 |
| Technicians | $775 | $682 | 14 |
| Transportation, moving | $728 | $525 | 39 |
| Total | $740 | $587 | 26 |

The difference between workers' compensation for union and nonunion workers is even more striking in areas of non-wage benefits such as health care, pensions, and disability. Figure 3.4 shows that union workers in 2000 received health care plans 22% more often than nonunion workers. Twice as many union members received disability coverage and almost four times as many had defined-benefit pension plans.

**Figure 3.4**   Percentage of Union and Nonunion Workers Receiving Benefits

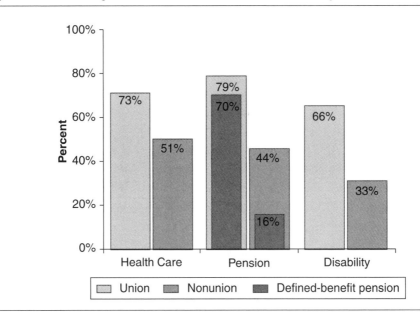

Source: Data from U.S. Bureau of the Census (2003a). *Current Population Reports,* Series P-60, no. 221. Income in the United States: 2002. Washington, DC: Government Printing Office.

Finally, this last figure (Figure 3.5) demonstrates another major change in the low-wage and low-skilled workforce. While the proportion of the low-wage workforce composed of white males declined from over three-quarters (77.2%) to just over one-half (55.4%) between 1980 and 2000, the percentage composed of Hispanic and Asian workers more than doubled, from 10.2% to 24.6% and 1.5% to 3.7%, respectively. This shift is probably a conservative snapshot, as the number of undocumented Hispanic and Asian workers continues to rise dramatically.

These numbers are especially significant when combined with previous figures to create a portrait of a contemporary labor force that is increasingly service sector based, with low wages and few benefits, working longer hours with fewer union protections, and highly vulnerable because of the workers' economic and social marginalization. To better understand these dynamics, it helps to place them in a historical context that explains how we got to such a point.

**Figure 3.5**   Percentage of Male Low Wage Labor Force by Race/Ethinicity (1980–2000)

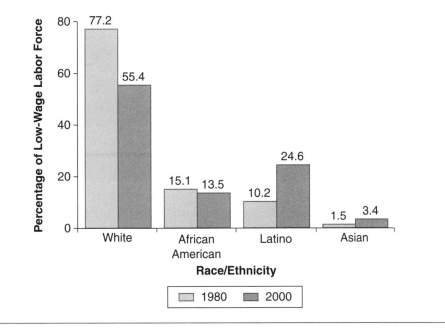

*Source:* U.S. Bureau of Labor Statistics (2004).

## FROM SUNUP TO SUNDOWN—A BRIEF HISTORY OF LABOR

**Feudalism** was an economic and social system that dominated Europe and elsewhere for almost six centuries between 900 and 1500 AD. Feudalism evolved from an agricultural system of production where land was controlled by monarchies and organized on a manorial basis. In essence, royal families gave land (known as *fiefs*) to lords who forced workers (or serfs, who were bound to the land by custom, debt, and law) to harvest crops primarily for the lords themselves. The centralization of wealth and power caused by feudal inheritance customs and patriarchal traditions eventually destabilized aristocratic families—there just was not enough land to go around. Similarly, increased European *colonization,* global trade, and financial markets created a rising "middle class" of merchants and bankers whose economic rise to power was often frustrated by monarchic rule. Anti-feudal and anti-monarchical movements grew rapidly throughout Western Europe in the 1600s and early 1700s (Bloch 1964).

Meanwhile, the rise of commercialism and international trade turned select port towns and market centers into thriving cities. Rapid *urbanization* even further destabilized feudalism as people found work in cities outside the fief system. The new urban labor force built ships, ports, houses, roads, commercial centers, and—eventually—parliaments, factories, and other businesses. Most importantly, though, they worked for wages. As the onset of the *industrial revolution* intensified these dynamics, a budding economic system (known as capitalism) firmly displaced feudalism. The **bourgeoisie,** composed mostly of factory owners, merchants, and financiers who owned the newly industrialized means of production, replaced the landed aristocracy as a power elite, and ultimately brought down monarchies in favor of more democratic systems of government. The **proletariat,** composed of the new working class of wage laborers, often fought alongside the bourgeoisie for new political rights, but usually found itself closed out of legislative power once the battles were over (Frank 1996).

As the bourgeoisie institutionalized their economic and political ascendancy, the new working class found that the industrial capitalist economy meant a significant shift in the nature of work itself. On the open market, workers had to sell their labor for wages, thus competing with other workers. This competition allowed factory owners and other employers to keep wages low as long as a **labor surplus** existed. To create this surplus, industrialists recruited workers from rural areas or other countries. In the United States, one of the first major sources of factory labor was young women from the New England countryside who left their farms to work at textile mills in places like Lowell, Massachusetts; Manchester, New Hampshire; and Pawtucket, Rhode Island. To persuade strict Protestant families to relinquish their daughters, factory owners created highly regulated boarding houses where "house mothers" and factory managers promised to shield young women from the "dangers and vice" of city life (Dublin 1981, 1995).

Encountering anything but the idyllic, "family-style" environment promised by recruiters, most young women found rules and enforcement oppressive. Similarly, factory life included long hours, poor health and safety conditions, physical and verbal abuse from male supervisors, and a variety of other hardships and indignities. As market instabilities impacted the textile industry, manufacturers increased hours, decreased wages, and clamped down on both industrial and social discipline. Young women responded to these conditions by organizing workers' associations, producing newspapers and magazines that told of their experiences, and eventually going on strike against mill owners. Suddenly, the shop floors and the boarding houses were not only places of alienation and exploitation, but they also became the sites where women had the opportunity to talk together, strategize, and develop the public discourse and private courage to protest. Between the 1820s and 1840s, "factory girls" around the Northeast organized to demand better wages, safer working conditions, and a sense of "liberty" (Eisler 1997).

### No More Shall I Work in the Factory

No more shall I work in the factory

To greasy up my clothes,

No more shall I work in the factory

With splinters in my toes.

It's pity me, my darling,

It's pity me, I say,

It's pity me, my darling,

And carry me away.

No more shall I hear the drummer wheels

A-rolling over my head;

When factory girls are hard at work,

I'll be in my bed.

No more shall I wear the old black dress,

Greasy all around;

No more shall I wear the old black bonnet,

With holes all in the crown

No more shall I see the super come,

All dressed up so fine:

For I know I'll marry a country boy

Before the year is round.

In the South, most agricultural production was provided by slave labor from the 17th century through the early and mid-19th century. While slavery became a racialized system, especially in the 18th century when states passed laws banning "white" slaves and discouraging the use of European "indentured servants," the South depended upon black slaves to supply the bulk of its inexpensive workforce up until emancipation in 1865. Even after Reconstruction, whites found ways to maintain their control over the cost of labor markets in the South by enforcing a racialized economic system. In particular, white landowners created a system of tenant farming and sharecropping that kept agricultural workers—primarily

**Image 3.1**   Young girl looks out window of a North Carolina textile mill, 1908.
*Source:* Copyright © Corbis.

former slaves—in debt to landowners. Unable to pay off credit used to buy food, supplies, and so on, tenants and sharecroppers became bound to the land much like feudal serfs. Meanwhile, the criminalization of ex-slaves and other young black men resulted in burgeoning prison populations. Southern prisons leased convict labor to big landowners for agricultural work as well as to both private and public developers to build the roads and factories that industrialized the South (Lichtenstein 1996).

By the middle of the 19th century, Northern industrialists had found a new surplus of labor provided by the first massive waves of immigrants from Eastern Europe. These workers experienced factory conditions just as hard and exploitive as the young women before them. Yet immigrants also suffered from discrimination and were often given the lowest wages for the most difficult and dangerous work. Meanwhile, their lives outside the factory were made even more challenging by poor housing; ethnic prejudice; and an overall lack of city services to address the urban problems of sanitation, fire, crime, and disease. Mid- and late 19th-century immigrants, especially those from agrarian economies in "the old country," found their lives inside and outside the factory segregated, impoverished, confusing, and always on the verge of collapse.

Manufacturers, on the other hand, determined early on that industrial production required two important elements. First, factory owners would have to develop an **industrial morality** or work ethic among laborers who had little factory experience. Second, they had to create an *industrial efficiency* that would infuse maximum production into the design of the labor process. Early work habits infuriated owners who "revoked grog privileges" and "forbade spirituous liquors, smoking, or any kind of amusement" (Gutman 1977). Preindustrial workers had much more freedom over their labor during the workday. Eating and drinking customs and rest periods may not seem efficient to our 21st-century sensibilities, but hard and challenging work was once somewhat mediated by custom and cultural traditions. Yet these were the very habits and norms that 19th-century industrialists wanted to change in order to create a "new" worker with the industrial capitalist values of strictly regulated tasks and obedience.

Railroad car magnate **George Pullman** went so far as to construct his own company town in an effort to control every aspect of workers' lives. Not only could he enforce an industrial morality from early schooling through mandatory church services, but he also found a way to profit by overcharging people for housing, water, and other services and commodities. Workers eventually organized and went on strike, complaining of both Pullman the owner and Pullman, the town he erected. One worker explained it this way:

> Pullman, both the man and the town, is an ulcer on the body politic. He owns the houses, the schoolhouses, and churches of God in the town he gave his once humble name. The revenue he derives from these, the wages he pays out with one hand—the Pullman Palace Car Company, he takes back with the other—the Pullman Land Association. He is able to bid under any contract car shop in this country. His competitors in business, to meet this, must reduce the wages of their men. This gives him the excuse to reduce ours to conform to the market. His business rivals must in turn scale down; so must he. And thus the merry war—the dance of skeletons bathed in human tears—goes on and it will go on, brothers, forever, unless you, the American Railway Union, stop it; end it; crush it out. ("Statement of the Pullman Strikers" 1894: 87–88)

While few manufacturers matched Pullman's totality of control, instilling industrial discipline in workers remained a crucial aspect of labor relations throughout the 19th and early 20th century. Even as late as 1910, the International Harvester Corporation indoctrinated its Polish workers with the following brochure entitled "Lesson One":

**Image 3.2**

*Source:* © Photos.com/ Thinkstock.

### Lesson One

I hear the whistle. I must hurry.

I hear the five-minute whistle.

It is time to go to the shop.

I take my check from the gate board and hang it on the department board.

I change my clothes

and get ready for work.

The starting whistle blows at five minutes of starting time.

I get ready to go to work.

I work until the whistle blows to quit.

I leave my place nice and clean.

I put my clothes in the locker.

I must go home.

Although workers did adapt to an industrial morality, they also found both formal and informal ways to resist it. On a formal level, workers organized collectively; formed unions; and used solidarity as a weapon to struggle against owners' efforts at complete control over wages, conditions, and work inside the factory, and their social and cultural life outside the factory. On an informal level, workers acted both individually and in groups to maintain more flexibility over time at work and their lives in town. Inside the factory, some workers used sabotage or "soldiering" (working collectively at a slow pace) to regulate the pace of work. In the community, some workers continued to observe holidays and festivals that often resulted in their missing work. This history of the labor movement is also the history of workers' struggles to control the parameters of an evolving industrial landscape. Eventually, workers assimilated to the world of the factory, but never completely, and rarely without dissatisfaction or protest.

Assimilating to industrial morality also involved what Harry Braverman (1974) called the "deskilling and degradation of labor." In other words, part of the history of labor under capitalism has been workers' diminishing control over the work process. Capitalists owned the tools and controlled relationships with consumers. They determined industrial design and owned the technology that took the skills and knowledge from workers and infused them into machinery and the production process. This phenomenon not only gave management the ability to control workers, but it also enabled them to pursue maximum efficiency. Much of this process became known as **scientific management**.

The most famous progenitor of scientific management was Frederic Winslow Taylor. The son of a wealthy Philadelphia lawyer, the prep school–educated Taylor spurned Harvard and took a job in a steel plant. He quickly worked his way up from machinist and clerk to become a gang boss in charge of the lathe (machine used to cut and shape metal) department. As a new manager, Taylor began a long career of trying to maximize the production and efficiency of his workers. Eventually, he would develop three main principles for achieving such goals:

1. "The managers assume . . . the burden of gathering together all of the traditional knowledge which in the past has been possessed by the workmen and then of classifying, tabulating and reducing this knowledge to rules, laws, and formulae";

2. "All possible brain work should be removed from the shop and centered in the planning or laying-out department";

3. "The most prominent single element in modern scientific management is the task idea. The work of every workman is fully planned out by management [in] written instructions describing . . . not only what is to be done, but how it is to be done and the exact time allowed for doing it." (Taylor, quoted in Braverman 1974:112)

According to Harry Braverman, the essence of scientific management would always be management's need to control labor "through control over the decisions that are made in the course of work" (p. 107).

Soon, a **knowledge-based economy**, where the production, distribution, and management of information drove capitalist growth, displaced industrial production as the prevailing force in the U.S. economy. But the **professional managerial class** that produced much of this knowledge eventually felt the same sting of increasing standardization and bureaucracy in the workplace. From Sinclair Lewis's *Babbitt* (1922), W. H. Whyte's *Organization Man* (1956) and C. Wright Mills's *White Collar* (1952) to Barbara Ehrenreich's *Fear of Falling* (1990) and recent books about the corporatization of colleges and universities (Soley 1995; White 2000), middle-class workers have found that even "mental labor" and the overall lives of "knowledge producers and supervisors" could be transformed by scientific management. In place of Pullman town came **Levittowns**, named for builder William Jaird Levitt, complete with mass-produced homes, TV dinners, and strip mall marketplaces. By the 1970s, study after study of the U.S. working and middle classes depicted an unhappy, apathetic, and increasingly unproductive labor force. Union membership was declining, and worker concessions to management were on the rise. Meanwhile, leisure time and activity became the social space where people sought meaningful experiences and identities, as neither workplaces nor domestic sites seemed to offer creative or passionate outlets.

But the 1970s also witnessed the advent of deindustrialization and the rise of a **service economy.** Deindustrialization represents the movement of industrial production away from "first world" countries to previously less developed regions of the world like Latin America and Southeast Asia. The relocation allowed corporations to save billions of dollars by paying foreign workers lower wages, offering no benefits, and avoiding costly environmental regulations. Meanwhile, most jobs in previously developed nations are now classified as service jobs relating to finance, administration, retail, residential, and education services. Recently, even white-collar jobs ranging from computer help lines to highly skilled software development have been outsourced overseas. Most workers in the United States rely on the service sector for jobs, and thus find themselves competing with an international labor force on all levels (Amin 1994; Bluestone and Harrison 1982).

Most of these phenomena exemplify what sociologists and economists call **globalization.** New technologies, including the Internet, have allowed both manufacturing and service sector corporations to spread production sites around the globe. At the same time, the demand for low-wage service work, as well as day laborers in construction, landscaping, and other manual jobs, has induced new waves of immigrants, particularly from Central and South America, Southeast Asia, and Africa, to postindustrial countries in North America and

Europe. On the one hand, globalization has increased the surplus of labor for white-collar technical and professional workers as well as blue-collar manufacturing and craft workers. On the other hand, unskilled and manual laborers from the underdeveloped countries of the South now leave their homes to find decent wages in the developed countries of the North. But the conditions they find are often no different from those faced by poor, immigrant workers over a century ago.

## THE DISAPPEARING WORKING CLASS ON TV

Working-class characters once dominated the TV screen, from the *Honeymooners'* bus driver Ralph Kramden (Jackie Gleason) and sewer worker Ed Norton (Art Carney) to the immigrant working families featured in shows such as *Mama* and the *The Goldbergs*. In the 1970s and 1980s, the category of working-class heroes expanded to encompass African Americans in *Sanford and Son, Good Times,* and *Roc,* as well as women in *Roseanne* and *Grace Under Fire.* Now, however, the only place to find working-class people on TV is either in animated characters such as Homer Simpson, the *Family Guy,* or the gang on *King of the Hill,* or on reality shows such as *Dirty Jobs, Ice Road Truckers,* or *Deadliest Catch.* Apparently, workers no longer capture the mainstream media's imagination, unless they are cartoons or risking life and limb.

**Image 3.3a and Image 3.3b**     More for less: From the Honeymooners to the Simpsons, working class families on TV usually ignore structural inequalities and focus on get-rich schemes in their search for happiness.

*Sources:* 3.3a © John Springer Collection/CORBIS; 3.3b AP Photo/Lennox McLendon.

# CASE STUDY #1

### Mobilizing Resources in the Fields—Student Action With Farm Workers

As early as the 1960s and 1970s, student activists responded to the problems of poverty in the United States by trying to organize and support low-income people in both urban and rural areas. Some of these student groups focused specifically on migrant farmworkers, especially in the South and Southeast. Many of these projects responded not only to the low wages and poor working conditions of farm labor, but also to the related issues of dilapidated housing and facilities, inadequate health care, employer fraud, and violations of civil and human rights. By the 1970s and 1980s, some of this work had inspired more formal organizations such as the North Carolina/South Carolina Student Action with Farmworkers (SAF). This organization continues to address a variety of economic and social issues by linking students and faculty to farmworkers and their families.

While many problems related to migrant farmworkers trace back to the late 19th and early 20th century, recent changes in demographics, governmental deregulation, economic policies, and the rebirth of anti-immigrant ideology in the United States have resulted in a new wave of hardships. Since 1989, the proportion of foreign-born farmworkers has risen from 10% to 81% (mostly Mexican), over three-quarters of whom earn less than $10,000 a year. SAF has produced a fact sheet (see www .saf-unite.org/learn/factsheet.htm) outlining some of the basic problems faced by migrant workers. Aside from poverty, these include the following:

- Farm work is the second most dangerous occupation in the United States.

- Farmworkers suffer from the highest rate of toxic chemical injuries of any workers in the United States.

- Farmworkers suffer higher incidences than other wage earners of heat stress, dermatitis, influenza, pneumonia, urinary tract infections, pesticide-related illnesses, and tuberculosis.

- Infant mortality rates are considerably higher among migrant farmworkers than in the rest of the U.S. population.

- Children of migrant farmworkers have high rates of parasitic infections, malnutrition, and dental disease. They are also less likely to be fully immunized than other children.

- Few, if any, migrant farmworkers have health insurance, and very few are covered through Medicaid.

- Substandard farmworker housing conditions result in increased prevalence of lead poisoning, respiratory illnesses, and diarrhea.

While transportation, accessibility, cost, and language difficulties remain barriers to adequate health care, the primary stumbling block for migrant workers remains the complete lack of political power to change their conditions. According to Neil Hasser (2003), an outreach worker for the Virginia Farmworkers' Legal Assistance Project, most workers don't know their legal rights and are often afraid to fight for them. Undocumented workers face especially difficult situations because they fear deportation or other kinds of reprisals from employers.[1]

In essence, farmworkers face a number of problems related to contemporary economic changes and social conditions. Poverty in their own countries, recently intensified by global trade agreements like the North American Free Trade Agreement (NAFTA) and the Global Agreement on Tariff and Trade (GATT), has forced them to seek work in wealthier countries of the North. Although the jobs they find in the United States are better than most in Latin America, migrant workers still receive low wages and few benefits. They also get poor-quality food, housing, and health care. Similarly, their ethnicity, language, and legal status allow employers to discriminate against them without fear of reprisals, as enforcement is sparse and workers rarely know their legal rights. The most recent increases in anti-immigrant sentiment among the U.S. population have resulted in little sympathy and greater hostility from neighboring communities. Meanwhile, workers often lack the solidarity necessary to fight collectively to educate the general public or improve conditions through their own efforts.

*Resource mobilization theory* (RMT) is a sociological paradigm that tries to understand why and how social change occurs. Essentially, it posits that collective behavior to change social conditions is more successful when groups can mobilize financial, political, cultural, and communication resources. Partly based on conflict theory's attention to power, RMT stresses the need for groups to build their capacity for developing and coordinating networks of communication, access to media, legal support, educational materials, and a variety of other resources. These resources result in increased membership; more legitimacy in, and therefore more support from, the general public; and an overall ability to pressure sites of economic and political power. Eventually, resources create a critical mass of power and support that can challenge the fundamental system of economic production and cultural mainstream often responsible for exploitive conditions.

Because farmworkers have so little of these resources, much of the work that SAF does is directed at producing more and more organizational capacity. Each of the following programs addresses different aspects of farmworkers' lives, to strengthen the possibility that they may be able to organize and demand their rights.

### Project Levante

Project Levante develops the leadership of migrant youth in rural North Carolina through leadership retreats, tours of colleges and universities, youth empowerment, art, and college preparation workshops. Through Project Levante, SAF has coordinated College Days for over 2,000 migrant youth and provided over 100 college student mentors for migrant youth. SAF partners with the North Carolina Migrant Education Program to develop leadership among migrant students in the state and has created over 50 Action, Inspiration, Motivation (AIM) clubs to encourage academic excellence and leadership among migrant youth.

*(Continued)*

---

[1] A great source is Oxfam America, 2004, "Like Machines in the Field: Workers Without Rights in American Agriculture." The report states that most of the 2 million U.S. farmworkers labor without basic rights, and 1 million earn less than $7,500 a year. An estimated 300,000 of these farmworkers suffer pesticide poisoning each year.

(Continued)

## Into the Fields

SAF's annual Into the Fields Summer Internship and Leadership Development Program provides opportunities for 30 bilingual (Spanish/English) college students to support farmworkers as they address health and safety concerns, educational barriers, unfair immigration policies, and discrimination in the workplace. SAF interns represent migrant families, historically black colleges and universities, private and state-supported universities, and community colleges. Since SAF's inception in 1992, over 350 Into the Fields alumni have spent their summers working with over 70,000 farmworkers and their families to improve farm labor conditions. Each year, at least one-half of these interns are from farmworker families.

## Sowing Seeds for Change

Sowing Seeds for Change is SAF's national program linking students with farmworkers. SAF provides workshops and trainings on farmworkers and the student movement. The program provides materials on developing campaigns and college courses on farmworker issues, coordinates technical support and events for Farmworker Awareness Week, and provides information on internship and volunteer opportunities with farmworkers through the online Internship Directory.

## From the Ground Up

Through the From the Ground Up program, SAF raises awareness of injustices in the agricultural industry. Through actions, presentations, publications and e-mail alerts, SAF informs and mobilizes students and community members around current legislation, consumer boycotts, and other justice efforts initiated by farmworkers.

These projects have obvious benefits for farmworkers, as they address some of the worst social problems they face. But SAF also gives students invaluable lessons that integrate a variety of academic disciplines and scholarship with practical experience. More notable is how such lessons simultaneously teach students what social problems are, why they exist, and what things can be done to ameliorate some of those conditions.

## Case Study Questions

1. What kinds of resources can programs such as those of SAF actually mobilize, and what kinds of changes do you think are possible with such strategies?

2. What kinds of resources already existed and what types of resources are new ones created by the collaboration of students and workers?

3. Think about workers' struggles in your communities. What kinds of resources do they have, and what kinds of resources might student and community supporters help them acquire?

## CASE STUDY #2

### Who Cleans the Knowledge Factory? Southampton College Coalition for Justice

On February 14, 1997, the custodial workers at Southampton College of Long Island University (LIU) were contracted out to LARO Service Systems, a firm that specialized in providing maintenance to large corporate facilities such as the Port Authority building in New York City and Kennedy Airport in Brooklyn. Custodians suddenly found themselves forced to fill out new job applications for positions some had held for almost 30 years. LARO supervisors told custodians that no one's job would be guaranteed, and changes in workforce, schedules, and procedures would soon follow. Although their union immediately negotiated a contract addendum that protected jobs for the last year and a half of the existing contract, custodians lost access to their retirement programs, emergency loans, college tuition remission, job tenure, overtime, and vacations. They traded in their green LIU uniforms for blue LARO overalls and an uncertain future. As one custodian told the local press, "we felt like dogs kicked onto the sidewalk" (Dolgon 2005:157).

Outsourcing has become a common part of today's business lexicon. In essence, it is the process of a company hiring an outside contractor to provide services or complete tasks that were once done "in house." Outsourcing has increased exponentially, as globalization resulted in two dynamics amenable to the practice. First, a variety of services can now be addressed via phone or the Internet from anywhere around the world. Thus, many companies have outsourced work to places where wages and benefits are lower. Second, increased emigration from underdeveloped countries has created a large surplus of low-wage workers in first world countries looking for service workers. Management companies, specifically in service industries like maintenance and security, offer lower-cost options for companies who can now avoid paying previously agreed-upon wages and benefits by contracting with outside agents. These practices are especially useful for employers trying to force out unionized workers.

Over the past two decades, colleges and universities have adopted private sector business practices in almost every aspect of their administration. The outsourcing of Southampton College's custodians fit this trend. The custodians, however, told a meeting of supportive faculty, staff, students, and local residents that they were also victims of racial prejudice. The custodial unit was composed mostly of people of color (African American and Native American), but not one person of color had ever been promoted in the school's 30 years of operation. Recently, a new shop steward had pressured the institution to create a promotional pipeline so that custodians would have a clear path to achieve advancement. Instead of responding, the college outsourced the whole unit. Many people on campus and in the community were outraged (Dolgon 2002).

A group's outrage or other forms of social upheaval often "shake up" a community's sense of norms and values, but sociologists argue that it takes more than just an upheaval for significant changes in culture and institutions to occur. *Frame analysis* is a theory derived from symbolic interactionism that focuses on how people's experiences are organized and defined. As in W. I. Thomas's "definition of a situation" (see Chapter 1), social change occurs when people think and act in coordinated ways

*(Continued)*

(Continued)

that challenge traditional structures of power and belief. For a small campus in a small town, the outsourcing caused people to question the decision. However, the college provost's claim that he only wanted to improve services, and the community's general sense that he was a "good guy," led many to believe that nothing further should or could be done. The framing of the event had to be significantly altered for people to think and act in a more defiant way. In part, the more successful a group is in reframing an event and its consequences, especially for those who might get involved in an organization or movement, the more likely the group is to succeed.

The meeting of supportive campus and community members eventually evolved into a group called the Southampton Coalition for Justice (CFJ), which developed strategies for pressuring the college's administration to terminate the LARO contract and rehire the custodians directly. CFJ decided to hold a campus rally to educate students and the community on the issues and build up support for the custodians. The rally attracted over 100 students and other campus workers, and received vast local and regional press coverage. CFJ met every week to discuss organizing strategies and tactics, but more importantly, each meeting strengthened a multicultural and interclass alliance among committed students, faculty, community activists, and the custodians themselves. Each meeting began with a custodian recounting the events of the outsourcing, and then others in the group adding in what CFJ had done so far to counter it. Thus, newcomers were brought up-to-date, but regular attendees also developed a greater sense of solidarity and commitment. One student wrote in her academic journal,

> Through meeting with the custodians and those faculty and students who had taken an interest, I was beginning to feel what it was like to be a community. This was a feeling different than any that I had felt here [on campus] before. We were discussing issues that, according to the usual run of the campus, should not have included us. However, even though the coalition of people came together with a common goal, stopping the custodians' outsourcing, we discussed things in the context of all of our lives. (Dolgon 2002:245)

Thus, through the ritual acts of congregating and telling stories, a diverse group of people created an organization capable of addressing social problems through direct action, despite the lack of a formal mechanism that included their voices or opinions. The coalition had reframed both the issues and the political landscape.

The Friends World Program, a former Quaker college that had become a division of Southampton College, attracted many active and politically engaged students because of its focus on experiential education and on "making the world's problems the subject of its curriculum" (Dolgon 2002). In March of 1997, the program offered a mini-course in "activism" taught by former civil rights leader Bob Zellner. Zellner allowed many of the students who were involved in CFJ to use their work as part of their course work. He explained, "this element of the course addressed the Friends World emphasis on experiential education and, more importantly, forced students to contemplate the practical and emotional dynamics of political work" (quoted in Dolgon 2002:247). Students used the opportunity to develop informational flyers and a variety of other educational activities.

The next year, the activism course was expanded to a full semester, and more students became involved in CFJ's efforts to get custodians back into their green uniforms. In fact, on Parents' Weekend, CFJ put together an informational flyer for visiting families and asked parents to wear green ribbons in support of custodians. In learning about the civil rights movement from Zellner, students decided to take more direct action and planned a sit-in in the provost's office. When students raised both the economic issues and claims of institutional racism, the provost would only say the decision was "administrative," and that he was not a racist. Meghan White, a Friends World student, responded by explaining what institutional racism was and that, even though one did not intend to act in racist ways, one's action could still be racist if he or she accepted or reaffirmed institutional policies that are racist. She claimed that the provost needed to challenge or change traditional practices. Otherwise, he was simply reinforcing institutionalized racism (Dolgon 2002).

Interestingly enough, the sit-in demonstrated how powerful the framing process had become. Some students felt bad for the provost and later defended his position as "administrative" and non-racist. While they disagreed with the outsourcing, they accepted the provost's framing of the event. Yet most of the students who attended the sit-in agreed with Meghan White's interpretation and contended that the institution continued to create employment structures that discriminated against low-wage workers of color. After Zellner spoke to both groups of students, it became clear that the major distinction between them was whether they had regularly attended the coalition meetings and participated in other activities with custodians. In other words, the coalition's work had not only impacted politics on campus and in the community, but it had also seriously reshaped the ways in which students thought about power and privilege.

The sit-in and other demonstrations began to take their toll on the administration, and they agreed to meet with representatives of CFJ. After the meeting, they made a number of concessions, which included giving custodians tuition remission options again. But the LARO contract remained intact, and CFJ continued to protest it. Meanwhile, the meetings not only had an impact on the students, but also on the custodians themselves. After years of bickering and infighting, often intensified by their own racial and ethnic divisions, the custodians had unified enough to kick out their union representatives who had allowed the outsourcing and join the much stronger and more militant Teamsters Union. The combination of CFJ activities and the prospect of dealing with the Teamsters finally weighed too heavily on the college administration, and they terminated the LARO contract. While the provost explained that they were dissatisfied with the company and that CFJ should not see the change as a "victory," custodians at a CFJ meeting said, "it feels like a victory to us" (Dolgon 2005:192).

This struggle highlighted many historical and contemporary social problems related to labor, including traditional racial and ethnic prejudices and job segregation. It also demonstrated the impact of new dynamics such as outsourcing and the changes in international labor migrations and service sector wage markets. It even exposed the demise of traditional business unionism and the pervasiveness of corporate ideology in the public sector. But CFJ's efforts also represented new forms of labor organizing from a community perspective. Students and others came together to challenge discriminatory policies and unfair labor practices, as well as socially restrictive identities that limit both community and democracy. Finally, students learned much about the social problems of work and what it takes to address them, as well as how diverse groups of people can decide what kind of community they want to live in.

*(Continued)*

(Continued)

Case Study Questions

1. What types of strategies and tactics helped CFJ create a new *frame* for understanding the issues facing college custodians?

2. In what ways did this new frame impact both the community at large and the members of the coalition itself?

3. How might framing issues in particular ways be compared to the need for groups to mobilize resources for change?

4. Think of a current conflict on your own campus or in your community, and describe how different groups frame issues differently. Who seems more successful and why?

## VOICES FROM THE FIELD

### Interview With Cassie Watters, SOCM Assistant Director and Lead Organizer

Cassie Watters was a junior at Southampton College when she got involved with the Coalition for Justice. Cassie became a leader of the group, went on to become class president, helped establish the college's first sexual harassment policy, and eventually became a lead organizer for student labor solidarity as a staff person with Jobs With Justice in Massachusetts. She is now Assistant Director and Lead Organizer for the group SOCM (Save Our Cumberland Mountains) in Knoxville, Tennessee.

| | |
|---|---|
| Corey Dolgon: | What were the main issues for students involved in the coalition? |
| Cassie Watters: | I thought the major issue was job protection for the custodians, but students felt very strongly that we needed to build community. We needed to see each other as interdependent members who do not sit idly when some of us were threatened because of our vulnerability. |
| CD: | What impact did your efforts have? |
| CW: | We created a lot of press that shook up both the campus and community by calling attention to issues not normally reported on like labor and race. I believe the college administration would have been much less willing to consider responding if press had not been generated through our actions. We showed them that decisions were not made in a vacuum. I also believe the coalition's efforts gave the custodians some hope. The experience entirely changed my concept of a community to include those that are often invisible. By leveling the hierarchical model we are all taught by introducing me to the janitors and by us forming a relationship through this effort. One of my cohorts went on to be an organizer for student issues on college campuses out West. |
| CD: | How would you say your experiences shaped your later work organizing students? |
| CW: | It really inspired me to want to do organizing work, especially based on the coalition model. It inspired me to seek work at a nonprofit such as Jobs with Justice, and the formation of SLAP [Student Labor Action Project] remain the most fulfilling work of mine to date. I think the revival of a national student activist network was influenced by local activism such as ours. |

*Source:* Reprinted with permission of Cassie Walters.

## CASE STUDY #3

### Conflicts on the Edge of Globalization: The Pomona Day Labor Center

Pomona is a relatively small city located on the northeastern border of Los Angeles County. Like the rest of the county, Pomona has changed rapidly over the past few decades as deindustrialization and the rise of a service sector have radically altered the region's economic landscape. Gone are most of the steel, automobile, tire, and aerospace manufacturers. Instead, Southern California now thrives on the computer, software, and other high-tech industries, along with the information producers that service the knowledge economy such as finance and media. New wealth and changing consumption

*(Continued)*

(Continued)

patterns have resulted in a huge demand for workers in restaurants and retail as well as residential construction, landscaping, and other related services.

Meanwhile, immigration laws (such as the Hart-Celler Act of 1965, which abolished quotas for immigrants of different national origins) and more recent political conditions and trade policies have inspired increased immigration to the region, initially from Mexico and now from all over Latin America. In fact, the City of Los Angeles is so dominated by increases in the immigration population, not just from Latin America, but also from Southeast Asia, that author David Rieff has called it the "Capital of the Third World." The combination of increasing demand for flexible, low-wage service workers and growing numbers of immigrants has created a situation where a large surplus of day laborers now exists throughout the Los Angeles region. On any given day, around 20,000 laborers (over three-quarters of whom are Mexican and the rest mostly Central American) congregate on street corners and outside of convenience stores and building supply centers waiting to get picked up for work.

Many communities in Southern California responded to these conditions by passing ordinances outlawing the solicitation of work in public spaces. Pomona's City Council approved an ordinance that punished anyone seeking employment in a street, public area, or parking lot with fines up to $1,000 and as much as 6 months in jail. While labor organizations and immigrant support groups have opposed such legislation in California and around the country, few groups have successfully organized the day laborers themselves. Immigrant day laborers, like many farmworkers, face threats of deportation and concerns over being labeled as "troublemakers." Meanwhile, language barriers and ignorance over legal rights combine with transience and fear flamed by anti-immigrant sentiments to make organizing efforts among day laborers quite difficult.

In Pomona, however, the city created a day labor center in 1998. Although the site's primary goal is to provide a safe and regulated space for employers to hire workers, the center also became a place for Pitzer College students to conduct language training classes, help with health care referrals, and counsel people about immigrant rights services. According to Professor José Calderón, some students taking his Restructuring Communities class began organizing with day laborers against the initial ordinance. Student research demonstrated that, counter to claims by the city council, many day workers were legal residents. The research also demonstrated that hiring centers were a more proactive way of addressing public solicitation problems than punitive ordinances that blamed low-wage workers. Although they lost the battle against the ordinance, they succeeded in convincing the city to fund a labor center. The city even appointed Professor Calderón and some of his students to the center's board.

The center experienced a variety of difficulties that included inadequate services and a lack of funding. Professor Calderón urged students at the college's Center for California Cultural and Social Issues to write grants that might support the center at the same time that the center would provide a source for ethnographic and participatory research. Calderón and the students decided to employ participant observation and collaborative action research methods where "both researchers and community participants collaborate to produce knowledge with the express purpose of taking action to promote social change and analysis" (pp. 81–82). Students soon discovered that the day center directors had failed to meet the need of day workers, and many of the center's "clients" had become frustrated and disillusioned. The center's directors had focused on the employers' agenda of making the hiring process more efficient and effective. However, they ignored the workers' own desires to empower themselves not only as employees, but also as human beings demanding education, health care, and civil rights.

In many ways, these conflicts can be analyzed by using functionalist and conflict theoretical approaches. The directors took a more functional approach to the problem, believing that the day center's purpose was to address systemic dysfunctions caused by rapid economic changes and the inability of institutions and local culture to address them. In their eyes, the center would help restore order and reduce conflict in the community. On the other hand, students wanted to adopt a program whose structure and activities challenged the systemic inequalities they believed were at work in disempowering and marginalizing day laborers. In opposition to the center directors' practices, a group of students and day workers introduced a model of day center programming advocated by the Coalition for Humane Immigrant Rights of Los Angeles (CHIRLA). CHIRLA proposed that labor centers not only facilitate workers getting jobs efficiently, but that they also ensure basic worker, civil, and human rights. At dozens of labor centers around the region impacted by CHIRLA, organizers and laborers worked together to learn about and protect the rights of clients. CHIRLA also called for developing new employment opportunities through outreach and marketing strategies created by the workers themselves. Finally, CHIRLA promoted civic engagement opportunities by having the centers organize neighborhood cleanups, housing rehabilitation, and even soccer leagues. Pitzer College students, and workers from the center, pressured the directors to employ CHIRLA's model. Instead, the directors eventually resigned.

A new leadership team began by initiating English as a Second Language (ESL) courses at the center. More importantly, they instituted an "assets-based model" (Bobo and Kendall 2001) of organizing that encouraged community development stemming from the group's strengths (hard work, creativity, skills, passion, and commitment) instead of focusing on addressing its deficiencies (poverty, disenfranchisement, etc.). To promote this strategy, students and workers used focus groups to identify needs as well as potential new leaders. The ESL classes themselves were designed to use workers' experiences and needs as the foundation for lessons and literacy skills. Subsequently, the courses helped draw more opinions from workers about the center and enhanced greater leadership development.

*(Continued)*

(Continued)

Quickly, the center's new leadership team recognized that workers faced difficult health care issues. The center created a partnership with the Western University of Health Sciences. Over 30 doctors and interns from the university's Pomona Community Health Action Team attended a health fair at the center, and over 50 workers received physical exams (some for the first time in many years). Eventually, students expanded the health project to include eye and dental care. Hundreds of workers now receive checkups, services, and information on preventive care through the day center's programming.

Students also recently helped launch an immigrant rights project at the center. They organized a workshop on immigration laws and available services led by a local immigration rights lawyer. Some student interns even worked on various legal cases. According to Professor Calderón (2004) one case involved an employer who refused to pay three workers $3,000 each for a job they had worked. By educating workers about the legal rights available to them, and by training them how to prepare and file small claims court paperwork, all three workers eventually got their money.

The day center continues to evolve and develop new programs and policies as determined by the collaboration of students and workers. Calderón (2004) argues that such partnerships demonstrate that no contradiction need exist "between the use of education as a service and an organizational form that is inclusive of day workers' voices and leadership" (p. 81). Workers have gained new power to control and determine the most crucial aspects of their work and their lives. Students have learned not only about the social problems emanating from economic and social transformations, but also about how people can solve some of the worst aspects of those problems by combining academic and professional resources with the experiences and knowledge of workers themselves. As Calderón concludes, "the collaboration between Pitzer College and the Pomona Day Labor Center, although confronting many obstacles, has advanced the development of a coalition between the day laborer and campus communities, a culture of participation and decision-making by all the partners involved, and a connection between the needed services of day laborers and an organizational form to advocate for their rights" (pp. 81–82).

## Case Study Questions

1. In what ways might different theoretical paradigms (such as functionalism or conflict theory) influence different approaches to understanding problems and various solutions to them?

2. How do groups like CHIRLA play a role in supporting student worker coalitions?

3. Can you think of workers on your own campus or in your own community who seem "invisible" to the mainstream public and might benefit from research and support on the issues they face? How might students go about approaching such an issue?

## VOICES FROM THE FIELD

José Calderón, Professor of Sociology and Chicano Studies, Pitzer College

 In the fall of 2004, I taught a class, Restructuring Communities, where students studied diverse perspectives on the meaning of democracy as applied to the plight of new immigrants, particularly Latin American undocumented workers in the United States. With an outlook to connecting our classroom studies with lived experiences in the community, we carried out service learning projects with day laborers at the Pomona Day Labor Center including: develop[ing] English classes, health workshops, and immigration rights projects. In the course of carrying out these service projects, the students worked alongside the workers to build a day labor organization run by day laborers and in taking up the larger policy issues that threatened the day laborers' rights as human beings.

Moving beyond service, a group of students and day laborers researched the question of why countries throughout the world enjoy the use of cheap immigrant labor but refuse to allow them basic human rights. In providing initial answers to this question, the students relied on their class readings and library research while the workers developed their analyses from Spanish newspapers and their lived experiences. This class was an example of connecting history to civic engagement for social change. In order for the students to get engaged, they first had to know some of this country's history when it came to issues involving immigration. We used the book *Harvest of Empire* by Juan Gonzalez to understand how the United States' "success was due in large measure to the unique brand of representative democracy, the spirit of bold enterprise, the respect for individual liberty, and the rugged devotion to hard work that characterized so many of American settlers." At the same time, my syllabus also included literature on one of Gonzalez's other contentions that "there was another aspect to that success . . . the details of which most Americans knew nothing about, but which was always carried out in their name. It was a vicious and relentless drive for territorial expansion, conquest, and subjugation of Native Americans, African slaves, Latin Americans, and others . . . one that our leaders justified as Manifest Destiny for us."

In this context, students were more equipped to understand the contemporary debates over immigration, free trade, globalization, and the many myths that have been created regarding the immigrant's taking of jobs, importing disease and crime, and the stealing of social services. Many of my students had not thought about these issues before. Hence, one practice of providing students with the knowledge and commitment to be socially responsible citizens had to include a curriculum that allowed them to learn the many sides of [the United States'] practice of democracy, both good and bad.

*(Continued)*

(Continued)

In many of our institutions, there is still a tendency to separate the content of the curriculum and practice of service learning in our communities. The best type of learning is where the reading materials in the classroom are helping the students to learn about the history of the communities that they are working with. The two should help build on each other. In working with immigrants, students carry out service but they also attend weekly meetings with the workers. It is in these meetings that dialogue occurs and where the issues that workers are concerned about come to the forefront. It is here where action research is used in finding solutions to these problems. It is here where the practice of democracy advances to the level of civic engagement. It is here where the immigrant and student participants join together in common actions to raise their voices and to ensure that their voices are heard. In this context, critical pedagogy and a democratic student-centered classroom join with a participant-centered site in implementing a deliberate framework of service that advances a culture of social change steeped in the voices of all the participants.

*Source:* Reprinted by permission of José Calderón.

## SUMMARY

In the 1960s, free speech movement activist Mario Savio (1964) critiqued the "university as corporation" model, suggesting that, if colleges were knowledge factories then students were the commodities they produced. In response, he argued that

> when the operation of the machine becomes so odious, makes you so sick at heart, that you can't take part . . . you've got to put your bodies upon the levers, upon all the apparatus and you've got to make it stop. And you've got to indicate to the people who run it, to the people who own it, that unless you're free the machine will be prevented from running at all. (retrieved from www.fsm-a.org)

While some students still remain critical of the corporate model of education (see Chapter 6), many no longer do. Yet this chapter shows that groups of students from around the country are investigating the social problems that emanate from the world of economic production and labor. Through educational curricula that includes service learning and action projects, students are engaging with issues such as migrant labor, outsourcing, and day labor, and learning how global economic transformations create social problems. But they are also learning how to work with those people affected to participate in solutions to those problems.

# SUMMARY QUESTIONS

1. How has work and labor changed historically? Why has it become a "social problem"?

2. What is deindustrialization? What is a service economy? Describe the major aspects of service sector jobs and how they have changed the lives of workers in the United States.

3. What is resource mobilization theory (RMT)? How does RMT explain strategies for changing workers' conditions?

4. What is social "framing"? Describe the ways in which framing issues create different ways of understanding and addressing social problems.

5. Describe what an "asset model" is for addressing social problems. How does it differ from other approaches to providing services or organizing workers.

# GLOSSARY

Alienation: According to Marx, the alienation of labor occurs when workers do not control their own means of production and therefore have no control over what they produce and the conditions under which they produce them.

Bourgeoisie: This is the ownership class under capitalism.

Deindustrialization: The loss of manufacturing facilities and jobs from industrialized Western nations to newly industrializing nations in China, South America, and elsewhere.

Feudalism: An economic system in Western Europe during the Middle Ages that preceded capitalism. Under feudalism, large landholders (lords) controlled their workers (serfs) not as property themselves, but as bound to the land they worked by custom, debt, and law.

Globalization: The major economic, political and cultural changes that have occurred primarily since the 1960s and 1970s. They include the intense saturation of a market economy, the rise of international governing bodies that regulate global political conflicts as well as world trade, and the international dominance of commercial and consumer cultures (especially as seen through the media, the Internet, etc.).

Industrial Morality: The values necessary for capitalists to get as much production from labor as possible, regardless of actual wages and working conditions. Capitalists enforced and persuaded workers to adopt these values as a way of demonstrating their loyalty to the company and to the capitalist system.

Knowledge-Based Economy:  Considered by some to be a "postindustrial revolution," the knowledge economy recognizes that much of what drives the modern economy is the production of information for computers, media, finance, and so on. Others argue that even the production of knowledge still requires industrial production to facilitate the creation and distribution of that knowledge.

Labor Surplus:  The necessary stock of unemployed workers that help capitalists manage labor supply and demand, thus keeping wages at a minimum. When unemployment decreases, a tighter labor market gives workers more bargaining power.

Levittowns:  Small, cookie-cutter homes built for the rising suburban middle class during the post–World War II period in the United States. These homes revolutionized the building industry, but also rapidly changed working-class culture and its sense of the "American Dream" as suburban middle-class homeowners.

Outsourcing:  When companies take labor originally done by their own workers "in house" (factories, offices, campuses, etc.) and either farm work to somewhere outside the establishment (often overseas) or simply hire management companies to bring in their own workers.

Professional Managerial Class:  Often considered the prototype of the middle class, this class has grown from the original realm of plant managers, lawyers, and so on, to include anyone who controls a certain production and flow of information, from mid-level accountants to media producers and directors.

Proletariat:  This is the working class under capitalism.

Pullman, George:  The great 19th-century railroad magnate who developed the Pullman train car. He experimented with creating a whole community connected to his factory in which all aspects of social and economic life were controlled by him and his corporation.

Scientific Management (Taylorism):  A system championed by Frederick Winslow Taylor, by which a clear-cut division of mental and physical labor is established throughout a factory. It is based on the precise time and motion analysis of each job in isolation and relegates the entire mental part of the task to the managerial staff.

Service Economy:  The result of deindustrialization in Western nations where the majority of employment available to workers resides in industries that no longer produce commodities like textiles and automobiles, but now provide for the distribution of food, information, entertainment, and so on.

Solidarity:  The act of workers coming together and uniting to struggle for some control over their own labor and the means of production. While this is normally done by forming unions, any act of collective bargaining or behavior by workers can be defined as solidarity.

## WEBSITES TO LEARN MORE ABOUT WORK, LABOR, AND STUDENT ACTION PROJECTS

AFL-CIO Organizing Institute: http://www.aflcio.org/aboutus/oi/main.cfm

Bureau of Labor Statistics: http://www.bls.gov/

The Coalition of Graduate Employee Unions: http://www.cgeu.org/

Fair Labor Association: http://dev.fairlabor.org/

Jobs with Justice: http://www.jwj.org/

Labor Heritage Foundation: http://www.laborheritage.org/

Labor Notes: http://labornotes.org/

Starbucks Union: http://www.starbucksunion.org/

Student Worker Solidarity Resource Center: http://www.livingwageaction.org/

Student/Farmworker Alliance: http://www.sfalliance.org/

U.S. Department of Labor: http://www.dol.gov/

United Students Against Sweatshops: http://www.studentsagainstsweatshops.org

Worker Rights Consortium: http://www.workersrights.org

## REFERENCES

Amin, Ash, ed. 1994. Post-Fordism: A Reader. New York: Wiley/Blackwell.

Benitez, Andrew. 2007a. "Students Launch Fast for Guards." *Harvard Crimson.* May 4. Retrieved January 14, 2010 (http://www.thecrimson.com/article/2007/5/4/students-launch-fast-for-guards-around/).

———. 2007b. "Students Rally for Workers." *Harvard Crimson.* April 5. Retrieved February 18, 2010 (http://www.thecrimson.com/article/2007/4/5/students-rally-for-workers-over-80).

Best, Joel. 2001. *Damned Lies and Statistics:* Untangling Numbers From the Media, Politicians, and Activists. Berkeley, CA: University of California Press.

Bloch, Marc. 1964. *Feudal Society, Volume 2: Social Classes and Political Organization.* Chicago, IL: University of Chicago Press.

Bluestone, Barry and Bennett Harrison. 1982. *The Deindustrialization of America*: Plant Closings, Community Abandonment, and the Dismantling of Basic Industry. New York: Basic Books.

Bobo, Kim and Jackie Kendall. 2001. *Organizing for Social Change: A Manual for Activists in the 1990s* (3rd ed.). Santa Ana, CA: Seven Locks Press.

Braverman, Harry. 1974. *Labor and Monopoly Capital: The Degradation of Labor in the Twentieth Century.* New York: Monthly Review Press.

Calderón, José. 2004. "Lessons From an Activist Intellectual: Participatory Research, Teaching, and Learning for Social Change." Latin American Perspectives, 31:81–94.

_____. 2008. Partnership in Teaching and Learning: Combining the Practice of Critical Pedagogy with Civic Engagement and Diversity Diversity & Democracy, 11:7–9.

Calderón, José and Gilbert Cadena. 2007. "Linking Critical Democratic Pedagogy, Multiculturalism, and Service Learning to a Project-Based Approach." Pp. 63–80 in Race, Poverty, and Social Justice: Multidisciplinary Perspectives Through Service Learning, edited by José Calderón. Herndon, VA: Stylus.

Dolgon, Corey. 2002. "Building Community Amid the Ruins: Strategies for Struggle From the Coalition for Justice at Southampton College." Pp. 220–232 in Forging Radical Alliances Across Difference: Coalition Politics for the New Millennium, edited by Jill Bystydzienski and Steven Schacht. Lanham, MD: Rowman & Littlefield.

Dolgon, Corey. 2005. The End of the Hamptons: Scenes from the Class Struggle in America's Paradise. New York: New York University Press.

Dublin, Thomas. 1981. Women at Work: The Transformation of Work and Community in Lowell, Massachusetts, 1826–1860. New York: Columbia University Press.

_____. 1995. Transforming Women's Work: New England Lives in the Industrial Revolution. Ithaca, NY: Cornell University Press.

Ehrenreich, Barbara. 2002. Nickel and Dimed. New York: Henry Holt.

Eisler, Benita. 1997. The Lowell Offering: Writings by New England Mill Women (1840–1845). New York: Harper Torchbooks.

Featherstone, Liza. 2002. Students Against Sweatshops: The Making of a Movement. New York: Verso.

Frank, Andre Gunder. 1996. The World System: Five Hundred Years or Five Thousand. New York: Routledge.

Gould, Elise. 2005, October 20. "Prognosis Worsens for Workers' Health Care: Fourth Consecutive Year of Decline in Employer-Provided Insurance Coverage." EPI Briefing Paper #167. Retrieved January 14, 2010 (http://www.epi.org/publications/entry/bp167/).

Gutman, Herbert. 1977. Work, Culture, and Society in Industrial America. New York: Vintage Books

Hamper, Ben. 1992. Rivethead: Tales From the Assembly Line. New York: Warner Books.

Hasser, Neil. 2003. "The Struggle for Farmworkers' Rights" Humanity and Society, 27.

Iverson, Torben and Anne Wren. 1998. "Equality, Employment, and Budgetary Restraint: The Trilemma of the Service Economy." World Politics, 50:507–546.

Lichtenstein, Alex. 1996. Twice the Work of Free Labor: The Political Economy of Convict Labor in the New South. New York: Verso.

Morris, Martina and Bruce Western. 1999. "Inequality in Earnings at the Close of the Twentieth Century." Annual Review of Sociology, 25:623–657.

Savio, Mario. 1964, December 3. "Mario Savio's Speech Before the FSM Sit-In." Retrieved February 19, 2010 (http://www.fsm-a.org/stacks/mario/mario_speech.html).

Schor, Juliet. 1992. The Overworked American: The Unexpected Decline of Leisure. New York: Basic Books.

Skocpol, Theda. 1997. Boomerang: Health Care Reform and the Turn Against Government. New York: Norton.

Soley, Lawrence. 1995. Leasing the Ivory Tower: The Corporate Takeover of Academia. Boston, MA: South End Press.

Stand for Security Coalition. 2007, April 30. "Who We Are." Retrieved February 18, 2010 (http://stand4security .blogspot.com/2007/04/who-we-are.html).

"Statement From the Pullman Strikers (June 15, 1894)." 1985. U.S. Strike Commission, Report and Testimony on the Chicago Strike of 1894. Washington, DC: Government Printing Office, 87–88.

Taylor, Frederick W. 1911. The Principles of Scientific Management. New York: Harper.

White, Geoffrey. Ed. 2000. Campus, Inc.: Corporate Power in the Ivory Tower. San Francisco, CA: Prometheus Books.

# CHAPTER 4

# Finding Ourselves

*Race, Gender, Sexuality, Multiculturalism, and Identity*

*You have to deal with the politics of why [service] is needed. . . . Built into it is an implicit way of saying that people in community A aren't up to dealing with the needs that they have. People in these areas rarely get the money to do the things they need. Some foundations easily give money to white people to do work in black communities and find it difficult to give money to black people to work in their own communities. . . . I'm not saying that people who are white can't work in communities of color at all. I'm saying that to the extent that there isn't thinking through of the implications of what you are perpetuating, there's a problem. Service without critical analysis and organizing is not service. It's a perpetuation of the dominant culture.*

—Mel King, organizer and educator (1999)

*My view is that in order to understand our commonalities, it is important to recognize our historical* differences *and why those differences exist. Then I think real unities develop, not just unities developed on superficial, feel-good levels, but unity based on understanding of each other and where we do have commonalities.*

—José Calderón, professor and activist (2004)

Janet Eyler and Dwight Giles (1999) conducted a pilot study to measure the impact of service learning on students' **prejudices.** According to one student who worked with youth in a service agency, she had "expected them to be very bad children who didn't want to accomplish anything except to be thugs." Instead, she came to see them as "intelligent and kind, and I made some great friends when I got to know them personally and stop stereotyping" (pp. 29–30). Another student at a different community site explained that "people are people! Like when you read 'of the Latino community, or the low-income community,' you're really setting yourself apart. When you're there, they're normal, just like you and me" (pp. 29–30). Eyler and Giles concluded that their students' experiences changed their prejudices against others and gave them a greater sense of tolerance and empathy. Yet the humanizing impact of a "just like me" revelation does not address the structural differences that inspired those **stereotypes** to begin with. In other words, it's one thing to overcome personal prejudices and stereotypes; it's another to know how they came to be in the first place, and how to change the inequalities they breed.

On the other hand, some students do gain a much richer sense of identities (their own, others', and the notion of collective identities) when their work in communities is more integrative. Sociologist Rick Battistoni (1997) offers a comment from a student engaged in a service learning project with a long-term community partner:

> I am now aware of what is happening around me. New Brunswick extends beyond the [campus] bus route. It is filled with people who need aid, people who give aid, people who cannot be bothered to give aid, and people who, like me, don't realize they are citizens at all. . . . One of the most instrumental facets of my experience was simply my walk to the building [where I worked] each day. Every time I went I became more aware of my surroundings. I now see the city differently. I'm no longer scared walking to the site—far from it. I feel like I know that small portion of the city. Now when I pass people on the street, some say hello to me and call me by name. Through my work . . . I've gotten to know people and they've gotten to know me. I enjoy my community service. It has opened my eyes as to the role I play as a citizen in my community. (p. 150)

Battistoni argues that an awareness of citizenship and democracy infuses service learning projects with insights into "collective identities." Thus, as students encounter community people from different racial or class identities, they not only learn about the humanity of "the other," but also of their own humanity, their own racial and class position, and the need to create **collective identities** that break down isolation, alienation, and inequality.

The Women's Studies Program at Rutgers University incorporates service learning and civic education through a variety of courses. According to faculty members Mary Trigg and Barbara Balliet, "feminist community service tests students' abilities to reach across boundaries of difference, and to move between the borders separating theory and practice, classroom and community, and their own conception of themselves as private individuals and public citizens" (p. 97). Feminist pedagogy, as a framework for service learning, challenges students to focus on the issues of identity and difference from a critical perspective, at the same time that their ideas are challenged and reshaped by their engagement with diverse groups of people.

For many students in the program, acknowledging prejudices and committing to reflection and change are major accomplishments. One student, who worked with the New Jersey Women and AIDS Network, acknowledged her need to "confront her own homophobic attitudes." She wrote in her journal,

I just know I feel (and have always felt) uncomfortable around homosexuals, because I don't understand the whole phenomenon. . . . Since the internship consists of 4 lesbians and 3 straights working in the office, I find it necessary to confront my own homophobic attitudes and deal with them. I'm sure it will be a difficult process, since I hate racists, sexists, and others who can't accept difference. I may be one of those people. (p. 94)

Other students recognized not only their own prejudices, but also their privileges. One white, middle-class student who worked at the American Civil Liberties Union noted a "contradiction" as she entered the agency's inner-city office. She explained,

I had to walk up to the third floor past Superior Cleaning . . . a temporary worker agency with a staff mainly made up of Latina and Black women (the rest are Latino and Black men). I was in stark contrast to them. There I was, a middle-class white student learning, thinking and working for credits. Not only was I not getting paid, but I was paying to be there. They showed up every morning looking for assignments that break their backs and do not pay well so they can feed themselves and their families. . . . I am continually questioning how I am using the privilege I have to work on creating a society without racist and sexist institutions and without such economic disparity. (Trigg and Balliet 2000:97)

This student's recognition of difference has been transcended by the recognition of inequality and injustice that make differences of race, ethnicity, gender, and class determining factors in who has privileges and resources and who does not. As Trigg and Balliet conclude, "women's studies' focus on gender and diversity and service learning's emphasis on what community means in contemporary American society and have the potential to enhance conversations about community, responsibility, citizenship, diversity, rights, and democracy" (p. 101). At their best, service learning projects offer students experiences with diversity, the analytical tools to understand the impact of different identities on social relationships and structural inequalities, and the opportunities to transcend rigid identities and inequalities toward the potential of creating new collective identities shaped by democracy and social justice.

Individual and collective identities are some of the more important social facts that impact people and society. Who we imagine and make ourselves out to be; who our families, coworkers, and classmates perceive us to be; and who social systems and institutions claim we are mark a point of convergence between individual agency and social structures—how we make ourselves and how the world makes us. Yet these social, cultural, and political categories such as race, gender, ethnicity, and sexual orientation have historically determined massive *inequalities* in power and privilege. Biological and physiological differences such as sex, skin color, or physical disabilities have been translated as, or manipulated to become, reasons for condescension, condemnation, discrimination, segregation, or outright violent repression. While identities are experienced as the most intimate and personal of social facts, they represent a host of complex social and political dynamics of power and inequality.

This chapter begins by looking at how sociologists define various categories of identity such as race, ethnicity, gender, sexual orientation, and physical ability. We also look at the link between these identities and different types of social inequalities by examining a variety of statistical portraits. Next, we investigate the ways in which historical and political movements change how societies and individuals create their identities. Finally, the chapter presents three case studies where students working with community organizations experienced how identities shape people's lived conditions and how working together to change those conditions actually helps to reshape identities on both individual and social levels.

## DEFINING IDENTITIES BY THE NUMBERS: A STATISTICAL LOOK AT IDENTITIES AND DIFFERENCE

Identities such as race and gender seem easy and given. After all, one's physical makeup (inside and outside) seems the most basic element of any person's identity. Man or woman, black or white seem to be biologically determined and, therefore, the most natural and primal of categories. Although biological differences among people do exist, what sociologists are most concerned with are the social and cultural *meanings* assigned to these differences. We know that men and women have some distinct physical features and internal organs, biological and chemical processes, and so forth, but what social and political significance do those differences acquire? Similarly, while some racial groups do have different features and genetic compositions,

> evidence from the analysis of genetics (e.g., DNA) indicates that most physical variation, about 94%, lies *within* so-called racial groups. Conventional geographic 'racial' groupings differ from one another only in about 6% of their genes. This means that there is greater variation *within* "racial" groups than *between* them. . . . Throughout history whenever different groups have come into contact, they have interbred. The continued sharing of genetic materials has maintained all of humankind as a single species." (American Anthropological Association 1998: n.p.)

Thus, social scientists distinguish between sex and gender, and between skin color and racial identities.

### Gender

**Sex** refers to the actual biological composition of a person, while **gender** refers to the cultural meanings that such a composition has in any given society. Sex is generally considered immutable, while gender changes with historical, cultural, and political conditions.

Discrimination and oppression based on these differences are called **sexism.** Women's rights in the United States have changed remarkably in the last century, altering the very nature of women's social roles and political power. Beliefs that women were intellectually or socially inferior by nature have proven to be myths, fueled by **patriarchal** ideology. Even many of the physical distinctions thought to be natural have shown to be cultural or political (Lorber 1993; Marini 1990). For example, with appropriate nutrition, training, and resources, women continue to excel in physical strength and speed, closing the gender gap in athletic achievements once thought to be natural and immutable.

If we look at male and female performance in the same sport, we can see how rapidly women have closed the gender gap. Table 4.1 shows the Boston Marathon finishing times for male and female champions from 1966 (the year of the first woman participant, although officially women were not permitted to participate until 1972) to the 2005 race. With better training, nutrition, economic support, and cultural encouragement, women have significantly reduced the difference in winning times from just over an hour in 1966 to less than 14 minutes in 2005. The increasing ability of women to perform at levels comparable to men in a variety of sports led some social scientists to contend that most gender and sex distinctions were far from natural and that women would eventually be able to equal men in most sports (Dworkin 2001; Fausto-Sterling 1985). While some biological

**Table 4.1**   Boston Marathon Winning Times for Men and Women, 1966–2005

| | Women | Men | | Women | Men | | Women | Men | | Women | Men |
|----|---------|---------|----|---------|---------|----|---------|---------|----|---------|---------|
| 66 | 3:21:40 | 2:17:1 | 76 | 2:47:10 | 2:20:19 | 86 | 2:24:55 | 2:07:51 | 96 | 2:27:12 | 2:09:15 |
| 67 | 3:27:17 | 2:15:45 | 77 | 2:48:33 | 2:14:46 | 87 | 2:25:21 | 2:11:50 | 97 | 2:26:23 | 2:10:34 |
| 68 | 3:30:00 | 2:22:17 | 78 | 2:44:52 | 2:10:13 | 88 | 2:24:30 | 2:08:43 | 98 | 2:23:21 | 2:07:34 |
| 69 | 3:22:46 | 2:13:49 | 79 | 2:35:15 | 2:09:27 | 89 | 2:24:33 | 2:09:06 | 99 | 2:23:25 | 2:09:52 |
| 70 | 3:05:07 | 2:10:30 | 80 | 2:34:28 | 2:12:11 | 90 | 2:25:24 | 2:08:19 | 00 | 2:26:11 | 2:09:47 |
| 71 | 3:08:30 | 2:18:45 | 81 | 2:26:46 | 2:09:26 | 91 | 2:24:18 | 2:11:06 | 01 | 2:23:53 | 2:09:43 |
| 72 | 3:10:26 | 2:15:39 | 82 | 2:29:33 | 2:08:52 | 92 | 2:23:43 | 2:08:14 | 02 | 2:20:43 | 2:09:02 |
| 73 | 3:05:59 | 2:16:03 | 83 | 2:22:43 | 2:09:00 | 93 | 2:25:27 | 2:09:33 | 03 | 2:25:20 | 2:10:11 |
| 74 | 2:47:11 | 2:13:39 | 84 | 2:29.28 | 2:10:34 | 94 | 2:21:45 | 2:07:15 | 04 | 2:24:27 | 2:10:37 |
| 75 | 2:42:24 | 2:09:55 | 85 | 2:34.06 | 2:14:05 | 95 | 2:25:11 | 2:09:22 | 05 | 2:25:13 | 2:11:45 |

differences between men and women remain, the meaning and impact of them continue to be debated and changed.

According to Andrew Tatem, Carlos Guerra, Peter Atkinson, and Simon Hay (2004), women sprinters are closing the gap with men at an even faster pace and, by 2156, women may actually have a faster time in the 100 meters than men—8.079 seconds to the men's 8.098.

## TITLE IX

In 1972, President Richard Nixon signed the Education Amendments of 1972 to the Civil Rights Act of 1964. Title IX of these amendments states that "no person in the United States shall, on the basis of sex, be excluded from participation in, or denied the benefits of, or be subjected to discrimination under any educational program or activity receiving federal assistance." While the law is broad in scope, school sports have been the area of the most controversy, as many institutions were forced to invest in women's sports on an equitable level with men's sports.

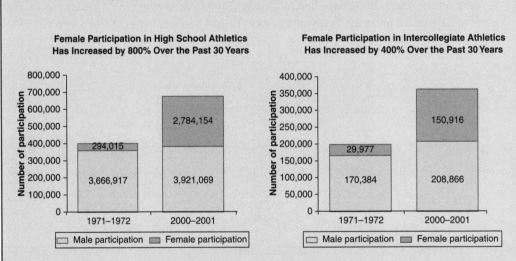

Female Participation in High School Athletics Has Increased by 800% Over the Past 30 Years

Female Participation in Intercollegiate Athletics Has Increased by 400% Over the Past 30 Years

*Source:* "Equal Opportunity for Women in Athletics: A Promise Yet to Be Fulfilled," August 2002, National Women's Law Center, p. 5 (http://www.nwlc.org/pdf/EOforWomeninAthletics_APromiseYettobeFulfilled.pdf).

The graphs above demonstrate the significant increase in women's participation in organized high school and college athletics. While many studies show that funding levels, staffing, publicity, media coverage, and a variety of other dynamics related to sports still remain dominated by men's sports, women's sports programs have now flourished in the United States and demonstrated that with relatively equal opportunities and support, the athletic prowess of men and women are more similar than once thought.

In the area of economics, women have historically been denied access to property ownership, inheritance, education, professional associations, apprenticeships, and skilled crafts. Even when they have gotten access to the same jobs as men, women were paid less. In 1963, the U.S. Congress passed the Equal Pay Act, which made it illegal to pay men and women different wage rates for equal work on jobs that require equal skill, effort, and responsibility and are performed under similar working conditions. Figure 4.1 illustrates that such legislation and other political and social forces did increase the relative wages of women.

However, despite legislation, social movements, and a variety of gains in positions of political and financial power, women continue to average almost 25% less than men working in similar jobs with similar job performance. Progressive social and economic policies have significantly changed the meaning of gender in the United States. Educational, political, and cultural opportunities now allow women more autonomy and resources for shaping

**Figure 4.1**   Women's Earnings Relative to Men, 1970–2002

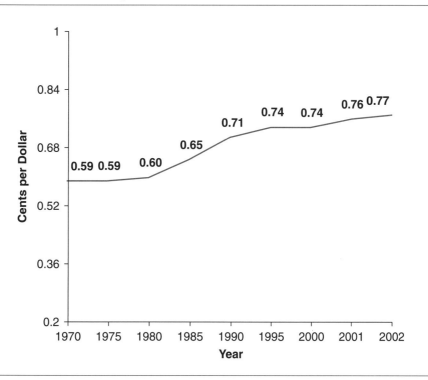

*Source:* "Women and Men in the United States," March 2004, U.S. Census Bureau.

new identities as athletes, professionals, and breadwinners. But discrimination based on gender continues to restrict those possibilities.

## Race

**Race**, too, has shown itself to be a flexible category. Despite claims about its biological deter-mination, the category has shifted both in definition and significance. In the United States, for example, the seventh federal census, in 1850, had a question about color with choices includ-ing "white," "black," and "mulatto" (or mixed). Thirty years later, the 10th census had expanded the color choices to "Indian" and "Chinese." The 1910 U.S. census divided the "Native Born" white population into three categories: Native white persons of Native Parentage, Native white persons of Foreign Parentage, and Native white persons of Mixed Parentage. The current cen-sus not only offers new categories such as Filipino, Korean, Japanese, Vietnamese, Native Hawaiian, and so forth, but it also has a question asking if respondents are "Spanish/ Hispanic/Latino." Thus, although race's biological link seemed natural and immutable, it has proven to be much more political and malleable (Lee 1993; Waters 1990).

Just as racial designations have changed, so, too, has discrimination based on race, or what is called **racism.** Historian Ronald Takaki (1993) traces the origins of race and racism in the United States back to European encounters with Native Americans. As Europeans sought to permanently expand their economic interests in the "New World," Native American communities became obstacles. As competition for land and resources intensi-fied, European collaboration with American Indians gave way to conquest over them; new ideologies arose to rationalize domination. As Takaki writes,

> What emerged to justify dispossessing [Native Americans] was the racialization of Indian 'savagery.' . . . This process of Indian dehumanization developed a peculiarly New England [Puritan] dimension as the colonists associated Indians with the devil. Indian identity became a matter of 'descent': their racial markers indicated inerasable qualities of savagery. (p. 38)

Gone were the stories of Chief Massasoit, Squanto, and Samoset who had helped early Pilgrim settlements and broke bread at the first Thanksgiving. Instead, Native Americans became a *race* perceived of as naturally lazy, unredeemable savages who needed to be pushed off their land to allow for an economic expansion "blessed by God." Racism resulted in poverty and **genocide** for Native Americans.

Regardless of whether racism emanated from economic competition, the impact of racism on economic outcomes remains significant. Figure 4.2 shows the median income differences between white and African American households from 1967 to 2002. In 1967, black households earned 60% of the nation's median income and 58% of what white American households earned. Twenty-five years later, in 1992, these percentages remained

**Figure 4.2**   Median Household Income by Race (1967–2006)

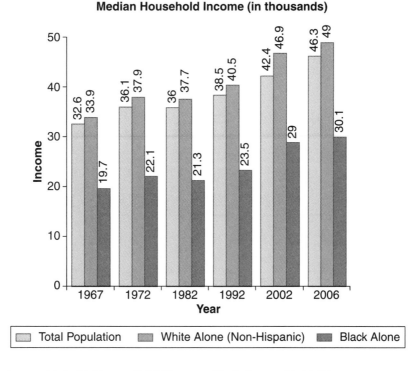

Source: "Income, Poverty and Health Insurance Coverage in the United States: 2006," August 2007, by Carmen DeNavas-Walt, Bernadette D. Proctor, and Jessica Smith, Current Population Reports (http://www.census.gov/prod/2007pubs/p60-233.pdf).

virtually the same. Only in the decade between 1992 and 2002 did African American households gain significantly, earning over 68% of the median household and almost 62% of white households. By 2006, these numbers had dropped again, as black households earned only 65% of the median and 61% of what white households earned.

Despite numerous civil rights–era laws, from affirmative action to equal opportunity employment, the actual income of black households remains less than two-thirds of white households.

As was stated in Chapter 2, economic inequality by race is even more notable in the area of wealth. Figure 4.3 shows that African Americans' median net worth lags behind that of white Americans by over 600%, average home equity by over 300%, and average stock ownership by almost 2000%. According to the organization United for a Fair Economy (UFE), the racial wealth gap persists even during times of economic growth. Thus, while the

**Figure 4.3** Racial Wealth Gap, 2001

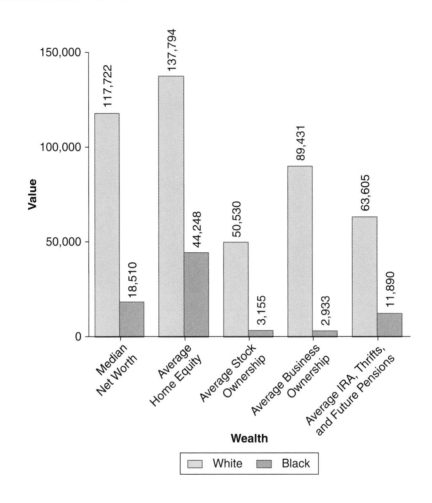

*Source: The Wealth and Inequality Reader*, 2004, United for a Fair Economy, Cambridge: Dollars & Sense.

1990s saw unprecedented periods of prolonged economic growth and African Americans did make up some ground in the area of income disparity with whites, the overall wealth of African American families actually declined.

UFE (2004) concludes that the "intransigent wealth gap is the product of a long history of discrimination in the United States, and is perpetuated by family inheritance patterns that pass accumulated advantages and disadvantages from one generation to the next" (p. 14). Again, despite numerous changes in social policies and achievement levels, race remains a determining force in the distribution of economic resources.

## Ethnicity

Unlike race, **ethnicity** has no real biological pretensions, although some members of the same ethnic group may share physical features such as skin color or hair texture, and some prejudices seem bolstered by claims that certain ethnic groups are *naturally* one thing or another. Instead, ethnicity is defined as shared cultural characteristics among groups usually of common national origin and often considered to be subcultures within a dominant majority population. For example, most Chicanos (Mexican American immigrants in the United States) share a common heritage; have a common language; practice a similar religion (Catholicism); and often enjoy similar music, foods, and so on. None of these emanates from biological sources, but as cultural indicators they distinguish some groups from others. For many ethnic groups, cultural markers were interpreted by white society (policy makers, corporate executives, and civic leaders) as signs of natural, biological, or cultural inferiority.

In the area of education, for example, Native American youth were believed incapable of higher learning and intellectual skills. Industrial boarding schools played a pivotal role in the Bureau of Indian Affairs' plan to push for comprehensive Indian education in the late 1800s. The policy's advocates, like Bureau Commissioner Thomas Morgan, believed that forced removal from reservations and relocation to boarding schools to learn marketable skills and crafts would "Americanize" young Native Americans and solve the "Indian problem," turning "savages into citizens" (Trennert 1987). Aside from developing industrial skills to enter the labor force, the crux of Indian education attacked Native American cultural practices and traditional values. According to David Wallace Adams (1995), school officials cut children's hair; changed their dress, diets, and names; and subjected them to militaristic regimentation and discipline. Teachers also forbade the use of tribal languages, dances, and other religious practices, and sought to replace them with English, Christianity, athletics, and patriotism. Students also learned the industrial and domestic skills and values suitable to mainstream American gender roles. Eventually, Native Americans would resist such acculturation and regain certain traditional practices and values to empower social and cultural movements during the civil rights era. But the damage done by the cultural and psychological warfare of forced assimilation continues to take its toll on Native American communities.

To Americanize Mexican Americans, California officials centered their attention on women. Historian George Sanchez (1990) stated that women were seen as "responsible for the transmission of values in the home . . . [and] the homekeeper creates the atmosphere, whether it be one of harmony and cooperation or dissatisfaction and revolt" (p. 289). While officials stressed changes in diet, cleanliness, family planning, and other cultural practices, eventually the need for domestic servants, seamstresses, laundresses, and other service workers dominated most efforts to educate Chicano women. In both the Native and Mexican American cases, government officials believed that cultural differences could be obliterated and a hardworking, amenable labor force could be created. But to "become

Americans" required that each group shed its language, culture, and traditions at the same time that they accept a status as an industrial or domestic working class. Such economic and social segregation continues to have its impact.

In the area of education, Figures 4.4 and 4.5 chronicle the percentages of U.S. residents who have attained high school and college degrees from 1940–2000. Black, Native American, and Hispanic high school graduates have continued to lag behind white and Asian/Pacific Islander graduates. Hispanics fare especially poorly, as barely half the population holds high school diplomas as compared to almost three-quarters of all other groups. Still, the data show that all groups (including whites) have benefited from massive infusions of resources into public education following World War II, as all numbers rose from 1940–1970. However, the data also show that white and Asian/Pacific Islander

**Figure 4.4**   Percentage of People 25 Years or Older With High School Diploma or Higher (by Race and Ethnicity)

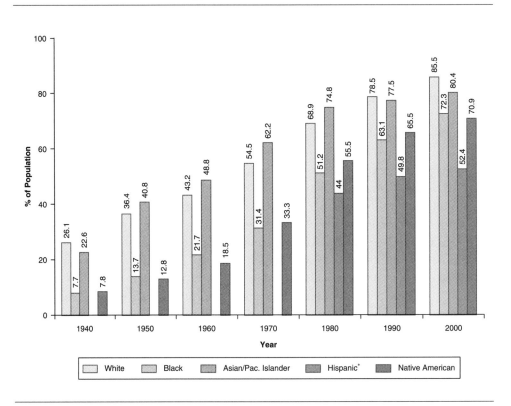

Source: "Educational Attainment of the Population 25 Years and Over: 1940 to 2000," U.S. Census Bureau, Current Population Survey (http://www.census.gov/population/www/socdemo/educ-attn.html).

Note: Hispanic not included until 1980.

populations benefited disproportionately during this period. It wasn't until affirmative action and the enforcement of desegregation during the 1970s that blacks, Hispanics, and Native Americans began making up ground.

A similar story is presented in this second graph (Figure 4.5) on the numbers of people holding college degrees. Major expansions in institutions of higher education and the demands of a changing economy based on advanced information technology have influenced large increases in college enrollment and degrees since the 1950s. These increases, however, remained small for blacks and Native Americans until the 1970s and the onset of affirmative action policies. Affirmative action has made a notable difference in the college attainment of non-whites. Still, Native and African Americans, as well as Hispanics, lag far behind the college degree attainment of whites and Asian/Pacific Islanders.

**Figure 4.5**   Percent of People 25 Years or Older With Bachelor's Degrees or Higher

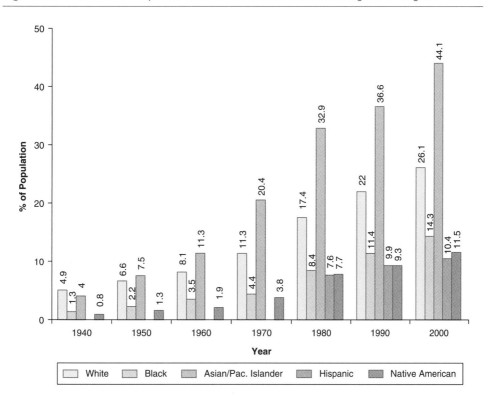

*Source: "Educational Attainment of the Population 25 Years and Over: 1940 to 2000,"* U.S. Census Bureau, Current Population Survey (http://www.census.gov/population/www/socdemo/educ-attn.html).

An important area where race, ethnicity, gender, education, and the economy intersect relates to unemployment. As the economic crisis of 2008 and 2009 deepened, the overall unemployment rate reached 10%—a figure not seen since 1983. Yet, as an instructive *New York Times* piece explained, "not all groups have felt the recession equally" (Carter, Cox, and Quealy, 2009:n.p.). Despite similar ages and education levels, non-whites fare worse economically than whites, with African Americans experiencing the greatest hardships.

As of September 2009, the highest unemployment rates for all racial, ethnic, and gender groups are among youth ages 15–24 without high school diplomas, as shown in Figure 4.6. African American men in this age and education category comprise the highest of all levels at 48.5%—almost half. The unemployment rate for black men and women in this age and education group is only slightly lower at 42.7%. But for Asian and American Indian people

**Figure 4.6**  Unemployment Rates, Ages 15–24 Without High School Degree

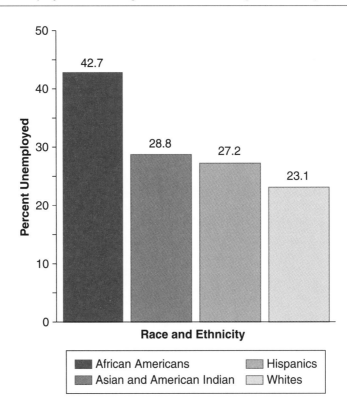

*Source:* "The Jobless Rate for People Like You," November 6, 2009, by Shan Carter, Amanda Cox, and Kevin Quealy, *New York Times* (http://www.nytimes.com/interactive/2009/11/06/business/economy/unemployment-lines.html?emc = eta1).

of more than one race in the same age and education category, unemployment is at 28.8%, almost 14% lower than for African American young people. For Hispanics in the same category, unemployment is slightly lower at 27.2%. However, for whites of the same age with the same lack of a high school diploma, unemployment is at 23.1%. While unemployment affects all young people tremendously, blacks in this age group without a high school diploma are almost twice as likely as similar white young people to be unemployed (Carter et al. 2009:n.p.).

The racial and ethnic difference is even more striking when African American men with high school and college degrees are compared to white men without them (see Figure 4.7). Black men without any degree have a 30.9% unemployment rate, but that gets cut almost in half, to 16.2%, when they have a high school degree. Yet white men without a high school

**Figure 4.7**   Unemployment Rates for African American and White Males

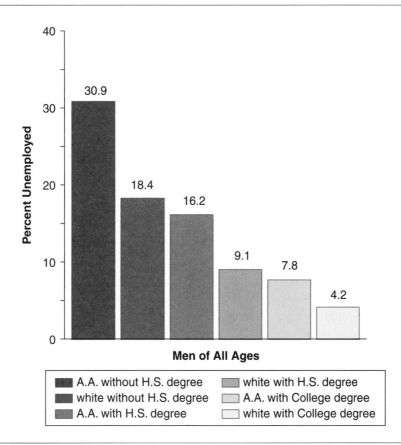

*Source:* "The Jobless Rate for People Like You," November 6, 2009, by Shan Carter, Amanda Cox, and Kevin Quealy, *New York Times* (http://www.nytimes.com/interactive/2009/11/06/business/economy/unemployment-lines.html?emc = eta1).

degree have an unemployment rate of 18.4%—only 2.2% higher than black men *with* a degree (Carter et al. 2009:n.p.).

For white men with a high school diploma, their unemployment rate goes down to 9.1%. But this rate is only 1.3 % higher than for African American men with a *college* degree, who have an unemployment rate of 7.8%. For white men with a college degree, unemployment rates drop to 4.2%. In all cases, African American men have an unemployment rate over 40% higher than white men with similar educational attainment, while only a slightly lower unemployment rate than white men with significantly *less* educational attainment. In all situations, race and ethnic identities play a definitive role in who suffers the worst in economic hard times (Carter et al. 2009:n.p.).[1]

## THE MODEL MINORITY MYTH

The data above demonstrate that, unlike African, Latino, and Native Americans, Asian Americans have succeeded in education on an equal and sometimes even higher level than whites. The educational, professional, and economic success of Asian Americans has resulted in their cultural status as a "model minority." The stereotype is simple: Asian Americans work hard, follow the rules, are naturally good in math and science, and their educational achievements have resulted in financial success and social acceptance. The downside of this myth is that it is usually used to challenge programs (such as affirmative action), as critics argue that if Asian Americans have succeeded on their own, why can't other non-white racial or ethnic groups? Far from being discriminated against by structural or institutional racism, Asian Americans would seem to show that any group that works hard can succeed.

Yet social scientists have been able to challenge this model minority image in a variety of ways. First of all, sociologists explain that the Asian American population remains so small that differentiations appear much larger as compared to African Americans, Latinos, or whites. Second, a majority of Asian American immigrants (especially Korean, Japanese, and South Asian Indian) came to the United States with advanced educational levels and often from middle-class backgrounds with economic resources. In fact, comparisons between Korean, Japanese, and South Asian, and newer Southeast Asian immigrants from Vietnam, Indonesia, and Thailand show that the latter groups actually challenge the model minority myth, as their levels of educational attainment and poverty rates are much closer to those of other minority groups than the former group. In other words, the success of *some* Asian Americans is more likely due to the educational and economic resources they had before arrival than because they exhibited "model" cultural behavior or beliefs.

---

[1]Go to the *New York Times* website to get an amazing interactive tool that compares late 2009 unemployment statistics among many demographic groups (www.nytimes.com/interactive/2009/11/06/business/economy/unemployment-lines.html?emc=eta1).

Finally, even within the group of Asian Americans who have been successful, they face what sociologists have called a "glass ceiling." According to law professor Mylinh Uy (2004) of the University of Dayton, "Asian-American men born in the United States are 7 percent to 11 percent less likely to hold managerial jobs than white men with the same educational and experience level. Median income for Asian-Americans with four years of college education is $34,470 a year, compared with $36,130 for whites, according to the U.S. Census Bureau." Still, the model minority argument remains an effective trope for those who want to claim that racial and ethnic discrimination no longer impacts levels of minority group achievement. In the end, the model minority idea may tell us more about the people who use it than the people it supposedly represents.

## Institutional Versus Attitudinal Discrimination

All of the economic and educational data presented above demonstrate that the historical impact of gender, race, and ethnic identities is integrally connected to a variety of forms of discrimination and inequality. As we suggested earlier, inequalities often come from the ways in which identities are established and enforced, sometimes legally restricting economic or political opportunities and other times promoting greater access and equalities. For example, by custom and law, women in the United States were once denied equal employment, wages, access to property ownership, as well as the political rights to vote and hold most legislative offices. To be a woman was to be a *second class* citizen. Similarly, African Americans (or Negroes or Coloreds or Blacks as they were once referred to) were slaves, the property of white landowners. By law, African Americans had no access to property, suffrage, or education. Even after slavery, laws (especially in the South) denied them equal access to political, educational, and social institutions. On a structural and institutional level, identities related to race and sex resulted in severe discrimination and repression. The history and persistence of these forms of inequality are called institutionalized discrimination.

**Institutionalized discrimination** is defined as systematic methods, policies, or laws that limit a particular group's wages, political enfranchisement, housing opportunities, education, and so forth. But the impact of such discrimination can remain long after the actual policies. Although slavery ended in 1865, the result was that African Americans had little or no economic resources with which to exercise their freedom. Segregation and other Jim Crow laws only further delayed black Americans' abilities to compete fairly. While civil rights legislation and policies such as affirmative action seem to have made some impact in rectifying generations of structural discrimination, a variety of institutional barriers such as culturally-biased standardized tests (Sacks 1999) and racially and ethnically discriminatory loan practices (Ross and Yinger 2002) continued a legacy of structural and institutional discrimination.

On a social and cultural level, however, the stigma related to identities also results in a variety of other forms of discrimination and alienation. Unequal rights for women were supported by an ideology that labeled women as intellectually inferior, emotionally unstable, and physically weak (often despite evidence to the contrary). Similarly, white stereotypes labeled African Americans as intellectually simple and lazy (again, despite evidence to the contrary). Today, in spite of equal rights legislation and a greater social acceptance of gender and racial equality, studies demonstrate that teachers have lower expectations of female students (Tiedemann 2002). Even when they excel academically, women are directed away from hard sciences and professions such as engineering, law, and medicine. Instead, they are encouraged to become teachers, nurses, social workers, and other nurturing professionals (Jacobs 1996). Many black and Latino students are similarly stereotyped as they are disproportionately subjected to placement in special education classes and more severe disciplinary action than their white cohorts (Agbenyega and Jiggetts 1999; Emihovich 1982). Inequalities based on individual prejudices and stereotyping are called attitudinal discrimination.

**Attitudinal discrimination** is defined as actions taken against a subordinate group based on individual prejudices or culturally-influenced biases. While these acts are often overt, direct, and visible, increasingly sociologists have looked at more subtle ways in which attitudinal discrimination impacts institutional outcomes for nonwhites. For example, in the year 2000, almost 80% of all states had a disproportionate representation of minority students in all forms of special education classes, including speech impairment programs, learning disabilities programs, and mental retardation programs (President's Commission on Excellence in Special Education 2002). Table 4.2 shows the 10 worst states in regard to this dynamic.

While some researchers have argued that student referrals to special education may also be influenced by structural conditions such as inadequate budgets, culturally-biased diagnostic tools such as IQ tests, and administrative strategies to hide poor-performing students' test scores, the attitudinal biases of predominately white teachers and administrators continue to result in young students of color being labeled as "emotionally disturbed," "retarded," or "learning disabled." According to Agbenyega and Jiggetts (1999),

> The consequence of "inappropriate referrals" into Special Education has been the stigmatization of a large number of minority children and of a continuing perception that this population is a racial underclass even in spite of the vast successes and progress of blacks in the nation. Such "irrational" placements of minority children into Special Education lend credibility to the charge of systematic bias and racism, and unfair cultural bias even when real medical and psychologically diagnosed disabilities have been factored out of placement decision-making. (p. 619)

Table 4.2   Percentage of Minority Students in Special Education Programs

| State | % of Minority Children in General Population | % of Minorities in Special Education Programs | Difference |
|---|---|---|---|
| New York | 42.65 | 61.57 | 19.12 |
| District of Columbia | 78.62 | 96.43 | 17.81 |
| Delaware | 32.38 | 46.59 | 14.21 |
| Louisiana | 44.26 | 54.76 | 10.48 |
| South Carolina | 39.99 | 50.25 | 10.26 |
| Mississippi | 47.50 | 55.68 | 8.18 |
| Alabama | 35.55 | 43.19 | 7.64 |
| Alaska | 35.60 | 42.98 | 7.38 |
| North Carolina | 34.09 | 41.25 | 7.16 |
| Oklahoma | 26.83 | 33.79 | 6.34 |

*Source:* "*A New Era: Revitalizing Special Education for Children and Their Families,*" 2002, President's Commission on Excellence in Special Education. Washington, DC: U.S. Department of Education.

## Sexual Orientation

**Sexual orientation** is a relatively new term used to describe whether a person is **hetero-sexual** (predisposed to or prefers physical relations with opposite sex), **bisexual** (predisposed to or prefers relations with either sex), or **homosexual** (predisposed to or prefers relations with the same sex). Recently, the term **transgender** has entered the sexuality lexicon to refer to people who claim a gender identity different from their given biological sex. There is ongoing debate about how much of one's sexuality is determined by biology or chemistry and how much is culturally or socially constructed, or perhaps even a personal choice. Historical and contemporary levels of violence and discrimination against gay men, lesbians, and those of other nonmainstream sexual orientations make it unlikely that most simply "choose" to be different. Yet scientific research exploring the existence of what some call the "gay gene" is in its early stages, and the evidence is far from conclusive.

From a sociological standpoint, we must remember that just because something lacks a biological or chemical cause, it does not mean one is *free* to choose without influence from a variety of social and cultural factors. In other words, one's sexuality may be learned or acquired from a variety of complex sources similar to other preferences (like taste for certain food or belief in God) without much active or conscious choice being made. Research points toward a highly complex interweaving of social, cultural, and individual conditions and experiences that converge to influence the ways in which individuals navigate their sexual identities. The significant questions about identity are not so much what causes difference (race, ethnicity, gender, or sexual orientation), but how such identities are linked to inequality, discrimination, and sometimes violent repression. Negative behaviors toward nonheterosexuals are often caused by **homophobia,** an irrational fear of different sexual orientations held by some heterosexuals.

While colleges and universities are often believed to be progressive and tolerant institutions, gay, lesbian, bisexual, and transgendered (GLBT) people report significant levels of harassment. In a study by the Policy Institute of the National Gay and Lesbian Task Force (Rankin 2003), over a third of the undergraduates surveyed experienced some form of harassment based on their sexual identities. Table 4.3 shows how many campus employees and residents reported experiencing harassment ranging from derogatory remarks and verbal threats to graffiti, denial of services, and outright physical attacks.

To address the issues of harassment and other forms of discrimination, over 125 colleges and universities have established administratively staffed and recognized offices to address GLBT issues. According to Warren Blumenfeld, author of *Making Colleges and Universities Safe for Gay, Lesbian, Bisexual, and Transgender Students and Staff* (1993), institutions can make a serious difference in preventing harassment by creating safer environments for GLBT people. His recommendations include enacting nondiscrimination policies, infusing diversity training into all forms of orientation programs, publicly supporting GLBT student organizations, and offering equal benefits and services to all students and employees regardless of sexual identity.

Table 4.3    Percentage of Campus Faculty, Staff, and Students Surveyed Who Experienced Harassment in 2002

|  | Yes | No |
|---|---|---|
| Undergraduate Students | 36 | 64 |
| Graduate Students | 23 | 77 |
| College Staff | 19 | 81 |
| College Faculty | 27 | 73 |
| Non-Degree Students | 32 | 68 |

*Source: Campus Climate for Sexual Minorities: A National Perspective, 2003, by Susan Rankin. New York: National Gay and Lesbian Task Force Policy Institute.*

## THE FIVE SEXES

In a controversial article by Anne Fausto-Sterling (1993), she argues that the existence of *hermaphrodites* and the range of possible physiological makeups mean that even the biological determination of sex may not be without its cultural and political influence. As Fausto-Sterling suggests, "For some time medical investigators have recognized the concept of the intersexual body. But the standard medical literature uses the term *intersex* as a catch-all for three major subgroups with some mixture of male and female characteristics: the so-called true hermaphrodites, whom I call herms, who possess one testis and one ovary (the sperm- and egg-producing vessels, or gonads); the male pseudohermaphrodites (the "merms"), who have testes and some aspects of the female genitalia but no ovaries; and the female pseudohermaphrodites (the "ferms"), who have ovaries and some aspects of the male genitalia but lack testes. Each of those categories is in itself complex; the percentage of male and female characteristics, for instance, can vary enormously among members of the same subgroup. Moreover, the inner lives of the people in each subgroup—their special needs and their problems, attractions and repulsions—have gone unexplored by science. But on the basis of what is known about them I suggest that the three intersexes, herm, merm and ferm, deserve to be considered additional sexes each in its own right. Indeed, I would argue further that sex is a vast, infinitely malleable continuum that defies the constraints of even five categories" (p. 2). In response to her article, many advocates for intersex people argued her theories were wrong and her terminology minimized the complexity of intersexuality. But the sociological argument here is one that challenges the determinative power of biology and contends that social, political, and other power relations shape even our understandings of what is natural or biological.

## Disabilities

People with **disabilities** are also a more recent identity group. Defined as those with permanent physical or mental conditions that restrict daily life activities, this group may include a wide range of people with diverse disabilities. Historically, many people with disabilities were fully dependent and marginalized in institutions or at home. Medical technology, changes in public policy, and cultural awareness have made the lives of such people remarkably different in the past few decades. Advanced biotechnology has increased the mobility and dexterity of people once limited by physical challenges. The **Americans with Disabilities Act** (see below) and other policies have opened up economic and social opportunities. Media attention and public awareness, especially through public figures such as actress Marlee Matlin and scientist Stephen Hawking, have decreased the stigma of disabilities. As we will see in the next section, social movements and policies have significant influence on changing identities and their related inequalities.

In 1990, President George H. W. Bush signed the American with Disabilities Act (ADA) into law. The act prohibits commercial, educational, or employment discrimination against people with disabilities. To achieve a nondiscriminatory climate, ADA makes clear the kinds of accessibility and related issues that must be established by public and private agencies and institutions. In a recent study completed by the Job Accommodation Network of West Virginia University (2009), the group found the following benefits reported by most employers from a variety of industrial sectors: Valued employees with disabilities were retained, their productivity increased, and the company saved money that would have been spent on training new employees for those positions (see Table 4.4).

**Table 4.4**  Benefits of Job Accommodations for Employees With Disabilities

| Direct Benefits | |
|---|---|
| Company retained valuable employee | 86% |
| Company promoted an employee | 10% |
| Company hired a qualified person with a disability | 18% |
| Employee's productivity increased | 71% |
| Eliminated costs associated with training a new employee | 56% |
| Increased the employee's attendance | 49% |
| Saved worker's compensation or other insurance costs | 39% |
| Diversity of the company increased | 42% |
| **Indirect Benefits** | |
| Improved interaction with coworkers | 67% |
| Increased overall company morale | 58% |
| Increased overall company productivity | 56% |
| Improved interactions with customers | 43% |
| Increased workplace safety | 41% |
| Increased overall company attendance | 34% |
| Increased profitability | 32% |
| Increased customer base | 16% |

*Source:* "Workplace Accommodations: Low Cost, High Impact: Annually Updated Research Findings Address the Costs and Benefits of Job Accommodations," 2009, Job Accommodation Network of West Virginia University (http://www.jan.wvu.edu/media/LowCostHighImpact.doc).

The complete findings presented in the table above are a testament to the impact of ADA. Yet people with disabilities continue to face both attitudinal and institutional discrimination in the workplace and the public sector.

This social stigmatization impacts people not only on a structural and cultural level, but also on a personal and psychological level. We've already discussed how the "social construction of the self" works to give people a sense of their individuality as shaped by their social relations and structural positions. W. E. B. Du Bois (1903) explained how this process impacted African Americans in a nation where racism resulted in their feeling simultaneously included and excluded. He wrote that black Americans were

> Born with a veil, and gifted with second-sight in this American world,—a world which yields him no true self-consciousness, but only lets him see himself through the revelation of the other world. It is a peculiar sensation, this double-consciousness, this sense of always looking at one's self through the eyes of others, of measuring one's soul by the tape of a world that looks on in amused contempt and pity. One ever feels his twoness,—an American, a Negro; two warring souls, two thoughts, two unreconciled strivings; two warring ideals in one dark body, whose dogged strength alone keeps it from being torn asunder. (p. 45)

Such a dynamic could be said to affect all groups subject to collective forms of discrimination based on their identity. Regardless, many identity groups not only suffer from restricted access to economic, political and cultural resources, but the social and ideological stigma associated with their discrimination can result in legitimizing an individual's own psychological sense of alienation and even inferiority.

## WHITENESS

Over the past two decades, numerous social scientists have developed a subfield of examination called by some "whiteness studies." According to Ashley "Woody" Doane (2003), whiteness studies reverse "the traditional focus of research on race relations by concentrating on the socially constructed nature of white identity. . . . [I]n contrast to the usual practice of studying the 'problem' of 'minority groups,' the whiteness studies paradigm makes problematic the identity and practice of the dominant group" (p. 7). Thus, scholars have looked at how white identities have been shaped by law, history, cultural assimilation, and so on. For instance, Roediger (2007) has argued that many immigrant groups started out as "non-white," but eventually gained white status and identity—some by changing names,

*(Continued)*

(Continued)

language, religious practices, and so forth. Most often, though, Roediger and others have maintained that whiteness is won by juxtaposing one's immigrant status to that of African Americans or blacks. In other words, the essence of white identity is its status as a dominant and privileged racial category in opposition to and domination of nonwhites, and especially black Americans.

Peggy McIntosh (2004) has likened the absence of talking about race as part of the "invisible knapsack" of privilege that white people carry with them. She writes that, "As a white person, I realized I had been taught about racism as something that puts others at a disadvantage, but had been taught not to see one of its corollary aspects, white privilege, which puts me at an advantage. I think whites are carefully taught not to recognize white privilege, as males are taught not to recognize male privilege. So I have begun in an untutored way to ask what it is like to have white privilege. I have come to see white privilege as an invisible package of unearned assets that I can count on cashing in each day, but about which I was 'meant' to remain oblivious. White privilege is like an invisible weightless knapsack of special provisions, maps, passports, code books, visas, clothes, tools and blank checks. Describing white privilege makes one newly accountable. As we in women's studies work to reveal male privilege and ask men to give up some of their power, so one who writes about having white privilege must ask, 'having described it, what will I do to lessen or end it?'

After I realized the extent to which men work from a base of unacknowledged privilege, I understood that much of their oppressiveness was unconscious. Then I remembered the frequent charges from women of color that white women whom they encounter are oppressive. I began to understand why we are justly seen as oppressive, even when we don't see ourselves that way. I began to count the ways in which I enjoy unearned skin privilege and have been conditioned into oblivion about its existence." (p. 191)

## A HISTORICAL LOOK AT SOCIAL MOVEMENTS AND CHANGING IDENTITIES

In the early 1950s, Bob Sigmon (Stanton, Giles, and Cruz 1999), a white high school student in Charlotte, North Carolina, participated in the American Friends Service Committee's interracial relations project. As a way to challenge segregation and support fledgling civil rights activities, the project brought black, white, Catholic, Protestant, and Jewish high school leaders from around the city together to learn about each other's lives. As he remembers, "Where I was raised, Catholic and Jews were more feared and more to be hated than Blacks. It was a remarkable setup. It's a theme that led me to what I've worked on all my life" (p. 36). As a student at Duke University, Sigmon worked with law students and others from the historically black North Carolina Central University to defeat segregation. He remembers,

> They were my friends. They took me in and taught me a lot about discrimination—about my own history and my own separation. I saw institutional racism at Duke in ways that I've never forgotten. It drove another wedge into me to say, "That's something I've got to pay attention to—my own complicity as a white man in that business of cultural segregation, ugliness, and oppression." That's deeply rooted. Those guys taught me a lot just by being with them in the way that they accepted me, loved me and took me to their homes, fed me in their homes, introduced me to their families. That's something white boys in 1954 and 1955 didn't get to do. (p. 37)

Sigmon's understanding of racial identities (both his black colleagues' and his own whiteness) shifted as he participated in local political activities that reshaped the larger landscape of race relations in the South.

Sociologists Michael Omi and Howard Winant (1994) have argued that the civil rights movement fundamentally transformed racial identities in the United States. New "collective identities" inspired by shared activism and political triumphs offered participants a "different view of themselves and their world" (p. 93). Omi and Winant call this process a "rearticulation" that produces "a new subjectivity" for participants, combining older elements of culture and tradition with new experiences of collective and individual empowerment. In other words, as people participated in the civil rights movement, they experienced a sense of social solidarity and political power that allowed them to envision and create new senses of self. These new identities replaced the kind of inferiority and alienation that Du Bois argued plagued African Americans.

Chuck McDew (1966) was a leader of the Student Nonviolent Coordinating Committee (SNCC)—the most important youth-led civil rights group of the 1960s. He explains how this rearticulation process occurred for many activists struggling against segregation:

> [B]y the time he comes to college, the Negro student is in dire need of faith which he can practice as a part of his growth and his daily adventure. The sit-ins offered students a chance for the "word to become flesh," as it were. The sit-ins promoted a challenging philosophy of love overcoming hate, of nonviolence conquering violence, of offering oneself as a sacrifice for a valuable cause. The sit-ins offer[ed] adventure and an opportunity to live out the demands of decency and dignity. The sit-ins inspired us to build a new image of ourselves in our own minds. (p 57)

For many African American students, the experience of working in the civil rights movement challenged society's dominant racial ideologies and changed their own self-identity. To be African American did not mean being inferior or marginalized, but instead symbolized the struggle for equality and dignity, and the courage it took to succeed.

## AFFIRMATIVE ACTION

In 1961, President John F. Kennedy first used the term "affirmative action" to pressure contractors on federally funded projects to hire non-white employees. Executive Order 10925 states that contractors should "take affirmative action to ensure that applicants are employed, and employees treated during their employment, without regard to race, creed, color, or national origin." The 1964 Civil Rights Act a few years later not only expanded laws against racial discrimination in hiring, but also created mechanisms such as the Equal Employment Opportunities Commission to enforce such laws. In setting up the affirmative action rationale, President Lyndon B. Johnson (1965) explained, "You do not take a person who, for years, has been hobbled by chains and liberate him, bring him up to the starting line of a race and say, 'you are free to compete with all the others,' and still justly believe you that you have been completely fair.... We seek not just freedom but opportunity, not just legal equity but human ability—not just equality as a right and a theory, but equality as a fact and as a result" (n.p.). Johnson further ordered that all government contractors and subcontractors use affirmative action to *expand* job opportunities for minorities, and created the Office of Federal Contract Compliance (OFCC) in the Department of Labor to administer the order.

President Richard Nixon was the first to implement federal policies designed to guarantee minority hiring. Responding to continuing racial inequalities in the workforce, in 1969 the Nixon administration developed the Philadelphia Plan, requiring that contractors on federally assisted projects set specific goals for hiring minorities. Federal courts upheld this plan in 1970 and 1971. Nixon later directed federal agencies to develop comprehensive plans and specific program goals for a national Minority Business Enterprise (MBE) contracting program. While Nixon and his aides were always careful to distinguish between diversity goals and targets on the one hand, and quotas on the other side, affirmative action as we know it came into its primacy fruition during the early 1970s.

The late 1970s and 1980s witnessed a backlash against affirmative action, as mostly whites decried such targets and goals as unconstitutional and amounting to what they defined as "reverse discrimination." Most famous was the 1978 Bakke case *(Regents of the University of California v. Bakke),* where the Supreme Court determined it was unconstitutional for schools to establish a rigid quota system by reserving a certain number of places in each class for nonwhites. Still, the court did uphold the rights of colleges and universities to consider race among a number of categories for consideration in enrollment. As more and more conservative judges were appointed to the Supreme Court during the Reagan and Bush Sr. administrations (1980–1992), the Court found fewer and fewer cases that justified affirmative action policies of any kind, thus supporting the claims that any law or policy favoring one group over another—even if it was to make up for past injustices—was "reverse discrimination." LBJ may have thought this disingenuous, but clearly the Reagan Supreme Court did not, or did not care if it was.

Of course, as sociologists like Ira Katznelson (2005) have explained, there has indeed been a long history of affirmative action for whites. The 17th-, 18th-, and early 19th-century slave codes created a racialized system that gave whites rights to public education, property, voting, and so forth, and denied them to nonwhites. The Naturalization Act of 1790 permitted only a "white person" to become a naturalized legal citizen. Even later policies such as the 1935 Social Security Act and the formation of the Federal Housing Authority (FHA) promoted white affirmative action. The Social Security Act gave millions of workers a post-employment safety net by granting retirees a guaranteed income. This benefit did not include agricultural and domestic workers—most of whom were African American and Latino. The FHA set up mortgage programs that offered working-class people the opportunity to buy homes and create wealth, but the appraisal system specifically targeted integrated and mostly non-white neighborhoods as too risky for mortgages, thus de facto excluding almost all non-white candidates. Post–civil rights affirmative action did turn this historical white affirmative action on its head and could be called "reverse discrimination," but only in the same way that imprisoning someone for kidnapping could be referred to as "reverse kidnapping."

Perhaps the most damaging aspect lingering from affirmative action is the myth of its stigma. Nowadays, many argue against affirmative action based on the contention that such policies stigmatize non-whites who succeed because whites believe they only did so *because* of affirmative action. According to this line of reasoning, affirmative action is to blame for this stigma. Again, the historical reality is that, in fact, many non-whites would *not* have succeeded in educational institutions or businesses or in homeownership, and so on, had affirmative action not mandated that they be given admission and opportunity. In other words, affirmative action actually had a positive impact on diminishing discrimination against non-whites and in increasing their opportunities. That non-whites used these opportunities is more a sign of their already existing skills, talents, and intellect, and not evidence that they couldn't achieve on their own. The irony is that this argument blames affirmative action when the real stigma comes from whites' attitudes, not the policy. It is the "reverse discrimination" narrative that claims non-whites have taken positions and admissions that *should* have gone to whites, as if whites are *entitled* to power and privilege. In the end, affirmative action has come under fire for being a successful policy that actually challenged historical and structural racial discrimination against non-whites and gave them opportunities once restricted to whites in America.

African American women, both young and old, have also experienced transformations. They often overcame stereotypes and discrimination based on both race and gender. Fannie Lou Hamer, a middle-aged African American woman from Mississippi, overcame a lifetime of prejudice and discrimination to join the SNCC and the civil rights movement. Claiming she was just "sick and tired of being sick and tired," Hamer decided that "we just got to stand up as Negroes for ourselves and our freedom." Despite being sharecroppers, her mother had taught her to "respect herself as a Black child . . . and a Black woman" (quoted in Giddings 1984:287–290). Hamer took that legacy of survival and dignity, despite years of racism and poverty, and turned it into a force for social justice.

For younger women like JoAnne Byron (née Chesimard), joining black community struggles over local schools and public services inspired a new sense of power and significance. She describes the experience of just such a demonstration in Brooklyn, New York, during the mid 1960s:

An energetic sea of Black faces. Proud, alive, angry, disciplined, upbeat, and most of all, with that sisterly and brotherly kinship I loved. Several of the parents spoke to the crowd, along with the Black principal the parents had insisted on hiring. A

Black teacher, head wrapped in a galee [African headdress], talked about the importance of Black people controlling our schools. She made sweeping gestures with her bangled arms as she spoke. Everybody dug what she said. It seemed like a kinetic dance was in the air. There aren't too many experiences that give you that good, satisfied feeling, that make you feel so clean and refreshed, as when you are fighting for your freedom. (Shakur 1987:182)

Later she joined the Black Panther Party, then left it to join the Black Liberation Army, at which time she changed her name to Assata Shakur. Eventually, she became one of the highest ranking women in the Black Power movement.

While the civil rights movement created a social process and paradigm for changing African American identities, white identities changed, too. White activist Bob Zellner (2008), the first white field secretary for the SNCC, believes his work completely changed his sense of who he was and who he could be as a white man. Perhaps more notable, however, was the way in which these movements impacted white women's identities. In part, this dynamic had a historical precursor. The 19th-century founders of the women's movement such as Elizabeth Cady Stanton and Lucretia Mott were internationally recognized abolitionists. In 1840, however, they were refused delegate status at the exclusively male World Anti-Slavery Convention in London. They returned to establish the first national convention on women rights, at Seneca Falls, New York. In the convention's final report, delegates wrote,

when a long train of [government] abuses and usurpations, pursuing invariably the same object, evinces a design to reduce them under absolute despotism, it is their [citizens'] duty to throw off such government, and to provide new guards for their future security. Such has been the patient sufferance of the women under this government, and such is now the necessity which constrains them to demand the equal station to which they are entitled. (Rife 2002:18)

In the 1960s, white women also built on their experiences working for desegregation and against racism to begin defining their own liberation movement. In part, women were inspired by the same kinds of passions, commitments, and visions that McDew and Shakur described. Yet, at the same time that they participated in protests against discrimination, they felt themselves discriminated against within the movement. Through women's workshops and, eventually, consciousness-raising sessions, these activist women shared experiences and frustrations. According to one participant,

Women frequently get relegated to "female" types of work—dish washing, cooking, cleaning, clerical work, etc. At national conferences, conventions, or council meetings, the problems of women become part of the general problems of prestige within the organization. . . . In an atmosphere where men are competing for prestige, women are easily dismissed, and women accustomed to being dismissed, come to believe their ideas aren't worth taking the time of the conferences; in short, they accept the definitions men impose on them and go silent. (Evans 1979:169)

Women challenged these role expectations within the movement and, as they built their own movement, challenged the institutional forms of sexism that relegated women to second-class citizenship in the rest of society.

The civil rights movement eventually expanded to include the Chicano movement, led by groups like La Raza, which fought discrimination against Latinos and established school programs from bilingual education to increased multiculturalism (Munoz, 2003). The American Indian Movement (AIM) also gained inspiration from the civil rights movement and struggled through the 1960s and 1970s to reclaim Native American lands stolen centuries ago (Churchill 2001; P. Smith and Warrior 1997). Although they failed in armed efforts to retake land, they inspired a rebirth of interest in cultural heritage and other legacies. Gay and lesbian rights efforts also gained legitimacy and inspiration from other movements during this time, eventually leading to a major uprising at a gay bar in New York City (D'Emilio, Turner, and Vaid 2002; Duberman 1994). This period in American history witnessed identities that had once been sources of stigma and discrimination become sources of pride, power, and collective movements for social justice. With these movements came a new sense of identity for both participants and the system of social relations around them. But the efforts of people working together to change social inequalities based on identities continue.

## STONEWALL AND THE HISTORY OF GAY RIGHTS ACTIVISM

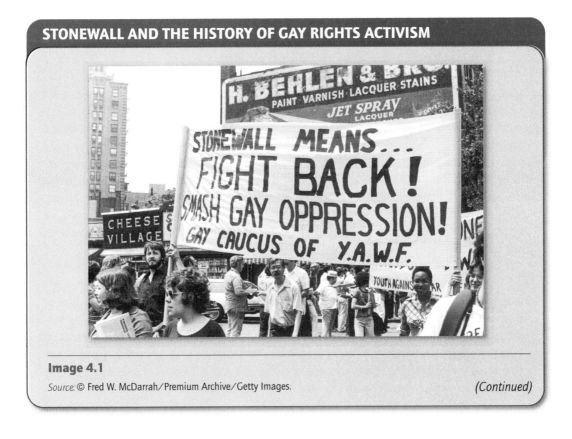

**Image 4.1**

*Source:* © Fred W. McDarrah/Premium Archive/Getty Images.                    *(Continued)*

(Continued)

In the early morning of June 27, 1969, police raided the Stonewall Inn, a gay bar in New York City. Police had routinely raided gay bars in the city and used the opportunity to destroy property, beat up clients, and arrest people for a variety of criminal offenses related to *indecency.* Historically, arrestees could find their names in local newspapers. Historian John D'Emilio (D'Emilio et al. 2002) has argued that Stonewall may have been targeted because its clientele was not only gay, but primarily black and Latino as well. On June 27, however, clients resisted police, and a riot ensued between clients and sympathizers who fought back against police, created barricades in the streets, and demonstrated that they would no longer submit to harassment and discrimination. Inspired by the civil rights movement and the women's and ethnic pride movements, gays and lesbians began a challenge to laws and conventions that had criminalized their identity and closeted their self-expression. The poster above, from 1994, celebrates that struggle's many successes, as well as its continued challenges as represented by groups like ACT UP and other AIDS activists; Queer Nation, which is fighting to end homophobia; and the movement toward equal rights in antidiscrimination status and the right to gay marriage.

## CASE STUDY #1

### Junior Arts Motivators: Expanding Identities Through the Arts

In 2004, the Greater Cincinnati Arts Education Center gave money from a federal Community Arts grant to a project designed by an AmeriCorps VISTA worker, Siobhan Taylor. The AmeriCorps VISTA program provides full-time workers to nonprofit community organizations and public agencies to create and expand programs that might ameliorate poverty (see www.americorps.org/about/programs/vista.asp). Taylor had been discussing possible arts projects with students from the city's School for Creative and Performing Arts. They didn't want to just work on one art project here and another one there. Instead, they wanted to start an organization that brought youth together from all over the city to talk about what kinds of projects they wanted to do and then work together to accomplish them. They also wanted to inspire others to get involved and realize that the arts were not just for artists, but for everyone in the community who wanted to be active and creative. They used the grant money to start the Junior Arts Motivators, or JAM.

Throughout 2005, the group met weekly to brainstorm ideas. They began with projects that took less work but would have an impact on the community and bring more and more people together. They held a reception for the SPCA ballet, *Dracula.* They also wanted to do intergenerational work, so they organized Christmas caroling with senior citizens from local assisted living centers. In the fall of 2006, Kris Donnelly was hired by the Arts Education Center to be JAM's new facilitator. Donnelly had herself been an AmeriCorps worker at a public arts project in Baltimore. She returned to her hometown to study community art and education at the University of Cincinnati. As facilitator, she participated in brainstorming sessions that eventually produced a much more ambitious plan—the idea of painting murals in the community.

Murals have long been an important element of public art and communities' expressions of identity. From cave paintings to urban street corners, artists and nonartists composed images that not only document the everyday lives of people in communities, but also reframe (literally) the difficulties and challenges of those lives as heroic efforts. During the 1970s and 1980s, a community mural movement spread throughout the United States. Sometimes these murals celebrated the ethnic cultures of neighborhoods, demarcated important social or political events in communities, or commemorated the deaths of people believed to be emblematic of a neighborhood's spirit (Cockcroft, Weber, and Cockcroft 1977/1998). According to Glenna Boltuch Avila, former director of the City Wide Mural Project, Los Angeles, "Murals are about people having an effect on their cities, taking responsibility for their visual and physical environment, leaving records of their lives and concerns, and in the process transforming neighborhoods, reducing vandalism and graffiti and creating new artists out of the youth of our communities" (quoted in Cockcroft et al.:36). The students in JAM wanted to accomplish some of these same things in their community.

The Emanuel Community Center provided the first site for JAM. The center is located in Cincinnati's Over-the-Rhine neighborhood and provides many social services to one of the city's poorest, mostly minority communities. The center had a space near the cafeteria that would make a good location for artwork. The cafeteria hosted free meals and snacks for local youth who used the center for educational and recreational activities. JAM's brainstorming sessions produced a design that would be

**Image 4.2**  A map, painted by JAM artists, of the United States and its food sources. Watermelon from Montana and potatoes from Idaho are painted along with Kool-Aid in Nebraska (where it was invented) and peppermint candy in Oregon.

*Source:* Reprinted with permission of Kristine Donnelly, former Greater Cincinnati Arts and Education Center Community Coordinator.

*(Continued)*

(Continued)

both educational and appealing. They chose to paint a map of the United States that depicted a food indigenous to each state. According to facilitator Kris Donnelly, students discussed how simply putting up images of food associated with different parts of the country might reinforce simple stereotypes and negative images. JAM members decided to do research and find out what food products really came from different areas and focused not on popular misconceptions but on agricultural products and industrial food production. Eventually, the mural provided lessons in culture and geography for both the youth entering the cafeteria as well as the youth who designed the mural. The result was so impressive that the center asked JAM to do a larger mural inside the cafeteria itself.

JAM decided to do a mural composed of a group of children from a variety of ethnic and racial groups enjoying a summer day at an outdoor café. They also chose to dress the youth in adult clothing. In part, JAM's mural shows the kids at the center that, despite racial, ethnic, and gender differences, they could find commonality in many of the things they enjoyed (food, pets, dance). But JAM also sends a message of empowerment to youth by giving them the status of full-fledged adult citizens: caring for pets, purchasing meals, and acting as ambassadors for their neighborhood. Finally, by bringing these different images of kids together, the mural also offered the visual representation—a vision—of new identities for the youth, ones that recognized the distinctions of race, ethnicity, and gender, but not as sources of separation and inequality, but as parts of larger identities created by the mixing of peoples, their cultures, their ideas, and their joy.

**Image 4.3**   Café scene painted by JAM in the Emanuel Community Center cafeteria. JAM members say that as much as they like knowing the youth who eat and play there like the mural, they get the biggest kick out of hearing how much the cafeteria workers like it.

*Source:* Photo of murals courtesy of Kristine Donnelly, former Greater Cincinnati Arts and Education Center Community Coordinator.

But the mural's *product,* that of a transformative image of new identities, is also representative of the mural's *process* as a collective work that already accomplished what the image represents. According to Tim Drescher (1977/1998), a historian of the international mural movement, "when a mural project integrates process and product, then not only does the finished image help people understand something, but the process helps them to grasp their own potential for doing something about it" (p. 248). In JAM's case, the process of planning and producing the mural—from brainstorming ideas to cleaning the brushes—reinforced the group's own sense of collective engagement. The youth's differences based on previously given and experienced identities such as race, ethnicity, disability, or gender no longer isolated or segregated them from each other. A new solidarity was created through the rituals and celebrations that reinforced the creative expressions of each individual. From a symbolic interactionist perspective, JAM created a new primary group that reinforces positive and empowering individual identities at the same time that it develops strong collective identities that transcend the limits of racial, ethnic, or gender categories. As one student expressed it, "People can be so different and yet come together to do and create great things" (personal communication with Kris Donnelly, May 10, 2008).

## Case Study Questions

1. What about the process by which JAM was created and carried out its projects might relate to how mainstream identities get questioned?

2. Although not a civil rights group per se, how could you consider JAM to be an organization that challenges forms of discrimination against different identity groups?

3. According to symbolic interactionism, what is the significance of students working together in JAM to create images of multiculturalism?

## VOICES FROM THE FIELD

### Young Women's Action Team (YWAT): Gaining Respect Through Action

We, the Rogers Park Young Women's Action Team, came together to address the very serious problem of street harassment in our community. We started in July 2003 by conducting some research. We asked girls who were our age about whether they felt that street harassment was a problem for them. We surveyed 168 girls between the ages of 10 and 19. We also interviewed 34 other teen girls. [A total of] 58% said that they had been harassed by men or boys [, and] 54% said that they never responded to the catcaller or harasser. The finding that was the most surprising to us was that 53% of the girls that we surveyed said that there was "NOTHING THEY COULD DO TO STOP STREET HARASSMENT."

*(Continued)*

(Continued)

We are teenage girls between the ages of 11 . . . [and] 21 who disagree with the idea that there is nothing we can do about street harassment. Although, we don't believe that we will be able to STOP street harassment, we do believe that we can do something to lessen it and to educate people about its negative effects on girls. We do this work as a team. We get support from each other and we believe that we are already making [a] difference in our community. We have met with our elected officials to share with them the results of our research and our recommendations; we have organized community forums and launched a RESPECT Campaign in Rogers Park [Chicago].

*Source:* YWAT website (http://www.youngwomensactionteam.org/).

## CASE STUDY #2

### Community Diversity From Community Action: Creating Diverse Social Capital

Cleveland, like many manufacturing cities in the United States, watched changing racial demographics, suburbanization, and deindustrialization in the 1950s and 1960s devastate its residential neighborhoods. Racist real estate practices (known as "redlining") and white flight left behind highly segregated enclaves. According to Smith and Reichtell (1997), "This pattern continued in the 1970s as families left to avoid court-ordered busing intended to integrate public schools. Today, many of Cleveland's neighborhoods maintain either a 'black' or 'white' identity, with very few truly stably integrated" (p. 58). The loss of affordable housing and other economic changes in the 1980s, however, resulted in new demographic shifts, especially in the Broadway and St. Hyacinth neighborhoods, which had long been majority white enclaves.

The Broadway Area Housing Coalition (BAHC), founded in 1980, took on the task of improving the area's image by rehabilitating existing housing, building affordable homes, and providing services to local residents. However, by producing 456 new housing units (rental and single residency), they attracted a low-income, minority, and immigrant population seeking inexpensive but good quality housing. Thus, BAHC facilitated many of the demographic changes that its primarily white membership had concerns about. While the BAHC had been successful in maintaining housing values and vacancy rates, racial and ethnic tensions were high, and fears about neighborhood change persisted.

Janet Smith, then a graduate student at Cleveland State University, met with Bobbie Reichtell of the BAHC to discuss how research might help the nonprofit organization promote stable change and diversity in the neighborhood. The BAHC board decided to support a research agenda that would assess community conditions and provide an overview of possible means for addressing racial change. Rather than focus explicitly on racial changes, the researchers examined how "grassroots strategies could build relationships among new and old residents, regardless of their race, ethnic heritage, or economic status" (Smith and Reichtell 1997:61). While project leaders did not *ignore* race and ethnic differences, they believed that the needs and desires that residents shared (regardless of their racial or ethnic identities) would prove more important than identity differences. If they could build relationships as collaborative residential partners in improving the neighborhood, perhaps new identities promoting unity and community could transcend the tensions brought on by fear and prejudice.

The first recommendation from the researchers was that BAHC emphasize *process*—the final visions of what BAHC would accomplish would have to incorporate all residents, thus reinforcing the ownership of new residents and the willingness of older ones. As the organization expanded its decision-making processes, some of its longer-term goals shifted from the "bricks and mortar" of revitalizing older homes and building new ones. Increasing "neighborhood capacity" for political participation and empowering residents to become their own agents for change took priority. When the BAHC accepted the researchers' proposals and had settled into a new decision-making process, the first proposal they enacted was the hiring of an organizer to help develop community participation and collaboration. This effort has already succeeded in developing several "block clubs" in the neighborhood, and these clubs have developed new leaders and added to the community's capacity for collaboration.

Although these efforts did not emphasize race and ethnicity, they still had a significant impact on addressing the tensions that existed. As Smith and Reichtell (1997) have written,

> This capacity was evidenced in a racial incident involving teenagers who firebombed the home of an African American family moving into the neighborhood.... Residents quickly responded by putting up money for a reward for the criminals, who were turned in after less than 48 hours. In addition, residents circulated a statement regarding their commitment to a peaceful, open neighborhood, which many neighbors signed. The statement was given to the family as well as published in the weekly neighborhood paper. Soon after, the Mayor of Cleveland issued a commendation to the residents, and the family stayed in the home once it was repaired. Although a negative event, the sense is that if it had happened prior to the work of an organizer, it most likely could have taken a very different turn. (p. 63)

*(Continued)*

(Continued)

The community has begun a difficult process of collaboration that may ultimately create new identities that transcend older ones that had been based on race, ethnicity, prejudice, and discrimination. New identities will be developed in the process of building neighborhood capacity and collaborative decision making. But the most important steps, those of repudiating prejudice, hatred, and violence and establishing solidarity based on mutuality and respect, have already been taken.

Sociologists such as James Coleman (1988) and Robert Putnam (2000) have popularized a theoretical concept known as social capital. This term refers to the value given to social networks and the assumption that the more networks and organizations individuals have, the more social capital they have, and therefore the more likely they are to have access to political and economic capital. For communities, the more neighbors participate in local organizations, the more likely they are to have the capacity to control the political and economic future of their town or city. But, as Putnam (2007) has noted in his recent work, the more diversity there is in communities, the less likely they are to develop collective participation in groups and create social capital. One way to think about BAHC's success is that the organization's ability to create connections among neighbors, despite their diversity and initial fragmentation, helped create the social capital necessary for them to control local development and maintain much of the neighborhood's population and integrity.

### Case Study Questions

1. What forms of social capital may have existed before BAHC organized?

2. How does BAHC represent the kind of new or at least different identities that local organizers and activists have created?

3. Can you think of any organizations in your community or on your campus that help develop diverse forms of social capital?

## CASE STUDY #3

### From Challenging Labels to Becoming Leaders: Service Learning Takes on Homophobia

Students and faculty at Eastern Oregon University (EOU) noticed that, despite campuswide efforts to promote tolerance and responsibility in "a diverse and interconnected world," a negative campus attitude toward LGBTQ (lesbian, gay, bisexual, transgendered, or questioning) students persisted. In particular, EOU students, faculty, and staff identified several factors contributing to the negative campus climate for LGBTQ students including: lack of administrative support for the GSA [Gay Straight Alliance]; a shortage of mentors for LGBTQ students; insufficient funds for educational resources; no office space for the GSA; and the consequences of placing untrained administrative personnel in charge of anti-discrimination policy enforcement. (Thomas and St. Germain 2005:n.p.)

Gender Studies faculty believed that many of these problems were the result of a local campus and community culture steeped in homophobia.

According to EOU faculty (Thomas and St. Germain 2005), LGBTQ people on campus faced devastating treatment in a variety of situations. For example,

One lesbian student commented on the lack of resources for LGBTQ students, including having no campus "safe space" program, no annual institutionalized staff "diversity" training, and no resource center, thereby creating "a desperate situation." Another student reflected that having no readily identifiable resources for gay students contributed to the feeling that there is no one and nowhere to turn to in times of need. Students have been ostracized in the classroom for "looking gay," and LGBTQ students report verbal harassment, including one lesbian student who has had to endure comments like "do you have a penis?" According to a gay student, the LGBTQ community "feel[s] like an underground community that everyone involved in knows [about], but if you are not involved [in it] then you have no idea." Further, LGBTQ students often claim they are not "completely free to voice opinions or feelings in many classes on campus due to the fact that many students are very traditional and hyper-hetero." Thus, LGBTQ students opt not to speak up in class "about homosexual topics" due to "not knowing how one or more people would react" and not "having the energy to fight the battle." (n.p.)

To address these challenges, EOU Gender Studies faculty designed a service learning course to help LGBTQ students develop the leadership and organizing skills necessary to create open and safe spaces for them to claim their identities and express themselves. By proclaiming a voice and visibility, faculty believed that students themselves could

persuade both administrative leadership and their own student government to include them fully and proudly in the campus community. Teaching LGBTQ students the skills they need to become student leaders in an environment that seeks to keep them invisible and silent is the challenge; feminist-based service learning is the solution. (Thomas and St. Germain 2005)

*(Continued)*

(Continued)

Faculty created a campus project for their introductory gender studies class that required students to work in groups and organize an "open mic" event on campus. They used the book, *That Takes Ovaries!* by Riva Soloman, a work that argues for women's empowerment and includes stories about "out" lesbians. Soloman also encourages girls and women to "organize and hold 'speak outs' in their community as part of a larger 'grassroots movement' to raise awareness of the conditions for all girls and women, creating essentially a human rights community forum" (Thomas and St. Germain 2005:n.p.).

The event was scheduled late in the term so students could first read and discuss course work on the social construction of gender, race, class, and heterosexism. In particular, they took on the problem of negative stereotyping and "one-dimensionalism" propagated by the national media and hate groups. As was presented earlier in this chapter with the idea of W. E. B. Du Bois' "double consciousness," LGBTQ students often internalize these negative images and struggle with discrimination and prejudice openly in the community, but also quietly within themselves. According to EOU teachers, "classroom engagement with sexuality (and other) issues raises awareness in students and helps to 'situate' the problems 'within local, national, and global political realities'" and not within themselves (Gilbert 2000, quoted in Thomas and St. Germain 2005:n.p.). Students first challenged preconceived notions about sexual orientation in class and then tested these ideas experientially through the open mic project.

As professors Thomas and St. Germain (2005) present, students expressed complex, almost besieged feelings before the event. One student felt that "people identify me in a negative way," while another labeled herself as "bad" and felt she needed to "live a lie" to gain acceptance. Such poor self-perceptions prevent LGBTQ students from "coming/being out" and actualizing their identity. The teachers argued that "student development in the form of scholarship and leadership can, and often does, suffer as a result of poor self-perception, because—as research has repeatedly shown—classroom experiences often marginalize LGBTQ students" (n.p.).

But the open mic project challenged these dynamics and had what the professors called a "ripple effect" that moved even beyond the students in the class. As Thomas and St. Germain (2005) explain,

> The LGBTQ students in the course passed the word to their friends on campus and in the Gay Straight Alliance (GSA). Leaders in the GSA saw an opportunity to make the wider community aware of their presence on campus in a positive way. These juniors and seniors spoke about being LGBTQ students, partners, parents, and friends, and told their stories with pride and confidence at the open mic, serving as role models for other LGBTQ students in the audience. These "bold and brazen" stories told by lesbian and bi-sexual students included tales of coming out to family members, mothering as a same sex partner, or asking a friend out for the first time. They gave the audience powerful examples of the pain that enforced heterosexism can cause in the lives of their friends and classmates. Gay men spoke about how much it meant to them to have strong and accepting women in their lives from mothers, to aunts, to classmates—again reinforcing for the audience the power of being and having "allies" in the face of heterosexist discrimination. One student "came out" publicly at the event and was clearly excited and empowered by the act of

telling her story. The event set a new standard for openness on campus, and allowed LGBTQ students their "space" for the first time in an organized and public way. (n.p.)

Ultimately, the service experience of the students in this gender studies course permitted marginalized LGBTQ students to find their voices, speak out, and take their space in the classroom and in the community—while becoming student leaders in the process. These students now carry on in a variety of ways to challenge the status quo of institutional practices as well as the arrogance or just plain social apathy represented by customs of homophobia.

## Case Study Questions

1. What issues face gay, lesbian, bisexual, and transgendered students who want to be open about their sexual identities?

2. How do social movements, large or small, impact the surrounding community's sense of people's identities and what they mean?

3. How might other issues of inequality—economic, social, or political—be impacted by groups proclaiming their identity and their equality?

4. Can you think of any groups on your campus or in your community that could benefit from being able to claim their identities or their issues more openly?

## VOICES FROM THE FIELD

### Bob Zellner

Interview with Bob Zellner, the first white field secretary (organizer) for the Student Nonviolent Coordinating Committee (SNCC) in 1963, and author of *The Wrong Side of Murder Creek: A White Southerner in the Freedom Movement.*

Corey Dolgon:  Bob, tell us how you got started in the civil rights movement.

Bob Zellner:  Well, I was a sociology undergraduate at Huntingdon College in Montgomery, Alabama, and my sociology professor assigned us a paper on race relations. My classmate and I knew that the Reverend Martin Luther King Jr. was holding a meeting at a black church in the city, and we thought that the best way to research the subject was to go see him and talk to him. We got a chance to see him but within minutes he took us to the basement

*(Continued)*

(Continued)

and said that someone had notified the police that we would be there and they wanted us turned over or they would storm the church. Dr. King explained that he would have to turn us over. We asked if he could simply let us "escape" out the back door. We needed to be able to tell our parents that at least we had tried to get away. We did. But the next day we were expelled. I learned then that the white South had much to hide and that I had much to learn from those in struggle against the kind of hypocrisy and arrogance of white supremacy. When we asked our sociology professor why we were expelled, he said he hadn't agreed with the decision but he never intended for us to go speak with civil rights activists—"I just wanted you to go to the library."

CD: What lessons about race and identity do you think you learned in the movement?

BZ: I guess the most important is that a lot of people in power have an interest in keeping those without power separated from one another. But I found I had more in common—values, dreams, love—with the people of color I worked with, struggled with, were imprisoned and beaten with, than with those whites who used religion or politics to try and justify segregation and violence. They often saw me as a white traitor, and to some degree I was because I fought against the political power and ideology of white supremacy. To them, I was no longer white and that was fine with me.

## SUMMARY

In all of these case studies, we have witnessed how students of all ages have worked to produce the visual images and policy recommendations needed to maintain and empower various communities' diversity. And in each case, students' work simultaneously led to their own challenging of rigid and alienating identities. Service learning requires that research and knowledge be used to *do* something. As Phil Nyden (1991), the Director of the Policy Research and Action Group (PRAG) explains, his own attraction to sociology came in the 1960s when he says, the discipline "dealt with social change, doing real things. Looking at real problems, and having a real impact" (p. 397). By engaging not only the problems of the world as the content of curriculum but also the people experiencing those problems as a source of collaborative research and solutions, the service learning projects discussed in this chapter have taken on the difficult but crucial work of understanding the relationship between identities and inequality while trying to simultaneously transcend them.

## SUMMARY QUESTIONS

1. What is gender? How does it differ from sex? How might the notion of "five sexes" challenge such a distinction?

2. What is race and ethnicity? How do they impact economic, social, and political inequalities?

3. What is the difference between attitudinal and institutional discrimination?

4. What is sexual orientation? How has the social construction of gender impacted the relationship between sexual orientation and inequality?

5. Describe the impact that social movements have had on the meaning of different identities and the levels of discrimination based on those identities.

6. Explain the ways in which the arts represent a way to challenge and re-envision identities.

## GLOSSARY

**Americans with Disabilities Act:** The Americans with Disabilities Act (ADA) gives civil rights protections to individuals with disabilities that are like those provided to individuals on the basis of race, sex, national origin, and religion. It guarantees equal opportunity for individuals with disabilities in employment, public accommodations, transportation, State and local government services, and telecommunications.

**Attitudinal Discrimination:** Actions taken against a subordinate group based on personal prejudices or culturally influenced biases. While attitudinal discrimination often seems to be the most overt, institutional forms of discrimination remain the most powerful and predictive, despite their becoming less obvious over time in the United States.

**Bisexual:** Having strong physical and emotional attractions to individuals of both dominant sexes.

**Civil Rights:** Those inalienable entitlements or freedoms bestowed on individuals by a government or other civil entity.

**Collective Identities:** The status and solidarities created by groups of people through group actions and collective behavior such as social movements.

**Disabilities:** According to the Americans with Disabilities Act, a disability is a physical or mental impairment that substantially limits one or more of the major life activities of an individual.

Ethnicity: A social identity or status that refers to a cultural or historical heritage or set of social practices and beliefs. Ethnic groups generally exist in contrast to a dominant or mainstream identity or status group.

Gay: Historically referred to as homosexual, it describes someone who has strong emotional or physical attraction to individuals of the same sex.

Gender: Refers to the cultural meanings that sex differences have in any given society. These characteristics change with historical, cultural, and political evolution.

Genocide: The systematic killing or displacement of a particular status or identity group, usually based on ethnicity, race, religion, or nationality.

Heterosexual: Predisposed to or preferring sexual relationships with the opposite sex.

Homophobia: The irrational fear of homosexuals and other nonheterosexual people.

Homosexual: Predisposed to or preferring sexual relationships with the same sex.

Institutionalized Discrimination: The systematic methods and structural implementation in the form of policies, laws, and customs that limit a particular group's wages, political enfranchisement, housing opportunities, social status, education, and so forth.

Patriarchal: Describes a system in which gender relations are highly stratified, and males possess a monopoly over economic, social, and political power with the legitimate use of physical force to maintain it. Women are held to be inferior in intellect and in moral capacities, and thus in need of control and guidance by males.

Prejudice: An attitude or disposition (negative or positive) toward a particular group based on a presumed identity (racial, ethnic, gender, sexual orientation, etc.).

Race: A socially constructed category depicting an identity, generally based on some physiological or cultural characteristics that are deemed "natural." While scientific knowledge often proves the naturalness of these characteristics to be dubious at best, many societies persist in creating, maintaining, and exploiting racial identities. Yet there remains only one human species—Homo sapiens.

Racism: The discrimination or oppression against people based on their perceived racial differences or historical backgrounds. Such mistreatment of people from particular ethnic groups is often lumped into the category of racism.

**Sex:** Refers to the actual biological composition of a person. One's sex is generally considered immutable except through surgery or other direct changes to physiology, while gender changes with historical, cultural, and political conditions.

**Sexism:** The discrimination or oppression of women based on their sexual identity or their gender. While the amount of innate biological differences between men and women is debated, sexism generally refers to unequal treatment and access to resources based on cultural stereotypes and social beliefs or norms, not on physiological difference.

**Sexual Orientation:** A relatively new term that may include gender identities, gender roles, and sexual preferences. It is generally used to describe whether a person is heterosexual, bisexual, homosexual, or transgendered.

**Social Capital:** According to sociologist Robert Putnam, this refers to the features of social life—networks, norms, and trust—that enable participants to act together more effectively to pursue shared objectives through social connections.

**Stereotypes:** Rigid, oversimplified assumptions or beliefs that are applied to all members of a social group. Labeling theory explains how such stereotypes become ensconced in cultural practices and even begin to impact the behavior of affected groups.

**Transgender:** Describes a person who crosses gender boundaries, or a man or woman who adopts the attributes of the opposite sex. The sexual preference of transgendered people will vary. A subset of transgendered people would be those who are *intersexed*—born with mixed sexual physiology.

## WEBSITES TO LEARN MORE ABOUT CIVIL RIGHTS AND ANTIDISCRIMINATION PROJECTS

Adapt: http://www.adapt25.org/

American Civil Liberties Union: http://www.aclu.org/

American Anthropological Association: Public Education Project on Race: http://www.aaanet.org/resources/A-Public-Education-Program.cfm

Colorlines: http://www.colorlines.com

Crossroads Anti-Racism Organizing & Training: http://www.crossroadsantiracism.org/

Dream Activist: http://www.dreamactivist.org/

Feminist.com (a clearinghouse for women's organizations and issues): http://www.feminist.com/

Hearts and Minds: Information for Change (list of many anti-racist groups): http://www.hearts andminds.org/links/racelinks.htm

Human Rights Campaign: http://www.hrc.org/

International Gay and Lesbian Youth Organization: http://www.iglyo.com/

National Association for the Advancement of Colored People: http://www.naacp.org

National Organization for Women: http://www.now.org/

SEED—Students Envisioning Equality through Diversity: http://www.olemiss.edu/orgs/seed/

U.S. Commission on Civil Rights: http://www.usccr.gov/

# REFERENCES

Adams, David Wallace. 1995. *Education for Extinction: American Indians and the Boarding School Experience, 1875–1928*. Lawrence, KS: University Press of Kansas.

Agbenyega, Stephen and Joseph Jiggetts. 1999. "Minority Children and Their Over-Representation in Special Education." *Education,* 119:619.

American Anthropological Association. 1998, May 17. "AAA Statement on Race." Retrieved February 24, 2010 (http://www.aaanet.org/issues/policy-advocacy/AAA-Statement-on-Race.cfm).

Battistoni, Richard. 1997. "Service Learning and Democratic Citizenship." *Theory Into Practice,* 36:150–156.

Blumenfeld, Warren. 1993. *Making Colleges and Universities Safe for Gay, Lesbian, Bisexual, and Transgender Students and Staff.* Boston, MA: The Governor's Commission on Gay and Lesbian Youth.

Calderón, José. 2004. "Lessons From an Activist Intellectual: Participatory Research, Teaching and Learning for Social Change." *Latin American Perspectives,* 31:January.

Carter, Shan, Amanda Cox, and Kevin Quealy. 2009. "The Jobless Rate for People Like You." *New York Times.* November 6.

Churchill, Ward. 2001. *Agents of Repression:* The FBI's Secret Wars Against the Black Panther Party and the American Indian Movement. Boston, MA: South End Press.

Cockcroft, Eva, John P. Weber, and James Cockcroft. [1977]1998. *Toward a People's Art: The Contemporary Mural Movement.* New York: Dutton.

Coleman, James. 1988. "Social Capital in the Creation of Human Capital." *American Journal of Sociology,* 94:S95–S120.

D'Emilio, John, William B. Turner, and Urvashi Vaid, eds. 2002. *Creating Change: Sexuality, Public Policy, and Civil Right.* New York: Stonewall Inn Editions.

DeNavas-Walt, Carmen, Bernadette D. Proctor, and Jessica Smith. 2007. "Income, Poverty, and Health Insurance Coverage in the United States: 2006." *Current Population Reports,* August.

Doane, Ashley "Woody." 2003. "Rethinking Whiteness Studies." Pp. 3–20 in *White Out: The Continuing Significance of Racism,* edited by Eduardo Bonilla-Silva and Ashley "Woody" Doane. New York: Routledge.

Du Bois, W. E. B. 1903. *The Souls of Black Folk.* New York: A.C. McClung.

Drescher, Tim. [1977]1998. "Afterword: The Next Two Decades." Pp. 281–312 in Eva Cockcroft, John P. Weber, and James Cockcroft, *Toward a People's Art: The Contemporary Mural Movement.* New York: Dutton.

Duberman, Martin B. 1994. *Stonewall.* New York: Plume.

Dworkin, Shari. 2001. "Holding Back: Negotiating a Glass Ceiling on Women's Muscular Strength." *Sociological Perspectives,* 44:333–350.

Emihovich, Catherine A. 1982. "The Color of Misbehaving: Two Case Studies of Deviant Boys in a Magnet School." *Journal of Black Studies,* 13:259–274.

Evans, Sara. 1979. *Personal Politics: The Roots of Women's Liberation in the Civil Rights Movement and the New Left.* New York: Vintage.

Eyler, Janet and Dwight E. Giles, Jr. 1999. *Where's the Learning in Service-Learning?* San Francisco, CA: Jossey-Bass.

Fausto-Sterling, Anne. 1985. *Myths About Gender: Biological Theories About Women and Men.* New York: Basic Books.

____. 1993. "The Five Sexes: Why Male and Female Are Not Enough." *The Sciences,* March/April:20–24.

Giddings, Paula. 1984. *When and Where I Enter: The Impact of Black Women on Race and Sex in America.* New York: William Morrow.

Jacobs, Jerry A. 1996. "Gender Inequality and Higher Education." *Annual Review of Sociology,* 22:153–185.

Job Accommodation Network of West Virginia University. 2009. "Workplace Accommodations: Low Cost, High Impact: Annually Updated Research Findings Address the Costs and Benefits of Job Accommodations." Retrieved February 24, 2010 (http://www.jan.wvu.edu/media/LowCostHighImpact.doc).

Johnson, Lyndon B. 1965. "President Lyndon B. Johnson's Commencement Address at Howard University: 'To Fulfill These Rights,' June 4, 1965." Retrieved February 24, 2010 (http://www.lbjlib.utexas.edu/johnson/archives .hom/speeches.hom/650604.asp).

Katznelson, Ira. 2005. *When Affirmative Action Was White.* New York: Norton.

King, Mel. 1999. Chain of Change: Struggles for Black Community Development. Boston, MA: South End Press.

Lee, Sharon. 1993. "Racial Classification in the U.S. Census, 1890–1990." *Racial and Ethnic Studies,* 17:75–94.

Lorber, Judith. 1993. "Believing Is Seeing: Biology as Ideology." *Gender and Society,* 7:568–581.

Marini, Margaret M. 1990. "Sex and Gender: What Do We Know?" *Sociological Forum,* 5:95–120.

McDew, Chuck. 1966. "Spiritual and Moral Aspects of the Student Nonviolent Struggle in the South." Pp. 51–57 in *The New Student Left,* edited by Mitchell Cohen and Dennis Hale. Boston, MA: Beacon Press.

McIntosh, Peggy. 2004. "Unpacking the Invisible Knapsack." Pp. 188–193 in *Race, Class, and Gender in the United States: An Integrated Study,* edited by Paula Rothenberg. New York: Worth.

Munoz, Jr., Carlos. 2003. *Youth, Identity, Power: The Chicano Power Movement.* New York: Verso.

National Women's Law Center. 2002, August. "Equal Opportunity for Women in Athletics: A Promise Yet to be Fulfilled." (Report to the Commission on Opportunity in Athletics). Retrieved February 24, 2010 (http://www.nwlc.org/pdf/EOforWomeninAthletics_APromiseYettobeFulfilled.pdf).

Nyden, Philip. 1991. "Teaching Qualitative Methods: An Interview With Phil Nyden." *Teaching Sociology,* 19:396–402.

____. 1997. *Building Community: Social Science in Action.* Thousand Oaks, CA: Pine Forge Press.

Omi, Michael and Howard Winant. 1994. Racial Formation in the United States: From the 1960s to the 1990s. New York: Routledge.

President's Commission on Excellence in Special Education. 2002. *A New Era: Revitalizing Special Education for Children and Their Families.* Washington, DC: U.S. Department of Education.

Putnam, Rober. 2000. *Bowling Alone: The Collapse and Revival of American Community.* New York: Simon & Schuster.

____. 2007. "E Pluribus Unum: Diversity and Community in the 21st Century." *Scandinavian Political Studies,* 30, 1: June.

Rankin, Susan. 2003. *Campus Climate for Sexual Minorities: A National Perspective.* New York: National Gay and Lesbian Task Force Policy Institute.

Rife, Douglas. 2002. *History Speaks: Seneca Falls Declaration of Sentiments and Resolutions.* Washington, DC: Teaching & Learning.

Roediger, David R. 2007. Wages of Whiteness: Race and the Making of the American Working Class. New York: Verso.

Ross, Stephen L. and John Yinger. 2002. The Color of Credit: Mortgage Discrimination, Research Methodology, and Fair-Lending Enforcement. Cambridge, MA: MIT Press.

Sacks, Peter. 1999. Standardized Minds: The High Price of America's Testing Culture and What We Can Do to Change It. New York: Da Capo Press.

Sanchez, George. 1994. "Go After the Women: Americanization and the Mexican Immigrant Woman, 1915–1929." Pp. 250–263 in *Unequal Sisters,* edited by Ellen Carol DuBois and Vicki Ruiz. New York: Routledge.

Shakur, Assata. 1987. *Assata: An Autobiography.* London: Zed Books.

Smith, Janet and Bobbi Reichtell 1997. "Changing Neighborhoods and Research for Diversity in Cleveland." Pp. 58–64 in *Building Community: Social Science in Action,* edited by Phil Nyden, Anne Figert, Darryl Burrows, and Mark Shibley. Thousand Oaks, CA: Pine Forge Press.

Smith, Paul Chaat and Robert Allen Warrior. 1997. Like a Hurricane: The Indian Movement From Alcatraz to Wounded Knee. New York: The New Press.

Stanton, Timothy, Dwight Giles, and Nadine Cruz. 1999. *Service-Learning: A Movement's Pioneers Reflect on Its Origins, Practice, and Future.* San Francisco, CA: Jossey-Bass.

Takaki, Ronald. 1993. *A Different Mirror: A History of Multicultural America.* Boston, MA: Back Bay Books.

Tatem, Andrew J., Carlos A. Guerra, Peter M. Atkinson, and Simon I. Hay. 2004. "Momentous Sprint at the 2056 Olympics?" *Nature,* 431:525.

Thomas, Cierra Olivia and Tonia St. Germain. 2005. "Bridging Differences Through Feminist Service Learning." *On campus With Women, 34.* Retrieved February 24, 2010 (http://www.aacu.org/ocww/volume34_3/from whereisit.cfm?section = 2).

Tiedemann, Joachim. 2002. "Teachers' Gender Stereotypes as Determinants of Teacher Perceptions in Elementary School Mathematics." *Educational Studies in Mathematics,* 50:49–62.

Trennert, Robert A. 1987. "Selling Indian Education at World's Fairs and Expositions, 1893–1904," *American Indian Quarterly,* 11:203–220.

Trigg, Mary and Barbara J. Balliet. 2000. "Learning Across Boundaries: Women's Studies, Praxis, and Community Service. Pp. 87–102 in *The Practice of Change: Concepts and Models for Service-Learning in Women's Studies,* edited by Barbara J. Balliet and Kerrissa Heffernan. Washington, DC: Stylus.

United for a Fair Economy. 2004. *The Wealth and Inequality Reader.* 2nd ed. Boston, MA: Dollars & Sense.

Uy, Mylinh. 2004. "Tax and Race: The Impact on Asian Americans." *Asian Law Journal,* 11:129–138.

Waters, Mary. 1990. *Ethnic Options: Choosing Identities in America.* Berkeley, CA: University of California Press.

Zellner, Bob. 2008. *The Wrong Side of Murder Creek: A White Southerner in the Freedom Movement.* Montgomery, AL: New South Books.

# Be It Ever So Humble

*Changing Families in a Changing World*

*I'd go see these kids and there would be rain pouring in through the roofs. The houses were falling apart. The children with low reading skills are the same ones living in these houses, so I wanted to fix that.*

—Jennifer Hamm, AmeriCorps volunteer,
Southern Appalachian Labor School

Jennifer Hamm's statement is a telling portrayal of the conditions many poor, rural American families face. Low-income families struggle with child care, housing, health care, and other basic needs. These challenges often result in special hardships for children and the elderly. Poor communities lack access to day care, after-school care, and summer programs for children as well as extended care and recreational programs for senior citizens. Community centers around the country make an important difference for these families by offering what would otherwise be unaffordable or inaccessible services.

Jennifer worked with the Southern Appalachian Labor School (SALS), a nonprofit community center in Beards Fork, West Virginia. Once a thriving coal town, Beards Fork is today one of hundreds of small Appalachian communities characterized by struggling families with few economic opportunities. SALS operates local projects that provide after-school programs, health care, food assistance, and summer camps. The organization's housing efforts rebuild and weatherize hundreds of substandard homes every year (Baker 2005).

Service learning programs at SALS allow students to experience the multiplicity of social problems faced by families. In West Virginia's coalfields, many families have few economic resources, limited access to institutional infrastructure or public services, and are geographically isolated. In addition, the area has lost many skilled workers and professionals to other regions resulting in some families having to split up as workers follow skilled jobs, while those who remain have fewer opportunities for good wages. SALS has effectively addressed some of these problems by integrating outside volunteers into these poor communities. SALS enlists many college students to provide services that other local agencies and institutions cannot, thus meeting the needs of some of the nation's poorest families. Youth development programs, for example, are especially important as they give children and teens structured activities and help develop social skills and self-discipline in a supportive environment (Nicholson, Collins, and Holmer 2004). College students provide the bulk of the staff and volunteers for these youth programs through SALS.

Meanwhile, college students learn that families face challenges that transcend the individual abilities or behavior of a parent or child. The social problems plaguing most families reflect larger social policies and the resources that communities can (or cannot) offer. Service learning projects break down the isolation that poor families feel while also breaking down the stereotypes that more privileged college students often have about such families and their individual traits. Students' experiences in the projects reinforce an ethic of care, a deep sense of responsibility, and feelings of empathy toward the recipients of services (Everett 1998; Rhoads 1997).

**Image 5.1**  Dilapidated house in Fairmont, West Virginia.

*Source:* ©Istockphoto.com/ Lawrence Sawyer.

Working in Appalachia's traditional and rural cultures often means changing one's view of what a community is as well as how it works. Rural mountain culture values self-reliance. Yet people accept assistance from kinship networks and neighbors as part of their sense of "self" identity (Baker 2005; Beaver 1986; Everett 1998). The community center approach to family social problems addresses many of the challenges that these families in crisis face, without harming their sense of dignity or pride. Even though we often think of family problems as a by-product of what goes on in a marriage or a household, issues such as teen pregnancy, domestic violence, lack of child care, stress from role overload, and so forth are linked to changes in social conditions and social policy. Structural changes such as the disappearance of affordable housing, the lack of adequate and affordable health care or education, and the rise of low-wage job markets all reduce a family's ability to provide basic needs for its members.

Volunteers in SALS housing programs learn about poverty and social disorganization firsthand while they come to know local people in West Virginia's tight-knit communities (Baker 2005). Students in AmeriCorps and service learning programs at housing sites put a face on poverty without blaming that face. They get to know families challenged by low wages and overburdened schedules. As one student remarked,

> The owners of the houses in Mossy and Page [towns in Fayette County] have thanked us for their now beautiful homes. They are now living in homes with roofs that will not cave in, walls that will not crumble, and wires that will not catch fire. I enjoy getting direct results from our work. We have created a house that will be nice to live in out of a shanty. (Quoted in Baker 2005:345)

For many students, experiencing rural communities is also a lesson in cultural diversity. SALS focuses on developing and empowering local communities by working from their own cultural integrity and collective assets. By doing so, the group not only facilitates a community version of "self-help," but it also breaks down stereotypes of the region's culture. The multicultural reality that participants from different regional cultures, religions, and socioeconomic classes experience challenges the provincial social life of both locals and visitors. Students working within this milieu gain experiences outside of the hypersegregation often found in educational institutions throughout the United States. Mountain communities also offer a connection with nature and the environment that is lost to many who have grown up in suburban landscapes. Volunteers engage in self-reflection while helping others:

> The most important thing that I did while I was here was to take a look at my life. I asked myself a lot of different questions concerning a lot of different aspects of my life. I might not have come up with all the answers but I did some re-prioritizing of the important things in my life. (Quoted in Baker 2005:344)

As another volunteer put it,

There were lessons every day I was there. From when to keep my mouth shut . . . to appreciating the moon and the stars, mountains, and land, or how I need to simplify my life." (p. 344)

An estimated 1,608 volunteers visited SALS in 2006. Colleges utilizing SALS programs for alternative spring breaks and service learning send student groups throughout the year. Denominations and churches sending volunteers include Presbyterian, Lutheran, Catholic, Episcopal, Methodist, and Church of Christ. The amount of students varies from a van load to the 300 students from the Pennsylvania Christian Endeavor program. The students come to build new homes, rehab substandard houses, and mentor children. Volunteers at SALS often take a whitewater raft ride down one of West Virginia's nearby rivers. The community center is operated by a multicultural staff who, with the exception of the director, John David (who is Jewish and from Michigan), finds its leadership among those who are indigenous to the area. Women serve as construction supervisors, education and health services program directors, housing specialists, directors, and grant writers. The center's chair and vice chair are African American, its former treasurer was a Catholic nun in her eighties, and its secretary has Cherokee heritage. Utilizing community capital, staff members draw on social networks to involve family members and assess the needs of community members, especially the elderly, the infirm, and single mothers and children (Baker 2006).

This chapter addresses the main problems faced by American families. Inequality perhaps has its greatest impact on these social groups. The root causes of their problems and the possible solutions to them exist in multiple contexts. However, most of these social problems are not limited to poor families. Social scientists point to a variety of family crises characterized by role overload, limited child care, overburdened working parents, power and violence in the family, and the inability of family units to adapt to rapid social change. Still other sociologists point to a decline in the family as an institution and cite this "breakdown" as the basis for social problems. These analysts often blame changing value systems for the institutional decline. While debating and analyzing the causes for these problems help us rethink and recreate policies and practices to ameliorate such conditions, this chapter also presents examples of how students engaged in projects to help families learn to analyze problems from a *practical* perspective. These students gain critical experiences in changing those conditions, improving the lives of others and themselves. While this chapter traces some of the sociological debate over the causes of family social problems, we also describe how active community organizations and service learning projects help address the difficult issues faced by America's families.

# FAMILIES BY THE NUMBERS:
# A STATISTICAL PORTRAIT OF FAMILY PROBLEMS

Contemporary mass media depictions of the American family in crisis blur the complex reality faced by the nation and its households. The assumption that the family has changed dramatically for the worse hides the institution's historical complexity. Yet, before we look at the historical evolution of the family in the United States, we should describe what some of the common challenges are to more traditional notions of family structure and function today.

## Divorce

Perhaps the most basic element blamed for the "breakdown of the family" is divorce. **Divorce** is the legal ending of a marriage contract. Since World War II, divorce rates have more than doubled, reaching their peak in 1980. The graph below demonstrates that since 1980, divorce rates have actually dropped by almost one-third, from a high of 5.2 per 1,000 people in 1980 to 3.6 in 2005. Overall, about 20% of all adults in the United States divorce at least once. Despite the significant increases in divorce rates during the latter half of the

**Figure 5.1**   Marriage and Divorce Rates, 1920–2004

*Source:* U.S. National Center for Health Statistics, and *Historical Statistics of the United States.*

20th century, marriage as an institution remains surprisingly strong. For example, the average length of marriages that end in divorce is 8 years, and over two-thirds of those who divorce eventually remarry. Meanwhile, only 12.2% of adult women and 17.4% of adult men have never been married (Benokraitis 2008). The fact that gays and lesbians are fighting legal and political battles to win the right to marry indicates that the institution of marriage is sought after even by groups often marginalized by those proclaiming to represent mainstream values and norms. Regardless of your position on this issue, the institution of marriage is far from over.

Claims for why divorce rates had increased range from conservative attacks on the women's movement, increasingly tolerant moral values, and liberal divorce laws to progressive claims that greater economic independence, education, support services, and social acceptance allow people (especially women) to escape bad marriages. Although each of these ideological perspectives offers important insights into the actual factors influencing divorce rates, the degree and type of impact are more complex.

For example, while increased education among women has resulted in a greater focus on career and delayed interests in marriage, divorce rates are lower for 4-year college graduates than for non–college graduates. The education gap in divorce is growing. By the 1990s, women with a 4-year degree were only about half as likely as other women to experience marital dissolution in the first 10 years of marriage (see Table 5.1 below). In fact, Martin (2004) found that for the majority of U.S. men and women with no 4-year college degree, divorce rates have not declined at all since the 1970s.

**Table 5.1**  Divorce Rates by Education for Women

| Level of Education | Percent Divorce |
| --- | --- |
| No High School Diploma | 39.7 |
| Non–College Graduates | 35.7 |
| Undergraduate Degree | 16.7 |
| Master's Degree | 15.5 |

*Source:* "Growing Evidence for a 'Divorce Divide': Education and Marital Dissolution Rates in the U.S.," 2004, by Steve P. Martin (Working Paper, Russell Sage Foundation Series on Social Dimensions of Inequality).

The social implications of divorce are complicated. Sociologists and social critics interpret divorce differently. Conservative theorists are pessimistic about such changes. They are troubled by the rising number of single-parent families and alternative family forms and bemoan a perceived "death of the traditional family." Below we offer a history of the family as an institution that challenges any simple notion of "traditional" family forms. However, some writers contend that divorced parents, single-parent families, and gay and lesbian households are flawed and incapable of reproducing the kind of social and moral values necessary to address social problems (Bellah et al. 1985; Blankenhorn 1995; Hackstaff 1999; Popenoe, Elshtain, and Blankenhorn 1996). Conservative sociologists and commentators believe the solution to family social problems is found in better individual moral choices and social policies that restrict family breakups (Furstenberg 2005).

Many sociologists, however, argue that divorce and other alternative family compositions result from rapid changes to economic and social institutions, and lay beyond the scope of individual decisions and traditional practices (Coontz 1992, 2005). Changes in work patterns and wages, the dual-earner household, as well as deindustrialization and globalization have shifted previous patterns of family life. Post–World War II, middle-class Americans entered the labor market early in life and created families around stable job opportunities, affordable housing and health care, and stable public school systems. Expanding domestic production and unionization made even most industrial factory workers middle class. Since the mid-1970s, however, an increasingly unstable economy has dissuaded young people from entering adulthood in a single step after high school. The modern global economy discourages young nuclear families. Early marriages now leave couples vulnerable to economic insecurity and family instability, especially for those without college degrees. Many young adults are waiting longer to leave their parents' home, marry, and launch careers (Skolnick and Skolnick 2005).

Meanwhile, feminist social scientists point to a lack of institutional supports for families, especially those facing increased economic instability, as a cause of changing family structures (Giele 1996). For instance, Coontz (1992) argues that the largest increase of marital breakup and single parents in the 1980s occurred in neighborhoods where populations were more vulnerable to poverty, regardless of family composition. She points out that simply comparing contemporary families with traditional ones misses the complexity of the modern experience: "Marriages are much more likely to be ended by divorce today, but marriages that do last are described by their participants as happier over many years" (p. 259). Critical of the traditional patriarchal family structures, feminists also point toward a greater self-determination for women able to escape restrictive and sometimes violent marriages. At the same time, women are free to pursue individual and professional fulfillment (Aulette 2002; Coontz 1992, 2005; Geiger 2002; Stacy 1991).

Evidence does suggest, however, that children and adolescents of divorced parents have greater risks for adjustment, including behavioral, social, and academic problems (Hackstaff 1999). The children of divorced parents are more likely to later divorce themselves. While a greater proportion of children of divorced parents have more problems than those of married parents, this does not mean that all children from divorced families fare worse than those from two-parent families. Many two-parent families do not provide a happy or supportive environment for parents or for children. Meanwhile, the majority of children of divorced parents are well-adjusted and do not suffer long term from the separation. Key factors in how a divorce affects family members over the long term (especially children) include issues of who gets custody and the economic and social stability of that parent. Another factor is the ability of the divorced parents to communicate effectively about children's needs and parental responsibilities. Children adjust to divorce best when they feel close to both parents. They are also better off when conflict is absent and they have adequate adult supervision (Hackstaff 1999).

Women get custody of their children after divorce 86% of the time. However, one study (Peterson 1996) shows that women see a decline in their standard of living of as much as 27% after divorce. Economically, women who are single parents are worse off due to typically low-paying jobs and the low number of fathers who pay child support. **Child support,** or payments supporting children in divorce, most often goes to women (83.8%). However, only 57.3% of custodial parents are awarded child support. Of these, only 46.9% receive the full amount and 22.8% receive none (see Table 5.2 below). Studies show that only half of all fathers pay court-mandated child support. The other half, the so-called "deadbeat dads," contribute to a lack of parental participation with children of divorce as well as other social problems (Hewlett and West 1998; Kelly and Emery 2000; Peterson 1996). The problem with divorce may not be the divorce itself, but the inadequate support networks available for divorced parents (mostly women) to provide economic stability, adult supervision, and an emotionally nurturing environment for their children.

**Table 5.2**  Child Support Received, 2005

| Child Support Due/Paid | Percentage |
| --- | --- |
| Full amount of child support paid | 46.9% |
| Partial amount of child support paid | 30.3% |
| No amount of child support paid | 22.8% |

*Source:* "Custodial Mothers and Fathers and Their Child Support: 2005," 2006, by Timothy Grall, *Current Population Reports,* U.S. Department of Commerce Economic and Statistics Administration.

## Changing Family Forms

Divorce is not the only factor responsible for the significant evolution of family structure. Changing family forms are a product of historical changes in economic and cultural institutions as well as social practices and individual choices. Family composition responds to growing inequalities in wealth as well as growing tolerance for nontraditional relationships among men and women. Increases in single-parent households; cohabitation and married couples without children; same-sex marriages and parenting; custodial aunts, uncles, and grandparents; and the burgeoning international adoption network all reflect new trends toward variety in family forms.

In 2005, for the first time, unmarried households in the United States outnumbered married households (Jayson 2005). For a number of reasons, more people are living alone or forgoing marriage by cohabitating. Overall, marriage rates have declined 50% since 1970, from 76.5 married women per 1,000 to 39.9 (Jayson 2005). The number of people living alone is also rising. Over 31 million people in the United States live alone, reflecting the growing number of single young adults and elderly widows and widowers in American society. Couples are more often living together before, or even instead of, marrying. An estimated 1 in 10 couples living together is unmarried—a statistic enhanced by the inability of most gay and lesbian couples to enter the institution. Between 2000 and 2005, the number of male couples rose 24% and female couples rose 12% (Roberts 2006).

**Table 5.3**   Households and Families, 2005

| Households | In Millions |
|---|---|
| Total Households | 111.1 |
| Married-Couple Households | 55.2 |
| Married Couples with Children | 35 |
| Unmarried Households | 55.8 |
| Female-Headed | 14 |
| Male-Headed | 5 |
| Cohabitating | 5.2 |
| Living Alone | 27 |

*Source:* "United States Households and Families" (2005 American Community Survey), U.S. Census Bureau (http://factfinder.census.gov/).

In 2005, an estimated 51% of women in America were living without a spouse, as compared to 49% in 2000 and 35% in 1970 (Roberts 2007). Analysis of racial differences shows that Asian American women are more likely to be married, while less than one-third of black women are married (see Table 5.4). Some of these women eventually marry, with many marrying later than in the past or living with unmarried partners for longer periods.

Table 5.4   Percentage of Women in the United States Who Are Married, by Race, 2005

| Race | Percent Married |
| --- | --- |
| White | 55 |
| Black | 30 |
| Hispanic | 49 |
| Asian | 60 |

*Source:* "51% of Women Are Now Living Without Spouse," 2007, by Sam Roberts, *New York Times,* January 16.

Coontz summarizes the trend, "This is yet another of the inexorable signs that there is no going back to a world where we can assume that marriage is the main institution that organizes people's lives" (quoted in Roberts 2007:1).

Another important trend in the American family is the increase in custodial grandparents with no parents present. Coupled with the rise of the field of social gerontology, research on aging has produced a new focus on social problems faced by the elderly, especially those who are caregivers (Putney, Ailey, and Bengtson 2005). In 2000, a total of 6 million children, or 1 in 12, lived with a grandparent or other relative who was the head of the household. Likewise, research suggests that 1 in 10 grandparents cares for a child for at least 6 months of the year (Cox 2000, 2002; Goyer 2006). While overall research has not found that caring for grandchildren adds significant stress to grandparents' health (Hughes, Waite, LaPiere, and Luo 2007), children in such households have a greater tendency toward behavioral problems, lower test scores, poverty, and so forth. While all races and classes are seeing more grandparents responsible for children, historically, communities of color have been more likely to exhibit grandparental involvement in child rearing (Minkler and Fuller-Thomson 2005). Therefore, children of color face social problems associated with these arrangements with even greater frequency.

## WORK AND ROLE OVERLOAD

According to the National Partnership for Women and Families (2005), families in the United States increasingly must put together solutions on their own to solve the time crunch created by financial demands and job stress. The United States is behind other developed nations in support for vacation and personal time to meet basic physical, emotional, and logistical needs. **Role overload** refers to the stress experienced when an individual has too many role expectations. The role overload of the average American dual-earner household has been well-documented. Overall, women are more likely to take up the slack created by role overload (Gerson and Jacobs 2004; Hochchild 1989). Arlie Hochschild, in her book *The Second Shift* (1989), reveals the extra work involved in married couples' having two jobs and maintaining a household. After working full days, the brunt of maintaining the household still tends to fall on women, thus becoming their **second shift.**

Subsequent researchers have found that women of all socioeconomic classes spend less time on housework and more time on child care than in the past. They have adapted to changing circumstances to ensure that they preserve their family time and provide adequately for their children. While more men do more housework—from 15% of housework in the 1960s to almost 30% in 2004—women still do over twice as much of the housework that is done. Similarly, men spend more time with children, as do women, reflecting new values placed on direct interaction and parental care (Fisher, Egerton, Gershuny, and Robinson 2007). Changes in workload have followed changes in work. In 1965, an estimated 60% of all children were in households with a breadwinner father and a stay-at-home mother. Today, only 30% follow that pattern (Bianchi, Casper, and King 2005; Bianchi, Robinson, and Milkie 2006).

**Figure 5.2**   Changes in Women's Workload, 1965–2000

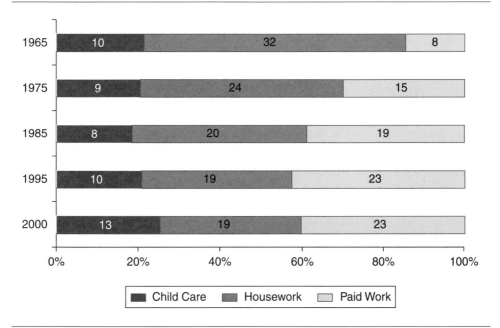

*Sources: Work, Family, Health, and Well-Being,* 2005, by Suzanne M. Bianchi, Lynne M. Casper, and Roselind Berkow King, Mahwah, NJ: Erlbaum; *Changing Rhythms of American Family Life,* 2006, by Suzanne M. Bianchi, John P. Robinson, and Melissa A. Milkie, New York: Russell Sage Foundation; "9 of 10 Nursing Homes Lack Adequate Staff, Study Finds," February 18, 2002, by Robert Pear, *New York Times.*

Research suggests that American families struggle more with balancing work and family when compared with other industrialized nations (Gornick 2005). Surveys suggest that working parents would prefer a work week of between 30 and 40 hours, yet 27% of men and 11% of women worked over 50 hours per week in 2000 (p. 66). With housing, health care, and especially child care costs on the rise, single parents (especially women) face tremendous hardships. Mothers and fathers have less time to monitor and bond with children after school and at other developmentally crucial or socially vulnerable times (Gerson and Jacobs 2004; Shor 1992). Another group facing a time crunch is that of single parents, who make up 25% of all households, most of which are headed by women. Women's annual salaries are lower than those of their male counterparts, usually requiring single mothers to work longer hours. In fact, Barko (2000) argues that, "if men and women were paid equally, over 50 percent of low-income U.S. households would rise above the poverty level" (p. 61).

Another important concern is the amount of time new parents have to spend with newborns. **Parental leave** in the United States is covered through the **Family and Medical Leave Act (FMLA)** of 1993. FMLA offers a very small safety net for working families who take care of infirm family members or have children. *Parental leave* refers to time off for new parents to care for an infant or a newly placed foster or adopted child. Workers in firms of over 50 employees are eligible for 12 weeks of unpaid maternity leave in the United States, whereas many countries provide longer periods of time off with full or partial salary provided by employers or the state. For instance, Heyman, Earl, and Hayes (2007) found that "out of 173 countries 169 offer guaranteed leave to women in connection with childbirth; 98 of these countries offer 14 or more weeks paid leave" (p. 1). According to the United Nations (see Table 5.5), the United States trails the rest of the world in providing leave for workers who have children. The European Union (EU) in its 1993 "Working Time Directive" requires all EU countries to provide at least 20 days of paid leave for all workers. Research suggests that Americans work longer with fewer vacation days along with less time for family leave (Ray and Schmitt 2007). For instance, Scandinavian countries such as Denmark provide 18 weeks with pay of up to 90% of wages. Table 5.5 also reveals that even many poor countries do better than the United States when it comes to taking care of working families.

Concerns over the U.S. approach to family leave center on employees in private firms where many employees lack basic protection (Gielow 2002). FMLA makes no provision for workers in small enterprises or without full-time employment. Only 60% of workers are covered by FMLA, and over 41 million Americans are without any parental leave (Leon-Guerrero 2005). Only five states offer wage replacement following childbirth or adoption. The U.S. approach to family leave often pressures new mothers to return to work as quickly as possible over financial and career concerns. The dilemma of work and the family for many American families increases the risks associated with inadequate day care and after-school monitoring. Reduced supervision can contribute to teen pregnancies, delinquency, and neglect.

**Table 5.5**   Maternity Leave Benefits: Selected Countries, 2004

| County | Length of Maternity Leave | Percent of Wages Covered |
| --- | --- | --- |
| United States | 12 weeks (50 or more employees only) | None |
| Mexico | 12 weeks (all employees) | 100 |
| China | 90 days (all employees) | 100 |
| Bulgaria | 135 days (all employees) | 90 |
| Iran | 90 days (all employees) | 67 |
| Italy | 5 months (all employees) | 80 |
| Denmark | 18 weeks (all employees) | 90 |
| Japan | 14 weeks (al employees) | 60 |
| Switzerland | 98 days (all employees) | 80 |
| Spain | 16 weeks (all employees) | 100 |

*Source:* "Statistics and Indicators on Women and Men," 2005, Table 5c, United Nations Statistics Division (http://unstats.un.org/unsd/demographic/products/indwm/).

The growing number of working hours in the United States (see Chapter 3) also contributes to role overload. Overtime is becoming more common for many Americans who are increasingly in debt (Warren and Tyagi 2004). According to Presser (2005), 40% of Americans work nonstandard hours. Night and swing shifts can lead to many hardships for families. The complex scheduling sometimes works for child care sharing, but the added stress of irregular and fewer off hours can contribute to a number of problems as well. Night shift workers face issues around getting enough sleep, finding child care, and increased physical and mental strains (Rubin 1994).

The effects of the time crunch are not equal across all classes, either. For upper-middle-class and wealthy families, poor women's domestic work in their household makes dealing with time poverty easier. The nation's nannies and maids, often women of color and immigrants, provide a low-wage labor force for upper-middle-class families (Erhenreich and Hochchild 2002). Working-class families are affected not only by the time crunch but also by declining wages and America's low minimum wage (Stacy 1991). Once again, a study of social problems demonstrates the intersectionality of inequality as wages and work hours impact workers as individual employees, but also as mothers and fathers.

## SOCIAL AND INDIVIDUAL SOLUTIONS TO FAMILY PROBLEMS

Approaches to solving family social problems vary from community group–based, to organizational or agency-based, to individual efforts. When it comes to divorce, some states are devising policies with incentives for couples to stay together and previously unmarried married parents to legally unite. In 1999, the state of Oklahoma began a program to train couples in building a strong and lasting marriage and put in place advertising to promote the value of marriage as an institution. Other states are following similar policies including West Virginia, which allots single female welfare claimants $100 more a month if they get married (Murphy 2004). These policies are in response to social science research that shows that single parents are more likely to be under the poverty line and their children more likely to abuse drugs and alcohol, commit crime, and experience teenage pregnancy. The George W. Bush administration followed these states' lead by funding the $150 million Healthy Marriage Initiative (HMI) in 2005. HMI programs promote marriage education, marriage skills training, public health campaigns, high school education, marriage mentoring, and responsible fatherhood. Critics of these programs point to potential problems such as encouraging marriage for people who are best off not being together, and maintaining marriages in which domestic violence or spousal abuse is present. These critics also argue that the state should not be in the business of promoting marriage at all. Marriage itself may not be the problem; rather, being poor could be the real issue for many who do not marry (Murphy 2004).

To address other problems such as role overload, social theorists suggest policies that will help resolve time pressures on families. Gerson and Jacobs (2004) focus on the work environment of families, suggesting "revising regulations on hours of work and providing benefits protects more workers, moving toward the norm of shorter work weeks, creating more family-supportive workplaces that offer both job flexibility and protections for employed parents, and developing a wider array of high quality, affordable child care options" (p. 29). Beyond changes in work, others take an approach centered on changes to the social system. More generally, Furstenberg (2005) argues that America will best be served by investing in children directly. He states, "By directing more resources to low-income children regardless of the family form they live in, through such mechanisms as access to quality child care, health care, schooling, and income tax credits, it may be possible to increase the level of human, social, and psychological capital that children receive" (p. 80). Combined with increasing support for young parents in the form of tuition and job support, these resources do more than protect children from low parental resources; they can increase access to higher-paying jobs and marital stability.

Other theorists point to the inadequacy of policies and programs for father- and grandparent-headed households. Hewlett and West (1998) argue that parenting, and fathering in particular, are under attack in America. They call for a **Parents' Bill of Rights**, which includes pro-marriage legal policies supporting stronger marriage, support for fathers, and adoption assistance. Cox (2000, 2002) surmises that empowerment for grandparents requires a focus on existing strengths in the family. Successful programs should draw on the problem-solving skills of individuals, which often extend to the community. Existing programs work best when they strengthen parenting skills and develop community peer educators. Furthermore, in order to be successful, programs assisting grandparents of all races and backgrounds must address legal matters and entitlement, access to agencies, and communication issues. Key concerns for counseling grandparents center on their special needs around issues such as AIDS, incarceration, grief counseling, abuse, and the loss of children's parents.

# FAMILY VIOLENCE, ABUSE, AND NEGLECT

Social theorists link violence and abuse in the family to a number of causes. Male domination, or patriarchy, is an overriding factor as well as poverty. **Domestic violence** is a behavior in which one person in a relationship seeks to maintain power and control over his or her partner or other family member. Legally, domestic violence is most often defined as criminal acts of battery, sexual assault, kidnapping, imprisonment, stalking, or types of criminal harassment. Acts of domestic violence may also be described as situational and occasional violence, acts of self-defense, intimate terrorism (often of long duration), or mutual violent control involving both partners (Durfee and Rosenberg 2004). Research on intimate partner violence (IPV) indicates that 25% of couples reported experiencing one or more episodes of partner violence in the last year (Benokraitis 2008). Race is also a factor in domestic violence. African American women are more likely to experience extreme partner violence than are white women. Also more likely to be low-income, Native American exhibit a higher rate of intimate partner violence than other groups.

Table 5.6   Average Annual Nonfatal Intimate Partner Victimization Rate by Race, 1993–2000

| Race | Victims per 1,000 Persons |
|------|---------------------------|
| White | 6.3 |
| Black | 8.2 |
| Hispanic | 6.0 |
| Asian | 1.5 |
| Native American | 18.2 |

*Source:* "Intimate Partner Violence Declined Between 1993 and 2004," 2006, Bureau of Justice Statistics (http://www.ojp.usdoj.gov/newsroom/pressreleases/2006/bjs07007.htm).

While both men and women commit partner aggression, male-to-female violence has more detrimental effects than female-to-male violence. Females are more likely to suffer physical injuries, require medical attention, and take time off due to abuse. In addition, females are more likely to suffer mental and emotional symptoms and effects such as anxiety and depression, suicide, posttraumatic stress disorder, substance abuse, and spousal homicide (Stuart, Moore, Gordon, Ramsey, and Kahler 2006).

While all social classes experience domestic violence, poor people have higher incidences of domestic violence and abuse. Gelles and Cornell (1990) found that unemployed men are twice as likely to abuse their wives as employed men. Contributing factors to domestic violence include low income, social and structural stress, and social isolation. Benson, Wooldredge, Thistlethwaite, and Fox. (2004) found that community context is more important in determining abuse than race. Specifically, family violence is more likely to occur in black families in disadvantaged communities. Rural victims of domestic violence are more prone to geographical isolation, especially poor ones. Women most at risk are those who are isolated from kinship systems and support agencies. Abusers use tactics such as checking car odometers, monitoring phone calls, and stranding victims during the day (Cantrell 1991). Websdale (1997) found that rural patriarchal social values and local politics often create a revictimization of domestic violence victims in the court system. Women in such circumstance often must deal with men who not only know their abusers, but sympathize with abusers and belittle the victim's plight.

The question of why victims do not leave abusers is frequently asked. In answering this question, Ferraro (2006) and Goetting (1999) found that in order to leave an abuser, a woman must have the following: a positive self-concept and belief that she deserves better, adequate independent resources, a sense of legitimacy in breaking with tradition, and a support network. Victims must also perceive and name what is happening as abuse, and conclude that the abuser will not change (Henslin 2007). Domestic violence has received considerable attention in the United States in the last 30 years, particularly as a result of the women's movement. The main approach to domestic violence has been to criminalize it by requiring medical and social service professionals to report suspected violence.

**Figure 5.3**  Types of Child Maltreatment

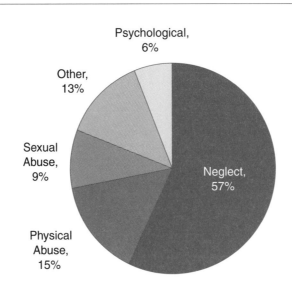

Source: *Marriages and Families: Changes, Choices, and Constraints,* 6th ed., 2008, by Nijole V. Benokraitis, Upper Saddle River, NJ: Prentice Hall.

Every year, 3 million reports of child abuse occur in the United States, with over 900,000 cases confirmed (Henslin 2007). Child neglect is more common than other types of child abuse. *Neglect* means failure to provide basic needs and can include physical harm, emotional abuse, or failure to enroll a child in or ensure that he or she attend school (Leon-Guerrero 2005). Child neglect is more likely to occur on the part of parents who are inexperienced, are teenagers, engage in substance abuse, or are subject to time pressures and role overload.

## VIOLENCE AGAINST WOMEN ACT

According to the United Nations, between 20% and 50% of all women globally are abused (Innocenti Research Centre 2000). The research findings by social, legal, and medical scholars on family violence help us to better understand different risk factors within the ecological systems defining the social worlds of victims and abusers. From a medical perspective, family violence has been called a public health issue of epidemic proportions by the World Health Organization (WHO). Social workers and other social service providers point to the role of poverty and discrimination in abuse. Abuse has also drawn United Nations directives and declarations resulting in framing abuse from an international human rights perspective. The most comprehensive international attempt to systemically address domestic violence was the 1994 Violence Against Women Act (VAWA), which was expanded in 1998 and 2004. Originating from the 1993 United Nations Declaration on the Elimination of Violence Against Women, VAWA was designed to provide women with broad protections against violence in a number of settings including homes, communities, and society (Innocenti Research Centre 2000). Scholars of domestic violence point out that societies around the world have been slow to adapt VAWA to men's abuse (see Hines and Malley-Morrison 2005). Nonetheless, as a result of the 1994 VAWA in the United States, changes to policies have occurred addressing abusers and victims. There has been a 51% increase in the reporting of domestic violence since 1994 in the United States. The legislation has created more intervention programs such as those for children who have witnessed domestic violence and for immigrants. The act has led to expanded legislation creating more databases on abusers, legal assistance for victims, and privacy protection. It has also meant improved access to housing for victims of domestic violence, dating violence, and sexual assault and stalking (National Network to End Domestic Violence 2006).

**Domestic elderly abuse** refers to any form of maltreatment of an older person by someone who has a special relationship with him or her (usually a spouse or child), and can include forms of physical, psychological, or financial exploitation (Leon-Guerrero 2005). Among the most invisible forms of abuse, domestic violence against custodial grandparents is also a growing phenomenon (Kosberg and MacNeil 2003). **Institutional elder abuse** refers to forms of abuse that occur in residential facilities for older people. Elderly people in nursing homes tend to be older, with many over age 85 and confined to wheelchairs and walkers. Elderly abuse in institutional settings is reflective of the general condition of the nation's nursing homes. A recent congressional study found that 90% of facilities are under-staffed and have high worker turnover (Henslin 2007; Pear 2002).

# A BRIEF HISTORY OF THE FAMILY IN THE UNITED STATES: STRUCTURE AND CULTURE

The contemporary family is a complicated and diverse social institution, in many ways not all that different from in the past. For example, social policy, power, and public criticism have always pointed to families with different cultural values or behaviors as "deficient" or "abnormal." Yet debates on traditional family values focused on "family breakdown" lack historical or sociological specificity. Such discourse often sheds more heat than light. Stephanie Coontz (1992), for example, points out that many people say they would like to return to the traditional family but are confused about which one. She explains that the "ideal" family many imagine is a combination or amalgam of structures, values, and behaviors that never really existed together at the same time or in the same place. Thus, she writes, "pessimists argue that the family is collapsing; optimists counter that it is merely diversifying" (p. 1). But the American family has always been shifting in size and structure and function, sometimes collapsing, sometimes expanding, and always incredibly diverse.

As historian Ronald Takaki (1994) has demonstrated, America was a multicultural nation from the outset. Thus, its families have always featured different backgrounds, had different values, and faced different realities. Colonialism and genocide, slavery and segregation, bigotry and internment have significantly impacted Mexican, African, Asian, and Native American families (Coontz 1992; Cox 2000, 2002; Ruiz 2004). The impact of slavery on African American families has been well-chronicled (Gutman 1976; Stevenson 1997). Forced assimilation to patri-archal political systems and cultures also altered historical gender relations and family systems among Native Americans. Prior to European settlement, Native American women had power through the control of land and food production. Family descent also went through the female line and the mother's clan. Native women controlled the household living, communally sharing child care duties (Jensen 1981; Purdue 1988). Following European settlement, and even-tual economic and political domination, Native Americans were forced to adopt the gender dynamics of those in power. Land deals and socialization policies promoted male-headed households, property ownership, and second-class citizen status for women.

Similarly, the "familism" and patriarchy of Mexican American and other Hispanic families relate to challenges they faced as U.S. social policies and reformers were bent on "Americanizing" them as units of economic and cultural production. The history of the American family is one of adaptation to social change regardless of race and class. We have discussed the impact of forced education on Latinos in Chapter 4. The colonial Puritan family featured extended family enclaves dictated by strict value systems. Economic roles were generally divided by gender, with occupational differences between families determining relationships. Families were divided according to craft production and agricultural work. Despite gender distinctions, the household remained the locus for economic production. Regardless of class, preindustrial colonial families settled in small villages with arranged marriages and interrelated property systems maintaining a provincial and intimate feeling throughout communities (Benokraitis 2008).

Arising in the 1830s, the Victorian family developed as wage work replaced household production, leading to a new division of labor among the middle class. As men went into the professions, the breadwinner model created new domestic roles for middle-class women and a prolonged childhood for their children. Despite this middle-class family icon of separate and strictly gendered spheres, working-class families often experienced the need for women and children to work for wages. The history of early industrialization in the United States demonstrates that many women and children comprised the lowest paid workers in the newly built New England textile mills and the Appalachian Mountain coal mines, as well as indentured servants and slaves in the fields and plantation houses of the South. In fact, professional and upper-class households often used working women and children as servants, thus building their own stable and ideal family structure on the backs of others (Coontz 1992).

The 20th-century family experienced the rise of fathers' wage labor, and public education, as well as the decline of the extended family (Hernandez 2005). Legislation passed during the early 1900s "age of reform" restricted the labor exploitation of women and young children, and created social welfare policies to influence a more stable "nuclear family." Yet, according to Mimi Abramowitz (1988/1996), the new social welfare system focused on the values and assumed deficiencies of poor women. She points out that the history of social welfare policy is full of examples of how poor women have been blamed for social problems linked to the family. These dynamics were intensified in the early 20th century as massive immigration and rapid urbanization increased the economic and cultural challenges facing poor women.

## WHAT WORKS TO REDUCE TEEN PREGNANCY

While the U.S. teen pregnancy rate has declined since the early 1990s, it is still the highest among industrialized nations with 435,436 births to mothers aged 15–19 in 2006. Of these births, two-thirds were to girls under 18 and most were unintended (Centers for Disease Control and Prevention 2009).

Populations most at risk for teen births are those from low-income and disadvantaged communities, teens who are emotionally distressed and have low attachment levels to parents, and those with certain family beliefs. Research on what works to reduce teen pregnancy shows that programs focusing on reproductive health such as sex and HIV education programs reduce

*(Continued)*

(Continued)

the prevalence of sex for teens, decrease the number of sexual partners, and delay the onset of sex (Kirby 2001). Programs focusing on youth development also reduce the teen pregnancy rate. Research suggests that programs incorporating service learning are effective in assisting teens to do well in school and have educational and career plans, which are goals shown to reduce teen pregnancy. Service learning engaged in by at-risk teens creates a sense of competency with adults along with the empowerment that comes with knowledge and control of their lives (Vincent, Clearie, and Schluchter 1987). Kirby articulates, "Service learning programs may have the strongest evidence of any intervention that they reduce teen pregnancy rates while the youth are participating in the program" (p. 13). Youth development organizations using service learning and community service provide a safe and supportive place for teens to face tough issues related to growing up (Nicholson et al. 2004).

The Depression era brought a new set of realities for America's families. The stress of overwhelming poverty and unemployment negatively reduced the nation's birthrate, but triggered increases in family-related violence. Massive poverty, alienation, and dislocation led to a reaffirmation of the family as an economic unit, and the popular culture of the period still reinforced the importance of family cohesion. The reemergence of three-generation households meant families entertained themselves rather than seeking entertainment elsewhere (Coontz 1992). The advent of World War II forced many working and middle-class women back into the factories. Unlike previous periods, however, these women were heralded as heroes, and images of Rosie the Riveter became famous around the country.

After the war, men returned to being sole breadwinners and most women went back to the home to raise children and tend the household. Marriage rates and birthrates boomed, home ownership rose, and the suburban picket fence became the geographical site for a reinvigorated nuclear family. The enduring, stereotypical images of *Leave It to Beaver* and *Father Knows Best* became engraved in the historical consciousness of American popular culture. By the mid-1960s, however, the stereotypical family became less common as a postindustrial economy generated nonunion service sector jobs that employed married women and mothers. The growing number of middle-class, college-educated women in the labor market coincided with lifestyle changes, once again altering the nature and shape of the family. Increasing divorce rates and cohabitation rates inspired more diverse family structures.

Class and race differences again determined whether women worked for wages or hired domestic help. For example, many poor and minority women worked as domestic servants (Coontz 1992) or entered the labor force as custodial, food service, or low-level health care workers in the public sector (Jones 1985). Thus, despite the 1950s and 1960s dominant image of a middle-class nuclear family owning a home in the suburbs and thriving on the father's professional salary, many working-class, poor, and families of color experienced a much different set of economic and social circumstances. Meanwhile, social welfare policies—this time linked to President Johnson's war on poverty—targeted poor, single mothers struggling to make ends meet. Yet these programs severely discriminated against African American and other nonwhite families, as the cultural, class, and racial bias of caseworkers, administrators, and local politicians affected the disbursement of welfare funds. As women went to work and gained more rights in the 1970s, families adapted to economic and social transformations (Nadasen 2005; Quadagno 1994).

The modern family is characterized by diverse behaviors reflecting two centuries of social changes. The complex sets of arrangements that make up the contemporary family are unlikely to change anytime soon to accommodate previous family forms. Contemporary families are characterized by the accumulation of these changes, including a growing number of singles as well as blended (reconstituted families from divorce), gay and lesbian, and other alternative families. What is perhaps most distinctive is the diversity of lifestyles as families work more and utilize more technology. As discussed in this chapter, the nation's lack of paid vacation and leave means less time for family. What seems consistent is that issues of economic and social inequality continue to influence or increase the social problems impacting families. Armed with an understanding of the historical and sociological dynamics of changes in family structure and function, faculty and students can engage in efforts to address social problems in a critical and effective way.

## MEDIA BOX: PUBLIC PERCEPTIONS OF DOMESTIC VIOLENCE

Exposing the contradictions inherent in blaming the victim for domestic violence is a key concern for advocates of victims of abuse. Ironically, the civil rights movement in the 1960s and the recent self-help movement have focused attention on women as victims of domestic violence and away from abusers, ignoring their role in abuse. Sociologists and social activists point to the important role the mass media has played in perpetuating myths about family violence. News programs, talk shows, movies, and other venues frame a discourse that leads us to believe that women alone have individual responsibility for domestic violence and should leave abusive relationships, defending themselves and their children. With an overriding focus on domestic violence as a private problem, talk shows promote individual responsibility while often ignoring the political, social, and cultural context within which the violence happens. This leads us to ignore the role of the abusers, even assuming they are not part of the problem. Sociologist Nancy Burns, in her book *Framing the Victim: Domestic Violence, Media, and Social Problems* (2004), has been at the forefront of exposing how the mass media's depiction of domestic violence continues the victimization of women in violent relationships. Her research shows that framing the victim has been the overriding focus of stories of domestic violence: "Most media stories focus on the victim. The victim is celebrated for having the courage to leave the abusive relationship or, conversely, blamed for staying and letting the abuse to continue. He or she is accused of provoking the abuse and held responsible for ending the abuse" (p. 3). Popular media talk show hosts such as Dr. Phil often overemphasize the role of the victim in domestic violence. Burns argues that the approach taken by the media plays an important part in how the public understands domestic violence and in turn shapes public policy. Would an increased focus on abusers lead to better results from advocates? How do abuse victims appear to you in the mass media?

## CASE STUDY #1

### Community Development Corporations: A Functionalist Approach to Family Problems

Community development corporations (CDCs) allow communities to draw on multiple sources to assist families challenged by social problems. They often create strategies for bringing communities together around solving problems. When CDCs integrate resources, they are keeping families and communities together in much the same way that functionalist sociologists suggest institutions lead to the survival of society. In many cases, CDCs work in urban areas overseen by a representative community board of directors. As with functionalist theory, CDCs emphasize the resolving of conflicts within communities and families (Stoecker 2005). An example of how CDCs address social problems in the family and community is the New York City–based Women's Housing and Economic Development Corporation (WHEDCo) in a number of Bronx communities.

Founded in 1991 with $75,000, WHEDCo is in one of the nation's poorest congressional districts. By 2003, the organization had grown to a $5 million operating budget with 10 programs serving 3,000 people. The organization operates programs in day care, fitness, and job training and placement, as well as a low-income housing program. Funding for the organization comes from multiple sources. In addition, it has over 25 partners. WHEDCo integrates a number of programs and services to change lives. The center is dedicated to alleviating poverty by providing people with the tools and support they need to enter and succeed in the economic mainstream. Family programs at the organization are integrated with a number of other programs in an effort to solidify the relationship between family roles and responsibilities and the various projects themselves.

For example, WHEDCo's Family Day Care network helps local women establish neighborhood-based child care enterprises by providing training, tax and licensing assistance, access to start-up funds, and other resources. In the last 10 years, the network has grown to include 180 business owners, collectively generating $6.1 million in annual gross revenue while caring for over 1,000 children annually in safe, affordable, and educational facilities. In addition to training providers, the program helps parents secure child care as they seek employment or education. Family Day Care businesses allow parents to maintain steady jobs no matter what their hours of employment. At the same time that some women gain business skills, other women in the community acquire affordable child care.

The CDC also operates a youth education program for Grades K–8 providing out-of-school activities and an Early Childhood Development Center for 104 children yearly. This program works with parents providing parenting skills and literacy to individuals representing 14 languages (see www.whedco.org/headstart.php). These programs reinforce family stability for their participants. Parents acquire skills that help them to function in society, while children are given a head start in their education. Increased exposure to education for both parents and children helps them to operate in social institutions. Ideally, the programs are able to assist people who would not otherwise gain resources and services. As we saw at the beginning of the chapter, helping with housing for people is also a way to address multiple social problems faced by families. At its Urban Horizons apartment complexes, WHEDCo assists with low-income housing, moving homeless people and families in substandard shelters to sustainable living arrangements (see www.whedco.org/urbanhorres.php).

Family education programs are another effective way to solve multiple social problems. Workshops and counseling at WHEDCo center on topics such as financial literacy, legal issues, public benefits, domestic violence, and family planning. Most low-income people in need of social services must navigate a rigid and unforgiving system. CDCs can make the system work for each individual's unique situation. Drawing on functionalist analysis, we can see that when integrated, institutions can work to reduce social problems related to families. Accessing available resources is a fundamental challenge for low-income urban residents. However, when resources are accessible, they lead to life-changing scenarios. Take the case of Cheryl Wilson, for example. Homeless with three children, Cheryl attended WHEDCo seminars on work and personal budgets, and obtained housing through the organization. She also received counseling, with her 18-year-old daughter helping her keep the family together (White, Nauer, Lerner, and Glenn 2005).

Single mothers like Cheryl face difficult odds. Their success or failure, however, as with anyone in society, is dependent on how well social institutions work to stabilize families. CDCs like WHEDCo are part of our society's commitment to the well-being of our nation. Providing skills and services to at-risk families solves a number of immediate as well as future social problems. Having healthy institutions means developing paths for everyone in society to access them.

## Case Study Questions

1. What barriers do poor urban families face in obtaining resources?

2. What is unique about CDCs for providing resources and services?

3. Looking at the case of WHEDCo, what advantages occur for addressing social problems when social institutions are integrated?

## CASE STUDY #2

### Symbolic Interaction and Multiagency Approaches to Domestic Violence and Abuse

As we explained in Chapter 1, some social problems that exist today also existed in the past but were often not discussed by families or society in general. Benokraitis (2008) offers that, "Until the 1970s, few people ever talked or wrote about child abuse, incest, domestic violence, marital happiness, sexual harassment, or gay bashing. Many families lived in silent misery and quiet desperation because these issues were largely invisible" (p. 14). The symbolic interactionist approach to social problems highlights the role of social construction in defining an act as a social problem. Domestic violence is one of the best examples of how social movements have changed how people think, leading to a redefining of a problem.

*(Continued)*

(Continued)

Much of the contemporary focus on domestic violence resulted from the successful consciousness-raising and educational work inspired by the women's movement in the 1960s and 1970s. The first attempt to address domestic violence in the United States occurred in the 1880s with Chicago's Protective Agency for Women and Children, which provided legal aid, court aid, and personal assistance to victims of domestic violence. But it wasn't until the 1960s that battered women were offered direct assistance from state legislators and state agencies. By the late 1970s, shelters, hotlines, and volunteer host homes had been developed in the United States, Canada, and Great Britain. From 1977 to 1990, the number of shelters for battered women increased from 89 to 1,250 (Roche and Sadoski 1996). Because of the increases in the reporting of domestic violence in recent years, it is difficult to determine how much it has been reduced. However, we know that the number of intimate partner homicides has declined significantly in the last 30 years (National Network to End Domestic Violence 2006).

Other solutions to domestic violence can be found in the everyday work lives of professionals in fields such as health care. For example, the history of shame and silence around hidden domestic violence made treating its impact almost impossible. At Idaho State University, the school's nursing program now utilizes partnerships with agencies in order to assist undergraduate nurses to better address domestic violence in their jobs. By taking a symbolic interactionist approach, we can understand how involvement with service learning can help nurses identify domestic violence and construct effective treatments.

Addressing domestic violence is complicated because of the shame and power involved in the behavior and the victimization. As society's understanding and perception of domestic violence changes, so too does the impact from stigmatization and negative stereotyping. Research suggests that nurses often lack the training and skills to intervene with families that experience domestic violence (Hayward and Weber 2003). In fact, because of negative labels and lack of experience, health professionals often misdiagnose or mistreat abuse victims. Through service learning projects, nursing students have gained greater familiarity with health problems related to abuse, and acquire a more integrated sense of how to address particular problems. As Idaho State students worked with the Family Services Alliance (FSA) of Southeast Idaho and local law enforcement agencies, they developed a variety of projects to address victims' needs. Students developed appropriate first aid resources for a women's shelter, wrote policies and protocol for addressing elderly abuse, and created a permanent wellness teaching area at the shelter where people could get important information on HIV prevention and other issues of importance.

Examples of student responses to the program reveal a lot about what service learning students take away from serving their community. They made the following comments:

"I am now more aware of how big a problem domestic violence is."

"Many victims are unaware of the resources. The outreach program is excellent."

"I had many clients express gratitude and relief that there are places to turn for help"

"This project is vital to the community. Every professional needs this experience."

"I plan to get involved again when I relocate after graduation." (Hayward and Weber 2003:6, 7)

Student gains from the program are both practical and developmental. Service learning in a community setting is a form of professional development for nurses. As nurses learn to socially construct their role in countering domestic violence, they are using their sociological imagination as a tool to solve social problems (Hayward and Weber 2004). Even with the gains from the women's movement, domestic violence is often still known as a silent epidemic. According to symbolic interactionists, "blame the victim" mentality is still prevalent in society. Informed health care workers can help victims get over the psychological, social, and legal stigmas of being victimized.

## Case Study Questions

1. What was the basis of the silence about domestic violence before the 1970s?

2. What barriers do health care professionals have in addressing domestic violence?

3. How does symbolic interactionism help us understand the reluctance to address domestic violence in the health care fields?

4. How can service learning break down the stigma of domestic violence?

## VOICES FROM THE FIELD

### An Interview with Dianne Levy From SafeSpace

The empowerment of abused women has increased in the post-1960s era. The feminist and women's movements, disabled rights movement, and civil rights movement set in motion legal and organizational strategies behind the empowerment of disenfranchised groups. Battered women face great barriers, which are often worse when women are poor or isolated. An example of how community-based organizations can address local social problems is the organization SafeSpace. With a number of centers across the United States, SafeSpace programs emerged as local communities fought to transform how domestic violence is perceived and addressed. Rural areas lag behind in empowering women due to isolation and patriarchal attitudes. SafeSpace of East Tennessee is one such example of this struggle.

*(Continued)*

(Continued)

SafeSpace began in the mid-1970s as an informal network of private homes providing safety to domestic violence victims. The leaders of SafeSpace envisioned it as a place for women and children who experience domestic violence (Couto 1999). The organization began when its creator Dianne Levy became aware of the plight of a neighbor who would eventually kill her abusive husband. The neighbor spent most of her time in a nearby empty block building, which served as an isolated community grocery store. Levy eventually found out the building's purpose.

   "This store that she called a store had a dozen onions. It had three cans of beanie weenies and a couple packs of cigarettes.... She had maybe $50 worth of groceries in the store. On another occasion, I said "Gosh, is this really worth your time? To sit here all day? How much business are you actually doing? She said, 'Ah, I'm not here to make money. See this building?' (It is a block building, very small, and it had two front windows and a door, no back door, had a wood stove in there and bare floor.) "Do you see this building? See that door? See that steel door? See, the windows have bars on them. This is made so he can't burn this place down. He can't get to me here. I can lock ourselves in here."

Levy drew on her experiences with her friend and other abused women in the community to begin to form a task force that eventually became SafeSpace. She says, "After about a year, I called many of these people who had been calling me asking me to help. I said to them, 'We need to have a meeting.' We formed a task force, that was in about '79. There was a group of about ten people that came together. That was the core." Levy was intent on creating a change-based organization.

   "We were looking into social change, and we were clear that providing temporary shelter to families was necessary and important, but we had to impact the entire community and the state to see change" (quoted in Couto 1999:189–190).

   SafeSpace eventually engaged in a number of efforts to empower abused women in rural East Tennessee. Dianne Levy's experiences were behind the group's designation as a nonprofit in 1981 and the opening of a full-time shelter in 1985. Today, SafeSpace serves three counties. The centers provide emergency shelter, advocacy, resources, referrals, and counseling.

*Source:* ©Istockphoto.com/Stock Photo NYC.

## CASE STUDY #3

### Community Partnerships, Domestic Violence, and Engaged Faculty

Community partnerships between universities and agencies can enhance learning opportunities and help provide solutions to social problems. Addressing family violence requires more than just locking up abusers in the criminal justice system. When a domestic violence case enters the system, it typically involves the county courts, public defender, women's shelters, law enforcement, probation, schools, health and human services department, and health providers. Often, these agencies have trouble working with one another for a number of reasons. Seeking solutions to coordinating agencies requires working cooperatively.

One California community, Stanislaus County, is a good example of how service learning can be used to solve the problem of coordination between agencies. For over 10 years, the Stanislaus County Domestic Violence Coordinating Council has addressed domestic violence by connecting agencies dedicated to its victims and those who serve them. The partnership between the county's agencies could not have been possible without those involved in service learning in the Department of Sociology and Criminal Justice at California State University (CSU) at Stanislaus. Initially, students did surveys to determine the public's attitudes toward, and knowledge about, domestic violence. Once surveys were tabulated and analyzed, the city's Domestic Violence Task Force partnered with CSU Stanislaus to conduct a forum to better educate the campus and community. In 1995, the task force and CSU Sociology Department cosponsored a forum entitled "Domestic Violence and Intimate Abusive Relationships." Held at the university, the campus and community were invited in an attempt to better educate people about domestic violence.

Students in service learning classes at CSU Stanislaus now have greater access to community agencies. Following their initial involvement, the Sociology and Criminal Justice program has developed courses on domestic violence and routinely integrates speakers from the council (Rhodes 1996). One professor, Cecil Rhodes (1996), had become a member of the task force. He explained the impact of the community partnerships and the students' ability to immerse themselves in such community work:

> Students were required to participate in a service learning project, by working in a community agency involved with domestic violence. Students committed to a "Service Learning Agreement" and engaged in volunteer service at criminal justice agencies and social service agencies in Stanislaus and surrounding counties. They were required to take field notes, which often became the basis for their assigned research projects.
>
> Students learned that not only was it possible for various organizations to work together cooperatively in dealing with domestic violence and abuse, but that it was also, in fact, happening in their community. The students also received information directly from various members of the council, including prosecutors, women's shelter administrators, and probation officers who volunteered to participate as guest lecturers in my class. (p. 1)

*(Continued)*

(Continued)

Throughout much of the 20th century, institutions and professional doctrine prescribed that faculty avoid relationships with the subjects they researched, wrote, and taught about. Unlike the history of engaged work that had shaped sociology (as noted in the introduction to this text), mainstream social science eschewed social and political involvement for the sake of objectivity and neutrality. But Rhodes' participation in the task force and his developing relationships with community organizations and agencies has enhanced his knowledge of domestic violence and its impact. These connections have also made student experiences with these groups richer and more integrated with their texts, lectures, and assignments.

Meanwhile, the county now has a mechanism for addressing the connections among agencies involved with domestic violence. The centralized services integrate the public defender's office, court judges and the police department, crisis referral services, family services, the Haven Women's Center, county mental health facilities, and health services. The council has a working group that addresses problems in the system and supports continual collaborations and partnerships between agencies. Victims of domestic violence can now more easily navigate the maze of support services and the legal requirements necessary to rebuild their lives and the lives of their children. And students now have opportunities to experience the reality that it takes a village—not just to raise a child, but to support families.

## Case Study Questions

1. Despite the legislation and services available to support victims of domestic violence, what systemic challenges still face these victims?

2. What kinds of resources can faculty and students bring to bear on these issues?

3. Think about the variety of agencies and organizations in your community—their goals and their strategies. How might your faculty or student cohort help maximize their success?

# SUMMARY

Debates over social problems and the family in the social sciences leave a number of questions unanswered. However, by taking an approach to the family that incorporates the gains of community programs and service to community, we can see how to solve problems faced by America's families in crisis. Changing family forms, rapid social change, and limited support for parents mean role overload and pressure reduce the quality of life for many of the nation's families. Social problems related to the unequal distribution of power in society are evident in domestic violence and abuse. Research reveals that investing in after-school programs, summer programs, and families has a payoff for both families and society. Youth development programs reduce teen pregnancy and delinquency. Service learning is playing a greater role in the operation of programs for families and becoming a larger part of public policy solutions. Community-based organizations and development corporations also revealed in this chapter solve social problems by providing direct services and empowerment.

## SUMMARY QUESTIONS

1. How do social scientists view changes in the contemporary American family? What are the policy implications of the differing views?

2. What is role overload and how does it affect the contemporary family? What is the Family and Medical Leave Act?

3. What are the main family forms? How do they affect the contemporary family?

4. What are the types of domestic violence? What are the impacts of social movements and community-based organizations on how society addresses domestic violence?

5. How have class differences shaped the American family in the past, and how do they shape it in the present?

## GLOSSARY

**Child Support:** Payments from one divorced spouse to the other, to support the children.

**Divorce:** The legal ending of a marriage contract.

**Domestic Elderly Abuse:** Refers to any form of maltreatment of an older person by someone who has a special relationship with him or her (usually a spouse or child), and can include forms of physical, psychological, or financial exploitation.

**Domestic Violence:** Refers to the behavior of a person in a relationship who seeks to maintain power and control over his or her partner or other family members through either actual or threatened physical abuse or mental and emotional manipulation.

**Family and Medical Leave Act (FMLA):** This legislation allows time off for the care of infirm family members or for all new parents to care for an infant or a newly placed foster or adopted child.

**Institutional Elderly Abuse:** Refers to forms of abuse that occur in residential or assisted living facilities for older people.

Parents' Bill of Rights: A document and movement that call for pro-marriage legal policies supporting stronger marriage, support for fathers, and adoption assistance.

Role Overload: This refers to the stresses experienced when an individual experiences stress as a result of being expected to do too many jobs or tasks within a period of time.

Second Shift: Term coined by author Arlie Hochschild, refers to the role overload faced by women who have both a full-time paid job and do the overwhelming majority of maintaining a household.

Violence Against Women Act (VAWA): This legislation provides women with broad protections against violence in a number of settings including homes, communities, and society.

## WEBSITES TO LEARN MORE ABOUT FAMILY SOCIAL PROBLEMS AND RELATED SERVICE LEARNING PROJECTS

American Association for Retired People (AARP): http://www.aarp.org/

Annie E. Casey Foundation: http://www.aecf.org/

Center for a New American Dream: http://www.newdream.org/

Center for Marriage and Families: http://center.americanvalues.org/

Child & Family Services: http://www.child-familyservices.org/

Childhelp: http://www.childhelp.org/

Children's Defense Fund: http://www.childrensdefense.org/

Community Organizing and Family Issues: http://www.cofionline.org/

Court Appointed Special Advocates (CASA): http://www.casaforchildren.org/site/c.mtJSJ7MPIsE/b.5301295/k.BE9A/Home.htm

Crittenton Women's Union: http://www.liveworkthrive.org/

Energize: http://www.energizeinc.com/index.html

Florida Bureau of Family and Community Outreach: http://www.fldoe.org/Family/learnserve.asp

National Center on Elder Abuse: http://www.ncea.aoa.gov/ncearoot/Main_Site/index.aspx

National Coalition Against Domestic Violence: http://www.ncadv.org/

National Domestic Violence Hotline: http://www.ndvh.org/

National Public Sex Offender Registry: http://www.nsopw.gov/Core/Conditions.aspx?AspxAutoDetectCookieSupport = 1

NeighborWorks America: http://www.nw.org/network/home.asp

U.S. Department of Labor—Family and Medical Leave Act: http://www.dol.gov/whd/fmla/index.htm

Working Families Party: http://www.workingfamiliesparty.org/

## REFERENCES

Abramowitz, Mimi. [1988]1996. *Regulating the Lives of Women: Social Welfare Policy From Colonial Times to the Present*. Boston, MA: South End Press.

Aulette, Judy Root. 2002. *Changing American Families*. Boston, MA: Allyn & Bacon.

Baker, Chris. 2005. "Collaborations for Change: Who Is Playing and Who Is Winning in Community-Based Organization Led Development in Rural Appalachia." *Humanity & Society*, 29.

Baker, Chris. 2006. "The Southern Appalachian Labor School (SALS): Communities of Difference and Development in Southern West Virginia." *Now and Then*, Fall/Winter.

Barko, Naomi. 2000. "The Other Gender Gap." *The American Prospect*. June 19, pp. 61–63.

Beaver, Patricia D. 1986. *Rural Community in the Appalachian South*. Lexington, KY: University Press of Kentucky.

Bellah, Robert, Richard Madsen, William M. Sullivan, Ann Swidler, and Steven M. Tipton. 1985. *Habits of the Heart: Individualism and Commitment in American Life*. Berkeley: University of California Press.

Benokraitis, Nijole V. 2008. *Marriages and Families: Changes, Choices, and Constraints*. 6th ed. Upper Saddle River, NJ: Prentice Hall.

Benson, Michael, John Wooldredge, Amy B. Thistlethwaite, and Greer Litton Fox. 2004. "The Correlation Between Race and Domestic Violence Is Confounded With Community Context." *Social Problems*, 51:326–342.

Bianchi, Suzanne M., Lynne M. Casper, and Roselind Berkow King. 2005. *Work, Family, Health, and Well-Being*. Mahwah, NJ: Erlbaum.

Bianchi, Suzanne M., John P. Robinson, and Melissa A. Milkie. 2006. *Changing Rhythms of American Family Life*. New York: Russell Sage Foundation.

Blankenhorn, David. 1995. *Fatherless America Confronting Our Most Urgent Social Problem*. New York: HarperCollins.

Burns, Nancy. 2004. *Framing the Victim: Domestic Violence, Media, and Social Problems*. New York: Aldine de Gruyter.

Cantrell, Peggy. 1991. "Victims of Their Families." *Now and Then*, 8:6–8.

Centers for Disease Control and Prevention. 2009. "Adolescent Reproductive Health: About Teen Pregnancy." U.S. Department of Health and Human Services. Retrieved February 14, 2010 (http://www.cdc.gov/reproductivehealth/adolescentreprohealth/AboutTP.htm).

Coontz, Stephanie. 1992. *The Way We Never Were: American Families and the Nostalgia Trap*. New York: Basic Books.

____. 2005. *Marriage, a History: How Love Conquered Marriage*. New York: Penguin.

Couto, Richard. 1999. *Making Democracy Work Better: Mediating Structures, Social Capital, and the Democratic Prospect*. Chapel Hill, NC: University of North Carolina Press.

Cox, Carole B. 2000. "Empowering Practice Implications for Interventions With African Americans and Latina Custodial Grandparents." *Journal of Mental Health and Aging*, 6:385–397.

____. 2002. "Empowering African American Custodial Grandparents." *Social Work,* 47:45–54.

Durfee, Alesha and Karen Rosenberg. 2004. "Domestic Violence in the United States: Current Research." Pp. 72–80 in *Agenda for Social Justice: Solutions 2004,* edited by Robert Perrucci, Kathleen Ferraro, JoAnn Miller, and Paula C. Rodríguez Rust. Knoxville, TN: Society for the Study of Social Problems.

Ehrenreich, Barbara and Arlie Russell Hochchild. 2002. *Global Women: Nannies, Maids, and Sex Workers in the New Economy.* New York: Metropolitan Books.

Everett, Kevin D. 1998. "Understanding Social Inequality Through Service Learning." Teaching Sociology, 4:299–310.

Ferraro, Kathleen. 2006. Neither Angels Nor Demons: Women, Crime, and Victimization. Lebanon, NH: University Press of New England.

Fisher, Kimberly, Muriel Egerton, Jonathan I. Gershuny, and John P. Robinson. 2007. "Gender Convergence in the American Heritage Time Use Study (AHTUS)." *Social Indicators Research,* 82:1–33.

Furstenberg, Frank. 2005. "Can Marriage Be Saved?" *Dissent,* Summer:76–80.

Geiger, Brenda. 2002. "From Deviance to Creation: Women's Answer to Subjugation." *Humanity & Society,* 26:226.

Gelles, Richard J. and Claire P. Cornell. 1990. 2nd edition. *Intimate Violence in Families.* Newbury Park, CA: Sage.

Gerson, Kathleen and Jerry A. Jacobs. 2004. "The Work-Home Crunch." *Contexts,* 3:29–37.

Giele, Janet Z. 1996. "Decline of the Family: Conservative, Liberal, and Feminist Views." Pp. 89–115 in *Promises to Keep: Decline and Renewal of Marriage in America,* edited by David Popenoe, Jean Bethke Elshtain, and David Blankenhorn. Totowa, NJ: Rowman & Littlefield.

Gielow, Erin. 2002. "Equality in the Workplace: Why Family Leave Does Not Work." *Southern California Law Review,* 75:1529–1551.

Goetting, Ann. 1999. *Getting Out: Life Stories of Women Who Left Abusive Men.* New York: Columbia University Press.

Gornick, Janet C. 2005. "Overworked, Time Poor, and Abandoned by Uncle Sam." *Dissent,* Summer: 65–69.

Goyer, Amy. 2006, February 1. "Intergenerational Relationships: Grandparents Raising Grandchildren." American Association for Retired Persons (AARP). Retrieved February 14, 2010 (http://www.aarpinternational .org/resourcelibrary/resourcelibrary_show.htm?doc_id = 545720).

Grall, Timothy S. 2006. "Custodial Mothers and Fathers and Their Child Support: 2005." *Current Population Reports.* Washington, DC: U.S. Department of Commerce, Economic and Statistics Administration.

Gutman, Herbert. 1976. *The Black Family in Slavery and Freedom.* Pittsburgh: University of Pittsburgh Press.

Hackstaff, Karla B. 1999. *Marriage in a Culture of Divorce.* Philadelphia, PA: Temple University Press.

Hayward, Karen and La Mae Weber. 2003. "A Community Partnership to Prepare Nursing Students to Respond to Domestic Violence" *Nursing Forum,* 38:5–10.

Henslin, James M. 2007. *Sociology: A Down-to-Earth Approach.* Boston, MA: Pearson.

Hernandez, Donald J. 2005. "Changes in the Demographics of Families Over the Course of American History." Pp. 13–35 in *Unfinished Work: Building Equality and Democracy in an Era of Working Families,* edited by Jody Heyman and Christopher Beem. New York: The New Press.

Hewlett, Sylvia Ann and Cornel West. 1998. *The War Against Parents.* New York: Houghton Mifflin.

Heyman, Jodi, Alison Earl, and Jeffery Hayes. 2007. "The Work, Family, and Equity Index: How Does the United States Measure Up?" Montreal, Quebec, Canada: McGill University, Institute for Health and Social Policy. Retrieved September 9, 2009 (http://www.mcgill.ca/files/ihsp/WFEI2007.pdf).

Hines, Denise A. and Kathleen Malley-Morrison. 2005. *Family Violence in the United States: Defining, Understanding, and Combating Abuse.* Thousand Oaks, CA: Sage.

Hochschild, Arlie Russell. 1989. *The Second Shift: Working Parents and the Revolution at Home.* New York: Viking.

Hughes, Mary Elizabeth, Linda J. Waite, Tracy A. LaPiere, and Ye Luo. 2007. "All in the Family: The Impact of Caring for Grandchildren on Grandparents' Health." *Journal of Gerontology,* 62:108–119.

Innocenti Research Centre. 2000. *Domestic Violence Against Women and Girls.* United Nations Children's Fund (UNICEF). Florence Italy: Author.

Jayson, Sharon. 2005. "Divorce Declining, But So is Marriage." *USA Today* July 18. Retrieved July 9, 2010: (http://www.usatoday.com/news/nation/2005-07-18-cohabit-divorce_x.htm)

Jensen, Joan. 1981. *Native American Women and Agriculture.* New York: The Feminist Press.

Jones, Jacqueline. 1985. *Labor of Love, Labor of Sorrow: Black Women, Work, and the Family From Slavery to the Present.* New York: Oxford University Press.

Kelly, Joan A. and Robert E. Emery. 2000. "Children's Adjustment Following Divorce: Risk and Resilience Perspectives." *Family Relations,* 52:352–362.

Kirby, Douglas. 2001. *Emerging Answers: Research Findings on Programs to Reduce Teen Pregnancy.* Washington, DC: National Campaign to Prevent Teen Pregnancy.

Kosberg, Jordon and Gordon MacNeil. 2003. "The Elderly Abuse of Custodial Grandparents A Hidden Phenomenon." *Journal of Elderly Abuse and Neglect,* 25:1005–1025.

Leon-Guerrero, Anna. 2005. *Social Problems: Community, Policy, and Social Action.* Thousand Oaks, CA: Pine Forge Press.

Martin, Steve P. 2004. "Growing Evidence for a 'Divorce Divide': Education and Marital Dissolution Rates in the U.S." (Working Paper, Russell Sage Foundation Series on Social Dimensions of Inequality).

Minkler, Meredith and Esme Fuller-Thomson. 2005. "American Indian/Alaskan Native Grandparents Raising Grandchildren: Findings From the Census of 2000 Supplementary." *Social Work,* 50:131–129.

Murphy, Clare. 2004. "Wedded to the Value of Marriage," *New York Times.* January 15.

Nadasen, Premilla. 2005. *Welfare Warriors: The Welfare Rights Movement in the United States.* New York: Routledge.

National Network to End Domestic Violence. 2006. "The Violence Against Women Act of 2005 Summary of Provisions." Washington, DC: Author. Retrieved February 14, 2010 (http://nnedv.org/docs/Policy/VAWA2005FactSheet.pdf).

National Partnership for Women and Families. 2005. *Expecting Better: A State-by-State Analysis of Parental Leave Programs* (National Partnership for Women and Families and the Anne E Casey Foundation).

Nicholson, Heather Johnston, Christopher Collins, and Heidi Holmer. 2004. "Youth as People: The Protective Aspects of Youth Development in After-School Settings." *The Annals of the American Academy of Political and Social Science,* 591:55–71.

Pear, Robert. 2002. "9 of 10 Nursing Homes Lack Adequate Staff, Study Finds." *New York Times.* February 18.

Peterson, Richard 1996. "A Re-evaluation of the Economic Consequences of Divorce." *American Sociological Review,* 61:528–536.

Popenoe, David, Jean Bethke Elshtain, and David Blankenhorn. 1996. *Promises to Keep: Decline and Renewal of Marriage in America.* Lanham, MD: Rowland & Littlefield.

Presser, Harriet. 2005. *Working in a 24/7 Economy: Challenges for American Families.* New York: Russell Sage Foundation.

Purdue, Theda. 1988. "Cherokee Women and the Trail of Tears." *Journal of Women's History,* 1:14–30.

Putney, Norella M., Dawn E. Ailey, and Vern L. Bengtson. 2005. "Social Gerontology as Public Sociology in Action." *The American Sociologist,* 36:88–104.

Quadagno, Jill. 1994. *The Color of Welfare: How Racism Undermined the War on Poverty.* New York: Oxford University Press.

Ray, Rebecca and John Schmitt. 2007. *No Vacation Nation.* Washington, DC: Center for Economic Policy.

Rhoads, Robert. 1997. *Community Service and Higher Learning: Explorations of the Caring Self.* Albany, NY: State University of New York Press.

Rhodes, Cecil A. 1996. "Domestic Violence and Abuse: Creating and Learning From University/Community Partnerships." *Family Law,* 12(1). Retrieved February 15, 2010 (http://www.abanet.org/publiced/focus/f96domv.html).

Roberts, Sam. 2006. "To be Married Means to Be Outnumbered." *New York Times.* October 15.

____. 2007. "51% of Women Are Now Living Without Spouse." *New York Times.* January 16.

Roche, Susan E. and Pam J. Sadoski. 1996. "Social Action for Battered Women." Pp. 13–30 in *Helping Battered Women: New Perspectives and Remedies,* edited by Albert R. Roberts. New York: Oxford University Press.

Rubin, Lillian B. 1994. *Families on the Fault Line.* New York: HarperCollins.

Ruiz, Dorothy Smith. 2004. *Amazing Grace: African American Grandmothers as Caregivers and Conveyors of Traditional Values.* Westport, CT: Praeger.

Shor, Juliet. 1992. *The Overworked American: The Unexpected Decline of Leisure.* New York: Basic Books.

Skolnick, Jerome and Arlene Skolnick. 2005. *Family in Transition.* Toronto, Ont., Canada: Allyn & Bacon.

Stacy, Judith. 1991. *Brave New Families: Stories of Domestic Upheaval in the Late Twentieth Century.* New York: Basic Books.

Stevenson, Brenda. 1997. *Life in Black and White: Family and Community in the Slave South.* New York: Oxford University Press.

Stoecker, Randy. 2005. *Research Methods for Community Change: A Project-Based Approach.* Thousand Oaks, CA: Sage.

Stuart, Gregory L., Todd M. Moore, Kristina Coop Gordon, Susan E. Ramsey, and Christopher W. Kahler. 2006. "Psychopathology in Women Arrested for Domestic Violence." *Journal of Interpersonal Violence,* 21:376–389.

Takaki, Ronald. 1994. *A Different Mirror: A History of Multicultural America.* New York: Backbay Books.

U.S. Census Bureau. 2005. "United States Households and Families" (2005 American Community Survey). Retrieved February 22, 2010 (http://factfinder.census.gov).

U.S. Department of Justice, Bureau of Justice Statistics. 2006. "Intimate Partner Violence Declined Between 1993 and 2004." Retrieved February 14, 2010 (http://www.ojp.usdoj.gov/newsroom/pressreleases/2006/bjs07007.htm).

Vincent, Murray L., Andrew F. Clearie, and Mark D. Schluchter. 1987. "Reducing Adolescent Pregnancy Through School and Community-Based Education." *Journal of the American Medical Association,* 257:3382–3386.

Warren, Elizabeth and Amelia Warren Tyagi. 2004. *The Two-Income Trap: Why Middle-Class Parents Are Going Broke.* New York: Basic Books.

Websdale, Neil. 1997. *Rural Women, Battering, and the Justice System: An Ethnography.* Boston, MA: Northeastern University Press.

White, Andrew, Kim Nauer, Sharon Lerner, and Beth Glenn. 2005. *Spanning the Neighborhood: The Bridge Between Housing and Supports for Families.* New York: Center for New York City Affairs, The New School. Retrieved February 14, 2010 (http://www.newschool.edu/Milano/nycaffairs/documents/Spanning Neighborhood_Report.pdf).

# Who Breathes Easy?

*Protecting and Designing Our Environments*

> *I propose a different ranking system for colleges based on whether the institution and its graduates move the world in a more suitable direction or not. Do four years at a particular institution instill knowledge, love, and compassion toward the natural world, or indifference and ignorance?*
>
> —David Orr, *Ecological Literacy* (1992)

> *Nature is the timekeeper.*
>
> —Lester R. Brown, *Plan B 2.0* (2006)

## INTRODUCTION: COLLEGES GOING GREEN

Social problems linked to industrial production, mass consumption, waste disposal, and energy use collectively threaten our future. Many of these large-scale problems have solutions that are rooted in the everyday life of individuals and the policies of social institutions. Polls reveal that Americans are concerned about environmental issues, yet individually most continue consuming massive amounts of energy to enjoy ecologically unsustainable lifestyles. Some colleges and universities, however, have taken the lead in supporting more sustainable environmental practices and encouraging ecologically responsible lifestyles on their campuses.

The Environmental Protection Agency (EPA) ranks institutions on how much green power they use to meet electricity needs. Their findings show a number of schools using wind energy and small hydro sources to provide power. The University of Pennsylvania, for example, obtains 46% of its energy from wind, while universities in Western Washington and Central Oklahoma obtain *all* their electricity from wind (EPA 2010). Meanwhile, a number of liberal arts colleges have students developing master plans for environmentally sustainable campuses. By changing habits and infrastructure to conserve and recycle, these colleges educate students in sustainable living and the benefits of social action.

Bates and Bowdoin Colleges in Maine, Berea College in Kentucky, and Connecticut College have addressed on-campus energy use and recycling as both sustainable environmental practices and economic strategies and educational tools. Bates, for example, prides itself on taking an active approach to green space preservation, as well as being the first collegial member of the Green Restaurant Association. With one of the earliest Human Ecology programs, begun in 1969, Connecticut College works to create a model society with shared governance. The school has invested in solar energy along with organic gardens and sustainable building practices. And one of the nation's most honored colleges, Berea College, has a philosophy that intertwines ecological, social, and educational goals. For the last 5 years at Berea, a complex of 50 apartments, a child development laboratory, and a commons building has utilized its Ecovillage ecological machine (naturally recycling industrial and sewage waste) and a demonstration building for environmental studies (Berea College Ecovillage). Currently, the machine is being converted for *aquaponics* use, integrating the raising of fish and vegetables into an ecologically efficient process. The project has wide applications for ecological waste treatment for rural Appalachian communities along with real-world situations for chemistry students (http://senshouse.org/blog/catfish-and-tilapia-coming-to-the-ecovillage/).

Located in Brunswick, Maine, Bowdoin College is a private school in an environmentally conscious state. Bowdoin's Office of Sustainability and its green programs allow students to participate in making the school an environmentally progressive institution. The college's initiatives include a goal of 100% renewable electricity use on campus, green-certified buildings, dining service collaborations with an on-campus organic garden and local food providers, a campuswide recycling program, and student-based drives to reduce electricity and water consumption. Bowdoin and other ecologically conscious colleges convey that individuals and institutions can reduce the impact of their resource use on the surrounding environment. From a social problems and service learning perspective, the campus's environmental approach creates opportunities to learn about social issues while simultaneously addressing social problems on campus, and developing a sense of citizenship in the larger community.

## BOWDOIN COLLEGE ENVIRONMENTAL MISSION STATEMENT

The environment within and beyond Bowdoin College is one of the fundamental aspects of our community and one that we, as members of the College, have in common. In keeping with Bowdoin's bicentennial motto, "The College and the Common Good," the opportunity exists to reaffirm our commitment to the history and future of Bowdoin's relationship with the environment.

Both the institution as a whole and individuals in the Bowdoin community have an impact on the environment and therefore should commit themselves to understanding their personal responsibility for the local and natural environment. In consideration of the common good, Bowdoin recognizes its responsibility to take a leadership role in environmental stewardship by promoting environmental awareness, local action, and global thinking. Because sustainability reaches beyond the Bowdoin campus, choices made by the College in its operations shall consider economic, environmental, and social impacts. Members of the Bowdoin community shall orient new faculty, staff, and students to the campus-wide environmental ethic and conduct research and teaching in a sustainable and responsible fashion. As a way to capture this ethic, the following Environmental Mission Statement has been developed:

"Being mindful of our use of the Earth's natural resources, we are committed to leading by example to integrate environmental awareness and responsibility throughout the college community. The College shall seek to encourage conservation, recycling, and other sustainable practices in its daily decision-making processes, and shall take into account, in the operations of the College, all appropriate economic, environmental, and social concerns" (Bowdoin College 2010:n.p.).

Bowdoin's "Environmental Mission Statement" above, and its overall approach to green citizenship, counters the logic of American consumer culture. They also show how vision and commitment can lead to innovation. The school's new dorms are certified by the U.S. Green Building Council's Leadership in Energy and Environmental Design (LEED) program (see www.usgbc.org). The buildings have reduced costs by saving water, maximizing light and geothermal energy, and centralizing recycling. Dorm designs encourage bicycles with easy access for storage. These practices lead to healthy indoor environments and improved air quality on campus. In many ways, Bowdoin College's environmental practices reflect Maine's overall approach to energy use: Maine requires 30% of all electricity sold in the state to be from renewable sources.

Bowdoin also infuses green practices into their service learning programs. One project involves the community partner Maine Energy Investment Corporation and its work on the Maine Green Power Connection (MGPC). The MGPC has linked over 50 businesses and individuals to green power from one of the state's 111 renewable energy facilities. The nonprofit has assisted seven of the state's colleges and universities, including the University of Maine, to shift over to partial use of green power. Environmental sociology students at Bowdoin devised a course project to research and assess available green energy options for the Harraseeket Inn in Freeport, Maine. By working with the owner, students were able to show the benefits and challenges of various power sources. Thus, students developed applicable skills regarding energy use and conservation, acquired a greater understanding of green energy issues for local economies, and provided a small business with valuable information it could not have afforded to collect on its own. Service learning projects in

environmental sociology offer an opportunity for students to support local sustainable practices while mastering their field (Pallant 1999).

Human beings face enormous environmental problems caused by a host of issues including fossil fuel dependency, modern consumption patterns, pollution, global warming,
poverty, militarization, and a growing water crisis. Solutions to these problems will require
a number of political, economic, and social responses, both local and global. The most powerful changes must occur on a structural level to limit the damage caused by industrial production and the energy that fuels factories and the global distribution of goods. Many
approaches to addressing environmental hazards relate to lifestyle changes in the way people
consume goods; construct their physical environment; and procure, use, and conserve
energy. However, while our consumer-driven culture intensifies environmental degradation,
it also obfuscates historical and contemporary examples of how groups and individuals have
successfully challenged status quo energy policies and consumption practices.

In particular, grassroots social movements have led the way in protecting communities
from dangerous practices and redirecting how society uses resources (Cable and Cable 1994).
Such forces have also raised the environmental consciousness of mainstream America. Thus,
despite the overwhelming saturation of commercial culture and its insatiable appetite for
energy use, Gallup polls show that 64% of Americans are concerned about the quality of
drinking water; 58% are worried about the contamination of rivers, reservoirs, and soil by
toxic waste; and over half believe the environment is "only fair" or "poor" (American
Sociological Association 2004). In addition, many Americans believe that a change in energy
policy is desirable. Polls show that in 2006, over 77% of Americans said that developing alternative energy should be the "top priority" for U.S. energy policy (Byrne et al. 2007).

This chapter begins with a general portrait of the problems facing our environment and
some of the possible alternatives to energy production and consumption practices that
might positively impact our ecological landscape. Next, we examine a brief history of energy
use, policy, and the environmental movement in the United States. Finally, we look at various case studies where students engaged in service learning projects or social action efforts
have been able to impact environmental change. Integrating a sociological imagination with
a commitment to civic engagement holds the possibility that students and their communities will be able to address environmental problems with critical strategies for change.

## THE ENVIRONMENT BY THE NUMBERS: A STATISTICAL PORTRAIT OF ENVIRONMENTAL CHALLENGES

Environmental problems in the United States are inextricably linked to lifestyle and
energy use. Fossil fuel use has become a major concern as the U.S. struggles with foreign
oil dependency in general and with particular issues such as the price of heating oil and

gas. Mass consumption and an automobile-based culture contribute to these issues. Few economists, political scientists, or other scholars would dispute that such dependency is at least indirectly related to (if not a direct cause of) conflicts in the Persian Gulf. The United States must compete with other countries (especially the rapidly growing consumer nation of China) for control over energy resources. The increased militarism around the world not only impacts the environment because of the amount of pollution and degradation it creates, but growing militarism itself is often a result of the need to compete for fossil fuels.

Because the stakes of environmental safety and security are so high, people in the United States (and around the world) are beginning to see the importance of environmental security. A good sign of this changing mentality is the growing effort to invest in renewable energy. For example, the proposed 2010 U.S. energy budget shows the growth in support for alternative energy research and use (see Table 6.1). Still, many critics of fossil fuels and their environmental impact argue that contemporary energy use patterns are completely unsustainable. Moreover, the United States continues to use more oil than any other country, by far.

The average person in the United States uses 459 gallons of petroleum annually, as compared to the average German (second highest) who uses 140 gallons in a year (Morris 2005). Today, humans use 3 times more water than 50 years ago and produce 4 times more carbon dioxide from the burning of fossil fuels (Brown 2005). **Fossil fuels**—defined as any fuel made from the burning of hydrocarbon deposits found in the Earth's crust such as oil, coal, gas, and propane—supply 85% of the energy consumed in the United States. While the major demand for these fuels comes from internal combustion engines, hydrocarbons are also the major power source for producing electricity (see Figure 6.1).

**Table 6.1**   U.S. Department of Energy Proposed Funding for 2010 Fiscal Year

| Energy Type | Dollars in Thousands | Percent Change from 2009 |
|---|---|---|
| Fossil | 881,565 | −20.6% |
| Nuclear | 884,632 | −37.8% |
| Solar | 175,000 | 82.9% |
| Wind | 75,000 | 36.4% |
| Geothermal | 50,000 | 13.6% |

*Source:* "FY 2010 DOE Budget Request to Congress," U.S. Department of Energy (http://www.cfo.doe.gov/budget/10budget/start.htm#Detailed Budget Justifications).

**Figure 6.1** Fuel Sources for United States Electricity Generation, 2008

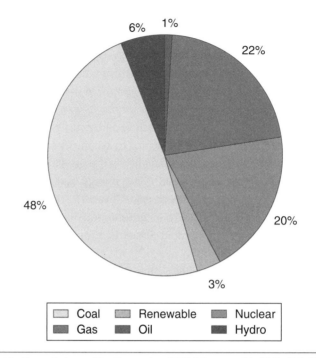

6% 1%

22%

20%

48%

3%

| ☐ Coal | ☒ Renewable | ▩ Nuclear |
| ▩ Gas | ▩ Oil | ▩ Hydro |

*Source:* "U.S. Electric Power Industry Net Generation 2008," January 21, 2010, U.S. Energy Information Administration (http://www.eia.doe.gov/cneaf/electricity/epa/figes1.html).

Even more alarming is that the United States imports over half (62%) of its petroleum, and this dependence on foreign sources is increasing. The two largest suppliers of oil to the United States include Canada and Mexico (U.S. Energy Information Administration 2010).

Since the U.S. economy is so closely tied with petroleum products and oil imports, small changes in prices or disruptions in production can have an enormous impact on our economy. The long-term supply of oil has been a concern of U.S. presidents and scientists since the First World War. Today, some commentators claim that the age of oil is rapidly nearing the end. Decades ago, Hubbert (1956) predicted that U.S. oil production would peak in the 1970s. Although oil exploration has expanded since the 1970s, demand continues to outpace new sources. The most striking evidence of oil's precarious future comes from the explosive demand for fossil fuels from Asian countries—especially China. Peak oil was also recently addressed in the Al Gore film *An Inconvenient Truth* (see also Brown 2006; Hubbert 1956; Strahan 2007). Similar to the 1970s oil embargo, recent oil price spikes are also destabilizing the U.S. economy. But the biggest threat to human survival comes from the ecological hazards created by massive fossil fuel consumption.

# FOSSIL FUELS AND GLOBAL WARMING

We've mentioned the many problems related to oil consumption, but natural gas and especially coal have proven equally difficult to manage and just as hazardous to the environment. Most dangerous is their causative relationship to global warming. **Global warming** refers to a gradual increase in the Earth's surface temperature. Since the 1950s, the Earth's surface temperature has risen anywhere from a half to a whole degree Centigrade. While seemingly a minor change, such small shifts have already intensified the melting of glaciers and the polar ice caps and raised sea levels significantly. Scientists unanimously consider this planetary overheating to have reached dangerous levels. If global warming continues unchecked, scientists predict that it will result in unimaginable instability as weather patterns will change drastically, major flooding and earthquakes will increase, and the basic resources of clean water and air necessary for survival will diminish.

The primary human-made cause of global warming is carbon dioxide in the atmosphere, and the primary source of carbon dioxide is fossil fuel consumption: burning oil, coal, and natural gas. As carbon dioxide accumulates in the atmosphere, the result is the **greenhouse effect.** Carbon dioxide allows less heat to escape, trapping solar radiation and thus heating the Earth's surface. The result is a warming effect on the Earth's surface, creating rising temperatures. Theorists suggest that the oil production of the Organization of Petroleum Exporting Countries (OPEC) will have to double by 2030 to meet growing global demand (Sieminski 2005). The United States emits more energy-related carbon dioxide than any other Organisation for Economic Co-operation and Development (OECD) country. Current estimates reveal that energy-related carbon emissions could rise 54% above 1990 levels by 2020 (Byrne et al. 2007).

The United States has 600 coal-fired plants, which produce 52% of the nation's electricity. The average 500-megawatt plant burns 1.4 million tons of coal each year. Coal pollutes when it is mined, transported to the power plant, stored, and burned. The same plant produces 125,000 tons of ash and 193,000 tons of sludge from a smokestack scrubber each year. Chemicals released into the atmosphere include arsenic, mercury, chromium, and cadmium. The typical coal-fired plant uses only 33% to 35% of its heat for electricity. The rest is released into the atmosphere or into cooling water (Union of Concerned Scientists 1999). Oxides and sulfur dioxide from coal-burning power plants are a major cause of **acid rain**—acidic precipitation from vehicle emission and burning coal, which can destroy forests and other ecosystems as well as seriously damage clean water and fresh air supplies

Because the cost to update coal-fired plants is in the billions of dollars, many companies have been reluctant to update them until recently. The process of extracting coal is also destructive to the environment and increasingly dangerous for the industry's workers.

From 1985 to 2001, a total of 724 miles of streams were buried under mining waste. Meanwhile, in an effort to meet consumption demands, the federal government reduced coal industry regulation and enforcement. The number of miners killed or injured in subsequent accidents has risen dramatically in the past few years, from 22 in 2005 to 47 in 2006 to 60 in 2007. Yet coal mining continues to be a major source of energy, with 50 new mines opening every year between 2004 and 2007 (Broder 2007; Union of Concerned Scientists 1999, 2007).

## Automobile Culture

The continuous sprawl of suburban highways, shopping malls, and housing developments along with the lack of adequate public transportation helps explain why the United States uses more oil than any other country. As automobile industries became more powerful after World War II, they helped to shape public policy that included major investments in public highway systems and the dismantling of public transportation systems. Today, Americans drive everywhere, even in the face of gridlock, air pollution, and road rage. Ironically, as sport utility vehicles (SUVs) have become a larger part of the U.S. auto market, the average vehicle is less efficient than the Model T of 80 years ago (Global Health Council 2006). According to the Environmental Defense Fund (2006), car makers produce a greater amount of carbon emissions than U.S. electric companies (see Figure 6.2).

**Figure 6.2**   Automakers vs. Electric Utilities for Carbon Emissions, Million Metric Tons (MMTc), 2004.

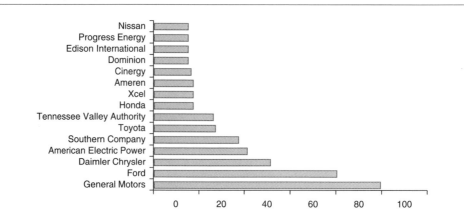

*Source:* "Global Warming on the Road: The Climate Impact of America Automobiles," 2006, by John DeCicco and Freda Fung. Environmental Defense Fund (http://www.edf.org/documents/5301_Globalwarmingontheroad.pdf).

Car culture is expensive. The United States spends $20 billion a year on routine road maintenance, clearing snow and filling potholes; $48 billion on traffic and parking coordination, law enforcement, and accident response teams; and an estimated $100 billion on highway congestion. Auto accidents kill 45,000 Americans each year, injure 5 million, and disable another 1.8 million. The estimated cost of auto accidents is $358 billion annually (Morris 2005). The number of Americans killed in auto accidents every year accounts for 44% of all accidental deaths and is equal to the number of Americans killed in the Vietnam War (Garling and Steg 2007). According to the World Health Organization (WHO), road crashes kill 1.2 million people and injure 50 million around the world each year (cited in Global Health Council 2006). Car culture also shapes the nation's natural landscape. Morris (2005) estimates that between 60% and 70% of the country is designed to accommodate cars in the form of highways, streets, and parking lots.

## CONSUMERISM AND A "THROWAWAY" CULTURE

Many of the environmental issues in the world today are linked to overconsumption and mass consumerism. Mass consumerism and its attendant "throwaway" mentality do create huge profits and jobs as corporations produce disposable commodities and people keep buying them. Overconsumption has contributed to a number of environmental problems such as resource depletion, water scarcities, global warming, and issues around solid waste management (Worldwatch Institute 2004). Ecologists point out that overconsumption can lead to the undermining of an entire species' life support system as well as individual human psychological problems such as obesity and perpetual dissatisfaction (Princen, Maniates, and Cenca 2002). Conflict sociologists note that consumption and the negative effects of production are not evenly divided across populations within the United States or across the world (Ćapek 2009; Foster 2002; Schnaiberg and Gould 1994). Critics of mass consumerism observe that the corporate goal of maximizing profit is not about satisfying needs, but persuading purchasers to buy regardless of need. Humans give meaning to the environment by transforming nature into cultural products (Fine 1998). Symbolic interactionists point out that one of the goals of advertising is to create dissatisfaction and a sense of inadequacy in order to increase sales (McGrane 1994). In *Born to Buy: The Commercialized Child and the New Consumer Culture* (2004), Juliet Shor articulates that children who are more involved in consumer culture are much worse off psychologically, more depressed and anxious, and have less self-esteem than other children. Begg (2000) contends,

Everywhere in the West, people are driven to purchase things they cannot afford, do not need, do not understand or are ignorant of the source of, trying to satisfy themselves as fast as advertisers can breed dissatisfaction. It seems that we can never have enough of the product that yesterday would bring eternal happiness, is today mundane and commonplace, and tomorrow will be obsolete and inadequate. (p. 78)

While the energy needed to manufacture goods is partly responsible for resource depletion and global warming, the solid waste produced by overproduction and consumption is another major cause of pollution. Packaging and plastic waste from products often end up in landfills where they destroy the environment. The average American produces 7 pounds of garbage a day, or 2,600 pounds a year. Americans throw away 80% of products after one use. With only 4.6% of the world's population, the United States produces 10 billion tons of solid waste per year, or 33% of the global total (Taylor and Morrissey 2004). By-products of mass consumption such as plastics, containers, and packaging make up the largest amount of garbage in the United States (see Figure 6.3).

**Figure 6.3**  Products Generated in Municipal Solid Waste, 2005

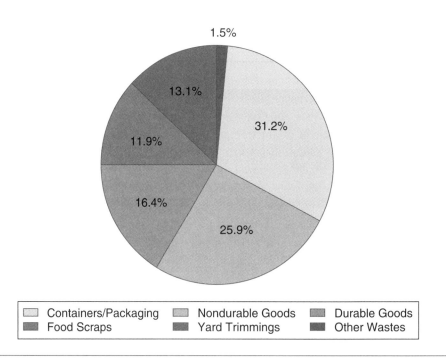

*Source:* "Municipal Solid Waste Generation, Recycling, and Disposal in the U.S.: Facts and Figures," 2005, U.S. Environmental Protection Agency.

The nation's communities fail to recycle large amounts of their waste, with 95% of plastic, 66% of glass containers, and 50% of aluminum cans not being recycled (Rogers 2005). The United States was once a country of vast open space. Today, the country requires more and more expansive land for its large volume of unrecycled garbage (see Figure 6.4). It takes 1 acre of land to store 40 tons of garbage. New York City alone produces 11,000 tons of garbage each day. Some of its trash is driven as far as 300 miles away to states like Pennsylvania, Virginia, and New Jersey (Brown 2002). With little open land left for waste dumps, European countries have been recycling effectively for 25 years. Denmark banned one-way soft drink containers in 1981. When the same trucks haul recycled containers back to the plant, they reduce traffic, congestion, and costs. Brown estimates New York City alone uses 550 rigs with 20 tons each to haul away its unrecycled trash each day—a convoy of trucks 9 miles long. Once, many goods were made to last a lifetime. Today, the same commodities are made to be quickly disposed of and then purchased over and over again. This set of economic and cultural behaviors slowly led—and now rapidly leads—us toward the brink of ecological disaster.

Some U.S. municipalities have instituted recycling and other similar programs. Aided by policies initiated by the Environmental Protection Agency in the 1990s, communities increased curbside recycling and composting. The result was a significant decrease in solid waste in those municipalities. Between 1988 and 2000, the number of landfills declined from 7,924 to 1,654. In 2005, the United States operated 8,550 curbside recycling and 3,470 composting programs (EPA 2005).

**Figure 6.4**   Percentage of Municipal Waste Recycled, 1960–2005

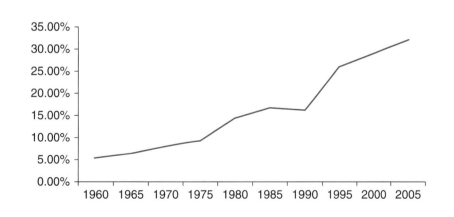

*Source:* "Municipal Solid Waste Generation, Recycling, and Disposal in the United States: Facts and Figures, 2005," U.S. Environmental Protection Agency.

# WATER SCARCITY AND WATER WARS

As economic growth has occurred, industry and agriculture have become principal users of the world's available water. Water supplies throughout the world are threatened by 2 million tons of industrial waste and chemicals, human waste, agricultural fertilizers, and pesticides yearly (Global Health Council 2006). Water use has increased in the last 50 years to the point where it has become a major global threat. The United Nations estimates that two-thirds of the world's population will live in water-scarce regions of the world by 2025. With the green revolution diverting water to agriculture and population increases since the 1950s, water scarcity has become common on almost every continent. Since 1950, over 45,000 dams have been built concentrating water flow leaving some areas without access to water. Over 97% of fresh water is stored in aquifers underground. The increased use of synthetic chemicals in the last 50 years is endangering these water supplies. From 1935 to 1995, the number of tons of chemicals used in the environment expanded from 150,000 to 150,000,000 tons (Global Health Council 2006).

Increasing agriculture production means the use of more water. Over 70% of available water sources are used in agriculture. Less than 1% of fresh water is available for human consumption (Thums 2004). Water is also threatened by development. Rainwater is polluted with pesticides from farms, houses, and industrial sites. The built environment also destroys water supplies with toxins as they run off into parking lots, sewers, and onto pavement.

According to the World Wildlife Fund (2004), only 4% of U.S. aid goes to water projects. This is evident when one looks at how water is distributed among the poor. Globally, 1.1 billion people do not have access to clean drinking water and 2.4 billion do not have proper sanitation.

In the United States, water wars are becoming commonplace. North Georgia competes for water with Atlanta, while California struggles with several other southwestern states for access to the Colorado River (Thums 2004). In the Middle East, a land viewed as rife with conflict over oil, water scarcity produces more serious interregional tensions as Israel, Palestine, Jordan, Turkey, Syria, Iraq, and Egypt all compete for the limited amount of fresh water. Several African countries constantly suffer from drought and water scarcity. China, too, is plagued by water degradation as an estimated 300 million Chinese lack access to clean drinking water due to industrial pollution. Industrial runoff and the burning of fossil fuels threaten rivers, lakes, and underwater aquifers in China's rural communities (Liv 2006). Contaminated water is the world's greatest killer, with 2.1 million people dying every year from a lack of water for drinking, sanitation, and hygiene. Children comprise 90% of those killed by water pollution (Global Health Council 2006).

Solutions to the water crisis, like other types of pollution, are found in altering consumption levels for both human populations and industry. Environmental organizations like the World Wildlife Fund (WWF) (www.worldwildlife.org) suggest that saving the planet's water supply must involve focuses on multiple partnerships. Focuses on local action must involve holding industry and agriculture more accountable for efficient use of water along with paying more for its availability. Individual efforts must also increase in order for water conservation to work. For instance, Thums (2004) estimates that a single flush of a Western toilet uses as much water as the average person in the developing world uses for a whole day for washing, drinking, cleaning, and cooking. Many Americans still use toilets made prior to the advent of the low-flush model.

## CORPORATE AGRICULTURE, AQUACULTURE, AND THE ENVIRONMENT

The rise of the factory farm is having a dramatic impact on the environment and health of rural areas. Critics contend that large industrial agricultural systems consume fossil fuels, water, and topsoil at unsustainable rates and introduce health hazards in the form of food-borne pathogens and occupational respiratory diseases (Horrigan, Lawrence, and Walker 2002). Because of the concentration of agriculture by a handful of corporations, agricultural policy in the United States is largely determined by these companies' practices (Food & Water Watch 2007). According to a report by Food & Water Watch, a Washington, DC-based nonprofit watchdog group, corporate farms are threatening human health and the environment in rural communities nationwide. Over 500 family farms in the United States close every week, while the majority of farm subsidies go to corporate and large farms. Critics say these Confined Animal Feeding Operations (CAFOs) raise hundreds of thousands of animals in unclean and inhumane environments. The concentration of production, meatpacking and slaughter, and animal operations into the hands of a few corporations means fewer farmers are involved in producing dairy, beef, pork, and poultry in the United States. The report found that four companies slaughter 80% of beef cattle and 60% of hogs. Today, half of all livestock is produced by 5% of the country's corporate farms. For some critics, these emerging political and economic consequences make industrial agriculture unsustainable (Edwards and Ladd 2000; Horrigan et al. 2002; Kimbrell 2002).

The concentration and mass production of farm animals reflect large companies' ability to control markets and take advantage of government farm subsidies. Corporate farms are exempt from clean air laws in many states, allowing them to concentrate animal waste in "lagoons," which become health hazards. The report cites numerous cases where concentrations of waste in lagoons have produced fish kills and other human health hazards such as E. coli outbreaks. One of the most reported stories is the June 2005 case where an 8-acre waste lagoon from a North Carolina hog factory burst, sending 25 million gallons of untreated swine feces and urine into the North Carolina New River, closing off 364,000 acres of fishing and recreational waters. This was followed by other spills and flooding from Hurricanes Dennis and Floyd, killing 30,000 hogs and flooding 50 waste lagoons (Food & Water Watch 2007). Corporate agriculture is linked to health hazards as well, including the overuse of antibiotics to promote growth and prevent disease in farm animals.

Likewise, over 1,000 inland aquaculture-based fish farms have emerged, mainly in southern states, to satisfy America's hunger for low-fat and high-protein catfish, tilapia, trout, and sea bass. Global marine fish stocks are increasingly stressed due to overfishing and growing demand. Studies on global marine ecosystems show that as many as 29% of species currently fished are near collapse (Dean 2006). In response to shrinking availability, inland fish farms are thriving. These new enterprises are

*(Continued)*

(Continued)

able to produce large amounts of fish in small tanks using wild fish food and circulating water systems. The runoff from fish farming can be dangerous for surrounding waterways. Fish farmers use *piscicide* (fish pesticide), *formalin* (for fungus control), and hormones (Food & Water Watch 2007). Like corporate livestock production, these farms change local ecosystems and alter the balance of nature.

## NUCLEAR POWER

One energy alternative to fossil fuels is even more controversial because of its potential environmental impact—**nuclear power,** which is produced by enriching uranium. Unlike coal, nuclear power does not lead to global warming through carbon emissions. However, hazards related to production and storage of nuclear waste threaten the health and safety of whole regions, not just local communities. Nuclear power plants produce high-level radioactive waste that is extremely toxic to organisms and can remain active for thousands of years. These plants emit high-level radiation and produce fuel rods, which must be stored away from populations. Contamination from nuclear waste is so powerful, far reaching, and long lasting, that finding adequate storage is a major problem: Few areas are considered safely isolated enough, few can build facilities strong enough to contain the radiation, and few can guarantee the storage safety for the generations that such waste remains dangerous. Thus, another problem is the hazard of transporting nuclear waste to storage facilities, as the only current permanent site for storing high-level nuclear waste is at Yucca Mountain near Los Vegas, Nevada, and even Yucca Mountain remains dangerous as it sits on an inactive volcano and earthquake fault line (Cable and Cable 1995; MacFarlane and Ewing 2006). Currently, there are 104 or so nuclear power plants making up 21% of total U.S. energy sources and 19% of electricity (see Table 6.2). European countries have been more reliant on nuclear power, with France generating 75% of its power from such sources. Globally, there are 440 nuclear plants producing 16% of electricity and plans to build 24 new plants worldwide—15 in the United States and United Kingdom (Guinnessy 2006).

Despite its present and potential dangers to the environment, some consider nuclear power to be a more environmentally friendly alternative than fossil fuels, and despite the memory of a major accident like the one at Chernobyl in the Ukraine or the "partial melt-down" at Three Mile Island in Pennsylvania, huge economic and political interests in nuclear energy remain. Critics, however, point out that new nuclear plants will require large amounts of uranium and that the waste from nuclear generators will last from 100,000 to 200,000 years (Byrne and Toly 2006).

**Table 6.2**   Percentage of Electricity Produced by Nuclear Energy by Country, 2008

| Country | Percent |
|---|---|
| France | 76.2 |
| Belgium | 53.8 |
| Sweden | 42 |
| South Korea | 35.2 |
| Switzerland | 39.2 |
| Hungary | 37.2 |
| Czech Republic | 32.5 |
| Finland | 29.7 |
| Germany | 28.3 |
| Japan | 24.9 |
| United States | 19.7 |
| Spain | 18.3 |
| Canada | 14.8 |
| United Kingdom | 13.5 |
| Mexico | 4 |

*Source:* "Nuclear Share Figures, 1998–2008," 2009, World Nuclear Association (http://www.world-nuclear.org/info/nshare.html).

## NUCLEAR ACCIDENTS AND A RISK SOCIETY

Nuclear power has often been described as the solution to the world's energy problems. However, in its history, it has been characterized as both an important energy source and a dangerous gamble leading to disaster. In fact, nuclear power in the 1950s was described as being too "cheap to meter" in the future. But by the 1970s and 1980s, huge cost overruns and a number of disasters halted the building of plants. In 1980, only 55% of plants were online. Today, the United States and various other countries are set to build new plants as a clean energy source. The new plants cost $4 billion each and will not be online for 10 years (Schoen 2007). The current push brings up a number of questions about the safety of nuclear power.

*(Continued)*

(Continued)

The German sociologist Ulrich Beck (1992) coined the term risk society to describe modern societal attitudes toward dangerous technology. He argues that humans now live in fear of losing control of their technologies. The social debates and fear over dangerous technology are part of living in a risk society. Debates over nuclear power are one such reality. In the United States, the 1979 Three Mile Island disaster is the nation's most dangerous nuclear accident to date. Located on the Susquehanna River near Middletown, Pennsylvania, and 100 miles from Washington, DC, the Three Mile Island nuclear generating station partially melted down on March 28, 1979. The plant malfunctioned, sending 32,000 gallons of coolant and radiation into the environment around the plant. After the accident, government officials released a statement advising pregnant women to leave the area. This was followed by the voluntary evacuation of 150,000 people. While contamination around Three Mile Island was thought to be minimal, the cleanup cost millions of dollars. The plant sits empty and unfueled today, serving as a reminder that nuclear power is not without danger and cost. The Three Mile Island incident led to an extensive public debate over the safety of nuclear power, bringing about sweeping changes to the industry and emergency management (Bell 2004; Cable and Cable 1995).

In April of 1986, the Chernobyl meltdown occurred, which was the worst nuclear disaster in history. Located near the town of Pripyat in the Ukraine, the Chernobyl accident forced the evacuation and relocation of 330,000 people and contaminated additional land areas in Germany, Scandinavia, Austria, Belarus, Russia, Poland, Slovakia, Hungary, and Romania. The fire that melted the core of the plant lasted for 10 days, releasing large amounts of radioactive iodine-131 and caesium-137 and contaminating an area containing 5 million people. The accident left an "exclusion zone" of an area that had contained about 116,000 people around the plant. The long-term impacts of the Chernobyl disaster include relocation trauma and increased incidents of thyroid disease. Along with radiation, the economic damage to the countries of Belarus and the Ukraine has been dramatic. In 1991, Belarus spent 22% of its national budget on the accident. The accident removed 784,320 hectares of agricultural land from production (Bell 2004; International Atomic Energy Agency 2005).

The two accidents described above show the reality of a risk society. While the debates surrounding nuclear energy have led to improvements in safety, tragedies still occur. As countries launch new plants, these incidents and debates are reminders of the real costs of nuclear power.

## RENEWABLE AND SUSTAINABLE RESOURCES

The movement to replace fossil fuels with renewable energy sources in the United States has come mainly from environmental groups but also from states (see Figure 6.5). **Renewable energy** describes energy sources that are not depleted and have less impact on the environment and in some case no impact at all. The main form of renewable energy resource used today is hydro, or water, power. However, increased research, a growing demand, and energy policies are behind the expanding use of biomass, solar, and wind energy. As of 2007, a total of 41 of 50 states are pursuing policies for renewable energy and energy efficiency market development, and 23 states have renewable electricity standards requiring a minimum percentage of power from clean energy sources, or what is termed a *renewable portfolio standard* (RPS). According to the U.S. Department of Energy (U.S. Energy Information Administration 2009), consumption of renewable fuels is growing by 3.3% per year, much faster than the 0.5% annual growth in total energy use. Nationally, over 600 utility companies in 36 states use *green pricing*. These programs allow consumers to purchase green energy (Byrne et al. 2007; Union of Concerned Scientists 2007). According to the U.S. Department of Energy (2009), "The primary goals of the National Energy Policy are to increase our energy supplies using a more diverse mix of domestic resources and to reduce our dependence on imported oil" (n.p.).

The Office of the Biomass Program's activities directly support the overall mission and priorities of the Department of Energy, Office of Energy Efficiency and Renewable Energy, and the government's National Energy Policy by contributing to the creation of a new bioindustry and reducing U.S. dependence on foreign oil by supplementing the use of petroleum for fuels and chemicals.

**Figure 6.5**  Total U.S. Energy Sources, 2005

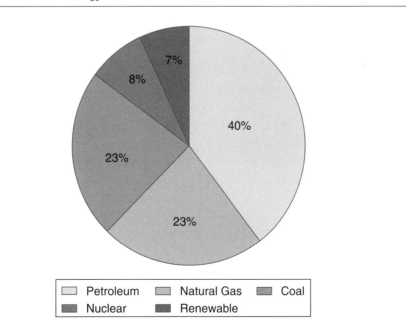

*Source: Renewable Energy Trends in Consumption and Electricity,* 2005, Energy Information Administration, U.S. Department of Energy.

As a domestic, renewable energy source, biomass offers an alternative to conventional energy sources and provides national energy security, economic growth, and environmental benefits. *Biomass* energy forms are made up of any organic material from plants or animals. Biomass can come from domestic resources such as agricultural and forestry residues, municipal solid wastes, industrial wastes, and terrestrial and aquatic crops (U.S. Department of Energy 2006). **Biofuels,** fuels produced from biomass materials such as grain crops, soy and corn, and non-food crops such as switchgrass and woody crops, include ethanol, methanol, biodiesel, biocrude, and methane. Biofuels are essentially nontoxic and they biodegrade readily. Every gallon of biofuel used reduces the hazard of toxic petroleum product spills from oil tankers and pipeline leaks. In addition, using biofuels reduces the risk of groundwater contamination from underground gasoline storage tanks and runoff of vehicle engine oil and fuel. The U.S. transportation sector is responsible for one-third of the country's carbon dioxide ($CO_2$) emissions, the principal greenhouse gas contributing to global warming. While biofuels when they burn release $CO_2$, they also capture it because biofuels are made from live plants, which reduce CO emission as they grow.

> Modern, high-yield corn production is relatively energy intense, but the net greenhouse gas emission reduction from making ethanol from corn is still about 20%. Making biodiesel from soybeans reduces net emissions nearly 80%. Producing ethanol from cellulosic material also involves generating electricity by combusting the non-fermentable lignin. The combination of reducing both gasoline use and fossil electrical production can mean a greater than 100% net greenhouse gas emission reduction. (U.S. Department of Energy 2006:1)

Other growing energy sources in the United States are biodiesel and ethanol. The United States is second in the world in ethanol production with 91 million gallons in 2005. The use of these fuels has increased due in part to the availability of corn and soybeans. Ethanol is made from corn, and biodiesel is made from soybeans. Ethanol provides much of Brazil's fuel for vehicles. While still a small part of the U.S. fuel sources, these types of energy are expanding rapidly. Ethanol is expected to absorb 20% of the U.S. corn crop for 2006 (Burger 2006). More recently, gas prices and consumption increases have led to concerns about the impact on food supplies from turning corn and other agricultural products into fuel.

## WIND AND SOLAR ENERGY

Use of alternatives to fossil fuels is increasing as the cost of production declines and the demand grows. The 2005 U.S. Energy Policy Act requires that 3% of energy must come from renewable sources in 2007–2009, 5% by 2010–2012, and 7.5% by 2013 (Byrne et al. 2007). In addition, corporate investment in alternative energy is expanding. British Petroleum (BP), for example, is pushing alternative energy and investing heavily in both solar and wind energy as oil becomes more difficult to produce. Car companies are also moving into the alternative energy market with hybrid vehicles becoming increasingly popular alternatives. Critics of U.S. energy policy suggest that a shift in tax breaks from oil, coal, and gas industries toward sustainable and renewable sources producing no carbon emissions would do more to solve energy problems than continued investment in the environmentally destructive practices of fossil fuel use (Brown 2001).

The average cost of a kilowatt of wind power declined from 32 cents to 8 cents from 1980 to 2002 (Brown 2003). While the United States creates less than 3% of its electricity from wind, research on wind technology is increasing. Wind energy can make a significant contribution to a diversified energy policy. For instance, Denmark produces 20% of its electricity from wind turbines with a growth rate of 35% a year since 1997. Other countries have similar patterns, with Spain increasing wind energy 30% a year and Germany 68% a year since 1997 (Byrne and Toly 2006). Growth in wind energy use is a sign that a diversity of energy sources is occurring, as fossil fuels are linked to environmental destruction. Figure 6.6 shows the growing number of megawatts produced by wind power facilities in the United States.

Like wind energy, solar power makes up a small part of the U.S. energy equation, with less than 1% of U.S. energy currently coming from solar. Solar mainly has a small-scale energy potential, which some theorists see as an empowering potential. It is emerging as the energy of the future. A few dozen companies are investing in an already growing market. As the cost of solar energy declines, it is becoming closer in price to other fossil fuels.

**Figure 6.6**   Wind Energy Use in Megawatts, 1981–2005

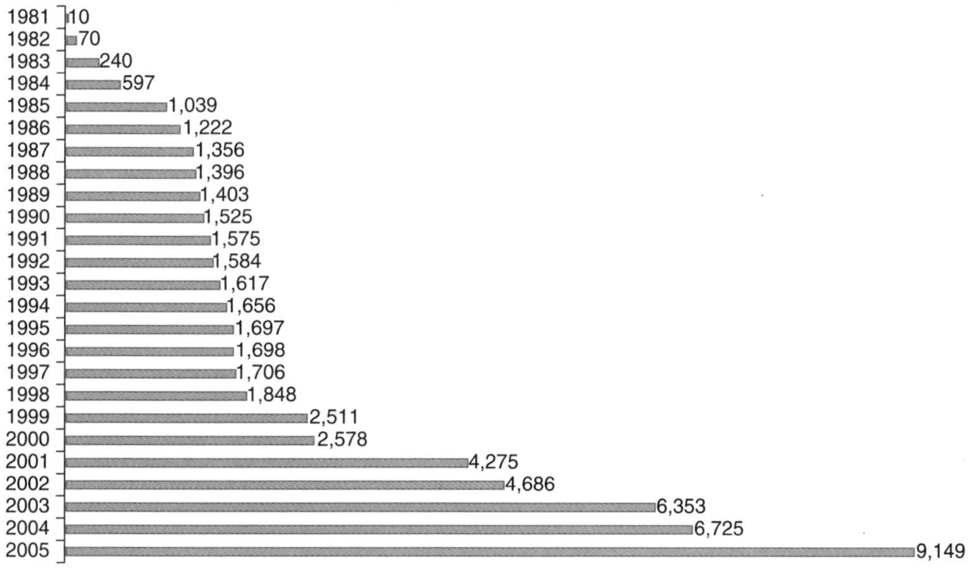

| Year | Megawatts |
|------|-----------|
| 1981 | 10 |
| 1982 | 70 |
| 1983 | 240 |
| 1984 | 597 |
| 1985 | 1,039 |
| 1986 | 1,222 |
| 1987 | 1,356 |
| 1988 | 1,396 |
| 1989 | 1,403 |
| 1990 | 1,525 |
| 1991 | 1,575 |
| 1992 | 1,584 |
| 1993 | 1,617 |
| 1994 | 1,656 |
| 1995 | 1,697 |
| 1996 | 1,698 |
| 1997 | 1,706 |
| 1998 | 1,848 |
| 1999 | 2,511 |
| 2000 | 2,578 |
| 2001 | 4,275 |
| 2002 | 4,686 |
| 2003 | 6,353 |
| 2004 | 6,725 |
| 2005 | 9,149 |

*Sources:* U.S. Department of Energy, Wind Energy Program and the U.S. Wind Energy Association.

Small-scale solar applications are well established throughout the world. Panels are used for water heaters, ovens, and other home uses such as lighting systems. Solar energy is also used for some large-scale electricity production. Small-scale solar heating is proving effective, especially in developing nations. Solar power is defined as either *passive* (space heating without the use of pumps or fans to distribute collected heat, such as through the use of solar panels on a home or greenhouse) or *active* (in which collection devices gather solar energy, which is transferred to liquid or air and stored). Active solar production of electricity involves solar thermal electric generation. Electricity is produced through protovoltaic (PV) solar cells, which transmit and store energy from sunlight (Byrne et al. 2007).

## RECYCLING AND GREEN ENERGY: THE CASE OF EUROPE

The United States can learn how to reduce its energy appetite and wasteful practices from other developed nations. Because of strong Green political parties, little room for landfill space, and limited amounts of fossil fuels, European countries have taken greater measures to prevent environmental degradation through recycling and putting pressure on industry and citizens to use less fossil fuels. With gasoline in European Union (EU) countries between $4 and $5 a gallon (U.S.), cars are smaller and use of public transportation is more common. EU countries have waste reduction as a national goal. The Netherlands is attempting to cut waste by 70% through pollution taxes and recycling. The country cut discharges of heavy metals into waterways by over 70% between 1972 and the mid-1990s (Sampat 2001). Instead of offering free plastic bags or paper bags, German grocery and other stores charge customers for bags if they do not have a personal one. Germany instigated its Package Ordinance in 1991, making manufacturers and retailers responsible for package recycling. As a result, most Germans carry a canvas bag to grocery stores for purchases. Many EU countries have provided good access to public transportation and strongly promote the use of bicycles. London buses carry 2 million people daily, as driving a vehicle into the city now costs $14 in "Congestion Tax" (Brown 2006).

Europeans have also begun to address industrial use of resources. In order to decrease the amount of energy and resources used by industry, Western European nations are shifting the focus of taxes away from income and toward the environment. The new taxes on environmentally destructive practices focus on taxing fuel use from cars, trucks, coal burning, and electricity along with waste production from garbage generation. Many European and Australian cities faced with congestion and smog have reduced air problems by taxing incoming drivers and investing the money in public transportation. Some countries are taxing low-fuel-mileage vehicles more than high-mileage ones. The taxes have a health benefit, which also saves money. Reducing air pollution from smokestacks and tailpipes decreases respiratory illnesses and lowers health costs. Other benefits of increasing use of renewable fuels are less congestion, safer roads, and rapid economic growth. The focus on alternatives to fossil fuels is also leading to investment in renewable sources of energy. Lester Brown (2006) describes the changes this way: "A four-year plan adopted by Germany in 1999 systematically shifted taxes from labor to energy. By 2001, this plan had lowered fuel use by 5 percent. It had also accelerated growth in the renewable energy sector, creating some 45,400 jobs by 2003 in the wind industry alone, a number that is projected to rise to 103,000 by 2010" (p. 2). Should the United States try to reduce the impact of production and consumption by taxing companies and retailers for the disposal of products? How should the United States increase the amount of green alternatives to its current unsustainable energy systems based on fossil fuel dependency and wasteful practices?

## A HISTORY OF ENERGY USE AND ENVIRONMENTAL MOVEMENTS

Energy is used for human survival. Historically, societies had little access to energy. Greater use of energy accompanied economic development in the 20th century. This greater energy use has meant more pollution and waste. As underdeveloped countries have begun to grow economically, the world faces increasing challenges. The 20th century also witnessed the rise of social movements to protect the environment. As we will see in this section, environmental activism is a major catalyst for change in the use of energy and its attendant environmental destruction.

Because energy was scarce, conservation of available energy has been crucial for survival. Even the early societies, however, had some impact on the environment. Redman (1999) has shown that these societies engaged in relationships with nature, some of which were sustainable and others destructive. Some societies lived in relative harmony with their environment, while others engaged in actions that led to the total depletion of resources. Pollution from deforestation and industrial development is not new. The beginning of industrialization in Europe was fueled by burning coal and wood. Early urban populations had no sanitation and little access to clean water. In Europe, and later in the United States, industrial by-products polluted cities and waterways and destroyed nearby countrysides.

Twentieth-century industrialization and expanding residential settlements led to clear-cutting of U.S. forests by the 1930s. Meanwhile, drought, erosion, and poor agricultural practices resulted in tragic "dust storms" in the South and Midwest. With the chemical revolution following World War II, large-scale agriculture and synthetic compounds led to mass consumption, particularly in the United States. From plastic consumer goods to pesticides, chemicals have changed the way people live. Increases in technology and personal transportation using inexpensive fossil fuels have expanded the global economy. During the last half of the 20th century, the amount of economic activity increased by sevenfold.

In the year 2000 alone, the growth of world economic activity was more than that of the entire 19th century (Kline 2000).

Following the Second World War, nuclear power and advances in hydroelectricity fueled massive growth. The Tennessee Valley Authority expanded electricity in the South, adding dams, nuclear power plants, and coal-fired steam plants. However, the use of chemicals and fossil fuels took a heavy toll on American communities. In 1948, toxic smog in the town of Donora, Pennsylvania, killed 20 people and sickened 6,000, or 43% of the population. Throughout the 1950s, urban air pollution killed thousands of people in London, New York, and Los Angeles (Layzer 2006). Improvements in environmental protection followed several well-publicized environmental catastrophes in the 1960s. By the time of Earth Day on April 22, 1970, there was a growing environmental awareness among even average Americans. The founder of Earth Day, Gaylord Nelson (2002), describes the nation's slow awaking to its legacy:

> It was a time when people could see, smell, and taste pollution. The air above major cities such as New York and Los Angeles was orange. Lake Erie was proclaimed dead, and backyard birds were dying from a chemical known as DDT. Public interest was further piqued by two environmental catastrophes that captured headlines from coast to coast earlier that year. The first was a large oil tanker spill offshore Santa Barbara that left the public with images of sea birds coated with oil. Then in June of 1969, the Cuyahoga River—slick with oil and grease and littered with debris—caught fire and shot flames high into the air in Cleveland. That image, widely circulated in the popular press, burned its way into the nation's collective memory as the poster child for the environmental atrocities of the time. (p. 6)

Yet it was the energy crisis of the mid-1970s that appeared to shock people into action, as ordinary citizens began to realize the potential impact of not looking for effective alternatives to oil and other fossil fuels. This "slow awakening" would speed up as environmental and nuclear disasters impacted peoples' environmental consciousness in the late 1970s and 1980s:

- In 1977, dangerous levels of toxic chemicals were discovered in backyards and parks at Love Canal, New York.

- In 1979, a nuclear reactor partially melted down at Three Mile Island.

- In 1984, in Bhopal, India, a Union Carbide gas leak killed 4,000 people right away and injured 30,000, a third of whom later died excruciating deaths.

- In 1986, a nuclear reactor in Chernobyl, Ukraine, exploded, resulting in 54 direct deaths and an estimated 10,000 related cancer deaths.

- In 1989, the oil tanker *Exxon Valdez* ran aground in Alaska, spilling 11 million gallons of crude oil into the ecosystems (Heran 2010).

- In 2010, the Deepwater Horizon, a British Petroleum (BP) oil rig, exploded in the Gulf of Mexico. It is estimated that 35,000 to 60,000 barrels have leaked each day in the 87 days since the explosion (current estimate as this book goes to press). The same amount of oil leaked every three days as the total amount leaked by the *Exxon Valdez* (Broder 2010).

These environmental crises resulted in changing trends in industrialized countries characterized by smaller cars and policies promoting protection of the environment. They also helped buttress an American environmental movement that had started growing early in the century, but had only begun to gather momentum in the late 1960s and early 1970s. Environmental legislation in the 1970s emerged as a response to the industrial dangers of the 20th century. The Environmental Protection Agency (EPA) was formed in 1970 with the charge of providing leadership in environmental science, research, education, and assessment (Leon-Guerrero 2004). It was followed by the Clean Air Act (1970), Endangered Species Act (1973), Toxic Substances Control Act (1976), and Clean Water Act (1977).

Early responses to industrialization and the desire to "conserve and protect nature," stirred early activists and made conservation a part of the early 20th-century reform movement in the United States. The Sierra Club, Audubon Society, and the Wilderness Society, along with the national parks movement, were responses to the impact of the expansion of capitalism on the environment in America (Kline 2000). But it was Rachel Carson's 1962 book *Silent Spring* that helped to foster a new consciousness of the effects of the chemical revolution and industrial pollution on society. Ecologists introduced the idea of the embeddedness of human affairs in the environment, critiquing the compartmentalizing of environmental problems and Western ideas in the control of nature (Schmidt 2005). James Lovelock's (1979) controversial "Gaia hypothesis" described the Earth as a self-balancing mechanism with the destruction of one location affecting other locations and processes. The science of ecology introduced the idea that the impact of human activity on the physical environment can serve as a delimiting factor of human societies and capitalism (Commoner 1992; Davis 1989; Lovelock 1979; Nolt 2005). European Green political parties organized in the 1960s created permanent pressure to enact green policies. In Germany, the Green Party effectively influenced the nation's policies on recycling and industrial and consumer waste management. The green movement encompasses conservation and counterculture groups. Research and policy groups include organizations such as the Worldwatch Institute and Lester Brown's Earth Policy Institute in Washington, DC (Cable and Cable 1995; Castells 2004). In the United States, conservationist groups collectively known as the Group of Ten merged politically to address wilderness preservation, urban sprawl, and other conservation causes. Many groups have emerged based on self-interest such as Not in My Backyard movements (NIMBYS). In other cases, more radical groups (Earth First, Greenpeace, ecofeminists) have partnered with conservation groups to counter development impacts on the environment (Castells 2004; Kline 2000).

In academia, environmental ecology and sociology, among other disciplines, grew out of the social turmoil of the 1960s. As a product of environmental social movements of that era, environmental sociology is a relatively recent field, concerned with investigating social interest in the human environment, its impact on society, and how it changes. Broadly, environmental sociology is the study of the interaction between the environment and society (Dunlap 1997). Understanding environmental social problems requires looking at how environmental concerns are identified, and like other social problems, how groups define a problem and what should be done to solve it (Buttel 1997). This includes studying how social movements influence social policy and the distribution of social justice (Bullard 1990; Cable and Cable 1995). Environmental sociologists and ecologists focus on the impact of human societies on the **carrying capacity** of the environment—how much life its natural resources can support. Adding to this approach are social theorists who use the idea of an **ecological footprint** left by human activities on the environment. All of these have in common the idea that energy use must be redefined in the context of its impact on the environment and that the scale of human economic expansion must not exceed the capacity of the biosphere (Chambers, Simmons, and Wackernagel 2000; Global Footprint Network 2009). This concept focuses on the ability of the environment to absorb human demand on it. Carrying capacity is threatened when the impact of human activities exceeds sustainable levels for the environment. There are numerous examples of humans exceeding the capacity of the environment today. For instance, when overfishing occurs, demand can destroy a species. Carrying capacity also refers to how much fish, trees, crops, air, and water can be extracted before the supply is damaged as a resource.

Sociologists are also concerned with consumption. *Consumption* is defined as the rate of resources used by a given population (Wallace 1998). Environmental sociologists point to the ever-increasing needs of humans and their impact on environmental systems in order to expand the economy for consumer goods and basic needs for growing populations. Inequality, in terms of the unequal impact of environmental degradation, is a central focus of environmental sociology (Schnaiberg and Gould 1994). The impacts of human activity on natural systems are depleting and damaging ecosystems. Yet, many of the issues addressed as social problems of the environment are controversial. The field includes analysis of energy policy, especially dependency on fossil fuels. Contemporary environmental social problems and lifestyle cannot be separated. Polluted water or air does not stop at political or state borders. While race and class play an important role in exposure to toxins, the future of all generations is at risk due to modern society's environmentally threatening practices. C. Wright Mills's (1959) idea that social problems involve the personal and the public as interwoven perhaps is best highlighted in looking at the environment. Key to changes in consciousness of the impact of humans on the environment was the emergence of local, regional, and international grassroots citizens' groups, community organizations, and nonprofit organizations (Brown and Mikkelson, 1990/1997; Cable and Cable 1995; Wade 2007).

## MEDIA BOX: THE RISE OF GREEN CONSCIOUSNESS

The mass media plays an important role in the public's consciousness of social problems. Multiple stake-holders ranging from environmental groups to energy companies use the media to attempt to shape consciousness and shape social policy (Cox 2006). Environmental groups throughout the 20th century used the media in effective ways to foster public consciousness, increasing visibility and mobilizing support for conservation and anti-pollution policies. Neuzil and Kovarik (1996) argue that prior to the 1960s environmental movement, the mass media was instrumental in generating debate over public land preservation, unleaded gasoline, and deadly air pollution. In her 2006 book *Communicating Nature: How We Create and Understand Environmental Messages,* Julia Corbett traces the rise of the environmental movement and then the movement of the idea toward a mass marketing ploy. She suggests, "From the 1970s onward, while the American public accepted the most basic premise of environmental protection, the very meaning of environmentalism and environmentalists was being appropriated. The percentage of citizens expressing support for the environment (which does not equate with support for the movement, however) is phenomenally high. This is due to the environmental movement's success—not its failure—in permeating its message into the public's psyche" (p. 306).

Today, the mass media is bringing environmental social problems into the mainstream's consciousness. Issues such as global warming and strip-mining are debated in the public's eye much the same as issues regarding public land were debated at the turn of the 20th century. Similarly, the media has increased its role in assessing environmental risks. Unlike the positive impact that media coverage of the environment has had on public consciousness, the media's "framing" of such problems is not always as enlightening.

The media's drive to combine information with entertainment in search of advertising revenue sometimes distorts the *daily* impact of so many environmental issues, instead focusing on the spectacular events such as Three Mile Island, or Bhopal, or Chernobyl. Critics argue that this focus comes at the expense of reporting on less entertaining and more everyday hazards such as hazardous waste dumping, the burning of fossil fuels, or even the growing use of plastic packaging (Allen 2000). In your experiences, what types of mass media information have provided the most input into your awareness of environmental problems?

## CASE STUDY #1

### Action Research, Lead Poisoning, and University/Community Commitments

Functionalist sociologists point out that the environmental crisis is a by-product of cultural values and technology. Conspicuous consumption is a part of the American mindscape. However, they also argue that past environmental problems were solved with laws cleaning up industrial pollution

*(Continued)*

(Continued)

(Mooney, Knox, and Schacht 2007). The basic premise of functionalism, (i.e., society is interconnected and change in one area leads to changes in other areas), guides their stance on the environment. Ideally, the interplay between forces in society can solve environmental problems as well as cause them. Functionalists also argue that capitalism will "turn green" as it becomes more profitable and, therefore, will do so in its own interest (Plumwood 2002). They point out that the negative impacts of technology are latent or hidden dysfunctions that eventually lead to social change. The rise of alternative energy can be seen as a proof that capitalism can address alternative energy sources if and when they become profitable. However, the latent dysfunctions have important negative consequences and are a major concern for public health. Service learning can be an important mechanism for finding solutions to the problems caused by past technology.

Lead in the human environment is a major public health concern. Found in houses built before 1978, lead in paint is a serious health concern for children who live in older houses. The post–World War II chemical revolution contributed to a greater quality of life but now is responsible for health hazards. Using functionalist analysis, we can also see how institutions can come together to solve the hazards from past development. Below, we look at an action research project involving the Lead Safe Omaha Coalition (LSOC) and service learning students at the University of Nebraska at Omaha. The collaboration shows how coalitions can emerge from different institutions to solve environmental problems in society.

Shireen Rajaram's service learning students in medical sociology at the University of Nebraska at Omaha (UNO) engaged in a project that let them see firsthand the impact of social forces on the health and well-being of the community. The project involved collecting baseline data and increasing awareness of lead poisoning in the eastern section of Omaha in Douglas County. Lead toxicity and contamination in older homes are dangerous problems in communities with aging homes. Because their bodies are small and still developing, children absorb 3 times as much lead as adults. Exposure can mean developmental delays, behavioral problems, and other physical and mental impairments. Exposure to lead comes from peeling and chipping of old paint in homes and also from contamination of air and water caused by industrial pollution. As is the case in many areas, African American children were most concentrated in the rentals and older homes with lead exposure in Omaha (Bullard 2005). Rajaram (2007) points out that Omaha was designated the largest residential site for superfund cleanup in the country in 2002.

The project involved coordinating a design for using research to address the problem with the Lead Safe Omaha Coalition. Organized in 1997, LSOC is a nonprofit, grassroots, community-based organization (CBO) made up of community members, grandparents, and child care givers. This is an example of action research, which addresses social problems through collaborations and partnerships valuing the specialized knowledge and work of community groups, researchers, and students (Greenwood 1998; Nyden, Figert, Shibley, and Burrows 1997). Unlike traditional research models, action research involves the community directly in the research, producing a collaboration that identifies and analyzes a problem, finds a solution by utilizing research methods, and tests the solution. UNO's collaboration also included the local health department. Participants coordinated research to map housing with high levels of lead content, assess how much people knew about the lead problem in their community, and discover the best method for disseminating information and raising awareness. The team produced a questionnaire and visited a total of 282 homes, distributing pamphlets and other information on lead poisoning. Follow-up surveys went to some 3,000 homes the following summer. Students and LSOC staff did door-to-door interviews in high lead-contaminated east Omaha neighborhoods. Also involved were AmeriCorps, Vista, EPA, and the city of Omaha planning department (Rajaram 2007).

Action research is designed to allow communities to take advantage of the skills and labor that universities have to offer. In this case, LSOC was able to do the outreach with the service learning students. Input for the community at every stage of the process helped to identify community problems and find solutions to those problems. Rajaram (2007) articulates that the program helps the nonprofit build trust, draw media attention, and better understand community needs. When college students become engaged in service learning with grassroots community groups, their activities often lead to social change. Importantly, the data revealed that people are not well informed about the hazards and that the homes contaminated had children under 6 years old who spent time in the house on a regular basis.

Students studying medical sociology look at the role of social forces in creating public health outcomes. Service learning provides an important opportunity to see these social forces in action. In this case, learning about the quality of substandard housing and lead contamination helped students make the connection between lead and children in low-income households. These new experiences provided students with concrete examples of the relationships between environmental forces and race and class. The project involved developing research skills including survey and communication techniques. The service learning class incorporated readings on lead poison prevention, presentations on the history of the LSOC, and experience with analyzing, interpreting, and presenting findings. Comments from student participants reveal they also developed a greater awareness of the sociological imagination:

> If someone watched a videotape of us going door-to-door each week, it would be hard to convince them that we were in the same city, not to mention less than a couple of miles from where we were before. Education, race, income and attitude were just a few obvious differences we found just from observation.

And as another student noted,

> I felt that I was able to look at the problems associated with lead contamination from the inside and see how the little intricate pieces fit and work together to make this a serious problem for children, the poor, and the uninsured. The problem of lead poisoning is very much social in origin. Although the physical aspect of lead is present, it is the social factors that produce the vulnerability to it. (Rajaram 2007:144)

Action research requires that colleges and community partners develop research projects that fit the needs of the community, not the needs of a researcher. The collaboration of the University of Nebraska at Omaha shows how social institutions can be integrated to solve social problems. In the case of LSOC and lead poisoning, service learning provides needed support to the community.

*(Continued)*

(Continued)

Case Study Questions

1. What is distinctive about action research?

2. Why was action research a good fit to address lead poisoning in communities in Omaha?

3. How do functionalists see causes of and solutions to environmental problems?

4. What did the students add to the community's quality of life in the LSOC project?

## ENVIRONMENTAL THREATS AND NATIVE AMERICANS: NAVAJO NATION ENVIRONMENTAL PROTECTION AGENCY

Responses to environmental threats in the 20th century are filtered through cultural lenses. Native American societies are especially affected by slow or limited response. Exposure to nuclear and toxic waste has plagued Native American communities since the Second World War (Adamson 2001; Bullard 1990; LaDuke 1999). Native communities have found themselves exposed to nuclear power and waste, military operations and waste sites, and industrial pollution. The Navajo Environmental Protection Commission was established in 1972 to provide a tribal mechanism to counter environmental degradation. It was not until 1995, however, that enabling legislation made the Navajo Nation Environmental Protection Agency (NNEPA) a separate regulatory entity within the executive branch of the Navajo Nation government. NNEPA is charged with protecting the human health, welfare, and environment of the Navajo Nation. In April 1995, the Navajo Nation Council passed the Navajo Nation Environmental Policy Act, which provides guidance for NNEPA and asserts the Navajo philosophy regarding the protection of Mother Earth (U.S. Environmental Protection Agency [EPA] 2006). The NNEPA has produced an inventory of actual and potential point source discharges on Navajo Nation land. The NNEPA Water Quality Program was set up to monitor and evaluate water quality problems on the Navaho Reservation in Window Rock, Arizona. The program looks after environmental quality issues on the reservation, which include overflowing sewer lagoons, indiscriminate dumping of septic tank waste, discharges of wastewater from oil field tank batteries, unchecked storm water runoff from both industrial and construction utility sites, as well as unpermitted off-reservation discharges impacting the Navajo Nation. The council provides education on factors affecting water quality and the value and function of wetlands. Through education, the value of conservation, restoration, and protection of the Navajo Nation watersheds can be realized for our children and their future (EPA 2006).

## CASE STUDY #2

### Changing the Way We See the Environment:
### Service Learning and Economic Development

The Allegheny College Department of Environmental Science seems like an odd place to find examples of economic solutions to job cuts. But this is what Professor Eric Pallant found when he began a service learning project in his junior seminars in environmental science called Sustainable Solutions. Pallant (1999) planned to grow fish in tanks warmed by heat waste at a former factory and use fish excrement from the aquaculture tanks to nourish vegetables (mainly tomatoes) and herbs in a greenhouse enterprise. His venture into aquaculture happened just as Allegheny College was becoming more involved in the surrounding town of Meadville, Pennsylvania. Meadville lost many of its main industries in the 1980s. As the town saw zipper maker Talon and other factories close, unemployment from deindustrialization affected its infrastructure. Like many rural towns across the country, Meadville is struggling in a postindustrial economy with poverty, job loss, and job creation. The county (Crawford) also has a legacy of *brownfields,* or abandoned industrial sites, left by heavy industry. Whereas much of the nation's investment in development occurs in the sprawling suburbs outside of inner cities and rural towns, finding sustainable economic solutions for these areas is perhaps America's most pressing development challenge.

Pallant (1999) researched how the hydroponic farming of fish could be sustainable, and in the fall of 1996, a group of 15 students investigated the feasibility of an aquaponics business in Meadville. The seminar consisted of designing the business through choosing the product and markets, calculating the energy requirements to heat fish tanks and pump water to greenhouse vegetables, and determining if the system could run off heat wasted by existing industry. The project ran over a single semester and into future service learning classes. Students produced a feasibility study that came to the attention of the Meadville Redevelopment Authority and the Crawford County Development Corporation (Pallant 1999). The class was difficult for the students and the professor to assess. However, their actions changed both the students themselves and the community. Pallant states,

> By the end of the semester, my original prediction stood unamended: It would be years before my class could have a reunion dinner of broiled Tilapia served on a bed of greenhouse lettuce. But the class was still a success, and for reasons I hadn't imagined. We introduced the business community of northwest Pennsylvania to sustainable development, and they loved it. (p. 94)

Changing the view of how the environment is linked to development is one of the goals of the environmental sciences. However, this is usually done in the context of the classroom and not the community.

*(Continued)*

(Continued)

By the end of the project, the business community along with engineers and the Small Business Administration were interested in the project, although it was only a proposal. Development officials used the project as a model for small businesses. The project also opened their minds to alternatives to "chasing smokestacks," or hard-to-find industrial jobs.

> Allegheny College's Environmental Science students have really influenced our thinking in making the environment a priority in whatever we do. Because our offices are at a site that was a Superfund site, we want to continue to work with companies that will keep the environment clean and healthy and not deplete resources. (Quoted in Pallant 1999:94)

The project influenced students' perception of how communities can move forward in a postindustrial economy. It also took academia to the front lines by applying classroom ideas and concepts. Student comments included the following:

> Our research was fully interdisciplinary and collaborative so that we had to learn everything from the thermodynamics of heat pumps to the biogeochemical cycling of fish crap and the business of advertising.

I was so tired of thinking because I had never thought as much as I had in that one class. It was not just memorizing notes but actually thinking, understanding, and putting the pieces together.

> I altered my feelings toward business. At the onset of the class, I viewed business as an evil entity hell-bent on making money regardless of the costs to society. After our class focus began to shift from how to make a sustainable, efficient, model business toward how to make a profit, I realized that my earlier thoughts were unfounded. (Pallant 1999:96)

Symbolic interactionists focus on the social construction of environmental problems and solutions. According to this perspective, issues such as nuclear power, wildlife preservation, and other environmental problems were negotiated in public discourse throughout the 20th century, often linked to events and emerging conditions. In addition, political mobilization within the environmental movement is a by-product of consciousness developed through struggles to link events to larger processes. This was evident in the 1960s as pollution endangered the health of urban residents (Yearley 2002). The project at Allegheny College is an example of how an environmental solution can be visualized as a solution to economic decline. In this case, sustainable development and environmental consciousness merged to change how local officials, residents, and students perceive environmental issues. One of the key lessons here is that success of a project may not depend on its completion but on the involvement of people in its conceptualization. As Pallant (1999) states, "Regardless of whether a Tilapia ever grows in Meadville, a profound change has occurred" (p. 97).

Case Study Questions

1. What are the causes behind economic decline faced by rural communities in Pennsylvania?

2. What sustainable use for brownfields did the project find?

3. How did the service learning project change how Meadville officials viewed development?

4. What types of changes did students experience due to the service learning project?

## CASE STUDY #3

Environmental Justice and Inequality:
Clark Atlanta University's Environmental Justice Resource Center

Conflict and critical sociologists argue that capitalism as a system based on the drive for endless accumulation and consumption presents a major threat to the environment (Commoner 1992; Pepper 1993). Critics of global capitalism point to the devastating environmental impacts of corporate practices on communities in both developed and developing nations (Karliner 1997). Conflict theorists focus on the relationships between environment and inequality, arguing that sustainability will come only with the transformation of capitalism to a more equitable system. John Bethany Foster (2002) makes the case that global corporate interests have determined how the United States addresses environmental issues. For example, he cites George W. Bush's withdrawal from the Kyoto Protocol as a direct effort to protect big business. Kyoto treaties would have undoubtedly forced corporations to curtail production of greenhouse gasses. The legacy of corporate pollution on American communities has been well documented (Lynch, Stretesky, and Burns 2004), and hundreds of small towns such as Love Canal in New York, Hinkley, California (of Erin Brockovich fame), and even Libby, Montana (where vermiculite strip mining resulted in what the EPA called "the worst case of industrial poisoning of a whole community in American history") stand as symbols of corporate greed supplanting human needs. Overall, Foster argues that big business's influence and power is the major reason environmental challenges remain unmet.

Other sociologists argue that the unequal impact of environmental outcomes on communities represents a form of race and class exploitation (Bullard 1990, 1994; Feagin and Vera 2001). Utilizing the conflict perspective, these sociologists draw on research methods and course work to influence environmental policy and create change in communities affected by contamination. They have developed the term environmental justice to refer not only to the unequal impacts on poor and minority communities, but also to the need for a "social justice" approach to such problems.

*(Continued)*

(Continued)

Social justice refers to the assessment of the collective benefit of a social practice. Social justice brings up the question of how a particular action leads to or reflects oppression or domination of a particular group by other groups (Feagin and Vera 2001). Environmental justice embraces the principle that all people have a right to equal protection under environmental, housing, transportation, health, land use, and civil rights laws, and that no one group of people should be singled out for environmental and health hazards (Bullard 1994). By using such an approach, sociologists have shifted the use of the social sciences to a focus on the right of all citizens to a clean and healthy environment.

To some degree, the movement for environmental justice grew out of civil and labor rights struggles among working-class people of color. The unequal protection of people of color in regards to environmental standards and policies has been well documented by sociologists (Agyeman, Bullard, and Evans 2003; Bullard 1990; Pena 2005a; VanWynsberghe 2002). Race and class play an important role in determining which social groups are most at risk for environmental social problems. Environmental racism refers to any environmental policy, practice, or directive that differentially affects or disadvantages (whether intended or unintended) individuals, groups, or communities based on race or color (Johnson 2005:289). The toxic and municipal waste produced by Americans disproportionately is located near poor and minority neighborhoods. Landfills, toxic waste dumps, garbage incinerators, and other noxious facilities are what Robert Bullard (1990) calls "locally unwanted land uses," or LULUs. These LULUs are located near poor communities that have less power to resist than wealthier communities.

In response to LULUs, grassroots groups have emerged to address environmental racism. The environmental justice movement further developed in the late 1980s to address the unequal protection from environmental hazards. Due to race and class segregation and racism, historically powerless neighborhoods have been designated as sacrifice zones for the dumping of toxic waste and the locating of polluting industries in inner cities, rural communities, and on or near Native American reservations. The risks of being exposed to urban and rural air pollution, landfills, industrial brownfields, toxic wastes sites, and chemicals in one's home or community are much higher for people of color, indigenous peoples, Native Americans, and poor communities than for the other social groups (Bullard 1992, 1994, 2005; Johnson 2005; Pena 2005a, 2005b; VanWynsberghe 2002). Poor and minority neighborhoods are also more likely to be negatively affected by urban sprawl and congestion.

One of the nation's foremost research institutions on environmental injustice is the Environmental Justice Resource Center (EJRC) at Clark Atlanta University, a historically black university in downtown Atlanta. The center promotes environmental justice, social justice, and leadership through service learning, internships, and community-based learning projects. Connected with the sociology department at Clark Atlanta University, the EJRC is a clearinghouse of academic resources for communities and researchers on environmental justice issues. The center offers training in geographical information systems to map out waste and hazards locations and track the social distribution of environmental and health risks. Working directly with communities, the EJRC also provides leadership in minority worker training, environmental restoration, and brownfield urban revitalization. In addition, the center produces research on community exposure to hazards and community efforts to resist contamination.

According to Robert Bullard (1994, 2005), the center's director, the location of hazardous plants and waste dumps follows the path of least resistance toward powerless communities. Environmental justice theorists argue that the current environment protection regulations place the burden of proof and protection on victims instead of polluting industries (Johnson 2005). Data by environmental sociologists and other researchers reveal the unequal distribution of pollution:

- Three out of five African Americans and Latino Americans live in communities with abandoned toxic sites (Bullard 2005).

- Air pollution is a contributing factor in rising asthma rates. Although African Americans represent 12.7% of the U.S. population, they account for 26% of asthma deaths. African American children are 5 times more likely to die from asthma than white children (Bullard 2005).

- Black children are 5 times more likely than white children to have lead poisoning.

- Nearly 1,200 public schools in Massachusetts, New York, New Jersey, Michigan, and California are located within a half mile of federal superfund or state-identified contaminated sites (Bullard, Johnson, and Torres 2005).

Utilizing critical perspectives and applied sociology, sociologists engaged in environmental justice work at Clark Atlanta do research and empower communities to address the environmental practices putting them at risk. EJRC theorists conduct research with communities and students to

- Identify environmental problems in the community;

- Examine how environmental problems impact quality of life;

- Utilize research to critically analyze environmental problems and provide advocacy;

- Mobilize grassroots leaders for social change (Johnson 2005) (see Voices from the Field box).

In EJRC's Applied Environmental Sociology program, undergraduate and graduate students experience community-based research. A key feature of such programs is not only advocacy work around issues of environmental racism, but also applying research to influence public policy and generate public participation in environmental decisions affecting communities. Students engaged in community research at EJRC are having important influences on the communities they serve. EJRC has influenced policy making in a number of areas. For instance, EJRC founder Robert Bullard was instrumental in creating the EPA Office of Environmental Justice and Executive Order 12898 obligating the government to incorporate environmental justice for minority communities into the practices of governmental agencies. More recently, he represented environmental justice initiatives at the 2009 United Nations Climate Change Conference in Copenhagen (Mock 2010).

Environmental justice activists transcend C. Wright Mills's (1959) idea of the sociological imagination as a greater consciousness of social problems. For them, a critical quality of mind must lead to social engagement and working for social justice. Social justice means finding the information and developing an analysis that aids those impacted by social injustice to seek redress.

*(Continued)*

(Continued)

While structural inequalities and corporate power may be the primary cause for their social problems, the EJRC provides knowledge to citizens in many communities as well as the tools to fight back (Feagin and Vera 2001; Langton and Kammerer 2005).

## Case Study Questions

1. How do race and class shape environmental problems and protection according to the environmental justice perspective?

2. What is a locally unwanted land use, or LULU?

3. What are the research tools environmental sociology uses to address social injustice in the distribution of environmental effects across populations?

4. What skills do students in environmental sociology gain working with the Environmental Justice Resource Center?

## VOICES FROM THE FIELD

### Service Learning and Environmental Justice: An Interview With Glen Johnson

Environmental justice coalitions bring together community groups, activists, and students to influence the decision-making process around lead contamination, transfer and storage of hazardous waste, public transportation, and other issues (Bullard and Johnson 1997) (see Case Study #3). Environmental sociologist Glenn Johnson has been at Clark Atlanta's EJRC for over 10 years. He teaches courses on the environment. He also works with communities at risk for environmental hazards across the United States.

Many are poor and minority neighborhoods that lack the political power and the information to determine the hazards that they face. Professor Johnson sums up the goals he has for students: "We strive to educate individuals to be good global citizens. Through service learning we want to offer undergraduate and graduate students an opportunity to participate in courses that link theory and practice. That is, we want them to apply what they learn in class to community problems. Students engage in a number of different types of research methods and are involved in multiple programs. They may collect trash as data and analyze what is in this trash or help a community to start a recycling program. Some of our students might do assessment on combined sewer overflows (CSOs). While they do this research they learn about pollution issues/environmental issues; they educate residents about issues and help offer solutions. Our students often engage in public meetings as advocates. We want them to become familiar with the policy-making process and how to impact it. Our students practice communication skills with residents. Their interviews may lead to action on a concern in the community. Our program does community studies in poor neighborhoods. Students engage in workshops drawing on experiential education and teaching. Community education on environmental issues requires engaging a cycle of action and reflection, using education to draw out environmental problems and solutions within the community context" (author interview with Glenn Johnson, August 19, 2006).

## SUMMARY

Environmental social problems concern everyone. However, as we have seen in this chapter, they are unequally distributed by race and class. A number of environmental problems are linked to the average U.S. lifestyle including car culture, fossil fuel energy use, and consumer goods. Environmental problems such as global warning and fossil fuel dependency will take large-scale global mobilization to solve. This chapter shows the consequences of industrialization and mass consumerism. It also offers an overview of the responses of scientists and citizens, including the environmental movement and the sociology of the environment paradigm. Important to our analysis are the actions of everyday citizens and students in addressing environmental degradation and influencing the public discourse. The examples of action and community research at Allegheny College and the University of Nebraska at Omaha reveal the effectiveness of these types of research methods for increasing participation and engaging the public in finding solutions to environmental problems. Along with these examples of student and community involvement, the case of students at Clark Atlanta University Environmental Justice Resource Center shows how service learning and community activism counter the race and class inequalities behind environmental wastes and exposure.

## SUMMARY QUESTIONS

1. What are the main energy challenges faced by the United States? How do they contribute to environmental problems?

2. How do fossil fuels contribute to environmental problems in the United States and around the world?

3. What role do consumerism and lifestyle play in the environmental challenges faced by the United States?

4. What do renewable sources of energy offer as solutions to environmental social problems?

5. What do the histories of energy use, environmental problems, and regulation in the United States tell us about solutions to current environmental social problems?

## GLOSSARY

**Acid Rain:** An acidic precipitation whose pollutants come mainly from vehicle emissions and burning coal.

**Action Research:** Research that addresses social problems through collaborations and partnerships that value the specialized knowledge and work of community groups, researchers, and students.

**Biofuels:** Energy sources produced by biomass such as grain crops, soy and corn, and non-food crops such as switchgrass and woody crops.

**Carrying Capacity:** The amount of life an ecosystem can support based on its natural resources.

**Confined Animal Feeding Operations:** Large farms raising animals in confined areas for commodity food production.

**Ecological Footprint:** The impact of a human activity on the environment.

**Environmental Justice:** A concept that embraces the principle that all people have a right to equal protection under environmental, housing, transportation, health, land use, and civil rights laws, and that no one group of people should be singled out for exposure to environmental and health hazards.

**Environmental Racism:** This term refers to any environmental policy, practice, or directive that differentially affects or disadvantages (whether intended or unintended) individuals, groups, or communities based on race or color.

**Fossil Fuels:** Any fuels made from the burning of hydrocarbon deposits found in the Earth's crust such as oil, coal, gas, and propane.

**Global Warming:** This term refers to the gradual increase in the Earth's surface temperature. Almost all scientists now agree that the Earth is warming up; most believe the increased temperatures are occurring at alarmingly fast rates.

**Greenhouse Effect:** The heating of the atmosphere due to carbon dioxide, primarily as a by-product of the burning of fossil fuels.

**Nuclear Power:** Power produced by enriching uranium.

**Renewable Energy:** Energy sources that are not depleted and have less impact on the environment, and in some cases no impact.

**Risk Society:** A society that must continually assess the risk of using dangerous technology.

**Social Justice:** The assessment of the collective benefit of a social practice.

## WEBSITES TO LEARN MORE ABOUT THE ENVIRONMENT AND SERVICE LEARNING PROJECTS

Carbon Footprint: http://www.carbonfootprint.com/

Center for Health, Environment & Justice: http://www.chej.org/

Center for Science in the Public Interest: http://www.cspinet.org/

Earth First: http://www.earthfirst.org/

Environmental Defense Fund: http://www.edf.org/home.cfm

Environmental Justice Foundation: http://www.ejfoundation.org/page231.html

Environmental Protection Agency: http://www.epa.gov/

Friends of the Earth: http://www.foe.org/

Greenpeace USA: http://www.greenpeace.org/usa/

National Service Learning Clearinghouse (articles on environmental projects): http://www.servicelearning.org/instant_info/bibs/he_bibs/environment

National Wildlife Federation (campus ecology program): http://www.nwf.org/campusecology/

Native American Environmental Protection Coalition: http://www.naepc.com/

Oak Ridge National Laboratory: http://jobs.ornl.gov/

Organic Consumers Association: http://www.organicconsumers.org/

Sierra Club: http://www.sierraclub.org/

Student Environmental Action Coalition: http://www.seac.org

U.S. Department of Energy: http://www.energy.gov/energysources/solar.htm

United Nations Environment Programme (UNEP): http://www.unep.org/

Worldwatch Institute: http://www.worldwatch.org/

## REFERENCES

Adamson, Joni. 2001. *American Indian, Environmental Justice, and Ecocriticism: The Middle Place.* Tucson, AZ: University of Arizona Press.

Agyeman, Julian, Robert Bullard, and Bob Evans, eds. 2003. *Just Sustainabilities: Development in an Unequal World.* London, UK: Earthscan.

Allen, Stuart. 2000. *Environmental Risk and the Media.* London, UK: Routledge.

American Sociological Association. 2004. "Global Warming and the Environment." *Contexts,* 3:62.

Beck, Ulrich. 1992. *Risk Society: Towards a New Modernity.* Newbury Park, CA: Sage.

Begg, Alex. 2000. *Empowering the Earth: Strategies for Social Change.* Foxhole, UK: Green Books.

Bell, Michael. 2004. *An Invitation to Environmental Sociology.* Thousand Oaks, CA: Pine Forge Press.

Berea College Ecovillage. [Home page]. Retrieved February 6, 2010 (http://www.berea.edu/sens/ecovillage/ecomachine/default.asp).

Bowdoin College. 2010. "Sustainability: Mission Statement." Retrieved February 15, 2010 (https://www.bowdoin.edu/sustainability/sustainable-planning/mission-statement.shtml).

Broder, John B. 2007. "Rule to Expand Mountaintop Coal Mining." *New York Times.* August 23.

———. 2010. "Obama Presses BP to Recover More Oil." *New York Times* July 8. Retrieved July 9, 2010: http://www.nytimes.com/2010/07/09/us/09spill.html?_r = 1&ref = gulf_of_mexico_2010

Brown, Lester R. 2001. *Eco-Economy: Building a New Economy for the Environmental Age.* New York: Norton.

———. 2002. "New York: Garbage Capital of the World." *Social Contract Journal,* 13(1). Retrieved February 6, 2010 (http://www.thesocialcontract.com/artman2/publish/tsc1301/article_1100.shtml).

———. 2003. "Wind Power Set to Become World's Leading Energy Source." Washington, DC: Earth Policy Institute. Retrieved February 6, 2010 (http://www.earth-policy.org/index.php?/plan_b_updates/2003/update24).

———. 2005. "Pushing Beyond the Earth's Limits." *The Futurist.* May/June.

———. 2006. *Plan B 2.0: Rescuing a Planet in Under Stress and a Civilization in Trouble.* New York: Norton.

Brown, Phil and Edwin J. Mikkelson. [1990]1997. *No Safe Place: Toxic Waste, Leukemia, and Community Action.* Berkeley, CA: University of California Press.

Bryne, John, Kristen Hughes, Wilson Rickerson, and Lado Kurdgelashvili. 2007. "American Policy Conflict in the Greenhouse: Divergent Trends in Federal, Regional, State, and Local Green Energy and Climate Change Policy." *Energy Policy,* 35:4555–4573.

Bryne, John and Noah Toly. 2006. "Energy as a Social Project: Recovering a Discourse." Pp. 1–32 in *Transforming Power Energy, Environmental, and Society in Society,* edited by John Byrne, Noah Toly, and Leigh Glover. Piscatawa, NJ: Transaction Publishers.

Bullard, Robert D. 1990. *Dumping in Dixie: Class, Race, and Environmental Quality.* Boulder CO: Westview Press.

———. 1992. *Confronting Environmental Racism: Voices From the Grassroots.* Boston, MA: South End Press.

———, ed. 1994. *Unequal Protection: Environmental Justice and Communities of Color.* San Francisco, CA: Sierra Club Books.

____. 2005. "More Blacks Overburdened With Dangerous Pollution: AP Study of EPA Risk Scores Confirms Two Decades of EJ Findings." The Environmental Justice Research Center, December 19. Retrieved February 6, 2010 (http://www.ejrc.cau.edu/BullardAPEJ.html).

Bullard, Robert D. and Glenn S. Johnson. 1997. *Just Transportation: Dismantling Race and Class Barriers to Mobility.* Gabriola Island, BC, Canada: New Society Publishers.

Bullard, Robert D., Glenn S. Johnson, and Angel O. Torres. 2004. *Highway Robbery: Transportation Racism and New Routes to Equity.* Boston, MA: South End Press.

____. 2005. "Addressing Global Poverty, Pollution, and Human Rights." Pp. 291-298 in *The Quest for Environmental Justice Human Rights and the Politics of Pollution,* edited by Robert D. Bullard. San Francisco, CA: Sierra Club Books.

Burger, Andrew K. 2006. "Green Energy, Part 2: Ethanol and Biodiesel." *E-CommerceTimes.* July 20. Retrieved February 6, 2010 (http://www.ecommercetimes.com/story/BPsMzVj2yrJAeP/Green- Energy-Part-2ethanol-and-Biodiesel.xhtml).

Buttel, Fredrick. 1997. "Social Institutions and Environmental Change." Pp. 40–54 in *The International Handbook of Environmental Sociology,* edited by Michael R. Redclift. Northampton, UK: Edward Elgar Publishing.

Cable, Sherry and Charles Cable. 1995. *Environmental Problems/Grassroots Solutions: The Politics of Environmental Conflict.* New York: St. Martin's Press.

Čapek, Stella. 2009. "The Social Construction of Nature." Pp. 11–23 in *Twenty Lessons in Environmental Sociology,* edited by Kenneth A Gould and Tammy L. Lewis. New York: Oxford University Press.

Carson, Rachel. 1962. *Silent Spring.* Greenwich, CT: Fawcett World Library.

Castells, Manuel. 2004. *The Power of Identity.* Oxford, UK: Blackwell.

Chambers, Nicky, Craig Simmons, and Mathis Wackernagel. 2000. *Sharing Nature's Interest: Ecological Footprints as an Indicator of Sustainability.* London, UK: Earthscan.

Commoner, Barry. 1992. *Making Peace With the Planet.* New York: The New Press.

Corbett, Julia. 2006. *Communicating Nature: How We Create and Understand Environmental Messages.* Washington, DC: Island Press.

Cox, Robert J. 2006. *Environmental Communication and the Public Sphere.* Thousand Oaks, CA: Sage.

Davis, Donald Edward. 1989. *Ecophilosophy: A Guide to the Literature.* San Pedro, CA: Miles & Miles.

Dean, Cornelia. 2006. "Study Sees 'Global Collapse' of Fish Species." *New York Times.* November 3.

DeCicco, John. 2006. *Global Warming on the Road: The Climate Impact of America's Automobiles.* New York: Environmental Defense Fund.

DeCicco, John and Freda Fung, with Feng An. 2006. "Global Warming on the Road. The Climate Impact of America Automobiles." Environmental Defense Fund. Retrieved February 16, 2010 (http://www.edf.org/documents/5301_Globalwarmingontheroad.pdf).

Dunlap, Riley E. 1997. "The Evolution of Environmental Sociology: A Brief History and Assessment of the American Experience." Pp 21–39 in *The International Handbook of Environmental Sociology,* edited by Michael R. Redclift. Northampton, UK: Edward Elgar Publishing.

Edwards, Bob and Tony Ladd. 2000. "Environmental Justice, Swine Production, and Farm Loss in North Carolina." *Sociological Spectrum,* 20(3):263–290.

Feagin, Joe R. and Hernan Vera. 2001. *Liberation Sociology.* Boulder, CO: Westview Press.

Fine, Gary Alan. 1998. *Morel Tales: The Culture of Mushrooming.* Cambridge, MA: Harvard University Press.

Food & Water Watch. 2007. *Turning Farms Into Factories: How Concentration of Animal Agriculture Threatens Human Health, the Environment, and Rural Communities.* Washington, DC: Author.

Foster, John Bethany. 2002. *Ecology Against Capitalism*. New York: Monthly Review Press.

Garling, Tommy and Linda Steg. 2007. *Threats From Car Traffic to the Quality of Urban Life: Problems, Causes, and Solutions*. Amsterdam, The Netherlands: Elsevier.

Global Footprint Network. 2009. Retrieved February 15, 2010 (http://www.footprintnetwork.org/en/index.php/GFN/).

Global Health Council. 2006. *Global Health Watch: An Alternative Report*. London, UK: Zed Books.

Greenwood, Davydd James. 1998. *Introduction to Action Research: Social Research for Social Change*. London, UK: Sage.

Guinnessy, Paul. 2006. "Stronger Future for Nuclear Power." *Physics Today,* 59:19.

Heran, Robert Emmet. 2010. *This Borrowed Earth: Lessons From the 15 Worst Environmental Disasters Around the World*. Palgrave Macmillan.

Horrigan, Leo, Robert Lawrence, and Polly Walker. 2002. "How Sustainable Agriculture Can Address the Environmental and Human Health Harms of Industrial Agriculture." *Environmental Health Perspectives,* 110(5):445–456.

Hubbert, Marion King. 1956. *Nuclear Energy and the Fossil Fuels in Drilling and Production Practice*. Washington, DC: American Petroleum Institute.

International Atomic Energy Agency. 2005. "The Chernobyl Forum: Chernobyl's Legacy: Health, Environmental, and Socioeconomic Impacts and Recommendations to Governments of Belarus, the Russian Federation, and the Ukraine." Retrieved February 6, 2010 (http://www.iaea.org/Publications/Booklets/Chernobyl/chernobyl.pdf).

Johnson, Glenn S. 2005. "Grassroots Activism in Louisiana." *Humanity and Society,* 29:285–304.

Karliner, Joshua. 1997. *The Corporate Planet: Ecology and Politics in the Age of Globalization*. San Francisco, CA: Sierra Club Books.

Kimbrell, Andrew. 2002. *Fatal Harvest: The Tragedy of Industrial Agriculture*. Washington, DC: Island Press.

Kline, Benjamin. 2000. *First Along the River: A Brief History of the U.S. Environmental Movement*. San Francisco, CA: Acada Books.

LaDuke, Winona. 1999. *All Our Relations: Native Struggles for Land and Life*. Boston, MA: South End Press.

Langton, Phyllis Ann and Dianne Anderson Kammerer. 2005. *Practicing Sociology in the Community: A Student's Guide*. Upper Saddle River, NJ: Pearson.

Layzer, Judith. 2006. *The Environmental Case: Translating Values Into Policy.* Washington, DC: Congressional Quarterly Press.

Leon-Guerrero, Anna. 2004. *Social Problems Community Policy and Social Action*. Thousand Oaks, CA: Pine Forge Press.

Liv, Yingling. 2006. "China's Drinking Water Situation Grim: Heavy Pollution to Blame." *Worldwatch Institute.* August 3.

Lovelock, James. 1979. *Gaia: A New Look at Life on Earth*. Oxford, UK: Oxford University Press.

Lynch, Michael J., Paul B. Stretesky, and Ronald G. Burns. 2004. "Slippery Business: Race, Class, and Legal Determinants of Penalties Against Petroleum Refineries, *Journal of Black Studies,* 34:421–440.

MacFarlane, Alison M. and Rodney Ewing. 2006. *Yucca Mountain and the Nation's High-Level Nuclear Waste*. Cambridge, MA: MIT Press.

McGrane, Bernard. 1994. *The Un-TV and the 10 MPH Cal: Experiments in Personal Freedom and Everyday Life*. Belmont, CA: The Small Press.

Mooney, Linda A., David Knox, and Caroline Schacht. 2007. *Understanding Social Problems.* 5th ed. Belmont, CA: Thomson/Wadsworth.

Mills, C. Wright. 1959. *The Sociological Imagination.* London, UK: Oxford University Press.

Mock, Brentin. 2010. "TheGrio's 100: Robert Bullard, Father of Environmental Justice, Inspires Next Generation." *TheGrio.* Retrieved February 16, 2010 (http://www.thegrio.com/topics/The-Grios-100).

Morris, Douglas E. 2005. *It's a Sprawl World After All.* Gabriola Island, BC, Canada: New Society Publishers.

Nelson, Gaylord. 2002. *Beyond Earth Day: Fulfilling the Promise.* Madison, WI: The University of Wisconsin.

Neuzil, Mark and William Kovarik. 1996. *Environmental Conflict: America's Green Crusades.* Thousand Oaks, CA: Sage.

Nolt, John. 2005. *A Land Imperiled: The Declining Health of the Southern Appalachian Bioregion.* Knoxville, TN: The University of Tennessee Press.

Nyden, Phillip, Anne Figert, Mark Shibley, and Darryl Burrows. 1997. "University–Community Collaborative Research: Adding Chairs at the Research Table." Pp. 3–13 in *Building Community: Social Science in Action,* edited by Phillip Nyden, Anne Figert, Mark Shibley, and Darryl Burrows. Thousand Oaks, CA: Sage.

Orr, David. 1992. *Ecological Literacy: Education and the Transition to a Postmodern World.* Albany, New York: State University of New York Press.

Pallant, Eric. 1999. "Raising Fish and Tomatoes to Save the Rustbelt." Pp. 89–98 in *Acting Locally Concepts and Models for Service Learning in Environmental Studies,* edited by Harold Ward. Washington, DC: American Association for Higher Education & Accreditation.

Pena, Devon G. 2005a. *Mexican Americans and the Environment: Tierra y Vida.* Tucson, AZ: The University of Arizona Press

____. 2005b. "Tierra y Vida: Chicano Environmental Justice Struggles in the Southwest." Pp. 188–206 in *The Quest for Environmental Justice: Human Rights and the Politics of Pollution,* edited by Robert D. Bullard. San Francisco, CA: Sierra Club Books.

Pepper, David. 1993. *Eco Socialism.* London, UK: Routledge.

Plumwood, Val. 2002. *Environmental Culture: The Ecological Crisis of Reason.* New York: Routledge.

Princen, Thomas, Michael Maniates, and Ken Cenca. 2002. *Confronting Consumption.* Boston, MA: MIT Press.

Rajaram, Shireen S. 2007. "An Action-Research Project: Community Lead Poisoning Prevention." *Teaching Sociology,* 35:138–150.

Redman, Charles L. 1999. *Human Impact on Ancient Environments.* Tucson, AZ: The University of Arizona Press.

Rees, William. 1992. "Ecological Footprints and Appropriated Carrying Capacity: What Urban Economics Leaves Out." *Environment and Urbanisation,* 4:121–130.

Rogers, Heather. 2005. *Gone Tomorrow: The Hidden Life of Garbage.* New York: The New Press.

Sampat, Payal. 2001. "The Hidden Threat of Groundwater Pollution." *USA Today.* July.

Schmidt, Gerald. 2005. *Positive Ecology: Sustainability and the "Good Life."* Hampshire, UK: Ashgate.

Schnaiberg, Allan and Kenneth Alan Gould. 1994. *Environment and Society: The Enduring Conflict.* New York: St. Martin's Press.

Schoen, John W. 2007. "Does Nuclear Power Now Make Financial Sense? *MSNBC.* January 26. Retrieved February 18, 2010 (http://www.msnbc.msn.com/id/16286304/ns/us_news-power_play/).

Sieminski, Adam E. 2005. "World Energy Futures." Pp. 21–50 in *Energy and Security: Toward a New Foreign Policy Strategy,* edited by Jan H. Kalicki and David L. Goldwyn. Baltimore, MD: Johns Hopkins University Press.

Shor, Juliet B. 2004. *Born to Buy: The Commercialized Child and the New Consumer Culture.* New York: Scribner

Strahan, David. 2007. *The Last Oil Shock A Survival Guide to the Imminent Extinction of Petroleum Man.* London, UK: John Murray.

Taylor, Ros and Kathy Morrissey. 2004. "Coping With Pollution, Dealing With Waste." Pp. 229–264 in *Global Environmental Issues,* edited by Frances Harris. New York: Wiley.

Thums, Shauna. 2004. "Report on the State of the World's Water." Retrieved August 3, 2006 (http://www.uaa.alaska.edu/modelun/).

Union of Concerned Scientists. 1999. "Powerful Solutions: 7 Ways to Switch America to Renewable Electricity." Retrieved February 15, 2010 (http://www.ucsusa.org/clean_energy/solutions/big_picture_solutions/powerful-solutions-7-ways-to.html).

_____. 2007. "Cashing in on Clean Energy." Retrieved February 6, 2010 (http://www.ucsusa.org/clean_energy/clean_energy_policies/cashing-in.html).

U.S. Department of Energy. 2006. "Biomass Program." Retrieved February 7, 2010 (http://www1.eere.energy.gov/biomass/environmental.html).

_____. 2009. "Annual Energy Outlook 2009: With Projection to 2030." Retrieved October 14, 2009 (http://www.eia.doe.gov/oiaf/aeo/execsummary.html).

_____. 2010. "FY 2010 DOE Budget Request to Congress." Retrieved February 15, 2010 (http://www.cfo.doe.gov/budget/10budget/start.htm#Detailed Budget Justifications).

U.S. Energy Information Administration. 2005. *Renewable Energy Trends in Consumption and Electricity.* Washington, DC: U.S. Department of Energy.

_____. 2008. "U.S. Electric Power Industry Net Generation 2008." 2010. U.S. Energy Information Administration. Retrieved February 15, 2010 (http://www.eia.doe.gov/cneaf/electricity/epa/figes1.html)

_____. 2009. "Annual Energy Outlook 2009: With Projection to 2030." Retrieved October 14, 2009 (http://www.eia.doe.gov/oiaf/aeo/execsummary.html).

_____. 2005. "Municipal Solid Waste in the United States: Facts and Figures 2005. Excutive Summary" Retrieved February 19, 2010 (http://www.seas.columbia.edu/earth/wtert/sofos/MSW_IN_THE_US.pdf).

_____. 2006. "Wastewater in Tribal Communities." Retrieved February 16, 2010 (http://www.epa.gov/owm/mab/indian/basicinfo.htm).

_____. 2010. "Green Power Partnership: Top 20 College and University." Retrieved February 15, 2010 (http://www.epa.gov/greenpower/toplists/top20ed.htm).

VanWynsberghe, Robert M. 2002. *AlterNatives Community: Identity and Environmental Justice on Walpole Island.* Boston, MA: Allyn & Bacon.

Wade, Ros. 2007. "Sustainable Development." Pp. 104–113 in *Teaching the Global Dimension: Key Principles and Effective Practice,* edited by David Hicks and Cathie Holden. London, UK: Routledge.

Wallace, Samuel E. 1998. *Social Problems: An Ecological Perspective.* Belmont, CA: Wadsworth.

World Nuclear Association. 2009. "Nuclear Share Figures, 1999–2009." Retrieved February 15, 2010 (http://www.world-nuclear.org/info/nshare.html).

Worldwatch Institute. 2004, January 2. "State of the World: Special Focus: The Consumer Society." [Press release]. Retrieved February 18, 2010 (http://www.worldwatch.org/node/1043).

World Wildlife Fund. 2004. "Promised But Not Delivered." Retrieved August 19, 2006 (http://assets.panda.org/downloads/csd12waterinitiativespaper.pdf).

Yearley, Steven. 2002. "The Social Construction of Environmental Problems: A Theoretical Review and Some Not-Very-Herculean Labors." Pp. 274–285 in *Social Theory and the Environment,* edited by Riley E. Dunlap, Frederick H. Buttel, Peter Dickens, and August Gijswijt. Oxford, UK: Rowman & Littlefield.

# Why Can't Johnny Read?

*Education in Crisis*

*The Great Books curriculum was good preparation for service-learning: in focusing on evaluative and interpretative questions (as opposed to factual ones), the students learned in the Fall 2004 semester "to see that reading is thinking, asking questions, and working together to gain meaning from a text."*

—Golden and Herman (2006)

*Democracy has never appeared more fragile and endangered in the United States than in this time of civic and political crisis. This is especially true for young people.*

—Giroux (2005)

Catherine Golden, Professor of English at Skidmore College, and Marjorie Herman, English Department Chair of Maple Avenue Middle School, developed a special service learning collaboration uniting college students and middle school students in an exploration of literature. Both schools are located in Saratoga Springs, New York, and are involved in "Saratoga Reads!"—a communitywide reading initiative designed to incorporate the entire community in shared conversations about books and contemporary issues. The Skidmore–Maple Avenue project joined 12 college students (ages 19–22) from an Honors Forum class on Great Books (HF 201) with middle school children in order to generate group discussions about books. One novel read by the group was *Parvana's Journey* by Deborah Ellis (2003), which tells the story of a young girl, disguised as a boy, in search of her mother in war-torn Afghanistan (Golden and Herman 2006). The book connects young students to larger global political and economic issues. They learn about Afghan Muslim culture and what life is like during war.

As part of their service learning project, Skidmore students worked with middle school youth and encouraged them to dramatize the book. Over the course of the semester, they created projects to visualize scenes, which increased all participants' understanding of world events and cultures. Students created images of communities caught in the chaos and tragedy of war through timelines, storyboards, and a story game (Golden and Herman 2006). They designed and wore Afghan costumes and wrote letters to soldiers in Afghanistan. Coming out of the stories were discussions about the Taliban and gender relations; life among land mines; children's kites; and other instances of international politics, regional cultures, and the everyday lives of children and families in a war-torn country.

This type of service learning initiative shows how schools and communities can broaden the curriculum for, and expand the imagination of, middle school children. At a time when budget constraints and a concentration on high-stakes tests increasingly narrow school curricula, arts and humanities courses often suffer. So, too, do efforts to train students in critical thinking, global awareness, and intercultural skills. As we will see in this chapter, critics claim the current policies established by No Child Left Behind legislation create an environment of high-stakes (and high-pressure) testing. Many school superintendents argue that these policies result in costly programs with unrealistic goals and punitive results if student performances fall short of standards (Hayes 2004). More and more, education in the United States has been given over to what Shapiro (2006) calls "test prep," where "schools offer little that can be taken as a source of personal meaning, as a stimulus for critical thought, or as the catalyst for imaginative interpretation of human experience" (p. 10). In contrast, service learning projects include, but also transcend, basic skill development to address a critical engagement of human experiences. Students *apply* basic skills to a sense of civic responsibility as they learn about the rights and responsibilities of citizenship, and envision what a more just society might look and feel like (Giroux 2005; Kenny, Simon, Kiley-Brabeck, and Lerner 2002). Instead of students stuck with teachers forced to "teach to the test," the Skidmore–Maple Avenue project of dramatizing and critically analyzing the text challenged middle school students to engage in enrichment activities outside the mandated school curriculum.

Meanwhile, Skidmore students got the opportunity to observe and teach eighth graders using a "Great Books Curriculum" (GBC). GBC's goal incorporates an entire community into the discussion of a common text—its ideas, significance, and implications. *Parvana's Journey* exposed school-aged children, teachers, parents, and college students to globalization, international conflict, and the ravages of war. Comments from those involved include the following:

> The older students wouldn't tell us what to do, but instead advised and guided us to get the best results. We had freedom to do what we wanted and also . . . the advice to make it the best project possible.

> We got to see two different views on the story, a view of a college student and a view of a middle school student. (Golden and Herman 2006:27, 25)

Service learning can have a powerful impact on how a student situates him- or herself in relation to others. It also fosters an ethic of care and a more pronounced concept of community (Rhodes 1997). The Saratoga collaboration put a face, or a number of faces, on the Saratoga Springs community, something students at a private liberal arts college like Skidmore don't always get (Golden and Herman 2006). Golden and Herman comment,

> [W]e recognize that average and less able learners would benefit from interaction with college students, who might spark their interest in reading and encourage them to consider college-bound career paths. Reciprocally, a more heterogeneous population of middle school students would expose college students to learners with a range of abilities and multiple learning modalities. (p. 29)

Service learning, as training for teachers in particular and citizens in general, allows students to understand the diversity of youth at the same time that they recognize the potential for achievement in all students.

Budget constraints and narrowly constructed curricula are only two of the major social problems facing education. Many critics and practitioners argue that education is an institution in crisis. In part, sociologists point toward the expanding functions of contemporary education. Once focused primarily on the "three R's" of reading, writing, and arithmetic, schools are now expected to teach citizenship and intercultural skills, computer and other basic technological skills, health and physical fitness, and even driver education and other vocational skills. In fact, schools have in some ways acquired the previous institutional functions of families and churches, professional organizations, and craft guilds; schools are expected to provide training in moral behavior and social values as well as occupational training and job skills. Early signs are that most schools cannot fulfill all of these expectations without a tremendous increase in economic and social resources.

High expectations for education are nothing new, though, as schools have always been considered the institution most likely to offer people economic and political opportunities. Public education has historically trained students with the skills and knowledge necessary to compete for better jobs and enhance their family's social mobility. At the same time, education has given students the citizenship tools and critical thinking necessary to participate in democratic self-government. Once again, schools in the United States are now expected to play a major role in solving social problems, not in reproducing them. The expansion and importance of educational functions have resulted in schools becoming lightning rods for a variety of public debates over economic and social issues. Creationism versus evolution, abstinence versus safe sex, tax cuts versus increased expectations, state and federal mandates versus local and parental control—all of these controversies play themselves out on the institutional landscape of education. Training our young people remains one of the most important social functions for any society. Despite these controversies, many of the social problems facing schools are related to the same problems of economy and social inequality that plague most contemporary institutions.

In this chapter, we look at the social problems faced by schools in the United States, and some of the ways in which students have helped to impact them on both local and national levels. First, we look at a variety of the problems through a statistical portrait of various issues. Next, we look at the history of public education in the United States, its evolving roles and debates, and how they set the stage for many of today's concerns. Finally, we examine some case studies of students working in the field, engaging youth, teachers, and communities in projects to improve our schools and change the lives of young people.

# EDUCATION BY THE NUMBERS: A STATISTICAL PORTRAIT OF SCHOOLS AND SOCIAL PROBLEMS

Inequality in education has always existed as a kind of blistering sore on the ideological body politic of America. After all, if education is supposed to be the primary institution responsible for fostering opportunities for economic equality and political democracy, one would hope that the institution itself could provide equitable resources in a nondiscriminatory way. In practice, however, our national educational systems and institutions are rife with inequalities.

The social problems of education can be broken down into two major categories: issues of inequality and access that impact whether or not certain groups get an education, and issues of institutional resources and curriculum that determine what *kind* of education is ultimately available. Whatever benefits schools may bestow upon youth, they cannot achieve much influence or provide necessary training and credentials when students don't go to class or finish degrees. Thus, one major problem impacting students and schools is the dropout rate.

## Dropout Rate

The following graph demonstrates that the overall dropout rate in the United States declined slightly between 1972 and 2002, but as of 2002, it still remained about 10%. However, many students, especially minorities, face steep odds when it comes to graduation. More recently, President Obama and Education Secretary Arne Duncan called the nation's worst high schools "dropout factories." These include the 2,000 high schools that graduate 60% or fewer of their students. They make up approximately 13% of all high schools in the United States (Almeida, Balfanz, and Steinberg 2009). While dropout rates for nonwhites remain disproportionately higher than for whites, the gap has been steadily decreasing: For blacks, the gap has diminished from just over 20% in 1972 to just over 10% in 2002, and for Hispanics it has gone down from over 30% to around 25%.

**Figure 7.1**   High School Dropout Rate by Race, 1972–2002

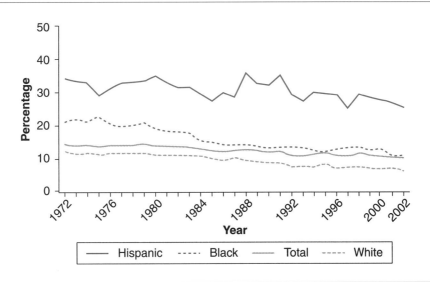

*Source:* Status Dropouts chart from *The Condition of Education*, 2005, U.S. Department of Education, National Center for Education Statistics (NCES 2005–094), Washington, DC: U.S. Government Printing Office.

*Note:* The status dropout rate reported in this indicator is one of a number of rates reporting on high school dropout and completion behavior in the United States. See *supplemental note 12* in *The Condition of Education,* cited below, for more information about the rate reported here. Due to small sample sizes for most or all of the years shown in the figure, American Indians/Alaska Natives, and Asians/Pacific Islanders are included in the total but are not shown separately. The erratic nature of the Hispanic status dropout rates reflects, in part, the historically small sample size of Hispanics. Black includes African American, and Hispanic includes Latino. Race categories exclude Hispanic origin unless specified. Some estimates are revised from previous publications.

Still, 10% is a large portion of youth without diplomas, ranking the United States 11th among industrialized nations for the proportion of students completing high school degrees. This statistic is even more significant when we measure the impact of dropping out. Figure 7.2 shows the strong link between level of education and unemployment.

Those without a high school diploma are almost twice as likely to be unemployed as those with a high school degree or some college education, and 3.5 times more likely to be unemployed than those with a college degree. When dropouts do get jobs, they earn almost 40% less than those with high school diplomas. Among adults age 25 or older, those who did not complete high school report having worse health than their peers who did complete high school, regardless of income. The impact of not having a high school diploma on unemployment and wages promises to get even worse as joblessness increases and wage rates continue to decrease during the current economic crisis (U.S. Department of Education 2002).

**Figure 7.2**   Unemployment by Level of Education, 2002

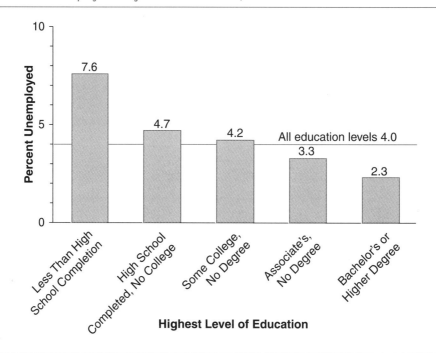

*Source:* National Center for Education Statistics (http://NCES.ed.gov/ssbr/pages/dropoutrates.asp).

The dropout problem, however, may be even more significant than these statistics demonstrate. The states determine how to measure dropout rates. Many states use different measures and have a variety of interests in showing rates to be lower than they might be. With so many flaws in the calculation system, researchers such as Harvard scholar Gary Orfield (2004) argue that the dropout rate is probably higher and much more serious than we know in the United States. He explains that the dropout *crisis* is "far beyond the imagination of most Americans" (p. 1) and results in mostly non-white and working-class children living lives of economic failure and emotional despair. According to Fernandes and Gabe (2009), over 1.5 million youth aged 16 to 24 were not in school or working in 2007.

It would be easy to blame youth themselves for dropping out, and many pundits and politicians do. From a sociological perspective, however, a high dropout rate does not simply indicate "personal troubles" caused by bad decisions or lifestyle choices, but social problems influenced strongly by social conditions. If we can predict what kinds of youth tend to drop out, we can get a sense of the root causes for their decisions and perhaps change those conditions to lower dropout rates. As we will see later in the chapter, service learning and civic engagement programs have demonstrated success at improving high school retention rates. But what *are* the root causes of dropping out?

According to a variety of researchers, the strongest predictors of who drops out are characteristics such as socioeconomic status, family structure, family stress (e.g., death, divorce, family moves), and the mother's age. As reported by *Education Week* ("Dropouts" 2004), an education journal that synthesizes myriad research studies, students who come from low-income families, are the children of single, young, unemployed mothers, or who have experienced high degrees of family stress are more likely than other students to drop out of school. But even the family-related causes of dropping out can be traced back to the powerful impact of socioeconomic inequality. Low socioeconomic status has been shown to have the strongest relationship to students' tendency to drop out, as youth from lower socioeconomic backgrounds dropped out at a rate that was 4 times higher than students from a higher socioeconomic status. Thus, while the national dropout rate may be about 10%, the dropout rate for poor and working-class students is much higher, and often a direct result of socioeconomic inequality. It may seem obvious, but one solution to the dropout problem might be to reduce levels of economic and social inequality throughout society ("Dropouts" 2004).

## Educational Inequality: Funding

The differences between private (especially what are called preparatory or "prep" schools) and public schools are legendary. Anyone who has seen *School Ties, Dead Poets Society, The Emperor's Club, Rushmore,* or any one of the plethora of films set in elite private schools understands the kind of resources, prestige, and privilege that these institutions bestow on their students. Students who attend private schools have large advantages through smaller class sizes, one-on-one advising and teaching, and a variety of college preparation activities. But, as educational scholar Martin Carnoy explains,

> We've done these studies, and other people have done these studies, and the findings are pretty clear. . . There is no significant difference between how kids do, given their socioeconomic background, their family background, in private schools and in public schools. What's crucial is family income. . . . In wealthy neighborhoods, public schools are just as successful as private schools in those neighborhoods. (Quoted in Wilkenfeld 2003:n.p.)

In fact, some of the worst inequality occurs among and between public schools. For example, in 1988, Mississippi spent an average of $2,548 per pupil, while Connecticut Public Schools spent an average of $6,230, about 2.5 times as much (Moser and Rubenstein 2002). The differences in public school funding can vary even more among districts within the same state. The gap between the richest and poorest districts in Texas in 1995, for example, was over $20,000 per classroom (Waldron 1997). A recent study by the Education

Trust found that unequal funding patterns for teacher pay in the 14 largest school districts in Ohio were significant. Poor school systems were found to have lower teacher pay than wealthier districts (cited in Wiener 2008). While the evidence is small and anecdotal, some studies do demonstrate that higher teacher salaries result in higher student performance (Figlio 1997; Hanushek, Rivkin, Rothstein, and Podgursky 2004).

Figure 7.3 shows the difference in funding per student between districts with the lowest child poverty rates and the highest child poverty rates in five states. The last column gives the average spending in districts with the lowest and highest poverty rates around the country.

**Figure 7.3**   The Education Trust Analysis, 2000

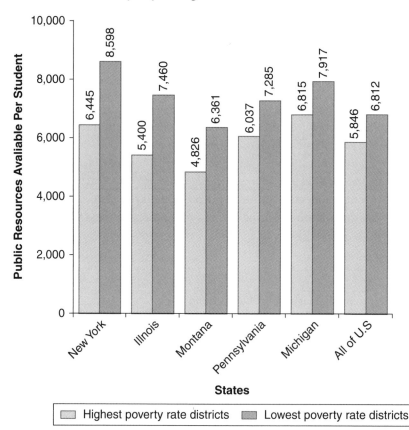

*Source:* The Education Trust. Analysis by Greg F. Orlofsky based on 1999–2000 Department of Education and U.S. Census Bureau data.

As Greg Orlofsky (2000) explains, this gap adds up quickly. In New York, for example, the difference of $2,153 per pupil becomes a gap of about $53,800 for a class of 25 students and over $860,000 for a typical elementary school of about 400 students.

Per-pupil spending derives from the funding formulas for most public schools, which are based on property taxes. Thus, communities with higher incomes generally spend more on their students and schools than do poorer communities. Meanwhile, Eitzen, Zinn, and Smith (2009) point out that average SAT (Scholastic Aptitude Test) scores for youth from families whose income was $70,000 or more is about 200 points higher than youth from families whose income is $10,000 or less. Pre-existing economic inequalities impact student success, as those whose families have money show up at the schoolhouse door with an advantage. But that advantage intensifies exponentially when the schools they attend are further stratified by communities' own collective economic resources and how much they spend on their schools. Far from an "equalizing" or "democratizing" force, most educational systems seem at least jerry-rigged, if not effectively designed, to increase social stratification and inequality.

## Educational Inequality: Segregation, Race, and Ethnicity

Economic inequalities are often intensified by racial and ethnic discrimination. Legal segregation **(de jure segregation)** through Jim Crow laws in the South or Indian boarding schools as mentioned in Chapter 4 resulted in non-white youth receiving inferior education that often trained them, at best, for basic industrial or domestic labor. The famous 1954 Supreme Court decision in the *Brown v. Board of Education* case made racial segregation unconstitutional. Despite desegregation, "white flight" from cities in the 1950s to early 1970s left urban public school systems "re-segregated," isolating non-white students in poorer urban districts (Coleman and Kerbo 2006). In fact, not only were these schools underfunded in general, but the concentration of poverty that surrounded them made it even more difficult for teachers and administrators to address youth problems (Anyon and Wilson 1997). Recent white and middle-class flight from certain suburban schools has resulted in similar dynamics, once again intensifying racial and class segregation and leaving underfunded schools to deal with myriad other social problems.

Figure 7.4 charts the increasing segregation of African American and Latino students from 1965 to 2005—a process that continued to intensify through 2005 and beyond.

A predominantly black and Latino school is one with 50–100% enrollment of black and Latino students. In a landmark study on race and education, the Applied Research Center (2003) found that "racially segregated schools are overwhelmingly

**Figure 7.4**   Percentage of Black and Latino Students in Predominantly Black and Latino Schools

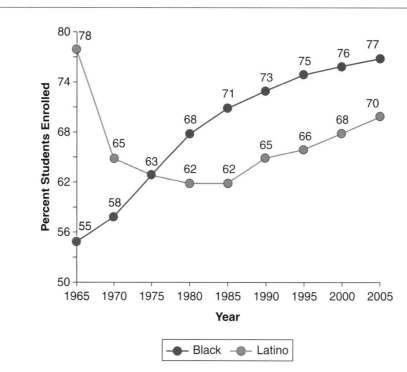

*Source:* Data from Applied Research Center (2003).

separated by socioeconomic status and by language proficiency as well (p. 12). The study continues,

> Students in these schools are not exposed to high-quality curricula, highly qualified teachers, or important social networks as often as students in wealthier, predominantly white schools. Where there is segregation, regardless of whether it is within or among schools or districts, numerous studies have found that racial disparities in achievement, school resources, discipline, and services between whites and students of color abound. (p. 12)

These disparities have resulted in conditions that educational scholar Richard Vogel (2005) refers to as a **de facto segregation** (not by law but by geographical or economic disparity) that insures inequality.

According to the U.S. Department of Education, in schools where "75 percent of the students were low income there were three times as many uncertified or out-of-field teachers in both English and science" (cited in Orfield and Lee 2005:7). Once they get more credentials, teachers at poor schools often move on to middle-class schools where they earn more money and work in better conditions. According to Obidah et al. (2007), city schools in the United States are hard-to-teach-in situations. The authors write,

> Urban centers of metropolitan cities suffer from debilitating social conditions such as poverty and its associated dysfunctions. When considering the political context, urban areas have a dwindling tax base and low voter turnout. As it relates to economic stability, there are high unemployment rates [and] limited employment opportunities. . . . Along with their students, African American teachers contend with poor working conditions, lack of materials and resources, and other structural barriers resulting from adverse economic, social, and political circumstances in urban centers, ultimately affecting the teaching and learning at these schools. The problems of urban education demonstrate a poignant convergence of racial, ethnic, and class inequalities. (p. 37)

## DESEGREGATION AND MIDDLE-CLASS FLIGHT: THE CASE OF KANSAS CITY

Court-ordered desegregation following the *Brown* decision did not end racial and class education inequality in U.S. cities. Throughout the nation, in city after city, attempts at desegregation have been countered by demographic trends (Rossell, Armor, and Walberg 2002). Difficult from the beginning, plans to integrate schools often resulted in mass exodus by white and middle-class residents to suburbs away from minority populations and inner-city schools. These demographic changes also redefined cities in other ways. The renewed racial isolation referred to earlier in the chapter reflects three key dynamics: (1) the relationship between class and geographical mobility; (2) an ideology that justifies parents' focus on their children's best interest, not the community in which they live; and (3) the pervading belief that desegregation by race and class negatively impacts educational quality and attainment. Some have argued that school desegregation has failed primarily because suburban sprawl facilitated white, middle-class exodus while saturating inner cities with low-income, minority populations (Caldas and Bankston 2005; Moran 2005).

Kansas City, Missouri's attempt to desegregate schools represents one of the nation's most ambitious efforts. In 1985, a federal judge ruled that the Kansas City Municipal School District and the state were liable for illegal segregation. Costing over $2 billion, the lawsuit was finally settled in 1997 after the district increased funding for students, decreased teacher–student ratios, built and remodeled schools and facilities, and relocated some students. Kansas City quickly became one of the nation's best-funded city school systems spending over $11,000 per pupil. However, the effort did not lead to desegregation, nor did it dramatically improve student test scores. Kansas City's experience occurred in city after city in the nation as school districts tried to desegregate students and improve education. Gotham (2002) argues that the investment by Kansas City was offset by the combination of the real estate market and Federal Housing Administration policies that supported white and middle-class flight at the same time the city tried to desegregate schools. Renewed residential segregation undermined the investment in new schools.

*(Continued)*

(Continued)

Debates over the effectiveness and desirability of desegregation focus on three areas. Commentators opposed to busing and racial quotas argue that mandatory reassignment and strict racial quotas are detrimental to communities. Some even argue that money is wasted on efforts to improve schools for minorities (Ciotti 1998). Others focus on the impact of desegregation efforts on communities. For instance Rossell et al. (2002) promote an approach based on financial assistance to low-income families instead of racial quotas. Still others argue that desegregation fails because of continued residential segregation and white flight from urban communities (Street 2005). Renewed racial segregation begs the question of how schools are funded and how inner cities will promote student success in the future. Kansas City remains a city with schools that are negatively affected by uneven development and racial isolation. Should we attempt to desegregate schools? How could we equalize school funding?

**Image 7.1**   An African American mother and daughter celebrate the Brown v. Board of Education decision. Over half a century after *Brown v. Board of Education of Topeka* provided the legal ruling necessary to desegregate schools in the United States, Kansas remains a controversial site for battles over equality in education.

*Source:* © Bettmann/CORBIS.

Given the economic inequalities of families and neighborhoods and the conditions for and quality of teachers and educational facilities in segregated schools, it should come as no surprise that race and ethnicity are important predictors of differences in overall school performance as well. School performance indicators show that white students have higher scores in reading, math, and science than black and Hispanic students (Eitzen et al. 2009). Table 7.1 shows just how much of an impact race and ethnicity have on math scores. Black students continue to lag behind other racial groups, although they have made gains between 2000 and 2007 relative to whites.

**Table 7.1**   National Math Scores for Fourth and Eighth Graders, 2000 and 2007

|  | Fourth Grade | | Eighth Grade | |
|---|---|---|---|---|
|  | 2000 | 2007 | 2000 | 2007 |
| White | 234 | 248 | 284 | 291 |
| Black | 203 | 222 | 244 | 260 |
| Hispanic | 208 | 227 | 253 | 265 |
| Asian/Pacific Islander | * | 253 | 288 | 297 |
| Native American | 209 | 228 | 259 | 264 |

*Source:* U.S. Department of Education, National Center for Education Statistics, National Assessment of Educational Progress (http://www.childstats.gov/americaschildren/edu2.asp).

*Data unavailable.

Many new immigrants face the same unequal schools and segregation as other minorities. First-generation families often have problems linked to learning English as a second language (ESL). Bilingual households often have lower levels of support at home (Portes and Rumbaut 2005). English language learners (ELL) have lower scores in math and reading than non-ELL students. (ELL students are those in the process of acquiring English language skills and knowledge.) Along with language barriers, poor counseling, tracking, and immigration status have been found to impact Latino school performance (Collatos, Morrell, Nuno, and Lara 2004). Table 7.2 shows the math and reading scores of ELL students compared to non-ELL students.

**Table 7.2**   National Reading Scores for Fourth and Eighth Graders: Non-English
Language Learners and English Language Learners, 2007

|  | Fourth Grade | | Eighth Grade | |
| --- | --- | --- | --- | --- |
|  | Math | Reading | Math | Reading |
| Non-ELLs | 242 | 224 | 283 | 265 |
| ELLs | 217 | 188 | 246 | 223 |

*Source:* U.S. Department of Education, National Center for Education Statistics, National Assessment of
Educational Progress (http://www.childstats.gov/americaschildren/edu2.asp).

## Education Inequality: Higher Education

Social class plays an important part in allowing access to higher education, especially
entrance into elite and private colleges and universities. Haycock (2007) articulates, "By
age 24, 75 percent of young people from families earning more than $80,000 a year
earn a bachelor's degree, while the corresponding figure for those in families earning less
than $25,000 a year is 9 percent" (p. 18). In many ways, the inequality that exists previ-
ous to higher education simply manifests itself after high school graduation. Even before
students set foot in the hallowed halls of academe, those from higher-income families
have taken advantage of college test-prep courses, college recruiting firms, college application specialists, and study skills trainers. The Century Foundation estimates that in the
146 top U.S. elite colleges, 74% of students came from upper-middle-class families and
wealthy families, and 5% from families with incomes of $35,000 or less. For many
working-class families with eligible children, dealing with financial aid, grants, and
loans is a difficult task (cited in Tyre 2003). Two-thirds of all graduates of 4-year colleges
now finish with sizable loans. Between 1995 and 2005, student debt rose by 50%. Public
college graduates now owe an average of $16,000, while private college graduates owe
an average of $20,000 (Gertner 2006). According to the Advisory Committee on Student
Financial Assistance (2006), 400,000 academically qualified students fail to pursue a post-
secondary education because they cannot afford it.

The free market movement toward privatization has meant a shift from government subsidies and grants (through taxes) to individual debt accumulation in the form of loans. While
grants have been cut and do not keep up with inflation, college tuition has been rising (Tyre
2003). Social theorists are beginning to note that the current costs of a college education
may threaten social mobility for future generations, especially for middle- and lower-class
college graduates. Pell grants, the federal government's principal aid program for low-
income students, went from covering 75% of college costs in 1979 to only 33% in 2005
(Haycock 2007). According to the Education Trust,

Between 1995 and 2003, flagship and other public research universities actually decreased aid by 13 percent for students from families with an annual income of $20,000 or less while they increased aid to students from families who make more than $100,000 by 406 percent. (cited in Campbell 2007)

As costs rise, college obtainment by race continues to be a cause for concern. African Americans make up 13% of the U.S. population, but they receive only 6.5% of college degrees (Campbell 2007). Ironically, while cost increases play a major role in restricting the accessibility of higher education for nonwhites already disproportionately impacted by economic inequality, changes in national and institutional policies toward race have also seriously influenced college access for minority youth. Looking at the effect of desegregation and affirmative action in the 1960s and 1970s, Carnoy (1994) has argued that national policies to increase access to higher education for minority youth have actually worked. Table 7.3 shows dramatic increases in educational attainment among black and Mexican-origin workers.

Table 7.3   Native-Born Mexican Origin and Black Workers, 25- to 34-Year-Old Males, by Level of Education

| Level of schooling | Mexican Origin | | | Black | | |
|---|---|---|---|---|---|---|
| | 1960 | 1970 | 1980 | 1960 | 1970 | 1980 |
| Less than 12 yrs | 78.1 | 45.8 | 31.0 | 68.8 | 47.4 | 23.4 |
| High school grad. | 12.8 | 35.2 | 33.8 | 19.2 | 37.9 | 39.2 |
| Some college | 3.8 | 12.3 | 22.9 | 7.0 | 9.7 | 24.3 |
| College degree | 2.8 | 2.5 | 5.8 | 3.2 | 3.0 | 8.1 |
| Graduate school | 2.4 | 4.2 | 6.4 | 1.9 | 2.3 | 4.9 |

*Source:* Department of Commerce, Bureau of the Census, cited in *Faded Dreams: The Politics and Economics of Race in America,* by Martin Carnoy, Cambridge, UK: Cambridge University Press.

Yet, while the ability to obtain an education, especially for African Americans, improved dramatically in the 1960s and 1970s, attainment stagnated in the 1980s and decreased in the early 1990s. Three major factors caused this trend:

1) The increased per pupil resources made available by pressure from civil rights groups and the War on Poverty policies of the 1960s leveled off and then decreased in real dollars in the 1980s and early 1990s; 2) Programs that improved student performance in school, such as Head Start [see following box] and back to basics instruction, expanded in the 1970s, but not in the 1980s and 1990s; and 3) Grants and government guaranteed loans for low-income college students expanded rapidly in the 1970s but not in the 1980s [or 1990s]. (Carnoy 1994:133)

By the early 1990s, a retrenchment in the support for economic resources inspired by the civil rights movement, the war on poverty, and affirmative action policies resulted in the slowing down of educational achievement and college access for nonwhites.

In fact, affirmative action itself became one of the most controversial domestic policies in the 1980s, and by the early 1990s, colleges and universities had begun dismantling their support for actively recruiting minority students to meet affirmative action goals. Table 7.4 documents this decrease in both public and private higher educational institutions.

**Table 7.4**  Percentage of Special Recruiting Activities Targeting Individual Subgroups of Students, 1992 and 2000

| Group | Four Year Private | | Four Year Public | |
|---|---|---|---|---|
| | 1992 | 2000 | 1992 | 2000 |
| Racial/ethnic minorities | 65 | 54 | 91 | 66 |
| Disadvantaged | 24 | 24 | 44 | 37 |
| Students with disabilities | 12 | 10 | 21 | 12 |
| Students with special talents in arts, music | 59 | 57 | 71 | 54 |
| Part-time students | 29 | 21 | 25 | 21 |

*Source:* "Socioeconomic Status, Race/Ethnicity, and Selective College Admissions," 2004, by Anthony P. Carnevale and Stephen J. Rose, pp. 101–156 in *America's Untapped Resource: Low-Income Students in Higher Education,* edited by Richard Kahlenberg, New York: The Century Foundation.

Carnevale and Rose (2004) explain that attacks on affirmative action and its effectiveness have resulted in decreased representation of non-white students on college campuses of all types. While most colleges and universities (especially elite schools) suggest that admissions is based primarily on merit, Carnevale and Rose found that, of students admitted whose qualifications based on high school grades, test scores, and recommendation letters did not meet posted standards, twice as many were white. Unlike a racial, ethnic, or gender identity that might have given students an affirmative action boost, these white students had two primary characteristics: 1) athletic prowess and/or 2) strong connections to faculty or administrators, alumni, politicians, or major donors. In other words, there exists another level of "affirmative action"—one for the wealthy sons and daughters of people connected to colleges and universities (especially elite ones). While affirmative action for non-whites and other nontraditional students is being dismantled, special entitlements for students of elite or well-connected parents continue to thrive.

## CULTURAL WARS AND EDUCATION

Cultural debates over the role of public schools and the content of curriculum are important forces shaping education policy. Historically, public schools promised equity at the same time that they reflected local belief systems. Thus, while the early push for an efficient, pragmatic, and math and science–based curriculum met industrial needs, communities often used schools to promote conservative religious and social values as well. These dual purposes ultimately resulted in major cultural controversies such as the Scopes Monkey Trial in 1926. The case's featured conflict between creationist theology and evolution/scientific paradigms continues to represent a powerful schism playing itself out in classroom curriculum debates today.

Increased curriculum standardization since World War II has been accompanied by a host of other cultural debates. In the 1960s, conflicts over multiculturalism in classes and textbooks highlighted the previously ignored roles of women, African Americans, Latinos, Native Americans, and gays and lesbians in American History. Whereas multiculturalism reflected new disciplines and theoretical frameworks, the conservative backlash of the 1980s generated controversies over the Pledge of Allegiance, the role of prayer and the Bible in schools, and whether the state or local communities should control textbooks and curriculum. Diane Ravitch (2003) asserts that by the 1980s, these warring factions had impacted special interest groups, textbook companies, and school boards. Critics argued that they were censoring educators and actually "dumbing down" American education (Gatto 1991). By screening out topics that could possibly be considered offensive, those involved in the cultural wars sacrificed truth and quality. Such screening has led to the banning of classic books and a fear-driven approach to providing children with knowledge and critical thinking skills.

Recently, sex education has again become an area of extreme conflict in U.S. schools. Since 1999, over 100 federally funded abstinence-based sex education courses are once again triggering controversy. With over 60% of youth having sex by the 12th grade, sexual activity in school-age children is a major concern for parents and educators. Social problems linked to teen sex include pregnancy, sexually transmitted diseases, and HIV/AIDS. Supported by conservatives and fundamentalist Christian groups, abstinence-only programs generally don't talk about contraception and they take negative approaches to sex before marriage. However, in some parts of the country, other controversial sex education programs are introducing contraception at an early age. These more comprehensive approaches inform students about *both* abstinence and the use of contraceptives (Irvine 2002; Sternberg 2002). What is your perspective on these cultural debates? What types of sex education are best for school-aged children?

## A HISTORY: U.S. EDUCATION PAST AND PRESENT

Early colonial education was based primarily on Protestant biblical teachings, vocational training, and apprenticeships. Class, race, and gender often determined access to basic literacy skills, as well as to formal or higher educational institutions. Most African Americans, poor children, and women were excluded from education, either by law in the South or by cost or custom in the North. Wealthy whites had access to private academies and also to the more prestigious religious schools. Yet, as American society developed, educational reformers, as well as manufacturing elites, realized that the promise of extending education to the middle and working classes could address a variety of agendas.

In 1841, Homer Bartlett, agent of the Massachusetts Cotton Mills, explained that "the owners of manufacturing property have a deep pecuniary interest in the education and morals of their help . . . [and that] the [factory,] which has the best educated and most moral help[,] will give the greatest production at the least cost per pound" (quoted in Bowles and Gintis 1976). Early advocates of mass public education argued that economic expansion would be best served by a workforce with basic literacy and arithmetic skills, as well as training in a new industrial work ethic that preached hard work, obedience, efficiency, and self-discipline. Michael Katz (1970) quotes an article written for *Massachusetts Teacher* magazine in the mid-1800s:

> The habit of prompt action in the performance of a duty required of the boy, by the teacher, at school, becomes in the man of business confirmed; thus system and order characterize the employment of the day laborer. He must begin each half day with as much promptness as he drops his tools at the close of it; and he must meet every appointment and order during the hours of the day with no less precision. . . . Thus, what has been instilled in the mind of the pupil, as a principle, becomes thoroughly recognized by the man as of the first importance in the transaction of business. (p. 87)

From the perspective of the economic elite, education could instill the kind of industrial discipline and corporate values necessary for a productive and deferent workforce, the kind of attitudes and behaviors discussed at length in Chapter 3.

But most reformers, including Horace Mann, envisioned education's reach as broader than just the shop floor. The growing textile towns and increasingly immigrant labor force posed threats to older agrarian values, Yankee culture, and provincial customs. While conflict and disruption threatened manufacturers, industrialization and urbanization also undermined once-stable and deferential communities, "rapidly ushering in an era of conflict, contention, and possible social disruption" (Bowles and Gintis 1976). Mann fought to expand compulsory education to all citizens, arguing that youth needed training in the morals and practices of a democratic society, because "the great moral attribute of self-government cannot be born and matured in a day; and if children are not trained to it, we only prepare ourselves for disappointment if we expect it of grown men" (quoted in Bowles and Gintis 1976: 170–171). Self-control, public propriety, respect for authority, and a dedication to hard work would be necessary for a democratic public as well as an expanding bottom line. Education would provide the basic literacy skills for working- and middle-class youth to enter the labor force and participate in public debates, at the same time that employers would get workers already indoctrinated with an industrial discipline that taught them to be on time, follow the rules, and adhere to a capitalist work ethic.

Americans in the late 19th and early 20th century witnessed great strides in education. In 1857, half of all school-aged children went to school; by 1918, it was 75%, in part as a result of every state establishing laws that made schooling mandatory for all children up until the age of 16. But the character of the growing system continued to respond primarily to the interests of the economic and political elite. Major industrial expansion employing millions of new immigrant workers required a massive system to train people in the skills and behaviors needed for factory and service work. Meanwhile, economic and political elites wished to quell the urban and industrial conflicts they believed stemmed from the huge influx of non–English-speaking people with different cultural practices and values. Schools became the most powerful tool available to indoctrinate new immigrant groups into the economic and social systems of the United States. As Pai and Adler (1997) write, "Schools in America went through many changes during the years from 1870 to the early 1920s, yet the belief that minority cultures represented deficit conditions to be eradicated by the schooling process remained unquestioned" (pp. 60–61). In other words, schools evolved as the primary institution for Americanizing immigrant youth and preparing them to work in an expanding industrial economy.

Schools also trained black, Latino, and Native American children for various segments of the working class. As mentioned previously, Native American children were forced into industrial or mission schools, while many Mexican children (mostly girls) were sent to learn the practices and values necessary to do domestic work for middle-class and wealthy whites in the American Southwest. Similarly, "normal" schools developed as early teacher and vocational prep schools for African Americans. These normal schools coexisted with the doctrine of "separate but equal," training the children and grandchildren of former slaves to handle brooms, work in industry, or teach in segregated schools themselves. At the same time that education acquired a cultural moniker as "the great equalizer," the education for non-white and immigrant working-class youth remained unequal at best and discriminatory at worst.

Reform movements did occur to make education more balanced, to empower poorer youth with critical knowledge and not simply train them to be obedient and efficient workers. The progressive movement led by John Dewey (1916/1944) pushed education in the direction of **pragmatism,** encouraging the values of citizenship and classes in life skills such as economics, wood shop, and family living. Such studies were not, for Dewey, about vocational or citizenship training, per se. Instead, he saw the "ideal aim of education [as the] creation of self-control" (p. 64) where, given the freedom and tools to perform real democracy, people and their communities would flourish. Dewey advocated for an "experience-based" education that offered students the critical intellectual and physical knowledge to be active creators of their own lives, as well as substantive participants in shaping the communities around them. As the educational system in the United States evolved throughout the late 19th and early 20th century, it remained what sociologists call a "contested terrain" where different groups with different values fought to establish their own agendas: some intent on maintaining a strictly stratified yet effective economic and social system; others interested in expanding middle-class economic and cultural opportunities; and others envisioning a different, more substantively democratic and equal society.

Another movement to improve the quantity and quality of education in the United States began after the Second World War. Access to higher education changed remarkably in 1944 with the Servicemen's Readjustment Act. This so-called "GI Bill of Rights" included housing and unemployment allotments, but the most important elements gave free or partially paid tuition and living stipends to over half of the 5.5 million veterans who returned from World War II and Korea. Combined with increasing government and corporate investments in university-based scientific research, both private and public universities burgeoned in the late 1940s and 1950s as the enrollment of college-bound students increased from 1.2 million in 1944 to 2.7 million in 1950 (Geiger 2004).

For African Americans and other minorities, desegregation and the war on poverty ultimately resulted in passage of the Civil Rights Acts of 1964, which, aside from outlawing discrimination in employment, public facilities, and so forth, also empowered the U.S. Attorney General to enforce the *Brown* antisegregation decision by bringing suits against school districts for plaintiffs free of charge. Similarly, the act charged the Department of Education with collecting data on school enrollments by race. These aspects of the 1964 Civil Rights Act led to a major study of American education in 1966 known as the **Coleman Report** or *Equality of Educational Opportunity*. The Coleman Report suggested that the large achievement gap between black and white students was due in part to a lack of educational tools and interventions in homes and communities for African Americans. The report also pointed to inequalities throughout black schools related to teacher accreditation, resources, and facilities (Coleman 1966; J. Jackson 2007). Despite desegregation and massive infusions of public monies into education for the working and middle classes, the institution and implementation of education remained steeped in inequalities.

The rise of community colleges in the 1970s represents one of the nation's most effective policies to address access to higher education. Community colleges or 2-year colleges currently enroll 44% of all U.S. college students. The United States' 1,000 community colleges offer technical programs and allow access to higher education for many working, low-income families and dislocated workers. Today, 2-year colleges provide skills that are needed in emerging green job and technical sectors of the economy (Zeidenberg and Van Noy 2009).

Community colleges may have addressed access and economic downturns in the economy, but the last part of the 20th century witnessed increased calls for reform in education. While the 1960s and 1970s hosted progressive reforms in the form of Head Start programs (see the following box), multicultural curricula, and affirmative action, the late 1980s and 1990s saw cuts to such programs; calls for "traditional" degree programs; and challenges to ethnic, racial, and gender studies. As the economy changed rapidly from domestic and industrial to global and "postindustrial," schools were called on to improve scientific and technological training, as well as provide an understanding and awareness of world history, culture, and geography. Meanwhile, intense crime and poverty (especially in the nation's urban centers) and rising rates of youth violence, teenage pregnancies, and drug use resulted in communities and politicians calling on schools to teach values, morals, and other basic socialization skills once thought the purview of families and religious institutions. By the end of the 1990s, more students had received college and high school degrees than ever before, yet complaints and controversies over the quality and ideology of schools and their curricula had reached a fever pitch.

Recent approaches to and conflicts over public education have been shaped by the **No Child Left Behind Act (NCLB)** of 2001. NCLB focuses on public school standardization in grades 3 through 8 and high school. The act requires all schools receiving federal aid to give annual performance tests, offering incentives to catch up with national averages and sanctions if a school does not perform well enough over time. NCLB is dependent on **standardized testing,** or the use of norm-referenced tests to determine the performance of individual students, the grade and school achievement levels, and the progress of students from one year to the next (Ebert and Culyer 2008). NCLB is designed to use testing to determine what is wrong with schools, but more importantly, it sets forth strategies and punishments for schools that don't improve. NCLB can be understood as a way in which functionalist theory has informed recent educational policy. By establishing standards of achievement and mechanisms for improvement and enforcement, society is reshaping educational institutions to fulfill the explicit function of making children competent in basic math and reading skills. Both individual children and institutions as a whole can be socialized to meet basic expectations through positive and negative reinforcement.

Mandated testing, however, impacts curriculum in substantive ways. Brem and Kyle (2004) argue that national standards should be developed with the reality that multiple intelligences exist—that is, students learn in different ways. An overreliance on standardized testing results in many students who don't "test well" becoming labeled as poor students, despite the fact that they may in fact be mastering materials but cannot demonstrate such knowledge on tests. Similarly, schools that fail to raise test scores adequately are referred to as "failing schools." From a symbolic interactionist perspective, once these students and schools acquire the label of "poor" or "failing," they are closely watched and punished for their inability to meet standards. Given that these schools generally exist in the poorest economic communities with the fewest resources, the social stigma created by NCLB actually further alienates many students. Meanwhile, "teaching to the test" has forced many schools (especially those with meager resources) to cut back on arts, music, physical education, and other aspects of a liberal arts curriculum (Kozol 2005).

Other critics of NCLB worry about the ideological indoctrination and possible privatization stemming from the legislation. Kincheloe (2006) argues that the reduction of curriculum to low-level thinking skills and away from critical inquiry and expression tends to indoctrinate students with conservative and corporate values. Such a conflict perspective also notes that schools failing to meet standards find themselves threatened with privatization. Studies on how to reform NCLB point out that the act has substantially underfunded dropout prevention and intervention components. High numbers of failing school systems have also undermined the act (Harris and Tsoi-A-Fatt 2007).

In many districts around the United States, charter schools and educational corporations such as EdisonLearning, Inc. (formerly known as Edison Schools Inc.) have literally taken control of public school systems, not just individual schools. School choice proponents promote the use of **vouchers** that allow parents to use public dollars to send students to charter and other private schools. Vogel (2005) argues that the school choice movement has its roots in urban gentrification, where affluent newcomers want the advantages of city life but feel compelled to avoid city schools. While choice allows some people to choose "successful" schools for their kids, it is often at the expense of further degrading public schools for the majority.

## MEDIA BOX: EDUCATION POLICY AND THE "MAKING" OF A CRISIS

Education policy is shaped by politics and corporate influence which are often translated to the public by the mass media. This chapter reveals that the history of public education has been influenced by political and social movements, often leading to debates over education priorities. The role of the mass media has increased as society relies more and more on media messages for its basic information. In the case of education, federal policies were introduced in the Elementary and Secondary Education Act (ESEA) of 1965, which addressed civil rights, disabilities, and inequalities (Manna 2006). Many of these programs are still in place. The policies represent the public view that led to the war on poverty and the nation's attempt to integrate schools. More recently, the No Child Left Behind policies were an attempt to make schools responsible for student failure, ignoring many of the social forces such as child poverty that ESEA was trying to address. The shift in policy reflected the rise of neoliberalism as a political reality and the move to privatize social institutions. Critics point out that NCLB policies were an attempt to limit the power of teachers' unions and strengthen corporations. The role of the mass media in NCLB policies has been well documented. In "What You Don't Know About School Is Hurting You and the Country," Kincheloe (2006) argues that No Child Left Behind policies were constructed around media messages that portrayed the nation's education as failing with horrific schools and inefficient bureaucracy. These policies put forth that the solution was privatization in the form of vouchers, school choice, and standardized testing. The marketing of the idea of schools in crisis has been called a misinformation campaign by a number of critics (see Manna 2006). The supporters of NCLB policies assert that schools can achieve regardless of levels of funding and support. They point out that competition and innovation are important for school success, ideas often promoted by NCLB policy makers quoted in the mass media. The politics of school reform reveal differences in approach to schools. Both making schools responsible for student performance and addressing the social forces behind underachieving schools will continue to shape policy. What are your ideas on school reform? How has the mass media shaped your perspective?

## CASE STUDY #1

### Tutoring for Reading and Education Success: The "Hidden Curriculum" of Poverty

English composition students involved in Arizona State University's (ASU's) service learning project fill heavy shoes. These students work with children who live in environments that put them at risk for academic failure. Emanating from ASU's Department of English and its Writing Across the Curriculum program, the program's internships provide one-on-one tutoring, reading development, educational enrichment workshops, and learning readiness programs for children in the Roosevelt School District (RSD), one of Phoenix's poorest areas. Students who live in the RSD face great adversity both within school and outside it. RSD's 18 schools rank only in the 30th percentile on national standardized tests. The district is a "majority minority" district with its student population composed of 68% Hispanic; 24% African American; and 8% white, Asian, and Native American young people. Outside of school, these children experience high levels of poverty and crime, a lack of adequate parks and recreational facilities, and a lack of English-language proficiency. They also experience extreme residential mobility (frequently moving in and out of homelessness, living in subsidized housing, or staying with relatives). Thus, they also move from school to school and have little or no ongoing relationships with peers or school faculty and staff.

Sociologists point out that the social environment not only indicates what kind of resources a school has, but it also influences what has been called the **hidden curriculum**. While the hidden curriculum has been defined broadly as the "ways in which pupils learn to accept the denial and interruption of their personal desires and wishes" (P. Jackson 1968, p. 78), conflict theorists emphasize the unwritten and indirect role that inequality plays in teaching poor students that they have unequal opportunities and face almost insurmountable obstacles. Apple (1979), for example, points toward a network of assumptions that, when internalized by students, establishes the boundaries of legitimacy for what they can and can't accomplish. In school, tracking, vocational training, and other practices that label and limit (often from very early on) students' potential characterize the impact of a hidden curriculum. But even more subtle conditions such as class size, the quality and quantity of books and other resources, the amount of attention given by teachers, and so on, all shape the educational expectations and attitudes of young people regarding their own intellectual possibilities. According to Brack and Hall (1997),

> The principal reason for the children's lack of appropriate academic development is an environment that puts them at great risk of failure. The South Mountain precinct of the Phoenix Police Department, which includes the RSD, reports the highest incidence of drive-by shootings and the highest homicide rate in the state of Arizona. The district averages a 16 percent dropout rate (approximately 1,700 students) and a 19 percent rate for juvenile detention referrals (approximately 2,200 students). Without significant one-on-one help, it is virtually impossible for many of the children and youth in the RSD to achieve grade-level performance. (p. 137)

*(Continued)*

(Continued)

The ASU service learning project matches college students with a very specific community problem: the impact of a poor community and a poor school district on young students. While the project takes college students from a variety of majors, upper-division classes that require more highly skilled students choose only among nursing and speech and hearing majors (to help with health screening and nutrition skills) and education majors (Brack and Hall 1997). Working with students ages 3–14, the service learners in the English classes prepare a customized lesson and activities for every tutoring session for each child.

Researchers find that service learning in the right setting can increase educational success for children from communities with few economic or social resources (Coleman 1966; Coleman and Kerbo 2006; Halpern 2005). Mentoring has an especially powerful potential to bridge gaps between students and the kinds of social or cultural capital often necessary for success. Effective guidance can play an important role in helping at-risk youth avoid the damaging effects of extended periods without adequate education or housing. Moreover, service learning–based mentoring can significantly boost academic performance and reduce dropout rates from school (Johnson 1999). Along with poor communities and poor schools, ASU mentors encountered children with physiological problems, low levels of self-esteem and other psychological impairments, and little optimism about their future education. Katie Davis, one such college student, wrote the following about working with her very young student:

> Monday and Friday from 11:30–2:30 I tutor a precious little girl named Alisha at the Salvation Army. This amazing child always gives me a new challenge or surprise. Minute after minute and hour after hour I struggle to teach this little girl everything I can. There comes a period in the day in which I become emotionally and physically exhausted, yet I continue to feed her information that will hopefully make her life a little easier. . . . Alisha is a four-year-old . . . who like many of the children with Fetal Alcohol Syndrome has a difficult time paying attention. Compared to other children around her she is developmentally delayed. . . . She struggles with questions I ask her and rarely can sit through an entire lesson. It is very typical for Alisha to become overstimulated. Everything in the room distracts her . . . including other people in the room, music, voices, and myself. The best way to teach her is to remain in a quiet, calm, and orderly room. (Brack and Hall 1997:142)

Studies show, however, that similar children do respond to the kinds of personal and intimate relationships that such one-on-one tutoring can establish. It is obvious that Katie has already learned the importance of creating the right environment and that the style and structure of lessons may be just as important as the content for a young learner like Alisha.

For the college students themselves, Brack and Hall (1997) suggest that those who engage in service learning write with a purpose related to their community experiences. Beyond witnessing the learning difficulties faced by the children, they are forced to engage the variety of social problems behind poor academic performance such as poverty and homelessness, gangs, drugs and crime, parental imprisonment or addictions, domestic violence and racial or ethnic discrimination, and so forth. ASU faculty uses an electronic forum to allow participants to discuss mutual concerns, talk about practical matters, and strategize about conditions and individual cases to improve tutoring. Many of these students will become teachers in the future. As Brack and Hall summarize, "Too often the 'research' done in such courses is seen by students as an empty exercise, a means of learning how to use the library or how to use correct citation, not as an avenue for changing someone's mind or making a difference in the world" (p. 143). ASU students go on to become professionals, but the fields they specialize in are no longer simply academic or service oriented in nature. They now recognize the complexity of those served and the conditions they live in, embracing the need to challenge larger structures of inequality at the same time they address the impact of the hidden curriculum on each student.

## Case Study Questions

1. What did the mentors learn about social problems through mentoring at ASU?

2. What is the hidden curriculum?

3. What are the differences pointed out in the case study between tutoring and library research?

4. How does mentoring help students become future teachers?

## CASE STUDY #2

### The Futures Project: Disrupting Education Inequality

This chapter reveals the roles that race, class, and ethnicity play in educational inequality in America. Intervention programs designed to assist minority youth to go to college are often ineffective because they address only the perceived problems students have and not the education system itself (Collatos and Morrell 2003). Drawing on critical sociology, social theorists at UCLA's Department of Education began to address college attainment for low-income students of color and disrupt the system that perpetuates underachievement in their high schools through the Futures Project. Located in the school's Institute for Democracy, Education, and Access, the program involves college and high school faculty in mentoring high school students to do better in high school and go to college. The Futures Project calls on students to become researchers for one class of each of their 4 years of high school. The project's basic research questions asked why students with their background did not go to college; the project's goal was to change those outcomes (Oakes, Rogers, and Lipton 2006). The students often later become college mentors themselves, assisting students from the same low-income, minority high school from where they came. Two of the programs involving UCLA were held in the late 1990s and 2000 for students at Woodrow Wilson and James Madison High Schools in Southern California. The students had weak educational backgrounds, had limited access to social resources, and were from low-income families. At Wilson, the participants were students of color, with 20 Latinos, 9 African Americans, and 1 Southeast Asian. Created by UCLA professors in collaboration with Woodrow Wilson teachers and administrators, the Futures Project drew on the idea that educational systems often shape how students see their potential.

*(Continued)*

(Continued)

Symbolic interactionists view the impact of school hierarchies, between administrators and teachers, teachers and students, and even among students themselves, from the perspective of the reflective self and social expectations. Low-achieving students experience school as a **self-fulfilling prophecy** where failure is expected by teachers, administrators, and peers. Once labeled and treated as failures, students find it more comfortable and—in perverse ways—even more rewarding to meet these low expectations. Labeling occurs in the process of tracking, or placing students into ability categories based on test scores. Tracking works as just such a label, where students are immediately treated in particular ways, introduced to particular curricula, and encouraged in particular directions based on initial determinations of their potential for success or failure. Increasingly, education's sorting function has determined the success or failure of an individual child entering the system. Functionalist theorists such as Kingsley Davis and Wilbert Moore valued the role that sorting played in education because it prepared individuals for a meritocracy and guaranteed society would fulfill its needs for professional elites and unskilled workers alike. Conflict theorists, however, see sorting as a way to reproduce class and cultural inequality by boosting the self-esteem and resources granted to elite students who are "expected to succeed," while restricting the potential and self-image of poor and working-class students predicted to fail. Regardless of the theoretical paradigm, the process of tracking and sorting, of labeling and stereotyping, have a major impact on the educational outcomes of economically and socially marginalized students.

As alluded to earlier in the chapter, the negative impacts many Latinos face in the education system can create a self-fulfilling prophecy of failure, especially when the education system does not address students' cultural heritage or social relationships (see Valverde 2005). The Futures Project began with a goal of altering how students see college and their own abilities. The students were age 14 when they began the project, working alongside university professors doing research in the sociology of urban education. In the spirit of John Dewey (1916/1944), the goal of the project was to bring the students in vital contact with caring communities. The project worked to bond students and staff.

> To speak of communities of practice and apprenticeships does not capture the "direct and vital contact" that takes place in an authentic community of caring adults and young people who are eager for learning, schooling, and emotional support. As the students studied their regular schoolwork together, as they worked together on the Futures research, and as they hung out together, they developed strong relationships. These bonds buffered the conflicts that arose when they tried to act like college-bound high school students simply did not know how, or felt it was impossible. (Oakes et al. 2006:51)

The program took students on college visits and provided computers along with the opportunity to build social networks. Amazingly, many of the subjects they discussed were college theories or "college knowledge." Students developed plans of study and worked toward college admission requirements, including studying for the SAT and ACT. In summer seminars at UCLA, students in the project looked at perspectives in the sociology of education.

By the time they were seniors, the Futures students had developed a strong critique of the "facts" about school achievement, college preparation, and college admissions. Alongside their inescapable induction into mainstream social, political, and economic thinking in which competition, merit, strong individualism, and so on, constituted the "even playing field" of American democracy, the project introduced the Futures students to critical social theory that would, at least, allow them to consider alternative explanations of disparities among groups of students. (Oakes et al. 2006:58)

The progress made by students participating in the experiment were in several areas. By the end of their high school career and the Futures Project, the participants outpaced the school average with all but one student graduating. 97% of the students who participated in the experiment graduated, while only 75% of the comparison group graduated. Their cumulative GPA was 2.52 compared to 2.37 for the comparison group. Many Futures Project students also took advanced placement (AP) classes (Oakes et al. 2006). They learned to counter the negative labels and self-doubt while their skills and self-esteem improved. More importantly, they came to understand the system of education—how it worked against them in some ways and how it could work for them in other ways. According to one student, "This shift was quite different from 'increased confidence' to take demanding courses." Learning to think critically is evident in the student responses to the program: "[Futures] is really preparing me to survive in this world, especially in a country like this one because there's a lot of injustice. There's really nothing that had been done to repair all the damage. Being aware and knowing what your rights are [is preparation]" (Oakes et al. 2006:59). Futures participant Alejandro Nuno went on to the University of San Francisco, at which time he became a mentor for other high school students.

Because of my experiences as a critical researcher, I learned navigational strategies that enabled me to develop a college-going identity and retain my culture while taking rigorous courses. Futures established a difference between knowing all the requirements to attend a 4-year university and knowing how to access them. Even though I had a 4.0 grade point average, a teacher or counselor never encouraged me to enroll in Advanced Placement courses. Before Futures, no school representatives ever informed me about SATs, ACTs, or SAT IIs or practice courses I could utilize to prepare for such high-stakes tests. (Collatos et al. 2004:164)

The Futures Project shows that students can adopt "college-going identities" that enable them to utilize resources and navigate obstacles. The key is a change in expectations. This work demonstrates that systemic inequality can be overcome through changing the orientation of students.

## Case Study Questions

1. How is race linked to self-fulfilling prophesies for Latinos in American high schools?

2. What assumptions did UCLA professors make about minority youth in the Futures Project?

3. What were the educational outcomes for youth involved in the Futures Project?

4. What are the implications of the Futures Project for U.S. education?

## VOICES FROM THE FIELD

### Jonathon Kozol

Source: © AP Photo/Steven Senne.

Harvard graduate and Rhodes scholar Jonathon Kozol gave up a lucrative career to teach in the Boston public school system. His experiences led to books such as *Death at an Early Age*, *Rachel and Her Children*, *Savage Inequalities*, and *Amazing Grace*, which document the impact on children of America's class and race segregation and inequality in its school systems. His 2005 book, *The Shame of the Nation: The Restoration of Apartheid Schooling in America*, chronicles the reemerging of racial segregation of America's schools and the impact of NCLB on poor schools in the inner city. Elana Berkowitz (2005) interviewed him in 2005 about involvement in educational equality.

EB:  How do we activate liberally minded young people who may graduate with a lot of debt and who are wavering between Teach for America and a lucrative career at Goldman Sachs? What do you say to students?

JK:  First of all, I think there's a myth most college students are selfishly inclined to earning money quickly or so determined to make their way in the corporate world that they don't have any time or inclination to go out and do the decent things that are needed to change the world. In fact, I find thousands of college students, tens of thousands, wherever I go, packing the auditoriums wherever I speak, and then typically 200 of them will keep me up for another two hours asking me exactly where they're needed. They are not willing to suppress their sense of justice or postpone their activism until some later time in life until after they've established a lucrative career. They want to do it now and they're right to have that feeling because if they postpone the moment of ethical action for another five years, the likelihood is that they'll never return to it. Once they go on to law school or whatever career it may be, they almost never return to that state of mind where they're willing to take risks for the cause of justice.

Source: "Five Minutes With: Jonathan Kozol" by Elana Berkowitz. This material was published by the Center for American Progress, (online). Created by the Center for American Progress (www.americanprogress.org)" (print). Copyright © American Progress.

## CASE STUDY #3

### Girls, Math, Water, and Lead: Challenging the Gender Gap in Science and Math Education

The Mother Caroline Academy (MCA) is an independent, urban school for low-income girls in Dorchester—a predominantly poor neighborhood of Boston, Massachusetts. The school was founded in 1993 by the School Sisters of Notre Dame and serves around 75 girls in grades 4 through 8 who are almost entirely first-generation children of immigrant parents. According to Farah and Heffernan (2000), "Mother Caroline Academy parents place a high value on education and are genuinely concerned with the educational success of their daughters" (p. 140). In the mid-1990s, faculty and students from Lasell College, what was then a small, all-women's school (the school went coed in 1998), began a variety of service-related initiatives with MCA including twice-weekly tutoring, weekly after-school enrichment projects, a speakers program, and a scholarship program. As Lasell students and faculty worked with MCA teachers and youth, the relationships deepened. Eventually, conversations ensued that challenged the tutor-student model. As Farah and Heffernan explain,

> Academy faculty felt that the college student tutors needed to model math efficacy for the Academy students. This required the student tutors to reflect on and discuss the role of a tutor. Student tutors met with Academy faculty and discussed the ways they could model *how* to be a math and science student. As a result, the tutors transformed the evening study sessions into collective study sessions to which they brought their own coursework so they could study alongside the Academy students. During these sessions, the Academy students were encouraged to rely on their peers as well as the college student tutors when they needed assistance and to reason through problems collectively. Academy faculty reported that these collective study sessions were extremely helpful to the schoolchildren and helped change those students' initial assumptions that intellectual pursuits were nonrelational, individual pursuits and that the role of a tutor was simply to provide answers. The children also articulated a sense of pride in the active role they played in the study sessions and began to think of themselves as scholars. (p. 141)

The evolving relationship between Mother Caroline Academy and Lasell students and faculty allowed the programs and projects to change based in many cases on a feminist research paradigm.

Feminist research (Feminist research) in sociology has many principles, but the most important for this case and for the study of social problems in general are the following:

- Feminist research is contextual, inclusive, experiential, involved, socially relevant, complete but not necessarily replicable, open to the environment, and inclusive of emotions and events as experienced (Nielsen 1990; Reinharz 1983, 1992).

*(Continued)*

(Continued)

- It assumes that men and women differ in their perceptions of life due to their social status; therefore, it puts gender in the center of social inquiry (Harvey 1990).
- It employs engaging and value-laden methods and procedures that bring the researcher closer to the subject.
- It aims to enlighten the community to the factors that generate this phenomenon and disclose distortions related to women's experiences.
- It proposes ways that can help alleviate the problem and empower women and gives them a voice to speak about social life from their perspective (Sarantakos 1998).

While feminist sociology emphasizes the centrality of gender in research and analysis, it does so in a way that promotes social change that establishes more equitable systems for both men and women. The case of the Lasell College/Mother Caroline Academy project is an excellent case for examining these dynamics.

Many of the problems faced initially by the Lasell tutors related to the gendered experiences of young girls' relationship to science and math. Much educational research has demonstrated that many girls do not see science and math as "appropriate" disciplines, and by middle and junior high school shift their focus to language arts and social studies (Bruner 1996). Parents' and teachers' perceptions of math skills are especially gendered and tend to conclude that boys are more competent and successful than girls in mathematics and related fields (Yee and Eccles 1988). For MCA students, their own attitudes toward math and science led them to believe that girls and boys had different aptitudes and that girls were better suited for other kinds of knowledge. Only by addressing the gendered experiences and ideologies of the students (and the society around them) could the Lasell tutors impact the potential learning capacity of MCA youth.

Similarly, feminist approaches often critique individualism and stress the more mutualistic or collective realities that underlie the creation of knowledge in particular and social reality in general. Whether examining the history of the civil rights movement (Giddings 1984; Ransby 2005) or the history of ideas in general (Fullbrook and Fullbrook 1994), researchers have demonstrated that our focus on "great men" often mythologizes and fetishizes individual male achievements and overlooks the role that women have played in working collectively to produce social movements and other historical innovations. Some feminists have argued that women's approaches are "naturally" more mutualistic, while others argue these social dynamics are more a result of historical conditions than biological instinct. In either case, however, feminist research and scholarship emphasize the role and power of social networks and group production. In the MCA/Lasell project, tutors helped youth recognize the collective efforts necessary to create knowledge.

Lasell tutors also noted that MCA students' difficulties with math and science seemed related to their lack of laboratory facilities, hands-on projects, and other resources. Together, student tutors and Lasell faculty developed a 10-week science project for seventh-grade girls at the Mother Caroline Academy. Through grant writing and donations of lab equipment from the college, the Lasell group provided the academy with a small lab. But the project also included a weekly lab session at the college. The initial project focused on environmental science and addressed water quality in the Dorchester community in order to give students a sense of science's applications and relevancy to their own lives. The project succeeded to some degree, but in evaluating the effort, student coordinators determined that a more "overtly relational" topic was needed to "encourage girls to take greater interest in outcomes" and that they would be "more inclined to participate in the exercise if the problems to be addressed were presented as a human drama" (Farah and Heffernan 2000:146).

The next project took on the problem of lead contamination and was designed to solve the scientific question, "What made Carlos ill?" Academy students learned about lead contamination, the impact of lead on the body, and the various tools and procedures necessary to test for lead. They also studied mathematics and the types of measures, as well as other uses of statistics. Academy students also visited a public health lab and learned to use a data set that demonstrated lead contamination levels in communities throughout the Boston area. While most testing ultimately demonstrated no lead contamination, some groups did find significant levels in drinking water, and site owners were contacted in writing and advised to contact the Department of Health to discuss testing and cleanup. Academy students also produced a pamphlet on the dangers of lead contamination to be shared with their local community.

Academy student evaluations demonstrated that almost all participants showed higher interests in chemistry and math and wanted to do more laboratory work and other hands-on exercises. For the Lasell students, the program gave them experiences that helped them "reconceptualize their interest in math and science." They wrote that "prior to this experience they had experienced both math and science as dry and pedantic. . . . [The Academy project] allowed them to examine the possibilities math and science held for solving community problems." They also began to understand the impact of social conditions on learning and gained new insights into the impact of economic and gender inequalities. As one student wrote, "prior to participating in this project I always believed that math was a gift you were born with. . . . Now I see that it can be taught and it can be learned" (Farah and Heffernan 2000:146).

For some Lasell students, the experience proved even more powerful, as aspects of feminist research led them to a greater sense of community and identity. As one non-white tutor explained,

> When I work with the Academy girls I am reminded that I have a responsibility to try and better the chances of other blacks and other women. I think service is more personal in the black community. They [Academy students] are not just helping this community but they are helping themselves and each other. It's more of a shared thing. . . . I think with a lot of service . . . and the way I hear people talk about service, it's like we're helping this foreign, different community and for a lot of black organizations, it's not us and them—it's we—and we are helping each other and this is our obligation to each other. (Farah and Heffernan 2000:145)

For Lasell students, service learning demonstrated a collective form of education that addressed issues of resource inequality, as well as the possibility that working together could challenge inequalities of race, gender, and class and result in creating new kinds of commitments and relationships.

*(Continued)*

(Continued)

Case Study Questions

1. What does feminist research add to the analysis of tutoring at Lasell?

2. What problems do students have to overcome related to gender and math at the academy?

3. What are the differences in how women and men were seen as historical actors?

4. How did community service lead to a different view of math and science for girls at the academy?

## SOLUTIONS IN YOUR OWN BACKYARD: THE BENEFITS OF MENTORING

Working with at-risk schoolchildren is a way for college students to change the odds in the U.S. education system. Schargel and Smink (2004) point out that regardless of the format, structure, or institutional host of the program, mentoring is a community development program. Mentoring and tutoring have many positive effects and benefits. Programs designed for youth mentoring such as AmeriCorps and Big Brother/Big Sister are low-cost, low-tech strategies to address multiple social problems. Extracurricular programs mediate the negative effects of disadvantaged family and poor neighborhoods.

Mentoring reduces truancy, improves grades, and improves family relationships. Mentors provide role models who enhance self-esteem, instill a sense of responsibility, and reinforce the efforts of schools and teachers (Schargel and Smink 2004). Service learning programs help develop relationships between colleges and communities (Cashel, Goodman, and Swanson 2003).

One mentoring program, GEAR UP (Gaining Early Awareness and Readiness for Undergraduate Programs), is put on through the U.S. Department of Education (DOE) and is designed to increase the number of students from low-income communities who are prepared to enter and succeed in postsecondary education. DOE grants are available to middle and high school students. The Washington, DC, GEAR UP school is partnered with one of seven colleges including Georgetown University, Howard University, Southeastern University, Trinity College, and the University of the District of Columbia.

The Trinity College Sociology of Education 201 course is a good example of the application of sociological principles to service learning. While covering the basic questions and issues in the field of sociology of education, students use *community-based learning* (CBL) as a strategy for mentoring in the GEAR UP program. CBL helps students to uncover the dynamics and problems of the education system as they mentor disadvantaged youth. CBL requires that course participants reflect on the service activity while they integrate course materials with their service learning experience. Sociology majors engaged in mentoring through service learning are in a unique position to be participant observers. Working with students helps social science majors develop skills related to critical evaluation, communication, and writing.

## SUMMARY

This chapter examined social problems in education with an emphasis on race, class, and gender. According to conflict theorists, many of the problems of the current system are linked to continued inequality in economic and social conditions. High levels of educational inequality are dysfunctional for society, as education increasingly plays a more pronounced role in the reproduction of opportunities in a postindustrial, global economy. The research presented in this chapter points out that segregation remains a fundamental block to educational opportunities for low-income and minority students. In addition, these groups face higher dropout rates and enter college less often than wealthy and middle-class Americans.

We also presented a historical context to try and understand what social and political dynamics have shaped the current conditions in our education system. Most contemporary issues in K–12 education are significantly impacted by the set of policies known as No Child Left Behind. A number of school systems across the country are struggling to address problems related to funding deficits and helping English language learners while facing increasing standards. While NCLB represents an attempt to reform education societywide, the legislation has failed to seriously improve public schools or the impact school systems have in communities throughout the United States.

Yet the chapter has also indicated that there are many instances where people have effected positive changes in education. College students working with their own faculty and institutions have provided powerful examples of how carefully designed projects can change the lives of children in schools. While service learning has a long-lasting impact on the students and faculty who participate, these case studies also demonstrate that schools can become agents of improvement when education itself becomes a living and breathing practice of social change, not a stagnant and frayed institutional husk reproducing systemic inequalities.

## SUMMARY QUESTIONS

1. What are the impacts of students dropping out of high school? What groups are more likely to drop out and why?

2. How do class and race influence educational outcomes?

3. What are the goals of the U.S. education system?

4. How does the self-fulfilling prophesy influence educational outcomes?

5. How do standardized testing and recent No Child Left Behind policies influence education programs and the addressing of social problems related to education?

## GLOSSARY

**Coleman Report:** A 1966 report that suggested the large achievement gap between black and white students was due in part to a lack of educational tools and interventions in homes and communities for African Americans.

**De Facto Segregation:** Segregation not by law but by geographical or economic disparity that insures inequality.

**De jure Segregation:** Legal segregation.

**English Language Learners (ELLs):** ELL students are those in the process of acquiring English language skills and knowledge.

**Hidden Curriculum:** Ways in which pupils learn to accept the denial and interruption of their personal desires and wishes.

**No Child Left Behind Act (NCLB):** Set of federal policies that focuses on public school standardization in Grades 3 through 8 and high school.

**Pragmatism:** Encouraging the values of citizenship and classes in life skills such as economics, wood shop, and family living.

**Self-Fulfilling Prophecy:** Phenomenon where failure of certain students is expected by teachers, administrators, and peers. Once labeled and treated as failures, students find it more comfortable and—in perverse ways—even more rewarding to meet these low expectations.

**Standardized Testing:** Use of norm-referenced tests that determine the performance of individual students as well as grade and school achievement levels, and chart progress over time.

**Tracking:** Stratifying students based on particular curricula.

**Vouchers:** System in which parents can use public dollars to send students to charter and other private schools.

## WEBSITES TO LEARN MORE ABOUT EDUCATION AND SERVICE LEARNING PROJECTS

Afterschool.gov: http://www.afterschool.gov/

American Educational Research Association: http://www.aera.net/

FairTest: http://www.fairtest.org/

Gay, Lesbian and Straight Education Network: http://www.glsen.org/cgi-bin/iowa/all/home/index.html

National Association for Multicultural Education: http://nameorg.org/

National Center for Education Statistics: http://nces.ed.gov/

National Dropout Prevention Centers: http://www.dropoutprevention.org/

National Education Association: http://www.nea.org/

National Institute for Literacy: http://www.nifl.gov/

Public School Insights: http://www.publicschoolinsights.org/

Rethinking Schools: http://www.rethinkingschools.org/

Teaching for Change: http://www.teachingforchange.org/

U.S. Charter Schools: http://www.uscharterschools.org/pub/uscs_docs/index.htm

U.S. Department of Education: http://www.ed.gov/index.jhtml

## REFERENCES

Advisory Committee on Student Financial Assistance. 2006. *Mortgaging Our Future: How Financial Barriers to College Undercut America's Global Competitiveness*. Washington DC: Author.

Almeida, Cheryl, Robert Balfanz, and Adria Steinberg. 2009. "Dropout Factories: New Strategies States Can Use." *Education Week*. December 16. Retrieved February 16, 2010 (http://www.edweek.org/login.html?source=http://www.edweek.org/ew/articles/2009/12/16/15almeida.h29.html&destination=http://www.edweek.org/ew/articles/2009/12/16/15almeida.h29.html&levelId = 2100).

Anyon, Jean and William Julius Wilson. 1997. *Ghetto Schooling: A Political Economy of Urban Education Reform*. New York: Teachers College Press.

Apple, Michael. 1979. *Ideology and Curriculum*. New York: Routledge.

_____. 1993. *Official Knowledge: Democratic Education in a Conservative Age*. New York: Routledge.

Applied Research Center. 2003. *Reporting on Race, Education and No Child Left Behind: A Guide for Journalists*. Oakland, CA: Author.

Berkowitz, Elana. 2005. "Five Minutes With: Jonathan Kozol." *Campus Progress*. September 19. Retrieved February 21, 2010 (http://www.campusprogress.org/features/552/five-minutes-with-jonathan-kozol).

Bowles, Samuel and Herbert Gintis. 1976. *Schooling in Capitalist America: Educational Reform and the Contradictions of Economic Life*. New York: Basic Books.

Brack, Gay W. and Leanna R. Hall. 1997. "Combining the Classroom and the Community: Service-Learning in Composition at Arizona State University." Pp. 134–152 in *Writing the Community: Concepts and Models for Service Learning in Composition* (Service Learning in the Disciplines Series, American Association for Higher Education & Accreditation), edited by Linda Adler-Kassner, Robert Crooks, and Ann Watters. Sterling, VA: Stylus Publishing.

Brem, Robert J. and Ken Kyle. 2004. "Equity in Education." Pp. 1–10 in *Solutions: Agenda for Social Justice*, edited by Robert Perrucci, Kathleen Farraro, JoAnn Miller, and Paula C. Rodriquez Rust. Knoxville, TN: Society for the Study of Social Problems.

Bruner, J. 1996. *The Culture of Education.* Cambridge, MA: Harvard University Press.

Caldas, Stephen and Carl Bankston. 2005. *Forced to Fail: The Paradox of School Desegregation.* Westport, CT: Praeger.

Campbell, Claire. 2007. "Engines of Inequality: Diminishing Equity in the Nation's Premier Public Universities." [Press release]. Washington, DC: The Education Trust. Retrieved February 9, 2010 (http://www.edtrust.org/dc/press-room/press-release/engines-of-inequality-diminishing-equity-in-the-nation%E2%80%99s-premier-public-).

Carey, Kevin. 2004. *The Funding Gap 2004: Many States Still Shortchanging Low-Income and Minority Students.* Washington, DC: The Education Trust.

Carnevale, Anthony P. and Stephen J. Rose. 2004. "Socioeconomic Status, Race/Ethnicity, and Selective College Admissions." Pp. 101–156 in *America's Untapped Resource: Low-Income Students in Higher Education,* edited by Richard Kahlenberg. New York: The Century Foundation.

Carnoy, Martin. 1994. *Faded Dreams: The Politics and Economics of Race in America.* Cambridge, UK: Cambridge University Press.

Cashel, Mary Louise, Clair Goodman, and Jane Swanson. 2003. Mentoring as Service-Learning for Undergraduates. *Academic Exchange Quarterly,* 7:106–110.

Ciotti, Paul. 1998. *Money and School Performance: Lessons From the Kansas City Desegregation Experiment.* Washington, DC: CATO Institute.

Coleman, James. A. 1966. *Equality of Education Opportunity.* Washington, DC: U.S. Government Printing Office.

Coleman, James A. and Harold R. Kerbo. 2006. *Social Problems.* 9th ed. Upper Saddle River, NJ: Pearson.

Collatos, Anthony M. and Ernest Morrell. 2003. "Apprenticing Urban Youth as Critical Researchers." Pp. 113–131 in *Critical Voices in School Reform: Students Living Through Change,* edited by Beth C. Rubin and Elena Silva. London, UK: Routledge.

Collatos, Anthony, Ernest Morrell, Alejandro Nuno, and Roger Lara. 2004. "Critical Sociology in K–16 Early Intervention: Remaking Latino Pathways to Higher Education." *Journal of Hispanic Higher Education,* 3:164–179.

Davis, Kingsley and Wilber Moore. 1945. "Principles of Stratification." *American Sociological Review,* 10:242–249.

Dewey, John. [1916]1944. *Democracy and Education.* New York: The Free Press.

"Dropouts." 2004. *Education Week.* September 10. Retrieved February 15, 2010 (http://www.edweek.org/rc/issues/dropouts/).

Ebert, Edward and Richard Culyer. 2008. *School: An Introduction to Education.* Belmont, CA: Thomson Wadsworth.

Edwards, Virginia B., ed. 2006. "Diplomas Count: An Essential Guide to Graduation Policy and Rates." *Education Week,* 25(41).

Eitzen, D. Stanley, Maxine Baca Zinn, and Kelly Eitzen Smith. 2009. *In Conflict and Order: Understanding Society.* 12th ed. Boston, MA: Allyn & Bacon.

Ellis, Deborah. 2003. *Parvana's Journey.* Toronto, Ont., Canada: Groundwood Books.

Farah, Kimberly and Kerrissa Heffernan. 2000. "The Urban Educational Initiative: Supporting Educational Partnerships With Young, Urban Girls." Pp. 139–151 in *The Practice of Change: Concepts and Models for Service-Learning in Women's Studies,* edited by Barbara J. Balliet and Kerrissa Heffernan. Washington, DC: American Association for Higher Education & Accreditation.

Fernandes, Adrienne L. and Thomas Gabe. 2009. "Disconnected Youth: A Look at 16- to 24-Year-Olds Who Are Not Working or in School." *Congressional Research Service.* April 22. Retrieved February 15, 2010 (http://www.fas.org/sgp/crs/misc/R40535.pdf).

Figlio, David. 1997. Teacher salaries and teacher quality. *Economics Letters,* 55:267–271.

Fullbrook, Kate and Edward Fullbrook. 1994. *Simone de Beauvoir and Jean-Paul Sartre: The Remaking of a Twentieth-Century Legend.* New York: Basic Books.

Gatto, John. 1991. *Dumbing Us Down: The Hidden Curriculum of Compulsory Schooling.* Gabriola Island, BC, Canada: New Society Publishers.

Geiger, Roger. 2004. Research and Relevant Knowledge: American Research Universities Since World War II. Piscataway, NJ: Transaction Publishers.

Gertner, Jon. 2006. "Forgive Us Our Student Debts." *New York Times.* June 11.

Giddings, Paula. 1984. *When and Where I Enter: The Impact of Black Women on Race and Sex in America.* New York: William Morrow.

Giroux, Henry. 2005. "The War Against Children and the Shredding of the Social Contract." Pp. 3–26 in *Communities of Difference,* edited by Peter Pericles Trifonas. New York: Palgrave Macmillan.

Golden, Catherine and Majorie Herman. 2006. "Reading and Learning as a Community-Wide Initiative." *Community Works Journal,* 8:23–29.

Gotham, Kevin Fox. 2002. Race, Real Estate, and Uneven Development: The Kansas City Experience, 1900–2000. Albany, NY: State University of New York Press.

Halpern, David. 2005. *Social Capital.* Cambridge, UK: Polity Press.

Hanushek, Eric A., Steven G. Rivkin, Richard Rothstein, and Michael Podgursky. 2004. *How to Improve the Supply of High-Quality Teachers.* Washington, DC: The Brookings Institution.

Harris, Linda and Rhonda Tsoi-A-Fatt. 2007. *Recommended Changes to the No Child Left Behind Act to Address Workforce Issues.* Washington, DC: Center for Law and Social Policy.

Harvey, Lee. 1990. *Critical Social Research.* London, UK: Unwin Hyman.

Haycock, Kati. 2007. "Closing College Doors: How Higher Education Sacrifices Opportunities to Privilege." *The American Prospect,* April 22:18–19. Retrieved February 9, 2010 (http://www.prospect.org/cs/articles?article=closing_college_doors).

Hayes, William. 2004. *Are We Still a Nation at Risk Two Decades Later?* Lanham, MD: Scarecrow Education.

Irvine, Janice. 2002. *Talk About Sex: The Battles Over Sex Education in the United States.* Berkeley, CA: University of California Press.

Jackson, Jerlando F. L., ed. 2007. *Strengthening the African American Educational Pipeline: Informing Research, Policy, and Practice.* Albany, NY: State University of New York Press.

Jackson, Phillip. 1968. *Life in Classrooms.* New York: Holt, Rinehart, and Winston.

Johnson, Amy. 1999. *Sponsor-a-Scholar: Long-Term Impacts of a Youth Mentoring Program on Student Performance.* Princeton, NJ: Mathematica Policy Research.

Katz, Michael. 1970. *The Irony of Early School Reform: Educational Innovation in Mid-Nineteenth Century Massachusetts.* 2nd ed. Boston, MA: Beacon Press.

Kenny, Maureen, Lou Anna K. Simon, Karen Kiley-Brabeck, and Richard M. Lerner. 2002. Learning to Serve: Promoting Civil Society Through Service Learning: A View of the Issues." Boston, MA: Kluwer Academic.

Kincheloe, Joe L. 2006. "What You Don't Know Is Hurting You and the Country." Pp. 1–30 in *What You Don't Know About Schools,* edited by Shirley R. Steinberg and Joe L. Kincheloe. New York: Palgrave Macmillan.

Kozol, Jonathon. 2005. *The Shame of the Nation: The Restoration of Apartheid Schooling in America.* New York: Crown.

Manna, Paul. 2006. *Schools In: Federalism and the National Education Agenda.* Washington, DC: Georgetown University Press.

Moran, Peter William. 2005. "Too Little, Too Late: The Illusive Goal of School Desegregation in Kansas City, Missouri, and the Role of the Federal Government." *Teachers College Record,* 107:1933–1955.

Moser, Michelle and Ross Rubenstein. 2002. "The Equality of Public School District Funding in the United States: A National Status Report." *Public Administration Review,* 62:63–72.

Nielsen, Joyce M. 1990. *Feminist Research Methods: Exemplary Readings in the Social Sciences.* Boulder, CO: Westview Press.

Oakes, Jeannie, John Rogers, and Martin Lipton. 2006. *Learning Power: Organizing for Education and Justice.* New York: Teachers College Press.

Obidah, Jennifer E., Tracy Buenavista, R. Evely Gildersleeve, Peter Kim, and Tyson Marsh. 2007. "Teaching in 'Hard to Teach in' Contexts": African American Teachers Uniquely Positioned in the African American Educational Pipeline." Pp. 37–52 in *Strengthening the African American Educational Pipeline: Informing Research, Policy, and Practice,* edited by Jerlando F. L. Jackson. Albany, NY: State University of New York Press.

Orfield, Gary, 2004. "Dropouts in America: Confronting the Graduation Rate Crisis." Pp. 1-12 in *Dropouts in America: Confronting the Graduation Rate Crisis,* edited by Gary Orfield. Cambridge, MA: Harvard Education Press.

Orfield, Gary and Chungmei Lee. 2005. *Why Segregation Matters: Poverty and Educational Inequality.* Cambridge, MA: The Civil Rights Project, Harvard University. Retrieved February 9, 2010 (http://bsdweb .bsdvt.org/district/EquityExcellence/Research/Why_Segreg_Matters.pdf).

Orlofsky, Greg. 2000. "New School Finance Data Analysis Shows Deep Inequalities, But Gaps in Some States Decreasing." *The Education Trust.* Retrieved February 15, 2010: (http://www.edtrust.org/dc/press-room/press-release/new-school-finance-data-analysis-shows-deep-inequities-but-gaps-in-some-).

Pai, Young and Susan Adler. 1997. *Cultural Foundations of School Reform.* Upper Saddle River, NJ: Prentice Hall.

Portes, Alejandro and Rubén G. Rumbaut. 2005. "Introduction: The Second Generation and the Children of Immigrants Longitudinal Study." *Ethnic and Racial Studies,* 28:983–999.

Ransby, Barbara. 2005. Ella Baker and the Black Freedom Movement: A Radical Democratic Vision. Chapel Hill, NC: University of North Carolina Press.

Ravitch, Diane. 2003. *The Language Police: How Pressure Groups Restrict What Students Learn.* New York: Knopf.

Reinharz, Shulamit. 1983. "Experiential Analysis: A Contribution to Feminist Research. Pp. 162–191 in *Theories of Women's Studies,* edited by Gloria Bowles and Renate Klein. London, UK: Routledge.

_____. 1992. "Neglected Voices and Excessive Demands in Feminist Research." *Qualitative Sociology,* 16:69–76.

Rhodes, Robert. 1997. *Community Service and Higher Education.* Albany, NY: State University of New York Press.

Rossell, Christine H., David J. Armor, and Herbert J. Walberg. 2002. *School Desegregation in the 21st Century.* Westport, CT: Praeger.

Salerno, Roger A. 2003. *Landscapes of Abandonment: Capitalism, Modernity, and Estrangement.* Albany, NY: State University of New York Press.

Sarantakos, Sotirios. 1998. *Social Research.* Palgrave Macmillan.

Schargel, Franklin and Jay Smink. 2004. *Strategies to Help Solve Our School Dropout Problem.* Larchmont, NY: Eye on Education.

Shapiro, H. Svi. 2006. *Losing Heart: The Moral and Spiritual Miseducation of America's Children*. Mahwah NJ: Lawrence Erlbaum Associates.

Sternberg, Steve. 2002. "Sex Education." *USA Today*. October 10.

Street, Paul. 2005. *Segregated Schools: Educational Apartheid in Post–Civil Rights America*. London, UK: Routledge.

Tyre, Peg. 2003. "Falling Through the Cracks." *Newsweek*. November 17. Retrieved February 9, 2010 (http://www.newsweek.com/id/60600).

U.S. Department of Education. 2002. "Dropout Rates 2002." Retrieved February 16, 2010 (http://nces.ed.gov/ssbr/pages/dropoutrates.asp?IndID = 27).

Valverde, Leonard. 2005. *Improving Schools for Latinos: Creating Better Learning Environments*. Lanham, MD: Rowman & Littlefield.

Vogel, Richard. D. 2005. "Insuring Inequality: The Privatization of Public Education in the U.S." *Monthly Review*. August 19.

Wiener, Ross. 2008. *No Accounting for Fairness: Equitable Education Funding Remains Elusive in Ohio*. Washington, DC: The Education Trust.

Waldron, John. 1997. "Education and Equality: The Battle for School Funding Reform." *Human Rights,* 24. Retrieved February 26, 2010 (http://www.abanet.org/irr/hr/summer97/waldron.html).

Wilkenfeld, Adam. 2003. "Public vs. Private Schools." *Connect with Kids*. Retrieved February 26, 2010 (http://www.connectwithkids.com/tipsheet/2003/115_mar12/school.html).

Yee, Doris K. and Jacquelynne S. Eccles. 1988. "Parent Perceptions and Attributes for Children's Math Achievement." *Sex Roles,* 19:317–333.

Zeidenbeurg, Matthew and Michelle Van Noy. 2009. "American Community Colleges in the Downturn." *Digital Learning,* June. Retrieved February 21, 2010 (http://www.digitallearning.in/articles/article-details.asp?articleid=2386&typ=COUNTRY % 20PERSPECTIVE).

# CHAPTER 8

# What Price Justice?

*Deviance, Crime, and Building Community*

*The U.S. court system is intoxicated with treating an entire class of people as inferior.*

—U.S. Supreme Court Justice Anthony Kennedy
(quoted in Hayden 2004)

*Nothing stops a bullet like a job.*

—Los Angeles Youth Minister
(quoted in Hayden 2004)

*The jury has spoken and they have sent an unmistakable message to boardrooms across the country that you can't lie to shareholders, you can't put yourself in front of your employees' interests, and no matter how rich and powerful you are you have to play by the rules.*

—Sean M. Berkowitz, Justice Department's Enron
Task Force (quoted in Barrionuevo 2006)

T he relationships among social problems, crime, and incarceration are complex. United States prisons are filled with individuals who face multiple personal and social issues, as well as strict and forbidding jail time. The prison population faces higher-than-average rates of poverty, dysfunctional families, illiteracy, domestic and sexual abuse, substance abuse, and mental illness. Most current prisoners grew up *at risk* for becoming delinquents—born and raised in environments composed of poor educational resources, few economic opportunities, and high rates of violence. Still, many used their intellectual and organizational skills to maximize the best opportunities available to them—drugs, gambling, and other forms of criminal activity. Many social theorists argue that addressing these realities remains crucial to actually solving the problem of crime and other social ills.

For most sociologists, addressing the social problems of crime begins, in part, with dismantling the myth that all crime is caused by those who simply lack the personal responsibility and the individual quality of character not to commit crimes. For college students, becoming involved in the lives of those convicted of crimes breaks down these stereotypes and produces a more accurate glimpse of the criminal justice system as a whole. Involving students in this system is often an unsettling process, but it leads to dramatic personal reflection and new ideas about what kinds of policies might be more effective in addressing social problems.

One example of how service learning projects recast the relationship between crime and social problems is in programs designed to provide inmates with various social and literacy skills. Students engaged in service learning in Sociology 389 at the University of Michigan (UM) became involved in a program called Project Community (PC) at the Washtenaw County Jail in Ann Arbor and at the federal correctional facility in Milan, Michigan. Course participants spent 3 hours a week to earn 2 credits or 6 hours to earn 3 credits. Students worked in a number of areas according to the needs of inmates and the interests of the student. In one effort, sponsored by the Washtenaw County Office of Correctional Services, students assisted inmates in therapy programs and a number of activities: art and creative writing, mother–child visitations, needs assessment, and pre-release counseling (Ross and Kellman 1993). PC provided a powerful sociological laboratory. As the course unfolded, the programs allowed students to personalize and clarify the criminal justice system for themselves. They found out what it is like to experience the loss of privacy and personal control. The program also exposed the social problems faced by inmates and what social dynamics had influenced or "structured" their decisions to commit crimes.

In addition, the service learning component demonstrated ways that social problems can be addressed effectively. While inmates learned how to live different lives, students made the connections among literacy, life skills, violence, and social problems. Literacy programs continue to be an important part of rehabilitation in America's prisons. With almost 70% of the nation's inmates illiterate, learning to read is a first step to change. The power of being able to read is evident, as studies have shown that recidivism rates are lower among ex-offenders who have acquired greater literacy skills while in prison (Alabama Department of Post-Secondary Education 1992; O'Neil 1990).

UM students involved in the PC's literacy program also experienced a transformation as their sense of values and understanding of racial, class, and gender identities changed dramatically. After working with the adult literacy program at Milan, one student, Scott, explained,

> Although we entered the prison as literacy volunteers, the issues raised by our experiences reached much further than how to communicate the rules of grammar and spelling. For many of us, the prison experience involved crossing lines of race and class as well as entering a correctional facility for the first time. Each of us had our own set of expectations, fears, and reasons for being there. Project Community allowed us a space where we fully realized our expectations. (Gray and Dent 1993:221, 224)

By working with inmates in the literacy program, Scott and others took away a different picture of Milan prison life as well as the prisoners themselves. Scott went on to declare that, "The creative writing of the inmates helped us break down the popular image of the men in prison as being barbaric, with nothing positive to offer to society; an image that dominated the orientation at Milan" (Gray and Dent 1993).

Much of popular cultural, political discourse, and public policy puts forth simplistic images of prisoners as bad people who make bad choices. From Scott's example, we can see how service learning can address the more complex reality of people in America's jails. But because of reductive images and draconian sentencing policies, prisoners enter an expanding criminal justice system for longer and longer periods. At the same time, those incarcerated increasingly come from poor schools and communities. Service learning projects, such as those in the Washtenaw jail, can make a difference in the lives of individual prisoners by giving them skills and new possibilities. But these programs also address students' own stereotypes and challenge them to consider alternative policies to address crime. The work of U-M students exemplifies how particular efforts can make a difference in keeping society safer while possibly changing the course of individuals facing numerous social problems.

No one in the United States would disagree that crime is a primary social problem. The nation has the highest murder rate in the developed world with its capital, Washington, DC, also being its murder capital. Anyone who has ever been to Tokyo, Japan, or Stockholm, Sweden, can detect a radical difference in the lower amount of crime and greater feelings of safety, compared to the U.S. capital. Still, crime remains a controversial subject, as scholars and politicians continue to debate the definitions, causes of, and potential solutions to crime. Drawing on sociological perspectives, this chapter explores different types of crime affecting U.S. society, policies of the criminal justice system, and projects that might decrease crime.

In particular, many sociologists have proposed that the solution to America's crime problems might not be found in the criminal justice system in general or in mass incarceration in particular. They point out that crime and social disorganization are products of the diminished capacities of poorer communities, the diminished investment in educational and cultural programs for youth, and the overall diminished opportunities so many individuals see for creating a better world for themselves and others. In some areas of the country, the policies behind the 1980s war on drugs and its ensuing mass incarceration are being challenged by new approaches to street crime that emphasize economic investment and capacity building in local neighborhoods. This chapter gives examples of how shifts toward prevention and away from harsh punishment make all of us safer.

Meanwhile, as we will see in this chapter, power and inequality play an important role in determining what behaviors are deemed "criminal" and what types of punishment are meted out for various crimes. Thus, we examine white-collar and corporate crimes such as the recent Ponzi scheme of Bernard Madoff and the Enron and WorldCom scandals of a few years ago. Historically, wealthy business executives escaped any serious consequences for financial shenanigans. Rises in the number and extent of corporate thievery have inspired renewed vigor for prosecution and punishment. Similarly, newly named crimes such as identity theft, cyber hacking, and other Internet scams threaten to create instability and reduce the quality of life for all individuals in modern society.

## CRIME BY THE NUMBERS: A STATISTICAL PORTRAIT OF WHO COMMITS WHAT AND HOW WE THINK ABOUT IT

As we will see throughout this chapter, the rise and decline of crime have to do with a number of factors. Sociologists point to the social forces behind *why* a society defines an act as a crime. Drug offenses and the "war on drugs" that began in the 1980s has taken up much of the public's consciousness of crime and the criminal justice system ever since. Yet white-collar crimes cost society much more economically and pose even greater long-term structural damage throughout society—as demonstrated by the recent economic crises of 2008 and 2009 and its links to unscrupulous and often illegal behavior by financial corporate executives. Likewise, who is arrested for what crimes and what punishments they receive often have more to do with race, class, gender, and other bases for preexisting inequalities than our supposedly objective and "blind" justice system would suggest.

An example of how the public's consciousness about crime remains remarkably askew from the data can be found in comparing these recent crime statistics versus people's perceptions. In the first three graphs below (Figure 8.1), we can see that violent crime rates, homicide rates, and even property crime rates declined significantly between 1993 and 2008.

**Figure 8.1**   Violent Crime, Homicide, and Property Crime Rates Since 1993

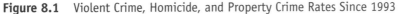

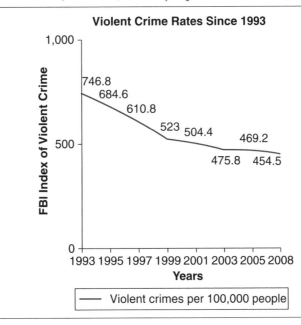

*(Continued)*

**Figure 8.1** (Continued)

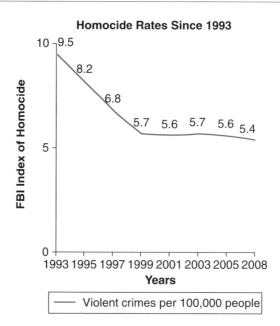

**Homocide Rates Since 1993**

FBI Index of Homocide

10 ─ 9.5
8.2
6.8
5.7  5.6  5.7  5.6  5.4
5

0

1993 1995 1997 1999 2001 2003 2005 2008
**Years**

── Violent crimes per 100,000 people

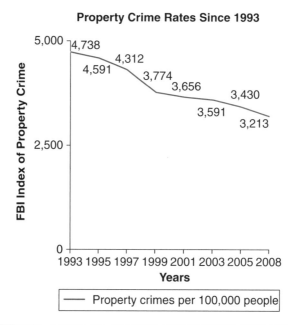

**Property Crime Rates Since 1993**

FBI Index of Property Crime

5,000 ─ 4,738
4,591    4,312
3,774
3,656
3,591    3,430
3,213
2,500

0

1993 1995 1997 1999 2001 2003 2005 2008
**Years**

── Property crimes per 100,000 people

*Source:* Data from "Crime in the United States, 2009: Preliminary Annual Uniform Crime Report—January to December," Federal Bureau of Investigation, Washington, D.C.

However, in the graph below (Figure 8.2), we can see that the percentage of people who say crime is going up has actually increased quite steadily, at least since 2001.

**Figure 8.2**    Percent of People Who Say Crime Is Increasing Between 1997 and 2009.

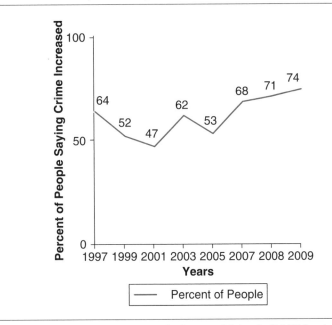

*Source:* Data from Jones (2009). "Americans Perceive Increased Crime in U.S." Princeton, NJ: Gallup.

Some sociologists refer to this divergence between statistics and perceptions as a pessimistic bias, or "the unshakable conviction that things are not only worse than they are, but worse than they used to be as well" (Keohane 2010, p. 1). But what social dynamics shape such pessimism about crime?

In part, many sociologists argue that a fear of crime is manufactured to maintain both the political interests of politicians who use "getting tough on crime" to scare up voter support (Beckett and Sasson 2004), as well as the economic interests of everyone from private prison corporations, to bail bondsmen, to local media whose news networks find that fear increases ratings (Gross 2006; Herivel and Wright 2003; Romer, Jamieson, and Adey 2003). But a look at some specific crime numbers also suggests that the public's obsession with drug-related crimes explains both the perception of crime increase as well as the real increase in prison populations, prison construction, and people subject to the criminal justice system. Table 8.1 shows that, except for drug-related violations, most other specific crimes have declined significantly in the last decade.

Table 8.1   Percent Change for Total Arrest, Selected Crimes, 1996–2005

| Offense | 1996 | 2005 | Percent Change |
|---------|------|------|----------------|
| Murder | 9,564 | 7,929 | −16.5 |
| Forcible Rape | 18,745 | 15,129 | −19.3 |
| Aggravated Assault | 315,405 | 282,003 | −10.6 |
| Burglary | 220,798 | 180,973 | −18.0 |
| Larceny Theft | 905,963 | 692,593 | −23.6 |
| Driving Under the Influence | 877,727 | 816,243 | −7.0 |
| Drug Abuse Violations | 830,684 | 1,034,844 | +24.6 |
| Fraud | 255,162 | 193,539 | −24.2 |
| Stolen Property | 91,832 | 82,771 | −9.9 |
| Weapons Offenses | 123,016 | 112,054 | −8.9 |

*Source: FBI Uniform Crime Reports,* 2005b, Table 32, U.S. Department of Justice, Federal Bureau of Investigation.

Thus, the only crimes to really increase over the past two decades have been drug-related crimes. But the large increases in sentencing for most drug-related crimes, even first-time minor offenses, have dramatically shifted prison demographics. According to Beckett and Sasson (2004),

> Between 1985 and 1997, the percentage of state prison inmates serving sentences for violent crimes fell from 54% to 47% and the percentage serving sentences for drug crimes rose from 9% to 21%. The shift was still more dramatic in the smaller federal system: the percentage of violent offenders declined from 28.1% to 15% and the percentage of drug offenders increased from 33.3% to 63%. (p. 168)

By 2005, drug-related offenses accounted for over 55% of the entire U.S. prison population—an increase of more than 1000% since the 1980s. Whether the fear of crime has influenced harsher sentencing or increased prison and ex-offender populations create a perception of higher crime rates, the prison-industrial complex, political campaigns, fear mongering, media hype about crime, and what some sociologists have called a "culture of fear" continue to distract Americans into spending trillions on the "crisis of crime" that simply doesn't exist.

Defining these crises related to crime and social deviance requires understanding how a particular society sees the world. **Deviance** is a violation of social norms. What is deviant for one society might be considered appropriate for another. Any type of deviance that violates society's laws is considered a **crime.** For example, most European countries have strict gun laws, but public nudity is not considered a public offence at beaches and parks. In America, the opposite is true. Crimes lead to formal **sanctions** or state-sanctioned punishment. Every society develops methods for ensuring conformity. The attempt to create conformity is what is known as **social control.** We often think of crime and punishment as somehow natural to society. However, even a universal crime such as murder is dealt with in a variety of ways throughout the world. The types of crime and crime rates vary not only between societies, but also within particular societies throughout history. For instance, prior to the turn of the previous century, the patent or legal drug business allowed opiates to be sold in an unregulated fashion. By the 1920s, alcohol prohibition led to underground bootleggers and helped organized crime to evolve in urban areas. Today, alcohol is legal in the United States and is the drug most often misused, while other drugs, such as opiates, have been criminalized.

Some crimes occur more often than others. Also, different classes and groups of people are more likely to be victims of a particular crime than others. Crimes are measured by using the FBI's Uniform Crime Reports (UCR). The UCR breaks down crime into **violent crimes** (such as murder, rape, robbery, and aggravated assault) and **property crimes** (such as burglary, larceny, and motor vehicle theft). Crimes are also divided into **felonies** (serious crimes) and **misdemeanors** (petty and less serious offenses). Felonies can lead to at least a year in prison or fines above $1,000. UCR crimes are often termed street crimes or *index crimes*. All other crimes are classified as non-index crimes. Another category refers to **victimless crimes**, those that involve violations of the law in which no victim steps forward or is identified. Prostitution, drug use, and illegal gambling are considered victimless crimes. In 2005, the FBI estimated that 14,094,186 arrests were made in the United States for all offenses (except for traffic violations), of which 603,503 were for violent crime and 1,609,327 for property crimes (Uniform Crime Reports 2005a).

The number of reported crimes that are *cleared* (perpetrators are found, arrested, and prosecuted, and cases are settled or decided) varies by the type of crime as shown in Table 8.2. Nationwide in 2005, 45.5% of violent crimes and 16.3% of property crimes were cleared by arrest or exceptional means. Examples of exceptional clearances include, but are not limited to, the death of the offender, the victim's refusal to cooperate with the prosecution after having identified the offender, or the denial of extradition because the offender committed a crime in another jurisdiction and is being prosecuted (Uniform Crime Reports 2005a). Of the violent crimes of murder and non-negligent manslaughter, forcible rape, robbery, and aggravated assault, murder had the highest percentage—62.1% of offenses cleared. Of the property crimes of burglary, larceny-theft, and motor vehicle theft, burglary was the offense least cleared with 12.7% cleared by arrest or exceptional means. Larceny is a common-law crime that includes theft and wrongful taking of property. Burglary is unlawful forcible entry or attempted entry of a residence. In 2005 across the United States, only 2.2% of arson offenses were cleared by arrest or exceptional means (Uniform Crime Reports 2005a)

**Table 8.2** Crimes Cleared by Arrest or Exceptional Means, 2005

| Type of Crime | Percent Cleared |
|---|---|
| Violent Crimes | 45.5 |
| Murder | 62.1 |
| Property Crime | 16.3 |
| Burglary | 12.7 |
| Arson | 2.2 |

*Source: Uniform Crime Reports,* 2005a, "Crime in the United States," U.S. Department of Justice, Federal Bureau of Investigation.

Another way data is collected on crime is through **self-report studies.** The National Crime Victimization Survey (NCVS) is the most important self-report study. The NCVS provides data on crimes that are not reported to the police and hence are not included in the UCR. Self-report studies provide more complete data on crimes likely to go unreported such as assault or sexual battery. The reporting of crime has a lot to do with how society, victims, and law enforcement interpret a particular criminal act. Some crimes such as auto theft must be reported to the police in order for insurance settlements to occur. Murders are also more likely to be reported and solved than most other crimes. Rape and sexual and other types of assault have historically been underreported. Similarly, white-collar and corporate crimes are not reported as often as most other types of crimes. The criminal justice system deals mainly with street crimes. As we will see below, the nation's mass incarceration of poor and minority youth reflect not only based on how crimes are perceived, but also differences in the amounts of power among the social classes in American society.

**Juvenile delinquency** falls into two categories: status offenses and delinquent offenses. Status offenses occur when a juvenile under age 18 commits an offense only a minor can commit, such as running away from home, truancy, or underage drinking. Delinquent offenses are adult crimes committed by juveniles (Mooney, Knox, and Schacht 2007). The number of cases handled in juvenile courts grew from 1.1 million cases in 1985 to 1.6 million cases in 2002. Officials in the U.S. Justice Department point out that the increasing number of teens in the system is straining the courts, programs, and resources. While violent offenses declined, drug cases increased from 12% of the total number of crimes in 1991 to 18% in 2002. Female delinquency cases rose from 19% of the total to 26% during the same period (Snyder and Sickmund 2006). Problem behavior cuts across race and gender (see Table 8.3).

**Table 8.3**   Problem Behavior Among Juveniles by Gender, Race, and Age
(Proportion of Youth Reporting Ever Engaging in the Behavior by Age 17)

| Type of Behavior | All youth | Male | Female | White | Black | Hispanic |
|---|---|---|---|---|---|---|
| Suspended from school | 33% | 42% | 24% | 28% | 56% | 38% |
| Ran away from home | 18 | 17 | 20 | 18 | 21 | 17 |
| Belonged to a gang | 8 | 11 | 6 | 7 | 12 | 12 |
| Vandalized | 37 | 47 | 27 | 39 | 33 | 34 |
| Theft less than $50 | 43 | 47 | 38 | 44 | 38 | 41 |
| Theft more than $50 | 13 | 16 | 10 | 12 | 15 | 14 |
| Assault | 27 | 33 | 21 | 25 | 36 | 28 |
| Sold drugs | 16 | 19 | 12 | 17 | 13 | 16 |
| Carried a handgun | 16 | 25 | 6 | 16 | 15 | 15 |

*Source: Juvenile Offenders and Victims,* 2006, by Howard Snyder and Melissa Sickmund, U.S. Department of Justice, Office of Justice Programs, Office of Juvenile Justice and Delinquency Prevention, p. 70.

## STREET CRIME

Conflict theorists point out that the capitalist system influences the criminal justice system by reinforcing the oppression of the working class while ignoring the damage corporate and white-collar criminals do to society. In this view, the criminal justice system works in favor of the capitalist class in part to maintain a marginal working class (Chambliss 1994; Michalowski and Carlson 2000). Studies reveal that inequalities in the criminal justice system are widespread. For instance, the United States' largest provider of civil legal services for the poor, the Legal Services Corporation (2008), estimates that 80% of low-income citizens needing legal assistance do not receive it. Roughly 1 million cases per year are being rejected because legal aid programs lack the resources to handle them. The United States leads the world in incarceration rates for a number of reasons, primarily due to reasons stated earlier such as drug sentencing laws, the economic interests of private prison and prison-related industries, and the propagation of a culture of fear (see Table 8.4).

**Table 8.4**   Top Ten Countries for Incarceration Rates, 2006

| Country | # of Inmates per 100,000 people |
|---|---|
| United States | 714 |
| Belarus | 532 |
| Russia | 532 |
| Bermuda | 532 |
| Palau | 532 |
| U.S. Virgin Islands | 490 |
| Turkmenistan | 489 |
| Belize | 420 |
| Ukraine | 417 |
| Maldive Islands | 416 |

Source: *World Prison Population List,* 2006, 6th ed., by Roy Walmsley, London, UK, King's College Centre for Prison Studies.

Crime control strategies in the form of get-tough laws, longer sentences, and mass imprisonment rekindle historical debates over racism and the desire for social control over the poor and working classes (Chambliss 1994; Chomsky 2003; Christie 1994). Conflict theorists point out the staggering economic and human toll of 30 years of policies centered on criminalizing particular populations. Low-income urban and working-class populations have borne the brunt of both gang violence and the nation's war on drugs. However, some criminologists, drawing on grounded theory in studying urban neighborhoods, point out the positive role of gangs in providing basic services and social bonds for poor youth (Kontos, Brotherton, and Barrios 2003). Below is an overview of the number of inmates in the United States in 2004 by race and gender.

**Table 8.5**   Number of Inmates by Race and Gender, 2008

| Total | Per 100,000 People |
|---|---|
| All Males | 952 |
| All Females | 68 |
| White Males | 487 |
| White Females | 50 |

| Total | Per 100,000 People |
|-------|:------------------:|
| Black Males | 3,161 |
| Black Females | 149 |
| Hispanic Males | 1,200 |
| Hispanic Females | 75 |

*Source:* "Bulletin: Prisoners in 2008," 2009, U.S. Department of Justice, Bureau of Justice Statistics.

## RACIAL PROFILING AS A SOCIAL PROBLEM

Symbolic interactionists remind us that perception of crime is an important component of policy making and policing. Mass media depictions of street crimes shape our conceptual map of crime. Fear of violence and gangs often leads to fear of poor communities and minorities. Racial profiling refers to situations where police use race, ethnicity, national origin, or religion to determine whom to stop and search. About 32 million Americans, or 11% of the population, have been victims of racial profiling. According to the U.S. Department of Justice, African Americans and Latinos are three times more likely than white drivers to experience force or threat of force during a police stop. In addition, Arab Americans are significantly more likely to experience racially-based policing since September 11, 2001, and the World Trade Center bombings. Profiling occurs in almost every context of people's lives. Most white Americans seldom if ever experience being treated as suspects while driving, shopping, going through airports, or at home. Racial profiling alienates communities and leads to mistrust between police departments and citizens (American Civil Liberties Union [ACLU] 2009; Amnesty International 1999; Del Carmen 2007).

One way racial profiling can be addressed is by understanding its systemic nature through service learning. Steve Cooper's Criminology 499 class at California State University at Long Beach is not your usual course. When students divide up into different races and genders, they often learn the varying experiences different social groups have with police and the criminal justice system. Course exercises include student ride-alongs with police officers and public seminars on profiling. Students experience what it is like to be profiled for one's racial and ethnic background. Course instructor Cooper comments, "In one hour we had tens of officers follow us, and we were stopped several times that night. This was most impressive for my white students that didn't accept the fact some minorities are profiled by the police" (personal communication, August 24, 2004).

In *Street Wars,* author Tom Hayden (2004) points to the negative effects on communities of seeing poor and troubled youth as simply superpredators without focusing on the context of their social environment. Hayden argues that instead of disinvestment, inner cities need a New Deal. In the final analysis, poor youth face a lack of capital and desperate odds in the labor market. What some have called a "war against youth" in America is fought against poor families with little political clout whose children are often victims of a misuse of the juvenile justice system. The United States lacks policies supporting working families and youth. Get-tough criminal justice policies reflect not only changing sentencing guidelines but also changes in policing tactics, the emerging prison industries, and the power of special interest groups.

Critics have argued for decades now that the drug war contributes to the violation of human rights and has opened up the criminal justice system to corporate abuse and conflicts of interests. Eric Schlosser (1998) calls the industries supporting mass incarceration the **Prison-Industrial Complex.** Overall, a number of industries are connected to this configuration of public policy made for and by private interests. Studies show that prison companies such as the Corrections Corporation of America, or CCA, donate large sums to political candidates in over half the nation's states (Bender 2000; Greene 2002; Schlosser 1998). Researchers have found that CCA lobbies for tougher sentences and privatization through lobby groups such as the American Legislative Exchange Council (ALEC) (Biewen 2007).

Sociological theories linking poverty, community, and delinquency date back to the 1920s. Drawing on the Chicago School of Cultural Ecology, an early generation of criminologists in the United States highlighted the relationship between juvenile delinquency and community-level processes. The work of social ecologists in the 1940s linked criminality and unstable community ties to weak social controls found in neighborhoods experiencing rapid transition (see Shaw and McKay 1949). A renewed focus on delinquency in urban areas emerged in the 1980s as cities began to transform around the loss of heavy industry, declining investment, and rising social problems. William Julius Wilson's (1987) work illustrates the impact of deindustrialization on poor minority youth in Chicago. His thesis asserts that a loss of sustainable employment in the 1980s led to an increase in social problems including crime. Since that time, both poor urban and rural communities have encountered higher incarceration rates. This perspective points to a prison population coming from areas that lack jobs but also social and human capital. Petersilia (2003) notes that only 60% of U.S. prisoners are high school graduates or have a General Educational Development (GED) certificate, while the national average is 85%. In addition, 11% have a learning disability.

New approaches to policing have led to higher incarceration rates and lower crime rates in the nation's cities. Sociologists George Kelling and James Q. Wilson (1982) argue that high-crime neighborhoods could only be fixed by weeding out criminal elements and then seeding the neighborhoods with pro-community programs. While Wilson's "weed and seed" idea was partially addressed, funding for drug policing overshadowed community initiatives in the 1980s and 1990s. The Weed and Seed program was followed by the Fixing

Broken Windows program in the 1990s. Drawing on Wilson's ideas, Kelling and Coles (1996) advocated an aggressive, get-tough confrontation of public disorder in its various forms: vagrancy, vandalism, panhandling, and so on. Their approach seemed to work in New York City's subways, where felonies dropped by 75% in the 1990s. Today, the program is being used to curb disorderly behavior in several American cities. Regardless of whether addressing small "quality of life" crimes like vagrancy and panhandling actually reduces larger and more violent crimes, what is clear is that addressing street-level crime has had a positive effect on communities. Nevertheless, as inequality remains the primary cause of poverty, perhaps the best way to reduce quality-of-life crimes would still be to reduce inequality and poverty, thereby reducing the need for people to panhandle or sleep outdoors.

## YOUTH

Similarly, even if Weed and Seed and Broken Windows programs can claim success, the nation's poorest children remain at risk for delinquency. Many children of single parents come home to an empty house after school, and studies show they may struggle with reading and math. These children are less likely to go to college and be employed. Add to these over a million and half children with at least one parent incarcerated. Especially for low-income youth, delinquency often lands them in the criminal justice system. Between 300,000 and 400,000 boys and girls cycle through youth detention centers each year in the United States (Coalition for Juvenile Justice 2003).

Many at-risk youth end up in detention facilities. The overriding focus on prison expansion has contributed to the neglect of basic mental health services for youth. A recent congressional investigation of 698 U.S. juvenile detention facilities reveals the widespread warehousing of mentally ill youth and the lack of mental health treatment options. The report found 33 states holding youth in juvenile detention facilities who were in need of mental health treatment and were charged with no crime, and 117 facilities holding children 10 years old and younger. The overwhelmed and ineffective facilities place children at an increased risk for suicide and harm (U.S. Senate Government Reform Committee, 2004). Other studies reveal the neglect of troubled youth by the nation. According to the Southern Poverty Law Center (2007), up to 85% of children in juvenile detention facilities have disabilities that make them eligible for special education services, yet only 37% had been receiving any kind of services in their school. Studies also have shown that children with emotional disturbances are particularly at risk for social problems. According to the Southern Poverty Law Center (2007), emotionally disturbed youth are

- Twice as likely as other students with disabilities to be living in a correctional facility, halfway house, drug treatment center, or on the street after leaving school;

- Almost twice as likely as students with other disabilities to become teenage mothers;

- More than three times as likely as other students to be arrested before leaving school.

In addition, 73% of emotionally disturbed students who drop out of school are arrested within 5 years.

These and other studies suggest a focus on the role that concentrated disadvantages play in the organization of poor neighborhoods. Looking at the nature of delinquency and other social problems among poor inner-city youth, some researchers (Sampson and Laub 1993, 2008; Sampson and Wilson 1995; W. Wilson 2006) argue that poor neighborhoods are often unable to provide social control and support for youth due to resource deprivation and racial segregation. Drawing on the idea of limited social capital and networks for success, Sampson and Laub (2008) make an argument for a renewed commitment to social institutions. Rather than incarceration, these authors suggest that in order to address criminality, society needs to focus efforts on involving youth in activities embedded in social networks that limit criminal persistence. These perspectives point to the important role of **mediating structures** (youth before- and after-school programs, community centers, family, and jobs programs) in providing social capital for poor youth. Successful programs not only make communities safer, they also lower the recidivism rate while improving the lives of their members. In fact, studies of findings on preventing crime show the most promise in community-level initiatives. The literature reveals that crime is reduced best by human capital investment in programs linked directly to families, communities, and schools (Reiman 2004; Stephens 1999). Reiman, in *The Rich Get Richer and the Poor Get Prison,* gives an overview of the crime prevention programs found to work best, which include

> family therapy and parenting training for delinquent and at-risk adolescents; teaching of social competency skills in schools and coaching of high-risk youth in "thinking skills"; vocational training for older male ex-offenders; extra police patrols in high-crime hot spots; monitoring of high-risk repeat offenders by specialized police forces as well as incarceration; rehabilitation programs with risk focusing treatments for convicted offenders; and therapeutic community treatment for drug-using offenders in prisons. (p. 54)

Likewise, Stephens (1999) found that what works best to prevent street crime are programs that focus on children's lives, (i.e., before- and after-school programs, family therapy, parent training, and school initiatives supporting self-control and life skills). He also reported that offenders are less likely to repeat offenses if they get therapy and training. His research suggests that incarcerating less active offenders works against community safety in the long run.

These findings lead us to concrete conclusions regarding the role of community action in reducing criminality in poor communities. First, they show the importance of examining crime from the locus of community-level organizations and the link between crime and other social problems, (i.e., poverty, social disorganization, and racial and class isolation). Second, investment in social capital and social institutions is crucial to delimiting criminal involvement among youth.

## WHITE-COLLAR CRIME

**White-collar crimes** are those committed by a person of respectability and high social status in the course of his or her occupation (Sutherland 1949). They include illicit acts that involve deceit and a violation of trust rather than direct physical acts against an individual or property (Leon-Guerrero 2005; Shover and Hochstetler 2005). In contrast to street crime, white-collar and occupational crimes often go unprosecuted. Examples of white-collar crimes include, among others, tax evasion, mail fraud, embezzlement, insurance fraud, and government and employee theft.

Corporate crime is a form of white-collar crime involving violations against the public by companies and their employees. These can include broad categories such as environmental crimes or securities fraud. White-collar crimes can put workers and the public at risk. For instance, substandard buildings and other labor violations kill and endanger many workers each year. According to the AFL-CIO (2006), 150 employees die each day in the workplace. Overall, 3.9 employees per 100,000 were killed or injured at work in 2006 (Bureau of Labor Statistics 2007). According to Richard Johnston (2002) of the National White Collar Crime Center, 1 in 3 Americans are victims of white-collar crimes, with only 41% reporting the incident to the police. One of the key barriers to prosecuting white-collar crimes is that they are often prosecuted by regulatory agencies that merely charge fines. Without the experience and stigma of serving time, white-collar criminals do not see their acts as crimes. Because of the lack of prosecution and the mild punishment, white-collar criminals often refuse to admit guilt and operate in an environment where they do not fear getting caught (Shover and Hochstetler 2005).

Widespread fraud in a number of key industries has led to destabilization of entire sectors of the economy. For example, the FBI (2007) estimates that between 3 and 10% of all medical billing in the U.S. health care system involves fraud. That is a large amount when you consider that the nation's health care expenditures were $2.16 trillion in 2006. Fraud directly hurts the economy. For instance, all U.S. households pay an estimated $300 annually as a result of insurance fraud.

Most recently, the world economy has been decimated by controversial and highly suspect practices within the Wall Street–led financial industry. While many dealings were in fact "legal," recent deregulation in many aspects of the industry led to what one critic called a "culture of banditry" where the line between legal and illegal, ethical and unscrupulous, was blurred by greed. Deregulation also led to poor oversight and few gatekeepers to guard those lines (Goldstein 2008). The result has been one of the largest international economic meltdowns in history (see following box).

## MADOFF, PONZI, AND THE NATURE OF WHITE-COLLAR CRIME

**Image 8.1**

*Source:* ©Chris Hondros/Getty Images News/Getty Images.

Most people have by now heard of Bernard Madoff, who was arrested in December of 2008 and convicted of running the largest Ponzi scheme in history—defrauding his investors of somewhere between $50 and $100 billion. Madoff received a 150-year prison sentence in June of 2009.

A Ponzi scheme is basically a financial fraud that works by paying off early investors with returns from the investment money of subsequent investors. Most of the money goes to the scheme's operator—in this case, Madoff and his family. Madoff offered investors a constantly increasing rate of return and by doing so, encouraged thousands of very wealthy individuals, institutions, and foundations to invest millions with his company. When the financial industry crisis hit, however, Madoff could no longer keep the scheme hidden. Since the Madoff case, dozens of smaller yet significant Ponzi schemes have been exposed and prosecuted: R. Allen Stanford ($8 billion) in Texas, Nicholas Cosmo ($380 million) in New York, and others. In all of these cases (especially the Madoff case), thousands of people lost their retirement and life savings, dozens of companies went out of business, and huge charitable foundations were forced to close up shop.

But as the high-profile cases came and went, less reported on were the ways in which the main-stream financial industry had been straddling the ethical and legal fault lines all along. According to derivative investment consultant Janet Tavakoli (quoted in Goldstein 2008), "the biggest Ponzi scheme of all may be the one that brought the world financial markets to its knees. And that's the scheme that united Wall Street bankers with mortgage lenders in a bid to funnel more and more money into the market for subprime home loans" (p. 1). She says the packaging of iffy home loans into securitized bonds that could be sold to institutional investors—many of them relying on borrowed money—was a system born to fail. "The largest Ponzi scheme in the history of the capital markets is the relationship between failed mortgage lenders and investment banks that securitized the risky over-priced loans and sold these packages to other investors—a Ponzi scheme by every definition applied to Madoff," says Tavakoli. "These and other related deeds led to the largest global credit meltdown in the history of the world" (quoted in Goldstein 2008:1). It may be that the nature of white-collar crime is greed, pure and simple—sometimes that greed is legal, and sometimes it is not.

Linked to the global economy, **cyber crimes** and **identity theft** are redefining how we see crime and societies' ability to counter it. The most cyber crimes occur in the area of credit card fraud, but such crimes also include other types of identity theft such as taking over another's professional identity. Through dumpster diving, "phishing," and skimming information, identity thieves engage in credit card, phone/utilities, bank, and government documentation fraud. These crimes are often committed "virtually," online. Many victims are unaware of whom to contact about identity crimes. Cyber crime can occur across national boundaries, making prosecution difficult. In addition, there are emerging virtual environments where people engage in hate crimes, child pornography, violation of property rights, and electronic harassment (Carrabone et al. 2004). The FBI (2007) estimates that 3.7% of U.S. adults are victims of identity theft, and that victims in the United States spend over 200 million hours attempting to recover from being victimized.

White-collar crime costs American society and the economy an estimated $650 billion a year, or 5% of the gross domestic product (Wells 2007). The financial cost of street crime is less than that of white-collar crime. Table 8.6 shows the estimated cost of street crimes such as property crimes versus the cost of fraud.

The number of corporate fraud cases pursued by the FBI (2007) increased from 291 in 2002 to 490 in 2006. A growing public outcry over corporate and white-collar crime in the 1990s reached a peak in 2002 with one of the most important cases of corporate fraud. The Enron stock fraud case led to the conviction of Kenneth Lay and Jeffrey Skilling, chief exec-utives of the Enron Corporation, for fraud and conspiracy in May of 2006. Convicted of mul-tiple counts of fraud, conspiracy, and insider trading, Lay and Skilling were found guilty of lying to investors, employees, and regulators about the value of Enron stocks in order to con-ceal their declining value. As Enron stocks became worthless, company employees and other

Table 8.6   Estimated Direct Cost of Selected Crimes, 2007

| Crime | Direct Costs to Victims |
| --- | --- |
| Violent Crimes | $427 million |
| Total Property Crimes | $15 billion |
| Telemarketing Fraud | $13.9 billion |
| Computer Crime | $67.2 million |
| Insurance Fraud | $40 billion |
| Identity Fraud | $56.6 billion |

*Source: 2007 National Crime Victims' Rights Week Resource Guide,* U.S. Department of Justice, Office of Victims of Crime.

investors lost billions of dollars (Barrionuevo 2006). The Enron case is one of a series of white-collar cases linked to the growing power of corporations in America since the 1980s.

Overall, corporate scandals contributed to a $5 trillion loss in market value due to stock fraud crimes in the early 2000s. Along with Enron, fraud perpetrated at companies like WorldCom and Adelphia destroyed the livelihood of thousands of retirees, employees, and investors. The Enron case alone led to the loss of 28,000 jobs and took 30 FBI agents and IRS investigators to prosecute it ("Corporate Crackdown" 2005; Drutman 2002). Conflict theory helps us to understand how this growing power has led to a culture of corruption in corporations. While justice was served in this case, thousands of innocent victims of Enron and other cases lost their pensions and their stocks due to these actions. Conflict theorists point out the differences in treatment received by white-collar criminals. For instance, unlike Madoff, whose 150-year sentence stands as a significant anomaly in such cases, many white-collar criminals are never prosecuted or held responsible for the direct costs to society of their actions. Even the recent uproar over million-dollar bonuses for financial industry fat cats most responsible for the 2008 economic collapse has done little to bring justice for the millions of middle- and working- (and even upper-) class people impacted by the boondoggle. This double standard reduces the effectiveness of the American justice system.

# RAPE

**Rape** is defined as a violent crime consisting of three elements: sexual penetration, force or the threat of force, and non-consent of the victim (Mooney et al. 2007). In 2005, the FBI documented 93,934 rapes in the United States, not including attempted rape or **statutory rape** (sex with a minor) (Macionis 2008). Mooney et al. estimates that as many as 80 % of rapes are **acquaintance rapes** (where the victim knows or is familiar with the rapist) as opposed to **classic rape** (where the rapist is a stranger). Acquaintance rape varies by social setting and the type of relationship between the victim and the perpetrator. Acquaintance rapists are typically neighbors, coworkers, or distant family members. **Marital or spousal rape** is when a man forces his wife to have sexual intercourse. A crime in all states since 1993, spousal rape prosecution varies state by state. In 30 states, there is a marital rape exemption, meaning that the act cannot be tried as marital rape if the man is living with a woman or if she is mentally or physically impaired, unconscious, or asleep (Bergen 2006, as cited in Benokraitis 2008). Spousal rapes are seldom prosecuted. Often, this type of rape is difficult to prove if a man used nonviolent coercive means against his spouse (Benokraitis 2008).

Rape varies among social settings as well as among the different types of victim–assailant relationships. College-age women are at a much greater risk of rape and sexual assault than any other group. Between 20 and 25 % of all the completed or attempted rapes of women occur while the victim is in college. Research also reveals that over 50 % of sexual assaults involve alcohol on the part of the victim and/or the rapist (Fisher, Cullen, and Turner 2000). Armstrong, Hamilton, and Sweeney (2006) terms rapes involving alcohol on or around campus housing as "party rapes" (p. 483). What is distinctive about party rapes is that the rape often involves supplying a woman with alcohol or targeting an intoxicated woman. **Date rape** occurs when the victim knows and socializes with the rapists. Drugs such as Rohypnol and GHB are dangerous drugs used to facilitate rape both on and off of college campuses. Banned in the United States, Rohypnol makes victims unable to fight back against sexual assaults. Often put into the drinks of victims, Rohypnol, or "roofies," are tasteless and colorless pills that leave victims incapacitated for up to 12 hours (Mooney et al. 2007). Sociologists point out that solutions to party rape must involve a change in campus environments and the social organization of student life, especially those that support men's coercive sexual strategies.

## Challenging Rape Culture

The first rape crisis centers in the United States emerged in the 1970s due to the activism of feminists involved in the second wave of the women's movement. The number of rape crisis centers in the country increased from 136 in 1975 to 1,200 in 1996 (Schmitt and Martin 2007). Consciousness of rape as a social problem arose as other changes affecting women came to the social forefront. Debates over rape, birth control, and abortion coincided with anti-rape social activism. The idea that the attitudes and behaviors of the police, the court, and the medical system often created a "second assault" accompanied the services to victims provided by the anti-rape movement (Brownmiller 1975). The influence of rape crisis centers spanned beyond immediate services to outreach, coordination of services, and lobbying efforts to create rape legislation and statutes. Schmitt and Martin note that the movement has helped eliminate victim-blaming laws. Martin (2005) points out that rape crisis centers are more responsive and see more victims than mainstream social institutions, even though they have far fewer resources. Rape crisis shelters are a good example of community-level solutions coming from social movements. The role of social movements in challenging rape culture reveals the importance of social action in defining an act as a crime and a social problem.

## WOMEN AND CRIMINAL JUSTICE

The rising number of women committing crimes and entering the criminal justice system reflects various social trends. Recent statistics show they are becoming more involved in gang and drug-related crimes (Mooney et al. 2007). Overall, men made up 68% of the total number of arrests and 82% of violent arrests in 2005. Women are more likely to commit money-related offenses such as fraud, embezzlement, prostitution, or commercial vice crimes; however, their involvement in more serious crimes is growing (Macionis 2008). Feminist criminologists make the case that not only do men and women often have difference experiences with crime, but not all women have the same experiences. Price and Sokoloff (2004) argue that, "Because social conditions and experiences of women's lives vary according to where they are located at the points of intersectionalities in societal systems of race, class, gender, nationality, and sexual orientation, the lives of women must be understood and examined in those contexts" (p. 4). Studies focusing on women in the U.S. criminal justice system point to a number of gender-based concerns for women inmates (Chesney-Lind and Pasko 2003). Young and Reviere (2006) found that 42% of women in prison who have children reported they were unemployed and 20% were homeless in the year before they were incarcerated. The American Civil Liberties Union (ACLU 2004) points out that women who are sentenced to death face many of the same problems as men on death row, (i.e., inadequate defense counsel, official misconduct, poverty, alcoholism, mental retardation, and mental illness). Women death row inmates, however, often suffered abuse and domestic violence before they entered prison. In a study of 66 women on death row, two-thirds were found to have experienced ongoing abuse as children and as adults. The same percentage was in prison for killing family members.

## A HISTORY OF THE PRISON AND THE PRISON-INDUSTRIAL COMPLEX

The criminal justice system in colonial America was a product of the frontier and the experiences of small, tight-knit communities shaped by consensus and social solidarity. Criminal justice agencies played minor roles in a society reliant on informal measures. There were fewer predatory crimes such as murder, rape, or robbery in pre–19th-century America than today. Colonial punishment emanated from a religious context, with shaming and corporal punishment rituals designed to reinforce community and religious authority (Walker 1998). The Puritans tried to create a model religious community, basing punishment on biblical scripture. Many of the acts of punishment were harsh and some included death, especially for disrespect of authority.

In Pennsylvania, the Quakers responded to the harsh codes by replacing corporal punishment with a prison system designed for isolation in order to rehabilitate inmates. Formal social control did not exist outside of the family, church, and town. Variations in social order such as the evolution of slavery in the South did not alter the fact that local power brokers and the community remained the main agents of the U.S. criminal justice system until the immigrations of the 19th century (Walker 1998).

The early courts were also prone to abuses. The poor and African Americans were subject to the power of wealthy white lawyers and the courts. Early prisons not only failed at the Quaker notion of rehabilitation, but also were failures when it came to social justice for all (Walker 1998). Prison systems remained marred by corruption, racism, and classism, especially in the South. In Southern states during Reconstruction, ex-slaves were governed by a set of laws known as the Black Codes between 1865 and 1866. Enacted to reaffirm white power, the Black Codes regulated civil and legal rights, making it illegal for a black laborer to leave the plantation or farm without a permit from his or her employer. The codes also made vagrancy a crime and required permits in order to engage in a skilled trade (See Du Bois 1903). Many of the harsh realities of the Black Codes would be replaced, in the Jim Crow era following the *Plessy v. Ferguson* (1896) case, by "separate but equal" doctrines (1896–1965) (Litwack 1998).

The national incarceration rate rose from 29.1 to 115.2 per 100,000 between 1850 and 1880 (Walker 1998). Blacks filled prisons in the South after the Civil War often due to violations of vagrancy laws under the Black Codes or trumped-up charges. In many ways, the chain gang found in most Southern states until after World War II was a reinstitution of slavery. The majority of individuals in prison in the early 20th century was under the age of 25 and had violated the public order (Banks 2003).

As a result of overwork, inadequate food, an almost total absence of health care, and exposure to rampant disease among other inmates, prisoners died at an extraordinarily high rate. In 1870, 41% of Alabama prisoners died; nearly 20% of prisoners had died in each of the two previous years. Tennessee reported a death rate of almost 15% in 1884. The official death rates were often lowered by pardoning inmates who were near death (Walker 1998:90).

The era of prison reform (1820–1900) encouraged the idea that prisoners were different from other people and were dangerous. Being few in number, women and juvenile offenders lacked separate facilities until the late 19th century. Removing prisoners and delinquents from society by placing them in prisons and reformatories became the norm. The brutality of earlier eras remained into the 1950s and 1960s, during which time growing numbers of prisoners were incarcerated. Prisons for both men and women were characterized by neglect and overcrowding.

# A HISTORY OF THE WAR ON DRUGS
# AND THE MODERN PRISON-INDUSTRIAL COMPLEX

**Drug addiction** refers to psychological or physical dependence on a substance. Substance abuse is linked to a number of social problems. Individuals who abuse drugs or alcohol are more at risk for domestic violence, automobile accidents, and early death. The estimated cost of illicit drug use in the United States is $181 billion. The cost of the abuse of all substances is over a half a trillion dollars annually in the United States (National Institute for Drug Abuse [NIDA] 2008). The lost productivity and health impacts of substance abuse reduce the quality of life for all Americans. Lost productivity for U.S. businesses due to substance abuse was estimated at $81 billion in 2002 (Leon-Guerrero 2005). The type of drug and its effect on individuals vary. The addiction to some drugs can lead to all-out loss of functions and one's livelihood, even resulting in homelessness, while other drug addictions can be easier to maintain. This section gives an overview of the types of drugs that are abused and the impact on society.

**Prescription drug abuse**—illegal and nonmedical use of prescription drugs—is a major health threat for teens and adults. According to NIDA (2004), 6.3 million Americans, or 2.7%, abuse psychotherapeutic drugs. Over 22.9 million Americans abuse pain medications. Abuse of prescription drugs runs the gamut of ages and can affect everyone from housewives to street dealers. Many get addicted after surgery or an accident. Some doctors also illegally prescribe medications for profit. Addictive drugs include opioids like Oxycontin, Vicodin, and Dilaudid. Opioids are an effective category of pain relievers. However, when abused by crushing and injecting, individuals receive in a few minutes what is supposed to be delivered through time release over a 12-hour period. Other categories include central nervous system depressants such as Valium and Xanax. This class of drugs is designed to reduce anxiety and tension, and to treat the symptoms of sleep disorders. When abused, these depressants become general anesthetics. Another category is stimulants designed to reduce hyperactivity disorders. These drugs include Ritalin and Dexedrine (NIDA 2004).

Alcohol is the most abused drug in the United States. **Alcoholism** is the continuous and excessive use of alcohol leading to dependence. Heavy drinking, including binge drinking, is the highest for youth. Addicts who drink heavily over time run the risk of chronic liver disease and cirrhosis. Groups most at risk for alcohol abuse include Native Americans and Alaska Natives. Men are more likely to abuse alcohol than women for any age or within any ethnic groups. Drinking alcohol at an early age (before age 15) is more likely to lead to dependency and abuse in later life. Youth who drink experience more problems at school and are at a higher risk for medical, social, and legal problems (Leon-Guerrero 2005).

**Marijuana** is also used by a relatively large number of Americans and is the most controversial of all illegal drugs. As the nation's most used illicit drug, marijuana has been used by half of high school students, with 60 % trying the drug in 1979 at its peak. Today, an estimated 15 million Americans use the drug. Marijuana has been called a *gateway drug,* meaning it often leads to the use of other harder drugs. Studies show that many people who use hard drugs began with marijuana. Also, drug users often use marijuana in conjunction with harder drugs. The medical use of the drug for cancer victims to control nausea has made its criminalization controversial. The negative effects of the drug include memory loss, brain damage, and lung damage (NIDA 2004). While hard drugs have a devastating impact on society, U.S. drug policies have focused on marijuana in its antidrug efforts (Jefferson 2005). What is your perspective on marijuana? Does it lead to use of other harder drugs?

**Cocaine** is also a controversial drug. One of the oldest known drugs, cocaine is made from coca leaves. A plant used for medicine in South America, coca is mixed with various chemicals to create cocaine. Another form of cocaine, **crack,** was invented in the mid-1980s by cooking hydrochloride with baking soda. Highly addictive, crack takes few tools or lab supplies to make. The drug is smoked, leading to what has been described as an "overall body orgasm" (Jacobs 1999). Because crack is profitable and addictive, it spread into criminal underground networks in the late 1980s. The drug led to devastation of many poor, inner-city communities. As one commentator put it, crack networks "would have made McDonald's proud" (quoted in Jacobs 1999:5). Crack possession became a main cause for the nation's mass incarceration of drug offenders as a result of the 1988 Anti-Drug Abuse Act, which created mandatory sentences for possession of 5 grams or more of the drug. The act created a disparity in sentencing between crack and powder cocaine. Mandatory sentencing for drugs is based on weight, with it taking 100 times more powdered cocaine than crack to result in the same mandatory minimum sentence (Leigey and Backman 2007; Young and Reviere 2006). As of this writing, the Obama administration is fighting to "close the gap" in prison sentences for possession of these two drugs (Meyer 2009).

The overall use of crack has declined, mainly because younger users are more reluctant in a changing environment. Changes in public welfare policy the 1990s (i.e., tougher requirements for public housing) have made it more difficult to maintain networks to acquire drugs, while the stigma of the drug has led to isolation of users. Cocaine and crack are distinctive because they are highly addictive. Pregnant women who are addicts compromise the health of their babies, causing low birth weight and developmental problems.

Driven by drug convictions, the U.S. incarceration rate rose to 192.3 per 100,000 in 1960, only to decline again in the 1970s. Between 1970 and 2000, the number of individuals who entered the U.S. criminal justice system increased 605 % (Macionis 2008; Walker 1998). Between 1986 and 1999, federal offenders incarcerated for drug-related offenses quadrupled from 14,976 to 68,360 (Leigey and Backman 2007).

As the United States entered the 1980s, the nation began to see social changes, including economic changes in urban areas that destabilized communities. Shifts in criminal justice policy, beginning in the early 1980s, initiated a large prison boom characterized by mass incarceration and increased spending on new prisons that has continued over the last 30 years. The Anti-Drug Abuse Act of 1986 was designed to eliminate disparities in sentencing, create transparency and fairness, establish proportional punishment, and increase crime control. While the approach focused on deterrence, incapacitation, and rehabilitation, mass incarceration has been the act's main outcome. The expanding prison population led to dramatic effects on the entire criminal justice system and society's approach to crime and punishment as a whole. By the late 1990s, as a way of "getting tough on crime," 26 states had passed "three strikes laws," giving felons 25 years to life for third-time convictions.

## A NATIONAL DRUG EPIDEMIC: METHAMPHETAMINE

Another drug that is highly addictive and destructive is methamphetamine, or meth. More than 12 million Americans have tried the drug, and as of 2005, 1.5 million were using methamphetamine. Unlike crack, meth labs are centered in rural areas and can be found in all 50 states. The epidemic of this drug is overwhelming the criminal justice and human services systems. Methamphetamine is made with cold medicine containing pseudoephedrine. The drug is "cooked up" from chemical components into a powder that is snorted, smoked, or injected. The cooking process leaves toxic waste that often costs law enforcement agencies thousands of dollars to clean up. The acid and other chemicals in the mixture destroy everything with which they come in contact. Highly addictive, meth causes individuals to have elevated blood pressure, and heavy use leads to permanent brain damage. Physically, addicts lose their hair and teeth, and they continually scratch their skin. The drug's seduction is its immediate and powerful high, which causes hyper-alertness and confidence. Especially appealing to younger men and women, the drug is often used to enhance sexual drive and for weight loss (Jefferson 2005).

A recent report on meth addiction by an emergency room doctor to state representatives in Tennessee sums up the drug's impact this way: "[M]eth is so addictive that users thrown in jail will drink their urine and eat their scabs to try to get some of the euphoria it produces" ("Can We Slow the Spread of Meth?" 2004:1). Often, methamphetamine addicts have to give up their children to social services or other relatives. The cost of a meth site cleanup is astronomical for law enforcement agencies already on tight budgets. For instance, in 2003, Tennessee removed 697 children from meth-related households. The state led the nation with a reported 1,253 labs and cleanups ("Can We Slow the Spread of Meth" 2004). Meth is increasing state prison populations. Tennessee's prison population increased 4.7% in 2003, which was also one of the highest increases in the nation. The devastation caused by meth is made worse by current economic crises and the reduction in treatment options for addicts. Meth arrests are leading to spikes in incarceration rates in other rural states as well. Montana and South Dakota witnessed nearly 8% increases in prisoners due to meth addiction in 2004 and 2005.

Southern states have seen the greatest increases in prisoners, with a large part of the growth due to the meth use. Meth is affecting society more than any other drug in recent history (Harrison and Beck 2005; "Jail, Prison Populations Rise" 2006; Stambaugh 2009).

**Image 8.2** Meth Lab

*Source:* ©Istockphoto.com/byllwill.

The federal Sentencing Reform Act of 1984 has led to the highest incarceration rates in America's history. Following a rise in street crime rates throughout the 1980s, the nation continued its path to mass incarceration. Since 1980, over 350 new prisons have been added to rural America, mostly in the South and in California. Texas built 49 rural prisons in the 1990s. Mississippi built 12, and south-central Georgia placed 14 prisons in rural counties during the same time period (Huling 2002). Building prisons in depressed rural counties with low crime rates has become common throughout the country. Schlosser, in *The Prison-Industrial Complex* (1998), points out that New York's North Country, including the Adirondack district, built 19 prisons between 1973 and 1998. By 2000, Pennsylvania had built 15 new prisons in the previous 13 years, most in its rural Appalachian counties, which are dependent on primary sector economic activities (those producing raw materials). The state's rural prison population grew 187% between 1990 and 2000 (Center for Rural Pennsylvania 2001).

Table 8.7 shows the predominance of arrests for individuals who use drugs compared to those who make or sell them. The effect of the war on drugs has been to take users off the street, with the bulk of arrests for using being centered on soft drugs such as marijuana. Marijuana users are more likely to be arrested than any other group in every part of the country. On the other hand, arrests for those who sell or manufacture drugs make up only 18.3% of arrests for drug abuse violations.

**Table 8.7**   Arrests for Drug Abuse Violations, Percent Distribution by Region, 2005

| Drug Abuse Violations | | United States total | Northeast | Midwest | South | West |
|---|---|---|---|---|---|---|
| **Total*** | | **100.0** | **100.0** | **100.0** | **100.0** | **100.0** |
| Sale/ Manufacturing: | Total | 18.3 | 23.7 | 18.5 | 19.5 | 14.6 |
| | Heroin or cocaine and its derivatives | 8.0 | 15.5 | 5.5 | 8.4 | 5.3 |
| | Marijuana | 4.9 | 6.0 | 7.3 | 4.6 | 3.8 |
| | Synthetic or manufactured drugs | 1.4 | 0.9 | 1.2 | 2.6 | 0.6 |
| | Other dangerous non-narcotic drugs | 4.0 | 1.4 | 4.4 | 4.0 | 5.0 |
| Possession: | Total | 81.7 | 76.3 | 81.5 | 80.5 | 85.4 |
| | Heroin or cocaine and its derivatives | 22.2 | 25.1 | 15.8 | 22.8 | 22.9 |
| | Marijuana | 37.7 | 42.0 | 47.5 | 44.7 | 24.3 |
| | Synthetic or manufactured drugs | 3.4 | 1.9 | 3.3 | 4.5 | 3.2 |
| | Other dangerous non-narcotic drugs | 18.3 | 7.3 | 14.9 | 8.6 | 34.9 |

Source: *Uniform Crime Reports,* "Crime in the United States," 2005a, U.S. Department of Justice.

*Because of rounding, the percentages may not add up to 100.0.

As we have seen, overall crime rates have declined significantly in the last 25 years, spurred on by the healthy economy of the 1990s. Changing demographics and the abortion rights movement have reduced the number of individuals who engage in street crimes (Hayden 2004; Hochstetler and Shover 1997). However, even as overall crime declined throughout much of the 1990s, incarceration continued to increase (Michalowski and Carlson 2000). As of 2005, there are 2.3 million Americans incarcerated in the U.S. prison system. The 30-year-old war on drugs has led to the incarceration of 1.4 million Americans in state and federal prisons, two-thirds of whom are in for status drug offenses or possession. Importantly, the success rate of the American prison system comes into question. The irony of mass incarceration is that violent and property crimes have dropped significantly since 1995 (Leon-Guerrero 2005). The U.S. criminal justice system has a high repeat offender or recidivism rate. Almost 2 out of 3 individuals who are released from U.S. prisons are repeat offenders. Another issue with the current system is the diverting of funds to prisons and away from other types of investment to address criminality. At a cost of over $300 billion in the last 15 years, the war on drugs has often overshadowed investment in other strategies for reducing crime such as rehabilitation and drug treatment programs (Chambliss 1994, 2006; Huling 2002).

Criminalization starts from the assumption that all drug use is a crime—there can be no legal use for pleasure or medical purposes. It precludes the idea that drug use can be a medical or health problem. The large rises in the U.S. incarceration rate are evidence of the criminalization approach to drug use. In the mid-1990s, debates on the nation's approach to drug use led to reforms, including suggestions that the country should focus on **decriminalization** (regulating and reducing the severity of penalties) and even **legalization** of drugs, or making them a legal controlled substance. More importantly, many critics of the drug war began to point to the futility of punishment for nonviolent drug use and promoted a focus on **drug treatment.** These policy makers and theorists argued that managing drug misuse is more important than trying to stop it altogether (Inciardi 1999; Leon-Guerrero 2005). Noam Chomsky (2003) offers the following:

> If we wanted to stop drug use in the United States there's an easy way to do it: education programs. They work very effectively, and they have made a difference to the extent they have been used. Among the more privileged sectors, my children, probably yours, the use of drugs has been declining for a long time and so has the use of every other substance. (p. 58)

Critics of mass incarceration point out that the prison system has emerged as one of the main responses to the nation's approach to development issues regarding human capital, substance abuse, illiteracy, mental illness, poverty, and social disorganization (Mauer and Chesney-Lind 2002). The impact on racial differences in the criminal justice system is evident when you take a closer look at who is more likely to make up the U.S. prison population. Echoes of past racism continue to haunt our prisons. In 2004, nearly 60% of prison and jail inmates were racial or ethnic minorities. In addition, the nation's poor continue to be more likely to enter the criminal justice system (Diaz-Cotto 2006). In sum, these debates point out that inequality in education and community resources plays an important role in criminality and incarceration.

## MEDIA BOX: CONTROLLING THE PERCEPTION AND DEPICTION OF CRIME

Symbolic interactionists hold that the social construction of social problems is a subjective process whereby people use knowledge obtained from the media to create a picture of their world, including images of crime. Sociologists point out that groups that have access to broadcasting through the mass media are able to manipulate public opinion to their own advantage. The mass media plays an important role in framing who and what is considered deviant and how it will be dealt with by society. With the advent of television, the media has been more able to create moral panics around emerging social trends, which shapes public opinion. Glassner's (2010) study provides evidence that the media's ability to frame issues has fanned American's fears of adolescents, crime, and minority groups while ignoring homelessness, child malnutrition, and other problems that are actually at the root of crime. This includes the media's ability to manipulate public opinion and make some issues more visible than others. As discussed in this chapter, the unequal distribution of punishment for different types of crime reflect issues of power often determined by differences in race and class. David Altheide (2002, 2006) argues that a discourse of fear has evolved as the mass media has manipulated public empathy in the last 30 years. Fear of crime, promoted by the mass media, has sparked public outrage leading to mass incarceration. A key symbol in the early years of the crack epidemic was the media's focus on inner-city mothers who used crack during their pregnancy (Litt and McNeil 1994). Crack babies became a symbol of the breakdown of social control and were connected with welfare mothers and eventually welfare reform in the 1990s. Humphries (1999) asserts, "such issues were so inflammatory that they intensified and extended the life of the war on drugs" (p. 11).

Conflict theorists point out that the power of corporations to manipulate the media has led to the "manufacturing of consent," resulting in their ability to avoid public scrutiny of illicit behavior (Chomsky and Herman 2002). Crime by the state is also subject to media manipulation. Altheide (2006) points out that after the September 11, 2001, attacks on the World Trade Center, the news media legitimated illegal government actions in the name of justice, which have reduced civil rights while violating the public trust. Examples of illegal activities in response to the 9/11 attacks include locking up foreign combatants in the Guantanamo detention center in Cuba and illegal wiretapping of U.S. citizens. These examples show the powerful role the mass media has played in creating criminal justice policy in the last 30 years. What current media approaches to social policy do you see as manipulation? What is your perspective on the general public's understanding of the relationship between crime and the mass media? How has the sociological perspective helped you be more conscious of how the media shapes social issues?

## CASE STUDY #1

Project Bridge—Prevention, Outreach, and Mentoring:
What Really Works in Addressing Gangs and Social Problems

As of 2005, there are an estimated 731,500 youth gang members in 21,500 gangs in the United States. Cities of 250,000 people or more all report a youth gang problem, while 87% of cities between 100,000 and 249,999 people report such a problem. Of law enforcement agencies surveyed, 26% reported an association between gangs and organized crime. The Federal Bureau of Prisons estimates that 11.7% of federal prison inmates belong to a gang (National Youth Gang Center 2005). Overall, gangs are at their lowest level in three decades. Gang membership declined from 850,000 to 760,000 from 1987 to 2007 (Jackman 2007). Studies find that most youth in gangs go through gang membership as a phase, and they will eventually age out of the culture. For those who stay, gang membership provides resources and social status (Greene and Pranis 2007). Gangs in the United States contribute to violent crime and delinquency, as well as drug use, manufacturing, and distribution. Yet, as functionalist sociologists maintain, gang memberships are fueled by the individuals' inability to enter mainstream society due to a host of other social problems.

Functionalist sociologists argue that crime can be "functional" for society because it can create solidarity and social change, and it affirms moral boundaries. Functionalists focus on the relationship between crime and the social bond. Early sociologist Émile Durkheim (1951) argued that deviance and crime were important for social systems. He claimed that deviance affirmed norms and moral boundaries, created social unity, and promoted social change within society. Later, functionalist social theorist Robert Merton (1953) developed what became know as *strain theory*. Merton argued that individuals who cannot achieve the goals of a society may become deviant. Blocked economic or social opportunities cause individuals to experience **anomie**, or a lack of normative guiding principles. According to Merton, strained individuals may innovate and try to achieve goals using alternative methods such as illegal activities. Others may reject cultural goals but continue to conform to expected behavior. This is called *ritualism*. According to Merton, individuals engage in **retreatism** when they reject cultural goals and the means to achieve them. Finally, the last category is individuals who rebel and challenge culturally accepted goals.

Social theorists focusing on the role of gangs in the community have also shown that gangs provide a number of social and material resources that are difficult to obtain in other ways for the poor in urban communities. Research on gangs draws on the idea of **illegitimate opportunity structures**. Cloward and Ohlin (1960) show that disadvantaged individuals will develop means to financial success even when they lack education, socialization, and other skills required in society. Recent studies (Henslin 2007) reaffirm Cloward and Ohlin's basic premise. Gangs provide a number of rewards for poor youth. Boys gain access to drugs, money, girls, and recreation. Beyond material benefits,

*(Continued)*

(Continued)

gangs defend communities and spearhead political change (Hayden 2004; Jankowski 1991; Kontos et al. 2003). Simply put, the presence of a gang shows that communities are not providing resources in other ways. Gangs are not new to America. Immigrant gangs have long been a feature of urban society. However, in an era when education plays an increasingly important role in the economy, investment in communities is of greater urgency.

Today, gangs in the United States reflect immigration and globalization. Historically, newly arriving immigrant communities have been ripe for gang activities. This is true today as well. Globalization is having a dramatic impact on U.S. gangs. Emerging international gangs are involved in extortion, murder, rape, assault, auto theft, fraud, and drug and gun trafficking. One of the faster-growing international gangs, MS-13, or Mara Salvatrucha, represents a violent and increasingly mobile street gang that is terrorizing communities in 33 states and the District of Columbia. MS-13, which started in Los Angeles in the late 1980s, has an estimated 8,000–10,000 members nationwide, mostly Salvadoran nationals or first-generation Salvadoran Americans, but also including Hondurans, Guatemalans, Mexicans, and other Central and South American immigrants. Members often wear clothing or sport tattoos incorporating MS-13 or the number 13. In order to combat the gang's cross-border activities, the FBI's Criminal Investigative Division linked with officials in El Salvador. In 2005–2006, the FBI's MS-13 National Gang Task Force coordinated a series of arrests and crackdowns in the United States and Central America that involved more than 6,000 police officers in five countries. Seventy-three suspects were arrested in the United States; in all, more than 650 were taken into custody (FBI 2006).

As we saw earlier in this chapter, the U.S. approach to drug use and crime is often ineffective due to an overemphasis on incarceration and after-the-fact measures. Recent research is finding the same reality for gangs. According to a number of studies, the failure of the United States to slow gang violence until recently is linked to its failure to establish effective public safety strategies. The Justice Policy Institute and others point out that heavy-handed suppression efforts can increase tensions, and they have a poor track record when it comes to reducing crime and violence (Greene and Pranis 2007; Jackman 2007; U.S. Department of Education 2007). These studies found that instead of suppression, gangs are reduced by promoting initiatives around jobs, education, and healthy communities. Preventative initiatives through schools and community outreach are proving the most effective way to keep at-risk children from joining gangs.

The main reason for the decline in gangs is the successful preventative approach some cities have taken to solving the gang problem. The most visible example of successful approaches includes the successes of Washington and New York City, which reduced its gang-related crimes to 520 in 2005 by taking comprehensive approaches to gangs. This is a dramatic decline when compared to Los Angeles, which for the same year experienced 11,402 gang-related crimes. Studies reveal that New York's success with its gangs is linked to an extensive use of social resources—job training, mentoring, after-school activities, and recreational programs. The city has succeeded by using street-level social workers and gang intervention, along with suppression (Greene and Pranis 2007; Jackman 2007).

In 2003, Washington police chief Charles Ramsey launched the Gang Intervention Partnership Unit, working with schools, neighborhood groups, and resident activists to reduce gang activity. Gang-related murders declined from 21 between 1999 and 2003 to zero between 2003 and 2006. On the other hand, Los Angeles remains the gang capital. Criminologists point out that the city's 25-year anti-gang effort has failed largely due to its reluctance to fund social programs, while New York has followed through on prevention measures. One Los Angeles gang outreach worker estimates that the city has just 61 gang intervention workers to handle 40,000 gang members (Jackman 2007).

In a similar vein, comparing programs across the United States, the Office of Juvenile Justice and Delinquency Prevention (OJJDP) (2000) found that approaches that target youth with a combination of measures such as community mobilization, job training, intervention, and other tactics are best used along with suppression tactics. Also, what happens after members are incarcerated is proving important for reducing gang membership. Research suggests that approaches targeting former gang members' reintegration into communities are effective in reducing gang activity (Spergel 1995). Prevention measures are an important part of emerging strategies. Research by the U.S. Department of Education (2007) shows **primary prevention** is an effective counter strategy to address youth violence. Primary prevention targets the entire community and the environment where gangs start, with programs dedicated to prenatal services and infant care, reducing truancy, anti-bullying, and dropout prevention. Researchers have found that some children join a gang to keep from being bullied. Anti-bullying efforts in schools reduce victimization and the ability of gangs to control school environments. **Secondary prevention** identifies young, at-risk children and provides them with services in order to reduce their movement toward gangs. Neighborhood community-based organizations and faith-based groups are best able to address these outreach efforts. Boys & Girls Clubs, for instance, target at-risk youth, providing them with experiences of success and resources. Comprehensive programs merge these efforts with law enforcement and juvenile justice systems (U.S. Department of Education 2007).

Most gang members are involved in gang activity by the age of 15, when prevention activities are no longer useful. Anthony, a former gang member and participant in the Project Bridge program in Riverside, California, shows how gangs provide resources and a social bond.

> By the time he was just 11 years old, the gang allowed Anthony to run with them. Soon, he was drinking, smoking pot, using methamphetamines, carrying a gun, and robbing bystanders, liquor stores and others. For a while he was selling drugs—anything to get money. But when asked about the appeal of the gang, he . . . says, "You had another family. Being a gang member, you always had to look over your shoulder. When you had your close friends in the gang, you had people looking out for you. You would have help for anything" (U.S. Department of Education 2007).

*(Continued)*

(Continued)

Project Bridge helps gang members to succeed in society instead of punishing them. The program provides social and human capital in the form of teaching gang members how to fill out a resume, fill out a job application, dress for a job, and interview effectively. As an incentive, participants who complete the program also receive a $225 stipend (U.S. Department of Education 2007). Gangs not only provide a survival strategy, but they also provide self-esteem and a feeling of accomplishment. Low-income communities are often unable to compete with gangs for the attention of their young people.

Other programs such as the Gang Reduction Program in Miami Beach, Florida; Los Angeles, California; Milwaukee, Wisconsin; and Richmond, Virginia take comprehensive approaches using former gang members as outreach workers focused on high-risk populations. These approaches take gang prevention into the schools, connecting at-risk youth with resources and coordinating key law enforcement officials, community outreach, and educators. Gang reduction programs address the lifeworlds of a student, not just gang involvement. Robert Tagle from the Houston Gang-Free Schools Project relates that he deals with home life, environment, and parent problems in his conversations with adolescents.

> When you start dealing with all the hurt and pain and all the things that they have buried all over the years, you're going to get gangs. . . . Sometimes [our work] is about breaking different cycles. If you are raised in an environment where that's all you see, if you've never been to a [Houston] Astros games, never been to the Holocaust museum or been to the zoo, you will think the world revolves around your neighborhood. (U.S. Department of Education 2007:n.p.)

These themes reveal the link between reducing gang membership and addressing the home life of at-risk youth. Functionalist sociologists make the point that criminal activity is embedded in the social structure. Changing the opportunity for youth to enter mainstream society is proving more effective than approaches that concentrate on criminalizing individuals.

## Cast Study Questions

1. What trends characterize gangs in the current era?

2. What have been the tactics to address gang crime until recently in the United States?

3. What social functions do gangs provide for youth?

4. What are primary and secondary prevention tactics?

## CASE STUDY #2

Drugs, Incarceration, and Rehabilitation:
Dismas House and Communities of Caring

Students in Worcester, Massachusetts, and elsewhere around the country have long been drawn to volunteer at Dismas Houses. According to Dismas, Inc., of Nashville, Tennessee, these nonprofit organizations provide "transitional housing and support services to men and women who have been recently released from prison or jail." They continue,

> Dismas provides a unique form of crime prevention by working with at-risk individuals to integrate them with community volunteers, college students, and staff. Dismas House recognizes that the cycle of crime can be reduced when men and women who have been incarcerated have assistance readjusting to society. To that end, Dismas House provides room and board, transportation, job referrals, life skills counseling, and drug and alcohol counseling referrals to help former offenders make a successful transition back into the community. (www.dismashouse.org)

Students have performed a variety of services at Dismas Houses, from helping with meals and maintenance to providing tutoring, job skills, and other capacity-building opportunities.

During the last few years, however, increased pressure to stop transitional housing programs from locating in residential areas has made providing this approach to crime prevention more difficult. In Worcester, Dismas House asked college students to help provide data that might help them in their local battles with homeowners who feared increased crime and reduced property values. While little evidence was found to support their fears, most opposed to Dismas House argued that released prisoners should not be given services and housing without having demonstrated their rehabilitation and "worthiness." Dismas House staff argue that most prisoners never have the opportunity to rehabilitate and develop their capacity to do so without housing and supportive services.

Conflict theorists point out that the criminal justice system reflects power relationships where people with power and privilege use their institutional resources to define what a crime is and what kinds of punishments should be meted out. As we have seen, minorities and the poor are most likely to be incarcerated and serve longer sentences for crimes that are similar to those of their white, wealthier counterparts. Meanwhile, white-collar and corporate crimes often go unpunished. The huge explosion of U.S. prison populations can be directly linked to the ways in which drug use has been criminalized and demonized by the so-called war on drugs. The incarceration of drug offenders has increased the number of prisoners in the United States but has not solved its drug problem. Investment in people who have drug problems is another option for dealing with substance abuse.

*(Continued)*

(Continued)

While the nation has filled its prisons to capacity with drug users, only 10% of the drug and alcohol treatment needs in the United States are being met. Ettner et al. (2006) show the positive impact of drug and alcohol treatment for reducing the costs of substance abuse. Their study of treatment centers in California reveals that for every dollar spent on substance abuse treatment, $7 worth of economic benefits are realized. On average, substance abuse treatment costs $1,583 per individual and is associated with a monetary benefit to society of $11,487. Drug treatment leads to increases in employment and the reduction of crime. Drug in- and outpatient treatment programs lead to reduced visits to emergency rooms and reductions in other health care costs. Most importantly, drug treatment reduces recidivism.

With the costs of incarcerating an inmate varying between $15,000 and $20,000 a year, other methods for drug addicts make more sense. According to their website (www.dismashouse.org), Dismas House, in Worcester, Massachusetts, is "a supportive community that provides transitional housing and services to former prisoners and real-life educational opportunities to students from area colleges, and from throughout the US and the world!" Opened in 1988, Dismas House in Worcester offers residents a place where they "work as a family, helping each other grow towards the goal of reintegration into society." According to Director Dave McMahon, Dismas gives ex-prisoners a "consensus-based, sober alternative to a return to the streets, and a return to incarceration. Our cooks, donors, board members and other volunteers help make reconciliation a reality" (www.dismashouse.org).

While Dismas House helps residents with everything from employment training to learning and study skills, McMahon acknowledges that drug and alcohol addictions are the primary handicap that individuals face when trying to reintegrate after prison. In fact, drug convictions are the primary cause for most residents' initial imprisonment. This should come as no surprise. Drug convictions made up 18% of the increase in prisoners in the 1990s for men and 36% for women. For those entering the criminal justice system for other offenses, 33% of state, 22% of federal, and 36% of local jail inmates were on drugs at the time of their arrest (U.S. Department of Health and Human Services 2001). Inequality of drug sentences has also played a role in increasing prison populations. Mandatory minimum sentencing has left more crack users in prison than cocaine users, who are more often white and living in the suburbs. As mentioned earlier in the chapter, mandatory sentencing policies incarcerating drug users for 5 years for 5 grams of crack, while it takes 500 grams of cocaine to elicit the same sentence, has meant a focus on incarcerating inner-city residents who are more likely to use crack (Chambliss 1994, 2006; Tonry 1995). The 1980s war on drugs set these forces in motion, yet despite the massive imprisonment of millions on drug charges, there is little evidence that overall drug use in the United States has dropped. In fact, recent studies show that certain drugs have different patterns of consumption based on economic forces, international policies and trade, and so forth, but that policing and punishment have little impact.

Still, according to McMahon, the greatest impact of the war on drugs, what he calls the "culture of punishment," has been its effect on people with addictions and especially ex-prisoners: "No one wants to actually help people overcome addictions or reintegrate into society—they just want to punish, longer and harder" (www.dismashouse.org). Yet Dismas House has demonstrated that it can be effective. While over 75% of prisoners return to jail after their initial release, Dismas House residents have a 75% success rate. The key, according to McMahon, is the phrase "Dismas is family." He explains,

> The success of the house is a collaborative effort. People living in the house pay part of the operating expenses. Students are given opportunities for internships in non-profit management and/or live-in positions in the Dismas community. There are simple rules, such as no violence, drugs or alcohol; and there are expectations, such as attendance at dinners, curfews, chores and participating in house meetings and activities. (www.dismashouse.org)

Despite its success, Dismas House (as well as a number of other transitional housing programs in the Worcester Main South neighborhood) has come under attack for "bringing the neighborhood down." A few vocal activists argue that transitional housing programs negatively impact property values and crime rates, and cause a general dissatisfaction in the quality of life among others in the community. McMahon didn't think these accusations were true, and from his work with the local Crime Watch and in the community gardens that Dismas House helped start, he knew that many in the community did not share those sentiments. He asked a local sociology professor, Corey Dolgon (coauthor of this book), if he and his students could help.

McMahon met with Dolgon and his students in a community research course, and they designed a neighborhood impact study that combined secondary research using other studies as well as primary research in four areas: Property Values, Crime Statistics, Neighborhood Attitudes, and Social Capital produced by Dismas and other housing programs. Student research demonstrated that the vast majority of studies showed that transitional housing programs had no negative impact on property values or crime rates. If anything, they seemed to help stabilize neighborhoods in transition, but for the most part, property values were linked to regional market trends and individual owner investment. Similarly, transitional housing programs seemed to decrease most crime by giving people who were most vulnerable to being victims or most desperate to commit crimes the kinds of support and resources they needed to avoid such fates.

The primary research done by the class seemed to confirm the secondary literature. Properties on the block on which Dismas was located and the blocks immediately surrounding it showed a significant increase in value between 2000 and 2006. In fact, the rate of increase was within 2–3% of the average

*(Continued)*

(Continued)

for the entire city. Similarly, by examining arrest records, students demonstrated that a miniscule number (less than .1%) of crimes committed in the area could be traced back to residents of transitional housing facilities. But perhaps the most startling finding was that, far from sharing the negative views of Dismas and other housing programs that were voiced by activists, most of the neighborhood supported its work and felt positive about its location in the neighborhood. It seems that much of this goodwill toward Dismas emanates from its very public presence in organizing local cleanups, the community gardens, a Crime Watch, and a variety of other events. The very same activities that help Dismas residents better reintegrate themselves into the community also help to integrate Dismas House itself into its neighborhood. While Dismas House is not a solution to the nation's drug problems, it does offer a powerful model of how the proper institutional and community support can positively impact dozens of people who once used or sold drugs, went to prison because of it, and likely would have gone back to such behaviors without the housing program opportunity.

## Cast Study Questions

1. What are the advantages of Dismas House over other methods of dealing with addicts?

2. What are the main differences between policies that criminalize drugs and those that address addiction?

3. How does the surrounding community contribute to the success of Dismas House?

4. How do the activities of Dismas House contribute to the surrounding community?

## CASE STUDY #3

### The Inside-Out Prison Exchange Program

The United States will be reintegrating 600,000 ex-convicts a year, with many returning to prison due to mental illness, illiteracy, and a lack of job skills. Clearly, the U.S. "get tough" laws are designed to deter street crimes. What happens to these ex-convicts will in part be determined by what types of training they receive in prison and when they get out. We can draw on symbolic interactionism to understand how ex-cons experience reentering society. The approached taken by symbolic interactionists to explain crime is based on the idea that people learn deviant behavior. Differential association is the term used to describe what happens when a person learns deviance from the groups he or she interacts with. According to these theories, deviance is learned within families, neighborhoods, and subcultures such as gangs (Laub and Sampson 2008; Sutherland, 1947). It can be learned in inner cities or corporate boardrooms. **Labeling** theories of crime draw not only on learning, but also on perception of oneself as a social deviant. Perception of an individual is important for symbolic interactionists. If a group is labeled as deviant, then the response to the label may shape the behavior of the group. In recent years, the perception of a group as deviant has led to racial profiling in the war on drugs, as described earlier in the chapter. Police and court discretion are often responsible for labeling individuals as deviant, especially those from poor backgrounds and areas (Chambliss 1994, 2006; Tonry 1995).

Another explanation of crime, based on socialization, is offered by Travis Hirschi (Gottfredson and Hirschi 1990). Hirschi expands on earlier ideals of what became known as **control theory** (Reckless 1973). He switched the focus of criminology to the question of why individuals do not commit crimes in order to understand why others take up deviant behavior. Control theory postulates that norms guide a person's behavior through attachments to commitment to conventional goals and means, involvement in conventional activities, and beliefs around acceptance of conventional goals and norms. Hirschi argues that instead of incarcerating criminals, the system should focus on the lives of youth and teenagers before they engage in acts related to low levels of self-control and a short-term view of their lives. Arguing that stiffer sentences will do little to reduce criminality, he recommends investing in young people before they enter the system. Hirschi argues that increasing support for families, promoting stronger families, and delaying pregnancy would do more to fight crime than other measures. Following Hirschi's ideas, social support for convicts reentering society is also crucial for their success.

Programs designed to assist reentry increasingly are drawing on college students in service learning programs. In Philadelphia, Temple University's Inside-Out exchange program allows criminal justice majors to have service learning opportunities inside of Pennsylvania prisons. The exchange links higher education and corrections systems while providing support for inmates. Since 1997, over 300 students and 400 inmates have participated in the program. The program is designed to change both individual and public attitudes toward prisoners and rehabilitation. Students apply social theory and methods in the exchange. They use their experiences to write papers and contextualize book materials. Class projects address issues such as the challenges faced by women in the criminal justice system and making the corrections system ideal for women's rehabilitation. The findings of these classes are presented to the prison administration. Projects at Graterford Prison address the basic educational needs of prisoners, transitional issues, and activities such as an art mural at the prison. This mural, entitled *Victims and Healing,* is one of 2,500 public works of art in Philadelphia sponsored and created by the Mural Arts Program, whose fundamental objective

*(Continued)*

(Continued)

uses mural making and art education as a means of combating and preventing crime and its impact on local communities. Other projects include creative writing workshops allowing inmates to publish their stories at Temple University.

As we saw in the beginning of the chapter with the Project Community example in Michigan, students who enter a prison system for service learning have a life-changing experience. Breaking down stereotypes is an important part of service learning. Growing as a person is another. One participant in the Inside-Out Program explains her transformation this way: "I didn't expect to grow and change as a result of the process. As I reflect on the power of this course, I am awestruck and humbled" (Inside-Out Program Introduction). Along with criminal justice courses at Temple, other classes involved in the program include Drugs in Urban Society and Parenting From Prison: Mothers on the Inside. Working with mothers in prison can be a powerful experience for students.

> This class has acted as the catalyst in my passion for life and human rights, and was the pivotal point where I realigned my own path. This program has brought me to a new understanding of life not just in prison, but in my own life. I have acquired the concrete knowledge of the true interworkings of the system, and at the same time come to realize my own captors in life. I have heard the stories, felt their smiles, and seen the tears of women who have been to hell and back and with them I have found a voice. (Temple University Program Participant, the Inside-Out Prison Exchange Program)

Connecting colleges and prisons not only raises the awareness of the needs of prisoners, but also provides services that will help ex-convicts to not become repeat offenders. These programs solve social problems as part of the education of both prisoners and college students. Investing in youth before they engage in delinquency is a better way to solve crime.

## Case Study Questions

1. How are individuals labeled in the criminal justice system according to labeling theories?

2. Drawing on control theory, Travis Hirschi argues that society should invest in what areas to reduce criminality in the long run?

3. What are some of the personal changes experienced by college students who work with prisoners in the Inside-Out project?

4. How might your future occupation address the reintegration of former prisoners into society?

## VOICES FROM THE FIELD

David McMahon, Codirector of Dismas House, Worcester, MA

According to David McMahon (personal communication, April and November 2006), "Dismas House residents stabilize and succeed at rates between 69% [and] 75%, in stark contrast to the general prison population, who return to jail at a rate of 75%. People living in the house pay part of the operating expenses. Students have internships in non-profit management and/or live-in positions in the Dismas community. People work together without distinctions based on class, race, gender, or even ex-offender status." McMahon believes this collective approach is the key to success—we're like a family. He articulates, "Former prisoners engage in the hard work of rebuilding lives, and rekindling hope for themselves and their families, but do so in the company of volunteer Board members and their families, live-in international students, and church and civic groups who work side-by-side, break bread, and create a community both within the house as well as in the surrounding neighborhood. Our residents work in community gardens, neighborhood watch and do local park clean-ups. Our model rebuilds individual lives but within a collective environment that stresses the importance of social and community relations to individual health and well-being."

## SUMMARY

This chapter shows that approaches to social problems vary. The work of sociologists and other community workers demonstrates that crime is linked to other social problems. The U.S. approach to its crime woes in the last 30 years has been at least in part unsuccessful. What *does* work with offenders and community members at risk for street crime are intervention strategies that provide skills and long-term self-control. Students engaged in service learning get more than satisfaction from providing skills. They question their perspectives on crime, policing, and the lives of offenders. In the program examples provided in this chapter, we see how activists and volunteers are addressing the needs of communities, families, and those incarcerated, along with their families and the victims of crimes.

The chapter also reveals that white-collar and corporate crime, while not historically prosecuted, are increasingly getting addressed in the criminal justice system, as society sees the threat that these crimes have for society. Globalization is also changing the types of prevalent crimes as well as who is involved in gangs.

## SUMMARY QUESTIONS

1. What are the types of crime? How is crime data reported and collected?

2. What approaches to street crime work best to reduce recidivism?

3. What is white-collar crime and why is it different from other types of crime?

4. What is the relationship between drug addiction and mass incarceration?

5. Describe sociological approaches to crime and criminality.

## GLOSSARY

**Acquaintance Rape:** Rape in which the victim knows or is familiar with the rapist.

**Alcoholism:** Continuous and excessive use of alcohol leading to dependence.

**Anomie:** A lack of normative guiding principles.

**Classic Rape:** Rape in which the rapist is a stranger.

**Cocaine:** Drug made from a mix of chemicals with the coca leaf.

**Control Theory:** Focus on why individuals do not commit crimes.

**Crack:** A form of cocaine made by cooking hydrochloride with baking soda and other chemicals.

**Crime:** Any type of deviance that violates society's laws.

**Cyber Crimes:** Crimes occurring in a virtual, Internet, or other computer environment.

**Date Rape:** Rape that occurs when the victim knows and socializes with the rapist.

**Decriminalization:** Regulating and reducing the severity of penalties for illegal drug use.

**Deviance:** Any violation of social norms.

**Differential Association:** Learning deviance from the groups people interact with.

**Drug Addiction:** Psychological and/or physical dependence on a substance.

**Drug Treatment:** Managing drug abuse by providing medical treatment.

Felonies: Serious crimes punishable by stiff penalties.

Identity Theft: Crime involving taking over another's professional or personal identity.

Illegitimate Opportunity Structures: Illegitimate means to financial success, developed when one lacks education, socialization, and other skills required in society.

Juvenile Delinquency: Crimes and offenses committed by young offenders, often school dropouts and those who are alienated from family and community supervision.

Labeling: Being treated as a criminal or deviant based on appearance, group associations, stereotypes, and so forth.

Legalization: Making drugs a legal controlled substance.

Marijuana: Drug used by a relatively large amount of Americans; the most controversial of all illegal drugs.

Marital or Spousal Rape: Rape that occurs when a man forces his wife to have sexual intercourse. In many time periods and places, marital rape has not been recognized as a crime.

Mediating Structures: Programs and opportunities providing social capital and opportunities for youth.

Misdemeanors: Petty and less serious offenses.

Prescription Drug Abuse: Illegal and nonmedical use of prescription drugs.

Primary Prevention: Prevention strategy to address gangs and youth violence that targets the entire community and the environment.

Prison-Industrial Complex: Private, corporate industries supporting and profiting from mass incarceration policies.

Property Crimes: Includes the offenses of burglary, larceny, and motor vehicle theft.

Racial Profiling: Official or unofficial use of racial, ethnic, national origin, or religion criteria to determine who should be stopped, searched, arrested, or otherwise addressed by law enforcement personnel.

Rape: Sexual penetration as a result of force or the threat of force and including nonconsent of the victim.

Retreatism: When someone rejects cultural goals and the means to achieve them.

Sanctions: State-sanctioned punishment.

Secondary Prevention: Identifies young, at-risk children and provides them with services in order to reduce their movement toward gangs.

Self-Report Studies: Collections of data created from self-reporting surveys, often outside of UCR reports.

Social Control: Any attempt to create conformity to authoritative values, norms, and laws.

Statutory Rape: When an adult has sex with a minor.

Victimless Crimes: These involve violations of the law in which no victim steps forward or is identified.

Violent Crimes: Physical and harmful in nature, these crimes include murder, rape, robbery, and aggravated assault.

White-Collar Crimes: Legal offenses committed by a person of respectability and high social status in the course of his or her occupation.

## WEBSITES FOR MORE INFORMATION ABOUT CRIME AND STUDENT ACTION ON ISSUES RELATED TO CRIME

Center for Community Corrections: http://centerforcommunitycorrections.org/

Center for Corporate Policy: http://www.corporatepolicy.org/issues/crime.htm

The Center for Victims of Violent Crimes: http://www.cvvc.org/

Death Penalty Information Center: http://www.deathpenaltyinfo.org/

Federal Bureau of Investigation—Uniform Crime Reports: http://www.fbi.gov/ucr/ucr.htm

Just Detention International: http://www.spr.org/

National Institute on Drug Abuse: http://www.nida.nih.gov/

Prison Activist Resource Center: http://www.prisonactivist.org/

Restorative Justice Online: http://www.restorativejustice.org/

Take Back the Night: http://www.takebackthenight.org/

U.S. Department of Justice—Reentry programs: http://www.reentry.gov/

Violence Prevention Institute: http://www.violencepreventioninstitute.org/gangs.html

Women and Prison: http://www.womenandprison.org/

## REFERENCES

Abu-Jamal, Mumia. 2003. "Sentenced to the Backwaters of Greene County, PA." Pp. 276–277 in *Prison Nation: The Warehousing of America's Poor,* edited by Tara Herivel and Paul Wright. New York: Routledge.

AFL-CIO. 2006, April. *Death on the Job: The Toll of Neglect—A National and State-by-State Profile of Worker Safety and Health in the United States.* Washington, DC: Author.

Alabama Department of Post-Secondary Education. 1992. *A Study of Alabama Prison Recidivism Rates of Inmates Having Completed Vocational and Academic Programs While Incarcerated Between the Years of 1987 through 1991.* Montgomery, AL: Author.

Altheide, David. 2002. *Creating Fear News and the Construction of Crisis.* Piscataway, NJ: Aldine Transaction.

_____. 2006. *Terrorism and the Politics of Fear.* Lanham, MD: AltaMira Press.

American Civil Liberties Union. 2001, July 24. *Bowing to ACLU Lawsuit, CT Officials Will Move Prisoners Out of Notorious Virginia "Supermax."* New York: The ACLU Foundation. Retrieved January 21, 2010 (http://www.aclu.org/prisoners-rights/bowing-aclu-lawsuit-ct-officials-will-move-prisoners-out-notorious-virginia-superma).

_____. 2004. *The Forgotten Population: A Look at Death Row in the United States Through the of Women.* New York: The ACLU Foundation. Retrieved April 9, 2007 (http://www.aclu.org/capital/women/10627pub20041129.html).

_____. 2009. *The Persistence of Racial and Ethnic Profiling in the United States. A Follow-Up Report to the U.N. Committee on the Elimination of Racial Discrimination.* New York: The ACLU Foundation.

Amnesty International. 1999, June 7. USA: *Cruelty in Control? The Stun Belt and Other Electroshock Equipment in Law Enforcement.* London, UK: Author. Index number AMR 51/054/1999. Retrieved January 21, 2010 (http://www.amnesty.org/en/library/info/AMR51/054/1999).

_____. 2004. *Threat and Humiliation: Racial Profiling, National Security, and Human Rights in the United States.* New York: Author.

Armstrong, Elizabeth, Laura A. Hamilton, and Brian Sweeney. 2006. "Sexual Assault on Campus: A Multilevel, Integrative Approach to Party Rape." *Social Problems,* 53:483–499.

Banks, Cyndi. 2003. *Women in Prison: A Reference Handbook.* Santa Barbara, CA: ABC-CLIO.

Barrionuevo, Alexei. 2006. "Two Enron Chiefs Are Convicted in Fraud and Conspiracy." *New York Times.* May 26.

Beckett, Katherine and Theodore Sasson. 2004. *The Politics of Injustice: Crime and Punishment in America.* Thousand Oaks, CA: Sage.

Bender, Edwin. 2000. *Private Prisons, Politics & Profits.* Helena, MT: National Institute on Money in State Politics.

Benokraitis, Nijole V. 2008. *Marriages and Families: Changes, Choices, and Constraints.* 6th ed. Upper Saddle River, NJ: Prentice Hall.

Bergen, Raquel Kennedy. 2006. "Marital Rape: New Research and Directions." National Online Resource Center on Violence Against Women. Retrieved July 9 2010: http://new.vawnet.org/Assoc_Files_VAWnet/AR_MaritalRapeRevised.pdf

Biewen, John. 2007. "The Story Behind 'Corrections, Inc.'" *American RadioWorks.* November 26. Retrieved November 30, 2007 (http://americanradioworks.publicradio.org/features/corrections/notebook.html).

Brownmiller, Susan. 1975. *Against Our Will: Men, Women, and Rape.* New York: Simon & Schuster.

Bureau of Justice Statistics. 2009. "Bulletin: Prisoners in 2008." U.S. Department of Justice. Retrieved February 13, 2010 (http://bjs.ojp.usdoj.gov/index.cfm?ty = pbdetail&iid = 1763).

Bureau of Labor Statistics. 2007. *Census of Fatal Occupational Injuries.* Washington, DC: U.S. Department of Labor.

"Can We Slow the Spread of Meth?" 2004. *Morristown Citizen Tribune.* March 2, p. 1.

Carrabone, Eamonn et al. 2004. *Criminology: A Sociological Introduction.* London, UK: Routledge.

Center for Rural Pennsylvania. 2001. "Just the Facts: Prison Population Growth." Retrieved February 15, 2010 (http://www.rural.palegislature.us/news1101.html#6).

Chambliss, William. 1994. "Policing the Ghetto Underclass: The Politics of Law and Law Enforcement." *Social Problems,* 34:187–212.

_____. 2006. *Power, Politics, and Crime.* Boulder, CO: Westview Press.

Chesney-Lind, Meda and Lisa Pasko. 2003. *The Female Offender: Girls, Women, and Crime.* Thousand Oaks, CA: Sage.

Chomsky, Noam. 2003. "Drug Policy as Social Control." Pp. 50–63 in *Prison Nation: The Warehousing of America's Poor,* edited by Tara Herivel and Paul Wright. New York: Routledge.

Chomsky, Noam and Edward S. Herman. 2002. *Manufacturing Consent: The Political Economy of the Mass Media.* New York: Pantheon.

Christie, Nils. 1994. *Crime Control as Industry: Towards Gulags Western Style.* London, UK: Routledge.

Cloward, Richard A. and Lloyd Ohlin. 1960. *Delinquency and Opportunity: A Theory of Delinquent Gangs.* New York: The Free Press.

Coalition for Juvenile Justice. 2003. *Unlocking the Future: Detention Reform in the Juvenile Justice System.* (Report for the Anne E. Casey Foundation). Washington, DC: Author.

"Corporate Crackdown: An Era of Accountability." 2005. *The Washington Post.* Retrieved January 22, 2010 (http://www.washingtonpost.com/wp-dyn/content/graphic/2006/05/26/GR2006052600174.html).

Del Carmen, Alejandro. 2007. *Racial Profiling in America.* Upper Saddle River, NJ: Prentice Hall.

Derber, Charles. 1998. *Corporate Nation: How Corporations Are Taking Over Our Lives and What We Can Do About It.* New York: St. Martin's Press.

Diaz-Cotto, Juanita. 2006. *Chicana Lives and Criminal Justice: Voices From the Barrio.* Austin, TX: Texas University Press.

Drutman, Lee. 2002. "The Top Financial Scams of the 2002 Corporate Crime Wave." *Multinational Monitor.* December 1.

Du Bois, W. E. B. 1903. *The Souls of Black Folk.* New York: Signet.

Ettner, Susan L. et al. 2006. "Benefit-Cost in the California Treatment Outcome Project: Does Substance Abuse Treatment 'Pay for Itself'?" *Health Services Research,* 41:192–199.

Federal Bureau of Investigation. 2006. *A Close-Up of MS-13: FBI Executive Visits El Salvador.* Washington DC: U.S. Department of Justice.

_____. 2007. *Fiscal Crimes Report to the Public, Fiscal Year 2006.* Washington, DC: U.S. Department of Justice.

Fisher, Bonnie, Francis Cullen and Michael Turner. 2000. *The Sexual Victimization of College Women.* Washington, DC: National Institute of Justice, Bureau of Justice Statistics.

Glassner, Barry. 2010. *The Culture of Fear: Why Americans Are Afraid of the Wrong Things: Crime, Drugs, Minorities, Teen Moms, Killer Kids, Mutant Microbes, Plane Crashes, Road Rage, and So Much More.* New York: Basic Books.

Goldstein, Matthew. 2008. "Ponzi Nation." *Business Week*. December 14. Retrieved February 8, 2010 (http://www.businessweek.com/investing/insights/blog/archives/2008/12/ponzi_nation.html).

Gottfredson, Michael and Travis Hirschi. 1990. *A General Theory of Crime*. Stanford, CA: Stanford University Press.

Gray, Jeanne and Scott Dent. 1993. "Prison Literacy." in *Praxis II: Service-Learning Resources for University Students, Staff, and Faculty,* edited by Joseph Galura, Rachel Meiland, Randy Ross, Mary Jo Callan, and Rick Smith. Ann Arbor, MI: University of Michigan, Office of Community Services.

Greene, Judith. 2002. "Entrepreneurial Corrections: Incarceration as a Business Opportunity." Pp. 96–113 in *Invisible Punishment: The Collateral Consequences of Mass Imprisonment,* edited by Marc Mauer and Meda Chesney-Lind. New York: The New Press.

Greene, Judith and Kevin Pranis. 2007, July 1. *Gang Wars: The Failure of Enforcement Tactics and the Need for Effective Public Safety Strategies*. Washington, DC: Justice Policy Institute.

Gross, Kimberly. 2006. "The Scary World in Your Living Room and Neighborhood: Using Local Broadcast News, Neighborhood Crime Rates, and Personal Experience to Test Agenda Setting and Cultivation." *Journal of Communication,* 53:411–426.

Harrison, Paige M. and Allen J. Beck. 2005. "Prison and Jail Inmates at Midyear 2004." *Bureau of Justice Statistic Bulletin,* April. Retrieved February 28, 2010 (http://bjs.ojp.usdoj.gov/content/pub/pdf/pjim04.pdf).

Hayden, Tom. 2004. *Street Wars*. New York: The New Press.

Henslin, James M. 2007. *Sociology: A Down-to-Earth Approach*. Boston, MA: Allyn & Bacon.

Herivel, Tara and Paul Wright. 2003. *Prison Nation: The Warehousing of America's Poor*. New York: Routledge.

Hochstetler, Andrew L. and Neal Shover. 1997. "Street Crime, Labor Surplus, and Criminal Punishment." *Social Problems,* 44:358–367.

Huling, Tracy. 2002. *"Building a Prison Economy in Rural America."* Pp. 197–213 in *Invisible Punishment: The Collateral Consequences of Mass Imprisonment,* edited by Marc Mauer and Meda Chesney-Lind. New York: The New Press.

Humphries, Drew. 1999. *Crack Mothers, Pregnancy, Drugs, and the Media*. Columbus, OH: The Ohio State University Press.

Jackman, Tom. 2007. "Social Programs to Combat Gangs Seen as More Effective Than Policy." *WashingtonPost.com*. July 18.

Inciardi, James. 1999. *The Drug Legalization Debate*. Thousand Oaks, CA: Sage.

Jacobs, Bruce. 1999. *Dealing Crack: The Social World of Street Corner Selling*. Boston, MA: Northeastern University Press.

"Jail, Prison Populations Rise 2.6 Percent." 2006. *CNN.com*. May 21. Retrieved February 28, 2010 (http://www.cnn.com/2006/LAW/05/21/incarceration.rate/index.html).

Jankowski, Martín Sánchez. 1991. *Islands in the Street: Gangs and American Urban Society*. Berkeley, CA: University of California Press.

Jefferson, David. 2005. "America's Most Dangerous Drug." *Newsweek*. August 8.

Johnston, Richard. 2002. "The Battle Against White-Collar Crime: 'The Exponential Growth of Technology and the Use of Computers Have Triggered a Purposeful Rethinking of the Tools Needed by Law Enforcement Organizations to Address Internet-Related Crime.'" *USA Today*. January 1.

Kelling, George and Catherine Coles. 1996. *Fixing Broken Windows: Restoring Order and Reducing Crime in Our Communities*. New York: The Free Press.

Kelling, George and James Q. Wilson. 1982 "Broken Windows." *Atlantic Monthly*. March:29–37.

Keohane, Joe. 2010, February 13. "Imaginary Fiends." *Boston.com*. Retrieved February 27, 2010 (http://mobile.boston.com/art/21//bostonglobe/ideas/articles/2010/02/14/imaginary_fiends/?single = 1).

Kontos, Louis, David Brotherton, and Luis Barrios, eds. 2003. *Gangs and Society: Alternative Perspectives*. New York: Columbia University Press.

Leigey, Margaret E. and Ronet Backman. 2007. "The Influence of Crack Cocaine on the Likelihood of Incarceration for a Violent Offense: An Examination of a Prison Sample." *Criminal Justice Policy Review*, 18:335–352.

Leon-Guerrero, Anna. 2005. *Social Problems: Community, Policy, and Social Action*. Thousand Oaks, CA: Pine Forge Press.

Litt, Jacquelyn and Maureen McNeil. 1994. "Crack Babies and the Politics of Reproduction and Nurturance." Pp.93–113 in *Troubling Children: Studies of Children and Social Problems*. New York: Aldine de Gruyter.

Litwack, Leon F. 1998. *Trouble in Mind: Black Southerners in the Age of Reconstruction*. New York: Knopf.

Macionis, John. 2008. *Society: The Basics*. Upper Saddle River, NJ: Prentice Hall.

Martin, Patricia Yancey. 2005. *Rape Work: Victims, Gender, and Emotions in Organizations and Community Context*. New York: Routledge.

Mauer, Marc. 1999. *Race to Incarcerate*. New York: The New Press.

Mauer, Marc and Meda Chesney-Lind, eds. 2002. *Invisible Punishment: The Collateral Consequences of Mass Imprisonment*. New York: The Free Press.

Merton, Robert. 1953. *Social Theory and Social Structure*. Glencoe, IL: The Free Press.

Meyer, Josh. 2009. "Obama Administration Urges Equal Penalties for Crack, Powder Cocaine Dealers." *Los Angeles Times*. April 30. Retrieved February 15, 2010 (http://articles.latimes.com/2009/apr/30/nation/na-crack30).

Michalowski, Raymond and Susan Carlson. 2000. "Crime, Punishment, and Social Structures of Accumulation: Toward a New and Much Needed Political-Economy of Justice." *Journal of Contemporary Criminal Justice*, 16:272–292.

Mooney, Linda A., David Knox, and Caroline Schacht. 2007. *Understanding Social Problems*. 5th ed. Belmont, CA: Thomson/Wadsworth.

National Institute for Drug Abuse. 2004. "Prescription Drugs: Abuse and Addiction." Washington, DC: U.S. Department of Health and Human Services, National Institutes of Health. Retrieved February 13, 2010 (http://www.drugabuse.gov/PDF/RRPrescription.pdf).

____. 2008. NIDA InfoFacts: Understanding Drug Abuse and Addiction. U.S. Department of Health and Human Services, National Institutes of Health. Retrieved February 13, 2010 (http://www.drugabuse.gov/infofacts/understand.html).

National Youth Gang Center. 2005. *National Youth Gang Survey*. Washington, DC: U.S. Department of Justice, Department of Justice Programs.

Office of Juvenile Justice and Delinquency Prevention. 2000. "Youth Gang Programs and Strategies." Retrieved February 13, 2010 (http://www.ncjrs.gov/pdffiles1/ojjdp/171154.pdf).

O'Neil, M. 1990. "Correctional Higher Education: Reduced Recidivism?" *Journal of Correctional Education*, 41:28–31.

Petersilia, Joan. 2003. *When Prisoners Come Home: Parole and Prisoner Reentry*. London, UK: Oxford University Press.

Price, Barbara Raffel and Natalie J. Sokoloff. 2004. *The Criminal Justice System and Women: Offenders, Prisoners, Victims, and Workers*. New York: McGraw-Hill.

Reckless, Walter. 1973. *The Crime Problem*. New York: Appleton.

Reiman, Jeffrey. 2004. *The Rich Get Richer and the Poor Get Prison: Ideology, Class, and Criminal Justice*. Boston, MA: Pearson.

Romer, D., Kathleen Hall Jamieson, and S. Adey. 2003. "Television News and the Cultivation of Fear of Crime." *Journal of Communication*, 53.

Ross, Randy and Jenny Kellman. 1993. "Student Involvement at the Washtenaw County Jail." *Praxis II: Service-Learning Resources for University Students, Staff, and Faculty*. Ann Arbor, MI: University of Michigan, Office of Community Services.

Sampson, Robert J. and John H. Laub. 1993. *Crime in the Making: Pathways and Turning Points Through Life*. Cambridge, MA: Harvard University Press.

_____. 2008. "A General Age-Graded Theory of Crime: Lessons Learned and the Future of Life-Course Criminology." Pp. 165–181 in *Integrated Developmental and Life-Course Theories of Offending: Advances in Criminology Theory, Vol. 14,* edited by David P. Farrington. Piscataway, NJ: Transaction.

Sampson, Robert J. and William Julius Wilson. 1995. "Toward a Theory of Race, Crime, and Urban Inequality." Pp. 37–54 in *Crime and Inequality,* edited by John Hogan and Ruth Peterson. Stanford, CA: Stanford University Press.

Schlosser, Eric. 1998. "The Prison-Industrial Complex." *Atlantic Monthly.* December:51–77.

Schmitt, Frederika E. and Patricia Yancey Martin. 2007. "The History of the Anti-Rape and Rape Crisis Center Movements." Pp. 29–30 in *Encyclopedia of Interpersonal Violence,* edited by Claire M. Renzetti and Jeffrey Edleson. Thousand Oaks, CA: Sage.

Shaw, Clifford and Henry McKay. 1949. *Juvenile Delinquency and Urban Areas.* Chicago, IL: University of Chicago Press.

Shover, Neil and Andy Hochstetler. 2005. *Choosing White Collar Crime.* New York: Cambridge University Press.

Snyder, Howard and Melissa Sickmund. 2006. *Juvenile Offenders and Victims.* Washington DC: U.S. Department of Justice, Office of Justice Programs, Office of Juvenile Justice and Delinquency Prevention.

Southern Poverty Law Center. 2007. "SPLC Launches 'School to Prison Reform Project' to Help At-Risk Children Get Special Education Services, Avoid Incarceration." *SPLC News.* September 11.

Spergel, Irving. 1995. *The Youth Gang Problem.* New York: Oxford University Press.

Stambaugh, J. J. 2009. "Officials Weigh Tougher Meth Laws After 40% Spike in Number of Labs Seized." *Knoxnews.* February 15. Retrieved February 27, 2010 (http://www.knoxnews.com/news/2009/feb/15/ending-meth-madness/).

Stephens, Gene. 1999. "Preventing Crime: The Promising Road Ahead." *The Futurist.* November:2–10.

Sutherland, Edwin H. 1947. *Principles of Criminology.* Philadelphia, PA: Lippincott.

_____. 1949. *White Collar Crime.* New York: Dryden Press.

Szuberla, Nick and Amelia Kirby. 2002. "From the Holler to the Hood: Stories From the American Prison Industry." Presentation for the 2002 Appalachian Studies Association, Unicoi State Park, Helen, GA.

Tavakoli, Janet. 2008. "Madoff Deserves Lots of Company." Retrieved February 15, 2010 (http://www.tavakolistructuredfinance.com/TSF11.html).

Tonry, Michael. 1995. *Malign Neglect: Race, Crime, and Punishment in America.* New York: Oxford University Press.

Uniform Crime Reports. 2005a. Crime in the United States: Persons Arrested. Washington, DC: U.S. Department of Justice, Federal Bureau of Investigation.

_____. 2005b. Table 32: Percent Change for Total Arrest Selected Crimes, 1996–2005. Washington, DC: U.S. Department of Justice, Federal Bureau of Investigation. Retrieved February 18, 2010 (http://www.fbi.gov/ucr/05cius/data/table_32.html).

U.S. Department of Education. 2007. *Youth Gangs: Going Beyond the Myths to Address a Critical Problem.* Washington, DC: Author.

U.S. Department of Health and Human Services. 2001, August. "Substance Abuse Treatment for Drug Users in the Criminal Justice System." Retrieved February 13, 2010 (http://www.cdc.gov/idu/facts/cj-satreat.pdf).

U.S. Senate Government Reform Committee. 2004. "Thousands of Children With Mental Illness Warehoused in Juvenile Detention Centers Awaiting Mental Health Services." (Report by the Special Investigations Division of the Minority Staff of the Government Reform Committee of the U.S. House of Representatives). Washington, DC: U.S. Government Printing Office.

Walker, Samuel. 1998. *Popular Justice: A History of American Criminal Justice.* New York: Oxford University Press.

Walmsley, Roy. 2006. *World Prison Population List.* 6th ed. London, UK: King's College Centre for Prison Studies.

Wells, Joseph T. 2007. *Corporate Fraud Handbook: Prevention and Detection.* New York: Wiley.

Wilson, William Julius. 1987. *The Truly Disadvantaged: The Inner City, the Underclass, and Public Policy.* Chicago, IL: University of Chicago Press.

____. 2006. "Social Theory and the Concept 'Underclass.'" Pp. 103–115 in *Poverty and Inequality,* edited by David Grusky and Ravi Kanbur. Stanford, CA: Stanford University Press.

Young, Vernetta D. and Rebecca Reviere. 2006. *Gender and Race in U.S. Prisons.* Boulder, CO: Lynne Rienner.

# CHAPTER 9

# An Apple a Day?

*Health and Health Care for All*

*Tobacco companies . . . marketed and sold their lethal product with zeal and deception, with a single-minded focus on their financial success and without regard for the human tragedy or social costs that success exacted.*

—Judge Gladys Kessler of the Federal District Court
of Columbia in a 1,742-page decision against the tobacco
industry for racketeering (quoted in Shenon 2006)

*You can't give away food without an emotional and spiritual component.*

—Steward Scofield, volunteer coordinator
who founded the Food for Thought food bank
after his partner died of AIDS

*What other industry says, 'Hey, look at us, our whole system is broken.'*

—Fredrick C. Blum, physician and president of
American College of Emergency Physicians on the state
of U.S. emergency care (D. Brown 2006)

## CAMPUS COMPACT AND TRIBAL SERVICE LEARNING IN MONTANA

The role of community groups in promoting primary health care, facilitating access to the health care system, and addressing disease is often ignored in the United States. While the United States represents the world's most advanced technology, its health care system focuses more on treating health problems with drugs or surgery than on preventing illnesses altogether. Meanwhile, treatment can be expensive, and an increasing number of American citizens cannot afford services or the medical insurance that would cover them. In many places around the country, communities have stepped in with a variety of methods to address both treatment and prevention. Clinics, community centers, and other community-based health care programs provide important health resources for millions of Americans. In this vein, community organizations (often with the help of student volunteers or those in service learning programs) play an important part in the success of health education and a variety of wellness efforts directed toward youth, seniors, and working-class and poor families.

Service learning in community health and educational settings has become common practice in the social sciences and in programs training health professionals including nursing, nutrition, pharmacy, social work, medicine, and public health (Maurana and Seifer 2000; Seifer 2000; Wolff, Young, and Maurana 2001). Such initiatives incorporate college students, advocates, professionals, and community members into programs that greatly improve the health and health care of families and children. In particular, service learning projects are in a position to assist local groups to meet changing health care needs. Simultaneously, students learn how health care–related issues are impacted by social phenomena such as class, race, gender, culture, and geography. Higher poverty rates, lower educational attainment, and social isolation intensify the health risks of people who are marginalized by poverty and discrimination and are less likely to have health insurance (Joe 2003).

Critics of the Western medical establishment point to its lack of cultural sensitivity in addressing health behavior, health promotion, and disease prevention (Airhihenbuwa 1995; Colomeda and Wenzel 2000). To counter this approach, indigenous teachers working with service projects in Native American cultures take the attitude that the service learning mission can only be successful if it addresses and incorporates culturally relevant strategies grounded in indigenous knowledge. Many indigenous societies approach health in the context of spirituality and a balance with nature, not simply as something achieved through doctor visits and prescription medicine. Tribal societies often address health issues through community "connectiveness" (Colomeda and Wenzel 2000; Herman-Stahl, Duncan, and Spencer 2003). Working with Native American populations requires understanding their traditions of reciprocity, extended family, and the role of the elderly as teachers and healers. Health care delivery for these groups occurs best when provided within existing support systems and cultural practices (Reimer 1999). Culturally sensitive approaches to health and other services draw on a culture's historical experiences, making scientific evidence and human services relevant and meaningful to the group's particular situation.

Good examples of culturally inclusive collaborations supported by service learning projects have occurred on reservations in conjunction with the Montana Campus Compact (MTCC). The nonprofit organization helps develop practices for community colleges on or near reservations that work to meet the needs of tribal members through service learning

(Ward and Grant 2006).[1] For example, the early childhood courses on the Blackfeet Reservation teach the nation's cultural heritage in classes. At Dull Knife Memorial, students on the Northern Cheyenne Reservation create oral histories of elders in their Writing Across Cultures English class. Students learn about cultural expectations by interviewing the elderly about events and disseminating stories across the reservation (Ward and Grant 2006). Some of these stories not only involve particular information about traditional medicine and community "health" practices, but also describe how issues related to health care and wellness were dealt with by local actors and systems. Among others, MTCC serves Salish Kootenai College and Flathead Valley, Blackfeet, and Fort Belknap Community Colleges. The Montana Campus Compact examples reveal how service learning can reinforce cultural values while solving community needs around health care.

Community-based health programs define health broadly to include not only mental and physical health, but also health from the context of aging, family, personal safety, literacy, economics, environment, and housing (Joe 2003; Reimer 1999). Community health advocates can improve the accessibility and quality of health care services, empower communities, and increase the relationships between community members and health care providers (Wolff et al. 2001). Other service learning programs at Montana's Native American colleges provide a greater understanding of the links between health and culture. College students participate in community events such as science fairs, summer youth camps, and early childhood initiatives. Students in Early Childhood and Native American Studies at Blackfoot Community College plan and administer a camp for youth that teaches them about Blackfoot culture and language. Mentoring youth serves the community while giving students hands-on experience (Ward and Grant 2006).

An example of how service learning can challenge health problems is found in Professor Lori Colomeda's Health in Ecological Perspective I course at Salish Kootenai College in Pablo, Montana. This interdisciplinary course focuses on how the environment impacts health for Native Americans. Economic and cultural exploitation have left most Native Americans poor and isolated, and disproportionately at risk for alcoholism and other addictions, accidents, and diabetes. Reservation residents also face overexposure to uranium mining and nuclear fallout, as well as other forms of environmental contamination and devastation primarily due to government policies of using reservation land for hazardous waste disposal.

As students address the challenges of native peoples, they learn the links among culture, politics, healing, and the environment. "When indigenous people speak about restoring health, they talk about restoring the land in the same breath. For indigenous people, health is linked to the health of the land, health of the culture, and health of the spirit" (Colomeda and Wenzel 2000:243). Colomeda's course addresses the health effects of contamination and pollution and health disruptions to indigenous people from diabetes and malnutrition

---

[1]Campus Compact is a coalition of over 1,000 college presidents representing over 5 million students. The goals of Campus Compact are to improve civil and social responsibility of students and increase democracy, citizenship, and community engagement (www.compact.org).

(Colomeda and Lambert 1998). Holistic approaches to health care used in these service learning courses reveal the complex sociological realities that health and health care entail. The course discusses the effects of nuclear contamination on the food chain while also discussing breast cancer in Native American women. By examining the Apache Nation's nuclear waste dump and possible effects of contamination, the course applies environmental, ecological, and political sciences to real-life issues faced by Native American communities.

Examples from Montana's Campus Compact reveal a number of social problems related to health care in the United States. Importantly, inequality blocks the distribution of health care for a large population in American society, especially the poor. Continued class and racial inequality and exclusion mean the problems associated with health care fall disproportionately on those least able to deal with them. In the world's most technologically advanced nation, poor and minority communities face third-world conditions when it comes to health care coverage and health outcomes. However, low-income and minority Americans are not the only victims of our health care system and the variety of health problems that face people in contemporary U.S. society.

Even as Americans spend more on health care than any other developed country, the nation is plagued with large uninsured populations and is experiencing epidemics of obesity, diabetes, and unhealthy lifestyles linked in part to a lack of preventive care. Finally, social changes, including an aging population, are outstripping the ability of the system to keep up with the demand for health care.

In this chapter, we will look at the main social problems associated with the U.S. health care system, including unequal access to health care, rising costs, and the growing crisis in the nation's hospitals and emergency rooms. We also address key concerns related to lifestyle, child health, and poverty. The way the United States changes the direction of health and health care will determine if it expands access and quality or continues to leave larger and larger chunks of its people unhealthy and unproductive. Fundamental changes will have to occur before the nation can address rising health costs and epidemics of obesity and diabetes. This chapter offers examples that show how the involvement of community groups and service learning initiatives are an important part of expanding care and rethinking prevention. But first, we offer a statistical portrait of many of the health and health care problems impacting the United States, as well as a historical look at the evolution of the nation's health care system.

## HEALTH CARE BY THE NUMBERS: A STATISTICAL PORTRAIT OF AMERICA'S HEALTH CARE SYSTEM

America's health care system is the most expensive in the world, but unlike all other developed nations, it leaves large numbers of people underinsured or uninsured. Most Americans believe that the nation's health care system is the best in the world, despite the United States' actual rank among industrialized nations. According to Russell (2006), though, "Americans acknowledge that the growing number of uninsured persons is a problem. But they are less likely to be aware that their expensive system ranks poorly in quality as well as coverage" (p. 124). Russell found that all 21 European countries rank higher than the United States in the quality of health care and the health conditions of its citizenry. A number of social problems (unhealthy populations, high mortality rates, etc.) are linked to a lack of health care caused by high costs of services and insurance. While the amount spent on health care has more than doubled between 1993 and 2009, from $916 billion to $2.1 trillion, more Americans are uninsured (46 million), and the costs for those that have insurance is rising faster than the rate of inflation (Sisko et al. 2009). The average hospital stay in the United States costs $1,300, the average doctor visit costs over $60, and the average emergency room visit costs almost $400. Perhaps even more alarming is that the percentage of the U.S. gross domestic product spent on health care rose from 13.3% in 2000 to 17.6% in 2009 (Kornblum and Julian 2007; World Health Organization [WHO] 2009b).

These costs exceed that of any other industrialized country. Table 9.1 shows a comparison between health care spending in the United States and in other industrialized nations. The paradox is that the United States spends more on health care both per

**Table 9.1**   Health Care Costs Per Capita for Developed Countries, 2004

| Country | Per Capita Cost | Percentage of GDP |
|---|---|---|
| United States | 6,096 | 15.4 |
| Switzerland | 5,571 | 11.5 |
| Norway | 5,404 | 9.7 |
| Sweden | 3,532 | 9.1 |
| Germany | 3,521 | 10.6 |
| France | 3,464 | 10.5 |
| Ireland | 3,234 | 7.2 |
| United Kingdom | 2,899 | 8.1 |
| Japan | 2,823 | 7.8 |
| Italy | 2,579 | 8.7 |

*Source:World Health Statistics,* 2009, WHO, Geneva, Switzerland.

capita and in percentage of gross domestic product, but it still fails to insure a large portion of its population.

Figure 9.1 shows that since 2000, the nation's health care costs have increased every year, from 9% in 2000 to a high of 15% in 2003. This situation has meant rising out-of-pocket costs for insured Americans. The expanding costs of copayments mean a burden for the middle and working class but also for companies and hospitals.

The large increases in overall health care costs have been accompanied by increases in employee contributions and out-of-pocket expenses. Figure 9.2 shows out-of-pocket costs going from an average of $1,350 in 2000 to $3,100 in 2006. This increase of over 100% reflects a trend that shifts health care costs from government and private sector employees to individuals. Rising health care costs are especially burdensome for working families. Decreases in union membership and the rise of smaller firms and service industries less likely to include health insurance as a benefit have resulted in working people and their families having to address higher costs with fewer resources. Even insured individuals are increasingly at risk of a major health event not being covered sufficiently, and eventually bankrupting their finances. The rising costs push smaller employers to cover fewer employees. For example, only 45% of employers with 3 to 9 workers offer employees health insurance, while only 60% of employers with 200 employees or less include health insurance as an employee benefit (Appleby 2007).

While rising costs themselves are a serious social problem, the fact is, higher costs are only a part of the problem. A primary cause of social problems in health care is inequality.

**Figure 9.1**   Estimated Annual Percent Increase in U.S. Health Care Costs, 2000–2006

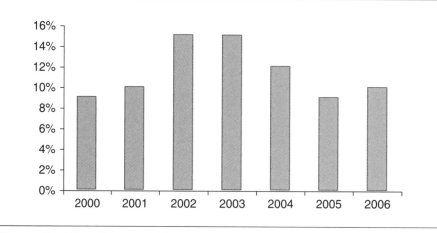

*Source:* "Care at a Cost," November 13, 2005, by Carly Harrington, *Knoxville News Sentinel.*

**Figure 9.2**   Estimated Combined Employee Contribution and Out-of-Pocket Health Costs, 2000–2006

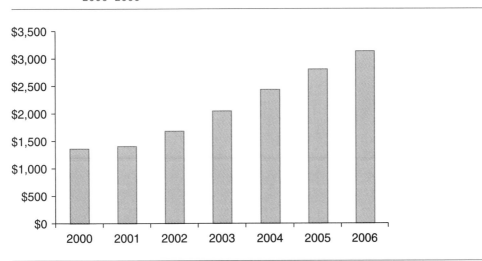

*Source:* "Care at a Cost," November 13, 2005, by Carly Harrington, *Knoxville News Sentinel.*

## POVERTY, HEALTH INEQUALITY, AND SOCIAL PROBLEMS

Health inequality is generated by differences in health status that are unnecessary, avoidable, and unfair. Individuals themselves cannot control either the cost or availability of most health care. While inequality impacts health in a variety of ways (the environmental degradation of Native American reservations and other minority communities around the country, for example), inequality in health care specifically refers to both health systems' inequality (access to technology and resources) and inequality of the medical care itself (access to doctors and other medical services). Many low-income people in the United States do not have private health insurance and rely on the **Medicaid** program for insurance. Medicaid provides insurance for low-income families, the elderly and disabled people requiring long term care services. Another program that covers mainly senior citizens is called **Medicare.** Other attempts at covering the poor include the 1997 State Children's Health Insurance Program (CHIP), created as an amendment to the Social Security Act in order to insure children. While these programs fill some of the gaps for low-income families, many working-class Americans often go without health insurance or coverage.

By the year 2000, an estimated 84.2% of Americans had health coverage of some sort, with about 75% covered through employer-sponsored plans (Kaufman 2004). But the skyrocketing cost of health care has reduced employer benefits, and governmental cuts reduced the numbers of those eligible for Medicare and Medicaid and the actual coverage for those who were eligible. People most at risk for lacking insurance are the poor, the working class, minorities, and those in depressed rural areas (Kornblum and Julian 2007).

According to Conrad and Leiter (2003), 34% of those below the poverty line are uninsured, compared to 9% of those making 200% of the poverty line income. Without insurance, the cost of even the most basic health services can devastate individuals and families. Some lose their homes, while others die without care. Sered and Fernandopulle (2007) estimate that between one-third and one-half of the people who filed bankruptcy in 2002 did so because of costs incurred from medical bills. More recently, Himmelstein (2009) found that 62% of all bankruptcies filed in 2007 were linked to medical expenses. Of those who filed for bankruptcy, nearly 80% had health insurance. Without health insurance, people are less likely to seek health care treatment, leading to future problems related to untreated conditions. Schwartz (2007) estimates that 1 out of 3 low-income parents spends less on food, heat, and other basic needs to pay for health care when needed for his or her children.

Many of the uninsured are working-poor families whose income places them above the level to receive Medicare or Medicaid, but whose earnings are still too low to pay for insurance. Overall, 4 of 10 low-income parents do not have health insurance in the United States (Schwartz 2007). Other populations that are uninsured include undocumented migrants who often work in jobs that don't provide health insurance. Studies suggest undocumented migrant workers use over $1 billion in health services because they lack coverage, work in some of the most dangerous jobs, live in unhealthy communities and living environments, and often lack the security of leverage to complain about unsafe conditions at work or at home. Still, undocumented people are as much as 50% less likely to use emergency rooms for care than documented citizens (Engels 2007). Regardless, the uninsured (who rarely have primary physicians and often cannot afford regular visits and prevention-based programs) rely heavily on expensive emergency care and other out-of-pocket services.

Failure to deliver health care has a devastating effect on the health of minorities and the poor in the United States. According to researchers writing in the *American Journal of Public Health,* black Americans are twice as likely to have diabetes as white Americans, have twice the risk of stroke, and are 23% more likely to die from cancer. The study concludes that failure to deliver standard care to America's black population cost nearly 900,000 lives between 1991 and 2000 (Woolf, Johnson, Fryer, Rust, and Satcher 2004). The Children's Defense Fund estimates that, of the nation's 13 million poor children, 9 million live in families that lack health insurance (Children's Defense Fund Action Council 2004). Figure 9.3 shows that blacks, Hispanics, and Native Americans are more likely to be uninsured. While whites make up 67% of the population, they make up only 48% of the uninsured. Meanwhile, Latinos—who are more likely to have jobs without insurance—make up only 15% of the population but 30 percent of the uninsured.

Finally, lacking health insurance also means individuals suffer when they are most vulnerable. According to the American Cancer Society (cited in Ward et al. 2007), uninsured individuals are 1.5 times more likely to die from cancer than insured individuals. The uninsured

**Figure 9.3**   Percent of Total Uninsured by Race, 2004

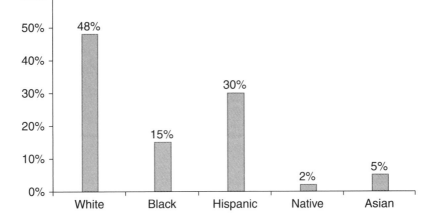

*Source:* "Overview of the Uninsured in the United States: An analysis of the 2005 Current Population Survey," September 22, 2005, *ASPE Issue Brief,* U.S. Department of Health and Human Services.

are more likely to forego treatment and preventive care. When the uninsured do seek treatment for illnesses such as cancer, they must pay "out of pocket." Thus, they seek medical attention at the expense of paying for rent or mortgages, food, heat and utilities, or other bills. These individuals become even more susceptible to risks of other illnesses due to poor nutrition, stress, and so forth (Ward et al. 2007).

## SYSTEM BREAKDOWN: IATROGENIC ILLNESSES AND EMERGENCY CARE IN CRISIS

Every year, between 44,000 and 98,000 Americans die from medical errors, or what are called **iatrogenic** illnesses, defined as sicknesses and deaths caused by doctors and the health care system. Using the lower estimate, deaths due to hospital errors exceed the number attributable to the eighth leading cause of death. The Centers for Disease Control and Prevention (CDC) estimates that 2 million people annually acquire infections while hospitalized, and 90,000 people die from those infections (Institute of Medicine 2000). Errors from everything from surgical site infections, to bad handwriting, to failure to check patient medicines for risks associated with medicine interactions kill patients almost routinely in America's health care system. A 2004 campaign by the Massachusetts nonprofit organization Institute for Health Care Improvement seeks to reduce iatrogenic illnesses

*(Continued)*

(Continued)

caused by hospital errors. The goals of the campaign are to save 100,000 lives by addressing hospitals' errors through training and awareness. According to Berwick, Calkins, McCannon, and Hackbarth (2006), hospitals that participate in the initiative focus on the following areas:

- Deploying rapid response teams

- Delivering reliable evidence-based care for acute myocardial infarction

- Preventing adverse drug events (ADEs)

- Preventing central line infections

- Preventing surgical site infections

- Preventing ventilator-associated pneumonia

## Children and Inequality

Meanwhile, a lack of emphasis on and funding for preventive health care lies behind much of the nation's poor record of child health outcomes. The children of families without insurance are 3 times more likely not to receive needed health care than those with coverage. They are 4 times more likely than the insured to rely on emergency rooms or to have no regular source of care (Karger and Stoesz 2005; Kornblum and Julian 2007). According to Karger and Stoesz, while young adults (ages 18–24) are the most likely to be uninsured (28%), 19.2% of poor children as opposed to 11.4% of all children were uninsured as of 2004. Minority youth make up 50% of the uninsured, despite various programs such as Medicaid and CHIP. According to the Robert Wood Johnson Foundation (2005), however, cuts during the George W. Bush administration resulted in 360,000 more children being without insurance in 2004. These numbers continued to rise until the most recent CHIP Reauthorization Act of 2009. President Obama's signature on the bill increased CHIP by almost $40 billion and is expected to expend coverage to 4 million more children, many of whom had lost coverage in the past few years alone.

Still, even death rates among children can be traced back to the poor health of America's poorest children. In developed countries, socioeconomic disadvantage is strongly associated with preterm birth and low birth weight babies. Poor pregnancy outcomes are most common among low-income rural and urban mothers. In the United States, black infants are more than twice as likely as white infants to be premature, have low birth weight, or die at birth (Collins, David, Handler, Wall, and Andes 2004). Figure 9.4 shows the infant mortality rate for various races. Blacks and Native Americans face child death rates that equal or exceed those in many less developed nations.

**Figure 9.4**   Infant Mortality Rate by Race, 2003

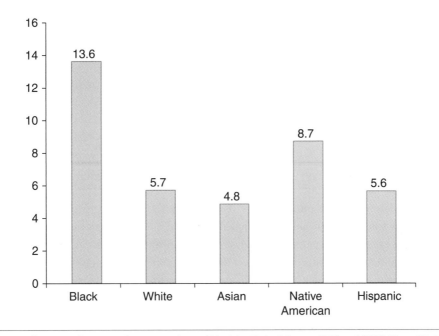

*Source:* "Infant Mortality Rates, by Maternal Race/Ethnicity United States, 1995 and 2003," June 23, 2006, *Morbidity and Mortality Weekly Report,* Centers for Disease Control and Prevention.

Inequality, including limited access to primary health care, is an important reason low-income families experience poor health care and outcomes in a nation with the most advanced health technology in the world (Zuberi 2006). Berkman (2004) explains,

> Even with all the neonatal technology in the United States, it ranks 25th in infant mortality among 38 developed countries. Neonatal intensive care units now regularly save small, low birth weight infants who years earlier would have died. Yet American infant mortality rates remain similar to those in the Czech Republic, Greece, Portugal, Belgium, and Cuba. Why? In the United States, less affluent mothers are more likely to smoke, and are less likely to get prenatal care, have health insurance, or vaccinate their children. Poor American women have limited resources for housing, nutrition, and transportation. Frequently, their jobs provide no sick leave. All of these factors contribute to poor health for their infants. (p. 39)

Life expectancy in poor communities—on Native American reservations, in Appalachia, and in inner-city minority communities—is much lower than the national average. On the Sioux Reservation in South Dakota, men live to be an average of only 64.5 years. In the poorest coalfield communities in West Virginia, children have the same life expectancy as those in poor, developing nations. Donnelly (2003) describes the health outcomes for children in West Virginia's McDowell County:

> The health of the residents of Appalachia has deteriorated so much that a boy born in McDowell County has a life expectancy lower than that of babies in 34 of the world's developing nations, among them some of the most impoverished—Tajikistan, Colombia, the Dominican Republic, Mongolia, and Vietnam. (p. 1)

Health outcomes among America's poorest communities and populations are dramatically different than for wealthier people in other communities. According to health researchers writing in the *American Journal of Preventive Medicine,* many of the poor not only can't afford health insurance, but because they have less healthy environments and spend more time on meeting basic needs, they suffer greater consequences when it comes to health practices and lifestyles. While we often assume that individuals maintain responsibility for their own health and the dietary and lifestyle decisions that circumscribe one's health, significant evidence exists that poor people have less access to health information, healthy food, and health care, and thus have little control over their own poorer health outcomes. From a sociological perspective, individuals have certain amounts of responsibility for the choices they make, but when their choices are so circumscribed by conditions beyond their individual control, the choices people have about their own health are clearly limited—especially for those marginalized by poverty and discrimination (Woolf, Johnson, and Geiger 2006). The diseases and unhealthy lifestyles responsible for some of these outcomes are also unequally distributed.

## Health and Disease

**Epidemiology** is the study of the patterns in the distribution and frequency of sickness, injury, and death across a population. Epidemiologists trace the movement of diseases within and between borders, providing primary data on diseases such as AIDS, influenza, and other conditions. Sociologists increasingly study the patterns of health and illness across borders as globalization leads to greater contact and interdependency among people. **Morbidity** refers to the illnesses, symptoms, and impairments that result from illness. Two of the most important institutions for producing health and disease research are the Department of Health and Human Services' Centers for Disease Control and Prevention (CDC) in Atlanta, Georgia, and the United Nations' health agency, the World Health Organization (WHO), located in Geneva, Switzerland. The CDC's research serves an important role in health surveillance by monitoring and preventing disease outbreaks. WHO traces not only poverty-based epidemics that affect developing nations, (e.g., cholera, malaria, and gastroenteritis), but also non-communicable diseases affecting populations across the globe such as heart disease, cancer, and diabetes (Alberti 2001).

By applying health research, the agencies are human society's number one defense against epidemics and pandemics. **Epidemics** are diseases that appear in a given population, at a given time, and at a rate that exceeds expectations. A **pandemic** is an epidemic that crosses many borders. The recent outbreak of swine flu quickly became an epidemic in Mexico, but many feared it could rapidly take on pandemic proportions. Both the CDC and WHO use health research to promote development, increase health security, and strengthen health systems. Like the CDC, WHO promotes health research and traces the occurrence of diseases at international levels. Recent pandemics are more troublesome given the increased flow of humans between border countries, which leaves communities with less time to prepare. Pandemics are dangerous due to their potential to reach millions of people. Historically, plagues and influenza have led to the near collapse of social systems. Today, WHO is involved in preparing for a number of major possible or existing global pandemics through its Epidemic and Pandemic Alert and Response Program (EPR) where it operates a global operations platform.

## PANDEMICS AND EPIDEMICS

| | |
|---|---|
| Avian Flu H5N1 | Noticed first in Asia in 1997, avian flu is linked to poultry production in Vietnam and Thailand. Having killed over 50 people, this strain of flu has meant the destruction of millions of poultry. Currently, the avian flu is transmitted by migratory birds, and experts predict that it most likely will bring the world closer to a flu pandemic than at any other time since 1968. Efforts by WHO have led to international preparedness including efforts to isolate and characterize the virus and make it available to vaccine makers (Pan American Health Organization [PAHO] 2005). |
| West Nile Virus | West Nile virus is a virus related to yellow fever and is found on all continents. The virus is fatal mainly for the elderly and infirm. Victims have included horses, birds, and humans. The virus reached the United States in 1999. The CDC operates a surveillance program focused on tracking incidences and prevention (CDC West Nile Virus, Division of Vector-Borne Infectious Diseases). |
| HIV/AIDS | An estimated 32.3 million people have HIV/AIDS globally. Working closely with the UNAIDS organization, WHO has been combating AIDS with country-by-country research. The CDC is at the forefront of developing AIDS prevention programs, testing, and tracking occurrences in the United States (UNAIDS 2008). (See Chapter 10 on globalization.) |
| SARS | The first outbreak of SARS was traced to Hong Kong and spread throughout Southeast Asia, Europe, and North America via individuals traveling to other countries. Early detection by WHO enabled the potential pandemic to be stopped. The aggressive approach was a response to the ineffective response to the AIDS epidemic in the 1980s (Leon-Guerrero 2004). |

*(Continued)*

(Continued)

H1N1/Swine Flu    The H1N1 virus mutated from pigs to humans, emerging in Mexico in the spring of 2009 and spreading to the United States and across the globe. H1N1 affects people whose immune systems are compromised such as those with diabetes and other diseases. It differs from seasonal flu strains due to its severity and high occurrences of severe respiratory failure requiring hospitalization. H1N1 also typically occurs in people under 65 (WHO 2009a).

Epidemiologists use databases to trace the main causes of death by looking at the rate of incidence in a population. The *rate of incidence* is defined as the number of cases in a population. The main killers in Western nations today are linked to old age and to lifestyle. **Acute illnesses** (abrupt, short-term, and sudden) such as the flu, diarrhea, or colds were once considered the main killers. Today, **chronic illnesses** (long-term, continuous) such as diabetes, stroke, heart disease, and conditions like arthritis are the main killers for most in developed nations. Table 9.2 shows that heart disease is the main killer for men and women, followed by cancer. In developed countries, smoking, overeating, accidents, and inactivity are contributing factors to death. The prevalence of cars, riding lawnmowers, and jobs not requiring physical activity has changed the way Americans get, or don't get, exercise. Declining physical activity and other poor health practices have resulted in the rapid increase in diabetes, heart disease, stroke, and lung cancer.

## Gender

Gender plays an important role in health outcomes. Women in the United States are more likely than men to seek routine health examinations and, therefore, live longer. In part, this is because treatable diseases that might cause death are found in earlier stages and can be eradicated or managed. However, although women live longer than men, they are at greater risk for diseases such as Alzheimer's. Minority women, led by black women, have poorer health status than white women. Black women are more likely to get diabetes and other potentially fatal diseases, and to not receive effective follow-up treatment. Native American women die in accidents at 3 times the national average and die of alcohol-related issues at 5 to 6 times the national rate (Leon-Guerrero 2004). Men are more likely to engage in risk-taking behaviors and be killed by unintentional accidents than women, and are also more likely to commit suicide. Accidents are the leading cause of death among men in the United States until middle age. Men are especially prone to workplace accidents and violence. The advances of our technological age not only have a "downside" when it comes to loss of physical activity, but they have increased the risk of accidents in certain ways. While previous populations in industrializing nations faced most physical injuries in the

**Table 9.2**   Leading Causes of Death in the United States for All Persons, Males and Females, 2003

| Rank | Causes of Death | All Persons | Causes of Death | Male | Causes of Death | Female |
|------|-----------------|-------------|-----------------|------|-----------------|--------|
| | **All causes** | **2,448,288** | **All causes** | **1,201,964** | **All causes** | **1,246,324** |
| 1. | Diseases of heart | 685,089 | Diseases of heart | 336,095 | Diseases of heart | 348,994 |
| 2. | Malignant neoplasms (cancer) | 556,902 | Malignant neoplasms (cancer) | 287,990 | Malignant neoplasms (cancer) | 268,912 |
| 3. | Cerebrovascular diseases | 157,689 | Unintentional injuries | 70,532 | Cerebrovascular diseases | 96,263 |
| 4. | Chronic lower respiratory diseases | 126,382 | Cerebrovascular diseases | 61,426 | Chronic lower respiratory diseases | 65,668 |
| 5. | Unintentional injuries | 109,277 | Chronic lower respiratory diseases | 60,714 | Alzheimer's disease | 45,122 |
| 6. | Diabetes mellitus | 74,219 | Diabetes mellitus | 35,438 | Diabetes mellitus | 38,781 |
| 7. | Influenza and pneumonia | 65,163 | Influenza and pneumonia | 28,778 | Unintentional injuries | 38,745 |
| 8. | Alzheimer's disease | 63,457 | Suicide | 25,203 | Influenza and pneumonia | 36,385 |
| 9. | Nephritis, nephrotic syndrome, and nephrosis | 42,453 | Nephritis, nephrotic syndrome, and nephrosis | 20,481 | Nephritis, nephrotic syndrome, and nephrosis | 21,972 |
| 10. | Septicemia | 34,069 | Alzheimer's disease | 18,335 | Septicemia | 19,082 |

*Source:* U.S. National Center for Health Statistics, *Health, United States, 2005* (http://www.infoplease.com/science/health/leading-causes-death-us-2003.html).

workplace from machine malfunctions, fires, and so forth, modern populations are more at risk away from work. Major causes of accidental deaths today are automobiles, motor-cycles, all-terrain vehicles, and guns. Fewer deaths at work due to declining fatalities in coal mines, factories, and farming have reduced the job-related accident rates. The leading cause of death for children and adults between 15 and 24 is accidents, followed by assault (Leon-Guerrero 2004).

# HEALTH STATUS, LIFESTYLE, AND PREVENTION

## Diet

Unhealthy practices or lifestyles are the main killers in developed nations, and the United States leads the way. Diet and a lack of exercise are major causes of poor health in America. Studies show the number of overweight Americans is 1 out of 2, while 1 out of 3 Americans can be classified as **obese**. Nutritionists point out that Americans' diets contain high levels of processed sugar, fatty foods, and carbohydrates while lacking in fiber, fruit, and vegetables. Americans' overall calorie intake has increased over 25% since 1970, and almost all new calo-ries come from refined grains (breads and cereals), oils and fats, and refined sugars (Cutler, Glaeser, and Shapiro 2003). Most of these refined grains, sugars, and fats come from our over-whelming reliance on fast and previously prepared foods. Between 1970 and 2000, the amount spent on fast food rose from $6 billion to $110 billion. Fast food plays a dominant role in the nation's diet, with 1 in 4 adults eating it at least once a day. Fast food contributes to obe-sity and chronic diseases because it is higher in polyunsaturated fats and has more empty calo-ries than other types of food (E Baker, Schootman, Barnidge, and Kelly 2006; Schlosser 2001).

Low-income communities are particularly susceptible to fast food, which is relatively cheap in cost and easily accessible. As discussed in the example of the East St. Louis Action Research Project in Chapter 2, poor communities often pay more for less because they lack access to healthy food. Due to limited transportation and corporate strategies for locating grocery stores in wealthier communities, poor communities depend on fast food, bodegas, and convenience stores. Corner markets are often stocked with junk foods and seldom carry healthy alternatives like fresh fruit. When they do, the markup on healthy items can be as much as 300% more than in larger grocery stores. A study of the Washington, DC, area reveals that low-income black neighborhoods have one grocery store for every 70,000 people, while wealthier white and mixed neighborhoods have one for every 12,000 people (Samuels 2006).

Diet and weight gain are directly linked to the growing epidemic of type 2 diabetes in the United States. From 1980 to 2005, the number of Americans with diabetes increased from 5.6 million to 15.8 million. People aged 65 years or older account for approximately 38% of those with diabetes (CDC 2007). Figure 9.5 shows the dramatic rise in the number of Americans with diabetes.

**Figure 9.5**   Number (in Millions) of Persons With Diagnosed Diabetes, U.S., 1980–2005

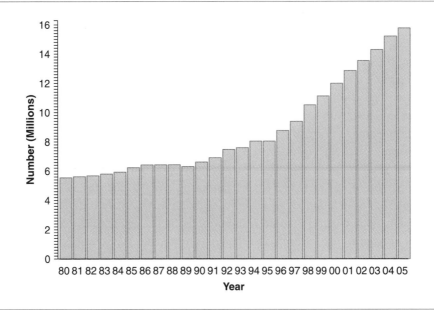

*Source:*"Diabetes Data and Trends," 2007a, Centers for Disease Control and Prevention (http://www.cdc.gov/diabetes/statistics/incidence/fig1.htm).

## Workplace Stress

Workplace stress is increasingly being linked to poor health in the United States. As the number of hours worked increases, so do related illnesses and health costs. Workplace stress costs the nation more than $300 billion each year in health treatment and missed work. Workers who report being stressed incur health care costs that are 46% higher, or an average of $600 more per person than other employees (Schwartz 2004). Because of low wages and the need to work more hours, poor people are also more likely to face health-debilitating job stress. Berkman (2004) argues that stressful social situations like job insecurity and the circumstances of the poor can lead to a "fight or flight" stress reaction, which leads to elevated blood sugar; higher blood pressure; and an increase in the risk of type 2 diabetes, cardiovascular disease, and stroke.

## Tobacco

Tobacco-related diseases have been called the single most preventable cause of death in the world by John Seffrin of the American Cancer Society (quoted in Nocera 2006). The World Health Organization estimates that globally, tobacco is responsible for the deaths of 1 in 10 adults, or approximately 5 million deaths a year. Worldwide, half of the people who smoke (650 million) will die of tobacco-related causes. Tobacco and poverty are linked. The world's poor smoking populations spend 10% of household income on tobacco. According to WHO (2006), the poor are more likely to smoke and less likely to quit. Studies suggest that low-income and uneducated smokers receive less preventive health care, including health education, both in developed and underdeveloped countries.

Citing the Department of Health and Human Services, Kornblum and Julian (2007) estimate that 57 million Americans are currently smoking. Overall, they make up 23% of Americans. Populations most at risk for smoking include those who are less educated such as teens and low-income individuals, as noted above. Every day, 3,000 teens and adolescents start smoking, with 1 in 3 eventually dying from smoking-related diseases. Smoking is the fourth leading cause of death in the United States, according to the American Lung Association (2008). An estimated 120,000 Americans die of lung disease, with 35,000 Americans currently having the disease. Smoking contributes to 440,000 deaths and 8.6 million serious illnesses a year. Furthermore, according to the surgeon general, secondhand smoke has been found to be dangerous to children and infants, increasing the likelihood of sudden infant death syndrome, respiratory problems, asthma, and ear infections. Linked to secondhand smoke, asthma is the leading chronic disease among American children. The smoke inhaled by adult nonsmokers increases their risk of heart disease by 25 to 30% and lung cancer by 20 to 30% (American Lung Association 2008; Coleman and Kerbo 2006).

Figure 9.6 reveals that race and gender are factors in who is more likely to smoke. Men are more likely to smoke than women of all races. Asian women are the least likely to smoke tobacco, while Native American men and women are most likely to smoke. Education also plays a role in determining who smokes. Individuals with 4 years of college are less likely to smoke (8%) compared to individuals with less than a high school degree (34%) (American Lung Association 2008).

**Figure 9.6** Percent of Smokers by Race and Gender, 2004

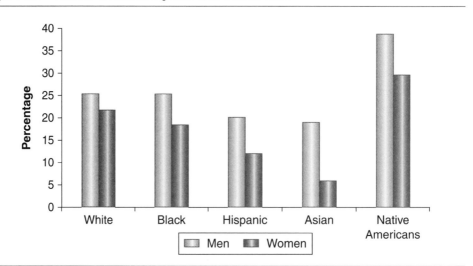

*Source:* "Statistical Fact Sheet: Populations," 2008, American Heart Association.

## COMPLEMENTARY THERAPIES AND PERSONAL CONTROL OF HEALTH

Modern Western medicine has been critiqued for its lack of focus on preventive health care. Many Americans tend to not have control over their personal health and are plagued with problems related to self-control such as obesity and chronic conditions. Conventional medicine often places less emphasis on the causes of disease rather than the cure. The system is relying more often on quick fixes, especially prescription drugs. This is evident when looking at the main causes of death in the United States. Heart disease, diabetes, cancer, and other diseases are linked to stress and other lifestyle factors such as diet and exercise. These illnesses are easily prevented by altering lifestyles and approaches to health. A number of people throughout the world combine Western-style medicine with alternative therapies that promote health rather than restore it. What are called CAM or Complementary and Alternative Medicines represent a large body of remedies that are based on self-help medicine.

Recent immigrants have brought alternative medicines from other cultures. Beyond drugs and surgery, alternative therapies address the body's ability to heal itself. The field of alternative medicine covers a number of interventions from cultures around the world. Introduced to the United States by the 1960s counterculture, most are holistic, incorporating the body, mind, and spirit making up the environment of a patient (Betz 2006; Ruggie 2004). Alternative therapies have also fostered paradigms based on wellness, organic foods, biofeedback, and the human potential movements. Preventive approaches include mind/body interventions—meditation, art/music/dance therapy, and prayer; biological therapy—as well as herbal and folk-based remedies.  Studies show that 60% of Americans will use a CAM therapy with usage of herbal and spiritual healing especially prevalent among Hispanics and Native Americans. Examples of alternative approaches are acupuncture, meditation, and chiropractic along with practices linked to cultural systems such as Chinese herbal medicine and Indian Ayurvedic medicine. Medical sociologists argue that CAM therapies for many are a search to promote and control one's own health (Betz 2006).

In 2002, the White Commission on Complementary and Alternative Medicine Policy found that "despite their diversity, there are some common threads that run among many traditional systems of health care as well as systems that have emerged more recently. These similarities include an emphasis on whole systems, the promotion of self-care and the stimulation of self-healing processes, the integration of mind and body, the spiritual nature of illness and healing, and the prevention of illness by enhancing the vital energy, or subtle forces, in the body."

Individuals who use CAM therapies are often disenchanted with conventional medicine. They are searching for ways to promote health. As seen in this chapter, exposure to hospitals and inconsistent medical care is often detrimental. Most that use CAM do it in conjunction with Western-style medicine. Theorists looking at Western medicine often claim it overlooks lifestyle. Many patients are seeking to take an active role in maintaining their health. The White Commission report goes on to state that "[t]here also is a growing

*(Continued)*

(Continued)

recognition within conventional health care that biopsychosocial and spiritual factors may play an important role in promoting health and preventing illness." Betz (2006) points out what is perhaps the most important point related to alternative therapies: "CAM calls for *active participation* from the consumer. Giving away personal power to 'experts' leads to dependency." CAM therapies do not replace the health care system. However, they do show how approaches to health are important components of health.

The relationship between socioeconomic class, race, and health status is complex. America's low-income citizens are not the only ones engaging in poor health practices. As discussed in Chapter 1, the practices noted earlier are played out in large-scale social and economic structures, and they reflect the interests of multiple actors, not just individuals in isolation. Next, we look at the history of the U.S. health care system and the role of the main players in shaping how health care is delivered and who receives it.

## HISTORY OF THE U.S. HEALTH CARE SYSTEM

The U.S. health care system is the most expensive in the world, but remains characterized by a paradox of top-notch care for those can afford it, and almost complete inaccessibility for those who cannot. The skyrocketing costs place more and more hospitals, clinics, and their patients in crisis as primary care is compromised in favor of cost reduction and profiteering. Meanwhile, the United States remains the only Western industrialized nation without a government-sponsored, comprehensive health care system. Because of its private, profit-driven paradigm, the U.S. health care system has been called the **medical-industrial complex**(Rellman 1980).

The system is made up of an agglomeration of public and private health care providers functioning autonomously in multiple and sometimes competing ways. Health and health care have been privatized and corporatized to maximize profits at the expense of the general public's health and welfare, all for the sake of an economic philosophy that argues that competition improves the quality of a product. But, at best, the highest-quality products and services are only available to those who can afford it. At worst, even those who believe they have adequate insurance often find they are not covered for the most dire or costly of procedures and treatments. While some aspects of medicine may advance because of laissez-faire competition, the provision of health care to poor, working-, and now even middle-class citizens has not. The U.S. health care system is dominated by multiple powerful actors: insurance companies, medical professionals, hospitals, pharmaceutical companies, and medical technology corporations whose interests in the health of all Americans are conflicted at best (Navarro 2003).

Historically, finite medical knowledge meant that doctors were able to handle almost all demands for health care in the home. In the 19th century, family, servants, or close friends cared for patients in the home with physicians making visits as needed. Poor people and immigrants received little formal health care and depended on regional or culturally-based herbal medicines and customary treatments passed on by families and communities. Prior to germ theory, public health innovations, and inoculations, infectious and communicable diseases such as cholera, pneumonia/influenza, tuberculosis, and intestinal disorders were the main causes of death. Life expectancy in the United States in 1900 was 47 years of age (Shrestha 2006).

Before the advent of modern medicine, various therapies often did more harm than good. Usually in pursuit of medical knowledge but sometimes based simply on fascination, scientists historically used slaves and other segments of a vulnerable black population to conduct experiments. The most famous example of such conduct occurred in the 1928 Tuskegee syphilis study, where over 400 African American men were purposely left untreated because researchers wanted to see how the disease progressed differently in blacks and study its devastating effects with postmortem dissections. Such cases, some having been conducted in the latter part of the 20th century, have left many in the black community with a legacy of fear and distrust of the medical system (Washington 2007). This legacy of abuse and the contemporary outcomes of lower health status and exclusion of a disproportionate number of African Americans from health care make up what author Harriet Washington calls "systemic medical racism" (Washington 2007).

Prior to the organization of medical associations, midwives typically attended births and provided prenatal care. The founding of the American Medical Association (AMA) in 1847 reflected exclusionary efforts to standardize medicine through medical training and standards for care. The AMA excluded midwives and other traditional "healers" from the creation of an "official" medical profession. From the outset, professionalized health care alienated traditional methods of treatment and prevention.

Early health care institutions focused primarily on care for incurable and chronic conditions. Prior to 1900, few people used America's mainly charity hospitals. Illness and disability were most often handled at home due to the lack of access to health care and fear of hospitals. The use of scientific principles and professional staff in hospitals accelerated after World War I when the AMA established medical schools, addressed medical fraud, and developed specialty boards for new areas of medical expertise (Guenter 1999). The AMA also benefitted from a historical and cultural trend toward expertise and professionalism during the first half of the 20th century. As American hospitals became central to medical training and doctor–patient interaction, the rights of patients diminished. According to Stevens, Rosenberg, and Burns (2006), in the 19th century, patients voted with their feet until they found doctors they trusted and liked. But, beginning in the late 1890s and continuing on until the 1960s, doctors and health care institutions controlled most relationships with patients by maintaining proprietary ownership over records and treatments.

In the 20th century, U.S. hospitals grew to serve the emerging middle class and its burgeoning financial capabilities. An increased reliance on technology led to the medicalization of society, and hospitals became the central location for fighting acute and curable conditions. The new public hospital merged with a new class of philanthropists who funded hospitals as displays of economic power. As the number of hospitals expanded, public expectation changed as their focus began to center on healing and recovery, not just major diseases. America's emerging private hospitals had private and semi-private rooms along with larger staffs and administrative personnel than European hospitals (Guenter 1999).

As the medical profession grew in status and power, the number of people who went to hospitals also increased. In the early part of the 20th century, developing technology, state licensing, insurance plans, and the growing number of nurses resulted in a better organized the system. Moreover, new technologies, drugs, and vaccines eliminated a number of illnesses. The first private health plans came to be in the 1930s. Indemnity payment, prepaid health plans, and health insurance emerged in 1934. The Hill-Burton Act of 1946 helped communities build more hospitals, while the creation of the National Institute of Health marked the first health research institute in the United States. Health insurance expanded following World War II as compensation paid to workers and as a condition subject to collective bargaining by organized labor (Hartman 2001; Reinert, 2001). The accelerated pace of research due to increased funding during and after the wars led to major gains in medical technology and advances in care, setting the stage for control of the health care system by powerful special interests.

## Stakeholder Mobilization and the U.S. Health Care System

In the past 60 years, research institutes, medical schools, and hospitals have increased dramatically the availability of medicines, procedures, and therapies. By the mid-1900s, doctors had begun to go beyond just diagnosis as the scope of available interventions increased. The early U.S. health care system had been almost completely based on individual payment. Since most people did not go to the hospital and few treatments were available, hospitals charged directly. While many poor people went without health care, charity was an important source of support. In 1940, an estimated 81% of health care was paid for by the individual or the family. As technology increased, health care financing became an issue.

Quadagno (2004) points to the role of powerful stakeholders in shaping the direction of the U.S. health care system after the Second World War. From the 1930s to the 1970s, employers, insurance companies, trade unions, and organized medicine sided with Republicans to oppose New Deal social welfare legislation, attempts at standardized national health insurance, or any government programs competing with the private insurance industries. Private insurance and the medical establishment pushed to keep health care privatized. In the South, the desire to maintain a racially segregated health system dominated public discourse and policy. American labor unions used their influence to redistribute health care thorough collective bargaining for benefits for workers after World War II. In the 1960s, the AFL-CIO helped create the Medicare and Medicaid programs for elderly and disabled populations. Quadagno (2004) argues that Medicare also removed the elderly as a politically worthy and deserving group that could get behind a national health insurance policy.

Across two-thirds of a century, physicians and their allies lobbied legislators, cultivated sympathetic candidates through large campaign contributions, organized petition drives, created grassroots protests, and developed new "products" whenever government action seemed imminent. (p. 28).

Between 1950 and 1973, the share of health care expenditure that was met by insurance more than tripled, from 12% to 41%. Attempts at creating a national health insurance program failed in the 1970s and in the 1990s. President Bill Clinton's 1993 Health Security Plan, ensuring universal coverage through employer mandate, was defeated after a lengthy planning period, which allowed opposition such as the Health Insurance Association of America to counter the proposal with a grassroots campaign proclaiming the plan as a move toward socialized medicine. Labor coalitions offered less-than-expected support for the plan, fighting instead the controversial North American Free Trade Agreement (Quadagno 2004). The failure of President Clinton's 1993 attempt to create universal care has not been followed up until recently by President Obama.

By 1997, third parties, including insurance, made up 81% of payments for health care. The federal government had become involved in providing a safety net with the introduction of Medicaid and Medicare in 1965 (Hartman 2001; Reinert 2001). Medicare increased the costs of health care while providing a profitable segment of the market for private insurers. Subsequent attempts to change the system led to the introduction of group insurance, health maintenance organizations (HMOs), and other for-profit health plans. HMOs emerged as an attempt to counter universal medicine for all people and the rising costs of the U.S. system for companies, individuals, and the public sector. Managed care, however, has often led to the loss of decision making for physician, the rationing of services, and powerful corporations becoming involved in health care debates (Quadagno 2004). Other attempts at covering the poor include the 1997 State Children's Health Insurance Program (CHIP), discussed earlier in this chapter, which was created as an amendment to the Social Security Act in order to insure children. By 2000, an estimated 84.2% of Americans had health coverage of some sort, with 3 of 4 covered through employer-sponsored plans (Kaufman 2004).

Health care costs are rising for a number of reasons, and they have risen for all groups. Increased costs of prescription drugs most severely affect the elderly, with average out-of-pocket costs of over $1,000 a year (Leon-Guerrero 2004). Other causes of spiraling costs include consolidation of insurance companies, more technology, and the increased use of prescription drugs. The cost of prescription drugs has emerged as a major issue in health care. According to the Congressional Budget Office, prescription drugs in the United States. cost between 35% and 55% more than in other countries such as Canada. According to the Kaiser Family Foundation (2010), the number of prescription drugs purchased in the United States expanded 68% between 1994 and 2004. Prices for these drugs increased 8.3% a year.

The use of prescription drugs has also expanded as new conditions are being defined in what Conrad (2007; Conrad and Potter 2000) calls the **medicalization of society**. Medicalization (by definition meaning "to make medical") has resulted in the overwhelming increase in diagnoses of new or once relatively rare illnesses. For instance, the number of diagnoses of bipolar disorder for young people increased from 20,000 in 1994 to 800,000 in 2003 (Carey 2007). Between 1990 and 1995 alone, the number of office-based visits documenting a diagnosis of Attention Deficit Hyperactivity Disorder (ADHD) increased dramatically. According to Robison, Skaer, and Sklar (2005),

> Between 1990 and 1995, the number of visits by girls diagnosed with ADHD rose 3.9-fold ($p < 0.05$), and the mean patient age increased by more than 1 year, from 9.7 in 1990, to 10.8 in 1995. The percentage of office-based visits resulting in a diagnosis of ADHD increased from 1.1% of all visits in this age group in 1990, to 2.8% by 1995. (p. 1497)

Thus, almost 3 times as many people were diagnosed with ADHD by the end of a 5-year period. As more and more Americans became diagnosed with illnesses ranging from ADHD and depression to bipolar disease and manic depression, the pharmacological response grew exponentially as well.

In fact, a variety of well-researched "exposés" have challenged Big Pharma's role in the burgeoning diagnoses and treatments of diseases such as depression. In David Healy's *Let Them Eat Prozac* (2004), the author explains how the pharmacology industry pushed a "simplistic 'biobabble' myth" claiming that depression resulted directly from a shortfall of the neurotransmitter *serotonin* in the brain. As Healy points out, "No such causation has been established, and the proposal is no more reasonable than claiming that headaches arise from aspirin deprivation" (quoted in Crews 2007:n.p.). Armed with this diagnosis, drug makers and sellers exploded the market with a class of drugs known as *selective serotonin reuptake inhibitors* (SSRIs) to increase serotonin and therefore "cure" depression with regular use. The ruse may have remained incredibly profitable but appeared no more hazardous than most superstitions— except that antidepressants could have severe side effects. In addition to serious bouts of dizziness, anxiety, nightmares, nausea, and constant agitation, the numbers of suicides and homicides committed by SSRI patients started to rise. Healy documents how drug companies not only pushed on to increase SSRI sales despite the body count, but also used a variety of disingenuous and manipulative arguments to try and avoid accountability. Frederic Crews (2007) explains,

> The drug firms, Healy saw, were distancing themselves from such tragedies by blaming depression itself for major side effects. Handouts for doctors and patients urged them to persist in the face of early emotional turmoil that only proved, they were told, how vigorously the medicine was tackling the ailment. So, too, dependency symptoms during termination were said to be evidence that the long-stifled depression was now reemerging. . . . Big Pharma's lawyers, parrying negligence suits by the bereaved, took this line of doubletalk to its limit by explaining SSRI-induced stabbings, shootings, and self-hangings by formerly peaceable individuals as manifestations of not-yet-subdued depression. (n.p.)

Eventually, Healy and others were able to challenge Big Pharma with some success in the courts and not only cost the industry millions in legal payouts, but also inspired doctors to stop prescribing as many SSRIs. The full impact of the expansion of drugs for patients with conditions such as depression and mood disorders, ADHD, and others is not yet known. One estimate finds that as many as 1.6 million children and teenagers are given at least two psychiatric drugs in combination per year, with 500,000 taking at least three such drugs for a number of conditions (Harris 2006).

Rising costs of health care and the destructive impact of having a large population uninsured have taken a heavy toll on emergency rooms, endangering the nation's emergency systems (see box on emergency care further down). The quality of the U.S. system also comes into question. As discussed in the box earlier in this chapter, errors in the health care system are an important problem. Iatrogenic illnesses, or illnesses caused by medical errors, kill between 44,000 and 98,000 Americans each year (American Iatrogenic Association 2003; Jost 2007). Chief among the causes are infections along with doctors' errors. In addition, medical malpractice laws have driven up the cost of health care. In response, doctors often practice defensive medicine, which also adds to the cost of health care. The high cost of health care for the country is also taking its toll on industry. General Motors claimed in the 1960s that it spent more on health care than on steel. The company's recent economic turmoil and downsizing are due in part to employee health care costs. Other companies incur similar costs—General Electric claims it currently spends $1.4 billion on employee medical needs (Marks 2004).

The current crisis in the U.S. system is a concern for the future. As 77 million *baby boomers* (individuals born between 1945 and 1962) reach retirement age, they are living longer and requiring more health care. Along with the changing health care needs of the elderly, declining births and fewer working-age adults signal a number of problems in paying for the current and future system. Health benefits have outstripped the growth in average income (Daniels 2008; Kotlikoff 2007). As individuals live longer, they are more likely to have chronic illnesses. Daniels lays out the reality that both developing and developed societies in the world face:

> The point is simple: No aging society, with or without public systems of support, escapes the problems created by societal aging for sustaining and improving institutions that provide care for elderly dependents. The increase in medical needs with societal aging is much broader than the problem of long-term care for frail elderly people. Aging increases the prevalence of cardiovascular disease, chronic pulmonary disease, diabetes, arthritis, and cancer, as well as Alzheimer's disease and other dementias. (p. 165)

Fixing health care is a controversial subject. Some conservatives claim the free market is the best solution. Those proposing a consumer-driven health care system claim that consumers should create savings plans to cover their own medical expenses and use insurance only for catastrophic medical events. They assert that high deductibles requiring individuals to pay for care will make them more selective and reduce the cost of their care for the system (Jost 2007). Critics point out that consumer-driven care will not reduce the problem of affordability or the cost of catastrophic care unless the individual is well off financially. They argue that in changing the system, the country must address universal coverage for all individuals. As we have seen in this chapter, inequalities of health care based on race and class are significant social problems. These are problems that affect the quality of life of a significant number of Americans (Daniels 2008; Jost, 2007; Kotlikoff 2007).

The current crisis in health care leaves millions of Americans in danger and raises questions about the future. Community-based organizations provide important information, as well as some clinical and other support services. Service learning supports communities who would not otherwise receive services. It also prepares individuals for their profession. As we will see in the next section, the experiences of working with individuals in need of care has a number of other outcomes, some of them life altering.

## MEDIA BOX: RACE-BASED HEALTH DISPARITIES

One of the key findings of this chapter is that unequal access to health care and health information based on race is a prominent feature of the U.S. health care system. Racial and ethnic minorities are less healthy; suffer more often from stroke, heart disease, diabetes, and cancer; and have higher infant mortality rates than the United States population as a whole (U.S. Department of Health and Human Services 2005). Obesity is higher among minorities and has increased dramatically among children in the last 30 years. Access to health information for minorities is a key concern for health practitioners and activists. African Americans are more likely to discover cancer in a later stage due to a lack of screening. Less access to care and preventive health information is a primary reason that minority and low-income families are more likely to smoke, fail to receive immunizations, and be obese. In addition, many racial and ethnic groups are more likely to have poor communication with their physicians. In addition, researchers find that the mass media pays less attention to diseases that affect minorities (Armstrong et al. 2006).

The mass media plays an important role in both America's poor health practices and racially-based health disparities. In addition to minorities and low-income families having less access to health information, evidence suggests that mass media campaigns by tobacco companies target both African Americans and Hispanic communities through billboards and advertisements (Hillier et al. 2009). According to the American Lung Association (2008), "Money spent on magazine advertising of mentholated cigarettes, popular with African Americans, increased from 13 percent of total ad expenditures in 1998 to 49" (n.p.).

Studies suggest the mass media has also contributed to rising obesity rates among children, especially minority children. During the same period that childhood obesity rates have increased, children's television shows and advertisements have multiplied. The average child in the United States spends the same amount of time watching television per week as an adult spends at work. Studies suggest that watching television has a negative effect on children—the more television a child watches, the more likely he or she will be obese, inactive, and eat less healthy food (Kaiser Family Foundation 2004).

*Source:* Thinkstock

## CASE STUDY #1

### Service Learning and Health Education

Health education is an important part of preventive health care. The ability to act on health concerns is determined by a number of factors. Service learning programs that incorporate training in the skills of health professionals can offer elementary schools valuable health resources for teaching health education. First-year medical students at Dartmouth Medical School in Connecticut have an option of teaching health in public elementary schools through service learning. The Partners in Health Education Program was designed by the C. Everett Koop Institute at Dartmouth, the Dartmouth Medical School Community Service Office, and local public schools. The program is designed to (1) increase quality health education lessons and frame basic science content in clinically relevant prevention messages; (2) assist future medical professionals in understanding the developmental level of children, identify appropriate messages and teach skills, and develop lesson plans; and finally, (3) foster an appreciation for the role that teachers and medical and community professionals play in community health (Walsh, Smith, Jernstedt, Reed, and Goodman2000). This program and others address preventive health care in the early grades.

*(Continued)*

(Continued)

If lifestyle issues are both a cause of and solution to significant health issues, then education is a vital source of building capacity for individuals and groups to improve their well-being. Functionalist sociologists point out that social structure is made up of integrated social institutions: What happens in one institution affects another institution. Functionalists also argue that many of the problems of the current system are caused by haphazard growth. The breakdown of the current system of health care is dysfunctional for society. Technology has led to a powerful system that can help people get well. However, according to the functionalist paradigm, the system is experiencing a cultural lag where rapid growth was unplanned and previous mechanisms for health care delivery no longer make sense and must evolve. Yet the idea that health care is a commodity continues to cause problems for the distribution of resources in the U.S. system (Coleman and Kerbo 2006).

Based on the work of Talcott Parsons, functionalists also point out that society's expectation of how an individual should act when facing an illness is termed a **sick role**. The sick role encompasses social exclusion from normal behavior; not being held at fault; the desire to get well; and finally, dependence on medical experts (Parsons 1951). Learning to be sick and learning to live with a health care system is part of socialization into an ongoing society, a society that we have already argued becomes more and more *medicalized*. Thus, there are problems with the dependency on health care systems. Leon-Guerrero (2004) notes that the powerful medical industry serves us well in technical and scientific advances. But as specialists, or those who treat a specific aliment, have replaced the general practitioner (GP, or family doctor model), a number of negative results occur. First, less attention is paid to prevention, as most medical practitioners focus on treatment. Second, these specialties focus on the malady and not the "whole" patient. Unlike the GP, specialists know little about the patient's family history, culture, lifestyle, and so on. Third, these trends increase costs and tax the whole health care system. Finally, the emphasis on expertise and specialty further isolates individuals, families, and communities from the kind of knowledge and sense of empowerment that could be powerful preventive tools. For example, lack of health education is linked to obesity, smoking, sexually transmitted diseases, and other health problems. As we have seen throughout this chapter, poor health is strongly related to Americans' unhealthy behaviors. A lack of health information and unhealthy lifestyles have emerged as a public health crisis.

Functionalists argue that with better social integration, healthy outcomes can occur. Health and education are good examples of how institutional integration can improve health outcomes and help maintain social stability by ensuring (or at least promoting) good health practices and knowledge of the health care system. In their service learning program, Dartmouth students draw on themes in the classroom such as "the human body," "nutrition and fitness," and "choices in health." Participants also sit in on three seminars that feature teaching and classroom management techniques, peer collaboration, and structured reflection. The program uses a number of forms of evaluation including surveys, classroom teaching videos, and patient video interviews (Walsh et al. 2000). According to Walsh et al., the findings of the program reveal that service learning increases elementary students' individual ability to act on health knowledge and college students' understanding of health practices including how to work with people.

Early results indicate that medical students move from standing in front of the class and lecturing the students on health topics to sitting among the students and acting as a resource for students to explore health topics as independent learners. We believe this change foreshadows similar important developments in the medical student's ability to communicate with patients as clerks and in practice as physicians. (p. 41)

According to functionalists, socialization into a particular culture is a latent function of schools. Incorporating medical students into the school systems serves a number of functions. Service learning is an effective way to show clearly the functions of education by highlighting the role of teachers and other community professionals in the development of healthy children and communities. In this example, both college and elementary students get interested in health education from the perspective of learning and teaching.

## Case Study Questions

1. What do functionalists claim is causing the current health care crisis?

2. What is the role of health education in addressing health needs?

3. What is a sick role, and what does it mean to a patient?

4. What gains do Dartmouth and local school students make from service learning?

## CASE STUDY #2

### Partnerships for Reducing Inequality:
### The Open Door Health Center

Nursing students in the South Central Minnesota area have the opportunity to participate in the Health Bond partnership linking Mankato State University and South Central Technical College with Arlington Municipal, Waseca Area Memorial, and Immanuel-St. Joseph's Hospitals. Drawing on funding from the Robert Wood Johnson Foundation and the PEW Charitable Trusts, Health Bond integrates family health care and integrates regional health services. The initiative has generated a faith-based healing ministry, a health clinic, a senior citizen center, and a continuing health care education council (Aadalen, Hohenstein, Huntley, and McBeth 1998). The initiative provides health care to an underserved rural population while training future nurses in real-world experiences. It is an example of how service learning can increase the effectiveness of the health care system and reduce the negative effects of inequality.

In the partnership, students participate in planning, implementing, strengthening, maintaining, and replicating community-based innovations in health care. Through the initiative, the Open Door Health Center serves patients and also refers patients to doctors and hospitals. Programs that expand nurse education and nurse practice into the community show promise for both strengthening nurses'

*(Continued)*

(Continued)

responses to consumer health care and increasing access to services for communities. The center not only coordinates services, but it also provides cost-effective treatment for individuals who would not otherwise receive it. As we have seen in the first part of the chapter, the uninsured often go without health care or must depend on emergency rooms for primary care. The Open Door Health Center is a good example of using student learning to reduce inequality in health care. Open Door is designed to meet the needs of underserved people, especially women and children.

Access to health care for communities in rural areas in the United States often depends on the availability of clinics and partnerships among multiple service providers. Inequality can include limited access to preventive care such as screenings, immunizations, and health information (Agency for Healthcare Research and Quality 2003). Participatory approaches involving multiple health care partners have been shown to be an effective research method for solving public health problems (Israel, Eng, Schulz, and Parker2005). Creating effective health service delivery for low-income, rural populations is a challenge that often requires creative organizational management. It also requires that individuals see the importance of using available services. Symbolic interactionists point out that health, illness, and medical responses are socially constructed (Leon-Guerrero 2004). Interpretations of health care are shaped by complex interactions among culture, race, class, and gender. Definitions of the health care system are also socially constructed, meaning they come from personal beliefs, institutional and professional definitions of the situation, and societal social norms. Emerging beliefs form the basis for how individuals interact with their health care system.

Rural residents often have difficulty accessing health care for a number of reasons. Beyond transportation issues are fears of going to the doctor and fear of costs. These perceptions may limit their desire to seek health care. The center described above provides a unique training opportunity for nurses to gain hands-on experience. It provides opportunities for faculty, students, staff, clients, and nurses to "get smart faster." Aadalen et al. (1998) describe how the future nurses see their service learning: "Nurses—including staff nurses, faculty, nurse clinicians, nurse practitioners, and students—relish the experience of practicing what they describe as *real* nursing at the center" (p. 18, emphasis original). The fee at the center is $5.00 per visit. Services include the taking of a health history, dental screening, throat culture, child and teen checkups, developmental screening, health education, vision and hearing screening, and immunizations. The center involves future nurses in interactive planning and consumer-driven services. It redefines health care by empowering both nurses and patients.

Beyond providing clinical health care, Health Bond service learning participants also are involved in elder care through the Living at Home/Block Nurse Programs (LAH/BNPs). The community-based programs draw on professionals, schools, churches, and volunteer support services to enable elderly residents to remain in their homes. The program also provides home health aides and nurses. The outcomes for nurses doing service learning are powerful. Working with Mankato means students have the opportunity to acquire, through these planned curricular experiences, a vision of how they will fulfill their own mission as a nurse where they live as well as where they work. Through these experiences, "students reflect on the importance to senior citizens of being able to remain in their homes, gaining all the while new appreciation of the meaning of 'activities of daily living' for people 65 years or older dealing with the health challenges of chronic disease" (Aadalen 1998:37).

Health Bond programs are redefining how community members and providers address health care. Service learning can change how future nurses perceive the community. At the same time, community health centers can alter the way low-income and at-risk rural community members see services and the health care system. By redefining service delivery, Health Bond programs are creating access to the U.S. system.

## Case Study Questions

1. Why do rural areas in the United States have difficulties providing health care?

2. How does symbolic interactionism explain health and medical practices?

3. What do participants gain from service learning experiences with Health Bond?

4. How does Health Bond increase autonomy for the elderly?

## EMERGENCY CARE IN NEED OF EMERGENCY CARE

Another result of not insuring all citizens and rising health care costs in the United States is the effect they have on the system. According to recent reports by the Institute of Medicine (2006a, 2006b), the strain incurred due to rising costs and the uninsured is beginning to seriously affect the ability of the nation's emergency rooms (ERs) to provide adequate emergency care. As many as half a million ambulances are turned away from emergency rooms each year due to overcrowding and are diverted to other hospitals in the area. Reports of patients routinely waiting 8 hours for treatment at emergency rooms reveal the inability of the current system to manage a growing crisis. Problems faced by ERs include not enough reimbursement from insurance companies and a lack of specialists on call. Researchers at the Institute of Medicine report that the U.S. system is in a precarious state. A major concern is the rising number of uninsured people who receive primary health care treatment inside of emergency rooms instead of doctors' offices and clinics. For hospitals, the cost of this care is often not reimbursed by the system. As much as 50% of emergency room costs go unpaid for. Nationally, unpaid hospital bills amount to $45 billion annually. While emergency room visits increased 27%, from 90 million in 1993 to 114 million in 2003, the United States lost 703 hospitals, 200,000 beds, and 425 emergency departments. Funding is a key issue in the crisis. For instance, emergency departments received only 4% of the $3.38 billion earmarked for emergency medical services by the U.S. Office of Homeland Security (Institute of Medicine 2006a, 2006b). The crisis in emergency medical care leads us to question how the current system will survive without a radical change in how health care is funded and distributed. It also is a concern for the growing number of elderly in the United States who will rely on emergency medical care now and in the near future. How do you think emergency medicine should be overhauled? What examples from your community reveal the pressures on the system? Do you think the nation's health care system is prepared to handle the growing elderly population?

## CASE STUDY #3

Participatory Research and Community-Based Health Work:
The East Side Village Health Worker Partnership

In Detroit, faculty and students from the University of Michigan's School of Public Health worked with neighborhood residents and activists to develop the East Side Village Health Worker Partnership (ESVHWP). According to participants, the ESVHWP is "a community-based participatory research partnership that uses a lay health advisor model to address social determinants of health on Detroit's East Side" (Schulz, Parker, Israel, Maciak, and Hollis 1998:11). Lay health advisors are individuals from within local communities or particular cultural groups who adopt healthy lifestyles and then promote health within their own families and communities. These "natural helpers" become vital role models and change agents within their communities, generating important research and knowledge that impact health provision resources and the field of public health in general.

The ESVHWP combines research and active intervention by gathering and analyzing data, providing education and services, and supporting community organizing and public policy initiatives. The group also incorporates the active participation of community partners in all phases of research and intervention. This process of research and action "brings together participants who represent a variety of perspectives and experiences to identify shared concerns, and to plan, implement, and evaluate actions taken to address those concerns." The partnership's purpose is to "mobilize resources to address the social factors that affect the health of East Side residents" (Schulz, Parker, Israel, Maciak, and Hollis 1998). It accomplishes this goal primarily by integrating residents' own knowledge, experience, and strategies with more academic and institutional forms of research.

For example, University of Michigan faculty and students initially helped design and implement research and evaluation questions to identify community strengths and resources, as well as risk factors and conditions challenging the health of the local community. As neighborhood health workers were recruited, these women analyzed and discussed the initial survey and interview results along with the ESVHWP steering committee (composed of Village Health workers, representatives from other community organizations, local health service providers, and members of academic institutions). These discussions eventually resulted in workers and steering committee members developing a list of five priority areas that included policing and safety, strengthening social support for parents, improving access to health care, addressing local economic insecurity and financial vulnerability through sustainable economic development, and addressing the overall community factors that resulted in higher risks of diabetes and cardiovascular disease in local residents (Schulz et al. 2005).

More importantly for the community, the constant collection of research data and discussion and analysis of the data also resulted in the group developing a variety of plans and possibilities for action. In the area of policing and safety, for example, health workers determined they could create better relationships with community police and attend local police precinct meetings to make their voices heard, as well as work with community officials to make sure burnt-out street lights are replaced. In other areas, project members realized they could build on current experiences and relationships to increase the neighborhood's capacity for improving support networks and resources, thus addressing some of the major factors affecting poor health: stress, depression, isolation, and alienation. For example, in-depth interviews among health workers demonstrated that some had received positive support from church groups that had mitigated certain stress factors. In response, one health worker organized an overnight retreat for women at her church designed to strengthen social support networks (Schulz et al. 2005).

The melding of research and action (or praxis, as it is sometimes called) as well as the desire for researchers and local residents or activists to develop more integrated relationships have been shaped both by emergent, community-based participatory research methods (CBPR) and feminist research methods (FR). From both fields, a focus on the power differentials between those doing research and those who are in many ways the subject of the research takes front stage. Working out these power dynamics of the various participants becomes part of the praxis involved. Researchers study how these power dynamics play a role in the research process, and activists consider redistributing the resources involved in knowledge production as part of their political action (Baker and Dolgon 2005; Minkler 2004; Nyden 1997). These challenges faced by researchers and activists are similar to those faced by any students doing service learning or other civic engagement and community-based work.

In the case of the ESVHWP, researchers like Amy Schulz (Schulz et al. 2005) believe that their work could encourage community residents in the form of Village Health workers to join the partnership because they believed it had the potential to influence positive community outcomes that would improve people's health. But part of the partnership among students and faculty, community organizations and neighborhood residents/activists is the relationships they develop and the ways in which these connections enhance both the research and practice of the partnership itself. As Schulz summarizes,

> Partnerships that seek to support and enhance the power of community residents must have as a first priority building and sustaining the relationships that provide an infrastructure or framework for a sense of common identity and reciprocal influence—a sense of community— within the partnership. These relationships—and the challenges, conflicts, and differences, as well as the commonalities embedded in them—provide the foundation for each partnership to determine how to most effectively integrate research with action to attain the fundamental goals of addressing inequalities that underlie health disparities. (p. 311).

As the following box (Figure 9.7) demonstrates, social and economic inequalities are major contributors to the causes of increased health risks for East Side Detroit residents. But what the ESVHWP also makes clear is that effectively understanding and addressing those inequalities takes a redistribution of resources as well as the creation of new commitments and identities that challenge rigid racial, gender, professional, and economic categorizations that contribute to both inequality and disempowerment or inaction.

*(Continued)*

(Continued)

**Figure 9.7**  Social Determinants of Health and Environmental Health Promotion

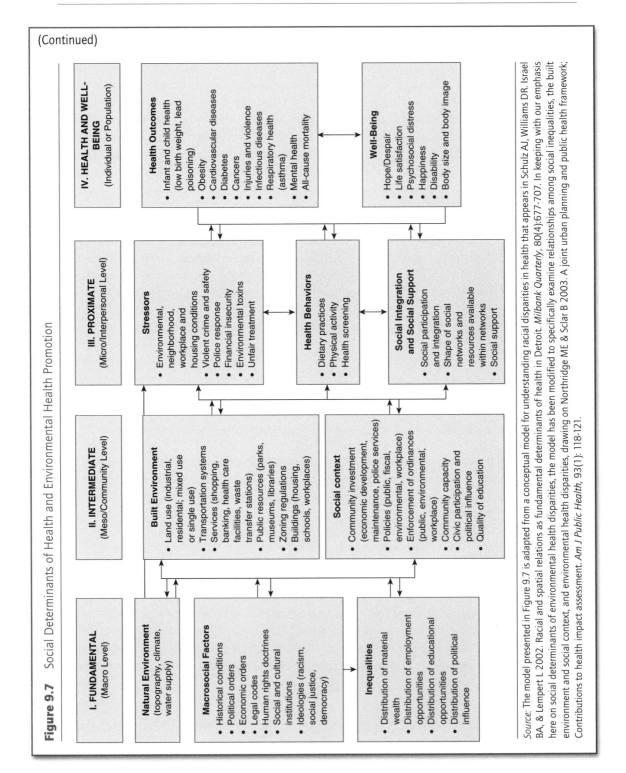

*Source:* The model presented in Figure 9.7 is adapted from a conceptual model for understanding racial disparities in health that appears in Schulz AJ, Williams DR. Israel BA, & Lempert L 2002. Racial and spatial relations as fundamental determinants of health in Detroit. *Milbank Quarterly,* 80(4):677-707. In keeping with our emphasis here on social determinants of environmental health disparities, the model has been modified to specifically examine relationships among social inequalities, the built environment and social context, and environmental health disparities, drawing on Northridge ME & Sclar B 2003. A joint urban planning and public health framework; Contributions to health impact assessment. *Am J Public Health,* 93(1): 118-12l.

Case Study Questions

1. What are the primary factors behind the health risks faced by Detroit's East Side residents?

2. How does the ESVHWP change the nature of the research into these factors?

3. How does the lay health advisor model shift the kinds of solutions suggested?

4. What are the key aspects of CBPR and FR, and how did they impact the design and success of ESVHWP? How might such approaches impact an issue in your community?

## VOICES FROM THE FIELD

**Amy Schulz, Associate Professor,**
**Health Behavior & Health Education**

Associate Director, Center for Research on Ethnicity, Culture and Health, University of Michigan

The evidence becomes clearer and clearer that we cannot separate the problem of health disparities among poor, non-white urban communities from the structural forms of discrimination and disinvestment that result in poverty and racism to begin with. Racial segregation and minimal economic resources negatively impact the physical environment (noise, air quality, parks), community infrastructure, and the social environment (street maintenance, police, fire and schools, hospitals and pharmacies, etc.). Even the lack of access to nutritious food and parks for physical activity increases health risks. For example, a heavy police presence along Detroit's greenways sends the message that these areas are dangerous and not to be used, but they are some of the only spaces available for walking, running, and other physical exercise. All of these conditions influence the basic elements of healthy lifestyles, choices, and opportunities such as diet, fitness and exercise, and even social suport networks. We cannot rectify these health disparities until people can change their structural access to adequate incomes, nutritious food and healthy environments, and decent and safe schools, and all without regard to race or ethnicity.

## SUMMARY

The current health care crisis is behind a number of social problems related to health in the United States. The growing number of uninsured, rising costs, and the crisis in emergency rooms are indicative of a systemic crisis. Moreover, the pain and suffering of those without access to the system are symptoms of a humanitarian crisis found not just in developing countries but also in the United States, one of the wealthiest countries in the world. The chapter also offers hope through service learning and community-based programs that reveal how getting involved in producing better health outcomes for disenfranchised populations produces better citizens, professionals, and persons. The examples challenge us to question the top-down health care system and see the value of participation from stakeholders other than those involved in the medical-industrial complex. The individuals, groups, and organizations involved in solving health-related social problems in this chapter will be redefining health care systems throughout the world in the future.

## SUMMARY QUESTIONS

1. How does the U.S. health care system create unequal access to resources?

2. What are the roles of the Centers for Disease Control and Prevention (CDC) and the World Health Organization (WHO) in understanding and preventing diseases?

3. Who are the stakeholders that shape the U.S. health care system?

4. How have the causes of death changed in the last 100 years? What health trends do these changes reflect?

5. What historical trends have led to the current crisis in the U.S. health care system?

## GLOSSARY

**Acute Illnesses:** Abrupt, short-term, and sudden illnesses such as the flu, diarrhea, or colds; were considered the main killers in the past.

**Chronic Illnesses:** Long-term, continuous illnesses such as diabetes, stroke, heart disease, and conditions like arthritis; these are the main killers for most in developed nations.

**Epidemics:** Diseases that appear in a given population, at a given time, and at a rate that exceeds expectations.

**Epidemiology:** The study of the patterns in the distribution and frequency of sickness, injury, and death across a population.

**Iatrogenic:** Describes illnesses caused by medical errors.

Medicaid: Federal program that provides insurance for low-income families, the elderly, and disabled people requiring long-term care services.

Medical-Industrial Complex: Phrase coined by Arnold Rellman; the United States' private, profit-driven health care system made up of an agglomeration of public and private health care providers.

Medicalization of Society: Term coined by Peter Conrad; to make a condition or behavior "medical" such as treating alcoholism as a "disease," not simply a behavior, has resulted in the overwhelming increase in diagnoses of new or once relatively rare illnesses.

Medicare: Federal insurance program that covers mainly senior citizens.

Morbidity: Refers to the illnesses, symptoms, and impairments, including death, that result from illness.

Obese: Describes a person whose weight is more than 20% above his or her ideal body weight.

Pandemics: An epidemic that crosses many borders.

Sick Role: Society's expectation about how an individual should act when facing an illness.

## WEBSITES TO LEARN MORE ABOUT SOCIAL PROBLEMS OF HEALTH AND RELATED STUDENT ACTION PROJECTS

American Medical Association: http://www.ama-assn.org/

American Public Health Association: http://www.apha.org/

California Center for Public Health Advocacy: http://www.publichealthadvocacy.org/gro.html

Centers for Disease Control and Prevention: http://www.cdc.gov/

Center for Community Health Education Research and Service: http://cchers.org/

Community-Campus Partnerships for Health: http://depts.washington.edu/ccph/index.html

Doctors Without Borders: http://doctorswithoutborders.org/splash.cfm

Heartland Centers for Public Health & Community Capacity Development: http://www.heartland centers.slu.edu/

Noble Prize for Medicine: http://nobelprize.org/nobel_prizes/medicine/laureates/2009/

The Obesity Society: http://www.obesity.org/

Occupational Safety & Health Administration: http://www.osha.gov/

Pain Management of America—Medical Marijuana: http://www.medicalmarijuana.net/

World Health Organization: http://www.who.int/en/

# REFERENCES

Aadalen, Sharon P., Mary Kay Hohenstein, Mary I. Huntley, and Annette J. McBeth. 1998. "Service Education Partnerships Create Community Service-Learning Opportunities in a Rural Region." Pp. 33–52 in *Creating Community-Responsive Physicians: Concepts and Models for Service-Learning in Medical Education,* edited by Serena D. Seifer, Kris Hermanns, and Judy Lewis. Washington, DC: American Association for Higher Education.

Agency for Healthcare Research and Quality. 2003. National Healthcare Disparities Report, 2003. Rockville, MD: Author. Retrieved February 14, 2010 (http://www.ahrq.gov/qual/nhdr03/nhdr03.htm).

Airhihenbuwa, Collins O. 1995. *Health and Culture Beyond the Western Paradigm.* Thousand Oaks, CA: Sage.

Alberti, Georg. 2001. "Noncommunicable Diseases: Tommorow's Pandemics." *Bulletin of the World Health Organization,* 79:907.

American Heart Association. 2008. "Statistical Fact Sheet: Populations." Retrieved February 25, 2010 (http://www.americanheart.org/downloadable/heart/1199397765814FS03AS08.pdf).

American Iatrogenic Association. 2003. [Home page]. Retrieved December 28, 2003 (http://www.iatrogenic .org/index.html).

American Lung Association. 2008. *The Future of Lung Health Annual Report.* Washington, DC: Author.

Appleby, Julie. 2007. "Employer-Provided Insurance Continues to Decline." *USA Today.* November 12.

Armstrong, Katrina, Abigail Rose, Nikki Peters, Judith Long, Suzanne McMurphy, and Judy Shea. 2006. "Distrust of the American Healthcare System and Self-Reported Health in the United States." *Journal of General Internal Medicine* 21:1525-1497.

Baker, Chris and Corey Dolgon. 2005. "Participatory Research Methods, Community-Based Organizations, and Service Learning: Introduction." Humanity and Society, 29.

Baker, Elizabeth A., Mario Schootman, Ellen Barnidge, and Cheryl Kelly. 2006. "The Role of Race and Poverty in Access to Foods That Enable Individuals to Adhere to Dietary Guidelines." *Preventing Chronic Disease,* July, 3.

Berkman, Lisa F. 2004. "The Health Divide." *Contexts,* 3:38–43.

Berwick, Donald M., David R. Calkins, C. Joseph McCannon, and Andrew D. Hackbarth. 2006. "The 100,000 Lives Campaign: Setting a Goal and a Deadline for Improving Health Care Quality." *Journal of the American Medical Association,* 295:324-327.

Betz, Michael. 2006. *Enriching Health: Pathways to Complementary Therapies.* Bloomington, IN: AuthorHouse.

Brown, David. 2006. "Crisis Seen in Nation's ER Care: Capacity, Expertise, Are Found Lacking." *The Washington Post.* June 15. Retrieved February 14, 2010 (http://www.washingtonpost.com/wp-dyn/content/article/ 2006/06/14/AR2006061402166.html).

Brown, Patricia Leigh. 2006. "A Rare Kind of Food Bank, and Just Maybe the Hippest, Flourishes." *New York Times.* September 26.

Carey, Benedict. 2007. "Bipolar Illness Soars as a Diagnosis for the Young." *New York Times*. September 4. Retrieved February 25, 2010 (http://ww.nytimes.com/2007/09/04/health/04psych.htm?_r = 1).

Centers for Disease Control and Prevention. 2006. "Twenty-Five Years of HIV/AIDS—United States, 1981–2006." *Morbidity and Mortality Weekly Report,* 55:585–589. Retrieved October 14, 2006 (http://www.cdc.gov/MMWR/preview/mmwrhtml/mm5521a1.htm).

____. 2007a. "Diabetes Data and Trends." Retrieved February 26, 2010 (http://www.cdc.gov/diabetes/statistics/incidence/fig1.htm).

Centers for Disease Control and Prevention. 2007b. "National Diabetes Fact Sheet, 2007. Retrieved February 26, 2010 (http://www.cdc.gov/diabetes/pubs/pdf/ndfs_2007.pdf).

Children's Defense Fund Action Council. 2004. *Where Is America Going? How You Can Make a Difference: An Action Guide.* Washington, DC: Author.

Coleman, James A. and Harold R. Kerbo. 2006. *Social Problems.* 9th ed. Upper Saddle River, NJ: Pearson.

Collins, James W., Richard J. David, Arden Handler, Stephen Wall, and Steven Andes. 2004. "Very Low Birthweight in African American Infants: The Role of Maternal Exposure to Interpersonal Racial Discrimination." *American Journal of Public Health,* 94:2132–2138.

Colomeda, Lorelei and Anne Lambert. 1998. *Keepers of the Central Fire: Issues in Ecology for Indigenous Peoples.* New York: HNA Books.

Colomeda, Lorelei and Eberhard R. Wenzel. 2000. "Medicine Keeper: Issues in Indigenous Health." *Critical Public Health,* 10:243–256.

Conrad, Peter. 2007. *The Medicalization of Society: On the Transformation of Human Conditions Into Treatable Disorders.* Baltimore, MD: The Johns Hopkins University Press.

Conrad, Peter and Valerie Leiter. 2003. "Introduction." *Health and Health Care as a Social Problem.* Boston: Rowman & Littlefield.

Conrad, Peter and Deborah Potter. 2000. "From Hyperactive Children to ADHD Adults: Observations on the Expansion of Medical Categories." *Social Problems,* 559–582.

Cutler, David M., Edward L. Glaeser, and Jesse M. Shapiro. 2003. "Why Have Americans Become Obese?" *National Bureau of Economic Statistics Bulletin of Aging and Health* (Working Paper No. 9446).

Daniels, Norman. 2008. *Just Health: Meeting Health Needs Fairly.* New York: Cambridge University Press.

Donnelly, John. 2003. "Losing Hope in Appalachia: As the Mines Shut Down, an Area's Health and Future Declined." *Boston Globe.* December 23.

Engels, Mary. 2007. "Study Finds Immigrants' Use of Healthcare System Lower Than Expected." *Los Angeles Times.* November 27.

Guenter, Risse B. 1999. *Mending Bodies, Saving Souls: A History of Hospitals.* New York: Oxford University Press.

Harrington, Carly. 2005. "Care at a Cost." *Knoxville News Sentinel.* November 13.

Harris, Gardiner. 2006. "Proof Is Scant on Psychiatric Drug Mix for Young." *New York Times.* November 23.

Hartman, Sherry. 2001. "Economics of Health Care." Pp. 156–185 in *Community Health Nursing Caring for the Public's Health,* edited by Karen Saucier Lundy and Sharyn James. Boston, MA: Jones and Bartlett.

Healy, David. 2004. *Let Them Eat Prozac.* New York: New York University Press.

Herman-Stahl, Mindy. Jessica Duncan, and Donna L. Spencer. 2003. "The Implications of Cultural Orientation for Substance Use Among American Indians." *American Indians and Alaska Mental Health Journal,* 11:46–66.

Hillier, Amy, Brian L. Cole, Tony E. Smith, Antronette K. Yancey, Jerome D. Williams, Sonya A. Grier, et al., 2009. "Clustering of Unhealthy Outdoor Advertisements around Child-Serving Institutions: A Comparison of Three Cities." *Health & Place,* 15:935–945.

Himmelstein, David U., Deborah Thorne, Elizabeth Warren, and Steffie Woolhandler. 2009. "Medical Bankruptcy in the United States, 2007: Results of a National Study." American Journal of Medicine, 122:741–746.

Institute of Medicine. 2006a. "Emergency Medical Services at the Crossroads." Retrieved October 21, 2006 (http://www.iom.edu/CMS/3809/16107/35010.aspx).

____. 2006b. "The Future of Emergency Care in the United States Health System." Retrieved October 21, 2006 (http://www.iom.edu/CMS/3809/16107/35007/35014.aspx).

Israel, Barbara A., Eugenia Eng, Amy J. Schulz, and Edith Parker. 2005. "Introduction to Methods in Community-Based Participatory Research in Health." Pp. 3–20 in *Methods in Community-Based Participatory Research for Health,* edited by Barbara A. Israel, Eugenia Eng, Amy J. Schulz, and Edith A. Parker. San Francisco, CA: Jossey-Bass.

Joe, Jennie R. 2003. "The Rationing of Healthcare and Health Disparity for the American Indians/Alaska Natives." Pp. 528–551 in *Unequal Treatment: Confronting Racial and Ethnic Disparities in Health Care,* edited by Brian D. Smedley, Adrienne Y. Stith, and Alan R. Nelson. Washington, DC: National Academies Press.

Jost, Timothy Stoltzfus. 2007. *Health Care at Risk: A Critique of the Consumer-Driven Movement.* Durham, NC: Duke University Press.

Kaiser Family Foundation. 2004. "The Role of Media in Childhood Obesity." Retrieved February 26, 2010 (http://www.kff.org/entmedia/upload/The-Role-Of-Media-in-Childhood-Obesity.pdf).

____. 2010. "Prescription Drug Costs." *Background Brief.* Retrieved February 15, 2010 (http://www.kaiseredu.org/topics_im.asp?id = 352&parentID = 68&imID = 1).

Karger, Howard and David Stoesz. 2005. *American Social Welfare Policy: A Pluralist Approach.* Boston MA: Allyn & Bacon.

Kaufman, Darren. 2004. "Health Care Provider." Pp. 250–251 in *The Encyclopedia of Health Care Management,* edited by Michael J. Stahl. Thousand Oaks, CA: Sage.

Kornblum, William and Joseph Julian. 2007. *Social Problems.* 12th ed. Upper Saddle River, NJ: Pearson.

Kotlikoff, Laurence J. 2007. *The Healthcare Fix: Universal Insurance for all Americans.* Cambridge, MA: MIT Press.

Leon-Guerrero, Anna. 2004. *Social Problems: Community, Policy, and Social Action.* Thousand Oaks, CA: Pine Forge Press.

Marks, Michael. 2004. "Employee Health." In *The Encyclopedia of Health Care Management,* edited by Michael J. Stahl. Thousand Oaks, CA: Sage.

Maurana, Cheryl. A. and Sarena D. Seifer. 2000. Key elements of community health advocacy. Family and Community Health, 23:vii–ix.

Minkler, Meredith. 2004. Community Organizing and Community Building for Health. 2nd ed. Piscataway, NJ: Rutgers University Press.

Montana Campus Compact. N.d. "Service Learning." Retrieved October 18, 2006 (http://www.mtcompact.org/servicelearning.htm).

Navarro, Vicente. 2003. "The Inhuman State of U.S. Healthcare." *Monthly Review,* 55. Retrieved February 25, 2010 (http://monthlyreview.org/0903navarro.htm).

Nocera, Joe. 2006. "If It's Good for Phillip Morris, Can It Also Be Good for Public Health?" *New York Times.* June 18.

Nyden, Phillip. 1997. *Building Community: Social Science in Action.* Thousand Oaks, CA: Pine Forge Press.

Pan American Health Organization. 2005. "WHO: Prepare Now for Influenza Pandemic." *PAHO Today,* April. Retrieved February 26, 2010 (http://www.paho.org/English/DD/PIN/ptoday05_apr05.htm).

Parsons, Talcott. 1951. *The Social System.* New York: The Free Press.

Quadagno, Jill. 2004. "Why the United States Has No National Health Insurance: Stakeholder Mobilization Against the Welfare State, 1955–1996." *Journal of Health and Social Behavior,* 45:25–44.

Reimer, Catherine Swan. 1999. *Counseling the Inupiat Eskimo.* Westport, CT: Greenwood Press.

Reinert, Bonita R. 2001. "Healthcare in Transition." Pp. 120-139 in *Community Health Nursing: Caring for the Public's Health,* edited by Karen Saucier Lundy and Sharyn James. Boston, MA: Jones and Bartlett.

Rellman, Arnold S. 1980. "The New Medical-Industrial Complex." *New England Journal of Medicine,* 22:19–48.

Robert Wood Johnson Foundation. 2005. *Going Without: America's Uninsured Children.* Washington, DC: Author. Retrieved February 25, 2010 (http://www.rwjf.org/files/newsroom/ckfresearchreportfinal.pdf).

Robison, Linda M., David A. Sclar, and Tracy L. Skaer. 2005. "Datapoints: Trends in ADHD and Stimulant Use Among Adults: 1995–2002." *Psychiatric Services,* 56:1497.

Russell, James W. 2006. *Double Standard: Social Policy in Europe and the United States.* Lanham, MD: Rowman & Littlefield.

Samuels, Robert. 2006. Healthful Foods Not an Option for Many: Poorer Areas Lack Access, Report Says." *The Washington Post.* July 13, p. DZ03. Retrieved September 24, 2006 (http://www.dchunger.org/Press/Articles/wpost7.13.06.html).

Schlosser, Eric. 2001. *Fast Food Nation: The Dark Side of the All-American Meal.* Boston, MA: Houghton Mifflin.

Schulz, Amy J., Edith Parker, Barbara Israel, Adam B. Becker, Barbara J. Maciak, and Rose Hollis. 1998. Conducting a Participatory Community-Based Survey for a Community Health Intervention on Detroit's East Side Public Health Management Practice, 4:10–24.

Schulz, Amy J., Edith Parker, Barbara Israel, Barbara Maciak, and Rose Hollis. 1998. "Detroit's East Side Village Health Worker Partnership: Community-Based Lay Health Advisor Intervention in an Urban Area." Public Health Management Practice, 25:24–45.

Schulz, Amy J., Srimathi Kannan, J. Timothy Dvonch, Barbara A. Israel, Alex Allen III, Sherman A. James, et al. 2005. "Social and Physical Environments and Disparities in Risk for Cardiovascular Disease: The Healthy Environments Partnership Conceptual Model." *Environmental Health Perspectives,* 113:1817–1825.

Schwartz, Kryn. 2007. *Spotlight on Uninsured Parents: How a Lack of Coverage Affects Parents and Their Families.* The Kaiser Family Foundation. Retrieved February 26, 2010 (http://www.kff.org/uninsured/upload/7662.pdf).

Seifer, Serena. 2000. "Engaging Colleges and Universities in Healthy Community Initiatives." *Public Health Reports,* 115:234–237.

Sered, Susan Starr and Rushika Fernandopulle. 2007. "Sick Out of Luck: The Uninsured in America." Pp. 290–296 in *Crisis in American Institutions,* edited by Jerome H. Skolnick and Elliot Currie. Boston, MA: Allyn & Bacon.

Shenon, Philip. 2006. "New Limits Set Over Marketing for Cigarettes." New York Times. August 18. Retrieved February 23, 2010 (http://www.nytimes.com/2006/08/18/washington/18tobacco.html).

Shrestha, Laura B. 2006. "Life Expectancy in the United States." Congressional Research Service, Library of Congress. Retrieved February 25, 2010 (http://aging.senate.gov/crs/aging1.pdf).

Sisko, Andrea, Christopher Truffer, Sheila Smith, Sean Keehan, Jonathan Cylus, John A. Poisal, et al. 2009. "Health Spending Projections Through 2018: Recession Effects Add Uncertainty to the Outlook." *Health Affairs,* 28:346–357.

Stevens, Rosemary A., Charles E. Rosenberg, and Lanton R. Burns. Editors 2006. *History and Health Policy in the United States: Putting the Past Back In.* Piscataway, NJ: Rutgers University Press.

UNAIDS. 2008. "2007 Aids Epidemic Update." April 16. Retrieved February 14, 2010 (http://www.unaids.org/en/KnowledgeCentre/HIVData/EpiUpdate/EpiUpdArchive/2007/default.asp).

U.S. Department of Health and Human Services. 2005. "Overview of the Uninsured in the United States: An Analysis of the 2005 Current Population Survey." *ASPE Issue Brief.*

Walsh, Joseph F., Jennifer Sage Smith, G. Christian Jernstedt, Virginia A. Reed, and Sara Goodman. 2000. "Partners in Health Education: Service-Learning by First-Year Medical Students." Pp. 35–75 in *Creating Community-Responsive Physicians: Concepts and Models for Service Learning in Medical Education,* edited by Serena D. Seifer, Kris Hermanns, and Judy Lewis. Washington, DC: American Association for Higher Education & Accreditation.

Ward, Elizabeth, Michael Halpern, Nicole Schrag, Vilma Cokkinides, Carol DeSantis, Priti Bandi, et al. 2007. "Association of Insurance With Cancer Care Utilization and Outcomes." *CA: Cancer Journal for Clinicians.* 11. Retrieved February 14, 2010 (http://caonline.amcancersoc.org/cgi/content/full/CA.2007.0011v1).

Ward, Kelly and Dana Grant. 2006. "Tribal Colleges: Responding to Cultural Needs." *Learn and Serve Higher Education: Disciplinary Pathways to Service Learning.* Retrieved December 15, 2006 (http://www.mc.maricopa.edu/other/engagement/pathways/tribal.html).

Washington, Harriet. 2007. *Medical Apartheid: The Dark History of Medical Experimentation on Black Americans.* New York: Doubleday.

White House Commission on Complementary and Alternative Medicine Policy. 2002. *Final Report.* Retrieved February 26, 2010 (http://www.whccamp.hhs.gov/).

Wolff, Marie, Staci Young, and Cheryl A. Maurana. 2001. "Community Advocates in Public Health." *American Journal of Public Health,* 19:1972–1973.

Woolf, Steven H., Robert E. Johnson, George E. Fryer, George Rust, and David Satcher. 2004. "The Health Impact of Resolving Racial Disparities: An Analysis of U.S. Mortality Data." *American Journal of Public Health,* 94:2078–2081.

Woolf, Steven H., Robert E. Johnson, and Jack Geiger. 2006. "The Rising Prevalence of Severe Poverty in America: A Growing Threat to Public Health." *American Journal of Preventive Medicine,* 31:332–341.

World Health Organization. 2006. "Why Is Tobacco a Public Health Priority?" Retrieved February 25, 2010 (http://74.125.155.132/scholar?q=cache:Hh49EN3vVr0J:scholar.google.com/+world+health+organization+who+2007+tobacco+and+poverty+&hl=en&as_sdt=8000000000000).

World Health Organization. 2009a. "Preparing for the Second Wave: Lessons From Current Outbreaks." *Global Alert and Response Geneva.* Retrieved February 14, 2010 (http://www.who.int/csr/disease/swineflu/notes/h1n1_second_wave_20090828/en/index.html).

World Health Organization. 2009b. *World Health Statistics.* Geneva, Switzerland: Author. Retrieved February 26, 2010 (http://www.who.int/whosis/whostat/2009/en/index.html).

Zuberi, Dan. 2006. *Differences That Matter: Social Policy and the Poor in the United States and Canada.* New York: Cornell University Press.

# The Whole Wide World Around

*Globalization and Its Discontents*

*That's why I define globalization this way: it is the inevitable integration of markets, nation-states and technologies to a degree never witnessed before—in a way that is enabling individuals, corporations and nation-states to reach around the world farther, faster, deeper and cheaper than ever before and in a way that is enabling the world to reach into individuals, corporations and nation-states farther, faster, and deeper, cheaper than ever before.*

—Thomas Friedman, *The Lexus and the Olive Tree* (1999)

*Never before has there been a system so ubiquitous, so destructive, and so well-managed. It is our creation.*

—Paul Hawken, *Blessed Unrest* (2007)

## AMIZADE AND GLOBALIZATION: SOLIDARITY AMONG THE RUINS

Following his own volunteer work in Brazil, Dan Weiss began a nonprofit organization called *Amizade* ("friendship" in Portuguese) to bring aid to poor communities around the world. Based on values of cultural exchange, volunteerism, and sustainability, Weiss premised his efforts on the notion that the source of social problems was the alienation and powerlessness of people in isolated communities. Amizade creates cross-cultural service learning experiences with the core philosophy that "bringing cultures together creates understanding, compassion, and a sense of purpose in people." The group explains, "As our world

becomes increasingly globalized, we are more aware than ever of the connection and commonalities among human beings the world over, but we often don't have the means to connect to each other in ways that go beyond the snapshot, the news article, or the clip on TV"
(www.amizade.org). Amizade offers students a deeper experience of people and cultures at
the same time that it partners with local service organizations to identify projects and programs (often "bricks and mortar" building efforts) that communities would otherwise have
difficulty developing.

A sample of Amizade's programs includes

- Building a vocational training center, children's health clinic, and a freshwater
  well-drilling center in the Tapajos region of Brazil;

- Building an orphanage and developing educational materials including a
  children's handbook on AIDS in Swahili in Tanzania;

- Building a new primary school, teaching computer courses and acting as
  counselors and tutors at a youth summer camp, and restoring houses for poor
  people in Jamaica.

Amizade has an especially deep-rooted relationship with the Universities of West
Virginia (UWV) and Pittsburgh (Pitt). Students from both institutions (and other colleges and universities as "visiting students") have participated in Amizade's program
in Northern Ireland where they learned about the history of the conflicts between
Protestants and Catholics while also helping in youth programs designed to support
young people who have experienced violence and family trauma. Some also worked
with Pitt biology and anthropology professor Linda Winkler to educate Tanzanian
children about AIDS, producing the children's handbook mentioned above. Professor
Reinhard Heinisch developed a political science course that began with 3 weeks of
traditional course work on campus studying the problems of development and
democracy in Andean society, Latin American political history, and the cultural and
historical elements of Andean peasant community life. The course then required
students to participate in a 3-week service learning project in Cochabamba, Bolivia,
where they partnered with a local government agency and helped construct a
perimeter wall for a local orphanage.

In 2000, Pitt faculty and students from the School of Education teamed with Amizade
and incorporated an extended spring break in Bolivia into a course designed to address
the pedagogical issues of international service learning. While the class discussed the
practical and theoretical issues involved in using service learning as a way of teaching
about international issues and cultures, faculty worked with Amizade to identify a suitable service project that students could do when "in country." According to instructors

**Image 10.1**   Dr. Reinhard Heinisch (University of Pittsburgh at Johnstown), his students, and residents of the Cochabamba community pose in front of the perimeter wall they built during a service project.

*Source:* Dr. Reinhard Heinisch.

in the International Service Learning Experience (ISLE) program, Maureen Porter and Kathia Monard (2001),

> Our criteria for a suitable project were: it must reflect actual and expressed needs of local people, the regional collaborating organizations must be well-integrated into the community, and the project could be accomplished in the very limited time available. Dr. Dan Weiss of Amizade [along] with local educators and grassroots community leaders revealed their priority on constructing the first adobe building of what would become an adult education complex. The labor promised to be muddy, physical, and engaging. We would be working hand-in-hand with local educators, activists, and residents. (p. 7)

Adult education was in great need, as increased globalization and a money-based economy required that this Bolivian community's adults acquire new skills that may have been unnecessary in the past. Local activists articulated the need for parents to have the literacy and technical skills to help their children learn as well.

Currently, Amizade's students receive credit through West Virginia University. A recent WVU graduate, Jonathan "Caleb" King participated in the Amizade program in Tanzania. His experiences led him to use an alumni association scholarship to return after the program and extend his travels into Uganda. After working in orphanages and hospitals in Uganda and helping to harvest rainwater in Tanzania, King explained the Amizade model: The group tries "to connect people across cultures . . . to make sort of an exchange, so that we can learn from (Africans), and they can learn from us. . . . I went over to Africa with a lot of American clothes on purpose. . . . We did sort of an exchange, I gave them some of my clothes, and they gave me some of theirs."

As the quotations that begin the chapter demonstrate, globalization has its triumphal boosters and its doomsday detractors. For some, globalization brings the promise of access to economic and informational resources around the world. As industries, jobs, computers, and the Internet spread consumer power and cultural diversity to every nook and cranny of the planet, globalization's advocates argue that all people will eventually acquire more economic, political, and cultural power. But for others, globalization is just a newer form of imperialism and exploitation where the poorest peoples in the world work harder, get paid less, and must struggle to survive in slum-ridden communities. At the same time these populations adapt to the end of their **indigenous economies,** they must also navigate challenges to their traditional social organizations and cultural practices—their identities and their ways of life. Regardless of overly optimistic or pessimistic portraits of globalization, the extent of recent technological changes in international economies, the global saturation of commercial culture and media images, and the rapidity with which indigenous traditions and ways of life are disappearing cannot be overstated.

Similar to the other social problems discussed in previous chapters, the basic elements of globalization may not be a problem per se, but the way in which they maintain or intensify inequalities and human suffering is. This chapter begins with a discussion of the definition of globalization; a description of its elements; and a statistical look at some of its impact on the world's economy, politics, and culture. We continue with a brief history of the World Trade Organization and the rise of the World Social Forum as a movement to challenge "corporate-led" globalization. Finally, we look at three case studies of students involved in various projects around the world addressing social problems related to globalization. Each case study takes on a major issue such as poverty, war, or global warming, but also offers an opportunity to look at how different sociological approaches inform practical efforts to address the social problems being examined.

But for students who have worked in Bolivia, the most powerful sociological lesson learned was the power of reciprocity and solidarity. As one student explained, "The more and more I worked, I realized that if we had . . . not actually worked side-by-side with the Bolivians it would have been a totally different experience. They showed us what Bolivia was about. I think we all learned something from each other" (Porter and Monard 2001:14).

Their teachers referred to this dynamic using the local language and tradition of ayni. According to the instructors, Porter and Monard,

> Simply, ayni is the exchange of comparable work or goods as part of an ongoing cycle of reciprocity. People enter into an ayni relationship with [others] to accomplish more than one group alone could manage. . . . [A]n ayni relationship indicates a shared responsibility to respond to mutual obligations and responsibilities. It is not a narrow, creedal statement of orthodox communal doctrine, but a covenant to unite and explore the meaning of community. It is also a promise that all parties will benefit as they, working together for the common good, serve a greater purpose than individual self-interest. (p. 7.)

For these faculty and students, the social problems of global poverty and illiteracy might be addressed, in part, by building schools and developing economies. But the larger issues of continued alienation and ignorance could only be addressed by building relationships. As another student wrote, "After experiencing everything that we did, I think that it will be hard not to feel that we belong to something bigger than just the University of Pittsburgh, ISLE, or even the Commonwealth of Pennsylvania, or even the United States of America, we belong as citizens of the world" (Porter and Monard 2001:14).

## GLOBALIZATION BY THE NUMBERS: A STATISTICAL PORTRAIT OF DYNAMICS AND PROBLEMS

From a sociological perspective, **globalization** refers to the major economic, political, and cultural changes that have occurred primarily since the 1960s and 1970s. These shifts include the intense saturation of a market economy, the rise of international governing bodies that regulate global political conflicts as well as world trade, and the international dominance of commercial and consumer cultures (especially as seen through the media, the Internet, etc.). The Global Policy Forum (2010) defines globalization this way:

> Human societies across the globe have established progressively closer contacts over many centuries, but recently the pace has dramatically increased. Jet airplanes, cheap telephone service, email, computers, huge oceangoing vessels, instant capital flows, all these have made the world more interdependent than ever. Multinational corporations manufacture products in many countries and sell to consumers around the world. Money, technology and raw materials move ever more swiftly across national borders. Along with products and finances, ideas and cultures circulate more freely. As a result, laws, economies, and social movements are forming at the international level. Many politicians, academics, and journalists treat these trends as both inevitable and (on the whole) welcome. But for billions of the world's people, business-driven globalization means uprooting old ways of life and threatening livelihoods and cultures.

While the economic impact of these trends seems the most dominant and notable, the political and cultural dynamics of globalization continue to change the very nature of people's everyday lives and the relative autonomy they have to control their own conditions. To better understand the scope of these changes, let's look at the three major elements of globalization: economic, political, and cultural change.

## The Economy

Most economists measure the impact of globalization by looking at how more and more countries around the world base more and more of their economic activity on international trade. In other words, the more a nation exports and imports commodities, provides both industrial and service sector jobs for multinational corporations, or increases the percentage of its gross domestic product (GDP) that is dependent on international trade, the more "globalized" that country becomes. Table 10.1 shows how these measures increased for almost all nations (rich, poor, and middle income) between the years 1990 and 2005. The figures represent the percentages of GDP that were dependent on global trade.

**Table 10.1**   Integration With the Global Economy

|  | Merchandise Trade | | Trade in Services | | Private Capital Flows | |
|---|---|---|---|---|---|---|
| Year | 1990 | 2005 | 1990 | 2005 | 1990 | 2005 |
| Low-income nations | 23.6 | 41.1 | 6.2 | 9.8 | 2.4 | 6.7 |
| Mid-income nations | 34.5 | 62.1 | 7.1 | 10.5 | 6.6 | 13.3 |
| Low/Mid income | 31.6 | 58.9 | 6.4 | 10.0 | 4.4 | 11.5 |
| Upper/Mid income | 38.3 | 66.4 | 8.0 | 11.1 | 7.9 | 15.7 |
| High-income nations | 32.3 | 43.9 | 7.9 | 11.1 | 11.0 | 37.2 |

*Source:* Adapted from World Bank data (http://siteresources.worldbank.org/DATASTATISTICS/Resources/table6_1.pdf).

Regardless of the wealth of the particular nation, almost all countries have seen their economies become significantly more intertwined with the global economy. *Merchandise trade* refers to the amount of exports and imports related to gross national product (GNP), while *trade in service* refers to how many services are imported or exported, which is also related to GNP. In each case above, these numbers have increased substantially, meaning that more and more countries have an increasing amount of their economic activities that are dependent on economic relationships with other countries.

Much of this trade has been fueled by the ability of manufacturers to shift production from wealthier industrialized nations (like the United States and France) to poorer industrializing nations (such as Mexico and China). While some of this shift has brought jobs to previously unindustrialized areas of the world, it has also destroyed indigenous economies and cultures. For example, in a rural region of Kerala, India, called Palakkad, farmers and their workers produced sustainable crops for local markets and coconut and rice for the national and international marketplace. In 2000, however, Coca-Cola built a bottling plant that provided almost 150 jobs for local people and thousands of dollars for the local economy. But plant operations require over 1.5 million liters of water a day, which has tapped most of the community dry. According to the London newspaper *The Independent* (Vallely, Clarke, and Stuart 2003),

> The cruelest twist is that the plant bottles a brand of mineral water while local people—who could never afford it—have to walk up to six miles twice a day to fetch water. The turbid, brackish water which remains at the bottom of their wells is now too high in dissolved salts to be healthy to drink, cook with or even wash in. (n.p.)

While local landowners have been hurt, the worst affected have been landless agricultural workers—some 10,000 of whom have lost their jobs. (Aiyer 2007)

The loss of indigenous economies and the simultaneous boom in the service sectors of wealthy nations have also set in motion labor migrations more extensive than at any other time in world history. And while the impact of such immigration for wealthy nations such as the United States has been discussed previously in Chapter 3, the most striking thing about contemporary migrations is that many poor workers migrate from one poor nation to another poor nation—just not as poor as their own. The chart in Figure 10.1 shows how poverty and other conditions (such as civil wars and violence in places like Colombia and Haiti) force people to seek work in Panama and Venezuela (for Colombians) and the Dominican Republic (for Haitians) even though these countries have relatively low standards of living themselves. In part, these are regional migrations that take advantage of nations whose economies became global earlier in the process of deindustrialization—Mexico, India, and Malaysia, for example. But these dynamics also reflect the political machinations of wealthier nations that find they must ratchet up restrictions on immigration. Some nations cannot provide the services necessary to support immigrants, while others have experienced strong anti-immigrant social movements and cultural prejudices. Whatever the internal forces, however, migrant workers from the poorest countries in the world are redirecting their strategies for seeking work in the global economy.

**Figure 10.1**  Migration of Workers to Poor, Developing Countries From Poorer, Even Less Developed Countries

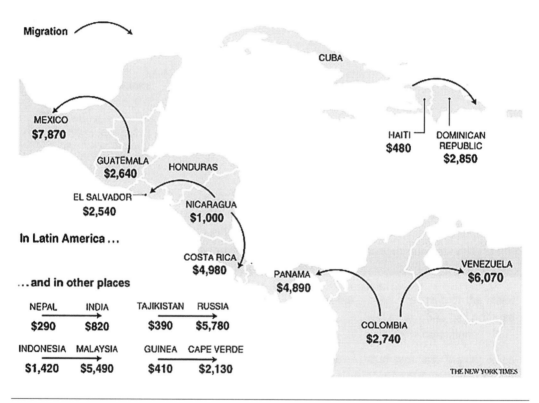

## Migrating to Poor Countries, Searching for a Better Life

Across the developing world, tens of millions of people move to poor countries from even poorer ones. Some move to neighboring countries where per capita incomes are many times higher. Below are some common origins and destinations, and the average per capita incomes of the countries involved.

Migration

CUBA

MEXICO
$7,870

HAITI — DOMINICAN
$480      REPUBLIC
         $2,850

GUATEMALA    HONDURAS
$2,640

EL SALVADOR
$2,540          NICARAGUA
                $1,000

In Latin America . . .

COSTA RICA
$4,980          PANAMA          VENEZUELA
                $4,890          $6,070

...and in other places

COLOMBIA
$2,740

| NEPAL | INDIA | TAJIKISTAN | RUSSIA |
|-------|-------|------------|--------|
| $290  | $820  | $390       | $5,780 |

| INDONESIA | MALAYSIA | GUINEA | CAPE VERDE |
|-----------|----------|--------|------------|
| $1,420    | $5,490   | $410   | $2,130     |

THE NEW YORK TIMES

*Source: New York Times,* December 27, 2007 (http://www.nytimes.com/imagepages/2007/12/27/world/20071227_MIGRATION_GRAPHIC.html).

Regardless of labor migration patterns and national strategies to become more competitive in the global economy, global inequality remains the most dominant social problem in the world. A recent study by the World Institute for Development Economics Research of the United Nations University, Helsinki (Nissanke 2006), shows that, in the year 2000,

- The wealthiest 2% of the world's households owned more than half its wealth;

- The richest 1% of adults (worth at least $500,000) controlled 40% of all assets;

- The richest 10% of adults (worth at least $61,000) owned 85% of all assets;

- The poorest 50% of adults (worth less than $2,200) owned barely 1% of assets.

The following map (Figure 10.2) demonstrates how uneven wealth per capita is on a global scale. The wealthiest nations have assets over $50,000 per person, while the poorest nations have less than $2,000 per person. But a more striking contrast is that almost three-quarters of the world possesses less than $10,000 per capita.

**Figure 10.2** World Wealth Levels, 2000

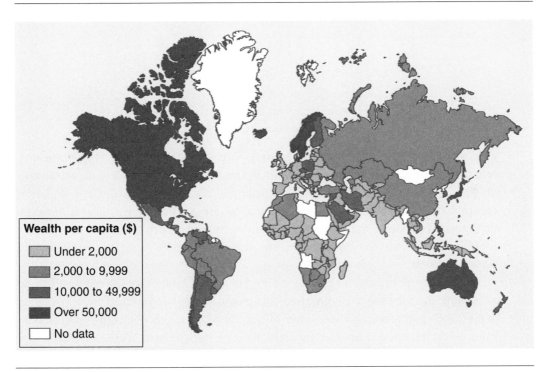

*Source: Impact of Globalization on the World's Poor,* 2006, by Machiko Nissanke, Helsinki, Finland: UNU-WIDER.

On a regional basis, this distribution of wealth is even starker. Figure 10.3 shows that North America, Europe, and the wealthiest countries of the Asia-Pacific region possess almost 90% of the world's entire wealth, while Africa, India and China (three of the

**Figure 10.3**  Global Wealth by Region

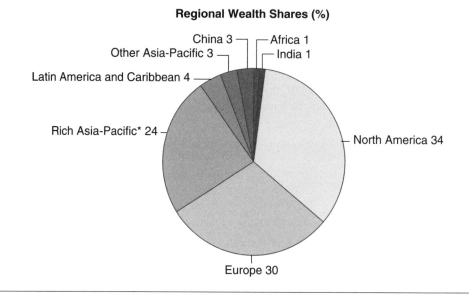

**Regional Wealth Shares (%)**

China 3 — ┌ Africa 1
Other Asia-Pacific 3 ┐ ┌ India 1
Latin America and Caribbean 4 ┐
Rich Asia-Pacific* 24 ┤ ├ North America 34
Europe 30

*Source:* World Institute for Development Economics Research of the United Nations (2006).

\* Rich Asia-Pacific includes Japan, Taiwan, and South Korea.

most populous areas in the world) control only 5%. Meanwhile, it is important to remember that within each nation, wealth is also highly stratified. As demonstrated in Chapter 2, within the United States, for example, the richest 10% of the population controls 70% of the wealth. Even in China, where globalization's biggest boosters point toward the democratizing influence and increased wealth created by the nation's rapid economic internationalization, the inequality index has risen dramatically since the 1980s.

According to globalization's optimists, time and market economies will eventually bring all nations into the same economic fold, and inequality will diminish as larger segments of the Earth's populations compete more effectively. As detractors point out, however, such gains would require that workers' incomes increase, not decrease. Yet the very dynamics of globalization have intensified competition between workers and among nations to such an extent that wages have been driven down around the globe. Originally, outsourcing and labor migrations impacted industrial and service jobs only. But today, even professional and highly skilled technological jobs are being outsourced from wealthy to developing nations, once again driving down wages for the middle class. For over a decade, sociologists and other critics have referred to this downward spiral of wages and working conditions as a **"race to the bottom"** for workers (Brecher and Costello 1998, emphasis added). Only strong international regulations would be able to guarantee workers decent wages and safer working conditions. However, just as globalization radically altered economic conditions, it has also changed the distribution of political power for international decision making and rule setting.

## Politics and Government

The beginning of the 20th century featured the initial efforts to bring about an international organization of individual countries. Two conventions (in 1899 and 1907) in the Netherlands resulted in the Hague Confederation of States, a global alliance for peacefully resolving disputes among nations. While these efforts resulted in effective rules for war and policies regarding war crimes (a direct predecessor to the Geneva Conventions of 1925), these meeting fell short of a comprehensive and enduring global body to negotiate among nations. Following World War I, the League of Nations was founded as a second attempt to create an international organization that touted disarmament, diplomacy, and the prevention of violence and conflict through negotiation and improving human conditions. Despite the support of major world leaders including U.S. President Woodrow Wilson, the League, too, failed to gain the consensus, power, and legitimacy necessary to shape global affairs. The outbreak of World War II exposed the League's weaknesses and the body disbanded (Rothe and Mullins 2006).

Following World War II, international leaders once again convened with the goal of creating a world organization of member states that could facilitate cooperation in international law and security, economic development, and human rights. Unlike previous efforts, however, the United Nations Organization succeeded in acquiring the necessary economic support and political legitimacy to establish itself as a credible source for international diplomacy and regulation. The **United Nations (UN)** eventually established three main areas of work: peace and security, human rights and humanitarian assistance, and social and economic development. The UN also maintains important world policy and regulation committees such as the World Atomic Energy Agency, the World Health Organization, the UN Educational, Social and Cultural Organization (UNESCO), and the World Bank. Despite numerous criticisms of the organization's inability to address political and military crises such as genocide in Rwanda, the Israeli–Palestinian conflict, or the U.S. invasion of Iraq, the UN remains the only viable international body that can effectively intervene in conflicts between nations and address the major health, environmental, poverty, and human rights issues around the world.

In 2000, the UN set eight Millennium Development Goals (MDGs) ranging from halving extreme global poverty to halting the spread of HIV/AIDS and providing universal primary education, all by the target date of 2015. According to the UN website, these goals (listed next) are "from a blueprint agreed to by all the world's countries and all the world's leading development institutions" (n.p.).

## UNITED NATIONS EIGHT MILLENNIUM GOALS

Goal 1: Eradicate Extreme Hunger and Poverty

Goal 2: Achieve Universal Primary Education

Goal 3: Promote Gender Equality and Empower Women

Goal 4: Reduce Child Mortality

Goal 5: Improve Maternal Health

Goal 6: Combat HIV/AIDS, Malaria and Other Diseases

Goal 7: Ensure Environmental Sustainability

Goal 8: Develop a Global Partnership for Development

*Source:* United Nations website (http://www.un.org/millenniumgoals/).

Former UN Secretary General Kofi Annan (2005) explained that reaching these goals could only be accomplished by breaking with "business as usual." He continued,

> Success will require sustained action across the entire decade between now and the deadline. It takes time to train the teachers, nurses and engineers; to build the roads, schools and hospitals; to grow the small and large businesses able to create the jobs and income needed. So we must start now. (n.p.)

The United Nations, however, was not the only post–World War II institution to impact global governance and affairs. In 1944, representatives from the 44 Allied Powers met in New Hampshire's Bretton Woods to develop an international monetary system of rules, institutions, and policies. This group established both the World Bank and the International Monetary Fund at these meetings. The **World Bank** focused on infrastructure and rebuilding following the war, but soon it also targeted undeveloped, poorer nations that never had much of an industrial infrastructure even before World War II. The **International Monetary Fund (IMF),** on the other hand, was given the responsibility of monitoring and facilitating international trade. Both groups have been responsible for lending trillions of dollars to countries around the world (Kenan 1994).

While some of these loans were effective in helping nations rebuild or innovate (especially those to already economically stable or successful countries), most loans to poorer or undeveloped nations merely increased their debt without giving them an effective way to repay them. These next two figures demonstrate the level of debt incurred by developing nations: Figure 10.4a shows the rapid increase in debt service

**Figure 10.4a**   Debt Service of Developing Countries

**Figure 10.4b**   Foreign Debt of Developing and Former USSR Countries

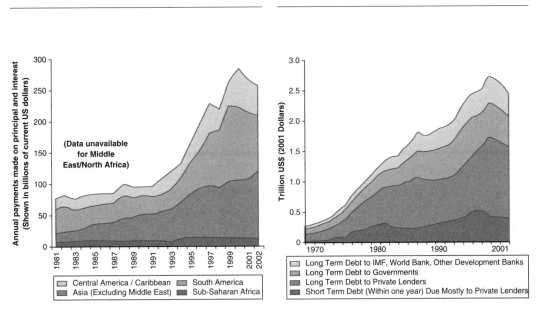

payments (made on principal and interest) owed by the poorest nations in four developing regions around the world. The chart in Figure 10.4b portrays the total debt owed by these nations (including the countries of the former Soviet Union) to other nations. While a small portion of this debt is short term, most of the debt is long term and is owed to other governments, private lenders, or the IMF or World Bank.

Building these mountains of debt created untenable situations for most developing nations, but the most salient point for understanding the impact of globalization on governance and politics is to look at who controls these international monetary organizations. Figure 10.5 demonstrates which nations have the lion's share of control in governing the IMF and World Bank. The chart shows that the United States has the most power in decision making, holding about 15% of the voting shares. While this is about twice as much as any other nation, it isn't necessarily a controlling share. Still, the countries of the G8 (Group of Eight, representing eight of the world's largest national economies) control over half of the organizations' operating shares. Thus, while the wealthiest nations of the world make decisions regarding loans, debt, and repayment services, the poorest nations have little if any control over the parameters of the loans they must ask for and the debt they consequently accrue.

**Figure 10.5** Voting Control of the IMF and World Bank, 2005

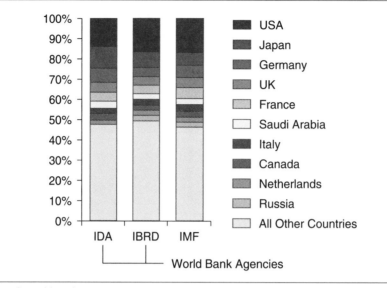

*Source:* © World Bank.

One major critique of these lending agencies has been the stipulations required of debtor nations called **structural adjustment programs (SAPs).** From the perspective of lenders such as the IMF and World Bank, structural adjustments were necessary for debtor nations to use loans successfully. After years of unsuccessful loans, these institutions believed that financial support was insufficient to boost the economies of poorer nations. Thus, they shifted to SAP loans that required countries to make significant policy changes to liberalize markets and promote entrepreneurism and privatization. In many poor countries, SAPs resulted in an end to government-run or -supported health care, work and poverty programs, government-owned industries, and a variety of other state-subsidized services (Easterly 2003).

Critics of SAPs argue that these policy changes have only deepened inequality by forcing poorer nations to end support and services to the poor. Instead, these governments devote resources to corporate enterprises focused on cash crops and export commodities. According to Kevin Danaher (1994), these policies allow foreign investors to swoop in and buy up industries previously operated by national governments. They also promote exports, especially in rural areas where poor people, who once grew crops primarily for subsistence and then small surpluses for local trade, now lose their land to large plantations growing cash crops for foreign markets or sell land to corporations looking to move large manufacturing plants to countries with few regulations and cheap land and labor. SAPs even encourage governments to impose use fees for services such as education and clean drinking water. Regardless of how small these fees may be, in poor countries such costs can be prohibitive. According to World Bank research (Dollar and Svensson 2000), SAPs have only succeeded in nations where policy changes were already taking place and reforms didn't devastate public services and poverty relief. But for critics, even in these so-called "successful nations," economic growth and stability has resulted in worse conditions for the poor.

The rise of the United Nations and economic agencies like the IMF and World Bank demonstrates some of globalization's dynamics as they represent the movement toward international decision-making and regulating agencies. While this is not in and of itself a social problem, the impact such changes have on the increased debt and poverty of poorer nations is a significant problem. The lack of power that these nations have in decision-making bodies and the decision-making process results in a loss of state autonomy and democracy within nations as well as between them. As we will see later in the chapter, the newest international regulating agency, the **World Trade Organization (WTO),** has only strengthened these dynamics, further centralizing power in the hands of wealthier nations and increasing the distance between rich and poor. At the same time that the politics of globalization place political power in the hands of organizations dominated by the wealthiest nations, the cultural aspects of global commercial markets have brought the cultural and aesthetic tastes of peoples from around the world into the living spaces and dining areas of every nook and cranny of civilization.

## GARBAGE AND RECYCLING IN DEVELOPING NATIONS: THE WASTE PICKERS

**Image 10.2**   La Chureca: Managua, Nicaragua's city waste dump.

(Continued)

Families and children routinely scavenge in landfills and on streets in many of the poorest nations around the world. Since most poor countries do not recycle, an informal economy of street workers called *waste pickers* plays a role in waste disposal and retrieval. Waste pickers can earn 3 times the minimum wage in an industry that is easily learned. In many developing countries, waste pickers are newly arrived immigrants or religious minorities. In Quezon City, the former capital of the Philippines, an estimated 1,500 children work with 13,000 other scavengers in landfills on a daily basis (International Labor Organization [ILO] 2002). W. Alexander Long's (2002) research on the Pepenadores in Xalapa, Mexico, exposes us to a world away from our kitchens and garbage cans. Over 600 waste pickers work in Guadalajara's largest dump. They make a living and provide a type of recycling service in a country without recycling. The Pepenadores risk serious health problems from handling and inhaling hazardous waste and other injuries by cleaning out landfills of sellable materials. Mexico's lack of recycling supports the waste pickers' industry, which has organized buyers and even a union that regulates the trade. Waste pickers pay the Department of Public Works a monthly fee in return for access to the site and a storage area. These waste pickers are not the poorest members of society. The materials they find and sell are anything from plastic milk containers to scrap metals. The United States also contributes to waste pickers and toxic waste overseas. According to "Exporting Harm: The High-Tech Trashing of Asia," a 2002 report by the Basel Action Network and the Silicon Valley Toxics Coalition (2002), the United States exports hundreds of thousands of supposedly recycled computers to China, India, and other poor Asian countries where they are most often dismantled for parts and burned. The fast turnover of new-model computers has led to the exporting of older models, which are leading to toxic waste dumps in countries without environmental standards. Should the United States charge consumers and producers to dispose of technology and "e-waste" to make disposal safer?

## Culture and Commercialism

One of the great progressive dreams of globalization is that the international marketplace will allow artists and other cultural workers to share their creativity with others around the world. The indigenous craftwork, dazzling music and dance, and fine cuisine from Asia and Africa, Latin America, and elsewhere would be available to consumers in the wealthier nations of Western Europe and the United States, while technology and media; advanced drugs and other medical treatments; and of course, Coke, McDonald's, and Starbucks would be available in even the most remote areas of poorer countries. To some degree, this dream has come true. International travel and especially the Internet have brought the world's great cultural diversity to the desktops of most working-class people in developed nations. As Fitzgerald (1997) has written,

Of course, some high-profile brands are global in nature—fast food chains, soft drinks and fragrances—and their international consumers are buying into a worldwide lifestyle concept. Modern communications and travel are allowing consumers across the globe to experience things once the preserve of the very few. Satellite dishes can now be seen in even the most remote South American and Asian villages. Those villages are no longer so remote; they see on their television screens what the developed world has to offer. (p. 742)

Moreover, some of the great advancements in technology and medicine have filtered (although more slowly) into the poorer countries of the world, making computers and prophylactic drugs more available. Globalization, as a force for democratizing technology and information and enriching lives with greater access to art, music, food, and world culture in general, cannot be denied.

Of course, not only have the medicines and technologies of industrialized nations seeped across the borders and into the consciousness of less developed nations, but so too have more pervasive and insidious commodities. The following map (Figure 10.6) demonstrates the saturation levels that international fast food and coffee companies have reached.

**Figure 10.6**   The Global Penetration of American Food Culture

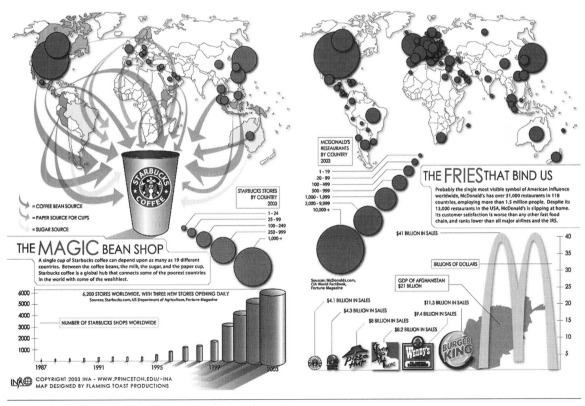

*Source:* Used with permission of International Networks Archive.

While Starbucks is small in comparison to McDonald's (and even Burger King and Wendy's), its startling growth in just the years 1999–2003 once suggested it was only a matter of time before lattes reached the global proportions of burgers and fries. The recent economic crisis, however, has impacted Starbucks' growth, resulting in many store closures and demonstrating that expensive coffee drinks may be more market precarious than cheaply made meat and potato products.

If these commodities were innocuous and only spread consumer choice around the globe, we might not consider this saturation a social problem. Unfortunately, these products come with high costs. As Eric Schlosser (2002) and others have examined, McDonald's and fast food companies like it change entire systems of food production around the world. This results in dangers to the global environment as well as to local, sustainable economies (see McLibel box on page 390). On a social level, they replace cultural food practices, usually resulting in greater health problems. For instance, increased consumption of fast food hamburgers and related foods like French fries, chicken nuggets/tenders, tacos, and so forth have proven to heighten risks of heart disease; liver disease; and other conditions related to high-fat, high-sugar, and high-carbohydrate diets. One of the most troubling health problems reaching epidemic proportions around the globe is obesity. As described in the previous chapter, the rising amount of fat in daily diets around the world threatens to introduce serious diseases and medical conditions once unknown to these countries.

One way to understand how corporate globalization and culture interact is to look at the correlation between obesity rates and the number of fast food restaurants in a nation. Table 10.2 presents the top 15 industrialized countries in terms of the number of McDonald's restaurants and their corresponding rank in obesity levels.

**Table 10.2**  Comparing the Relationship Between Nations' Obesity Rankings and Numbers of McDonald's Restaurants, 2008

| Country Rank in # of McDonald's | # of McDonald's | Rank in Obesity |
|---|---|---|
| 1. United States | 12,804 | 1 |
| 2. Japan | 3,598 | 28 |
| 3. Canada | 1,154 | 11 |
| 4. United Kingdom | 1,115 | 3 |
| 5. Germany | 1,091 | 14 |
| 6. France | 857 | 23 |
| 7. Australia | 701 | 6 |
| 8. Taiwan | 338 | below 30 |

| Country Rank in # of McDonald's | # of McDonald's | Rank in Obesity |
| --- | --- | --- |
| 9. China | 326 | below 30 |
| 10. Italy | 290 | 25 |
| 11. Spain | 276 | 12 |
| 12. South Korea | 233 | 29 |
| 13. Philippines | 235 | 30 |
| 14. Sweden | 227 | 21 |
| 15. Netherlands | 205 | 15 |
| 16. Mexico | 205 | 2 |

*Source:* Compiled from www.NationMaster.com with original data from McDonald's Corp. and the Organisation for Economic Co-operation and Development.

Most non-Asian countries with high numbers of McDonald's restaurants have some of the highest levels of obesity. But why do Asian countries with high numbers of McDonald's not have obesity problems of note? One reason is that, while these countries feature some of the standard McDonald's fare such as burgers and fries, much of the menu is composed of more regional cuisine with the majority of main items being fish based. In other words, the food itself is based more on local diets and tastes, which are low fat in nature. A second factor is that the social and cultural practices of the regions have shaped the ways in which people buy and eat McDonald's food in the first place. According to Watson (1997), many Japanese adults don't think of McDonald's as a place for a meal so much as a place for a snack, since to older Japanese, a meal must include rice. While adults rush in and out of McDonald's, many Japanese young people will remain for hours, sharing several orders of French fries and doing homework. Most meals are still eaten with families in large groups at home. In Asian countries where native cultures and economies are strong, even the pervasiveness of Western corporate commodities are significantly mitigated by regional conditions.

But in countries with weaker local economies and little political power, cultural ways of life are radically changed and the impact on health can be devastating. A prime example of this dynamic has occurred in many of the Pacific Island nations. Of all countries, industrialized and not, those with the highest levels of obesity are the Cook Islands, Micronesia, Nauru, Niue, and Tonga. Why? Because since World War II, these island nations have been colonial territories or trusteeships of industrialized nations such as the United States, Great Britain, Australia, and New Zealand. As such, they were inundated with Western commodities and a cash economy based on government employment funded by colonial protectors.

According to Curtis (2003), "For thousands of years, the inhabitants of the Pacific Islands were isolated from the rest of the world, allowing their social, cultural, and economic patterns to develop untouched" (p. 38). When European "explorers" did pass through sporadically in the 17th and 18th centuries, they noted the islands' "strong and muscular" people (Hughes 2003, cited in Curtis). As religious missionaries arrived in the 19th and early 20th centuries, some tried to change local customs and cultures, not only by preaching Christian religions, but also by teaching local women the "proper way" to feed their families. Island women were taught "[t]o bake tarts and serve a roast beef dinner in order to keep their families healthy" (Pollock 1992:182). Aside from the obvious health impact of increased fats and sugars, the only way for local islanders to get these products was by paying for imports with money. Pollock calls this a form of "dietary colonialism," a variation on the theme of **cultural imperialism** that refers to the spread of dominant countries' cultural products and values to less powerful nations, either by force or by market imperatives.

## MCLIBEL

In 1990, McDonald's sued five London Greenpeace activists for libel. The company based its suit on a leaflet that the activists were handing out as part of an annual International Day of Action against McDonald's. Three of the five Greenpeace members plea-bargained an agreement by reluctantly apologizing to the company, but two activists pursued their defense in court. Helen Steele and David Morris spent the next 15 years fighting the corporation on the grounds that their information leaflets were accurate and protected by free speech. After struggling through the longest civil trial in British history, the duo eventually succeeded in winning at least a partial victory in 1997, as the judge found suitable grounds for their claims "that McDonald's 'exploit children' with their advertising, falsely advertise their food as nutritious, risk the health of their most regular, long-term customers, are 'culpabably responsible' for cruelty to animals, are 'strongly antipathetic' to unions and pay their workers low wages" (www.mcspotlight.org/case/). They were, however, found guilty of libel on other claims where the court found "no basis" for arguments about McDonald's role in rainforest depletion and world hunger. Steele and Morris appealed the decision, and in 1999, three Lord Justices found McDonald's even more culpable than in the initial cases, handing the Greenpeace activists almost a complete victory. Steele and Morris's final triumph came when the European Court ruled that UK laws had failed to protect the public's right to criticize massive corporations whose business practices can affect people's lives, health, and the environment. The European Court has now agreed that the "McLibel" defendants were denied a fair trial due to the complex and oppressive nature of the UK libel laws, and the lack of legal aid and resulting imbalance in resources between them and McDonald's.

*Source:* http://www.mcspotlight.org/case/pretrial/factsheet.html.

(The material below is quoted from a factsheet called "What's Wrong With McDonald's," published by the Anti-McDonald's Campaign in Nottingham, UK.)

McDonald's spends over $2 billion every year worldwide on advertising and promotions, trying to cultivate an image of being a "caring" and "green" company that is also a fun place to eat. Children are lured in (dragging their parents behind them) with the promise of toys and other gimmicks. But behind the smiling face of Ronald McDonald lies the reality—McDonald's only interest is money, making profits from whoever and whatever they can, just like all multinational companies. McDonald's Annual Reports talk of "global domination"—they aim to open more and more stores across the globe—but their continual worldwide expansion means more uniformity, less choice, and the undermining of local communities.

### Promoting Unhealthy Food

McDonald's promotes their food as "nutritious," but the reality is that it is junk food—high in fat, sugar, and salt, and low in fibre and vitamins. A diet of this type is linked with a greater risk of heart disease, cancer, diabetes and other diseases. Their food also contains many chemical additives, some of which may cause ill-health, and hyperactivity in children. Don't forget too that meat is the cause of the majority of food poisoning incidents. In 1991 McDonald's was responsible for an outbreak of food poisoning in the UK, in which people suffered serious kidney failure. With modern intensive farming methods, other diseases—linked to chemical residues or unnatural practices—have become a danger to people too (such as BSE).

### Robbing the Poor

Vast areas of land in poor countries are used for cash crops or for cattle ranching, or to grow grain to feed animals to be eaten in the West. This is at the expense of local food needs. McDonald's continually promotes meat products, encouraging people to eat meat more often, which wastes more and more food resources. [A total of] 7 million tons of grain fed to livestock produces only 1 million tons of meat and by-products. On a plant-based diet and with land shared fairly, almost every region could be self-sufficient in food.

### Damaging the Environment

Forests throughout the world—vital for all life—are being destroyed at an appalling rate by multinational companies. McDonald's has at last been forced to admit to using beef reared on ex-rainforest land, preventing its regeneration. Also, the use of farmland by multinationals and their suppliers forces local people to move on to other areas and cut down further trees. McDonald's is the world's largest user of beef. Methane emitted by cattle reared for the beef industry is a major contributor to the "global warming" crisis. Modern intensive agriculture is based on the heavy use of chemicals which are damaging to the environment. Every year McDonald's use thousands of tons of unnecessary packaging, most of which ends up littering our streets or polluting the land buried in landfill sites.

*(Continued)*

(Continued)

**What You Can Do**

Together we can fight back against the institutions and the people in power who dominate our lives and our planet, and we can create a better society without exploitation. Workers can and do organise together to fight for their rights and dignity. People are increasingly aware of the need to think seriously about the food we and our children eat. People in poor countries are organising themselves to stand up to multinationals and banks which dominate the world's economy. Environmental and animal rights protests and campaigns are growing everywhere. Why not join in the struggle for a better world. Talk to friends and family, neighbours and workmates about these issues. Please copy and circulate this leaflet as widely as you can. (n.p.)

After World War II, however, such conditions expanded in a hurry as an influx of Western commodities, technology, and government spending flooded the Pacific Islands. According to Curtis (2003), "The traditional foods of the islands such as fresh fish, meat, and local fruits and vegetables have been replaced by rice, sugar, flour, canned meats, canned fruits and vegetables, soft drinks and beer. The diet is high in calories with little nutritional value." Their reliance on this nonlocal menu has had many important commercial and health impacts. First, retailers no longer stock locally grown or caught commodities and rely on imported, high-fat, high-density foods, thus destroying local markets and the foundation for any local economy. Meanwhile, the transition from agricultural and farming work to office or retail work has sharply decreased the physical activity of Pacific Islanders. As locals traded in canoes and walking for motorized boats and cars, the need to compete in a cash economy has also introduced stress and all of its health factors into their cultural mix. The current result for the Pacific Islanders from Micronesia, Nauru, Niue, Tonga, and the Cook Islands is the highest rates of obesity in the world (between 60 and 80% of the population) and accompanying problems with diabetes, heart disease, and so on.

Thus, while the **global integration** of culture and knowledge brings exotic commodities and culture from the world's newly discovered nooks and crannies to the kitchens and gardens of industrialized nations, and brings advanced medical and communication technologies to places where now-preventable and treatable diseases such as malaria and tuberculosis once killed millions, it remains a double-edged sword that cuts through the hearts and flesh of indigenous communities everywhere. The UN Commission on Human Rights explains that:

Indigenous or aboriginal peoples are so-called because they were living on their lands before settlers came from elsewhere; they are the descendants—according to one definition—of those who inhabited a country or a geographical region at the time when people of different cultures or ethnic origins arrived, the new arrivals later becoming dominant through conquest, occupation, settlement or other means. (UN Permanent Forum on Indigenous Issues, 2010:n.p.)

Globalization's threat to indigenous peoples became so notable that the United Nations declared 1993 as the Year of Indigenous Peoples to try and raise global awareness and economic and political support. Below (Figure 10.7) is a map produced by the International Forum on Globalization (IFG) that locates hundreds of the over 5,000 different indigenous groups recognized around the world, and lists the variety of different commercial, political and environmental problems attacking their cultural integrity and survival.

**Figure 10.7**   Impact of Globalization on Indigenous Peoples

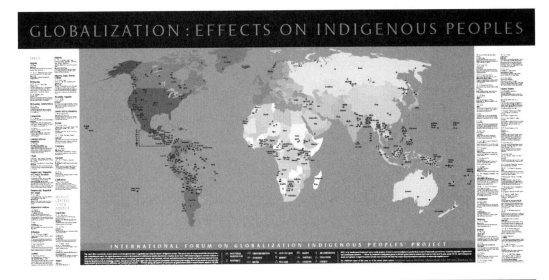

*Source:* International Forum on Globalization (full map available at www.ifg.org/programs/indig/IFGmap.pdf).

According to the IFG website (http://www.ifg.org/programs/indig.htm),

- Indigenous peoples throughout the world sit on the "frontlines" of globalization's expansion; they occupy the last pristine places on earth, where resources are still abundant: forests, minerals, water, and genetic diversity . . . and all are ferociously sought by global corporations, trying to push traditional societies off their land.

- New advances in technology, the reorientation toward export-led development, and the imperatives of pleasing global financial markets are all driving forces in the extermination of countless native communities which stand in their way.

- Traditional sovereignty over hunting and gathering rights has been thrown into question as national governments bind themselves to new global economic treaties.

- New trade agreements, which are opening up previously inaccessible territory to industrial extraction of natural resources, have forced indigenous peoples to defend their homelands under an invasion of unprecedented rate and scale: Big dams, mines, pipelines, roads, energy developments, [and] military intrusions all threaten native lands." (n.p.)

Globalization itself cannot be seen as inherently good or bad, as arguments made on either side will seem relative depending on particular interest groups or issues. But it is impossible to overlook the social problems either brought on or exacerbated by the scope, rapidity, and sometimes ferocity with which global markets, technology, and environmental devastation have occurred. For many, the main issue is not simply globalization, but whether globalization is led and shaped by powerful nations and corporations (from above) or by noncorporate and nongovernmental groups of citizens without traditional sources of power (from below). According to Brecher, Costello, and Smith (2000), "**Globalization from below** has emerged from diverse concerns and experiences" (environmentalists, poor people's movements, small farmers and their advocates, labor unions, women's movements, consumer movements, and college students), but despite "varied agendas, the movement's unifying mission is to bring about sufficient democratic control over states, markets and corporations to insure a viable future for people and the planet" (p. 180, emphasis added).

## GLOBALIZATION AND THE ENVIRONMENT

Globalization is altering the nature of environmental activism. Increasingly, international movements link environmental concerns with other social problems connected to development. Activists and scholars have created the concept of sustainable development to characterize this integration of social issues with environmental concerns (Bullard 2005; Elliot 2006). In fact, by initiating the idea of sustainable development, proponents hope to transcend the years of conflict between those who promoted economic development at the cost of environmental safety, and those who argue that one must protect the environment regardless of economic costs. Nowhere are these struggles more apparent than in developing nations, many of which believe they cannot worry about environmental hazards as they are being devastated by poverty. Developing nations' impact on the environment reflects their struggle to meet basic needs, escape the conditions of post-colonialism and militarism, and develop within the global economy.

As post-colonial nations began to develop after the Second World War, the green revolution (1960 to 1975) led to increases in food production on large land holdings due to high-yielding seeds and low-cost oil-based fertilizers, herbicides, pesticides, and tractor fuel. The percentage of people in developing countries without adequate food declined from 50% in 1960 to 20% in the mid-1970s (Shiva 1992). As more chemical fertilizers are used throughout the world, environmental pollution has become a concern.

The causes of pollution in developing nations are not only chemical use but also military production and conflict, population increases, and rapid urbanization. In urban areas, developing nations continue to use a variety of chemicals and materials that are no longer legal in developed nations. The continued use of asbestos, polychlorinated biphenyls (PCBs), and persistent organic pollutants (PCPs) endangers water supplies, fish stocks, and human health in many nations around the world. In addition to the use of dangerous technology, dumping from developed countries and export processing zones is also a cause of environmental problems due to few regulations. Communities and waterways near the *maquiladoras* exporting zone on the U.S.–Mexico border are exposed to dangerous chemicals such as xylene, which causes respiratory irritation; organ hemorrhages, and lung, liver, and kidney damage. Heavy metals, untreated sewage, and agricultural runoff contaminate water sources in watersheds on both sides of the border, endangering communities and wildlife. Corporations profit and their global consumers save money because of the lack of environmental regulations and low-wage labor.

The impacts of environmental problems are not equally distributed. The worst environmental effects are experienced by the poorest developing nations who face a daily struggle for water, food, education, and shelter. Bullard (2005) describes the world's water situation: "Dirty water is the world's deadliest pollutant. Lack of clean water and adequate sanitation contributes each year to approximately 2 billion diarrhea infections and 4 million deaths, mostly among infants and young children in developing countries" (p. 282). Globally, every year contaminated drinking water, untreated human excrement, and air pollution combined account for 7.7 million deaths, or 15% of the global death toll of 52 million. Air pollution kills 2.7 million worldwide each year (Agyeman 2005; Bullard 2005).

The struggle for survival leads individuals to sacrifice natural and sustainable processes of production and consumption in return for seeking the money or wages necessary to *buy* basic necessities. Development theorists suggest that water scarcity and quality will likely determine much about the future of human economic and societal security in developing nations. Social conflict over land and water has increased over the last two decades in India. Underdevelopment of its rural populations pushed India into a water crisis. Guha (1999) says that one-third of India's land area has been classified as unproductive wasteland due to erosion. Destroyed land and India's reduced ability to provide water led to a population of "ecological refugees" who must work harder to find firewood and water for crops and households. Increased military conflicts over resources will likely intensify as well, unless changes occur in who controls what for whom.

## GLOBALIZATION FROM ABOVE AND BELOW: A BRIEF HISTORY OF THE WTO AND THE WORLD SOCIAL FORUM

The World Trade Organization first met officially in 1995. It operates a system of trade rules that serve as a mechanism for nations to settle commercial disputes and negotiate agreements to reduce trade barriers. The WTO is not the first attempt by the world's economic powers to develop governing bodies and policies for international trade. As was detailed above, the IMF and the World Bank were two initial organizations established immediately after World War II, but neither group could negotiate or enforce trade regulations between or among nations. Thus, in 1947, 33 of the world's richest nations signed the Global Agreement on Tariff and Trade (GATT) in order to carry out trade talks and set international rules. Periodically, rounds of GATT talks were held to determine new policies such as cutting import tariffs or banning trade dumping (when a country sells a product to another country at an unfairly low price). By 1986, 123 nations had signed onto GATT and had agreed to create a more permanent and powerful governing body that would eventually become the WTO.

According to the WTO itself (www.wto.org), the institution has three main functions: 1) negotiations, 2) establishing rules, and 3) resolving disputes. First and foremost, the WTO is a place where member governments go to discuss problems they are having with each other or with global trade in general, in the hopes of designing effective policies and procedures to address concerns. Thus,

> at its heart are the WTO agreements, negotiated and signed by the bulk of the world's trading nations . . . [which] provide the legal ground-rules for international commerce. They are essentially contracts, binding governments to keep their trade policies within agreed limits. . . . The system's overriding purpose is to help trade flow as freely as possible—so long as there are no undesirable side-effects—because this is important for economic development and well-being. (n.p.)

Finally, the WTO recognizes that trade often represents conflicting interests and, despite having a set of rules to govern trade, rules often need to be interpreted and enforced. Mostly, however, the WTO is a place where conflicts can be resolved through discussion, negotiation, and—if necessary—peer pressure from other member states. As of 2007, a total of 143 countries have signed onto the WTO as members.

Yet the WTO is not an ideologically neutral body, as its primary agenda remains "liberalizing" trade policies around the world. Much like the World Bank's SAP requirements, the

WTO holds nations accountable to meet restrictions against government interventions into and regulations over markets. In other words, the WTO primarily represents the agendas of major corporations whose interests lie in permeating marketplaces around the globe. Ever in search of cheaper raw materials and labor, fewer environmental or labor restrictions, and friendly governments that help develop manufacturing infrastructures and neutralize attempts by workers to organize, the WTO quickly established a reputation as undemocratic, antithetical to environmental protection and labor rights, and more concerned with greater profits than people's well-being. Still, the WTO is in many ways the "only game in town," and in order to be competitive and receive "favored nation" trading status, most countries—big and small—believe they must participate in the organization and follow its rules.

While the coordination of economic efforts on a global scale is not necessarily a social problem in and of itself (though one could argue that such coordination will become increasingly important as communications and commodities continue to cross the globe ever more quickly and easily), the WTO's policies have come under attack for promoting some of the worst economic inequalities, political alienation, and cultural and environmental devastation around the world. For example, the European Union (EU) had a long-term custom of purchasing bananas from small Caribbean countries, a preference widely recognized as the EU's way of granting reparations to its former colonies and assisting the poor. But U.S.-based Chiquita Brands International claimed this market-oriented form of humanitarian aid was a barrier to free trade. Chiquita pressured the United States to file a WTO complaint, and the WTO ruled that the EU system constituted an unfair barrier, eventually forcing them to change their trading policies. Instead of encouraging smaller, developing nations to participate in trade, WTO policies further stifled their ability to compete with larger growers and lower prices.

On a political level, the WTO can intervene in disputes and pressure countries to override or dismantle human rights and environmental protections if they deem them "unfair" barriers to free trade. For example, in 1989, the U.S. Congress passed a law that requires government officials to certify that all shrimp imported to the country are caught with methods (such as use of "turtle excluder devices," or TEDs, that reduce the number of turtles and dolphins caught in shrimp nets by some 90%) that protect sea turtles, dolphins, and other sea life not specifically being hunted, from incidental drowning in shrimp trawling nets. In 1996, the United States expanded this embargo to almost 40 nations. Four South and Southeast Asian nations, India, Pakistan, Malaysia, and Thailand, lodged complaints against the United States, and the WTO found in these other countries' favor. In general, the WTO ruled that the U.S. legislation represented a unilateral measure that put unfair restrictions on other countries competing for shrimp sales to the United States. The ensuing pressure resulted in the policy's demise, and there is no longer a legislative imperative to keep turtles, dolphins, and other sea life safe from shrimp trawlers.

On a cultural level, WTO policies continue to threaten indigenous cultures and practices. Many indigenous cultural organizations site the continued impact of structural adjustment programs, corporate competition and ultimate control over lands once belonging to indigenous peoples, and even "biopiracy" stemming from the corporate patenting of traditional medicines and the indigenous plants they derived from as all having severe negative impacts on their survival. In 2003, representatives from indigenous groups around the world came to Cancun, Mexico, and gathered in conjunction with the 5th WTO Ministerial Conference. They produced "The International Cancun Declaration of Indigenous Peoples" in which they called on the WTO to do the following:

1. Recognize and protect our territorial and resource rights and our right to self-determination.

2. Stop patenting of life forms and other intellectual property rights over biological resources and indigenous knowledge.

3. Ensure Indigenous Peoples' basic right to health.

4. End the militarization of Indigenous Peoples' communities and stop the criminalization of protest and resistance actions of Indigenous Peoples against destructive industries, projects and programs.

5. Support and strengthen the sustainable trading systems which have existed for centuries between the Indigenous Peoples of the Americas (International Forum on Globalization 2003).

While these groups continue to press the WTO to meet demands, the impact of **globalization from above** threatens the cultural autonomy of people with the least amount of economic and political resources around the globe.

As this congregation demonstrated, however, globalization from above has not been without protest. Many groups throughout the 1980s and early 1990s expressed serious dissatisfaction with the IMF, the World Bank, and the rise of various regional and global trade agreements. In 1994, the 50 Years Is Enough coalition formed on the 50th anniversary of the formation of the Bretton Woods organizations. According to its platform, 50 Years Is Enough's network uses education and action to transform the international financial institutions' policies and practices, to end the outside imposition of neoliberal economic programs, and to make the development process democratic and accountable (Danaher 1994).

The year 1994 was also when a group of Mexican revolutionaries from Chiapas formed the *Ejército Zapatista de Liberación Nacional,* or EZLN, otherwise known as the Zapatistas. Taking their name from a hero of the Mexican Revolution, Emiliano Zapatista, the group took over the governance of major towns in Chiapas on January 1, 1994—the first day of the North American Free Trade Agreement's institution. They called for an end to neoliberalism and a return of power and autonomy to indigenous peoples. While much of their territorial gains were eventually taken back by the Mexican Army, the Zapatistas remain an icon of David challenging Goliath on the globalization landscape (Hayden 2001; Ramirez 2008).

But the most important protest against globalization at the turn of the 21st century came during late 1999 in Seattle, Washington. For almost 5 full days, from November 29 to December 3, over 75,000 people representing over 700 organizations took to the streets in an effort to shut down the third annual World Trade Organization Ministerial Conference. On November 30, support demonstrations occurred around the world, while major speeches by U.S. and global labor, environmental, and human rights leaders occurred at various rallies. Along with marches and rallies, direct action activists succeeded in creating enough disturbances that the WTO meetings were in fact cancelled for the day. The activists' success in shutting down the WTO temporarily did not stop it from meeting eventually, but the demonstrations (and the police violence that ensued) raised the level of awareness about the WTO and its policies. Since Seattle, the WTO has pledged transparency and greater democracy at its meetings. It has also made poverty alleviation its primary development goal (Cockburn and St. Clair 2000; Dicaprio and Gallagher 2006).

With a modicum of success under its belt, the anticorporate globalization movement changed part of its strategy from that of demonstrations against the WTO and other symbols of neoliberalism and global free trade to the search for alternative visions. In 2001, the first **World Social Forum (WSF)** was held in Porto Alegre, Brazil. Chosen because of its socialist government and its experimentation with an open assembly model of participatory democratic governance, Brazil hosted 12,000 official delegates from groups and institutions around the world. Over 60,000 people attended hundreds of speeches, workshops, and planning meetings focused on developing alternative visions of organizing global economies and communications based on noncorporate interests. The WSF has been held eight times since 2001, with 2008 set aside for regional forums (Fisher and Ponniah 2003a; Smith 2007)

The success of these WSF gatherings, along with a variety of protests and demonstrations held annually at WTO, G8, and other economic and political summits, is debatable. Many of the corporate projects and international systems of free trade and development continue unabated. The powerful role these systems play in creating massive levels of global inequality cannot be denied. But the triumph of globalization in its early stages was certainly the lack of seriously organized groups and expressions of opposition. The challenge to globalization from above is now clear. The Seattle protests, the WSF, and myriad other organizations and events have raised the level of awareness around neoliberalism and its policies to a heightened degree. Global economic and political decisions are now watched, understood, and critiqued by much of the world.

But divisions within the WSF and other movements present themselves as major stumbling blocks as groups search for alternative economic, political, and cultural organizing principles. Thomas Ponniah (Fisher and Ponniah 2003b), a scholar and activist who has attended, organized, and written about the WSF, explains that there are six major divergences within the movement:

> First, *revolution versus reform*. Some think that we should reform the WTO, the IMF and the World Bank, while others believe they are unreformable and should be replaced by decentralized pluralist global governance.

> Second, *environment versus economy*. Some call for a reduction of economic growth to preserve environmental sustainability while others want sustainable economic growth as the best form of guaranteeing resource distribution.

> Third, *human rights versus protectionism*. Labor groups from the North [industrialized and developed nations] want human rights legislation as part of trade agreements, while labor from the South [industrializing and developing nations] interpret a selective use of 'human rights' as disguised protectionism.

> Fourth, the question of whether *universal* values are *western* values. Some argue that we should return to the values of the French revolution—liberty, equality and fraternity—but broaden them out so they include women, marginalised groups, people of colour and so forth. Others argue these values were always laden with patriarchal and colonial assumptions, so why should they be the beacons for building another world?

> Fifth deals with the different scales of the proposed alternatives. Some call for a return to the local, some call for a return to the state as the mechanism for social redistribution, and others call for a new system of global governance.

> Sixth is a conflict between political parties and social movements. Parties tend to appropriate the aspiration of social movements. But at the same time they have been crucial for implementing many of the best ideas that political activists have brought forward. (n.p.)

Ponniah believes that these divergences may never be fully resolved, but he argues that the debates over disagreements further the overwhelming tasks of expressing, envisioning, and ultimately articulating and enacting new ways of organizing human life on the planet (Fisher and Ponniah 2003b).

## GLOBALIZATION IN THE MEDIA: INDYMEDIA—ALTERNATIVE VIEWS FROM BELOW

In response to the corporate media outlets that discuss globalization as either an uncritically positive process or at least as a fait accompli, the group Indymedia formed during the Seattle anti-WTO demonstrations to promote the international "antiglobalization from above" movement. According to Douglas Morris (2004), "Since its launch in Seattle in November 1999, Indymedia has multiplied itself, rhizomatically branching out into a decentralized global network of media collectives. The Indymedia network now comprises nonlocal media working groups and 104 affiliated local media centers (96 active and 8 new IMCs approved as of October, 2002, with over 60 more in formation). The network is very diverse. Media are created in over twenty languages across over thirty nations in various stages of technical development. Local, regional, and global organizing processes are engaged extensively over the Internet. A global media center, www.indymedia.org, and local IMC websites act as portals to the information, communications, media collectives, and projects of the network" (p. 329). To some degree, Indymedia offers people a democratic opportunity to report on the kinds of news that mainstream and for-profit institutions largely ignore. But as Carlos Fontes (2003) claims, the real power of Indymedia "comes from not only its reporting on social movements but in its existence as a kind of social movement in and of itself. It represents not only an important tool for people organizing global social movements against corporate hegemony, but it is itself a movement against such hegemony" (p. 155).

## CASE STUDY #1

### Bridging the Global Health Care Divide: The Assets of Understanding Culture

Bringing health care and resources to poor nations around the world is certainly an important service. But without proper training and knowledge, such efforts often fail to make much of a difference. First of all, people who lack access to and familiarity with various medications and treatments need information and training as well as resources. Second, those delivering services may not adequately understand the culture and may underestimate the capacity of people different from themselves, thus not preparing or even communicating effectively with local populations. Finally, without adequate institutional commitments and follow-up, programs lose their sustainability and the underlying causes of poor health and disease are left untreated.

The University of Memphis' Loewenberg School of Nursing tries to provide unique services while framing its efforts with proper institutional systems and academic training. In 2005, the school created a Nursing in Diverse Cultures program that sends groups of nursing students and faculty to

*(Continued)*

(Continued)

the Dominican Republic every semester. According to faculty member Lawrette Axley (2009), "The program is designed as a service-learning program with the goals of providing culturally competent healthcare and health teaching while working mano-a-mano 'hand in hand' with the community leaders, physicians, and teachers in the country" (p. 4).

Cultural competence is a relatively new term in health care, education, and other human service fields. Essentially, it is defined as a set of congruent behaviors, attitudes, and policies that come together in a system, agency, or among professionals and help them work effectively in cross-cultural situations (Cross, Bazron, Dennis, and Isaacs 1989; Isaacs and Benjamin 1991; Teal and Street 2009). "It integrates knowledge about individuals and groups of people into specific standards, policies, practices, and attitudes used in appropriate cultural settings to increase the quality of services, thereby producing better outcomes" (Kings, Sims, and Osher 2007, n.p.). Earlier, we discussed the importance of understanding cultural heritage and local customs in bringing health care to Native American populations. The Loewenberg program has adopted the mechanism for international work as well.

The places targeted by the program are isolated rural areas characterized by high levels of poverty and illiteracy. Students and faculty bring a number of medical and nonmedical supplies because access to even basic hygiene products, over-the-counter remedies, and preventive resources is rare. While students have prepared for the various health conditions in the Dominican Republic, textbook descriptions and the actual presentation of diseases and symptoms do not match up perfectly. As Axley (2009) explains,

> Most of the Dominican people have parasites, poor nutrition, and daily chronic pain, with little hope of ever seeing a doctor for treatment. . . . [N]ursing students see how health care is negatively impacted by inadequate nutrition and extremely poor economic situations of a third world country. (p. 4)

Regardless of a community's abject poverty and isolation, generations of survival and indigenous cultural practices result in a variety of local strengths or capacities. In fact, the nursing program's cultural competence approach is based on an asset-model theory of service provision, organizing, and development. This paradigm realizes that, while people may lack money and resources, they also have important strengths that have helped them struggle and survive adverse conditions (Kretzman and McKnight 1997). Thus, the nursing program works closely with a local nongovernmental organization (the Foundation for Peace, or FFP) and with the local people who assist in setting up supplies and organizing and conducting registration—which includes gathering brief demographic information, determining specific health needs, and addressing family concerns. Clinics may be makeshift and primitive by developed-country standards: fold-up tables, cotton bed sheets, twine, and safety pins laid out to form the waiting area and "consultoriums," or examination rooms, but they run effectively and relatively efficiently as local people help administer to their own friends and families.

The preparation for students begins right from the start with the application process. As Axley (2009) describes,

Each participant must reflect on personal and professional goals related to developing cultural competence. For first-time participants, the goals often relate to helping the underserved population in the Dominican. Returning participants spend more time visiting in the homes, experiencing the culture, and developing relationships with people in the communities. For many individuals, the concept of culture relates only to the difference in ethnicity, dress, diet, and language. In reality, cultural competence is multi-dimensional, requiring an understanding of cultural awareness, knowledge, skill, and personal encounters. Participants must take time to reflect on personal feelings and begin to recognize differences prior to their arrival. (p. 4)

While students bring better health services and knowledge about certain illnesses and treatments, they leave with new understandings about the interrelation of social conditions, cultural practices, and health. Axley (2009) quotes one student whose academic work on family structure in various Hispanic and Caribbean cultures reinforced her experience:

In the Dominican Republic, some of the people were unaware of the connection between unsafe drinking water and parasites. One thing I found interesting about this trip was the way families interacted with each other. The family unit was not just parents and children, but one big extended family with at least three generations coming to the clinic together. I remembered this about the Hispanic culture from our classes, but it was interesting to actually see it. (p. 5)

More notable was a second student's integrative understanding of conditions and agency among the Dominicans:

I have new respect for the Dominican people. To manage as well as they do with the poverty and adverse environmental conditions they must live with is remarkable. I could never have this respect and understanding without the experience of actually being there. A nurse can't fake respect and empathy. We can read about and talk about other cultures all we want, but in order to truly have the respect and understanding to deal with the immigrant population in the U.S. we need to know what they have grown up with and what they have left behind to get here. (p. 5)

Not only has this student succeeded in providing service, but in doing so she has become a better nurse and a better health care professional, prepared to make any community she enters a better place.

## Case Study Questions

1. What is cultural competence and why is it important for international work?

2. What aspects of preparation enable nurses to better reflect on their own identities in different cultures and communities?

3. What other local assets might help these nurses in providing the best possible health care?

4. Think of communities around your own campus. How many assets might be better used to address local social problems?

## CASE STUDY #2

Learning Languages, Learning Cultures:
Building Bridges One Word at a Time

Portland State University (PSU) in Portland, Oregon, is a national leader in community-based learning (a synonym for service learning). In June of 2003, two foreign language faculty members led a group of 14 students on an alternative study abroad program to rural Guatemala for 3 weeks. The program combined an interdisciplinary examination of national history and politics with local language and cultural immersion. But the centerpiece of the course was helping the rural communities with painting their schools and assisting teachers in the classroom. As one of the faculty leaders, Robert Sanders (2005), explains, the relationships established between students and communities created more of a "civic immersion" experience as "students became participants in the communities whose society they studied" (p. 183).

The students stayed in the town of Panajachel, a central Guatemalan tourist destination on Lake Atitlán. A local Peace Corps volunteer helped choose the schools and communities with whom the students worked and helped plan housing, transportation, and local excursions. The rural schools were bilingual, with Spanish and the local indigenous Mayan language (Quiché or Kaqchikel). Another school, Proyecto Semilla, was located in Panajachel and featured a special arts center for youth who could not attend normal classes at their local schools because their work obligations in restaurants, hotels, shops, and even as street vendors catering to the local tourist industry kept them in town. But the major problems faced by the rural schools remained the serious lack of resources and social isolation of the rural communities.

As is often the case, however, PSU students were quickly impressed by the creative strategies of local teachers. Lacking notebooks and other resources, teachers drew letters on pieces of paper and then pasted them to rocks collected by the students. According to Sanders (2005), "A few letters are added each day until each of the students has a complete, individual alphabet. The letters are taught phonetically, and spelling competitions using the rocks reinforce the old and new sounds studied" (p. 185).

Still, much of the teaching at these rural schools employed traditional methods of learning by rote memorization and call and response. Certainly, some of these pedagogical strategies reflected patriarchal customs and social relations, but even the teachers themselves agreed that more critical thinking skills "needed to be cultivated among their students, especially in writing" (Sanders 2005:183). Sanders reminds us that both economic poverty and educational rigidity have powerful causes and contours in Guatemala. He writes,

> The economic and educational problems in rural communities are not coincidental. They reflect a social context that lacks critical literacy, civic debate, justice, and economic development. There are constant reminders from the rural communities that Guatemala's civil war just ended in 1996. This was a counter-insurgency war by the military and paramilitary against rural populations that lasted 36 years and for which the Comisión para la Clarificación Histórica (Historical Truth Commission) has documented 626 massacres perpetuated by the Guatemalan government. After two generations of war, there is still great fear in the rural communities and a sense that they are isolated even within their own country. (p. 185)

To be critical, to ask questions, and to use writing and language as forms of self-expression and cultural inquiry remain acts of great risk in such a historical context.

Soon after arriving in the rural areas, PSU students began to express a kind of helplessness about their work in particular and the local peoples' situation in general. Certainly, the school supplies they brought would make an immediate and not unimportant impact in the lives of school children and their teachers, but the communities' needs were so great and PSU students' time and efforts so small in comparison. Even when it came to helping teachers consider innovative pedagogical strategies, none of the students were education majors or had experience with teaching young children. As one student wrote in her reflections, "The more I learned, the more depressed I felt, but it was good to feel that way" (Sanders 2005:188).

Students quickly learned that the teachers' creativity and resourcefulness was not the only strength that rural communities had in their struggles with present conditions. Sanders (2005) discusses the role that *colaboración* has in Mayan culture, as it emphasizes material and social solidarity around community interests and a greater sense of humanity. He explains, "Evidence of these values is ubiquitous in the sacred Mayan text *Popul Vuh,* and the need for discussion permeated daily decisions during our stay abroad" (p. 186). Sanders believes that at least a quarter of the time students lived in the communities was spent in conferences, planning almost every aspect of running the schools and even deciding each day's activities. He concludes that, far from discrediting local leadership, such methods of governing community resources and institutions demonstrate that reaching "consensus was far more important than the decisions themselves" (p. 187). It was solidarity and their sense of community that had helped them survive two generations of war and suffering, and it would be their connections to one another that would be crucial for any future success in education, local development, and cultural stability.

Ultimately, this demonstration of collaboration inspired PSU students. They wrote about a "globalization from below" that came from building relationships between themselves and the communities they visited. Students not only learned about the conditions that plagued these communities, but also the strengths and joys of the local cultures that helped them survive and even promised a renewal of sorts. As one student wrote,

> It really hit home to know what it's like growing up in the rural areas of a third-world country. There is no amount of book learning that can convey the smell of pesticides in the corn fields, the making of tortillas in the dim kitchen with a dirt floor, the personal life stories of real people, and the joy of handholding from the students. (Sanders 2005:187–188)

As more and more PSU students visit these communities over the years, one hopes a longer-lasting, institutional and personal commitment will continue to develop an even more powerful sense of collaboration. Sanders (2005) writes that PSU is committed to teaching exchanges that would bring some Guatemalan teachers to the United States and some U.S. teachers to the Panajachel rural areas. "The most important findings of the program," Sanders concludes, "are that we can significantly help a distant educational community despite our limitations and that the Guatemalan communities can help us improve our lives while increasing our knowledge" (p. 187).

*(Continued)*

(Continued)

## Case Study Questions

1. How do you think recent history has shaped the economic and educational strategies for local communities in Guatemala?

2. As in programs described in previous chapters, what kinds of social or cultural assets did local communities have that students might never have learned without engaging the people themselves?

3. Can you think of issues in your own community where collaboration might pose a more effective strategy for developing solutions to local problems?

## VOICES FROM THE FIELD

### Interview With Christiana Ochoa, Associate Professor of Law, Indiana University

Christiana Ochoa: I was involved with two projects with the Office of Community Service and Learning (OCSL) during 1992 and 1993, both of which granted sociology credits. The first was a migrant worker project in which class time was spent studying the demographics, history, and current situation for migrant laborers in the United States. The community service aspect of the project was teaching English as a Second Language to migrant workers on a Michigan cucumber and pickle farm. The second project focused on education of Latinos in the United States.

The classroom component (which I taught, or "facilitated") concentrated on issues of culture and education that impacted specifically on the Latino community (e.g., English-only initiatives, bilingual education, etc.). The service component required all students to provide tutoring to students at a specific Michigan high school which was populated by many Mexican families who had dropped out of the migrant stream and settled in this small Michigan town. When I left college, I traveled to Costa Rica to teach English as a Foreign Language to elementary-aged kids. Clearly, the experience and training I had received as an ESL teacher a couple years before were greatly beneficial while I was in Costa Rica. That job led directly into my next job, volunteering for a community development organization in Managua, Nicaragua, in which I helped to organize other volunteers and translated for medical delegations visiting Managua and neighboring towns. Both of these early volunteer jobs held much of the same components of the classes I took and the service I performed with the OCSL. All of these experiences were on a volunteer basis; all of them required that I perform volunteer services to Spanish-speaking communities in need of assistance. All of them also required that I understand the community with which I was working, and certainly contributed to that understanding. In each of them, I learned that the only way to fully understand a community is to study it academically at the same time as I engage with it personally and professionally. This lesson—that to come as close as possible to understanding a community and the problems which it faces one must study it through "traditional" academic media and also engage with it as personally as possible (through living within it, eating local food, attending community gatherings and parties, actively contributing to the alleviation of discrete problems)—is one of the most important lessons of my life to date.

Corey Dolgon:   And how have the initial service learning experiences influenced your career path?

CO:   The job in Nicaragua inspired me to attend law school. I had the great fortune of being accepted to and attending Harvard Law School. While I was in law school, I was as close to an activist as an HLS student can be. I worked for 3 years to assure that students who wanted to use their law degrees to do public service work could do so without being saddled with the unbearable burden of the debt an unfunded student incurs during 3 years of law school (at that time, nearly $100,000). I spent precious time on this because I know that an HLS degree holds real power and value and, though they are few, the students who leave HLS committed to working in the public interest have real potential to change the world they live in, or at least improve the lives of the communities they serve. While I was in law school, I had the opportunity to work for two human rights organizations in Brazil. Again, my experiences with living among the communities I was serving, and my knowledge of how to combine academic knowledge with firsthand experience were helpful to me personally and also

*(Continued)*

(Continued)

helpful to my work. I believe my empathy skills, if you will, are well developed as a result of all of these experiences, which started with the OCSL classes.

My primary reason for attending law school was to study human rights. During law school, perhaps my biggest disenchantment was that, while I was learning a good deal about human rights doctrine, I felt oddly disconnected and alienated from that doctrine. I felt a strong desire to work in a country in which human rights are a very pressing issue and had the wonderful opportunity to do so in Colombia. It is my time there that, upon reflection, demonstrates just how influential my work with OCSL has been for me. I went to Colombia to teach as a visiting professor and scholar for a law school in Bogotá. It was a wonderful opportunity to travel and work in a country which consistently experiences some of the most violent human rights and humanitarian law violations in the Western Hemisphere. Still, I felt detached and, almost as though it was second nature, sought out volunteer work with a human rights organization there—to see, to talk with, and to learn from some of the most active and influential human rights advocates in the country. I also had the invaluable opportunity to travel to a number of towns away from the capital, towns which I read about in the newspapers on a regular basis due to the violence they were experiencing. Many people thought I was crazy for going to Colombia in the first place, and many Colombians thought I was crazy for going to these rural communities. I knew there were risks involved in these travels. But I also knew there was knowledge and understanding waiting for me there. So, I couldn't stay away.

I suppose in some ways, my leaving Colombia to work at a global giant of a law firm was also the result of my desire to personally know and understand communities which I study academically. My project at the time was to find means by which transnational corporations could come to be held accountable when they engage in or facilitate human rights violations. But I had never worked in the private sector and felt very much a stranger to the business world. It was a mystery to me and, as such, I felt ignorant commenting on its responsibilities and obligations. Consistent with all my other experiential learning, my time with my law firm personalized the business community and helped me understand better the motivations of corporate actors. This knowledge and understanding created nuance and shades of gray where before I had seen the human rights/corporate social responsibility problem overly simplistically. I feel certain that this nuanced view is what facilitated the offer I received from Indiana University School of Law (where I now work) to teach business law classes as well as human rights classes. I now study the inter-relationship of human rights and international economic activity and am grateful for the understanding I gained from my volunteer work with communities affected by often irresponsible corporate activity as well as the time I spent serving corporate clients in a New York law firm.

The question you asked was how my service learning has shaped my life. The above story tells you that the lessons I learned with OCSL have stayed with me throughout. I believe that in order to understand a problem, it is best to see it for one's self. I believe social problems are much more complex and muddy than can ever be expressed on paper—they simply look different in person. They have a smell, a taste, a feel, an energy, and a life that can only be truly understood through personal experience. Perhaps my early service learning work has taught me to recognize my own ignorance and to seek out opportunities to see, to touch, and to engage with social problems, rather than to remain insulated from the dangers and discomforts I will surely face in doing so.

## SUMMARY

Collaboration (or *colaboración*) will be crucial to construct the knowledge necessary for envisioning a future world without social problems. Much of this book has been about how students who are engaged with communities—locally and around the world—develop such collaborative experiences. These experiences not only allow students an opportunity to feel useful, but a major theme throughout the book is that the intellectual knowledge that helps students analyze the contours of social problems is even further enhanced when combined with the local knowledge about those same problems. With each community-based experience, students brought information gained in the classroom to bear on local problems, and they also gained new perspectives and approaches for understanding those same issues. Even more importantly, students working with communities created new knowledge together, the kinds of experiences and opportunities, the visions and the hopes for being able to create a better world for all people. And that is, after all, the purpose of any sociological endeavor.

## GLOSSARY

**Cultural Competence:** A relatively new term in health care, education, and other human service fields that represents a set of congruent behaviors, attitudes, and policies that come together in a system, agency, or among professionals and help them work effectively in cross-cultural situations.

**Cultural Imperialism:** The spread of dominant countries' cultural products and values to less powerful nations, either by force or by market imperatives. These dynamics often result in the disappearance of more indigenous and traditional cultural practices and beliefs.

Global Integration: The amount of economic or cultural ties that one nation-state possesses with other nation-states. While major industrial nations have carried on international trade for centuries, less industrialized countries are demonstrating strong penchants or mandates to increase their global integration.

Globalization: The major economic, political, and cultural changes that have occurred primarily since the 1960s and 1970s. They include the intense saturation of a market economy, the rise of international governing bodies that regulate global political conflicts as well as world trade, and the international dominance of commercial and consumer cultures (especially as seen through the media, the Internet, etc.).

Globalization From Above: The dynamics of globalization as controlled and driven by a power elite to mazimize corporate profit and control, and maintain political power in the hands of international regulating agencies and the more powerful nation-states that comprise their leadership.

Globalization From Below: The dynamics of globalization that integrate and inform grassroots movements and their efforts to address the issues of poverty, environmental degradation, cultural imperialism, international labor issues and workers' rights, and a variety of other social problems intensified by globalization from above.

Green Revolution: Post–World War II research and technology that aided the agricultural development of wheat and other staple food crops in poorer countries such as India and Mexico.

Indigenous Economies: The ways in which people went about fullfilling the economic needs and demands of pre-indutrial society.

International Monetary Fund (IMF): Established at the same time as the World Bank, the IMF is currently an organization of 186 countries working to foster global monetary cooperation, secure financial stability, facilitate international trade, promote high employment and sustainable economic growth, and reduce poverty.

Race to the Bottom: The process by which countries, states, municipalities, and other regional development entities promise bigger tax breaks, free infrastructural support, and lower labor costs (including wages) in order to compete for corporate investments (new factories, retailers, etc.). As these entities promise more tax breaks and more tax dollars to pay for infrastructural development at the same time that they promise their workers will accept cheaper wages and fewer labor restrictions on health and saftey, and so forth. People and municipalities are essentially racing against each other to end up with worse jobs, poorer wages, and fewer community resources.

Structural Adjustment Programs (SAPs): These are programs that call for less government regulation or direct participation in national economic systems; greater liberalization of trade policies—more open markets and repeal of tariffs and taxes on international goods; and reduced government spending on services such as health care, education, and so on. These policies are generally implemented in order to qualify for IMF or World Bank loans and supposedly reduce the risk that governments will default on loan repayment. However, many critics argue that such spending reductions and trade liberalization hurt citizens (higher costs for health care, education, and other goods and services) and domestic production (as increased competition puts locals out of business). Sustainable Development: The production and distribution of goods that meets present needs without compromising future generations because of resource depletion or destruction.

United Nations (UN): Established in 1945, it replaced the League of Nations as a body whose purpose was to be a world forum for avoiding international military conflicts and addressing global problems related to poverty and development, human rights, and environmental devastation.

World Bank: Composed of both the International Bank for Reconstruction and Development (IBRD) and the International Development Association (IDA), this institution began in 1944 as the primary financial resource for post–World War II reconstruction. Today, its emphasis is on global poverty alleviation.

World Social Forum (WSF): First held in 2001 in Porto Allegre, Brazil, this almost annual gathering of activists and social movement organizations, nongovernmental organizations, and other grassroots groups focuses on developing the solidarity and communications networks necessary to develop stronger international campaigns for human rights and social justice issues. The WSF is often juxtaposed with the WTO as a representative of the most powerful and coordinated driving force behind the "globalization from below" movement.

World Trade Organization (WTO): The most current and comprehensive of the international trade regulation agencies, the WTO began in 1996 and has taken an increased role in coordinating and legislating international trade rules. The WTO is often cited as the most powerful and coordinated force behind the "globalization from above" movement.

## WEBSITES FOR MORE INFORMATION ABOUT GLOBALIZATION AND GLOBAL CITIZENSHIP

Amnesty International: http://www.amnesty.org/

Global AIDS Alliance: http://www.globalaidsalliance.org/

Global Exchange: http://www.globalexchange.org/

Global Policy Forum: http://www.globalpolicy.org/

Global Warming International Center: http://globalwarming.net/

Globalization 101: http://www.globalization101.org/

International Service Learning: http://www.islonline.org/

Jubilee USA Network: Global Debt Cancellation: http://www.jubileeusa.org/

Third World Traveler: http://www.thirdworldtraveler.com/

UNESCO—United Nations Education, Scientific and Cultural Organization: http://www.unesco.org/

Vermont Campus Compact—Fostering Global Citizenship in Higher Education 3rd Annual Conference: http://www.vtcampuscompact.org/2009/FGC/FGC09Post.htm

World Social Forum: http://www.forumsocialmundial.org.br/index.php?cd_language=2

YES: Youth for Environmental Sanity: http://www.yesworld.org/

# REFERENCES

Agyeman, Julian. 2005. *Sustainable Communities and the Challenge of Environmental Justice.* New York: New York University Press.

Aiyer, Ananthakrishnan. 2007. "The Allure of the Transnational: Notes on Some Aspects of the Political Economy of Water." *Cultural Anthropology,* 22:640–658.

Annan, Kofi. 2005, July 6. "Secretary-General's Address to St. Paul's Cathedral Event on the Millennium Development Goals." Retrieved February 23, 2010 (http://www.un.org/apps/sg/sgstats.asp?nid = 1558).

Axley, Lawrette. 2009. "Nursing in Diverse Cultures: An International Experience." *Tennessee Nurse,* 72:4–5.

Basel Action Network and the Silicon Valley Toxics Coalition. 2002. "Exporting Harm: The High-Tech Trashing of Asia." Retrieved February 17, 2010 (http://www.ban.org/E-waste/technotrashfinalcomp.pdf).

Brecher, Jeremy and Tim Costello. 1998. *Global Village or Global Pillage: Economic Reconstruction From the Bottom Up.* Boston: South End Press.

Brecher, Jeremy, Tim Costello, and Brendan Smith. 2000. *Globalization From Below: The Power of Solidarity.* Boston, MA: South End Press.

Bullard, Robert, ed. 2005. *The Quest for Environmental Justice: Human Rights and the Politics of Pollution.* San Francisco, CA: Sierra Club Books.

Cochburn, Alexander and Jeffrey St. Clair. 2000. *Five Days That Shook the World: The Battle for Seattle and Beyond.* London, UK: Verso.

Cross, T. L., B. J. Bazron, K. W. Dennis, and M. R. Isaacs. 1989. *Towards a Culturally Competent System of Care: A Monograph on Effective Services for Minority Children Who Are Severely Emotionally Disturbed.* Washington, DC: Georgetown University Child Development Center, CASSP Technical Assistance Center.

Curtis, Michael. 2003. "The Obesity Epidemic in the Pacific Islands." *Journal of Development and Social Transformation,* 1:37–42.

Danaher, Kevin. 1994. *Fifty Years Is Enough: The Case Against the World Bank and the International Monetary Fund.* Boston, MA: South End Press.

Dicaprio, Alisa and Kevin P. Gallagher. 2006. "The WTO and the Shrinking of Development Space: How Big Is the Bite?" *Journal of World Investment and Trade,* 7:781–805.

Dollar, David and Jakob Svensson. 2000. "What Explains the Success or Failure of Structural Adjustment Programmes?" *Economic Journal*, 110:894–917.

Easterly, William. 2003. "IMF and World Bank Structural Adjustment Programs and Poverty." Pp. 361–392 in *Managing Currency Crises in Emerging Markets*, edited by Michael Dooley and Jeffrey Frankel. Chicago, IL: University of Chicago Press.

Elliot. J. 2006. *An Introduction to Sustainable Development*. London, UK: Routledge.

Fisher, William and Thomas Ponniah. 2003a. *Another World Is Possible: Popular Alternatives to Globalization at the World Social Forum*. London, UK: Zed Books.

____. 2003b. "Under a Tree in Porto Alegre: Democracy in Its Most Radical Sense." *Open Democracy*. Retrieved February 24 (http://www.opendemocracy.net/globalization-world/article_954.jsp).

Fitzgerald, Niall. 1997. "Harnessing the Potential of Globalization for the Consumer and the Citizen." *International Affairs*, 73:739–746.

Fontes, Carlos. 2003. "A Passion for Peace and Justice: A Global Voice From Below." Pp. 152–170 in *Cyber Media Go to War*, edited by Ralph Berenger. Spokane, WA: Marquette Books.

Friedman, Thomas L. 1999. *The Lexus and the Olive Tree*. New York: Anchor Books.

Global Policy Forum. 2010. "Defining Globalization." Retrieved February 16, 2010 (http://www.globalpolicy.org/globalization/defining-globalization.html).

Guha, Ramachandra. 1999. *Environmentalism: A Global History*. London, UK: Longman.

Hawken, Paul. 2007. Blessed Unrest: How the Largest Movement in the World Came into Being and Why No One Saw It Coming. New York: Viking.

Hayden, Tom. 2001. *The Zapatista Reader*. New York: Nation Books.

International Forum on Globalization. 2003. "The International Cancun Declaration of Indigenous Peoples." Retrieved February 24, 2010 (http://www.ifg.org/programs/indig/CancunDec.html).

International Labor Organization. 2002. *Decent Work and the Informal Economy*. Geneva, Switzerland: Author.

Isaacs, M. R. and M. P. Benjamin. 1991. *Towards a Culturally Competent System of Care: Programs Which Utilize Culturally Competent Principles, Vol. 2*. Washington, DC: Georgetown University Child Development Center.

Kenan, Peter B. 1994. *Managing the World Economy: Fifty Years After Bretton Woods*. Princeton, NJ: Institute for International Economics.

King, Mark A., Anthony Sims, and David Osher. 2007. "How Is Cultural Competence Integrated in Education?" Retrieved February 24, 2010 (http://cecp.air.org/cultural/Q_integrated.htm).

Kretzman, John, and John McKnight. 1997. *Building Communities From the Inside Out: A Path Toward Finding and Mobilizing a Community's Assets*. Skokie, IL: ACTA Publishers.

Long, W. Alexander. 2002. "Marginalization and Waste in Mexico: The Pepenadores of Los Belenes." Pp. 102–128 in *Just Doing It: Popular Collective Action in the Americas*, edited by Gene Desfor, Deborah Barndt, and Barbara Rahder. Montreal, Quebec, Canada: Black Rose Books.

Mcspotlight. N.d. "The McLibel Trial Story." Retrieved February 24, 2010 (http://www.mcspotlight.org/case).

Morris, Douglas. 2004. "Globalization and Media Democracy: The Case of Indymedia." Pp. 325–352 in *Shaping the Network Society: The New Role of Civil Society in Cyberspace*, edited by Douglas Schuler and Peter Day. Cambridge, MA: MIT Press.

Nissanke, Machiko. 2006. Impact of Globalization on the World's Poor. Helsinki, Finland: UNU-WIDER.

Pollock, Nancy J. 1992. *These Roots Remain: Food Habits in Islands of the Central and Eastern Pacific Since Western Contact*. Honolulu: University of Hawaii Press.

Porter, Maureen and Kathia Monard. 2001. "Anyi in the Global Village: Building Relationships of Reciprocity through International Service-Learning." *Michigan Journal of Community Service-Learning,* 8:5–17.

Ramirez, Gloria Muñoz. 2008. *The Fire and the Word: A History of the Zapatista Movement.* San Francisco, CA: City Lights Books.

Ringrose, Helen and Paul Zimmet. 1979. "Nutrient Intakes in an Urbanized Micronesian Population With High Diabetes Prevalence." *American Journal of Clinical Nutrition,* 32:1334–1341.

Rothe, Dawn and Christopher W. Mullins. 2006. "International Community: Legitimizing a Moral Collective Consciousness." *Humanity and Society,* 30:254–276.

Sanders, Robert. 2005. "Community-Based Learning in Rural Guatemala." Hispania, 88:182–189.

Schlosser. Eric. 2002. *Fast Food Nation: The Dark Side of the All-American Meal.* New York: Harper Perennial.

Shiva, Vandana. 1992. *The Violence of Green Revolution: Third World Agriculture, Ecology and Politics.* London, UK: Zed Books.

Smith, Jackie. 2007. *Global Democracy and the World Social Forums.* Boulder, CO: Paradigm.

Teal, Cayla and Richard Street. 2009. "Critical Elements of Culturally Competent Communication in the Medical Encounter: A Review and Model." *Social Science & Medicine,* 68:533–543.

UN Permanent Forum on Indigenous Issues. 2010. [website]. Retrieved February 24, 2010 (http://www .un.org/esa/socdev/unpfii/index.html).

Vallely, Paul, Jon Clarke, and Liz Stuart. 2003. "In India, Impoverished Farmers are Fighting to Stop Drinks Giant 'Destroying Livelihoods.'" *The Independent.* July 25.

Watson, James L., ed. 1997. *Golden Arches East: McDonald's in East Asia.* Palo Alto, CA: Stanford University Press.

"What's Wrong With McDonald's?" N.d. [Fact sheet]. Nottingham, UK: Anti-McDonald's Campaign.

Zimmet, Paul. 1979. "Epidemiology of Diabetes and Its Macrovascular Manifestations in Pacific Populations: The Medical Effects of Social Progress." *Diabetes Care,* 2:144–153.

# Index

Note: In page references, p indicates photos, f indicates figures and t indicates tables.

# About the Authors

**Corey Dolgon** is a Professor of Sociology and Director of Community-Based Learning at Stonehill College in Easton, Massachusetts. Corey has been an activist/scholar for 15 years since graduating from the University of Michigan with a PhD in American Culture in 1994. He is Past President of the Association for Humanist Sociology (AHS) and was Founding Director of the Center for Service Learning and Civic Engagement at Worcester State College. He is also the author of the award-winning book, *The End of the Hamptons: Scenes From the Class Struggle in America's Paradise,* and he has served as Editor of *Humanity and Society*, the AHS journal. He is currently Assistant Editor for *Theory in Action*, the journal of the Transformative Studies Institute, and is Editor of an anthology entitled *Pioneers of Public Sociology: The First 30 Years of Humanity and Society.* Dolgon continues his engaged scholarship as an active member of area political and social organizations including Massachusetts Jobs With Justice; Brockton Interfaith Community; Dismas House; and a variety of other local, regional, and national organizations.

**Chris Baker** earned his PhD in Sociology from the University of Tennessee (1995). He has 14 years of teaching experience, including 4 years working at West Virginia Institute of Technology (1996–2000). Since 2000, he has been at Walters State Community College in Morristown, Tennessee. He teaches courses in Appalachian sociology, social problems, family, and cultural anthropology. Chris publishes articles in the areas of participatory research, social problems, community development, Appalachian studies, race, social movements, and service learning. He has held positions for the Society for the Study of Social Problems and is Editor of the *Appalachian Studies Syllabus Guide* for the American Sociological Association and a special edition on participatory research for *Humanity and Society*. He works with activist groups in the Appalachian region including collaborating with the Highlander Research and Education Center and the Southern Appalachian Labor School. His activist work focuses on rural working-class poverty and empowerment and Latino migrants in the rural South.